Lecture Notes in Computer Science 2757

Edited by G. Goos, J. Hartmanis, and J. van Leeuwen

D1717723

Springer
Berlin
Heidelberg
New York
Hong Kong
London
Milan
Paris
Tokyo

Bernhard K. Aichernig   Tom Maibaum (Eds.)

Formal Methods at the Crossroads

From Panacea to Foundational Support

10th Anniversary Colloquium of UNU/IIST
the International Institute for Software Technology of
The United Nations University
Lisbon, Portugal, March 18-20, 2002
Revised Papers

 Springer

Series Editors

Gerhard Goos, Karlsruhe University, Germany
Juris Hartmanis, Cornell University, NY, USA
Jan van Leeuwen, Utrecht University, The Netherlands

Volume Editors

Bernhard K. Aichernig
UNU/IIST, The United Nations University
International Institute for Software Technology
P.O. Box 3058, Macao, China
E-mail: bka@iist.unu.edu

Tom Maibaum
King's College London, Department of Computer Science
Strand, London WC2R 2LS, United Kingdom
E-mail: tom@maibaum.org

Cataloging-in-Publication Data applied for

A catalog record for this book is available from the Library of Congress.

Bibliographic information published by Die Deutsche Bibliothek
Die Deutsche Bibliothek lists this publication in the Deutsche Nationalbibliografie;
detailed bibliographic data is available in the Internet at <http://dnb.ddb.de>.

CR Subject Classification (1998): D.2, F.3, D.3, F.4

ISSN 0302-9743
ISBN 3-540-20527-6 Springer-Verlag Berlin Heidelberg New York

Springer-Verlag is a part of Springer Science+Business Media

springeronline.com

© Springer-Verlag Berlin Heidelberg 2003
Printed in Germany

Typesetting: Camera-ready by author, data conversion by Olgun Computergrafik
Printed on acid-free paper   SPIN: 10930748   06/3142   5 4 3 2 1 0

In Memoriam

Armando Martín Haeberer (1947–2003)

In Memoriam

Preface

This volume records the 10th Anniversary Colloquium of UNU/IIST, the International Institute for Software Technology of the United Nations University, held in Lisbon, Portugal, March 18–21, 2002. Armando Haeberer, then Chairman of the board of UNU/IIST, conceived the idea of an international meeting in celebration of the institute's 10th anniversary. He was working in Lisbon at this time and he proposed to hold the meeting there, not least because the Portuguese government had been one of the major sponsors of the institute, right from the very beginning. The aim of the meeting, organized by the Board of UNU/IIST, was twofold. First, the institute's research work should be re-assessed and disseminated. Second, the future role of UNU/IIST's research area, formal methods, should be discussed.

Role of Formal Methods. Over at least three decades of development, the conception of what role formal methods should play in software engineering seems to have changed dramatically, influenced by both advocates and detractors. Beginning with a fundamentalist view that contested the genuineness of any 'non-formal' practice, dismissing it as an inappropriate contribution to the as yet ill-defined corpus of so-called software engineering, the conception of what this role should be has apparently evolved to a less naive engineering viewpoint. Today, as these theoretical methods acquire a new maturity and breadth of use, many of their advocates appear to be questioning their direct application by software practitioners, often considering it to be nonmandatory, and sometimes even nonadvisable. It appears that, together with the said maturation of the theoretical results and constructions, the perspective of their role within a far more complex picture of the software development activity has also matured. Today, many specialists and advocates of formal methods consider them as the framework that, by underlying the corpus of the software development praxis, lifts its status from craftsmanship to engineering, as happens in more classic branches of technology.

Aim and Shape of the Colloquium. UNU/IIST itself is located in Macao, near Hong Kong, at the heart of one of the major cultural and commercial crossroads of the world. In keeping with this multicultural focus, a group of approximately 30 eminent researchers from 15 countries on four continents gathered in Lisbon to cross swords and initiate the arduous task of tackling the colloquium's theme: *Formal Methods at the Crossroads: from Panacea to Foundational Support.* The meeting served as a forum for a thorough discussion of the inflexion point in the history of formal methods at which we currently find ourselves and an exploration of the potential changes to its very character. In addition to the group of active senior international scientists working in the area of formal methods and their application to software and hardware engineering, a group of young researchers and Ph.D. students were invited to participate. The reason for the existence of the second group can be found in the very spirit of UNU/IIST, which is both a research and a training center of the UNU system.

The colloquium was organized as follows: First, the presentations were made and discussions took place among the best-known researchers, worldwide, in the area, interacting with young researchers and Ph.D. students. Second, the papers accompanying the presentations were discussed among the authors and the program committee while being written. Moreover, two scientists, who volunteered to do this, Profs. Carlo Ghezzi and Tom Maibaum, produced presentations to induce a couple of discussions that took place during the colloquium. In addition, the presentations and discussions were recorded and can be accessed at the postcolloquium site

http://www.iist.unu.edu/colloquium/

With satisfaction we see that the work initiated at this colloquium is currently being continued at a series of annual CUE workshops supported by agencies in China, Europe and the USA.

Contents of the Volume. The invited speakers at the colloquium and the participants from UNU/IIST were asked to submit a paper about the topic of their presentation. Most participants responded by indeed submitting said papers. Then, the tragic death of Armando Haeberer in February 2003 brought the process to a standstill for some time, as he had much of the material in his possession. It was subsequently agreed that we should proceed with the volume, but that some elements of Armando's vision could no longer be achieved, at least if we wanted to produce a timely volume. Hence, there are no introductory and concluding chapters by Armando, Tom Maibaum and Carlo Ghezzi, which were intended to be a commentary on and analysis of the contents of the papers and what was said at the colloquium. As the meeting was recorded, it had also been Armando's hope to integrate the transcription of the audio tapes into the volume itself, to provide further context and analysis for the papers. Again, unfortunately, we could not proceed with this. The submitted papers were reviewed by the participating invited speakers.

Hence, the volume is more conventional than had been intended. It is organized into 6 parts. The first paper in the volume is a recollection of Armando Haeberer's life by Tom Maibaum. The second part, entitled 'Work at UNU/IIST,' contains a paper by Zhou Chaochen, then Director of the Institute (and now retired) about the Institute, its history and its present work. Then there are several papers illustrating the research ongoing at the Institute. There is a paper by its newest Research Fellow, Bernhard Aichernig, about a formal-methods-based approach to testing. The idea of contracts, as seen in the work of Bertrand Meyer, amongst others, is extended to tests, seen as an operational contract. It is shown how tests can be derived via refinement techniques from specification contracts.

Chris George, now Director ad interim of the Institute, describes work on the RAISE tools and method. The focus is on deriving a design specification from the requirements. He Jifeng describes how the hardware specification language

VERILOG can be characterized algebraically and how this algebraic characterization leads to operational and denotational presentations of the language. Dang Van Hung then reviews the development of the Duration Calculus, which can be used to describe and analyze real-time systems. Tomasz Janowski then describes the language X2Rel and its semantics. The purpose of the language is to enable the description of many different kinds of binary relations between XML documents.

In the next section, entitled 'At the Crossroads,' we see a number of papers that tried to directly address the theme of the colloquium, i.e., the state of the art in software engineering and its basis in proper engineering/scientific principles. The title of the paper by Michael Jackson, 'Where, Exactly, Is Software Development?,' directly focuses on the problem of characterizing and analyzing the context of the software to be built. How can one formalize the context and its relationship to the software? Michael sees this as an important challenge for the subject. The paper by Astesiano, Reggio and Cerioli uses reflections by the authors of their experience and knowledge of practical software engineering to propose software development methods that more purposefully integrate the use of formal techniques. Tony Hoare proposes a challenge for software development: making a verifying compiler. The idea is that a compiler proves the correctness of a program before 'allowing it to run.' This is aided by assertions attached to the program and, of course, appropriate and automatic verification technology.

J Strother Moore puts forward another grand challenge for formal methods: to build and mechanically verify a practical software system, from the transistor level right to the application software. He sees this as being beyond the capacity of any single person or group and requiring both competition and collaboration. However, he sees the benefits to the subject as being of major proportions. Dines Bjørner addresses the problems and role of domain engineering and, in particular, the importance and role of infrastructure components and an associated notion of transaction script workflows. (He also devotes some space to reflections on the 10 years of UNU/IIST's existence.) The paper by Cliff Jones on the formalization of some dependability notions concludes the section. He identifies the concept of system as an important focus, together with the genesis of a system from other systems. He characterizes concepts such as fault, error and failure in the framework.

The section 'From Models to Software' begins with a paper by Manfred Broy on the role of models and views in program development. His paper includes a comprehensive family of software models as well as a discussion on how these models are related. The section continues with a paper by Thiagarajan and Roychoudhury on message sequence charts. Their concern is the establishment of a relationship between the language of message sequence charts and an executable language. They propose Cyclic Transition Processes to fill this gap. Ferrari, Montanari and Tuosto use hypergraphs and graph synchronization to model wide area network applications. Their longer-term objective is to provide software engineering tools for designing and certifying internetworking systems. The paper by Pavlovic and Smith rehearses the ongoing work at the Kestrel

Institute on support for the formal development of software, focusing on refinement concepts. The underlying mathematical framework is based on a category of higher-order specifications, and refinement is implemented via the construction of colimits.

Bailes and Kemp describe their 'totally functional approach to programming,' consisting of the representation of data structures in terms of 'platonic combinators,' which have some nice formal properties. The paper by José Fiadeiro concludes the section by describing the use of co-ordination technologies in support of the evolution of systems. The claim is that most systems are not built as new, but rather are evolved from some previous system. The key is the externalization of interaction between components so as to more easily assemble and extend systems built in this way.

The next section contains papers focusing on real-time systems. The paper by Yingxu Wang describes real-time process algebra. The language addresses operations, event/process timing and memory manipulation, and the paper also provides examples of its use. Chen and Lin describe a formalism based on communicating timed automata. The language enables the expression of real-time constraints and data communication, and the language has a graphical representation. The paper by David, Behrmann, Larsen and Wang Yi describes the architecture of a new implementation of the model-checking tool Uppaal. The design is based on a pipeline architecture and a single shared data structure. The design decisions are supported by experimental evidence.

The final section is on verification. The paper by Shankar looks at the problem of combining the effectiveness of model checking, with its limitations due to the size of state spaces, and deductive theorem proving methods, with their limitations on automation. The method proposed is based on abstracting from a specification a finite state approximation of the program that preserves the property of interest by using deductive methods. Then, model checking can be used to provide assurance of the proper working of the program with respect to that property. The paper by Manna and Zarba gives a survey of what is known about combining decision procedures, in particular in relation to combining theories over nondisjoint signatures. Kaltenbach and Misra address the problem of model checking progress properties of systems. These kinds of properties are usually difficult to check as they involve doubly nested fixed points. They propose the addition of 'hints,' expressed as regular expressions over the language of actions of a program. Finally, in his paper Naoki Kobayashi extends type systems to concurrent programs to analyze deadlock freedom, safe usage of locks, etc.

We hope that the readers of this volume benefit scientifically from these proceedings and also find it stimulating for clarifying the role of formal methods in their research.

July 2003

Bernhard K. Aichernig
Tom Maibaum

Keynote Speakers

The list of invited participants includes some of the most well-known researchers in the area of formal methods and their applications. They are:

- Prof. Egidio Astesiano (University of Genoa, Italy)
- Prof. Paul Bailes (University of Queensland, Australia)
- Prof. Dines Bjørner (Technical University of Denmark, Denmark)
- Dr. Dominique Bolignano (Trusted Logic, France)
- Prof. Manfred Broy (Technische Universität München, Germany)
- Prof. Fu Yuxi (Department of CS, Shanghai JiaoTong University, People's Republic of China)
- Prof. José Luiz Fiadeiro (ATX Software and University of Lisbon, Portugal)
- Prof. Carlo Ghezzi (Politecnico di Milano, Italy)
- Dr. Constance Heitmeyer (US Naval Research Laboratory, USA)
- Prof. Tom Henzinger (University of Berkeley, USA)
- Prof. C.A.R. Hoare (Microsoft Research, Cambridge, UK)
- Prof. Michael Jackson (Open University, UK)
- Prof. Cliff Jones (University of Newcastle upon Tyne, UK)
- Prof. Gilles Kahn (INRIA, France)
- Dr. Naoki Kobayashi (Tokyo Institute of Technology, Japan)
- Prof. Lin Huimin (Chinese Academy of Sciences, Beijing, People's Republic of China)
- Prof. Tom Maibaum (King's College London, UK)
- Prof. Ugo Montanari (Università di Pisa, Italy)
- Prof. David Parnas (McMaster University, Canada)
- Prof. Amir Pnueli (Weizmann Institute of Science, Israel)
- Dr. Natarajan Shankar (SRI International, USA)
- Dr. Douglas Smith (Kestrel Institute, USA)
- Prof. P.S. Thiagarajan (Chennai Mathematical Institute, India)
- Prof. Wang Yi (Chinese Academy of Sciences, People's Republic of China and Uppsala University, Sweden)
- Prof. Yingxu Wang (University of Calgary, Canada)

The following academic staff of UNU/IIST participated:

- Prof. Zhou Chaochen, Director
- Chris George, Senior Research Fellow
- Prof. He Jifeng, Senior Research Fellow
- Dr. Bernhard K. Aichernig, Research Fellow
- Dr. Dang Van Hung, Research Fellow
- Dr. Tomasz Janowski, Research Fellow

Program Committee

The organization of the colloquium was the responsibility of a program committee, isomorphic to the membership of the UNU/IIST Board at the time.

Chairman	Armando Haeberer (ATX Software, Portugal and King's College London, UK)
Vice-Chairman	Mathai Joseph (Tata Institute, India)
Members	Ibrahim Eissa (University of Cairo, Egypt)
	Hans van Ginkel (Rector of UNU, Japan)
	Gerard Huet (INRIA, France)
	Iu Vai Pan (University of Macau, China)
	Zohar Manna (Stanford University, USA)
	Pedro Manuel Barbosa Veiga (University of Lisbon, Portugal)
	Wu Ying Jian (Ministry of Science and Technology, China)
	Zhou Chaochen (Director of UNU/IIST, China)

Executive Committee

The program committee delegated the executive organization to the executive committee.

Members	José Luiz Fiadeiro (ATX Software and University of Lisbon, Portugal)
	Armando Haeberer

In addition, the following people helped particularly with the organization of the colloquium in various capacities:

Technical Organization	Miguel Costa (ATX Software)
Administrative Organization	Cristina Teles (ATX Software)
Organization at UNU/IIST	Hoi Iok Wa, Wendy
	Pun Chong Iu, Alice
	Ho Sut Meng, Michelle
	Chan Iok Sam, Kitty

Support

We are grateful for the support of the following organizations:
- ATX Software (Portugal)
- European Commission
- Fundação para a Ciência e a Tecnologia (Portugal)
- Gabinete de Relações Internacionais da Ciência e do Ensino Superior (Portugal)
- University of Lisbon

Table of Contents

From Models to Software

Real-Time Systems

Verification

In Memoriam

Armando Martín Haeberer

4 January 1947 – 11 February 2003

Tom Maibaum

King's College London
tom@maibaum.org

1 Introduction

The sudden death of Arrmando in February devastated his many friends and colleagues around the world. I had known him for almost twenty years and I cannot but remember him in very personal terms. Hence, this brief account of his life and work will be written in the first person singular and represents mainly my own impressions of him as a man and as a scientist/academic.

Armando was a true exemplar of the phrase *a force of nature*! He was a polymath in the tradition of Babbage. Whatever subject was being discussed, it appeared that not only did he know about the topic, but he had read extensively about it! His knowledge of world literature, world history, music, philosophy, epistemology, physics and chemistry, etc was unsurpassed by anyone I knew (other than a few professionals specializing in just one of these topics). Perhaps this depth of knowledge is best illustrated by an example: Armando recently found himself explaining the underlying musical patterns in *Swan Lake* and their meaning to a *prima ballerina* who had danced the main part(s) many times in one of the best companies in the world!

He was particularly fond of Byron and Oscar Wilde, and had an extensive collection of works by them and about them. Whenever he was in London, the first thing he did (after buying the champagne, more on this below) was look to see if one of Wilde's plays was on. He admired enormously Wilde's wit and his talent for a *bon mot*. I think he also admired both Byron's and Wilde's abilities to live life to the full. Armando certainly attempted to mimic them in this regard. He loved food, wine and travel and engaged in all of them fully and extensively. He was apparently known as *el gordo* by close friends from his days in Argentina, and with good reason! (However, he was extremely thin when in his teens and close friends from those days apparently called him *el flaco* (the thin one)!) He was a very large man indeed and lost 35 kilos on a diet he undertook 3 years ago! The diet also illustrated one of his other characteristics, namely his ability to focus on some target and not stop until he achieved it, or it was completely clear that it was impossible to do so.

Besides being a close collaborator, especially over the past 10 years, Armando was a very close personal and family friend. Over the past decade, he fell into the habit of buying champagne whenever there was an excuse for celebration. This turned eventually into any visit to our house being an excuse for a celebration. (I suspect that visits

B.K. Aichernig and T. Maibaum (Eds.): Formal Methods ..., LNCS 2757, pp. 1–25, 2003.
© Springer-Verlag Berlin Heidelberg 2003

to our house were not the only visits used as excuses for a celebration.) Indeed, on one of his last visits to us, my daughter arrived home and noticed two cases of champagne (Laurent Perrier was one of his favourites) on the counter in the kitchen and commented: Ah, Armando must be here!

On the other hand, Armando was a workaholic. He seemed to exist on hardly any sleep. (This became less true over the past few years. His daughter Ana writes: "Recently, I am pretty sure it was last year [2002], Pablo, my fiancée, and I were preparing a special sauce for dinner. It was around 9:30pm in Argentina and my father was still living in Lisbon, so it was around 12:30am for him. We were not being very successful with the sauce so we decided to e-mail him asking for help since he used to stay up working late. One hour, 6 e-mails and no answer later, we finally decided to eat whatever it was we had made. The following morning, when I got online, I received a message from my dad that said: "Dulcinea, sometimes at one o'clock in the morning I'm sleeping".)

Armando worked all hours of the day and night on his various projects and writings. He was able to cut himself off from work when appropriate, e.g., family holidays, social occasions, etc. But, when he was in work mode, it was 24 hours a day. Woe betide those of us who could not keep up! On the other hand, he had many colleagues and friends who were under his 'spell' and would perform superhuman efforts on his behalf. He induced much loyalty and devotion amongst his colleagues, friends and students. He demanded a lot, but was also very generous, and not just with the champagne! In recent years, with the very serious economic difficulties experienced by everyone in Argentina, Armando made sure that before the champagne was purchased, a very large part of whatever income was available at the time went to his extended family there. He was always ready and willing to help friends, colleagues and students in any way required when the need arose. He did not have any understanding of the concept of 'too much trouble'.

Armando was the best technical 'salesman' I have ever come across. He had an uncanny ability to explain serious technical ideas to the less knowledgeable and to sell ideas and projects to funding authorities and industry. He saw all of this as a kind of gambling game (and once told me off for not taking cognizance of some game in some discussion about a project). He enjoyed playing this game enormously. On the other hand, he was not always as good or as devoted to getting the resulting project organized and finished. He was already on to the next grand project. As a result, some of his ideas and initiatives did not get the reward that they might otherwise have deserved.

Living such a life may well have taken its toll on him in the end. He was unable to 'keep still', as instructed by his doctors and although feeling unwell after the angioplasty he had undergone after the first heart attack, he was back at work just two weeks later. On the day of his death, UNU/IIST was closed because it was an Islamic holiday and Armando was eager to find a replacement part in Hong Kong for one of his beloved Mont Blanc pens. He died on the jetfoil carrying him from Macau to Hong Kong, eager, as ever, not to waste an opportunity.

2   The Bare Personal and Professional Facts ...

Armando was born in Argentina on the 4th of January in 1947. His family tree had contributions from Italy, France and Germany. It was large and he seems to have had an extensive and happy family life in his youth. (His father was Armando Augusto Ricardo Haeberer (aka Bubi) and his mother, still alive, was Enriqueta Felicidad Meschio (aka Queta). Also, two very important figures in his early years were his aunts (Armando's father's sisters) Guillermina Haeberer (aka Mina) and Adelina Gregoria Haeberer (Nena, the smallest of the 4 siblings). Armando also has a brother working in Argentina as a medical doctor.)

His family was musical and his love of music started in the home. He was an accomplished pianist and might have had a career as a musician if he had not chosen science instead. His father was an engineer working on roads for the Argentine government. This may have had some influence on Armando's predilection for science and engineering. At university, Armando studied Physics, Chemistry and Operations Research. He also came across epistemology, a subject he never forgot and took up as a research theme later in his career.

After pursuing studies in Physics and Chemistry at Universidad Nacional de La Plata (and he also acquired a qualification in Operations Research), Armando worked first for the Argentine Federal Highway administration (Vialidad Nacional, VN), initially as a programmer and then as Head of the Analysis Division and as Head of the Computing Group in the Research Department. The first manifestation of his love for abstraction was Abstract Data Types, which he used to develop his home-grown DBMS for VN. In late 1973, he gave an initial presentation of this work under the auspices of SADIO, the Argentine Society for Informatics and Operations Research, the first evidence of what would become long lasting support of their activities. One of his first close friends in the discipline, Professor Jorge Aguirre, convinced him to work full time at the Jesuit Observatory in San Miguel, then a leading centre in numerical analysis, and a hot spot for computer scientists. Through his association with the Observatory, Armando met Jorge Boria, in a fortuitous encounter related to hardware limitations in Jorge's PDP-11 that caused him to spend time at the Observatory. Boria was working then at the Universidad de San Luis (UNSL), as the Computer Scientist in residence, where he was asked to prepare a three-year curriculum to train computer programmers. Boria recognised in Armando and Jorge Aguirre two like minds with whom to build the curriculum. Armando started travelling to San Luis frequently and cemented a friendship with Boria that survived the latter's expulsion from San Luis on political grounds in 1980. In the meantime, Armando had joined forces with Aguirre and other Observatory fellows and helped establish the company Soft-Lab S.R.I., where he served as Chief Executive Officer for the period 1976-81. His entrepreneurship flourished soon after once more: Starting in 1978, he became involved in setting up INFOS S.A., where he served on the Board, later becoming Vice Chairman, Technical Director and then Chief Executive Officer. Aguirre and some of his cronies from the days of the Observatory tagged along.

During this period, he married Alicia B. Luboz (1973) and had a daughter, Ana (1975). (Ana writes of this period: "[…] since you talk about his devotion to champagne at the beginning of your piece, [that] when I was a little baby, during celebrations or family reunions, he would dampen my pacifier in champagne and give it to me. Everybody said that I used to love it; my mother used to become really mad and my father used to enjoy it like hell. Anyway, he used to do exactly the same thing with Nati [Armando's second daughter] several years ago. The thing is, he led me into the "good" drinking and it was the same with music and reading. I have, now, these unconditional companions I can carry anywhere, anytime as it is music or a good book. My way of thinking, my approach to life, even when they are mine, have my father's imprint on them."

She continues: "When I was about six years old, my family (all four grandparents and my parents) rented a summer house for our vacations. It had a huge swimming pool, and lots and lots of rooms; at least this is how I remember it. My dad decided to give me an inflatable dinghy for Epiphany. By then, I was starting to be suspicious about the existence of the wise men and this made him think that he had to reinforce my beliefs somehow. Thus, on the night of Epiphany, he inflated the dinghy all by himself and, when it was finally done, he was so tired that he fell into the pool along with the boat as he tried to place it there for me to find in the morning. This is by itself a pretty funny story if you think about it, but what really captures my father's tone is the habit he later developed during that summer. I also had a life belt with a sort of t-shirt so that you could put it on like one and the life belt would be around your stomach hanging from this t-shirt kind of thing. The point is that my dad developed a new device by turning the life belt upside down so now the t-shirt would hang from the life belt. Finally, he would place a bucket full of ice cubes with a bottle of champagne inside this sort of floating basket he had created and he would get in the dinghy, laying back, after which he would proceed to spend the whole afternoon floating around the pool drinking champagne while listening to some Beethoven or Tchaikovsky or Chopin or whatever.

During all my childhood my mother worked on Saturday morning so I used to stay with my dad. We would go always to the same coffeehouse in my home town and always have the same breakfast, consisting in a sort of "dulce de leche" [doce de leite in Portuguese] muffin they used to make there and a special kind of chocolate whose name in English I do not know; it is called "submarino" (submarine) in Spanish. What they would do is serve you a tall glass of really hot milk and a bar of dark chocolate, which you would put into the milk at the moment of drinking it. Afterwards, we would perform some errand, visit some bookstore or whatever. The thing is that, while we were in the car, it was examination time. He would either whistle to me some classical piece and I had to give him the name of the piece and its composer or the other way around. When the exam was over he would give me 5 or 6 new pieces for me to learn for the next Saturday. Some people I know now think that this was crazy but I really enjoyed those Saturdays; they were just magical for a little girl. That was my father: He told me facts about classical composers' lives and when I asked him to tell me a story he would tell me Greek myths from "The Iliad" and "The Odyssey" or about the theory of colour (how black would absorb all the light so that it is black, etc, etc). Finally, I started to ask him to tell me "the colour story". I still enjoy reading Greek mythology and listening to classical music.")

Even with Boria out of the picture, the UNSL program quickly gained recognition in Argentina. Armando's academic seed had been planted for the first time. When the military regime succumbed to its own misdeeds, Boria was asked by another small University (UNCPBA of Tandil) to revamp their Information Sciences programme. Again Boria recalled Armando to the task and Armando gladly joined the team. It was here that Armando met Viviana Rubinstein, by then Jorge Boria's wife, in a professional capacity. The organiser of the team, Angel Orbe, was in love with the idea of a Summer School. At great personal expense (in the non monetary sense), Armando took the whole team and other prominent Latin American scientists to Tandil for eight weeks in January of 1983. Armando drove the Keynote speaker of the meeting, Carlos José Pereira de Lucena, who was already at the peak of his career in Software Engineering in Brasil, back to Buenos Aires. On that trip, the collaboration between the two countries, which has had an enormous and lasting impact in Latin America, was born. We cannot (i.e., Viviana, Boria and I) help but smile thinking of poor Carlos, being subjected to the irritating habit of Armando lifting his foot from the gas pedal and almost bringing the car to a halt when he was engrossed in an argument and it was his turn to speak! The trip certainly must have taken more than the normal four hours! It is also common knowledge amongst his friends that it was a bad idea to engage Armando in a serious discussion whilst walking anywhere. When it was his turn to speak, he just stopped walking until he had finished! I used to get very irritated at times and reminded him about the joke concerning, Gerry Ford, former US President, about whom it was unkindly said that he could not walk and chew gum at the same time!

Carlos and Armando gave birth to the Programa Argentino Brasileiro de Informatica, PABI for short. This required the backing of Argentina's government, and that came soon enough, with the election of Argentina's first democratic government later in 1983. Armando was immediately recognised as the ideal man the new government needed, even if at that time he was a business man, with a strong scientific background. (According to Viviana and Boria, he had already made a name for himself as the Leonardo Da Vinci of the twentieth century: an artist, playing piano like an angel, a profound reader, an astronomer, ... a knowledgeable guy! And likeable at that. Boria likes to say of him: "Armando lived like a character in a Russian novel: his was a life to be seen on the screen, rags-to-riches (professionally, that is), larger-than-life life".)

Attracted by Manuel Sadosky's nomination to Argentina's equivalent of the National Science Foundation, he left INFOS S.A. to take up the next major challenge in his life, namely the establishment of a unique adventure in higher education, the Escuela Superior Latinoamericana de Informatica, commonly referred to as ESLAI. It was created by a decree of the Argentine Minister of Science and Technology, and was sponsored by the Intergovernmental Bureau for Informatics (IBI), UNESCO, UNDP, the European Community, and the governments of Italy and France. Each year a selection of 35 students (20 from Argentina and 15 from other Latin American countries) were selected from approximately 500 applicants from all over Latin America. To be admitted to ESLAI, the student should have had two years of an undergraduate course in Exact Sciences, Engineering, Mathematics, or Informatics. The students had to sit an examination on Mathematics, Logic, and English. This examination took place each year on the same day, at all Argentine embassies in Latin America. The result was analysed by the ESLAI Academic Council, which chose the accepted students. The course at ESLAI took another three years, to obtain a Diploma in Informatics. The students lived in a residence belonging to the school and all of them received scholarships.

The students from the first three cohorts did their PhDs at universities like Chalmers (Sweden); Paris XI, Paris Sud, and Grenoble (France); Edinburgh (UK); Illinois (Urbana-Champaign) and Massachusetts (Amherst) (USA); Rome (La Sapienza), Pisa, and Politecnico di Milano (Italy); Ludwig-Maximilians in Munich, and Christian Albrecht in Kiel (Germany). Many of them have positions in well known universities or research centres around the world, for instance: at the École Normale Superieure (Paris), at the University of Paris-Sud, and at the VERIMAG Laboratory – CNRS- (France): at the Universities of Cambridge, Edinburgh and Sussex (UK); at Chalmers University, and at the Technological University of Halmstad (Sweden); at the University of California at Berkeley (USA); at the University of Genoa (Italy); at the Technische Universität München, and at the Forschungsinstitüt für Angewandte Softwaretechnologie, in Munich, (Germany); at the University of La República (Uruguay); and at the University of Buenos Aires, the National University of La Plata, and the University of Córdoba (Argentina).

Teachers at the university included Ugo Montanari (Italy), Carlo Ghezzi (Italy), Gregorio Klimovsky (Argentina), Jean Pierre Peyren (France), Michael Levy (France), Julián Araoz (Venezuela), Lia Oubinha (Argentina), and Roberto Cignoli (Argentina), Jean Raymond Abrial (France), Martin Wirsing (Germany), Helmut Parsch (Germany), Egidio Astesiano (Italy), Joseph Sifakis (France), Philippe Jorrand (France), and Giogio Aussiello (Italy). (No mean list!)

But, because of his involvement with ESLAI, the PABI was suffering. He had committed to organise, jointly with the Brasilian government, twelve summer courses and a software engineering seminar, each with its own published textbook. Five hundred students, one half from each country, would take these classes, and the textbooks would be used in courses across the two countries. This grand vision was being supported wholeheartedly by Brazil, and SADIO was helping in some of the arrangements. Armando again exhibited a characteristic that was a negative side of his personality, lacking in management follow-up of a grand idea: as on a number of occasions afterwards, Armando lacked the interest in following through to make the vision come to life. When he heard that Viviana Rubinstein was travelling to Brasil to attend her cousin's wedding, he made her an offer she could not resist: he would cover the cost of the trip if she would help organise the school. The collaboration grew into a President-Vice President relationship and lasted as long as the democratic government of Alfonsin in Argentina. When Armando found someone who would do the follow up for his ideas, there was nothing he could not accomplish!

(Viviana writes: I looked after the accounting of the PABI. Once, when the finances of the programme were in bad shape, Armando and Gabriel Baum had to travel to Rio from Buenos Aires, normally a three to four hour trip. Viviana bought them a ticket that took them through five cities and lasted eight hours! Armando, a gourmet, a bon-vivant who chose first class, Mont Blancs, champagne and oysters to macaroni and cheese and coach tickets, got wind of this too late. He almost cancelled the trip. But, he came back in a fantastic mood: thanks to the length of the trip, the two had completed three theorems that set the foundation for Armando's, and later Veloso's, Theory of Problems! When he retold this story, as often when he found something just too funny, tears welled in his eyes and laughter shook his prominent belly. There he was, a big Falstaff, merry beyond description because lack of funds had actually funded the initial steps of his research!)

During this period, Armando separated from Alicia and eventually they were divorced. From 1985-6 he was involved with a lady called Graciela (whose surname I do not know). They parted and he 'married' Maria Teresa Borchez. (Armando referred to these relationships as marriages though he did not officially marry anyone after Alicia.) They had a child, Natacha (Nati). Armando had wanted to call her Natajsa, from the Russian, but at this time Argentinians were allowed to name their children according to a prescribed list of allowed names. So, Armando had to settle for Natacha.

It was during this period that I met Armando. Our first encounter was in 1985 at an IBM sponsored seminar in Rio at IBM's Latin American Research facility there. I had been asked to give several of these week long seminars over the years and IBM paid for participants to come from all over South America, though most students were Brasilian. One of the crucial relationships established during this period was with Paulo Veloso, who worked on formal specification (with me, amongst others) at the Departamento de Informática of the Pontifícia Universidade Católica do Rio de Janeiro (DI/PUC) and who eventually became Armando's PhD supervisor.

Armando was the real 'father' of the ESLAI enterprise and many of the students I have talked to remember him and the school with great affection. Unfortunately, the political and economic situation altered for the worse after a change of government in Argentina and the future of the school was very much in doubt. Armando decided to abandon ship and go on leave to PUC in Rio to work with Paulo Veloso. He embarked on a PhD and quickly became a member of the academic staff. He eventually spent ten years in Rio and had several major achievements to his name. His PhD was about relational algebra and motivated by its applications in program derivation. More on this in the following section. In the early 90s, Armando procured some funding that enabled him to hire a secretary. He did the classic thing and fell in love with Marcia Ferreira and their on and off relationship lasted until his death. In fact, Marcia and her two children spent three weeks in Macau with Armando just before he died. And it was Marcia who went to Macau to clear up his personal affairs and to take his body back to Argentina for burial.

At this time, Brasil had a very interesting law. Basically, all IT companies were required to invest 5% of their turnover in research, of which 40% was to be invested in arms length laboratories. This resulted in a lot of funds being available for academic research with relevance to industry. Armando formed a very close relationship with the Director of a telecommunications division of Siemens in Curitiba in the south of Brasil. Armando had already started the Formal Methods Laboratory (Laboratório de Métodos Formais, LMF) to attempt to work with industry in the application of formal methods.

Quoting Armando: "The original intention of the laboratory was the generation of knowledge and its application to practical technological problems, in order to then use the acquired experience as a catalyst for the generation of new knowledge, in an unlimited progression. This commitment was captured graphically in the logotype of the laboratory, an abstraction of the well-known engraving Drawing Hands, by Mauritius Cornelius Escher (1948), in which one hand designs the other recursively.

The laboratory was the main partner of UNU/IIST in its collaboration with the CNPq, the Brazilian National Research Council ....

The rationale leading to the creation of the laboratory (according to Armando) was:

> "The interest in having an environment where data could be gathered and ideas tried out, for the research activities of the Formal Methods Group of the Department of Informatics of the PUC-Rio.
> The necessity of generating critical mass in the area, and
> The urgent need for alternative sources of funding to sustain development of basic research, at a time when the funding from governmental agencies was shrinking due both to local contingencies and to the utilitarian global trend in scientific research.
> Between 1995 and 1998 the laboratory grew fourfold in personnel, almost the same in terms of number of projects with industry, both national and international, as well as some thousands of times in terms of the annual turnover measured in US dollars."

As may be noted from the above, Armando certainly did not lack ambition and vision! He had an almost messianic need to sell formal methods to industry, as did several people in my experience who had spent some years in industry in the earlier parts of their careers and were frustrated by the limited application of scientific and engineering principles in every day software production. A number of people in Curitiba were very sympathetic and wanted to move the technological basis of the company forward. Furthermore, they had serious quality related problems at a time when CMM was just becoming really popular. The relationship between LMF and Siemens was very productive, with work started in a number of areas. There was a large project to build an object oriented environment based on formal methods for software development. There was a large project on software measurement, testing and quality control, built on a scientifically sound basis. And there were many other projects.

Unfortunately, the relationship began to deteriorate because of Armando's lack of attention to project management and the relationship began to sour. And, although he worked to prevent it, he did succumb to the classis mistake of having a 'single customer'. So, when in 1998 the global economy, and that of Brasil in particular, suffered serious traumas as a result of the crisis in Southeast Asia and because Siemens was itself having global difficulties, the relationship collapsed, as did LMF as then constituted. (It actually still exists, but on nothing like the scale seen in 1995-98.) Armando decided that it would be very difficult to start again in Brasil and that perhaps he should try his luck in Europe. He started off at Imperial College with a visiting fellowship I obtained for him (one of several we had used to work together). After 6 months in London, he went to Munich to work in Martin Wirsing's group, where he did some very original work on testing, using epistemological principles as a starting point. Again, there will be more on this in the next section.

He then moved to Lisbon where he worked for Oblog and/or ATX Software. (The changing interrelationships between these companies are too difficult to understand, let alone explain!) Basically, the companies provided software technology and services to one of the biggest financial and industrial groups in Portugal. Originally, there had been an intention to start a reverse engineering business based on transformational principles (see below), but venture capital for this was not procured. Armando worked on a number of projects during this period and eventually proved his point about reverse engineering when the financial group had a serious need for the technology to enable it to move to a web based operation. Armando designed and supervised the construction of a tool that used principles he had developed earlier and combined it with a creative use of slicing techniques. He enjoyed this engineering work enormously.

He became frustrated at not being able to devote himself more to his own research interests or directly to realizing the technical vision he had for a reverse engineering business. When the opportunity to become Director of UNU/IIST arose, he jumped at it. He had been a member of the Board of Governors for some years and then became its Chairman. He felt that the Institute needed redirection, but as Chairman of the Board he had limited leverage to affect change. As Director, he could develop the ambitious aims he thought were necessary for the growth and success of the Institute. He was indeed appointed and took up his post only in early November last year. Until Christmas he was busy settling in and clearing up his affairs in Europe. He really properly started in January when we met in Venice to begin implementing some of his plans. It was there that he had his first heart attack. (The meetings in Venice were part of a plan to put in place a European base for UNU/IIST activities. He had earlier had a courtesy meeting with the mayor of Venice, who had been on the UNU Board, and conceived the idea of the UNU becoming a member of the Venice International University and UNU/IIST using this as a basis for starting an UNU/IIST branch to serve the Middle East, Africa and Eastern Europe, as well as to enable UNU/IIST to participate more easily in EU funded projects. He also had the idea of starting in Venice a research centre on software intensive systems, with the model of the physics centre in Trieste in the back of his mind.)

It seems to have happened after a morning meeting attended by various people to discuss the idea of establishing an international research centre in Venice on the topic of Software Intensive Systems. After the meeting, in mid afternoon, Armando and I, together with Carlo Ghezzi, decided to visit the Scuola Grande di San Rocco to see the Tintorettos. (On the way, we were forced to stop in a café, Pasticceria Tonolo, which Carlo claimed served the best frittelle in Venice! Carlo and I had coffee with our frittelle, but Armando had a prosecco.) The building of the Scuola is large and on that day literally freezing cold.

Being otherwise of such a strong constitution, he first thought that the tightness and pain in his chest and arms was bronchitis brought on by the cold weather in Venice and, in particular, the freezing two hours he had spent in the Scuola. After suffering for two days and attending meetings, he saw a doctor who confirmed that bronchitis was the likely explanation. It was only several days later in Macau when he was still not feeling well that he again saw a doctor who immediately suspected a heart problem. He was stabilized in hospital over one week and then traveled to Hong Kong (under his own steam!) for treatment. This took place on a Tuesday exactly just one day short of two weeks after the initial heart attack. By Thursday, he was traveling home to Macau (again under his own steam) for two weeks' rest. It was 12 days later that he died on his way back to Hong Kong again.

3   The Technical Story

It would be wholly inappropriate to remember Armando without also recollecting his considerable technical achievements. He started his professional life as a scientist and amateur programmer. He spent many years working on software and hardware products in a commercial environment until he became frustrated at the seeming lack of scientific/engineering rigour in his work. He turned to academic software engineering and theory/formal methods to plug this gap. He then realized that the state of software engineering, even as an academic discipline, lacked the rigour he expected, based on his scientific training. He then attempted to ameliorate the situation by resorting to another area of interest and detailed knowledge, i.e., epistemology. In particular, he was a great believer in the work of Rudolf Carnap and the logical positivists, and what they had to say about the language of science. I participated in this work and we adapted Carnap's framework to engineering, in particular, software engineering.

3.1   The Early Commercial Years

During the period 1970-1976, first as programmer and then as director, he worked on the design and development of the Highway Inventory and Traffic Data System (Federal Highway Administration – Argentina). The system administered a huge database with the description of the Argentine road network. The resolution of the events in the network was 10m. The system had, in the time by which the first version was finished, 1.400.000 lines of code.

From 1976 to 1978, at SOFT-LAB S.R.L., he participated in the development of the basic software (operating system, assembly language, text editor, file system, and high-level language) for the Argentine computer lines MCA 3503 and 4503. Then, at INFOS S.A., between 1979 and 1983, he undertook in succession the direction of projects on:

> the design and development of a data acquisition system (including the design of an Intel 8085-based special purpose computer) for a solar energy concentrator for the National Atomic Energy Commission.
>
> the design and development of a Graphic Multiparametric Spectra Manipulator for the tandem linear particle accelerator of the project TANDSAR of the National Atomic Energy Commission – Argentina. (The development and implementation was done on a computer network consisting of a Vax-780, 2 PDP11/34s, a graphics processor and CAMAC data acquisition circuitry.)
>
> the design and implementation of the Integrated Oceanographic System of the ship ARA Puerto Deseado (which belongs to the Argentine National Research Council). It was a real-time control-system (both for navigation and for oceanographic experiments), consisting of a network of 5 HP100 Hewlett-Packard Computers, one special purpose computer, and 300 instruments. The software system had 1.300.000 lines of code.

Armando had a passion for astronomy, amongst many other passions(!). At some point during this period, he obtained a contract for the software to control a new telescope in Argentina. The payment was in hardware. That is, he obtained a twin telescope that was assembled and working at his home in Argentina. He wrote the software for the positioning and tracking. The main issue was to develop the tracking algorithms. He got them using some mathematical transformations but he introduced a bug. When the telescope was pointing to the top the software entered a loop and rotated the telescope *ad infinitum*. This was one early example pointing out to him the importance of software testing.

Yet another project was for the navy in Argentina. The idea was to simulate torpedo attacks. He wrote the soft simulation but when testing the system, he discovered that a torpedo never ever met a ship. After looking and looking he could not find what was wrong. Unfortunately, he had to deliver a demo and the system was still "buggy". Well, then he then decided to fake the demo! The navy officers were at some terminal creating the input and Armando was at another terminal typing the supposed output. Nobody discovered that it was absolutely a fake. Afterwards, with more time at his disposal, he discovered what was wrong. Actually nothing was wrong with the software. It was an input error: the coordinates for the submarine and the torpedo had to have a negative component, otherwise the torpedoes had to fly. Just modifying the input in this way, the output obtained was exactly what he had typed in the fake demo.

3.2   The Years in Rio and LMF

In 1989, Armando embarked on a PhD under the supervision of Paulo Veloso. (I had been working with Paulo since 1977 on formal specification. He is a profound scientific thinker about logic and programming and a rather unacknowledged, but very important contributor to specification theory.) They chose the topic of binary relations as a vehicle for specifying and developing sequential programs. (There was a large community of researchers and material devoted to this topic centred largely on the activities of IFIP Working group 2.1. The calculus of binary relations and issues related to it was also a topic of interest amongst algebraic logicians.)

At this point, a short historical and technical digression is necessary. I will quote and paraphrase extensively from *Fork algebras in algebra, logic and computer science* by Marcelo Frias, another Argentinean who went to Rio in the mid 90s to undertake a PhD under Armando's supervision. The references are from the above book and I will not reproduce them here.

"In 1941 Alfred Tarski [A. Tarski (1941)] introduced the elementary theory of binary relations (ETBR) as a logical formalization of the algebras of binary relations. The elementary theory of binary relations is a formal theory where two different sorts of variables are present. The set *IndVar* = $\{v_1, v_2, v_3, \ldots\}$ contains the so-called *individual variables*, and the set *RelVar* = $\{R,S,T, \ldots\}$ contains the so-called *relation variables*. If we add the *relation constants* 0, 1 and 1' [the empty relation, the universal relation and the identity relation on the underlying set, respectively] to the relation variables and close this set under the unary operators – and ˘ [complement and converse, respectively], and the binary operators +, · and ; [union, intersection and relational composition, respectively], we obtain the set of *relation designations*. Examples of such objects are, for instance, ˘R (to be read 'the *converse* of R') and R;S (to be read 'the *relative product* of R and S'). Atomic formulas are expressions of the form xRy (where x, y are arbitrary individual variables and R is an arbitrary relation designation) or R = S (with R and S arbitrary relation designations). From the atomic formulas, we obtain compound formulas as usual, by closing the atomic formulas under the unary logical constants ¬, $\forall x$, $\forall y$, ..., $\exists x$, $\exists y$ ... (x, y, ... individual variables) and the binary logical constants ∨, ∧, ⇒ and ⇔. We will choose a standard set of logical axioms and inference rules for our theory (see e.g. [H. Enderton (1972), Ch. 2.4]). As the axioms that explain the meaning of the relational symbols 0, 1, 1', –, ˘, +, · and ;, we single out the following sentences in which x, y, z are arbitrary individual variables and R, S, T are arbitrary relation designations. [...]

From the elementary theory of binary relations, Tarski [A. Tarski (1941)] introduced the *calculus of relations* (CR). The calculus of relations is defined as a restriction of the elementary theory of binary relations. Formulas of the calculus of relations are those formulas of the elementary theory of binary relations where no variables over individuals occur. As axioms of the calculus of relations, Tarski chose a subset of formulas without variables over individuals valid in the elementary theory of binary relations. The formulas Tarski chose as axioms are, besides a set of axioms for the logical connectives, the following: [axioms for a Boolean algebra and axioms characterizing ˘ and ; in terms of the other operations.]

... a result due to Korselt and whose proof is included in [L. Löwenheim (1915)] shows that the expressive power of the calculus of relations is that of a proper restriction of first-order logic. The logical counterpart of the calculus of relations – denoted by $L^\times$ in [A. Tarski et al. (1987)] – is equivalent (*equipollent* is the technical term) with a three variable fragment of first-order predicate logic (see [A. Tarski et al. (1987), Ch. 3.9] for a detailed proof of this). If we recall our mission of devising a framework suitable for system specification, such lack of expressiveness has a negative impact since first-order specifications of systems are not likely to have meaning-ful translations into the calculus of relations. In [A. Tarski et al. (1987), §3.4(iv)] Tarski and Givant present the following formula, which is not equivalent to any sentence of the calculus of relations:

$$\forall x \forall y \forall z \forall u \, (u0'x \wedge u0'y \wedge u0'z) \tag{2.4}$$

[0' = $\overline{1'}$, i.e., 0' is the complement of the identity relation.]

One way to convince oneself that this is indeed the case is by attempting to reduce this formula to a relational expression using the definitions of the relational operations. [...] For a more detailed study in the origin of relation algebras and the calculus of relations the reader is referred to [R. Maddux (1998); R. Maddux (1991)] and [C. Brink et al. (1997), Ch. 2]."

Further:

"Fork algebras [...] have their origin as the foundation of a framework for software specification, verification and derivation. In our view, specification languages – as modern graphical notations like UML [G. Booch et al. (1998)] – must allow for a modular description of the different aspects that comprise a system. These aspects include structural properties, dynamic properties, temporal properties, etc. Different formalisms allow us to specify each one of these aspects, namely,

> first-order classical logic for structural properties
> propositional and first-order dynamic logic for dynamic properties,
> different modal logics for temporal properties.

Many of the previously mentioned formalisms have complete deductive systems. Nevertheless, reasoning across formalisms may be diffcult, if not impossible. A possible solution in order to solve this problem consists on finding an amalgamating formalism satisfying at least the following:

> the formalism must be expressive enough to interpret the specification formalisms,
> the formalism must have very simple semantics, understandable by non mathematicians,
> the formalism must have a complete and simple deductive system.

In this book we propose the formalism called *fork algebras* to this end. The formalism is presented in the form of an equational calculus, which reduces reasoning to substitution of equals by equals. The calculus is complete with respect to a very simple semantics in terms of *algebras of binary relations*. Algebras of binary relations, such as the ones to be used in this book, have as domain a set of binary relations on some set (let us say A). Among the operations that can be defined on such domain, consider the following:

> the empty binary relation $\varnothing$,
> complement of a binary relation x with respect to a largest relation E, i.e., $\overline{x}$ – as the complement of x is denoted – is defined as $E\backslash x$,
> union of binary relations – denoted by $\cup$ –, and
> intersection of binary relations – denoted by $\cap$.

Notice that the previous operations are defined on arbitrary sets, independently of whether these are binary relations or not. Actually, a set of binary relations closed under these operations is an example of *set Boolean algebra*. However, there are other operations that operate naturally on binary relations but are not defined on arbitrary sets. Among these we can mention:

the identity binary relation on A – denoted by Id – ,
composition of binary relations – denoted by $\circ$ – , and
transposition of the pairs of a binary relation – denoted by $\overline{}$.

Unfortunately, a class of algebras containing these operations cannot be axiomatized by a finite number of equations [D. Monk (1964)]. [See above re Tarski's CR.] In order to overcome this important drawback, we add an extra binary operation on relations called *fork*. Addition of fork has two main consequences. First, the class of algebras obtained can be axiomatized by a finite (and small) number of equations. Second, addition of fork induces a structure on the domain on top of which relations are built, i.e., rather than being the arbitrary set A, it is a set $A*$ closed under a binary function $*$. The definition of the operation fork (denoted by $\underline{\nabla}$) is then given by:

$$R\underline{\nabla}S = \{\langle x,\, y*z\rangle : xRy \wedge xSz\}$$

[…] Whenever x and y are related via R, and x and z are related via S, x and $y * z$ are related via $R\underline{\nabla}S$. Notice that the definition strongly depends on the function $*$. Actually, the definition of fork evolved around the definition of the function $*$. From 1990 (when the first class of fork algebras was introduced) until now, different alternatives were explored with the aim of finding a framework which would satisfy our needs. In the definition of the first class of fork algebras [P. Veloso et al. (1991)], function $*$ produced true set theoretical pairs, i.e., when applied to values a and b, $*(a, b)$ returned the pair $\langle a,b\rangle$. Mikulás, Sain, Simon and Németi showed in [S. Mikulás et al. (1992); I. Sain et al. (1995)] that this class of fork algebras was not finitely axiomatizable. This was done by proving that a sufficiently complex theory of natural numbers can be interpreted in the equational theory of these fork algebras, and thus leads to a non recursively enumerable equational theory. Other classes of fork algebras were defined, in which $*$ was binary tree formation or even concatenation of sequences, but these were shown to be non finitely axiomatizable too. It was in [M. Frias et al. (1995)a] where the class of fork algebras to be used in this book came up. The only requirement placed on function $*$ was that it had to be injective. This was enough to prove in [M. Frias et al. (1997)b] that the newly defined class of fork algebras was indeed finitely axiomatizable by a set of equations."

This work on fork algebras was the main focus of Armando's technical work in the years from 1989 to 1997. As noted above, the work started with Paulo Veloso and mainly motivated by the problem of program construction. It turned into a kind of technical, mathematical challenge, with some controversy about the 'solution' to the so-called Monk-Tarski problem of finding an extension of CR that was equivalent in expressive power to first order logic and was finitely axiomatisable. Gabriel Baum from La Plata and Marcelo Frias joined the hunt and the project culminated in the ideas proposed in Marcelo's thesis. The 'solution' was not accepted by some, e.g., the Hungarian algebraic logicians who had been working on the problem for years, because it failed a technical requirement for a 'solution'. This was that the operations must be invariant under permutations of the base set on which relations are defined. Fork does not satisfy this property.

Marcelo said recently: "To be completely fair, the Monk-Tarski problem is stated in such a way that most probably there is no solution for it. The fork algebra solution was partial in that the fork operation is not "logical" (a condition in the Monk-Tarski problem). This is why the Hungarians do not accept this as a solution to this problem (they are probably right).

On the other hand, even if this is not a solution, it did generate a lot of noise in the Algebraic Logic community, and the Hungarians wrote at least three papers on fork algebras.

What is definitely true is that Armando and Paulo were the creators of fork algebras, which are still alive and kicking."

By this time, Armando had started working on projects with industry using formal methods and he conceived the idea of a laboratory associated with PUC that would give such work a higher profile and attract greater attention and funding. (It was by no means the first such laboratory at PUC, which has run such operations very successfully for almost two decades.) It was to be called the Laboratório de Métodos Formais (LMF) and included several other academic staff in the Department. There was no doubt, however, that Armando was the driving force. Marcia became the administrative manager of the laboratory and Armando's 'right hand man'. His first projects were on using program transformation methods to reverse engineer programs, in conjunction with Hermann Hausler and his students. These experiments were very successful and the ideas were demonstrated on systems with millions of lines of code. The idea of using transformation technology for this purpose was not that new (e.g., the work at Kestrel), but LMF had a new ingredient to add to it. In the past, transformations had been used to capture the semantics of the programming language in which the code to be translated is written, in terms of the semantics of the target language. Armando's and Hermann's idea was to capture the semantics of the *application*, including the semantics of the language(s) in which it is written. This proved to be a very effective insight. It was also the basis of Armando's later ideas on a reverse engineering business. The difficulty to be overcome in applying these ideas was the labour intensive nature of writing large numbers of transformations each time a different application was tackled. (However, there would be a large stable part if the application was written in a language already tackled before.)

The transformation idea was also exploited in projects building software engineering development environments. In particular, it was observed that executable code generated from (low level) designs by transformational methods instead of compilation might have several advantages:

> the code would be correct by construction with respect to the design,
> any errors observed in the running code (presumably due to requirements problems and not implementation problems!) could be traced back directly to the source in the design because of the direct transformational link. (The use of software libraries militated against this, as this code was not transformationally produced.)

This work on transformational code generation was part of a larger effort to produce an object oriented design environment for the Siemens division in Curitiba. It was called ARTS and consumed much of the resources in the laboratory.

With the spectacular growth of the laboratory, new premises were required. Space was made available by PUC and a lot of the money earned by LMF was invested in refurbishment and fitting out of this space. When the laboratory was opened, there was an official day of celebrations involving some senior guests from around the world.

During this period, the staff in Curitiba realized that their processes were not well defined and that they would come out badly in any CMM like assessment. This became a serious management concern and the Director turned to Armando for help. It was suggested by them that the use of function points as a measure should be a starting point for any attempt at improvement. Armando recoiled from this in horror, rejecting it as scientifically unsound. He conceived a project, MENSURAE, involving some knowledgeable people from the UK, to attack the overall problem of measurement and quality. Part of this work was the development of a formal language to describe business processes (including technical processes).

Armando was expanding the work of the laboratory in various directions, including work on smart card verification and certification for the São Paulo transportation system. But, then came the economic crises of 1998 and Armando's life in Rio came to an end.

3.3 In Europe

3.3.1 Testing and Epistemology

His move to Europe also brought a change of focus in his research. We had been working together for some time on what we had started referring to as the *epistemology of software engineering* (to be described below). In pursuing this work, Armando had come to the conclusion that the basis of software testing was not properly conceived and that modern developments in epistemology about the design and interpretation of experiments could be adapted to provide a scientifically sound framework. He started this work in London and completed it during his stay in Munich, collaborating there with a former student at ESLAI, Victoria Cengarle, who had recently obtained a PhD under the supervision of Martin Wirsing at Ludwig-Maximilians-Universität München. I quote (loosely) from a paper by them, with which I also had some association[1]:

"The *Statement View of Scientific Theories* (in short the Statement View) was developed by Carnap in the 38 years between 1928 and 1966. The version used is based on Carnap's presentation in [2][2], has a slight modification similar to the one proposed by Nagel [17], and is influenced by criticisms and by developments of other logical empiricists such as Mary Hesse [14]. On this background we settled the bootstrap strategy for relating theory and evidence due to Clark Glymour [10, 11]. Moreover, given that we address the Computer Science community, we have also modified the notation.

---

[1] On seeing a draft of this piece, one reader commented that the remainder of this section was very dense and might be boring for many readers. So, I hereby issue a health warning: skip or skim this part if you are not interested in the technical aspects of Armando's later work!

[2] The references are from M.V. Cengarle, A.M. Haeberer, "Specifications, programs, and confirmation". *Proc Workshop on Requirements, Design, Correct Construction, And Verification: Mind The Gaps!* F.A.S.T. GmbH- Munich April 2000. www.fast.de.

In the context of the Statement View, whenever we have an empirically inter-preted[3] theory ST_*, we have two disjoint subtheories of it, a theoretical (uninterpreted) one, whose presentation is $ST_T = (\Sigma_T^{ST}, Ax_T^{ST}))$, and a purely observational one, whose presentation is $ST_O = (\Sigma_O^{ST}, Ax_O^{ST}))$, related by a set of correspondence rules C_{ST}. Therefore, we have two languages generated by the vocabulary of ST_*, the theo-retical one (which we call ST_T) and the observational one (which we call ST_O). Ob-servable facts are stated in ST_O. We refer to such observable facts as *evidence*. The set C_{ST} of correspondence rules provides the only empirical interpretation of ST_T. This requirement preserves the safeness of observational consequences. That is, some theoretical symbols are given empirical interpretation, by the correspondence rules, in terms of the observational symbols. The theoretical symbols whose meaning is not definitionally given by the correspondence rules are not interpreted further. Their properties are given by relating them with the already interpreted theoretical symbols by means of the deduction mechanisms provided by the underlying logic, via the axioms of the theory. This means that there are more symbols in the theoretical lan-guage (which includes the observational language) than there are in the observational language. Therefore, it is easy to see that ST_T outstrips ST_O in expressive power. This difference is due, on the one hand, to the above mentioned 'difference in size' of the corresponding vocabularies, and on the other, and more importantly, to the logic underlying the theoretical and the observational segments of the theory. (The former reflects the ability to create universal laws, whereas the latter allows only so-called *empirical generalizations*, finitary generalizations from finite sets of finite observa-tions.)

When testing theoretical statements against evidence we face two problems. The first of these problems is what relations between observational statements, on the one hand, and theoretical statements, on the other hand, permit statements of the former kind to confirm statements of the latter kind. During the development of Science and the Philosophy of Science, at least four confirmation strategies were proposed, namely, *elimination of theory*, the *hypothetico-deductive method*, the *bootstrap method*, and *probabilistic strategies*. [...] we examine only two of them. First, we briefly describe the hypothetico-deductive strategy (abbreviated to 'HD strategy'), to provide a basis for our critical appraisal of [other specification based] approach[es]. Later, we base our proposed method for verification and validation testing on the bootstrap strategy. This first problem is the issue early work by Marie-Clude Gaudel, amongst others, tries to address with, for instance, her *exhaustive test set* and her *regularity hypotheses*.

To grasp the second problem, notice that there are no constraints on the logic un-derlying the theoretical segment, whilst the universal quantifier of the logic underly-

---

[3] Here 'interpreted' is related to the usual logical notion of interpretation (assigning models to theories). The difference in usage here is that this use by Carnap describes what would be called a partial interpretation in logic, assigning meanings in a structure to **some** of the sym-bols in the language of the theory. The 'some' in this case is that fragment of the language used to describe observations. Hence, it will act as a constraint on interpretations of scientific theories by constraining models of the theory to those which have the 'correct' observational part. So, not all models of the scientific theory will be allowed, but only those that reflect ob-servational phenomena correctly.

ing the observational segment is constrained to be of finite domain, i.e., equivalent to a generalised conjunction. The problem of how to 'lift' from the confirmation of a hypothesis by a single experiment (or a finite set of them), its confirmation for all the cases, is a problem of induction [3, 15]. Scientists are accustomed to relying on the regularity of natural phenomena for carrying out such induction. In Gaudel's proposal this issue is addressed by the so-called *uniformity hypotheses*.

In this paper we address only the first of these two problems. The term confirmation is not used here as meaning 'the experiment entails that this hypothesis is true on the basis of that theory,' it is used just in the sense of 'the experiment did not refute this hypothesis on the basis of that theory.'

We have a scientific (empirically interpreted) theory ST_*, presented by a presentation $ST = (\Sigma^{ST}, Ax^{ST})$ (a formal specification, for instance), a hypothesis H stated in the theoretical language L_T^{ST}, which we want to test w.r.t. the background theory ST, and evidence E^* stated in the observation language L_O^{ST}.

The question is, in Clark Glymour's words [10], *[: : :] how can evidence stated in one language confirm hypotheses stated in a language that outstrips the first? The hypotheses of the broader language cannot be confirmed by their instances, for the evidence, if framed in the narrower tongue, provides none. Consistency with the evidence is insufficient, for an infinity of incompatible hypotheses may obviously be consistent with the evidence, and the same is true if it is required that the hypotheses logically entail the evidence.*

In the HD strategy, first the hypothesis H in question and the background theory ST are used to derive a prediction in terms of an evidence E, and then it must be determined whether or not the prediction holds. The hypothesis H is stated partly in the theoretical language and partly in the observational one; the background theory ST_* is an interpreted theory containing its theoretical part, its observational part, and its correspondence rules; finally the evidence must obviously be stated in the observational language. A HD schema is a triple $\langle ST_*, H, E \rangle$ where ST_*, H, and E are as in our scenario above, and the following three conditions hold: (i) ST_* and H are mutually consistent, (ii) ST_*, H w E, and (iii) E is not derivable from ST_*. The reason for condition (i) is obvious, a hypothesis inconsistent with a theory cannot be confirmed or disconfirmed on its basis. What condition (ii) states is the heart of the strategy, i.e., the theory ST_* together with H must entail the evidence E. Condition (iii) prevents the confirmation (or disconfirmation) by E of any irrelevant H on the basis of a theory ST_*. The outstanding problems of the HD strategy are that, first, E can never confirm any consequence of ST_*; second, if H is confirmed by E w.r.t. ST_*, then so is $H \wedge \varphi$, where φ is any sentence whatsoever that is consistent with $H \wedge ST_*$, and third, if E^* is true and not valid and φ is any consistent sentence such that φ does not follow from E^*, then φ is confirmed by E^* w.r.t a true theory (namely $(\varphi \rightarrow E^*)$). The first difficulty might be tolerated were it not for the other two; together, they make the HD account untenable. Clark Glymour provided an alternative structural account of confirmation [10, 11] and also showed that attempts to save the HD strategy by adding additional constraints only leads to other disasters [9].

[...]

Bootstrap testing schemata were originally developed by Glymour in [10, 11] and are based on ideas of Carnap, Reichenbach, and Weyl. Here they are presented just for specifications over *existential equational logic EEQ⁺*.

Let $\mathcal{A} = \langle A, \leq \rangle$ be an algebra with a natural order. Let $T_T^{EEQ^+}$ be an equation or a system of equations, let H be an equation (or inequality), and let both be mutually consistent and stated in the theoretical language.

Let $E = \{\varepsilon_j: j \in J\}$ be a set of variables, and let $E^* = \{\varepsilon^*_j: \varepsilon^*_j \in A, j \in J\}$ be a set of values for the variables in E; these values are *observations* and constitute the *evidence*. Let C_T be a set of axioms or *correspondence rules* containing both theoretical and, non-vacuously, observation symbols. Let moreover the set of values E, once reinterpreted by the set of correspondence rules, be consistent with H and $T_T^{EEQ^+}$.

Bootstrap testing schemata are triples $\langle T_*, H, E^* \rangle$, where T_* is an empirically interpreted theory, H the hypothesis to be tested w.r.t. this theory, and E^* the evidence which can refute [or confirm] H w.r.t T_*. In general, to be considered a bootstrap testing schema, $\langle T_*, H, E^* \rangle$, must satisfy conditions (i) to (iv) below. The original proposal by Glymour included three schemata, each one with a variant for non-determinism, that differ only in what condition (iii) below states, as well as two schemata related to the concept of 'degree of confirmation,' a schema using Shafer's belief functions and a Bayesian one.

[The paper discusses mainly the first of these.]

Schema I. Given $\langle T_*, H, E^* \rangle$, for each $x \in Evar(H)$ [The set $Evar(U)$ of *essential variables* of U is the set of those in U that also occur in any theory equivalent to U.] let $T_x < T$ be such that:

i. T_x determines x as a function of a set of variables indexed by I_x, which is a subset of $E = \{\varepsilon_j: j \in J\}$ denoted by $x = f_{T_x}(C^T(\varepsilon_j : j \in I_x \wedge I_x \subseteq J))$. (Notice that we denote by f_{T_x} the function (determined by subtheory T_x) which assigns a value to the essential variable x as a function of the $\{\varepsilon_j : j \in I_x \wedge I_x \subseteq J\}$ translated by the set of correspondence rules C_T.)

ii. The set of values for the variables in $Evar(H)$ given by
$$x^* = f_{T_x}(C^T(\varepsilon^*_j : j \in I_x \wedge I_x \subseteq J))$$ satisfies H.

iii. There is no (in)equation K with $Evar(K) \subset Evar(H))$ such that $H,;\&T$ w K and $K, \&T$ w H. ($\&T \cong \bigcup_{x \in Evar(H)} T_x$)

iv. For all $x \in Evar(H)$, there is no (in)equation K with $Evar(K) \subset Evar(T_x)$ such that $H \cup T_x < K$.

If these conditions are met, E^* is said to provide a *positive test* of H w.r.t. T. The motivation for the conditions above is as follows:

Condition (i). The requirement that a value be determined for each quantity occurring essentially in H reflects a common prejudice against theories containing quantities that cannot be determined from the evidence. Given $\langle T_*, H, E^* \rangle$, when values for the basic quantities occurring in H have not been determined from the evidence E^* using some theory T_*, then E^* and the relevant fragment of T_* do not of themselves provide reason to believe that those basic quantities are related as H claims them to be.

Condition (ii). Obvious.

Condition (iii). Suppose there exists an (in)equation K such that $Evar(K) \subset Evar(H)$, $H, \&T$ w K and $K, \&T$ w H. Let $y \in Evar(H)$, $y \notin Evar(K)$. This means that y is essential to H, but not to H in conjunction with $\&T$. In other words, y could take any value, independent of the evidence $\{\varepsilon_j^* : j \in I_y \wedge I_y \subseteq J\}$. Therefore, the evidence E^* and the method $\{x = f_{T_x}(C^T(\varepsilon_j : j \in I_x \wedge I_x \subseteq J))\}_{x \in Evar(H)}$ of computing quantities in *Evar(H)* from the evidence would fail to test the constraints H imposes on y. Thus, a significant component of what H says would go untested.

Condition (iv). Consider the theory $T : \{x = y; c = d\}$ and the hypothesis $H : x = y$ with $E = \{x,y,c,d\}$. For simplicity, and because the theoretico-observational distinction is not relevant for this discussion, let us suppose that the correspondence rules are, in this case, identity functions (i.e., we identify observational and theoretical variables). The set *Evar(H)* is $\{x,y\}$, and a positive test of H w.r.t. T is any set $E^* = \{x^*,y^*,c^*,d^* : x^*=y^*\}$, because, applying conditions (i) to (iv), (i.e., the schema above), $T_x: x = x$ and $T_y: y=y$. This means that whatever values c and d take, the hypothesis $H : x = y$ will not be refuted w.r.t. theory T provided the evidence satisfies $x^*=y^*$. Notice that a $T"_x : x = y+(c-d)$ is rejected by condition (iv) because there exists $K : y = y+c-d$ with $Evar(K) = \{y,c,d\}$ included in $Evar(T"_x) = \{x,y,c,d\}$ such that $H \cup T'_x$ is equivalent to K. If we eliminate condition (iv) and, therefore, accept $T"_x: x = y+(c-d)$, then the evidence $E^* = \{x^*,y^*,c^*,d^* : x^* = y^* \wedge c^* \neq d^*\}$ will refute $H : x = y$ although T does not establish any link between variables x and y, on the one hand, and c and d, on the other.

[...]"

The rest of the paper, and related unpublished papers, including a tome of 100 pages with all the details, outline how the other Glymourian schemas differ from the above and how the ideas may be applied to software testing and validation, going beyond the limitations in other approaches alluded to by Armando in his analyses. The point of the above lengthy quote and summary was not to try and explain a very difficult technical development in a very short space, but rather to illustrate a number of important points about Armando. Firstly, Armando knew intimately the modern literature of epistemology and could call upon the ideas of various members of this community and explain the sometimes subtle differences in ideas and approaches. Secondly, he was not afraid to tackle technically difficult developments. Finally, he was able to understand where and how the ideas about science might find application in software engineering. (As to the last point, perhaps his experiences early in his career with astronomy and torpedoes might have prepared him well for the exploration of the discipline of software testing!) It would be a real loss to the scientific community if some of these papers did not eventually see the light of day.

3.3.2 The Epistemology of Software Engineering

Finally, I would like to take the opportunity to briefly describe some work that was dear to Armando's heart for well over a decade, what was referred to above as the *epistemology of software engineering*. He was disturbed, as were many of us, at the lack of a coherent framework of ideas supporting the subject of software engineering. However, unlike most of us, he had the arsenal with which to attack the problem, i.e., the Carnapian approach and its derivatives. (One of the main criticisms of the Carnapian approach by scientists was that practicing scientists did not work normally as Carnap idealized it. When I pointed out to him that, unlike science, engineering is a normative discipline (one is licensed as an engineer to follow prescriptive rules), Armando's doubts disappeared).

The beginnings of an explanation of the Carnapian approach are contained at the beginning of the segment on testing, referred to as the *Statement View*. In our study of this approach, we came to a deep understanding of it and its associated criticisms and achievements. We brought to it a fresh eye and we felt that we were able to rebut some of the criticisms of it by scientists and philosophers, by drawing on a discipline they were largely unaware of, i.e., computer science!

For example, one of the challenges to Carnap, which neither he nor his followers were able to overcome, was the provision of a crucial example to demonstrate the necessity of theoretical symbols and, therefore, the theoretical level of discourse. (The claim was not that the theoretical level was not useful, but that it was not *necessary*.) Of course, we have been familiar with the crucial example for many decades: the crucial difference between *termination* and *halting*. Because of what the halting problem tells us, we cannot design experiments to test whether a program (whose behaviour we can observe, in the sense of science) halts on some input or not, as we might have to wait forever for a negative answer. This is not a proper experiment. However, with a termination argument at the theoretical level of discourse, we can possibly predict how much time is required for a particular program to halt on some specific input and then we can design a (finite) experiment to test the hypothesis that the program will indeed halt on that input by executing the program on that input and waiting the requisite time (and a bit, just to make sure). We will then have either confirmation or a refutation. Clearly, without termination arguments, we cannot design the experiment. We assert that this is the answer to the question to Carnap about the crucial evidence. (We leave it to scientists to find a purely scientific example!)

Another challenge to Carnap was presented in the form of the so-called Ramsay sentence. The idea was that, if one were given a theory using theoretical and observational symbols, one could deskolemize the sentences and remove the theoretical symbols from the formula(e). What was not clear to the proponents of this challenge was that this deskolemization could only be done by using (at least weak) second order variables and quantifiers. Hence, there were still 'anonymous' theoretical terms in the theory. Moreover, crucially for engineering, these anonymous terms were the key to an understanding of the process of engineering. A design or requirement might use symbols about a hypothetical posit (the entity to be built) describing artifacts that did not yet exist. The process of realization might be described as deskolemizing the description and then finding witnesses for the second order variables using expressions in a language describing already existing artifacts, i.e., telling us how to build the hypothetical posit from known ingredients.

I want to close with one of Armando's famous diagrams describing the software engineering process, defining (not just by illustration, but by defining scientifically/mathematically everything that appeared in the diagram) the beginnings of the software engineering framework he had been looking for. Armando spent hours creating diagrams to illustrate ideas or designs, on the principle that a picture is worth a thousand words. Well, given the time he spent, perhaps several thousand words would not have cost more!

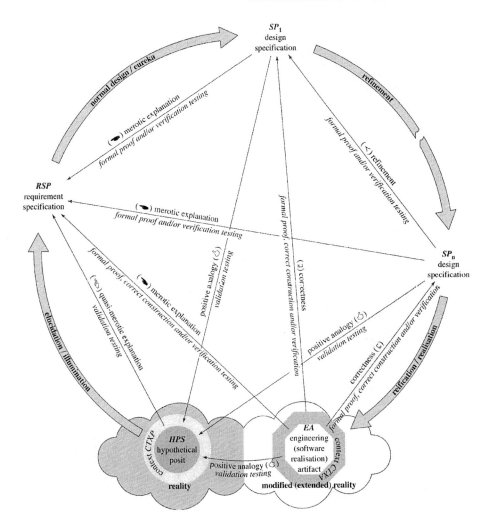

The diagram (and you are not seeing the full glory of Technicolor!) illustrates the software engineering process, its constituents and the relationships involved.

Perhaps the first matter to emphasize is that requirements and designs are theoretical artifacts, whilst the hypothetical posit and the engineering artefact (and their contexts) are at the observational level. (Of course, the former is only hypothetically observable!)

Some elements of the diagram should be familiar and others are not. There is no space to explain all the elements, but some guidance might be useful. (Otherwise, readers are referred to our ICSE'00 paper.) We have the usual elements of such a diagram:

> unformalised requirements, called the *hypothetical posit*, and referring to the conception motivating the construction of a new artefact, in the context of the posited reality in which it is to be embedded;

a formalized requirements specification, which may or may not completely separate what is to be built from the context in which it will function (and different requirements methods take different stances about this separation);

various abstract designs, the first of which is derived from the requirements, and which define what is to be built;

a realization of what is built as an abstract machine (misnamed for our purposes, as it exists in the observed world!), combining the resulting software, and the platform on which it is executed, in the context of the changed reality required to make it work.

Some of the relationships are also familiar: refinement and correctness. Some others are not so familiar and require some discussion/clarification:

Explanation is a term borrowed from epistemology and is used in the same sense: some theory providing the basis for explaining some observed phenomenon. Here, an *explanation* is a formal demonstration (in the framework of the Statement View) with the form:

$$\frac{\{some\ antecedent\ conditions\},\ \{some\ interpreted\ theories\}}{explanandum}$$

Above the line we have the *explanans*, consisting in some contingent conditions defining the specific context (e.g., experimental details, properties of the apparatus being used, environmental conditions, etc) and the scientific theories on which the explanation is based. The constituents of an explanation must satisfy the following logical (the first 3) and empirical (the 4th) *conditions of adequacy*: the explanandum must be a logical consequence of the explanans; the explanans must contain general laws, and these must actually be required for the derivation of the explanandum; the explanans must have empirical content, i.e., it must be capable, at least in principle, of test by experiment or observation; the sentences constituting the explanans must be true. In the diagram above, designs must explain, in this sense, the requirements. And realizations and their context must explain the requirements as well. The relationship between the hypothetical posit and the requirements specification is called a *pseudo-explanation* because the former is not formal, so the essential notion of proof cannot be applied. Note that all explanations 'point' to the requirements! in a very real sense, this 'incompatibility in direction' of explanation relationships, between the hypothetical posit, on the one hand, and the various designs and realizations, on the other, *constitutes the essential problem of engineering*.

In relation to intuition, we have the following from [Hem48]: *"Many explanations which are customarily offered, especially in pre-scientific discourse, lack this predictive character, however. Thus, it may be explained that a car turned over on the road 'because' one of its tires blew out while the car was travelling at high speed. Clearly, on the basis of just this information, the accident could not have been predicted, for the explanans provides no explicit general laws by means of which the prediction might be effected, nor does it state adequately the antecedent conditions which would be needed for the prediction."*

We would accept that the antecedent conditions $\{s_i\}_{1 \leq i \leq k}$ and the theories $\{sT_j\}_{1 \leq j \leq r}$ must be combined in a particular way to produce an explanation, be it some form of valid reasoning, be it some kind of logico-mathematical structure; so, we will write our scheme of explanation as

$$\Xi\left(\{s_\iota\}_{1\leq\iota\leq\kappa},\{{}_{\mathcal{S}}T_\varphi\}_{1\leq\varphi\leq\rho}\right)\Rightarrow E \quad (\mathcal{E})$$

where $\Xi_{()}$ represents the "application" of such a structure and $\Rightarrow$ is the symbol for explanation.

On the other hand, let us analyse the engineering artefact and its context $EA + CTXA$. Let us denote this expression by $_{CTXA}\{EA\}$, or simply $\{EA\}$, when there is no need to explicitly refer to the context.

The engineering artefact is usually a composite *system*

$$_{CTXA}\{EA\} = \underset{CTXA}{\Sigma}\left(EA_1^\Sigma,...,EA_m^\Sigma\right) \ C$$

Here, Σ denotes the structure[4] of the composition, which from $\{EA_1^\Sigma,...,EA_m^\Sigma\}$ yields $_{CTXA}\{EA\}$. In software engineering, $\Sigma()$ denotes compositional mechanisms, synchronising devices such as *contracts* [Fia99]. We qualified the composition symbol with the context for (we hope!) obvious reasons. In the contracts approach to co-ordination and composition, the context of such co-ordination imposes restrictions on the behaviour of the co-ordinated components.

An *engineering artefact* (in the context of a given framework produced by an instance of the Statement View, where ST is the set of the theories underlying our engineering and therefore, pertinent to our explanation) is an entity denoted by a symbol of the observational language that is the result of a constructive (engineering) activity. It must be connected with symbols in the theoretical language (obviously via correspondence rules). These symbols in the theoretical language are part of an extension of ST by means of symbols, which need a manufacturing process to have empirical interpretation[5].

RSP can be seen as the predicted behaviour of an object (the engineering artefact to be) which will be constructed and for which there is a symbol in an extension of the (language of the) pertinent theories of the science underlying our engineering together with an appropriate correspondence rule. Now, let us assume that an explanation for RSP has the form $\mathcal{E}$.

Notice hat the process we have in mind for devising a new engineering artefact is as follows. We have a requirement for a new artefact RSP. Therefore, we construct an extension of our underlying theoretical language (belonging to our underlying science and to the already existing engineering discipline) with the necessary symbols, etc., to enable us to show that what RSP describes (at this point only an *hypothetical posit HSP* and its context) is scientifically possible and that (if the status of our current technology makes its construction viable) the resulting engineering artefact EA will be in a positive analogy with HSP, i.e., $HSP \ \dot{o} \ EA$. Then, we construct EA, through a process of design and reification, which adds detail to the above said extension. Thus, at the end we have an artefact EA, but we have also constructed an explanation $\mathcal{E}$, because if we have constructed EA as C, then we have also extended the theoretical language with symbols relating each one of the components of EA via a correspondence rule, and, moreover, we have also defined a new correspondence rule $c(\Xi,\Sigma)$. Therefore, because we have correspondence rules and corresponding theoretical symbols for each one of the components, and we have for each composi-

---

[4] Here, we use the symbol Σ to denote composition due to the Greek word for compound, συνθετος (synthetos).

[5] This is called design, construction and deployment!

tion Σ, a theoretical construction Ξ, we can say that $EA+CTXA \blacktriangleleft RSP$, because $\mathcal{E}$, C and there exist a set of appropriate correspondence rules, including one $c_{(RSP, EA)}$. Thus, $\blacktriangleleft$ is based on explanation, $EA+CTXA \blacktriangleleft RSP$ means that the construction of the explanation of RSP was driven by the particular constructive process for EA, constructed from its parts and the explanations for its atoms (or the already accepted $\blacktriangleleft$s, for existing components with already existing corresponding theoretical symbols and correspondence rules). Thus, we will call $\blacktriangleleft$ a *merotic explanation*[6]. Notice that often, we do not use explicitly the induced explanation $\mathcal{E}$, and we just write $EA+CTXA \blacktriangleleft RSP$ and say that *EA explains RSP*. **Unfortunately, this use is misleading and leads to confusion amongst gullible amateurs/craftsman who, forgetting that some process, such as the one outlined above, is underpinning engineering construction, talk about *intuition, art,* etc.**

Traceability is often quoted as an important aspect of SE. In our framework, it is easy to see why this is the case. Explanation is facilitated if we have traceability. As we will see, the greater the level of traceability, the less burdensome will be the process of constructing explanations.

Traceability is an asymmetric and transitive binary relation between two artefacts in SW development pertaining to the ability to relate structural elements of one to those of the other so as to record how one design is derived from another.

Positive analogy is a relation between two entities ... consisting of a map between the two underlying ontologies (an interpretation between languages, in the sense used in specification theory), which correlates positive (in the sense of essential and not non-negative) properties of the source of the mapping with the positive properties of the target. We call the source an *iconic* model of the target. (Think of the planetary model of atoms.)"

The diagram is also annotated with various techniques and processes, which we will not detail here, but the concepts are given proper definitions and their roles can be explained, in the sense described above, on the basis of the defined framework. One of the interesting outcomes is a formal explanation of why validation testing is necessary throughout the design and realization process. For example, a refinement step may be correct and explain the requirements, but may still not be acceptable, as refinement introduces new details, corresponding to new properties of the abstract artefact that were not derivable from the abstract specification and therefore contradict the client's view of what is acceptable. (The requirements are themselves an 'abstraction' of the hypothetical posit and its context and therefore using it as the basis for development may not give us complete confidence about the result. Of course, we have no choice but to use the requirements specification as the basis of development, but we must be correspondingly careful.)

Such frameworks were intended by Carnap to formalize the assumptions and processes being used in some approach to science and our ambition, Armando's and mine, was to establish an acceptable framework of such a kind. Towards the end, Armando started looking at Turing computability from the epistemological point of view, hoping to see what a framework based on the distinctions between theoretical and observational languages might add to the accepted ideas about computability.

We had a lot of fun doing this work and felt like we were creating something new, interesting and, we felt, profoundly useful (at least to us)! Unfortunately, this ambi-

---

[6] From the Greek $\mu\varepsilon\rho o\varsigma$ (meros) part, piece.

tion is likely to remain unfulfilled, as the epistemological engine driving the enterprise is no longer in place.

4 Final Thoughts

On that fateful Tuesday morning, I was sitting at breakfast and awaiting the usual call from Armando. We had been speaking more or less every day, and sometimes more than once a day, about plans, tasks, and opportunities. He was still less than two weeks beyond his operation in Hong Kong and was already planning a trip to Shanghai for that Thursday to meet the mayor on UNU/IIST business. When the expected call did not come, I had this fleeting thought that something must be wrong for Armando not to have called. When I received an email 3 hours later from Michel Wermelinger in Lisbon that he had heard that Armando had died, I went into a kind of shock, as did many of his friends and family when hearing the news. The news of his death flashed around the world at a speed that seemed unreal.

Most mornings at breakfast I still have this vague feeling that something is amiss and that the expected call is coming any moment. I fully expect one day to receive such a call from Armando[7], wherever he is, ready to catch up on news, plan the next big project or initiative or just gossip about life and the universe ...

Acknowledgement

I would like to thank the various people who shared with me information about Armando and his life.

References

M. Frias. *Fork algebras in algebra, logic and computer science*. World Scientific 2002 (Advances in Logic, Vol. 2)

A. M. Haeberer, T. S. E. Maibaum. "Scientific rigour, an answer to a pragmatic question: a linguistic framework for software engineering". *Proc ICSE 2001 - 23rd International Conference on Software Engineering* Toronto. IEEE Computer Society Press, 2001.

M. V. Cengarle, A. M. Haeberer. "A formal approach to specification-based black-box testing". *Workshop on Modelling Software System Structures in a Fastly Moving Scenario*. June, 2000. Santa Margherita Ligure, Italia. *Proc of the...*
www.disi.unige.it/person/FerrandoE/MSSSworkshop.

M. V. Cengarle, A. M. Haeberer. "Specifications, programs, and confirmation". *Proc Workshop on Requirements, Design, Correct Construction, And Verification: Mind The Gaps!* F.A.S.T. mbH- Munich April 2000. www.fast.de.

A. M. Haeberer, T. S. E. Maibaum. "The Very Idea of Software Development Environments - A Conceptual Architecture for the ARTS Environment Paradigm". *International Conference on Automated Software Engineering* (ASE'98). Havaii, 1998.

M. V. Cengarle, A. M. Haeberer. "Towards an epistemology-based methodology for verification and validation testing". *Technical Report 0001*, Ludwig-Maximilians-Universität München, Institut für Informatik, January 2000
(www.pst.informatik.uni-muenchen.de/bibtex/bibtex.html).

---

[7] Completely independently, Viviana sent me an email as I was composing this conclusion that stated a very similar premonition!

UNU and UNU/IIST

Zhou Chaochen

The United Nations University
International Institute for Software Technology
P.O.Box 3058, Macau

Abstract. This Colloquium is to celebrate the 10th anniversary of the
United Nations University, International Institute for Software Technology (UNU/IIST), and this essay is to brief readers about UNU and
UNU/IIST. UNU is the only university of the United Nations. UNU/IIST
is a research and training center of UNU with a mission to strengthen
the capabilities of developing countries in software technology.

1   United Nations University (UNU)

The establishment of UNU was proposed in 1969 by the then UN Secretary-
General, Mr. U. Thant. In 1973 the UN General Assembly adopted the UNU
Charter and the UNU headquarters commenced its operation in 1975 in Tokyo,
Japan.

UNU is an academic institution within the UN systems, and has four key
roles:

- an international community of scholars;
- a bridge between UN and the international academic community;
- a think-tank for UN; and
- a capacity builder, particularly for developing countries.

The mission of UNU is formulated as:

> "to contribute, through research and capacity building, to efforts to
> resolve the pressing global problems that are the concern of the United
> Nations, its Peoples and Member States."

UNU has evolved considerably over the past quarter century from its initial
three programmes to a global network of thirteen research and training centers
and programmes (RTC/Ps). They are:

1. World Institute for Development Economics Research in Helsinki, Finland
2. Programme for Biotechnology in Latin America and the Caribbean in Cara-
   cas, Venezuela
3. Institute for New Technologies in Maastricht, the Netherlands
4. Institute for Natural Resources in Africa in Accra, Ghana
5. International Institute for Software Technology in Macao, China
6. Leadership Academy in Amman, Jordan

B.K. Aichernig and T. Maibaum (Eds.): Formal Methods ..., LNCS 2757, pp. 26–33, 2003.

7. Institute of Advanced Studies in Tokyo, Japan
8. International Network on Water, Environment and Health in Ontario, Canada
9. Programme on Comparative Regional Integration Studies in Bruges, Belgium
10. Food and Nutrition Programme for Human and Social Development in Ithaca, United States
11. Initiative on Conflict Resolution and Ethnicity in Ulster, United Kingdom
12. Geothermal and Fisheries Training Programme in Reykjavik, Iceland
13. Initiative on Science and Technology for Sustainability in Kwangju, Republic of Korea

Within the current two broad programme areas of *Peace and Governance* and *Environment and Sustainable Development*, the UNU headquarters and thirteen RTC/Ps identify their main thematic areas and conduct their research and postgraduate training projects. UNU does not have students, but offers MSc and PhD internship.

UNU is financed by the income from the UNU Endowment Fund and also by the operating and project contributions. The UNU Endowment Fund includes donations from member states of UN which are earmarked for individual units of UNU.

Please visit the UNU web site (http://www.unu.edu) for more information.

2   International Institute for Software Technology (UNU/IIST)

2.1   Mission and Programme

UNU/IIST is a research and training center of UNU. The official agreements to establish UNU/IIST were signed by UNU, the Governor of Macao and the Governments of China and Portugal on 12 March 1991. They contributed US$30 million to UNU/IIST through the UNU Endowment Fund. According to the agreements, Macao has further provided generous support in form of special operating contributions for 1991-1993, as well as temporary and permanent premises of UNU/IIST, furniture and fixtures, and subsidy of trainee accommodation.

UNU/IIST commenced its operation on 2 July 1992. Prof. Dines Bjørner was the founding director.

The mission of UNU/IIST as defined in its Statute is to assist developing countries in meeting needs and in strengthening capabilities for education, research and development of software technology.

Software technology is a wide field, while UNU/IIST is a small institute with seven to eight academic staff. We must have an institutional focus in order to generate a reasonable impact.

At present UNU/IIST research focuses on formal techniques. Formal techniques encompass both a scientific foundation for software engineering, and also techniques and tools that can be used in industry. Formal techniques have been taught in universities in developed countries, and adopted by industry there to complement traditional techniques, in order to develop medium and large scale systems and also safety critical systems. People believe formal techniques can fundamentally influence future software practice if we keep educating students and engineers for this.

Education capacity should be at the center of capacity building of developing countries. In developing countries, university computer science curriculum urgently needs to be created or updated, and computer science courses needs to be introduced or upgraded. UNU is also a university. Therefore universities in developing countries are our major constituency, and computer science curriculum development becomes another focal point of the UNU/IIST programme.

In summary, the UNU/IIST current programme is

> *"to assist developing countries in building up capabilities for education, research and development of software technology, focusing on formal techniques and university computer science curriculum."*

2.2   Institutional Structure

UNU/IIST has a Board which is entrusted by the UNU Council with the authority and responsibility for the governance of the institute. The Board formulates the principles and policies to govern the activities and operations of UNU/IIST and to ensure the attainment of the highest levels of scientific excellence. It also adopts and reviews the programme and budget of the institute. The current Board members are

1. Chairman: Prof. Armando Haeberer, Argentina
2. Vice-Chairman: Prof. Mathai Joseph, India
3. Prof. Ibrahim Eissa, Egypt
4. Dr. Gerard Huet, France
5. Prof. Iu Vai Pan, Macao
6. Prof Zohar Manna, United States
7. Prof. Pedro Veiga, Portugal
8. Dr. Wu Yingjian, China
9. Prof. J.A. van Ginkel (ex-officio), UNU Rector
10. Prof. Zhou Chaochen (ex-officio), UNU/IIST Director

The ex-members of the UNU/IIST Board include Prof. Dines Bjørner (ex-officio), Prof. Mario Nascimento Ferreira, Prof. Ivan M. Havel, Prof. Ji Fushen, Dr. Gilles Kahn, Prof. Kesav V. Nori, Prof. Margarita M. Pena, Dr. J. Soromenho-Ramos, Dra. Ana Regina Cavalcanti da Rocha, Prof. Hcrito Gurgulino de Souza (ex-officio), Prof. Maurice Tchuente and Prof. Zhou Ligao.

At present UNU/IIST has the following academic staff:

1. Bernhard Aichernig
2. Chris George

3. He Jifeng
4. Dang Van Hung
5. Tomasz Janowski
6. Zhiming Liu (July 2002)
7. Zhou Chaochen

The former UNU/IIST academic staff are Dines Bjørner, Cornelis Adam Middelburg, Richard Moore, Soren Prehn and Xu Qiwen. UNU/IIST personnel also includes eight administration staff and 10-20 trainees and visitors at any time. UNU/IIST trainees usually stay at UNU/IIST for a period of 3-12 months to do project under supervision of UNU/IIST academic staff.

3 UNU/IIST Projects

UNU/IIST has had 3 kinds of projects:

1. Research and advanced development projects;
2. Training projects; and
3. Local IT projects

3.1 Research and Advanced Development Projects

The objective of UNU/IIST research and advanced development projects is to:

- contribute to the international research community and develop UNU/IIST research excellence; and
- train professionals from developing countries in research and application of advanced software techniques.

At present UNU/IIST has the following 5 research and advanced development projects.

1. Formalising UML and object-oriented programming.
   This project aims to develop a method to support the formal use of UML in object-oriented software development, including formal definitions of the modelling units in UML, linking different models used at different stages, and defining relational semantics for object-oriented programming languages and algebraic properties of object-oriented programs.

2. Co-design of mixed hardware/software systems.
   It attempts to provide a tool-based design technique in support of design of mixed hardware/software systems, including models of the hardware description language, Verilog, tools such as interactive simulator, Verilog synthesiser (from Verilog to netlists), hardware compiler (from occam to verilog), implementation of communication protocols, and applications for digital signal processing and other asynchronous integrated circuit design.

3. Specification and design of hybrid systems.
   This will adopt the notation of the Duration Calculus (DC) in specifying
   and reasoning about real-time features of embedded computer systems. The
   development process is associated with various well-known formalisms (such
   as CSP and state-based specification notations). We will link Hybrid CSP
   (CSP+DC) with timed programming languages, emphasise applications to
   formalise the script language SMILE and communication protocols used in
   multi-media communication, and develop tools based on SPIN, DCVALID
   and the DC Model Checker.

4. Formal techniques for software development.
   The project aims to help institutions and enterprises in developing countries
   improve their capacity for software development through training their staff
   at UNU/IIST and through jointly developing requirements and design specifications.

   As part of this project, a continuing activity will be the further development
   of the RAISE (Rigorous Approach to Industrial Software Engineering) tools.
   In particular, a tool to provide a theorem proving capability through translation to PVS is implemented, and providing a link with the graphical UML
   notation is planned.

   A new theme in this project is specification-based testing. The aim is to
   investigate the relations of formal methods and testing. Systematic testing
   and test-automation should become a natural motivation for the use of advanced development methods in an industrial context.

5. Specifying XML-based enterprise software.
   This project will aim to analyse business models from a variety of institutions and enterprises, to specify them formally, and to develop tools and
   techniques to be used in automating relevant business processes. The emerging application fields of e-business and e-governance, and new technologies
   like XML, will be central to this. Again the emphasis will be on capacity
   building, with fellows being trained in the appropriate techniques.

3.2   Training Projects

The objective of UNU/IIST training projects is to introduce new subjects of
software technology and, in general, computer science into developing countries,
and to help universities in developing countries improve their computer science
education, in particular software engineering education.

At present UNU/IIST has the following 3 training projects:

1. Curriculum for formal software development.
   The project is assisting universities in developing countries to develop their
   ability to teach formal techniques. This has been a common feature of computer science curricula in developed countries but much rarer in the developing ones.

2. Development of computer science departments in developing countries.
   This project aims to strengthen all aspects of computer science teaching in universities in developing countries. Under this project we arrange for computer science lecturers from developing countries to learn new courses at partner universities in developed countries, at the same time provide them with the supporting course materials. The following twelve partner universities have helped UNU/IIST for this project: Calgary University, Kwangju Institute of Science and Technology, Leicester University, Macau University, National University of Singapore, Oxford University, Queen's University in Belfast, Queensland University, Swinburne University of Technology, Toronto University, Utrecht University and York University. UNU/IIST is exploring possibilities to expand this project to joint PhD programme with partner universities.
   UNU/IIST has also prepared a recommendation for undergraduate software engineering curriculum for developing countries.

3. IT training courses and schools in developing countries.
   The UNU/IIST course is to propagate awareness of and provide in-depth training in advanced software technology in developing countries. It is also to identify possible joint research and development activities with developing countries, and potential trainees to be trained through UNU/IIST projects. The UNU/IIST training courses have covered subjects such as RAISE, Duration Calculus, ACP and SDL, Logic of Programming, Relational Programming, Algorithmics, Software Project Management, UML and Object-Oriented Programming, SPIN and Model Checking, etc.
   UNU/IIST training schools are organised in selected institutions in developing countries and invite local or external qualified academics to lecture for participants from neighbouring developing countries.

3.3   Local IT Projects

The objective of the UNU/IIST local IT projects is to help Macao develop its IT education and industry, and establish its good relation with the host society. This project has included cooperation with local universities, in particular Macau University, training courses for local professionals, web sites design, etc.

3.4   Project Achievements

Since 1992 UNU/IIST has published 154 scientific papers in international journals and conferences, trained 242 people from 33 countries and organised 114 courses and schools in 37 countries. UNU/IIST has also published a book, *Specification Case Studies in RAISE* in the Springer-Verlag FACIT series.

4   UNU/IIST Experience

The UNU/IIST mission is unique. It is the first international institute concerned with the fundamental needs of developing countries in the area of software technology. It is also an international institute, located in and pursuing software technology research with people from developing world, but aiming for world class excellence. The UNU/IIST endeavour has lasted for ten years, and achieved its goal. Its experience is obvious. We hope the UNU/IIST experience will be gradually recognised and accepted by developing countries in developing their science and technology.

4.1   International Openness

Any international institute must operate *internationally*, if it seeks success.

International Staffing. An elite institute must be staffed by a group of elites. Any UNU/IIST recruitment has been announced internationally, and applications have been reviewed by international selection committee. The current UNU/IIST academic staff are from 5 countries.

International Board. As listed above, the UNU/IIST Board members are from 8 countries, and include representatives of its donors and constituency as well as worldwide well-known software technology experts. This Board is a governance body to review and recommend UNU/IIST activities. It also functions as a standing channel to connect UNU/IIST to the rest part of the world.

International Research. Although UNU/IIST is located in Macao, China, a developing country, its research aims at international excellence. It selects research topics in the forefront of the field, and only counts peer reviewed international publications. It seeks research cooperation and receives visitors from developed countries. In 2001, UNU/IIST arranged 29 seminars for visitors from 17 countries. It also organises international conferences such as the International Symposium for Software Industry in Developing Countries in August 2000, the 8th Asia-Pacific Software Engineering Conference in December 2001, and the International Conference for Formal Engineering Methods in October 2002.

4.2   Thematic Focus

"Software technology is a wide field. We could try to cover as much of it as possible (by having each of our academic staff a specialist in a different area) or instead have an institutional focus. The first option would be more costly, since staff cannot mutually support each other. Over a period we might hope to cover most areas in software, but not all could be covered at any one time. Having one or perhaps two institutional focuses, according to the feasibility with a small staff, is more attractive to staff because it offers them a better academic environment. It is also easier for the institution to generate a high profile, albeit limited to the focal area(s)."

The above is copied from a UNU/IIST strategic plan. It is quite often that new institute wants to cover all new subjects at a time. However, it is not always true that the larger coverage of subjects the better achievements of the institute.

4.3   Strong and Continuous Support

UNU/IIST has received an endowment fund of US\$ 30 million, which has supported UNU/IIST to continuously develop its programme and to become an internationally acknowledged research center.

Many developing countries are eager to develop their science and technology. However even distributed but weak funding cannot help growth of scientific research. Intermittent funding obstructs a research to reach advanced level that usually needs a long and continuous effort. Selecting focal subjects and concentrating funds may be helpful to the development of science and technology in developing countries.

Contract-Based Testing

Bernhard K. Aichernig

The United Nations University
International Institute for Software Technology (UNU/IIST)
P.O. Box 3058, Macau
bka@iist.unu.edu

Abstract. A tester relies on some sort of contract between the users and the implementers of a system. The contract defines the obligations of each part that are partially checked by selecting and executing test-cases. In fact, these test-cases are contracts, too, although in a rather operational form. In this article we define the general relationship between these two forms of contract and present a method how various test-selection strategies can be defined formally. More precisely, we demonstrate how test-cases can be calculated from contracts using a refinement calculus.

1 Introduction

Testing is not very prestigious. From a scientific point of view it is an inadequate tool for verification: "it can only show the presence of errors, not their absence" (E. Dijkstra). From a social point of view it does not have a high status: it is a beginner's job, usually assigned to newcomers in order to get familiar with a system. From a psychological point of view it is no fun: programmers rather like to construct new artifacts than analyzing existing ones. From a management point of view, it is always too late and takes too long. However, from a practical point of view it must be done.

In this paper we attempt to increase the reputation of testing by showing how advanced software development techniques can be applied to derive test-cases. Ironically, program synthesis, an area founded by Dijkstra, is used. These techniques demonstrate that adequate test-case synthesis is a design process that certainly requires the skills of well-educated test-engineers that are able to defend their findings and decisions on a scientific bases.

An adequate test-synthesis process must certainly involve some form of contract, either on specification level (black-box testing) or on implementation level (white-box testing), from which test-cases are derived systematically. Since practice shows that specification-level contracts with the needed preciseness are seldom available, a test-engineer must be able to model such contracts using, e.g., formal notations. This enables him to start his work right at the requirements level. Our industrial case-studies in the area of avionics have shown that a formal definition of a contract for testing purposes raises many questions that help to clarify the requirements and lead to test-cases of much higher quality [20, 1]. These case-studies have also shown that test-cases for non-trivial systems

B.K. Aichernig and T. Maibaum (Eds.): Formal Methods ..., LNCS 2757, pp. 34–48, 2003.

are rather complex procedures that have to be executed either manually by a tester, or by test drivers. It is not trivial to get these test-cases right. The work described in [20] uncovered an unacceptable low coverage of appr. 80 % in the existing test-cases. In the second project [1] we found that appr. 25 % of the previously designed test-cases were erroneous. However, incorrect test-cases are a major problem: a tester not relying on the designed test-cases will start his own interpretations with possible wrong conclusions. Furthermore, the validation of a contract with erroneous test-cases is impossible.

The idea of our framework is based on the derivation of test-cases T from a formal specification S. A test-case T should be correct with respect to S, and a program P that implements S should be tested with T. Thus, the derivation of T from S constitutes a formal synthesis process. In order to formalize a certification criteria for this synthesis process, the relation between T, S and P must be clarified. It is well-known that the relation between a specification S and its correct implementation P is called refinement. We write $S \sqsubseteq P$ for expressing that P is a correct refinement (implementation) of S. The problem of deriving an unknown P? from a given S is generally known as program synthesis: $S \sqsubseteq P$?. In [2, 6] we have shown that correct test-cases T can be defined as abstractions of the specifications S, or $T \sqsubseteq S \sqsubseteq P$. Consequently, test-case synthesis is a reverse refinement problem. The reverse refinement from a given S into an unknown test-case T? is here called abstraction, and denoted as $S \sqsupseteq T$?. Hence, formal synthesis techniques may be applied for deriving test-cases from a formal specification. This is the basic idea of our generalized view on testing techniques. Which test-cases to derive depends on the selection strategy. Our framework allows us to define different abstraction rules for different selection strategies. We use Back and von Wright's refinement calculus [7] in order to discuss the topic.

The following section introduces to the notion of contracts used throughout this paper. Next, Section 3 explains how test-cases can be considered as abstractions of specification contracts. In Section 4 we use this fact to define synthesis rules for calculating test-cases according to a certain test-strategy. Then, Section 5 defines the properties for interesting new test-cases under refinement. Finally, our concluding remarks are made in Section 6.

2   Contracts

2.1   Defining Responsibilities of Agents

The prerequisite for testing is some form of contract between the user and the provider of a system (component, class, etc.). It specifies what each part is supposed to do. In case of system-level testing usually user and software requirement documents define the contract. Formal methods propose mathematical languages for defining sound and unambiguous contracts. In our work the contract-language of the refinement calculus [7, 8] has been chosen as the most appropriate formalism. It is a generalization of the conventional pre- and post-condition style of formal techniques like VDM, B and Z in the sense that it permits reasoning about interaction, using demonic and angelic nondeterminism. It uses higher-order logic. In the refinement calculus the notion of contracts includes specifications as well as programs. A computation is seen as involving a number of agents (programs, components, users, here testers) who carry out actions according to a document, called contract.

A system described by a contract is modeled by a global state σ of type Σ denoted by $\sigma : \Sigma$. The state has a number of program variables $x_1, \ldots, x_n$, each of which can be observed and changed independently of the others. State changes are either expressed by functional state transformers f or relational updates R. A state transformer is a function $f : \Sigma \to \Gamma$ mapping a state space Σ to the same or another state space Γ. A relational update $R : \Sigma \to \Gamma \to$ Bool specifies a state change by relating the state before with the state after execution. For convenience, a relational assignment is available that generalizes assignment statements. For example, $(x := x'|x' > x)$ changes state σ to state σ' such that the value of x in σ' is greater than the value of x in σ.

A contract further distinguishes between the responsibilities of agents operating on the state space Σ. If agent a is responsible for changing the state $\sigma : \Sigma$ according to a relation R we denote it by $\langle R \rangle_a$. Operationally, this means that agent a resolves the nondeterminism by choosing an after-state σ' such that $R.\sigma.\sigma'$ holds. Functional state transformers are deterministic, and therefore no choice is involved. Thus, they are simply denoted by $\langle f \rangle$. An important special case of relational update $\langle R \rangle_a$ occurs when $R = (\lambda \sigma \sigma' \cdot \sigma = \sigma' \wedge p.\sigma)$ and $p : \Sigma \to$ Bool is a predicate. In this case, $\langle R \rangle_a$ is called an *assertion* simply written as $\langle p \rangle_a$. An assertion $\langle p \rangle_a$ in a contract does not change the state but agent a is responsible that p is satisfied.

Two contracts C_1, C_2 can be combined to form a new contract either by *sequential composition* $C_1; C_2$ or by a *choice* operator $C_1 []_a C_2$. Which of the subcontracts C_1, C_2 to be chosen in $C_1 []_a C_2$ is decided by agent a. In this contract language, traditional pre-postcondition specifications have the form $\langle p \rangle_u ; \langle R \rangle_s$, where u is a user (agent), s the system (agent), p is the precondition predicate, and R the postcondition relation.

For example, assume that we want to find an index i pointing to the smallest element in an array $A[1..n]$, where $n = len.A$ is the length of the array and $1 \leq n$ (so the array is nonempty). Using a predicate minat.$i.A$ that holds when the minimum value in A is found at $A[i]$, we can define a contract for this problem:

$$\text{minat.}i.A \triangleq 1 \leq i \leq len.A \wedge (\forall j \mid 1 \leq j \leq len.A \cdot A[i] \leq A[j])$$

$$\text{Min} \triangleq \langle 1 \leq len.A \rangle_u ; \langle i := i' \mid \text{minat.}i'.A \rangle_s$$

An interactive version of this contract models the user's action explicitly:

$$\text{Min}_I \triangleq \langle A := A' \mid 1 \leq len.A \rangle_u ; \langle i := i' \mid \text{minat.}i'.A \rangle_s$$

In order to express iteration, recursive contract statements with least- (μ) and greatest-fixpoint semantics (ν) are available. The syntax of the core language used throughout this paper is

$$C := \langle p \rangle_a \mid \langle R \rangle_a \mid C; C \mid C []_a C \mid \mu X \cdot C \mid \nu X \cdot C$$

With this basic notation more familiar concepts of programming languages, like loops and if-statements, as well as new commands can be expressed easily. Given an idea of this contract statements' meaning, now, we become more precise about their semantics.

2.2 Semantics: On Angels and Demons

Every contract statement has a *weakest-precondition* predicate transformer semantics. A predicate transformer $T : (\Gamma \to \mathsf{Bool}) \to (\Sigma \to \mathsf{Bool})$ is a function, mapping postcondition predicates q to precondition predicates p. Thus, $T.q = p$ (here, $T.q$ denotes function application $T(q)$). Following an established tradition, we identify contract statements with the predicate transformers that they determine.

Intuitively, the execution of a contract statement with the semantics of predicate transformer T is interpreted as a game between an *angel* and a *demon*. Given an initial state σ; if the angel can resolve its choices so that, regardless of the demon's choices, the postcondition q holds after execution, then the precondition $(T.q)$ holds in σ. Angelic choice between two predicate transformers is defined by $(T_1 \sqcup T_2).q \triangleq C_1.q \cup C_2.q$ and demonic choice by $(T_1 \sqcap T_2).q \triangleq T_1.q \cap T_2.q$. The two kinds of choices in relational updates are expressed by an angelic update $\{R\}.q.\sigma \triangleq (\exists \gamma \in \Gamma . R.\sigma.\gamma \wedge q.\gamma)$ and a demonic update $[R].q.\sigma \triangleq (\forall \gamma \in \Gamma . R.\sigma.\gamma \Rightarrow q.\gamma)$. Finally, the responsibility of the angel for satisfying an assertion predicate p is expressed by an *assertion* predicate transformer $\{p\}.q \triangleq p \cap q$. Dually, the demon has to ensure an *assumption* $[p].q \triangleq \neg p \cup q$. Sequential composition is defined as usual. In this semantics, the forced breach of a contract by the angel, means that the weakest-precondition is false. If the demon breaches a contract, the weakest-precondition is trivially true.

With this notion of angelic and demonic predicate transformers, the semantics of a contract involving a collection Ω of agents can be given as follows. We always take the point of view of a *coalition* $U \subseteq \Omega$ of users. In our work, a set of testers form also part of the coalition U. The system under test consists of the other agents $\Omega \setminus U$. Given a user coalition U, a contract statement C can be translated into a predicate transformer $\mathsf{wp}.C.U$ as follows:

$$\mathsf{wp}.\langle p \rangle_a.U \triangleq \begin{cases} \{p\} & \text{if } a \in U \quad \text{(assertion)} \\ [p] & \text{if } a \notin U \quad \text{(assumption)} \end{cases}$$

$$\mathsf{wp}.\langle R \rangle_a.U \triangleq \begin{cases} \{R\} & \text{if } a \in U \quad \text{(angelic update)} \\ [R] & \text{if } a \notin U \quad \text{(demonic update)} \end{cases}$$

$$\mathsf{wp}.(C_1 []_a C_2).U \triangleq \begin{cases} C_1 \sqcup C_2 & \text{if } a \in U \quad \text{(angelic choice)} \\ C_1 \sqcap C_2 & \text{if } a \notin U \quad \text{(demonic choice)} \end{cases}$$

The semantics expresses that a user agent $u \in U$ is considered as an angel, and the other agents behave like demons. Thus, we take the point of view of a user $u \in U$ and ask if he can satisfy his obligations in a contract C — he can if wp.$C.U \neq$ false. For further study, an operational semantics as well as a game theoretic semantics can be found in [8, 9].

2.3   Refinement and Abstraction

The refinement calculus provides a synthesis method for refining specification statements into programming statements that are executable by the target platform. The refinement rules of the calculus ensure that a program is correct by construction with respect to its specification. Formally, refinement of a contract C by C', written $C \sqsubseteq C'$, is defined by the pointwise extension of the subset ordering on predicates: For Γ being the after state space of the contracts, we have

$$C \sqsubseteq C' \triangleq \forall q \in (\Gamma \to \textsf{Bool}) \cdot C.q \subseteq C'.q$$

This ordering relation defines a lattice of predicate transformers (and thus of contracts) with the lattice operators meet $\sqcap$ and join $\sqcup$. For a detailed introduction to the foundations of this contract language we refer to [7]. A large collection of refinement rules can be found in [7, 23]. Abstraction is the reverse of refinement: $C \sqsupseteq C' \triangleq C' \sqsubseteq C$ and is used to emphasize the synthesis of abstractions instead of refinements. Note that in this article we have updated our previous results to the latest version of the contract language introduced in [8].

3   Test-Cases

In the following we will demonstrate that test-cases common in software engineering are in fact contracts — highly abstract contracts. To keep our discussion simple, we do not consider parameterized procedures, but only global state manipulations. In [7] it is shown how procedures can be defined in the contract language. Consequently, our approach scales up to procedure calls.

3.1   Input-Output Tests

The simplest form of test-cases are pairs of input i and output o. We can define such an input-output test-case $\textsf{TC}$ as a contract between a tester $t \in U$ and the system under test s:

$$\textsf{TC } i\ o \triangleq \langle x = i \rangle_t; \langle y := y' | y' = o \rangle_s$$

Intuitively, the contract states that if the tester provides input i, the state will be updated such that it equals o. Here, x is the input variable and y the output variable. The variable names x, y are arbitrarily chosen and other variable names will be used in subsequent examples without changing the definition of $\textsf{TC}$. In fact, such a test-case $\textsf{TC}$ is a formal pre-postcondition specification solely defined for a single input i. This demonstrates that a collection of n input-output test-cases TCs are indeed pointwise defined formal specifications:

$$\textsf{TCs} \triangleq \textsf{TC } i_1\ o_1\ []_t\ \ldots\ []_t\ \textsf{TC } i_n\ o_n$$

For example, the test-cases $TC_{1-3} \triangleq$ TC $[2,1,3]$ 2 $[]_t$ TC $[2,3,1]$ 3 $[]_t$ TC $[1,2,3]$ 1 form a contract that must be satisfied by Min and its refinements. Moreover, each of the test-cases is an abstraction of Min. The justification for this fact is that the precondition of Min has been strengthened to a single input state — and precondition strengthening is abstraction. A proof of this abstraction relation theorem between test-cases and specifications can be found in [3]. A simple version of this theorem, assumes that the input i and output o are specified by global states, thus $i, o : \Sigma$. Then, a test-case TC is an abstraction of a pre-postcondition specification $\langle p \rangle_u; \langle R \rangle_s$, iff

$$\langle p \rangle_u; \langle R \rangle_s \sqsupseteq \mathsf{TC} \ i \ o \quad \equiv \quad (p.i \wedge (R.i = o))$$

Note, that the tester t of a test-case contract and the user u are both in the same coalition: $t, u \in U$.

It can be easily observed from the second condition $(R.i = o)$ that $R.i$ must be deterministic for a test-case TC i o . This is reasonable, since one should not test with a deterministic test-case if several outputs may be possible. In general, a contract can permit more than one result. In this case, testing the requirements with simple input-output values is insufficient. Therefore, on the specification level, nondeterministic test-cases are needed. An output predicate $\omega : \Sigma \rightarrow$ Bool can be used for describing the set of possible outputs. We define such a test-case as follows:

$$\mathsf{TCp} \ i \ \omega \triangleq \langle x = i \rangle_t; \langle y := y' | \omega \rangle_s$$

For example, a test-case $T_4 \triangleq$ TC $[3,1,1]$ 2 for Min is not an abstraction of Min and thus not correct. The specification does not say which index should be selected if several minima exist. Thus, a correct and appropriate test-case for this input would be

$$T_4 \triangleq \mathsf{TCp} \ [3,1,1] \ (i = 2 \vee i = 3).$$

Designing a test-case for an interactive specification like $\mathsf{Min}_{\mathsf{I}}$ results in the notion of an interactive test-case TCI.

$$\mathsf{TCI} \ i \ o \triangleq \langle x := x' | x' = i \rangle_t; \langle y := y' | y' = o \rangle_s$$

Again the abstraction relation is preserved. Generally, in the refinement calculus abstraction is restricting the choices of the angel (here users and testers) and extending the demonic choices (here the system under test). Therefore, restricting a tester's choice to a single input is abstraction, as was the precondition strengthening. For example, a correct test-case for the interactive contract $\mathsf{Min}_{\mathsf{I}}$ is TCI $[1,2,3]$ 1 which has the same arguments than TC_3 for Min but different semantics.

A nondeterministic version of interactive test-cases is straightforward to define and therefore omitted. Furthermore, we have shown in [3] that test-partitions obtained by partition analysis are abstractions of specification contracts.

3.2   Test-Scenarios

When testing interactive systems, simple input-output interaction tests are insufficient for practical systems. Moreover, sequences of interactions, called scenarios, are necessary for setting the system under test into the states of interest. These scenarios, too, are abstractions of interactive systems. In [2] we have proved the abstraction relation by modeling interactive systems using the iterative choice statement, introduced in [7] and extensively discussed in [10].

$$\mathbf{do}\ \Diamond_i^n\ g_i\ ::\ S_i\ \mathbf{od}\ \triangleq\ (\mu X \cdot (\langle g_1 \rangle_u; S_1; X)[]_u \cdots []_u (\{g_n\}; S_n; X)[]_u \mathbf{skip})$$

In contracts of this form, a user agent u recursively selects possible interactions S_i with the system, enabled by guards g_i. skip models the user's choice of stopping the dialog. The contract above unfolds to skip $[]_u \{g_1\}; S_1\ []_u\ \{g_2\}; S_2\ []_u \{g_1\}; S_1; \{g_1\}; S_1\ []_u\ \{g_1\} S_1; \{g_2\} S_2\ []_u \ldots$ Hence, by definition of angelic choice $([]_u \triangleq \sqcup)$, any sequence of these interactions (the scenarios) are abstractions. Further abstracting the interactions results in concrete test-scenarios of input-output contracts.

For all the kinds of test-cases presented above, the abstraction relation to their specification must hold. The fact that test-cases are indeed formal specifications and abstractions of more general contracts explains why test-cases are so popular: First, they are abstract, and thus easy to understand. Second, they are formal and thus unambiguous. Currently, the *Extreme Programming* movement [11] is strongly promoting this view of test-cases as specifications. Similarly, scenarios are gaining more and more popularity in software engineering. The reasons are the same as for other test-cases: Scenarios are abstractions of interactive systems. For a comprehensive introduction to the different roles of scenarios in software engineering see [21]. In our work, the focus is on their role in validation and verification.

4   Calculating Test-Cases

This section shows that formal synthesis rules can be defined for calculating test-cases from contracts. Such rules guarantee correct test-cases by preserving abstraction. In fact, each rule represents a certain test-case selection strategy. The advantage of this test-case calculus is that quite different strategies, like structural and error-based ones, can be handled. Two traditional strategies, domain partitioning [16] and mutation testing [19, 15], will serve as demonstrating examples.

4.1   Structural Strategies

As an example of a structural selection strategy, we will use a domain partitioning technique that rewrites a model-based specification into its disjunctive normal form (DNF). Partition testing techniques are based on a uniformity hypothesis. This strategy assumes that a system shows the same behavior for a certain partition of input values. Therefore, once the equivalence partitions are selected, it is sufficient to test one case for every partition. DNF rewriting, first proposed in [16], is based on rewriting disjunctions with:

$$a \vee b \equiv (a \wedge \neg b) \vee (\neg a \wedge b) \vee (a \wedge b)$$

The proof of the following abstraction rule for this well-known strategy high-lighted a problem with this technique (see [6, 3]). In general, DNF-rewriting results in disjoint partitions. Applied to a relational specification it gives disjoint input-output relations, but the input partitions (the domain of the relation) may overlap. In such pathological cases, selecting a test-case for each partition is not correct. If test-cases are derived for overlapping domains and the specification is non-deterministic then two test-cases with the same input may define two different deterministic outputs. Therefore, the disjointness of the resulting input partitions $\mathrm{dom}.Q_i$ is assumed in the following synthesis rule, where a and b be arbitrary Boolean expressions and Q_1, Q_2, Q_3 be relations.

$$\frac{\langle x := x' | a \wedge \neg b \rangle_s \sqsupseteq \langle Q_1 \rangle_s,}{\langle x := x' | \neg a \wedge b \rangle_s \sqsupseteq \langle Q_2 \rangle_s,}$$
$$\frac{\langle x := x' | a \wedge b \rangle_s \sqsupseteq \langle Q_3 \rangle_s,}{\forall i, j \in \{1, 2, 3\} \, . \, i \neq j \Rightarrow \mathrm{dom}.Q_i \cap \mathrm{dom}.Q_j = \emptyset}{\langle p \rangle_u; \langle x := x' | a \vee b \rangle_s \sqsupseteq \langle p \cap \mathrm{dom}.Q_1 \rangle_t; \langle Q_1 \rangle_s \ [\!]_t}$$
$$\langle p \cap \mathrm{dom}.Q_2 \rangle_t; \langle Q_2 \rangle_s \ [\!]_t$$
$$\langle p \cap \mathrm{dom}.Q_3 \rangle_t; \langle Q_3 \rangle_s$$

The synthesis rule for test-cases yields three disjoint partitions, although a derived partition might be empty, thus $\mathrm{dom}.Q_i = \mathrm{false}$. The advantage of using the refinement calculus is that our rules are not axioms but theorems. Thus we are able to certify them via proofs. We can prove that each of these partitions is an abstraction of the original contract and that they cover the full input domain. Furthermore, it follows from the assumptions that for one partition more non-determinism can be introduced due to abstraction. This reflects the possibility of weakening certain tests. For example, the premise $\langle x := x' | a \wedge \neg b >_s \sqsupseteq \langle Q_1 \rangle_s$ indicates such a possible weakening of a test-case. This form of weakening a test-case is a further strategy for test-case design. The reason for this further abstraction of a partition might be that, either a tester does not wish to observe the (demonic) changes of the whole state space, or the whole state and thus its updates are not observable. Consequently, parts of the demonic updates of the state might be skipped in test-case specifications. Formally this is an abstraction process carried out by weakening a post-condition. It should be obvious that the synthesis rule has to be applied recursively to the resulting partitions if further sub-partitioning is needed.

Example 1. This synthesis rule is best illustrated by the following example, where the test partitions are calculated from a contract that specifies the minimum computation of two numbers:

$$\langle z := z' | (z' = x \wedge x \leq y) \vee (z' = y \wedge x \geq y) \rangle_s$$
$\sqsupseteq$ by the partitioning rule
$$\langle x < y \rangle_t; \langle z := z' | (z' = x \wedge x \leq y) \wedge (z' \neq y \vee x < y) \rangle_s \; []_t$$
$$\langle x > y \rangle_t; \langle z := z' | (z' \neq x \vee x > y) \wedge (z' = y \wedge x \geq y) \rangle_s \; []_t$$
$$\langle x = y \rangle_t; \langle z := z' | (z' = x \wedge x \leq y) \wedge (z' = y \wedge x \geq y) \rangle_s$$
$\sqsupseteq$ by simplification
$$\langle x < y \rangle_t; \langle z := z' | z' = x \rangle_s \; []_t$$
$$\langle x > y \rangle_t; \langle z := z' | z' = y \rangle_s \; []_t$$
$$\langle x = y \rangle_t; \langle z := z' | z' = x \wedge z' = y \rangle_s$$

As indicated in the partitioning rule, the post-conditions might be further abstracted, if the tester wishes. In the third partition of this example, a tester might choose to simply compare the new value z' with only one input variable, e.g. x, not with both.

$\sqsupseteq$ by weakening the post-condition in the third test-case
$$\langle x < y \rangle_t; \langle z := z' | z' = x \rangle_s \; []_t$$
$$\langle x > y \rangle_t; \langle z := z' | z' = y \rangle_s \; []_t$$
$$\langle x = y \rangle_t; \langle z := z' | z' = x \rangle_s$$
$\sqsupseteq$ by further abstraction to test-cases we might obtain
$$\mathsf{TC}\,(1,2)\,1\;[]_t\;\mathsf{TC}\,(2,1)\,1\;[]_t\mathsf{TC}\,(1,1)\,1 \qquad \square$$

An alternative to pure DNF-rewriting is to also take the syntax of a contract, either specification or implementation, into account. The advantage is to have more control over the partitioning process in order to reduce the number of partitions usually resulting from a pure DNF strategy. See, e.g., [12] for such a mixed strategy, tailored for the syntax of the B method. The same can be done in our framework as shown in [3]. The contract language allows us to define arbitrary specification or program statements on which abstraction rules can be defined.

4.2 Error-Based Strategies

A different class of strategies for selecting test-cases is rather based on covering typical errors than on covering the structure of a contract. Mutation testing is of this form. Mutation testing is a fault-based testing technique introduced by Hamlet [19] and DeMillo et al [15]. It is a means of assessing test suites. When a program passes all tests in a suite, mutant programs are generated and the suite is assessed in terms of how many mutants it distinguishes from the original program. If some mutants pass the test-suite, additional test-cases are designed until all mutants that reflect errors can be distinguished. A hypothesis of this technique is that programmers only make small errors. In [5] we have shown how mutation testing applies to contracts.

Mutant contracts are generated by a mutation operator m that injects an error into the contract. However, not all mutants are useful in the sense that they represent an error. Some are simply refinements. Consequently, a mutant C_i of a contract C is *useful* iff $C \not\sqsubseteq C_i$. Note, that abstractions are considered as useful mutations as will become clear in the example below.

In mutation testing, the strategy for selecting the test-cases is based on a hypothesis about faults in a program and consists of three parts:

1. a set of mutation operators M explicitly represents the knowledge of typical errors that occur in a program in a specific application domain.
2. usually, programmers create programs that are close to being correct: the small error assumption.
3. the *coupling effect*: test data that distinguishes all programs differing from a correct one by only simple errors is so sensitive that it also implicitly distinguishes more complex errors.

Based on this hypothesis, *adequate test-cases* are designed. A test-case for a contract C is defined to be *adequate*, with respect to a set of mutation operators M, if it is able to distinguish at least one useful mutant C_i, with $m.C = C_i$ for some $m \in M$. We write $C \sqsupseteq_M TC$ in order to denote an adequate test-case TC. Applied to executable contracts, usually called programs, adequacy is checked by test-execution. For general contracts, again the notion of abstraction can be used to check if a test-case is adequate. Given a contract C and a mutation C_i generated by applying a mutation operator m such that $m.C = C_i$ holds. Then a test-case TC is adequate iff it satisfies the synthesis rule

$$\frac{m \in M,\ m.C = C_i,\ C \not\sqsubseteq C_i,\ C \sqsupseteq TC,\ C_i \not\sqsupseteq TC}{C \sqsupseteq_M TC}$$

The rule formalizes the central criteria for an adequate test-case in mutation testing: a test-case must be an abstraction of the original contract but it must not be an abstraction of some useful mutant.

Example 2. Consider the previous example contract Min. A first test-case for Min might be chosen as follows:

$$T_1 \triangleq \mathsf{TC}\ [2,1,3]\ 2$$

How sensitive is this test-case? By inspection, we notice that if an error had occurred in the implementation of the relational operation $A[i] \le A[j]$ the test-case T_1 would have distinguished those errors. That means that for example, implementations of the following two mutants can be distinguished:

$$\mathsf{minat}_1.i.A \triangleq 1 \le i \le len.A \wedge (\forall j \mid 1 \le j \le len.A \bullet A[i] \ge A[j])$$

$$\mathsf{Min}_1 \triangleq \langle 1 \le len.A \rangle_u; \langle i := i' \mid \mathsf{minat}_1.i'.A \rangle_s$$

$$\mathsf{minat}_2.i.A \triangleq 1 \le i \le len.A \wedge (\forall j \mid 1 \le j \le len.A \bullet A[i] < A[j])$$

$$\mathsf{Min}_2 \triangleq \langle 1 \le len.A \rangle_u; \langle i := i' \mid \mathsf{minat}_2.i'.A \rangle_s$$

The mutant Min_2 is subtle since $minat_2$ is equivalent to false. Hence, the weakest-precondition $wp.Min_2 = $ false, which denotes the most abstract contracts in the hierarchy of contracts equivalent to abort. Since, like every contract, T_1 is a refinement of abort and $T_1 \neq$ abort, it cannot be an abstraction of Min_2. This proves that the test-case is able to detect this kind of error. This shows that our criteria based on abstraction also holds for the trivial case of non-terminating mutants. Similarly, the test-case detects a swapping of the index variables resulting in a mutated expression $A[j] \leq A[i]$. However, is T_1 able to detect a mutation in the range definition of j? Consider a corresponding mutation of minat:

$$minat_3.i.A \triangleq 1 \leq i \leq len.A \wedge (\forall j \mid 1 \leq j \boxed{<} len.A \cdot A[i] \leq A[j])$$

This mutation corresponds to a common implementation error in loops, where not the whole array is searched through due to an error in the termination condition. In fact, T_1 is not able to distinguish this kind of error, since the mutant Min_3 is a correct refinement of T_1 (or T_1 an abstraction of Min_3). In order to violate the abstraction relation, the minimum must be at the last position in the array. Thus, a second test-case is needed in order to distinguish implementations of Min_3:

$$T_2 \triangleq \text{TC } [2, 3, 1] \ 3$$

This test-case is an example that would not have been found by simple path analysis. It indicates that an error-based strategy is more efficient in detecting errors in commonly used data-centered applications than path-based strategies.

Similarly, an additional test-case for detecting an error in the lower bound of the array range must be designed.

$$T_3 \triangleq \text{TC } [1, 2, 3] \ 1$$

The test-cases T_2, T_3 also cover the typical one-off mutations effecting the range of i:

$$minat_4.i.A \triangleq \boxed{2} \leq i \leq len.A \wedge (\forall j \mid 1 \leq j \leq len.A \cdot A[i] \leq A[j])$$

$$minat_5.i.A \triangleq 1 \leq i \leq \boxed{(len.A - 1)} \wedge (\forall j \mid 1 \leq j \leq len.A \cdot A[i] \leq A[j])$$

One might think that test-case T_1 becomes redundant since T_2, T_3 can distinguish all mutants so far. However, we did not yet take a mutation of the assignment variable itself into account. Consider the mutation:

$$Min_6 \triangleq \langle 1 \leq len.A \rangle_u ; \langle i := \boxed{A[i']} \mid minat.i'.A \rangle_s$$

This contract represents the error that not the index, but the minimum itself is assigned to variable i. Only, test-case T_1 is able to detect this error, since its minimum does not equal the corresponding index. Of course, more clever values for $A[1]$ to $A[3]$ might be chosen such that T_1 can be excluded from the test-suite. However, having one typical case in addition to extreme values is considered to be good practice for demonstrating the basic functionality (see [13]).   □

5   Refining Test-Cases

This section focuses on finding new useful test-cases to be added under refinement. The contribution of [4] is the insight that this problem can be mapped to our above mutation testing approach.

The idea is that the new test-cases should be considered as useful if they are able to distinguish the original contract from its refined version. Hence, in our quest for useful new test-cases T'_{new} for a contract C' and $C \sqsubseteq C'$, we consider C as a mutant. Consequently, the new test-cases T'_{new} should be able to distinguish the abstract mutant C from its refinement C'. Hence, T'_{new} should be *adequate* mutation test-cases.

Thus, the criterion for useful new test-cases is an adaptation of the abstraction rule for deriving mutation test-cases: Given a contract C and its refinement C'. Furthermore, test-cases T for C have been correctly designed. Then the refined test-cases T' for testing C' have the general form

$$T' = (T \;[]_t\; T'_{new}) \;\text{ and }\; C' \sqsupseteq T'_{new} \;\wedge\; C \not\sqsupseteq T'_{new}$$

Alternatively an abstraction rule for producing useful new test-cases, denoted by $\sqsupseteq_u$, can be formulated as follows:

$$\frac{C \sqsubseteq C', C \sqsupseteq T}{C' \sqsupseteq T'_{new}, \; C \not\sqsupseteq T'_{new}}$$
$$\overline{C' \sqsupseteq_u (T \;[]_t\; T'_{new})}$$

It can be seen that $C \not\sqsupseteq T'_{new}$ is the central property for adding new test-cases that are able to distinguish between contract C and its refinement C' or between their implementations, respectively. Again the Min contract serves as the illustrating example of this fact.

Example 3. In the previous section, it is shown how three test-cases are derived by mutation testing. Note that only deterministic test-cases are used, although the specification of Min is non-deterministic. We would have to add a non-deterministic test-case

$$T_4 \triangleq TC \,[1,1,3]\,(i = 1 \vee i = 2)$$

in order to obtain a sufficient coverage.

Next, consider the following implementation (refinement) of Min using a guarded iteration statement:

```
Min ⊑ Min' ≜ begin var k := 2; i := 1;
                do k ≤ n ∧ A[k] < A[i] → i, k  := k, k + 1
                [] k ≤ n ∧ A[k] ≥ A[i] → k  := k + 1
                od
             end
```

What test-cases should be added in order to test the refinement? The corresponding synthesis rule points us to the answer, since a correct test-case of Min' should be found that is not an abstraction of Min. It is straightforward to reconsider the non-deterministic test-case T_4, since the implementation Min$'$ is deterministic. Hence, new test-cases should be able to distinguish the deterministic from the non-deterministic version (mutant):

$$\mathsf{T}'_{new} \triangleq \mathsf{TC}\ [1,1,3]\ 1$$

is such a useful test-case. Our framework actually allows us to prove this fact by showing that Min$' \sqsupseteq \mathsf{T}'_{new}$ and Min $\not\sqsupseteq \mathsf{T}'_{new}$. □

6   Concluding Remarks

Summary. In this article we have presented an overview of our recent research on testing. The novelty in our approach is to use a refinement calculus in order to derive test-cases from formal contracts. The contract language can explicitly express the interaction of a set of testers with a system under test. Once their responsibilities are defined in a formal contract, correct test-cases can be derived by following abstraction rules. Different rules represent different test-case selection strategies. Partition testing and mutation testing strategies served as demonstrating examples. In addition, test-case synthesis under refinement has been briefly covered.

Related Work. The synergy of formal methods and testing have become a popular area of research. In the last years, test-generation tools have been invented for almost every popular specification language. These tools work on model-based specifications, e.g. BZ-TT [22], on labeled transition systems, e.g. TGV [17], or on algebraic specifications, e.g. the tools of [14]. They are mostly tailored to a single test-case selection strategy for the formal notation in use. Gaudel and James [18] presents a unification of algebraic testing strategies and those for process algebras. Their selection strategies are purely structural. To our knowledge, only Stocks has applied mutation testing to formal specifications before [26]. In his work he extends mutation testing to model-based specification languages by defining a collection of mutation operators for Z's specification language. However, Stocks does not address issues like useful mutations, coverage or refinement. Nor does he discuss, why some test-cases are more successful in finding errors than others. To our current knowledge no other work has been published that uses a refinement calculus for deriving test-cases. Stepney was the first who made the abstraction relation between test-cases and object-oriented Z specifications explicitly [25]. Her group developed a tool for interactively calculating partition abstractions and to structure them for reuse. Our work can be seen as an extension of this view on testing. A summary of other work on formal methods and testing can be found in [6]. For an overview on testing concurrent systems consider [27].

Discussion. We consider most of the work on formal methods and testing as special purpose testing frameworks investigating specialized strategies for certain notations. The motivation of our work is to unify the different approaches, justify and compare them in our theory, and develop and evaluate new strategies. Then, with general scientific results, special purpose tools can be designed. It is the author's opinion that an abstraction calculus for testing, provides deeper insight into the methods of test-case derivation. Especially, the understanding of new black-box testing strategies is supported by reasoning about the synthesis process. The examined testing strategies showed that even existing techniques reveal interesting properties. New test-case generation techniques may be the result. An example is the presented synthesis rule for mutation testing which defines a novel method of assessing test-cases statically.

Perspective. We hope that the presented work stimulates further research on test-synthesis based on other program-synthesis approaches. Especially, the application of program synthesis and transformation tools for testing could be a promising topic of future research. We are happy to see that recently other colleagues seem to pick up our ideas and transfer the results to other frameworks and application domains like modal logics and security [24]. The work presented in this article should demonstrate that software testing is a complex engineering task. Like every engineering discipline it should apply advanced methods — based on mathematics.

References

1. Bernhard K. Aichernig, Andreas Gerstinger, and Robert Aster. Formal specification techniques as a catalyst in validation. In *Proceedings of the 5th Conference on High-Assurance Software Engineering, 15th–17th November 2000, Albuquerque, New Mexico, USA.* IEEE, 2000.
2. Bernhard K. Aichernig. Test-case calculation through abstraction. In *Proceedings of Formal Methods Europe 2001, FME 2001, March 12–16 2001, Berlin, Germany,* Lecture Notes in Computer Science. Springer Verlag, 2001.
3. Bernhard K. Aichernig. Test-Design through Abstraction – A Systematic Approach Based on the Refinement Calculus. *Journal of Universal Computer Science,* 7(8):710 – 735, aug 2001.
4. Bernhard K. Aichernig. The commuting V-diagram: On the relation of refinement and testing. Technical Report 254, The United Nations University, International Institute for Software Technology (UNU/IIST), P.O. Box 3058, Macau, May 2002.
5. Bernhard K. Aichernig. Contract-based mutation testing in the refinement calculus. In *REFINE'02, the BCS-FACS refinement workshop, Copenhagen, Denmark, July 20-21, 2002, affiliated with FME 2002,* Electronic Notes in Theoretical Computer Science, 2002. To appear.
6. Bernhard Aichernig. *Systematic Black-Box Testing of Computer-Based Systems through Formal Abstraction Techniques.* PhD thesis, Institute for Software Technology, TU Graz, Austria, Jannuary 2001. Supervisor: Peter Lucas.
7. Ralph-Johan Back and Joakim von Wright. *Refinement Calculus: a Systematic Introduction.* Graduate Texts in Computer Science. Springer, 1998.
8. Ralph-Johan Back and Joakim von Wright. Enforcing behavior with contracts. Technical Report 373, Turku Centre for Computer Science, November 2000.
9. Ralph-Johan Back and Joakim von Wright. Verification and refinement of action contracts. Technical Report 374, Turku Centre for Computer Science, April 2001.

10. Ralph Back, Anna Mikhajlova, and Joakim von Wright. Reasoning about interactive systems. In J.M. Wing, J. Woodcock, and J. Davies, editors, *FM'99: Formal Methods, World Congress on Formal Methods in the Development of Computing Systems, Toulouse, France, September 1999*, volume 1709 of *Lecture Notes in Computer Science*. Springer, 1999.

11. Kent Beck. *Extreme Programming Explained: Embrace Change*. Addison-Wesley, 1999.

12. Salimeh Behnia and Hélène Waeselynck. Test criteria definition for B models. In Jeannette M. Wing, Jim Woodcock, and Jim Davies, editors, *FM'99 — Formal Methods, World Congress on Formal Methods in the Development of Computing Systems, Toulouse, France, September 1999, Proceedings, Volume I*, volume 1709 of *Lecture Notes in Computer Science*, pages 509–529. Springer, 1999.

13. Boris Beizer. *Software Testing Techniques*. Van Nostrand Reinhold, New York, 2nd edition, 1990.

14. Huo Yan Chen, T.H. Tse, F.T. Chan, and T.Y. Chen. In Black and White: An Integrated Approach to Class-Level Testing of Object-Oriented Programs. *ACM Transactions on Software Engineering and Methodology*, 7(3):250–295, July 1998.

15. R. DeMillo, R. Lipton, and F. Sayward. Hints on test data selection: Help for the practicing programmer. *IEEE Computer*, 11(4):34–41, April 1978.

16. Jeremy Dick and Alain Faivre. Automating the generation and sequencing of test cases from model-based specifications. In J.C.P. Woodcock and P.G. Larsen, editors, *FME'93: Industrial-Strength Formal Methods*. Springer-Verlag, April 1993.

17. J.-C. Fernandez, C. Jard, T. Jéron, and C. Viho. An experiment in automatic generation of test suites for protocols with verification technology. *Science of Computer Programming*, 29(1–2):123–146, 1997.

18. Marie-Claude Gaudel and Perry R. James. Testing algebraic data types and processes: A unifying theory. *Formal Aspects of Computing*, 10(5 & 6):436–451, 1998.

19. Richard G. Hamlet. Testing programs with the aid of a compiler. *IEEE Transactions on Software Engineering*, 3(4):279–290, July 1977.

20. Johann Hörl and Bernhard K. Aichernig. Validating voice communication requirements using lightweight formal methods. *IEEE Software*, pages 21–27, May/June 2000.

21. Mathias Jarke and Reino Kurki-Suoni (editors). Special issue on scenario management. *IEEE Transactions on Software Engineering*, 24(12), 1998.

22. Bruno Legeard, Fabien Peureux, and Mark Utting. Automated boundary testing from Z and B. In *Proceedings of FME 2002, Formal Methods Europe, Copenhagen, Denmark, July 22–24 2002*, Lecture Notes in Computer Science. Springer, 2002.

23. Carrol C. Morgan. *Programming from Specifications*. Series in Computer Science. Prentice-Hall International, 1990.

24. Claus Pahl. Interference Analysis for Dependable Systems using Refinement and Abstraction. In *Formal Methods Europe 2002, Copenhagen, Denmark, July 22-24, 2002*. Springer-Verlag, 2002.

25. Susan Stepney. Testing as abstraction. In J. P. Bowen and M. G. Hinchey, editors, *ZUM '95: 9th International Conference of Z Users, Limerick 1995*, volume 967 of *Lecture Notes in Computer Science*. Springer, 1995.

26. Philip Alan Stocks. *Applying formal methods to software testing*. PhD thesis, The Department of computer science, The University of Queensland, 1993.

27. Jan Tretmans. Testing concurrent systems: A formal approach. In Jos C.M. Baeten and Sjouke Mauw, editors, *CONCUR'99*, volume 1664 of *Lecture Notes in Computer Science*, pages 46–65. Springer-Verlag, 1999.

The Development of the RAISE Tools

Chris George

UNU/IIST

Abstract. The use of a formal method is often seen in terms of (a) creating a formal description, or specification, that meets the requirements, and (b) refining that specification into code. More emphasis is commonly placed on (b) than on (a). This paper looks more at (a), particularly at means by which we can be more confident that a specification is correct. It considers the RAISE tools in terms both of their development and also in terms of the support they provide for gaining confidence in specifications, and hence in raising their quality.

1 Introduction

The RAISE Method and Specification Language (RSL) were originally developed by collaborative projects in the ESPRIT programme: the RAISE project ran from 1985–90 and LaCoS from 1990–95. The first project produced RSL [1], some basic ideas on the method, and some prototype tools. The successor project, LaCoS, concentrated on trying RAISE on a range of industrial projects [2] and from it came a book on the method [3] and a set of industrial quality tools [4].

RAISE has been the main formal method employed by the *Advanced Development* group at UNU/IIST since UNU/IIST's inception in 1992. A large number of projects have been carried out using it. Some have been collected in a book of case studies [5], and all are reported in technical reports available from UNU/IIST's web site http://www.iist.unu.edu.

The original tools were used successfully on projects at UNU/IIST for several years. But their main disadvantage was only being available to run on Sun workstations. The company that owns them, Terma A/S, allows them to be used free for education and research, but has no funds to port them to other platforms. UNU/IIST's mission is to help developing countries improve their capacity in software development. It trains "fellows", typically postgraduate students, academics, and software engineers, in research and in software development. These fellows come from institutions in developing countries, few of which have Sun workstations available. This made it hard for fellows to continue when they returned home, and also prevented us including tools when we taught courses on RAISE in developing countries.

Towards the end of 1998 we started investigating how to create a new set of tools for RAISE. Gentle [6] was recommended to us as a good compiler generation tool, and proved very effective: a type checker was written (part time) within 2 months. This type checker has formed the basis for a number of tools

B.K. Aichernig and T. Maibaum (Eds.): Formal Methods ..., LNCS 2757, pp. 49–64, 2003.

written as extensions to it: a pretty printer [7], extraction of module dependencies, generation of "confidence conditions", translators to Standard ML [8], to C++ [9], and to PVS [10]. A tool to generate RSL from from UML class diagrams has also been produced [11], plus a prototype tool to generate test cases automatically from RSL specifications [12].

This paper first (section 2) describes some of the features of RSL. Section 3 describes the tool functions, and section 4 discusses how it meets the requirements for tools to support the teaching and use of formal methods. Section 5 discusses some ways we can gain confidence in what we develop, and section 6 draws some conclusions, including what the experience with the tool tells us about the more general use of formal methods.

2   The RAISE Specification Language

We try not to be dependent in this paper on details of RSL, but here give some intuition. RSL is in several ways a "wide spectrum" language, intended to support a range of styles from the abstract to the concrete. It supports both the "algebraic" style of languages like OBJ, Larch, and CASL (in which types, or "sorts", are abstract and specifications are value signatures and axioms) and the "model-oriented" style of languages like VDM, Z, and B (in which types like sets, products and records are predefined and specifications are either explicit value definitions or implicit ones: signatures plus pre- and postconditions). These styles may be freely mixed in RSL. RSL also supports concurrent specifications by including the concepts of process algebra. So RSL specifications may be applicative or imperative, sequential or concurrent.

RSL is also a modular language. Modules may be "schemes", denoting classes of models, or "objects", denoting models. Schemes may be parameterised. A specification in RSL is therefore one or more modules, a "top-level" one and perhaps a number of others used by it. For example, a scheme may contain an object within it, and this object may be the instantiation of another scheme. Module dependencies may not be cyclic.

A recent addition to RSL is the inclusion of "test cases". These are described further in section 5.1.

3   The RAISE Tool

The basic tool has just a command-line interface, with different capabilities selected by options. Its normal use is from emacs, using a menu to access its capabilities and the "compile" facility of emacs to display output and provide a mouse-click means of, for example, relating error messages to their source. This approach avoids the need to develop a GUI that would also need effort to port it to different operating systems. The tool can therefore be built and executed in any operating system that supports the compilation and execution of C code, and has a basic development environment in any system where emacs is available. (This does not preclude creating a special GUI for the tool.)

The current tool has the following capabilities:

- Scope and type checking an RSL specification. The tool is presented with the top-level module and reads in others from its "context". The convention is that each module is in its own file with a `.rsl` extension. A "context" at the start of the file is a list of modules it depends on, which may include directory information in relative or absolute form.
- Display of the module dependencies as a textual tree.
- Display of the module dependencies as a graph using Visualisation of Computer Graphs (VCG).
- Pretty printing of a module. The pretty printed module is still in ASCII syntax, suitable for input to the tool (so you might consider this a "formatter" if your notion of pretty printing includes generating non-ASCII symbols). It preserves comments (which are removed from the original input when making the abstract syntax tree) by recovering them and pasting them back in during unparsing.
- Generation of confidence conditions. See section 5.2 for a description of these.
- Translation to C++. The tool is supplied with a number of C++ library files in source code format to allow the translator output to be compiled.
- Translation to SML. There is a file of SML definitions of RSL constructs that is loaded together with the translator output and executed by the SML system. Executing the translated code in emacs needs just the selection of a menu item.
- Translation to PVS. Again there is a supporting definition of basic RSL constructs in PVS that is loaded together with the translator output. A major aim is to discharge as many confidence conditions (see section 5.2) as possible automatically. Defining the appropriate strategies is ongoing work.
- Support for LaTeX documents. Within emacs, facilities are provided to include RSL files in LaTeX documents (including bold fonts for keywords, mathematical symbols, etc). The tool translates RSL files into `.tex` files which are then input to the LaTeX document. A "make" facility translates RSL files only as necessary to keep the document up to date.

A user and installation guide is available in postscript, pdf, and html.

Recent other work has been the development of a tool to convert UML class diagrams into RSL, and of an extension to automatically generate test cases from RSL specifications.

The tool works in three phases:

1. A "front end" does parsing and type checking. It does this by building an abstract syntax tree plus an "environment" containing information about all the identifiers defined in the input. This is in fact done by parsing plus 4 passes over the syntax tree: (a) to create the environment for objects, types, variables, and channels (b) to add type abbreviations, (c) to add value definitions with types to the environment, and (d) to do type checking. Module dependency and pretty printing are done after parsing, without environment creation or type checking.

2. A "resolve" pass adds to the environment versions of all types, defining value expressions, axioms, and test cases in which all occurrences of names are replaced with references to the environment.

3. Tools like the confidence condition generator and translators operate on the resolved terms in the environment. And most further extensions to the tool will take this as their main input. It is straightforward to add new information to the environment as this is found useful or created during processing, and so the environment acts as an intermediate representation suitable for various kinds of processing.

4   Tool Requirements

In this section we consider the main requirements for the RAISE tool. We start in section 4.1 with considering soundness, and its particular manifestations in type checking, translation, and theorem proving. Then in section 4.2 we consider various aspects of usability.

4.1   Soundness

The first requirement is that a tool should be sound, i.e. it should not support or generate a conclusion that is not supported by the semantics of the specification being processed by the tool. Soundness is of particular concern to theorem provers, of course, but essentially the same criteria can be applied to other tools.

Type Checking. In common with other specification and programming languages, an RSL specification is only defined to mean anything at all provided it meets certain checks that show that it satisfies the syntax and static semantics of its language definition. So soundness in this context means that the tool should not accept, i.e. should report errors in, any specification that does not satisfy the syntax and static semantics.

Checking the grammar seems straightforward. There is a grammar in BNF, and provided (a) the lexical and syntactic productions are properly coded, and (b) we can rely on tools like flex and bison, we can conclude grammatical soundness: that incorrect grammar will not be accepted.

There is a denotational semantics of RSL that includes the static semantics [13], and is generally accepted as the official definition. But the critical problem is that in a document of some 350 pages, almost entirely formal, there are inevitably mistakes. The document is probably sufficient to answer the main questions about such a project: "Is the whole thing consistent?", "Do the domains exist?" But to detailed questions like "Is the static semantics correct?" one has two possible answers, either (a) "Yes by definition, if this is the defining document." or (b) "In this much material there must be mistakes." Answer (b) is certainly true (we discovered an example in preparing this paper), but leaves open the question of not only what these mistakes are, but what the correct version would be. In practice, of course, correcting mistakes once they are found is mostly straightforward: only occasionally are questions of substance raised by them. But this does not affect the theoretical question of where the ultimate authority is to be found.

Any programmer, given a tricky piece of C or whatever and asked what it means, will compile it and test it to find out. Some may check the documentation as well. If compiler and documentation differ (or appear to: often it is a matter of interpretation) it is a moot point which will be considered definitive. Programmers are forced to live with their compilers; documentation can be annotated. We can find such problems even at the level of type checking. For example, the RSL to C++ translator uses templates to model RSL types like sets and tuples. There are several functions defined for all types, which means there is considerable overloading. It turns out that GNU's gcc compiler is much more successful at disambiguating functions defined in several templates than Microsoft's Visual C++ compiler is. We don't know if there is a definition of C++ that could resolve which compiler is correct, but it wouldn't help us much anyway. We need the translator to produce code that is accepted by the compilers people have.

Translation. There are currently translations of almost the same subset of RSL into Standard ML and C++. The SML translator is intended for use like an interpreter, the C++ translator for generating code for use in implementations. So, for example, the C++ code is meant to be readable and does not enforce complete translatability. A function defined implicitly by a postcondition, for example, will produce a C++ function prototype with a comment reminding the user that there is more to be done by hand to complete the C++ code.

What does it mean for a translator to be sound? An (informal) definition is that, provided the translator runs successfully without generating error messages, and the compiler likewise, executing the resulting code without errors occurring must not produce results inconsistent with the specification[1].

This definition begs the main question: what is "consistent"? The "formal" answer to this question is, presumably, to define (specify) a relation (probably a simulation) between the semantics of RSL and the semantics of C++ and then show that the translator implements a (subset of) this relation. Given the sizes of the semantic definitions, would anyone seriously contemplate undertaking this? If they did, would anyone else believe them? An alternative is to suggest that if the specification of the translator were executable, so people could test it, they would eventually start to believe it.

We don't see how to get an executable formal specification of the translator, which means that even if we wrote one we would have then to write an implementation. Then we would want, to be "formal", to show that it was an implementation. Again we see no practical way to do this. And basically we

---

[1] We try hard, of course, to find errors at translation time rather than silently produce code that the compiler or execution will complain about, but it is occasionally impractical or not worth the effort. For example, we don't check if user-defined identifiers in RSL are C++ keywords. And we don't check that arithmetic overflow will not occur.

have written the thing twice. For reasonably sized programs, who is going to do this? And even if they did, what are the chances that both versions would be maintained?

Another suggested approach [14] is to prove correct the output of the translator against its input, by establishing and proving a simulation relation between the two. This may be possible for small programs, but given that one typically has a term in a relation expression for every statement in the output it is difficult to see how this is feasible for programs of any reasonable size.

One also has to be aware that the correctness of an application depends not only on its code, but on the operating system, the compiler, libraries, usually a window system, and, increasingly often, other applications. One needs to pay attention to all of these in considering how to ensure correctness of final behaviour. And the vast majority will normally be out of our control.

So how can we construct a correct translator and demonstrate its correctness? An answer is to distinguish between the "conceptual" problems (which we need to avoid, because they will necessitate redesign) and the "typos", the errors of implementation rather than conception, which we hope to avoid but will in practice need to weed out by quality assurance. So we first identify the conceptual problems: What is the subset of RSL we can translate? How do we deal with modules? How do we model the RSL types? How do we deal with translating the mathematical types like **Int** in RSL to inadequate representations like **int** in C++? How do we deal with differences in allowed characters for names? How do we deal with overloading, for which the rules in C++ are different from RSL? Where does C++ not enforce left-to-right evaluation order like RSL does?

Answers may be pragmatic (such as restricting the subset we attempt to translate) and partial (such as advising that for most applications **int** will be adequate, but in cases where it isn't the user will have to define something special) or they may involve writing pieces of ready-made C++ (like the templates for sets, lists, maps, and tuples). For these templates there are effectively specifications in the RSL proof rules.

Once these conceptual issues are decided, the writing of the actual translator is mostly straightforward, at least in a high-level language like Gentle. Again, the RSL proof rules provide detailed guidance on some issues, but a complete specification of the translator did not seem worth while: Gentle is almost the same in terms of length of description as a specification would be, and is almost as abstract.

To give an idea of what was hard, we briefly describe three problems that we had in correcting and extending the C++ translator after its first version [9] was done by a UNU/IIST fellow.

Expressions with Effects. We do not translate concurrency (yet) but we do translate RSL variables, and value expressions can involve writing to variables: they can have (side) effects. The original version of the translator tried to deal with effects by translating all RSL expressions into sequences of C++ statements, with result values being lifted to **return** statements. But the solution was not always successful and was sometimes clumsy. A much better approach was to recall that the RSL denotational semantics represents value expressions as having effects (here writing to variables) and also results (values). The result type of the function `Translate`, that takes as an argument an RSL value expression, was changed from `Statements` to the pair `Statements` and `Expression`. The `Statements` component translates the effect, and the `Expression` component translates the result. This solved a number of problems, particularly with ensuring that the order of execution was correct, and one could say the improvement came from a good specification.

Local Functions. RSL has a **local** expression that allows in particular for functions and variables to be defined locally to others. This is not supported in C++: a local function has to be declared at the top level (where it can be put in a little namespace to prevent name clashes). But declaring it there changes its scope, and in particular puts it outside the scope of local variables (which are allowed in C++) and the outer function's formal parameters. The adopted solution is to copy the formal parameters and local variables into the outer scope. But this solution fails when there is mutual recursion between the outer and local function. Finding a solution that did not just ban local functions but that is sound was as much a case of experiment as theory. There was a similar problem with translating quantified and comprehended expressions. Provided the quantification or comprehension is over a finite set, list, or map, such expressions can be translated via template functions. The template functions take function parameters, and functions for these parameters have to be defined in the outer scope: C++ does not admit lambda-expressions!

Templates. Initial development of the translator was done in a Linux environment using GNU's gcc as the compiler. Testing it in Windows and using Microsoft's Visual C++ as the compiler produced a number of problems with the overloading of functions produced through instantiating templates. It is difficult to see how specification could have helped with this problem, which has been tackled entirely through experiment.

We see that the hard problems are often not at the detailed statement or expression level where most academic work tends to concentrate, but involve higher-level concepts like scope and visibility, recursion, and the environment in which the output should execute.

Theorem Provers. Here is where soundness seems most obviously to arise, but in fact (undetected) lack of soundness in any tool would be disastrous.

There is a formal definition of the proof rules for RSL [15], which effectively defines an axiomatic semantics. Whether this axiomatic semantics is consistent with the denotational one is a question for which the answer can only be "They are intended to be, but it has not and in practice cannot be demonstrated." The best approach is probably to say that the denotational semantics gives evidence that the semantic domains exist; for detailed questions the axiomatic semantics provides the easiest way to find answers.

There is an interactive theorem prover (called the "justification editor") in the original RAISE tools. It uses for its proof rules a language which is simpler than those in [15], but adequate for most purposes. There are some short cuts that can be taken, in particular the assumption that terms are well-formed (scope- and type-checked) rather than having to define when they are. In the book on the RAISE method [3] we were careful to separate out the "basic" rules from the "derived" ones that we believe follow as consequences. There are over 200 basic rules, while in the current version of the justification editor there are over 2000 rules altogether: the rules found most useful in proofs are rarely the basic ones. Proving that 90% of these rules follow from the other 10% was only attempted recently (for the applicative ones, using the PVS translator). Several erroneous rules were discovered.

How do we show that the justification editor is correct? In part we rely on transparency: the 2000+ rules are printed in a document that is produced directly from the files of rules input to the editor. But there are still some parts of the tool that are hard coded: the matching of terms to rules and the consequent instantiation of term variables; the instantiation of side-conditions to be proved when they don't simplify; the workings of the simplifier.

4.2   Usability

There are a collection of requirements that refer in general to the usefulness of a tool.

Speed. It is convenient when writing specifications to be able to check them frequently, especially when the specification language is unfamiliar. This requires that a small specification be type checked within a second or two on a standard PC. The tool meets this requirement easily (although it has never been optimised for speed). Neither has size proved a problem: modern machines have plenty of space.

Clear Messages. Messages should be clear and allow the user to identify the problem easily.
The original tools took the approach that the error messages should be as close as possible to the informal description of the static semantics in the book on RSL [1]. These descriptions aim for precision, but are not always very readable. The new tool gives a higher priority to comprehensibility, preferring, for example, "Values of type A and type B cannot be compared" to "Types A and B do not have a least upper bound".
It should be policy to report as many errors as possible (except perhaps for parse errors) and to avoid multiple error messages for a single cause. We try to prevent multiple messages from one error, and they seem to be infrequent.

Portability. One of the problems with the original tools was their restriction to Sun workstations. The new ones are required to run on as wide a range of machines as possible. Portability also includes the translators generating code that will work with common compilers for the target languages.

Finally, any third-party tools needed should be either free or very common. Gentle is written in C, and the tool is written mostly in Gentle's language plus a few files of C. So the tool can be built on any machine that allows C to be compiled. We have compiled and used the tool in Windows 95, 98, 2000, ME and NT, plus Sun Solaris and Linux. The tool is statically linked to remove the risk of library version problems. The (compressed) tool is under 800K bytes, and so can quickly be downloaded over a slow connection or put onto a floppy (which is very useful when teaching courses: participants can take the tool home or to work to load on a PC).

Portability and small size are enhanced by making the tool "command line": there is no GUI. A simple but quite effective user interface is provided through emacs. The emacs "compile" facility is used to run the tool. This puts messages in a separate window, and clicking on a message puts the cursor on the source of the error. All the tool components can be run from an emacs menu. There is a cut-down version of emacs available for Windows that provides all the facilities needed and that fits on one floppy disk.

emacs is not essential: the tool can be run from the command line in a shell. But switching between a shell window where errors are displayed and an editor to fix them is tedious and error-prone.

Most of the people we teach do not have the resources to buy much software. The RAISE tool itself is open source, distributed under the GNU Public License (GPL). It uses Gentle, which is free and places no restriction on tools generated with it. VCG is free. The SML translator is aimed at SML of New Jersey, which is free, and the C++ translator works with gcc (which is GPL) or Microsoft's Visual C++, which seems quite common. PVS is free (but it only runs in Linux on a PC or in Solaris on a Sun Sparc). The differences mentioned earlier between C++ compilers have been the biggest portability problem so far.

Extensibility. Development of the tool has been gradual, involving a number of UNU/IIST fellows, and is still continuing. It needs to be possible for someone to come to UNU/IIST and write a new component supervised by someone who knows the tool but without relying on some permanent project team, and this has been possible in practice.

Ease of Use. To be used on courses, the tool must be capable of being learned quickly by new users.

Users seem to use the tool quickly. emacs is typically new to Windows users, but there are menus for doing most things beyond basic editing. You can start to use emacs quickly without having to learn the myriad short-cuts that the experienced user employs.

It is interesting to compare emacs with the structure editor "eden" of the original RAISE tools. Structure editors were seen at the time those tools were developed as a new and exciting development, that would make it much easier to write texts in languages with formal grammars, since the tool would enforce the grammar. But in practice users find such editors clumsy and difficult to use: within a short time they input RSL into files with a text editor and only use eden as a batch checker.

The structure editor approach of eden was extremely successful, however, in creating the justification editor, the proof tool of the original RAISE tools. Here the tool does most of the creation of RSL expressions as proof rules are applied, and the structure editor supports the selection of sub-expressions, prevents users altering parts of proofs, provides a good pretty-printed display, etc.

Ease of Installation. To be used on courses, the tool must be capable of rapid installation in Windows and Unix/Linux environments, particularly the former. It should, for example, be possible to install it on every PC in a laboratory within an hour.

Installation is simple. There are differences between Windows and Unix/Linux, mainly because emacs is almost always already available in the latter, but usually has to be installed on the former. A "self installing executable" for Windows, and .deb and .rpm versions for Linux would be useful.

Ease of Maintenance. There is very little effort available for maintenance, so in particular the danger of proliferating features that are dependent on host environments needs to be minimised. Again, the C++ translator has proved to be the most problematic part in this respect.

5   Gaining Confidence in Specifications

If specifications of reasonable size contain errors, both "typo" and "conceptual", what effective means do we have for finding them?

The best means are undoubtedly mechanical, and syntax, scope, and type checking are very useful. But these are also the limits of purely mechanical aids, unless we also admit semi-decision procedures.

An obvious aid would be theorem proving. But this is in our experience a very expensive and inefficient way to find errors. It is hard to distinguish between the theorem that is not provable and the one that you haven't found a strategy for. It seems rare that a proof exposes an error by simplifying to "false" when you expect "true".

The advantage of proof, of course, is that the theorems you formulate and attempt to prove reflect your understanding of the problem, of the requirements, and failing to prove them can indicate errors that could never be found by analysing the specification on its own. That is, proof against requirements can expose the "external" errors that are failures to meet the requirements. Without such an external reference, or oracle, we can only find the "internal" errors that are failures to specify properly and consistently. Internal errors often in practice have their roots in external ones, but the relation is not a necessary one.

RSL (and the tool) supports the formulation of theorems about specifications through "theories". Theories may take the form of Boolean RSL expressions, or "implementation" (refinement) relations between classes (which may in turn be expanded into RSL expressions).

5.1   Testing

Testing specifications also has the advantage of (potentially) bringing external errors to light, provided the test cases are derived from the requirements rather than just from the specification. Generating test cases from a specification and executing them on the implementation is a useful way of gaining confidence in that implementation, but tells you nothing about external errors. Asking your user to check the test cases can do so, however (and they may well find them more understandable than the specification!). But directly testing specifications does require that those specifications be executable.

To support testing specifications, the **test_case** declaration was added to RSL. A **test_case** declaration consists simply of a series of value expressions, optionally tagged with identifiers. Semantically test cases are no more than comments. But they are indications to translation tools that code should be generated to execute them. In the C++ translator, for example, they cause a `main` function to be generated that will output the tags and values. Test cases are often written so that they should evaluate to **true**, which makes for easy checking as well as documenting as part of the specification what the expected results of expressions are, but values of any RSL type are allowed.

To take a simple example (designed to show properties of the C++ translator rather than the specification) consider the following specification

scheme A =
   class
      variable x : **Int** := 1
      test_case
         [t1] x = 1, -- check that x is correctly initialised
         [t2] (x := x + 1 ; x) = (x := x + 1 ; x − 1),
                          -- check order of evaluation is left-to-right
         [t3] x = 3   -- check that previous test case increased x twice
   end

Translating, compiling and running this example does, as expected, generate the output

```
[t1]  true
[t2]  true
[t3]  true
```

Test cases are evaluated in sequence, and so can be used to test scenarios in which there are several updates to an imperative state before observations are made.

Capturing scenarios as test cases indicates another feature of test cases: they can be seen as high-level descriptions of requirements, and hence as specifications, in fact as abstractions of the specification they are used to test. Bernhard Aichernig has developed this view of testing [16, 17].

Bottom-up testing of modular specifications is supported by a convention that test cases in lower level modules are ignored. So lower level modules can be tested through test cases and then included in larger specifications without being changed.

5.2   Confidence Conditions

Another technique that has proved useful is the generation of confidence conditions. Confidence conditions are conditions that should generally be true if the module is to be consistent, but that cannot in general be determined as true by a tool. There is a confidence condition generator as part of the RAISE tool that generates the following conditions:

1. Arguments of invocations of functions and operators are in subtypes, and, for partial functions and operators, preconditions are satisfied.
2. Values supposed to be in subtypes are in the subtypes. These conditions are generated for
   - values in explicit value definitions (i.e. constants);
   - result values of explicit function definitions;
   - initial values of variables;
   - values assigned to variables;
   - values output on channels.
3. Subtypes are not empty.
4. Values satisfying the restrictions exist for implicit value and function definitions (i.e. functions defined using **post**).
5. The classes of actual scheme parameters implement the classes of the formal parameters.
6. For an implementation relation, the implementing class implements the implemented class. This gives a means of expanding such a relation or expression, by asserting the relation in a theory and then generating the confidence conditions for the theory.

In theory, confidence conditions should be proved. Currently the advice is to check them carefully by hand. They can be regarded as an aid to effective specification reading. There is, however, a large "noise" level in checking them: given a reasonably proficiently written specification, few of them, typically less than 5%, will be false and these few can easily be overlooked. The PVS translator generates them as lemmas (unless they also occur as "type check conditions" (TCCs) when the translator's output is checked by the PVS tool) and we hope to discharge most of the true ones automatically.

Confidence conditions are only useful, of course, in checking for internal consistency: they cannot detect external errors, failures to meet requirements.

There is also a technical problem with proving confidence conditions. If the specification is indeed inconsistent then there is a danger that the inconsistency can allow the condition to be proved. For example, the declaration

value x : **Nat** $= -1$

generates the confidence condition

$$-1 \geq 0$$

which is obviously false, but which can also be proved true using the inconsistent declaration. This is not a problem if confidence conditions are inspected rather than proved, but a tool aiming to automate their proof needs to avoid such problems.

Of the confidence conditions enumerated above, 1 and 2 are included in the translators. That is, code is included to check them at run-time, and to generate warnings if they are not satisfied. In the case of the C++ translator, inclusion of the code is a compile-time option. Conversely, one can say that careful checking (or proving) of confidence conditions is a precondition for turning this option off. "Confidence conditions checked" (or "proved") is a useful attribute in a quality control system.

6   Conclusions

The development of the RAISE tool illustrates a number of practical problems in the development of non-trivial software systems. We have seen various problems arising, particularly concerned with soundness, that are more or less amenable to solution by a more formal treatment. We have also seen how the tool can provide support for activities like testing and confidence condition generation and analysis that help us gain confidence in specifications.

One can also consider what implications these experiences have on the use of formal methods in general. If we are concerned with the development of software applications which are of reasonable size and that are not safety- or mission-critical, there will be definite limitations on the resources that it is economic to use. So the main question is "Does the expected improvement justify the resources used?" For non-critical systems the tools and methods used are not intended in themselves to help convince some third party inspector that things are correct: they have to convince the users. They need to make the development process more efficient, more predictable, and more reliable, and to make the products more reliable and more maintainable.

First we need to consider if the RAISE tool is a typical example of software development. One way in which it is atypical is that it is an example in a well-studied domain: formal language analysis and processing. One should not underestimate the extent that early work on formalising languages has improved our ability to deal with them with confidence. Second, there was a formal description of most of what the type checker was to achieve, though not the translators. Third, the developer of the type checker at least was extremely familiar with the RAISE language, having worked on its development. But then many software developers work in particular domains with which they have become very familiar.

Another factor we think relevant is the high level of the Gentle language. It seems about as terse and almost as abstract as a specification would be. We think it unlikely we can persuade people to "write it twice" unless there is a very definite pay back.

Formal languages have two definite advantages over programming languages: formality and abstraction. Formality means we can reason about our descriptions, and in the design of these languages we place the emphasis on constructs that support reasoning, by having clean semantics and convenient proof rules. But ultimately the full power of formality depends on being able to do proof, and we are still some way from being able to do proof except at exorbitant cost on anything but small descriptions. And there are limits, particularly the inevitable dependence of any piece of software on other software that we have no control over, on being able to reason from the properties of what we write to the properties of the final system.

Abstraction does have definite advantages: in particular it allows us to defer the design of some parts while we concentrate on others. It may, as in RAISE, prevent us being able to execute the description for testing. But we also have the possibility of doing rapid prototypes of the abstract parts in order to test others via interpretation or translation. This also implies modularity, so we can isolate the abstract part, and replace it with a prototype for testing, without touching other parts.

Our suspicion is that abstraction has something to do with why graphical approaches are popular. There is truth in the old saying "a picture is worth a thousand words", and it is also noticeable that people use diagrams to emphasise certain concepts or issues while leaving out many others. People rarely, for example, include all the attributes or all the methods in a class diagram.

Abstraction also has a role to play in the generation of documents that can help in maintenance, since abstraction helps focus on what is critical.

Because people are typically producing software that needs to work with other software, or that will be extended later by further products, we believe that domain modelling, typically with a wider scope than the domain of the immediate problem, can be very useful. Abstraction allows us to do this, and perhaps we should also mostly do it in "sketch" mode where we define the domains in terms of types, but ignore most of the functions and operations we will need. This is how many users use UML class diagrams, concentrating on the entities and their relations.

We feel we can have little confidence in anything more than the fairly trivial without testing it. So it seems that being able to execute the specification in some way is critical to its use. The success of model checking also supports this, but we would also want to be able to produce code that is mostly good enough to use in the final product: we cannot persuade people to write much the same thing twice.

So there seem to be two modes in which specifications can be useful. One is the domain modelling mode where much is left incomplete. And there is no reason why this should not be generated from graphical input.

Second we can use a specification language as something like a high-level programming language, where we are able to test and translate to an implementation with little further cost, and maintain only the original description.

But both uses depend on our being able to show that this approach is more useful than other approaches. We have to find ways of exploiting the formal underpinnings of specification languages to create useful additional tools that can find errors earlier, do other analysis, produce better documentation, in general *add value* [18].

Acknowledgements

A number of UNU/IIST fellows have worked on the RAISE tool:

Tan Xinming, Wuhan Jiaotong University, China
Ms He Hua, Peking University, Beijing, China
Ke Wei, Chinese Academy of Sciences, Beijing, China
Univan Ahn, Kim Il Sung University, Pyongyang, DPR Korea
Ms Ana Funes and Aristides Dasso, University of San Luis, San Luis, Argentina
Li Dan, Guizhou Academy of Sciences, Guiyang, China

References

1. The RAISE Language Group. *The RAISE Specification Language.* BCS Practitioner Series. Prentice Hall, 1992. Available from Terma A/S. Contact jnp@terma.com.
2. B. Dandanell, J. Gørtz, J. Storbank Pedersen, and E. Zierau. Experiences from Applications of RAISE. In *FME'93: Industrial Strength Formal Methods*, volume 670 of *Lecture Notes in Computer Science.* Springer-Verlag, 1993.
3. The RAISE Method Group. *The RAISE Development Method.* BCS Practitioner Series. Prentice Hall, 1995. Available by ftp from ftp://ftp.iist.unu.edu/pub/RAISE/method_book.
4. P.M. Bruun et al. RAISE Tools Reference Manual. Technical Report LACOS/CRI/DOC/17, CRI: Computer Resources International, 1995.
5. Hung Dang Van, Chris George, Tomasz Janowski, and Richard Moore, editors. *Specification Case Studies in RAISE.* FACIT. Springer, 2002. Web site: http://www.iist.unu.edu/RAISE_Case_Studies.
6. Friedrich Wilhelm Schröer. The GENTLE Compiler Construction System, 1997. GENTLE is available from http://www.first.gmd.de/gentle.
7. He Hua. A Prettyprinter for the RAISE Specification Language. Technical Report 150, UNU/IIST, P.O.Box 3058, Macau, December 1998.
8. Ke Wei and Chris George. An RSL to SML Translator. Technical Report 208, UNU/IIST, P.O. Box 3058, Macau, August 2000.
9. Univan Ahn and Chris George. C++ Translator for RAISE Specification Language. Technical Report 220, UNU/IIST, P.O. Box 3058, Macau, November 2000.

10. Aristides Dasso and Chris George. Transforming RSL into PVS. Technical Report 256, UNU/IIST, P.O. Box 3058, Macau, May 2002.
11. Ana Funes and Chris George. Formal Foundations in RSL for UML Class Diagrams. Technical Report 253, UNU/IIST, P.O. Box 3058, Macau, May 2002.
12. Li Dan and Bernhard K. Aichernig. Automatic Test Case Generation for RAISE. Technical Report 273, UNU/IIST, P.O.Box 3058, Macau, February 2003.
13. R.E. Milne. The semantic foundations of the RAISE specification language. Technical Report RAISE/STC/REM/11, STC/STL, Harlow, UK, 1990.
14. A. Pnueli, M. Siegel, and E. Singerman. Translation validation. In Bernhard Steffen, editor, *TACAS'98: Tools and Algorithms for the Construction and Aanlysis of Systems*, volume 1384 of *Lecture Notes in Computer Science*, pages 151–166, Lisbon, Portugal, March/April 1998. Springer Verlag.
15. R.E. Milne. The proof theory for the RAISE specification language. Technical Report RAISE/STC/REM/12, STC/STL, Harlow, UK, 1990.
16. Bernhard Aichernig. *Systematic Black-Box Testing of Computer-Based Systems through Formal Abstraction Techniques*. PhD thesis, Institute for Software Technology, TU Graz, Austria, January 2001. Supervisor: Peter Lucas.
17. Bernhard K. Aichernig. Test-Design through Abstraction – A Systematic Approach Based on the Refinement Calculus. *Journal of Universal Computer Science*, 7(8):710 – 735, August 2001.
18. John Rushby. Mechanized formal methods: Where next? In Jeannette Wing and Jim Woodcock, editors, *FM99: The World Congress in Formal Methods*, volume 1708 of *Lecture Notes in Computer Science*, pages 48–51, Toulouse, France, September 1999. Springer Verlag.

An Algebraic Approach
to the VERILOG Programming

He Jifeng*

United Nations University
International Institute For Software Technology
P.O.Box 3058, Macau
jifeng@iist.unu.edu

Abstract. The semantics of a hardware description language is usually given in terms of how a simulator should behave. This paper adopts a different strategy by first listing a collection of equational laws expressing algebraic properties of VERILOG programs. It outlines some techniques of formal derivation of operational model and denotational presentation of the language VERILOG from its algebraic definition.

1 Introduction

Modern hardware design typically uses the hardware description languages to express designs at various levels of abstraction. A hardware description language is a high level programming language, with the usual programming constructs such as assignment, conditional and iteration, and appropriate extension for real-time, concurrency and data structures suitable for modelling hardware. The common approach is to first build a high level design, using programming constructs for hardware behaviour descriptions. The high level design is then refined using a subset of the description language which explores the underlying architecture of the hardware. This process may be repeated until the design is at a sufficiently lower level such that the hardware device can be synthesised from it. For ensuring correctness of the development, precise understanding of the hardware description languages is important.

Contemporary hardware description languages VHDL and VERILOG [18, 19, 23, 25] are an increasingly popular way to develop hardware industry as tool support improves and standards become established. The formal semantics of VHDL has been studied quite thoroughly, but that of VERILOG less so.

The computation of a VERILOG program is driven by events, which are either the change of the values of wires or registers, or an explicitly generated abstract signal. Like in CSP [16], the input mechanism in VERILOG is synchronous, i.e., an input event can happen only when the corresponding output event becomes available. However, the output in VERILOG is asynchronous; a

---

* On leave from East China Normal University, Shanghai, China. The work is also partially supported by the 211 Key Subject Project of the ministry of education of China.

B.K. Aichernig and T. Maibaum (Eds.): Formal Methods ..., LNCS 2757, pp. 65–80, 2003.

process can broadcast a message to its environment without consulting its partners. An event control construct $(\varrho(e)\,S)$ can be fired by the event output by the execution of its sequential predecessor. This means that communications can take place among both parallel components and sequential components.

The semantics of VERILOG is usually given in terms of how a simulator should behave. In contrast to many attempts to formalise semantics of the hardware description languages, this paper adopts a different strategy, which yields an even more precise characterisation of VERILOG programs. We start by listing a collection of laws expressing familiar properties of the chosen operators, and their mutual interactions. These laws are sufficiently powerful to reduce every program to a *head normal form*. Moreover, they also enable us to formalise a complete recipe for executing an arbitrary VERILOG program, and for reasoning about such execution. The paper also illustrates how to construct a *denotational* presentation for VERILOG from its algebraic definition.

The remaining of the paper is organised as follows. Section 2 discusses algebraic properties of VERILOG programs, and shows how to convert an arbitrary program to a head normal form using the equational laws. Section 3 derives a collection of transition rules from the algebraic presentation of VERILOG, which can be taken in execution of programs. Section 4 presents a definition of bisimulation, and demonstrates the soundness of the algebraic semantics with respect to the operational semantics. In Section 5, we outline some techniques of derivation of an observation-oriented semantics for VERILOG from its algebraic definition.

2   Algebraic Presentation

The simple version of VERILOG contains the following categories of syntactic elements:

1. Sequential Process:

$$S ::= PC \mid S; S \mid S \triangleleft b \triangleright S \mid b * S \mid g\,S \mid \textsf{always}\,S$$

where $PC ::= (x := e) \mid \textsf{skip} \mid \textsf{sink} \mid \bot$

and g is a guard used for scheduling

$$g ::= \#(n) \text{ (time delay)} \mid \varrho(\eta) \text{ (event control)}$$

$$\eta ::= \ \sim v \text{ (value change)} \mid \ \uparrow v \text{ (value rising)}$$

$$\mid \ \downarrow v \text{ (value falling)} \mid \eta\,or\,\eta \text{ (composite event)}$$

2. Parallel Process (Module): $P ::= S \mid P \| P$

We will use $P \equiv Q$ to indicate that P and Q are the same program. For convenience, the notation ϵ is used to model a terminated program in the later discussion.

This section examines each VERILOG construct in turn, and uncovers the laws governing it. The set of laws is not exhaustive; we restrict ourselves to the laws needed to translate programs to head normal forms. Other laws can be deduced from these laws, either by elementary manipulation, or by structural induction on head normal forms,

We define $Event =_{df} \{\uparrow x, \quad \downarrow x \mid x \in Var\}$, and let the notation τ to stand for the silent event, and $Event_\tau =_{df} Event \cup \{\tau\}$.

2.1   Guarded Choice

To facilitate equational reasoning, we add the guarded choice constructor $[\![$ to the language, which takes as arguments a number of guarded processes. A guarded process is a guard and a process $(g\ P)$

$$[\![\{g_1\ P_1, \ .., \ g_n\ P_n\}$$

Guards may be *simple* $\varrho(e)$, $\#(1)$, e and τ, or *composite* $\varrho(\eta_1\ or\ ...\ or\ \eta_n)$, $b\&e$ and $b\&\tau$ where b is a Boolean expression.

For an input guard $\varrho(\eta)$ we define $E(\eta)$ as the set of simple events in η

$$E(\varrho(\eta)) =_{df} \{\eta\} \quad \text{if } \eta \in Event$$
$$E(\varrho(\sim x)) =_{df} \{\downarrow x, \ \uparrow x\}$$
$$E(\varrho(\eta_1\ or\ \eta_2)) =_{df} E(\varrho(\eta_1)) \cup E(\varrho(\eta_2))$$

We adopt the convention $E(g) = \emptyset$ for delay and output guards.

A choice construct is *well-formed* if

1. $g_i = g_j = \#(1)$ implies $P_i \equiv P_j$, and
2. $E(g_i) \cap E(g_j) \neq \emptyset$ implies $P_i \equiv P_j$, and
3. The Boolean components of its output guards satisfy $\vee_i b_i = true$ or $\vee_i b_i = false$, where a simple output guard e should be seen as $true\&e$.

We will confine ourselves to well-formed choice constructs.

The order of arguments in a choice construct is irrelevant.

L1 $[\![\{g_1\ P_1, .., g_n\ P_n\} = [\![\{g_{\pi(1)}\ P_{\pi(1)}, .., g_{\pi(n)}\ P_{\pi(n)}\}$ for any permutation π.

The choice construct of no arguments is `sink`.

L2 $[\![\{\} = $ `sink`.

If a guarded process is already present, adding it again has no effect.

L3 $[\![\{g\ P,\ G\} = [\![\{g\ P,\ g\ P,\ G\}$

A guard with the Boolean component false is never activated.

L4 $[\![\{false\&e\ P,\ G\} = [\![\{G\}$

The Boolean component true of a composite guard can be removed.

L5 $[\![\{true\&e\ P,\ G\} = [\![\{e\ P,\ G\}$

If two timing events guard the same process, then they can be amalgamated.

L6 $[\![\{\varrho(\eta_1)\ P,\ \varrho(\eta_2)\ P,\ G\} = [\![\{\varrho(\eta_1\ or\ \eta_2)\ P,\ G\}$

L7 $[\![\{\varrho(\uparrow x)\ P,\ \varrho(\downarrow x)\ P,\ G\} = [\![\{\varrho(\sim x)\ P,\ G\}$

L8 $\|\{b\&e\ P,\ c\&e\ P,\ G\}\ =\ \|\{(b\vee c)\&e\ P,\ G\}$

An output guard can not rescue a chaotic process which it guards.

L9 $\|\{b\&e\ \bot,\ G\}\ =\ \|\{b\&\tau\ \bot,\ G\}$

L10 $\|\{b\&\tau\ \bot,\ b\&e\ P,\ G\}\ =\ \|\{b\&\tau\ \bot,\ G\}$

The guarded process $(\tau\ \bot)$ is the zero of the choice constructor.

L11 $\|\{\tau\bot,\ G\}\ =\ \bot$

A τ guard is always ready, and its execution has no effect other than to block the event control statement which it guards to be fired by the environment.

L12 $\|\{b\&\tau\ \|\{c_1\&e_1\ P_1,\ ..,\ c_m\&e_m\ P_m\},\ G\}=\|\{(b\wedge c_1)\&e_1\ P_1,\ ..,\ (b\wedge c_m)\&e_m\ P_m,\ G\}$

A guarded process can be dropped if its activation makes no progress, or its guard can never be fired.

L13 $\|\{\varrho(e)\ \|\{G\},\ G\}\ =\ \|\{G\}$

L14 $\|\{\#(1)\ \|\{G\},\ G\}\ =\ \|\{G\}$

L15 $\|\{\#(1)\ P,\ b_1\&e_1\ Q_1,\ ..,\ b_n\&e_n\ Q_n,\ G\}\ =\ \|\{b_1\&e_1,\ ..,\ b_n\&e_n,\ G\}$

provided that $\vee_i b_i = true$.

L16 $\|\{\tau\ \|\{G_1,\ G_2\},\ G_2\}\ =\ \|\{G_1,\ G_2\}$ if G_1 has no input guard.

2.2   Timing Control Statement

An event-control construct waits for an event to occur. Events do not model states, but their changes, and they may be interpreted as the arrival of a rising signal edge or an acknowledgement of another process. An event-control construct can be converted into a choice construct with simple primitive event guards using the following laws.

L1 $\varrho(\eta)\ P\ =\ \|\{\varrho(\eta)\ P\}$

L2 $\#(1)\ S\ =\ \|\{\#(1)\ S\}$

L3 $\#(n+1)\ S\ =\ \|\{\#(1)\ (\#(n)\ S)\}$

2.3   Conditional

$P\lhd b\rhd Q$ describes a program which behaves like P if the initial value of b is true, or like Q if the initial value of b is false.

L1 $P\lhd b\rhd Q\ =\ \|\{b\&\tau\ P,\ \neg b\&\tau\ Q\}$

This law in conjunction with the algebraic properties of the $\|$ constructor is strong enough to prove additional useful laws, as shown below.

Lemma 2.1

(1) $S_1\lhd b\rhd S_2\ =\ S_2\lhd b\rhd S_1$

(2) $S_1\lhd b\rhd (S_2\lhd c\rhd S_3)\ =\ (S_1\lhd b\rhd S_2)\lhd c\rhd (S_1\lhd b\rhd S_3)$

(3) $(S_1\lhd b\rhd S_2)\lhd c\rhd S_3\ =\ S_1\lhd b\wedge c\rhd (S_2\lhd c\rhd S_3)$

(4) $(S \lhd b \rhd S) = \texttt{skip}; S$

(5) $S_1 \lhd true \rhd S_2 = \texttt{skip}; S_1$

2.4 Sequential Composition

Sequential composition is associative, and it has $\bot$ as its left zero.

L1 $S_1; (S_2; S_3) = (S_1; S_2); S_3$

L2 $\bot; S = \bot$

It distributes backward through guarded choice.

L3 $[\!|\{g_1\, P_1, .., g_n\, P_n\}; Q = [\!|\{g_1\, (P_1; Q), .., g_n\, (P_n; Q)\}$

It also has $\texttt{sink}$ as its left zero, and distributes back through conditional.

Lemma 2.2

(1) $\texttt{sink}; S = \texttt{sink}$

(2) $(P \lhd b \rhd Q); R = (P; R) \lhd b \rhd (Q; R)$

2.5 Iteration

$b * S$ repeats the program S as long as b is true before each iteration.

L1 $b * S = (S; (b * S)) \lhd b \rhd \texttt{skip}$

$\texttt{always}\, S$ executes S forever.

L2 $\texttt{always}\, S = S; \texttt{always}\, S$

2.6 Assignment

The execution of the assignment $x := f$ may update the value of variable x, thereby generating an output event $\uparrow x$ or $\downarrow x$.

L1 $x := f = [\!|\{(x < f)\&(\uparrow x)\ \epsilon,\ (x = f)\&\tau\ \epsilon,\ (x > f)\&(\downarrow x)\ \epsilon\}$

L2 $\texttt{skip} = [\!|\{\tau\ \epsilon\}$

The events generated by an assignment can be used to awake its partners.

L3 Let $P = [\!|\{g_1\, P_1, .., g_n\, P_n\}$ where all input guards in $\{g_1, .., g_n\}$ are simple and distinct, then

$$b\&e\ (\epsilon; P) = \begin{cases} b\&e\ P \ \text{ if } \varrho(e) \notin \{g_1, .., g_n\} \\ b\&e\ P_k \ \text{ if } g_k = \varrho(e) \end{cases}$$

$\texttt{skip}$ is NOT the unit of sequential composition. For example, the execution of $(\varrho(\uparrow w)\ S)$ will be resumed after the arrival of a rising edge of w, but the event $\varrho(\uparrow w)$ in $\texttt{skip}; (\varrho(\uparrow w)\ S)$ can not be triggered before $\texttt{skip}$ is executed.

Definition 2.1
A sequential process is *event control insensitive* if it has the following forms

- $[\{g_1\,P_1, ..., g_n\,P_n\}$, where none of g_i is an input event guard.
- $(x := e)$, or skip, or sink, or $\perp$
- $S_1 \lhd b \rhd S_2$, or $b * S$
- $(S; T)$, or always S where S is insensitive.

Lemma 2.3 skip; $S \;=\; S$ if S is event control insensitive.

2.7   Parallel

Parallel processes interact each other via shared variables. The parallel operator is associative and symmetric, and has skip as its unit and $\perp$ as its zero.

L1 $P \,\|\, Q \;=\; Q \,\|\, P$

L2 $(P \,\|\, Q) \,\|\, R \;=\; P \,\|\, (Q \,\|\, R)$

L3 $P \,\|\, \text{skip} \;=\; P$

L4 $P \,\|\, \perp \;=\; \perp$

The following expansion rules permit us to convert a parallel construct into a choice one.

L5 Let $A1, B1 \subseteq Event_\tau$, and $A2, B2 \subseteq Event$.

(1) Let $P \;=\; [\{b_i \& e_i\,P1_i \,|\, e_i \in A1\} \cup \{\varrho(h_j)\,P2j \,|\, h_j \in A2\}$

and $Q \;=\; [\{\hat{b}_i \& \hat{e}_i\,Q1_i \,|\, \hat{e}_i \in B1\} \cup \{\varrho(\hat{h}_j)\,Q2_j \,|\, \hat{h}_j \in B2\}$

$$
P\|Q \;=\; [\ \left(\begin{array}{l}
\{b_i \& e_i\ (P1_i\|Q) \mid e_i \in A1 \setminus B2\} \cup \\
\{b_i \& e_i\ (P1_i\|Q2_j) \mid e_i = \hat{h}_j \in (A1 \cap B2)\} \cup \\
\{\hat{b}_i \& \hat{e}_i\ (P\|Q1_i) \mid \hat{e}_i \in B1 \setminus A2\} \cup \\
\{\hat{b}_i \& \hat{e}_i\ (P2_k\|Q1_i) \mid \hat{e}_i = h_k \in (B1 \cap A2)\} \cup \\
\{\varrho(h_j)\ (P2_j\|Q) \mid h_j \in A2 \setminus B2\} \cup \\
\{\varrho(h_j)\ (P2_j\|Q2_k) \mid h_j = \hat{h}_k \in A2 \cap B2\} \cup \\
\{\varrho(\hat{h}_j)\ (P\|Q2_j) \mid \hat{h}_j \in B2 \setminus A2\}
\end{array}\right)
$$

(2) Let $P \;=\; [\{\varrho(h_j)\,P2j \,|\, h_j \in A2\} \cup \{\#(1)\,P3\}$

and $Q \;=\; [\{\varrho(\hat{h}_j)\,Q2_j \,|\, \hat{h}_j \in B2\} \cup \{\#(1)\,Q3\}$

$$
P\|Q \;=\; [\ \left(\begin{array}{l}
\{\varrho(h_j)\ (P2_j\|Q) \mid h_j \in A2 \setminus B2\} \cup \\
\{\varrho(h_j)\ (P2_j\|Q2_k) \mid h_j = \hat{h}_k \in A2 \cap B2\} \cup \\
\{\varrho(\hat{h}_j)\ (P\|Q2_j) \mid \hat{h}_j \in B2 \setminus A2\} \cup \\
\{\#(1)\ (P3\|Q3)\}
\end{array}\right)
$$

(3) Let $P = \|\{\varrho(h_j)\,P2j \mid h_j \in A2\}$,

and $Q = \|\{\varrho(\hat{h}_j)\,Q2_j \mid \hat{h}_j \in B2\} \cup \{\#(1)\,Q3\}$

$$P\|Q = \|\begin{pmatrix} \{\varrho(h_j)\,(P2_j\|Q) \mid h_j \in A2 \setminus B2\}\cup \\ \{\varrho(h_j)\,(P2_j\|Q2_k) \mid h_j = \hat{h}_k \in A2 \cap B2\}\cup \\ \{\varrho(\hat{h}_j)\,(P\|Q2_j) \mid \hat{h}_j \in B2 \setminus A2\}\cup \\ \{\#(1)\,(P\|Q3)\} \end{pmatrix}$$

(4) Let $P = \|\{b_i\&e_i\,P1_i \mid e_i \in A_1\} \cup \{\varrho(h_j)\,P2j \mid h_j \in A2\}$ where $\vee_i b_i = true$

and $Q = \|\{\varrho(\hat{h}_j)\,Q2_j \mid \hat{h}_j \in B2\} \cup \{\#(1)\,Q3\}$

$$P\|Q = \|\begin{pmatrix} \{b_i\&e_i\,(P1_i\|Q) \mid e_i \in A1 \setminus B2\}\cup \\ \{b_i\&e_i\,(P1_i\|Q2_j) \mid e_i = \hat{h}_j \in (A1 \cap B2)\}\cup \\ \{\varrho(h_j)\,(P2_j\|Q) \mid h_j \in A2 \setminus B2\}\cup \\ \{\varrho(h_j)\,(P2_j\|Q2_k) \mid h_j = \hat{h}_k \in A2 \cap B2\}\cup \\ \{\varrho(\hat{h}_j)\,(P\|Q2_j) \mid \hat{h}_j \in B2 \setminus A2\} \end{pmatrix}$$

L6 $(x := f_1)\|(y := f_2) = \|\begin{Bmatrix} (x < f_1)\&\uparrow x\,(y := f_2),\ \ (x > f_1)\&\downarrow x\,(y := f_2), \\ (x = f_1)\&\tau\,(y := f_2),\ \ (y = f_2)\&\tau\,(x := f_1), \\ (y < f_2)\&\uparrow y\,(x := f_1),\ \ (y > f_2)\&\downarrow y\,(x := f_1) \end{Bmatrix}$

L7 Let $A1 \subseteq Event_\tau$ and $A2 \subseteq Event$.

and $P = \|\{b_i\&e_i\,P1_i \mid e_i \in A1\} \cup \{\varrho(h_j)\,P2_j \mid h_j \in A2\} \cup \{\#(1)\,P3\}$

$$P\|(x := f) = \|\begin{pmatrix} \{b_i\&e_i\,(P1_i\|x := f) \mid e_i \in A1\}\cup \\ \{\varrho(h_j)\,(P2_j\|x := f) \mid h_j \in A2\}\cup \\ \{(x < f)\&\uparrow x\,P \mid \uparrow x \notin A2\}\cup \\ \{(x < f)\&\uparrow x\,P2_j \mid \uparrow x = h_j \in A2\}\cup \\ \{(x > f)\&\downarrow x\,P \mid \downarrow x \notin A2\}\cup \\ \{(x < f)\&\downarrow x\,P2_j \mid \uparrow x = h_j \in A2\}\cup \\ \{(x = f)\&\tau\,P\} \end{pmatrix}$$

2.8   Head Normal Forms

The laws given in the previous sections permit us to convert a VERILOG program into a head normal form, which will be used to derive a labelled transition system for VERIOLG in the subsequent section.

Definition 2.2 (Head normal form)
A choice construct is in *head normal form* if

(1) All its input guards are simple and distinct.
(2) If the Boolean components $\{b_1, .., b_n\}$ of its output guards satisfy $\vee_i b_i = true$, then none of its guards is a delay guard.

We associate each VERILOG program with an equivalent head normal form shown as below

$$\mathcal{HF}(x := f) =_{df} \|\{(x < f)\& \uparrow x\ \epsilon,\ (x = f)\&\tau\ \epsilon,\ (x > f)\& \downarrow x\ \epsilon\}$$

$$\mathcal{HF}(\text{skip}) =_{df} \|\{\tau\ \epsilon\}$$

$$\mathcal{HF}(\text{sink}) =_{df} \|\{\}$$

$$\mathcal{HF}(\bot) =_{df} \|\{\tau\ \bot\}$$

$$\mathcal{HF}(\varrho(\eta)\ S) =_{df} \|\{\varrho(e)\ S \mid e \in E(\eta)\}$$

$$\mathcal{HF}(\#(n+1)\ S) =_{df} \|\{\#(1)\ (\#(n)\ S)\}$$

$$\mathcal{HF}(delay(1)\ S) =_{df} \|\{\#(1)\ S\}$$

$$\mathcal{HF}(S_1 \lhd b \rhd S_2) =_{df} \|\{b\&\tau\ S_1,\ \neg b\&\tau\ S_2\}$$

$$\mathcal{HF}(b * S) =_{df} \|\{b\&\tau\ (S; b * S),\ \neg b\&\tau\ \text{skip}\}$$

$$\mathcal{HF}(S_1; S_2) =_{df} \|\{g_1\ (P_1; S_2),\ ..,\ g_n\ (P_n; S_2)\}$$
$$\text{if } \mathcal{HF}(S_1) = \|\{g_1\ P_1, .., g_n\ P_n\}$$

$$\mathcal{HF}(\text{alway}\ S) =_{df} \|\{g_1\ (P_1; \text{always}\ S),\ ..,\ g_n\ (P_n; \text{always}\ S)\}$$
$$\text{if } \mathcal{HF}(S) = \|\{g_1\ P_1, .., g_n\ P_n\}$$

$$\mathcal{HF}(\|\{g_1\ P_1, .., g_n\ P_n\}) =_{df} \| \left\{ \begin{array}{l} \{g_i\ P_i \mid g_i \text{ is output guard}\} \cup \\ \{\varrho(e)\ P_j \mid e \in E(g_j)\} \cup \\ \{\#(1)\ P_k \mid g_k = \#(1)\ \wedge\ \vee_i\ b_i = false\} \end{array} \right\}$$

where $b_1, .., b_k$ are the Boolean components in $\{g_1, .., g_n\}$.

$\mathcal{HF}(P\|Q)$ is defined as the result of applying the expansion rules of the parallel constructor to $\mathcal{HF}(P)\|\mathcal{HF}(Q)$.

Lemma 2.3 $\mathcal{HF}(P)$ is in the head normal form.

Lemma 2.4 $P = \mathcal{HF}(P)$ is derivable using the algebraic laws presented in the previous section.

3   Operational Approach

A VERILOG program is composed by several sequential processes that are running in parallel. Its execution consists of interleaving transitions from the components. If there are several transitions enabled, one of them is selected non-deterministically for execution. Otherwise, time may advance until one process becomes enabled. Transitions are of the following form

$$C \xrightarrow{l} C'$$

where C is a pattern describing the state of an executing mechanism of VER-ILOG programs before an action l, and C' describes the state immediately after. In our case, the states are identified as pairs $\langle P, \sigma \rangle$, where

- P is a program text, representing the rest of the program that remains to be executed.
- σ defines the data state as a mapping form program variables to their values and will be referred by $\underline{state}(C)$ later. We use $\sigma(e)$ to denote the value of expression e on state σ.

A label l can be

(1) either an output event in the set $Event_\tau$,

(2) or an input event in $\{?e \mid e \in Event\}$

(3) or a clock event $\sqrt{}$

Definition 3.1 (Transitions)

Let $\mathcal{HF}(P) = \|\{g_1\, P_1, ..., g_n\, P_n\}$. Define

$$\langle P, \sigma \rangle \xrightarrow{?e} \langle Q, \sigma' \rangle \ =_{df} \left(\begin{array}{l} P = \|\{\varrho(e)\, Q, G\} \wedge \underline{rel}(\sigma, e, \sigma') \wedge \\ (\varrho(e) \notin \{g_1, .., g_n\} \Rightarrow (Q \equiv P)) \wedge \\ \forall i \bullet (\varrho(e) = g_i \Rightarrow (Q \equiv P_i)) \end{array} \right)$$

$$\langle P, \sigma \rangle \xrightarrow{e} \langle Q, \sigma' \rangle \ =_{df} \left(\begin{array}{l} P = \|\{\bigwedge_{v \in Var}(v = \sigma(v))\&e\, Q, G\} \wedge \\ \underline{rel}(\sigma, e, \sigma') \wedge \\ \{g_1, .., g_n\} \text{ contains output guards with event } e \end{array} \right)$$

$$\langle P, \sigma \rangle \xrightarrow{\sqrt{}} \langle Q, \sigma' \rangle \ =_{df} \left(\begin{array}{l} P = \|\{\#(1)\, Q, G\} \wedge \underline{rel}(\sigma, \sqrt{}, \sigma') \wedge \\ (\#(1) \notin \{g_1, .., g_n\} \Rightarrow (Q \equiv P)) \wedge \\ \forall i \bullet (\#(1) = g_i \Rightarrow (Q \equiv P_i)) \wedge \\ \forall b, e, i \bullet (g_i = b\&e \Rightarrow b = false) \end{array} \right)$$

where the predicate $\underline{rel}$ is defined by

$$\underline{rel}(\sigma, l, \sigma') \ =_{df} \left\{ \begin{array}{ll} \sigma' = \sigma & l \in \{\tau, \sqrt{}\} \\ \sigma(x) = 0 \wedge \sigma' = \sigma \oplus \{x \mapsto 1\} & l = \uparrow x \\ \sigma(x) = 1 \wedge \sigma' = \sigma \oplus \{x \mapsto 0\} & l = \downarrow x \end{array} \right.$$

This definition allows the following transition rules to be formalised as theorems, rather than being presented as postulates or definitions; they can be easily proved using the equational laws given in Section 2.

Theorem 3.1 (Assignment)

$$(1) \quad \frac{\sigma(f) > \sigma(x), \quad \underline{rel}(\sigma, \ \uparrow x, \ \sigma')}{\langle x := f, \ \sigma \rangle \xrightarrow{\uparrow x} \langle \epsilon, \ \sigma' \rangle}$$

$$(2) \quad \frac{\sigma(f) < \sigma(x), \quad \underline{rel}(\sigma, \ \downarrow x, \ \sigma')}{\langle x := f, \ \sigma \rangle \xrightarrow{\downarrow x} \langle \epsilon, \ \sigma' \rangle}$$

$$(3) \quad \frac{\sigma(f) = \sigma(x)}{\langle x := f, \ \sigma \rangle \xrightarrow{\tau} \langle \epsilon, \ \sigma \rangle}$$

$$(4) \quad \frac{e \in Event, \quad \underline{rel}(\sigma, \ e, \ \sigma')}{\langle x := f, \ \sigma \rangle \xrightarrow{?e} \langle x := f, \ \sigma' \rangle}$$

Theorem 3.2 (skip)

$$(1) \ \langle \texttt{skip}, \ \sigma \rangle \xrightarrow{\tau} \langle \epsilon, \ \sigma \rangle \qquad (2) \ \frac{e \in Event, \quad \underline{rel}(\sigma, \ e, \ \sigma')}{\langle \texttt{skip}, \ \sigma \rangle \xrightarrow{?e} \langle \texttt{skip}, \ \sigma' \rangle}$$

Theorem 3.3 ($\bot$)

$$\langle \bot, \ \sigma \rangle \xrightarrow{\tau} \langle \bot, \ \sigma' \rangle$$

Theorem 3.4 (sink)

$$(1) \ \langle \texttt{sink}, \ \sigma \rangle \xrightarrow{\surd} \langle \texttt{sink}, \ \sigma \rangle \qquad (2) \ \frac{e \in Event, \quad \underline{rel}(\sigma, \ e, \ \sigma')}{\langle \texttt{sink}, \ \sigma \rangle \xrightarrow{?e} \langle \texttt{sink}, \ \sigma' \rangle}$$

Theorem 3.5 (Input event control construct)

$$(1) \ \langle \varrho(\eta) \, S, \ \sigma \rangle \xrightarrow{\surd} \langle \varrho(\eta) \, S, \ \sigma \rangle$$

$$(2) \quad \frac{e \in E(\eta), \quad \underline{rel}(\sigma, \ e, \ \sigma')}{\langle \varrho(\eta) \, S, \ \sigma \rangle \xrightarrow{?e} \langle S, \ \sigma' \rangle}$$

$$(3) \quad \frac{e \notin E(\eta), \quad \underline{rel}(\sigma, \ e, \ \sigma')}{\langle \varrho(\eta) \, S, \ \sigma \rangle \xrightarrow{?e} \langle \varrho(\eta) \, S, \ \sigma' \rangle}$$

Theorem 3.6 (Delay control construct)

$$(1) \quad \langle \#(1) \, S, \ \sigma \rangle \xrightarrow{\surd} \langle S, \ \sigma \rangle \qquad (2) \ \langle \#(n+1) \, S, \ \sigma \rangle \xrightarrow{\surd} \langle \#(n) \, S, \ \sigma \rangle$$

$$(3) \quad \frac{e \in Event, \quad \underline{rel}(\sigma, \ e, \ \sigma')}{\langle \#(n) \, S, \ \sigma \rangle \xrightarrow{?e} \langle \#(n) \, S, \ \sigma' \rangle}$$

Theorem 3.7 (Choice construct)

Let $P = [\![\{g_1 \, P_1, ..., g_n \, P_n\}$

$$(1) \quad \frac{\underline{rel}(\sigma, \ e, \ \sigma'), \quad e \notin \cup_i E(g_i)}{\langle P, \ \sigma \rangle \xrightarrow{?e} \langle P, \ \sigma' \rangle}$$

$$(2) \quad \frac{\underline{rel}(\sigma, \ e, \ \sigma'), \quad e \in E(g_i)}{\langle P, \ \sigma \rangle \xrightarrow{?e} \langle P_i, \ \sigma' \rangle}$$

$$(3) \quad \frac{g_i = \#(1), \quad \vee_j b_j = false}{\langle P, \ \sigma \rangle \xrightarrow{\surd} \langle P_i, \ \sigma \rangle}$$

$$(4) \quad \frac{E(g_i) \neq \emptyset \ \text{ for all } i}{\langle P, \ \sigma \rangle \xrightarrow{\surd} \langle P, \ \sigma \rangle}$$

$$(5) \quad \frac{g_i = b \& e, \quad \sigma(b) = true, \quad \underline{rel}(\sigma, \ e, \ \sigma')}{\langle P, \ \sigma \rangle \xrightarrow{e} \langle P_i, \ \sigma' \rangle}$$

where $b_1, .., b_k$ are the Boolean components of output guards in $\{g_1, .., g_n\}$.

Theorem 3.8 (Conditional)

(1)
$$\frac{\sigma(b) = true}{\langle P \triangleleft b \triangleright Q, \sigma \rangle \xrightarrow{\tau} \langle P, \sigma \rangle}$$

(2)
$$\frac{\sigma(b) = false}{\langle P \triangleleft b \triangleright Q, \sigma \rangle \xrightarrow{\tau} \langle Q, \sigma \rangle}$$

(3)
$$\frac{e \in Event, \ \underline{rel}(\sigma, e, \sigma')}{\langle P \triangleleft b \triangleright Q, \sigma \rangle \xrightarrow{?e} \langle P \triangleleft b \triangleright Q, \sigma' \rangle}$$

Theorem 3.9 (Sequential composition)

If P is not an assignment, then

(1)
$$\frac{\langle P, \sigma \rangle \xrightarrow{l} \langle \epsilon, \sigma' \rangle}{\langle P;Q, \sigma \rangle \xrightarrow{l} \langle Q, \sigma' \rangle}$$

(2)
$$\frac{\langle P, \sigma \rangle \xrightarrow{l} \langle P', \sigma' \rangle}{\langle P;Q, \sigma \rangle \xrightarrow{l} \langle P';Q, \sigma' \rangle}$$

(3)
$$\frac{\underline{rel}(\sigma, e, \sigma[f/x]), \langle Q, \sigma \rangle \xrightarrow{?e} \langle R, \sigma[f/x] \rangle}{\langle (x := f);Q, \sigma \rangle \xrightarrow{e} \langle R, \sigma[f/x] \rangle}$$

(4)
$$\frac{\sigma(x) = \sigma(f)}{\langle (x := f);Q, \sigma \rangle \xrightarrow{\tau} \langle Q, \sigma \rangle}$$

where the state $\sigma[f/x]$ is the same as σ except that it maps variable x to the value of expression f on state σ.

Theorem 3.10 (Iteration)

(1)
$$\frac{\sigma(b) = true}{\langle b * S, \sigma \rangle \xrightarrow{\tau} \langle S;(b * S), \sigma \rangle}$$

(2)
$$\frac{\sigma(b) = false}{\langle b * S, \sigma \rangle \xrightarrow{\tau} \langle \texttt{skip}, \sigma \rangle}$$

Theorem 3.11 (Always construct)

(1)
$$\frac{\langle S, \sigma \rangle \xrightarrow{l} \langle S', \sigma' \rangle}{\langle \texttt{always } S, \sigma \rangle \xrightarrow{l} \langle S';(\texttt{always } S), \sigma' \rangle}$$

(2)
$$\frac{\langle S, \sigma \rangle \xrightarrow{l} \langle \epsilon, \sigma' \rangle}{\langle \texttt{always } S, \sigma \rangle \xrightarrow{l} \langle \texttt{always } S, \sigma' \rangle}$$

Theorem 3.12 (Parallel composition)

(1)
$$\frac{\langle P, \sigma \rangle \xrightarrow{\tau} \langle P', \sigma \rangle}{\substack{\langle P\|Q, \sigma \rangle \xrightarrow{\tau} \langle P'\|Q, \sigma \rangle \\ \langle Q\|P, \sigma \rangle \xrightarrow{\tau} \langle Q\|P', \sigma \rangle}}$$

(2)
$$\frac{\langle P, \sigma \rangle \xrightarrow{e} \langle P', \sigma' \rangle, \ \langle Q, \sigma \rangle \xrightarrow{?e} \langle Q', \sigma' \rangle}{\substack{\langle P\|Q, \sigma \rangle \xrightarrow{e} \langle P'\|Q', \sigma' \rangle \\ \langle Q\|P, \sigma \rangle \xrightarrow{e} \langle Q'\|P', \sigma' \rangle}}$$

(3)
$$\frac{\langle P, \sigma \rangle \xrightarrow{\tau} \langle \epsilon, \sigma \rangle}{\substack{\langle P\|Q, \sigma \rangle \xrightarrow{\tau} \langle Q, \sigma \rangle \\ \langle Q\|P, \sigma \rangle \xrightarrow{\tau} \langle Q, \sigma \rangle}}$$

(4)
$$\frac{\langle P, \sigma \rangle \xrightarrow{e} \langle \epsilon, \sigma' \rangle, \ \langle Q, \sigma \rangle \xrightarrow{?e} \langle Q', \sigma' \rangle}{\substack{\langle P\|Q, \sigma \rangle \xrightarrow{e} \langle Q', \sigma' \rangle \\ \langle Q\|P, \sigma \rangle \xrightarrow{e} \langle Q', \sigma' \rangle}}$$

(5)
$$\frac{\langle P, \sigma \rangle \xrightarrow{l} \langle P', \sigma' \rangle, \ \langle Q, \sigma \rangle \xrightarrow{l} \langle Q', \sigma' \rangle, \ l \in \{\sqrt{}\} \cup ?Event}{\langle P\|Q, \sigma \rangle \xrightarrow{l} \langle P'\|Q', \sigma' \rangle}$$

The correctness of each of these transition rules can be established simply. In effect, the rules constitute an operational semantics whose step is *defined* as the *least* relation satisfying Theorem 3.1 to 3.12. As so often in mathematics, the theorems of one branch become the axioms or definitions of some apparently distinct branch. Accordingly, we can regard Theorems 3.1 to 3.12 as a *definition* of the transition relation between machine states. The proof of these theorems is regarded as a demonstration of the *soundness* of the operational semantics to the algebraic semantics for VERILOG. The following theorem shows that this operational semantics gives a *complete* recipe for executing an arbitrary VERILOG program.

Theorem 3.13

$$
P \;=\; \|\left(\begin{array}{l}
\{\varrho(e)\,Q \mid \exists \sigma,\, \sigma' \bullet \langle P,\, \sigma \rangle \xrightarrow{?e} \langle Q,\, \sigma' \rangle\} \cup \\[4pt]
\{\wedge_{v \in Var}(v = \sigma(v))\&e\,Q \mid \langle P,\, \sigma \rangle \xrightarrow{e} \langle Q,\, \sigma' \rangle\} \cup \\[4pt]
\{\#(1)\,Q \mid \exists \sigma \bullet \langle P,\, \sigma \rangle \xrightarrow{\checkmark} \langle Q,\, \sigma \rangle\}
\end{array}\right)
$$

4   Equivalence

The operational semantics uses the actual text of programs to control the progress of the computation; as a consequence, two programs are equal if they are written in exactly the same way, so there cannot be any non-trivial algebraic equations. Instead, we have to define and use some reasonable *equivalence* relation (conventionally denoted $\sim$) between program texts. In fact, it is customary to define this relation first between machine states. Two programs will then be regarded as equivalent if they are equivalent whenever they are paired with the same data state. In this section, we will present a notion of equivalence for VERILOG processes, based on the idea that the distinction of two processes can be observed during the interaction between the environment of each of them.

Definition 4.1 (Delay event)

Define $\xrightarrow{\checkmark}\; =_{df}\; (\xrightarrow{\tau})^* \circ \xrightarrow{\checkmark}$

where $(\xrightarrow{\tau})^*$ denotes the transitive closure of $\xrightarrow{\tau}$.

Definition 4.2 (Output event)

Let $e \in Event$, Define

$$
\xrightarrow{e}_1 \;=_{df}\; (\xrightarrow{\tau})^* \circ (\{\langle P,\, \sigma \rangle \mid P \text{ is not assignment}\} \vartriangleleft \xrightarrow{e})
$$

$$
\xrightarrow{e}_2 \;=_{df}\; (\xrightarrow{\tau})^* \circ (\{\langle P,\, \sigma \rangle \mid P \text{ is an assignment}\} \vartriangleleft \xrightarrow{e})
$$

where for a binary relation R and a subset X of its domain, the notation $X \vartriangleleft R$ stands for the binary relation R restricted its domain to the set X.

Definition 4.3 (Divergent state)

A configuration C_0 is divergent (denoted by $\uparrow C$) if there is an infinite sequence of configurations $\{C_i \mid i \geq 1\}$ such that for all $n \geq 0$

$$
C_n \xrightarrow{e_n} C_{n+1} \quad \text{where } e_n \in Event_\tau
$$

Definition 4.4 (Bisimulation)

A binary relation S over configurations is a bisimulation, if it satisfies the following conditions

1. it is symmetric,

2. $C_1 \, \mathcal{S} \, C_2$ implies $\uparrow C_1 \Leftrightarrow \uparrow C_2 \; \wedge \; \underline{state}(C_1) = \underline{state}(C_2)$

3. if C_1 is not divergent, $C_1 \, \mathcal{S} \, C_2$ implies

   – for all $e \in Event$ whenever $C_1 \stackrel{?e}{\dashrightarrow} C_1'$, there exists C_2' such that

$$C_2 \stackrel{?e}{\dashrightarrow} C_2' \; \wedge \; C_1' \, \mathcal{S} \, C_2'$$

   – whenever $C_1 \stackrel{\surd}{\Rightarrow} C_1'$ there exists C_2' such that

$$C_2 \stackrel{\surd}{\Rightarrow} C_2' \; \wedge \; C_1' \, \mathcal{S} \, C_2'$$

   – whenever $C_1 \stackrel{\tau}{\rightarrow} C_1'$ there exists C_2' such that

$$C_2(Id \cup \stackrel{\tau}{\rightarrow})C_2' \; \wedge \; C_1' \, \mathcal{S} \, C_2'$$

   – for all $e \in Event$ and $i = 1, 2$ whenever $C_1 \stackrel{e}{\Rightarrow}_i C_1'$, there exists C_2' such that

$$C_2 \stackrel{e}{\Rightarrow}_i C_2' \; \wedge \; C_1' \, \mathcal{S} \, C_2'$$

Lemma 4.1

If each $\mathcal{S}_i$ is a bisimulation, so are the relations $\bigcup_i \mathcal{S}_i$ and $\mathcal{S}_i \circ \mathcal{S}_j$.

Definition 4.5 (Equivalence)

Configurations C_1 and C_2 are *equivalent* (denoted $C_1 \sim C_2$) if there exists a bisimulation $\mathcal{S}$ such that $C_1 \, \mathcal{S} \, C_2$.

Two programs P and Q are *equivalent*, written $P \sim Q$, if for all states σ, the configurations $\langle P, \sigma \rangle$ and $\langle Q, \sigma \rangle$ are equivalent

$$P \sim Q \;=_{df}\; \forall \sigma \bullet \langle P, \sigma \rangle \sim \langle Q, \sigma \rangle$$

Lemma 4.2 $\sim$ is an equivalence relation.

Theorem 4.1 (Congruence)

$P \sim Q$ implies $F(P) \sim F(Q)$ for all VERILOG constructor F.

Theorem 4.2 (Soundness of Equational Laws)

If $P = Q$ is provable using the equational laws of Section 2, then $P \sim Q$.

5   Observation-Oriented Semantics

As shown in the previous section, a VERILOG process can perform either an input event, or an output event, or a clock event. The set

$$Com \;=_{df}\; Event \cup {?}Event \cup \{\surd\}$$

consists only of the visible communication with environment. A trace $t \in Com^*$ is a finite sequence of events in which a particular process might participate with its environment. After engaging t, the environment may be unable to obtain output from the process. Usually this refusal arises because the process becomes idle and remains so, at least until either the environment supplies further input, or time makes advance. In this case, t is called a *quiescent* traces. However, a refusal may also arise because the process behaves chaotically. In this case, t is called a *divergence*. In either case, the trace t is a *failure* of the process. If P terminates after engaging in t, t is called a *termination trace*.

The behaviour of a VERILOG program P which starts in a state σ can be modelled by a triple of sets, the set $\mathcal{D}(P)_\sigma$ of all its divergences, the set $\mathcal{F}(P)_\sigma$ of all failures, and the set $\mathcal{T}(P)_\sigma$ of all termination traces:

$$\mathcal{D}(P)_\sigma =_{df} \{t \in Com^* \mid \exists s, Q, \sigma' \bullet s \setminus \{\tau\} \preceq t \wedge$$

$$< P, \sigma > \xrightarrow{s} < Q, \sigma' > \ \wedge \ \uparrow < Q, \sigma' >\}$$

$$\mathcal{F}(P)_\sigma =_{df} \mathcal{D}(P)_\sigma \ \cup$$

$$\{t \in Com^* \mid \exists s, Q, R, \sigma' \bullet t = s \setminus \{\tau\} \wedge$$

$$< P, \sigma > \xrightarrow{s} < Q, \sigma' > \ \wedge \ < Q, \sigma' > \xrightarrow{\checkmark} < R, \sigma' >\}$$

$$\mathcal{T}(P)_\sigma =_{df} \mathcal{D}(P)_\sigma \ \cup$$

$$\{t \in Com^* \mid \exists s, \sigma' \bullet t = s \setminus \{\tau\} \wedge \ < P, \sigma > \xrightarrow{s} < \epsilon, \sigma' >\}$$

where $\xrightarrow{s}$ is inductively defined by

$$\xrightarrow{<>} =_{df} Id$$

$$\xrightarrow{<l>s} =_{df} \xrightarrow{l} \circ \xrightarrow{s}$$

and $s \setminus \{\tau\}$ removes from s all the occurrences of τ, and the notation $t1 \preceq t2$ indicates sequence $t1$ is a *prefix* of sequence $t2$.

Theorem 5.1

$P \sim Q$ implies that for all $\sigma \in \Sigma$

$$\mathcal{D}(P)_\sigma = \mathcal{D}(Q)_\sigma, \quad \text{and} \quad \mathcal{F}(P)_\sigma = \mathcal{F}(Q)_\sigma, \quad \text{and} \quad \mathcal{T}(P)_\sigma = \mathcal{T}(Q)_\sigma$$

6   Conclusions

This paper explores an algebraic approach to the VERILOG programming. We extend the language by adding the choice operator, which enables us to convert any VERILOG program to a head normal form. We discuss the algebraic properties of the choice operator, and demonstrate how these laws can be used to prove the properties of the remaining VERILOG constructors. The paper identifies the link between the algebraic approach with the operational approach by defining the transitions as semantic-preserving transformation, and shows how the equation laws dominate the choice of transition rules. The paper has not addressed the issue of completeness of the algebraic laws, and it is expected to deliver a positive result soon. Finally, we construct an observational semantics from the operational semantics to complete the formalisation task for the VERILOG programming.

The operational semantics presented in this paper is very close to the simulator algorithm given in [7, 8]. The operational style of definition of a language is distinctive to the study of theoretical computing science, and it also plays an essential practical role. For example, the search for program efficiency and the study of abstract complexity are wholly dependent on counting the number of steps in program execution. In analysing the fault of an incorrect program, it is common to obtain information dumped from an intermediate step of the running program, and this can be interpreted only in the light of an understanding of an operational semantics. Furthermore, an operational semantics can allow non-determinism, which is also advantageous in a specification, but potentially problematic in a simulator where one execution path must normally be selected.

References

1. R. Bawankule. *Alternative Verilog FAQ.*
   URL: http://www.angelfire.com/in/verilogfaq/, 1997–1999.
2. B.C. Brock and W.A. Hunt. *Formal Analysis of the Motorola CAP DSP¿* in "Industrial-strength Formal Methods in Practice" 81–116, (1999).
3. J. Bowen. *Animating the Semantics of VERILOG using Prolog.* UNU/IIST technical Report 176, (1999)
4. J.P. Bowen and M.G. Hinchey. *High-Integrity System Specification and Design.* Springer-Verlag, (1999).
5. C. Delgado Kloos and P.T. Breuer (eds). *Formal Semantics for VHDL.* Kluwer Academic Publishers, (1995).
6. U. Golze. *VLSI Chip Design with Hardware Description Language VERILOG.* Springer-Verlag, (1996).
7. Mike Gordon. *The Semantic Challenge of VERILOG HDL.* in the proceedings of Tenth Annual IEEE Symposium on Logic in Computer Science (LICS'95), San Diego, California. (1995).
8. Mike Gordon. *Event and Cyclic Semantics of Hardware Description Languages* Technical Report of the VERILOG Formal Equivalence Project of Cambridge Computing Laboratory, (1995).
9. He Jifeng, I. Page and J.P. Bowen. *Towards a Provably Correct Hardware Implementation of Occam.* Lecture Notes in Computer Science 683, 214–225, (1993).
10. He Jifeng A Behavioural Model For Co-design. In Proc. FM'99 World Congress on Formal Methods, Toulouse, France, Springer-Verlag, Lecture Notes in Computer Science, (1999).
11. He Jifeng A Common Framework for Mixed Hardware/Software Systems. Proceedings of IFM'99, Springer-Verlag, 1–25, (1999).
12. He Jifeng and Xu Qiwen. An Advance Features of DC and their applications. In Jim Davies, Bill Roscoe and Jim Woodcock (eds) "Millennial Perspective in Computer Science", 133-147, (1999)
13. He Jifeng and Xu Qiwen. *An Operational Semantics of a Simulator Algorithm.* Proceedings of PDPTA'2000, 203–209, (2000).

14. He Jifeng, *An Integrated Approach to Hardware/Software Co-design.* Proceedings of 16th World Computer Congress 2000, 5–19, (2000)

15. He Jifeng, *Formalising VERILOG* Proceedings of the 7th IEEE International Conference on Electronics, Circuits and Systems (ICECS'2000), 412–416, IEEE Catelog number: 00EX445, (2000).

16. C.A.R. Hoare, *Communicating Sequential Processes.* Prentice Hall (1985)

17. C.A.R. Hoare and He Jifeng Unifying Theories of Programming. Prentice Hall, (1998)

18. IEEE Standard VHDL Language Reference Manual. IEEE Standard 1076-1993, URL: http://www.ieee.org/catalog/design.html#1076-1993.

19. IEEE Standard Hardware Description Language Based on the VERILOG Hardware Description Language. IEEE Standard 1364-1995, URL: http://standards.ieee.org/catalog/design/html#1364-1995.

20. J. Iyoda, A. Sampaio and L. Silva. *ParTS: A Partitioning Transformation System.* In Proc. FM'99 World Congress on Formal Methods, Toulouse, France. Springer-Verlag, Lecture Notes in Computer Science, (1999).

21. J. Iyoda and He Jifeng, *Towards an Algebraic Synthesis of Verilog.* Proceedings of the 2001 International Conference on Engineering of Reconfigurable systems and algorithms (ERSA'2001), 15–21, Las Vegas, USA, (2001)

22. Li Yong Jian and He Jifeng, *Formalising Verilog.* Proceedings of the International Conference on Applied Informatics (AI 2001), Innsbruck, Austria. (2001)

23. Open VERILOG International (OVI). VERILOG Hardware Description Language Reference Manual. Version 1, (1994)

24. Qin Shengchao and He Jifeng, *An Algebraic Approach to Hardware/Software Partitioning* Proceedings of ICECS2000, 273–277, (2000)

25. D.E. Thomas and P. Moorby. The VERILOG Hardware Description Language. Kluwer Publisher, (1991).

26. V.D. Tran and He Jifeng, *A Theory of Combinational Programs.* Proceedings of APSEC2001, (2001)

27. N. Wirth. *Hardware Compilation: Translating Programs into Circuits.* IEEE Computer, 31(6), 25–31, (1998).

28. Zhu Huibiao and J. Bowen and He Jifeng, *Deriving Operational Semantics from Denotational Semantics for Verilog.* Proceedings of CHARME'2001, Lecture Notes in Computer Science 2144, (2001)

Real-Time Systems Development with Duration Calculi: An Overview

Dang Van Hung

The United Nations University
International Institute for Software Technology
P.O.Box 3058, Macau

Abstract. In this paper we present the main achievements of UNU/ IIST during the project "Design Techniques for Real-time Systems" carried out since 1993 by its staff and fellows. Duration Calculus was originally introduced in 1991 as a powerful logic for specifying the safety of real-time systems. During the project, it has evolved to a set of calculi that can capture many important aspects in real-time systems development including techniques for specification, design, discretisation and verification. These techniques are discussed informally in the paper.

1 Introduction

Development of safety-critical systems has received a great deal of attention for long time, and has shown challenges to the researchers and developers. There is no doubt that formal methods have played a key role in response to these challenges. To assist developing countries with advanced software development techniques, UNU/IIST has its focus in formal methods. In this context, the research group in UNU/IIST has carried out the project *Design Techniques for Real-Time Systems* since its establishment in 1993. The aim of the project is to help researchers from developing countries to do research at the international standard. The approach taken by the group is based on real-time logics: starting from Duration Calculus developed in the ProCoS projects ESPRIT BRA 3104 and 7071 in 1990 by Zhou, Hoare and Ravn [6], the group has developed new techniques for specifying all kinds of requirements of real-time systems including functionality requirements and dependability requirements. In order to support the design and verification of real-time systems the language of Duration Calculus has been developed further to be able to describe systems at more detailed and lower levels of abstraction that can be translated directly into a programming language. This language is supported with refinement methods, a powerful proof system and tool support for deriving, reasoning and verifying designs. The main achievements of this project are summarised in this paper.

To motivate our work, for the rest of this section we describe some concepts and aspects related to real-time systems that we have to handle during their development. They are time, durations, requirements, phases, synchrony hypothesis and discretisation.

B.K. Aichernig and T. Maibaum (Eds.): Formal Methods ..., LNCS 2757, pp. 81–96, 2003.

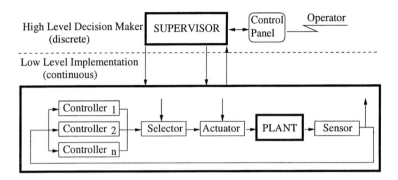

Fig. 1. Structure of Real-Time Embedded Systems

Time can be either continuous or discrete. Continuous time is represented by the set of non-negative reals, while discrete time is represented by the set of natural numbers. Although discrete time has been well accepted in computer science, we adopt continuous time. The reason for this is that for the purpose of specification, continuous time is easier to use and more familiar to the people who do not know computer science than discrete time is. Real-time systems have their behaviour dependent on time, and hence, can be presented as functions of time. For instance, a state P of a system can be considered as a Boolean value function $P : Time \rightarrow \{0,1\}$. $P(t) = 1$ says that state P is present at time t, and $P(t) = 0$ says that state P is absent at time t. Hence, the accumulated time for the presence of state P over a time interval $[b,e]$ is exactly $\int_b^e P(t)\,dt$. We call $\int_b^e P(t)\,dt$ the duration of state P over interval $[b,e]$. When the states of a system are modelled as Boolean valued functions of time, their durations can be a powerful concept for specifying the requirements of the system. For example, one requirement of a simple gas burner is that "for any observation interval that is longer than 60 seconds, the ratio between the duration of the state *leak* and the length of the interval should not be more than 5%". This requirement means that there must not be too much leak relative to the length of the observation interval. A language which is able to formally specify all kinds of requirements for real-time systems based on state durations would be useful. This led to the development of Duration Calculus and its extensions.

A commonly accepted structure of a real-time embedded system ([56, 50]) is shown in Figure 1.

A 'control program' (or supervisor) is the goal of the development of a real-time embedded system. The design process with the step-wise refinement method can be described as follows. Starting from the requirement $\mathcal{R}$ of the plant and the assumption $\mathcal{E}$ about the behaviour of the environment:

1. Derive a finer specification D for the plant such that $\mathcal{R}$ is provable from D under $\mathcal{E}$. Repeat this step with D in the role of $\mathcal{R}$ until we feel that D is detailed enough for implementation,

2. Derive a specification of the control program S such that D is provable from S under the assumption $\mathcal{E}$ and the assumption $\mathcal{I}$ about the interface between the plant and the control program including the assumption about the behaviour of the sensors, actuators and the controllers.

3. Refine S in the discrete world.

The first step involves the refinement in the continuous world. DC (with its extension) and its powerful proof system are a good formalism for supporting and reasoning in this step. There are some issues in carrying out Step 2. Since the sensors and actuators are working in discrete time, there is a delay (bounded by the distance between two ticks of clock) between the change of a state and the time it is observed (by the sensor). If a state changes very frequently (relative to the sensor's clock), some changes may not be observable. If we take this phenomenon into account, we need a technique for discretisation of time. In many cases, where we can assume that the clocks of the sensor and actuator are very fast, and that the plant is relatively stable, all the changes of the plant states are observable within a negligible time-delay. In the literature, most of the techniques are based on this assumption, and skip the discretisation step for simplicity. However, this assumption cannot be satisfied when the plant is also a computing device, such as a communication system at the physical layer.

In carrying out the third step, most of the techniques use the following hypothesis called synchrony hypothesis: the communication and computation take no time, only the explicit delays or waiting (for an event) take time. While this assumption makes it easy to handle the time features in real-time programming languages, it causes some problems for reasoning. For instance, if the command $x := 1; x := 2$ takes place instantaneously at a time point t then x has two values at the time t which is a contradiction in the model. A formal reasoning technique for handling this situation is needed. For example, to express a discrete change of the value of a state at a time point, a neighbourhood of the point has to be considered. When there are a few changes happening sequentially at a time point, the time moment has to be treated as a virtual time period.

In the following sections we will describe how these issues are treated by Duration Calculus and its extensions. In fact, they are motivations for the development of our design techniques for real-time systems.

2 Duration Calculus and Some of Its New Features

Research and development of Duration Calculus was initiated in [6]. In this section, we present some new main features of the development for specifying real-time systems.

As said in the previous section, a state of a real-time system is modelled by a Boolean valued function of the real-time. A duration term of a state P is denoted by $\int P$, and defined as a function of time intervals. The function $\int P$ when applied to an interval $[b, e]$ is the duration of P over that interval, i.e. $\int_b^e P(t)\, dt$. A formula (or sentence) of the language is just a constraint over state durations, which is a kind of statements about intervals. For example,

$20 * \int leak \leq \ell$ is a formula, where ℓ is a term to express the length of the interval to which the term ℓ is applied. This formula is satisfied by an interval $[b, e]$ iff $20 * \int_b^e leak(t) \, dt \leq e - b$ holds. A formula $\int P = \ell \wedge \ell > 0$ holds for an interval $[b, e]$ iff $[b, e]$ is not a point interval, and P holds almost every where in $[b, e]$. If this is the case, $[b, e]$ is called a phase of state P. The concept of phase here bears the same meaning as in the literature. For simplicity, a phase of P is denoted by $\lceil P \rceil$, and the formula $\ell = 0$ is denoted by $\lceil \ \rceil$. A more complicated formula is built by using classical logical connectives like $\vee, \neg, \exists$, etc., and the infix binary modality $\frown$ called the *chop* modality. Formula $\psi \frown \phi$ is satisfied by an interval $[a, b]$ iff for some $m \in [a, b]$, ψ is satisfied by $[a, m]$ and ϕ is satisfied by $[m, b]$. Formula $\Diamond \phi$ holds for an interval $[a, b]$ iff there exists a sub interval of $[a, b]$ that satisfies ϕ. On the other hand, formula $\Box \phi$ holds for an interval $[a, b]$ iff any sub interval of $[a, b]$ satisfies ϕ. So, $\Box \phi$ is the dual modality of $\Diamond \phi$, i.e. $\Box \phi \Leftrightarrow \neg \Diamond \neg \phi$.

A proof system consisting of axioms and inference rules has been developed and proved to be complete relative to the completeness of the real numbers [20]. This makes Duration Calculus a powerful formalism for specifying and reasoning about safety requirements of real-time systems. For example, the safety requirement of the gas burner [6] mentioned in the introduction of this paper is written simply as

$$\Box(\ell \geq 60 \Rightarrow 20 * \int leak \leq \ell),$$

or the performance requirement for a double water-tank system [50] is written as

$$\Box(\lceil W \rceil \wedge \ell > L_o \Rightarrow \int Steady \geq \gamma * \ell)$$

which says that if the water-tank system is observed longer than L_0 time units during its working time, the accumulated time for the steady state of the water level should be at least γ times the observation time. The expressive power of DC lies on the fact that it can specify a property of a system in term of time intervals and state durations, the concepts that could not be captured by any real-time logic before the introduction of DC.

While this language is good enough for the specification of the safety requirement of real-time systems in general, and for the first step of development outlined in the previous section, it cannot be used to specify liveness and fairness since a formula can specify only a property of a system *inside* an interval. This observation has led to the development of a Duration Calculus with infinite intervals [7] and a neighbourhood logic [5].

2.1   Neighbourhood Logics

In [5] Zhou and Hansen introduced a Neighbourhood Logic which is able to specify liveness and fairness with a powerful proof system. This logic is similar to Venema's CDT logic ([51]), but more powerful. Namely it can be used to reason about state durations. It extends the basic Duration Calculus with the neighbourhood modalities $\Diamond_l$ and $\Diamond_r$. For a formula ϕ, the formula $\Diamond_l \phi$ is satisfied by an interval $[a, b]$ iff there exists an interval which is a left neighbourhood of

a, i.e. $[m, a]$ for some m, that satisfies ϕ. On the other hand, the formula $\Diamond_r \phi$ is a formula which is satisfied by an interval $[a, b]$ iff there exists an interval which is a right neighbourhood of b, i.e. $[b, m]$ for some m, that satisfies ϕ.

The neighbourhood logic is very expressive. Each of the thirteen possible relations between two intervals can be represented by a formula in this logic. We refer readers to [5] for the expressiveness and (relative) complete proof system of the neighbourhood logic. It turns out that not only fairness and liveness properties can be specified, but more complicated properties like the limit of durations can be defined in the logic as well. For example, the statement about interval "the interval can be extended to the right to an interval that satisfies ϕ" is specified by

$$\exists x.(\ell = x \wedge \Diamond_l \Diamond_r(\phi \wedge (\ell = x^\frown true))),$$

where for a formula D, $\Diamond_l \Diamond_r D$ says that D holds for an interval having the same starting point. Let us denote this formula by $\mathbf{E}\phi$. So, $\mathbf{E}\phi$ expresses the liveness of ϕ. Fairness of formulas ψ means that any extension to the right of the reference interval has an extension to the right of it for which ψ. This means that ψ is satisfied infinitely often. This fairness of ψ is specified by $\neg\mathbf{E}\neg\mathbf{E}\psi$.

The fact that a Boolean-valued state S has divergent duration when the right end point of the reference approaches ∞ can be specified simply by

$$\forall x.(\mathbf{E}(\textstyle\int S > x))$$

This is abbreviated as $\lim \int S = \infty$ as in mathematical analysis.

The fact that state S takes v as the limit of its duration when the right end point of the reference approaches ∞ can be specified by

$$\forall \epsilon > 0.(\mathbf{E}\neg\mathbf{E}(|v - \textstyle\int S| \geq \epsilon))$$

This is abbreviated as $\lim \int S = v$.

Similarly, we can specify the absolute fairness of two states S_1 and S_2 by

$$\forall \epsilon > 0.(\mathbf{E}\neg\mathbf{E}(|\textstyle\int S_1 - \int S_2| \geq \epsilon))$$

This is denoted by $\lim(\int S_1 - \int S_2) = 0$ as usual. With this logic, the semantics of a real-time program P can be defined by a pair of formulas (S_f, S_i). The formula S_f specifies the termination behaviour of P, which is the specification of P for the interval from the time P starts to the time P terminates. The formula S_i specifies the nontermination behaviour of P, which is a specification of P for any prefix of the infinite interval starting from the time P starts. Because in general, a specification of the nontermination behaviour of P includes the liveness and fairness of P, S_i should preferably be a formula in the neighbourhood logic. The details of the technique are described in [23, 17, 48].

The synchrony hypothesis and handling the behaviour of a state at a time point have motivated several extensions of Duration Calculus: Duration Calculus with super-dense chop [19], Duration Calculus with projections [23, 17], Mean-Value Duration Calculus [10], Duration Calculus with Weakly Monotonic

Time [40] and Two-Dimension Duration Calculus [2]. The first two calculi use
the following idea to solve the problem arising with the synchrony hypothesis
mentioned in the previous section: in fact, the communications and computations do take time, and therefore the temporal order between the operations are
reflected by the real-time. Because the time spent in performing these operations
is negligible, it is hidden to the observers. The approach of implicitly hiding the
computation time is taken by the super-dense chop operator, and the approach
of explicitly hiding the computation time is taken by the projections over states.
The first approach is presented in the the following subsection.

2.2 Super-dense Chop

In 1996, Zhou and Hansen [19] extended the basic DC with the modality • called
super-dense chop. The idea can be seen in the following example. Consider the
command $x := x + 1$. The meaning of this command can be defined by a DC
formula $\ell = 0 \wedge \overleftarrow{x} + 1 = \overrightarrow{x}$, where $\overleftarrow{x}$ and $\overrightarrow{x}$ are functions of intervals which,
when applied to an interval, give the value of the variable x in the left and right
neighbourhood of the interval respectively (note that x is a piecewise constant
function of time having the finite variability, and hence $\overleftarrow{x}$ and $\overrightarrow{x}$ are defined).
Now consider the program $x := x + 1; x := x + 1$. This program is executed
instantaneously according to the synchrony hypothesis. The right meaning for
it is $\ell = 0 \wedge \overleftarrow{x} + 2 = \overrightarrow{x}$. How is this meaning derived from the meanings of $x :=$
$x + 1$ and sequential composition? We may assume that the composition ';' takes
a virtual time for passing the value of x from the first command to the second,
i.e. there is a virtual time interval between the two commands, the value of x in
this interval is exactly the output of the first command, and at the same time it
is the input for the other command. This interval is virtual, i.e. it is considered
as a point, and is treated as an interval only when necessary. This point is
expressed by •. So, a chopping point can be implicitly expanded (mapped) to
an interval to express the computation with negligible time for which the state
variables are kept unchanged (to express the on-going computation process).
Let Φ and Ψ be DC formulas. Then $\Phi \bullet \Psi$ is also a formula. The semantics for
this formula can be defined via higher order Duration Calculus. Higher order
Duration Calculus extends basic with quantifications over state variables and
with terms of the forms $\overleftarrow{s}$ and $\overrightarrow{s}$, where s is a piecewise constant function
of time having finite variability [4, 32] (for higher order DC, Zhan Naijun in
[38] has given a (relatively) complete proof system just like first order DC).
The operator • is defined as follows. For any higher order Duration Calculus
formulas $\Phi(V_1, \ldots, V_n)$ and $\Psi(V_1, \ldots, V_n)$, where $V_1, \ldots, V_n$ are all their free
state variables and real state variables,

$$\Phi \bullet \Psi \triangleq \exists x_1, \ldots, x_n, V_{l1}, \ldots, V_{ln}, V_{r1}, \ldots, V_{rn}.$$
$$(\Phi(V_{l1}, \ldots, V_{ln}) \wedge_{i=1}^{n} (([V_i = V_{li}] \vee \lceil \; \rceil) \wedge (\overleftarrow{V_i} = \overleftarrow{V_{li}}) \wedge (\overrightarrow{V_{li}} = x_i)))^\frown$$
$$\Psi(V_{r1}, \ldots, V_{rn}) \wedge_{i=1}^{n} (([V_i = V_{ri}] \vee \lceil \; \rceil) \wedge (\overrightarrow{V_i} = \overrightarrow{V_{ri}}) \wedge (\overleftarrow{V_{ri}} = x_i))))$$

Global variables x_k in this formula play the role of passing the values of the state variables V_k at the chop point. As said above, the operator $\bullet$ is introduced for giving precise semantics for sequential composition of programs under the synchrony hypothesis. Let $Sem[\mathcal{P}]$ be semantics of program P in higher order DC with $\bullet$. Then, we have

$$Sem[\mathcal{P}_1; \mathcal{P}_2] \,\hat{=}\, Sem[\mathcal{P}_1] \bullet Sem[\mathcal{P}_2]$$

Hence the logic can reason about both parallel composition and sequential composition in a very comfortable way: parallel composition corresponds to conjunction, and sequential composition corresponds to super-dense chop.

As an example, in this logic, we can prove that

$$Sem[x := x + 1; x := x + 2] \Leftrightarrow Sem[x := x + 3]$$

In fact, the semantics of the two sides is the formula $\overrightarrow{x} = \overleftarrow{x} + 3 \wedge \ell = 0$. So, the behaviour of the program at an instant is invisible, and is abstracted away by this logic. Logic with super-dense chop is convenient for reasoning about the abstract behaviour of programs. In reasoning about the behaviour of programs at the operational level, in some cases we may not want to identify the program $x := x + 1; x := x + 2$ with $x := x + 3$. We want to identify them only when we observe them at the higher level of abstraction. This is the idea for introducing the projection operator into the logic [23, 17].

2.3 Recursive Duration Calculus and Iteration

To capture the behaviour of recursive procedures and loops in programs, Recursive Duration Calculus (μHDC) has been introduced by Paritosh Pandya [41] and was developed further by Xu Qiwen, Wang Hanpin and Paritosh Pandya [42]. Later on, He Jifeng and Xu Qiwen studied the operator using an algebraic approach [32] and developed some algebraic laws for a sequential hybrid language developed by them. A thorough study was given later by Guelev [15] with a completeness result for a class of μHDC. A subclass of μHDC to handle iterations was introduced earlier in [27] and was studied later in [25]. Presentation of the recursion operator μ needs a formal definition of Duration Calculus and is rather technical which is out of scope for this survey paper. Therefore, we present here just the iteration operator, which is a simple form of the recursion operator.

The iteration of a duration calculus formula ϕ is a formula denoted by ϕ^*. The iteration formula ϕ^* holds for an interval $[a, b]$ iff either $a = b$ or $[a, b]$ can split into a finite number of intervals, each of which satisfies ϕ. Formula ϕ^* can be written using μ operator as:

$$\mu X.(\ell = 0 \vee X^\frown \phi)$$

The behaviour of the simple Gas-Burner depicted as a simple timed automaton in Fig. 2 can be written simply and intuitively by a formula with iteration

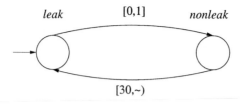

leak   [0,1]   nonleak

[30,~)

Fig. 2. Simple Design of Gas Burner

$((\lceil leak \rceil \wedge \ell \le 1)^\frown(\lceil nonleak \rceil \wedge \ell \ge 30))^* ^\frown (\lceil \, \rceil \vee (\lceil leak \rceil \wedge \ell \le 1) \vee ((\lceil leak \rceil \wedge \ell \le 1)^\frown \lceil nonleak \rceil))$ similar to the derivation of a regular expression from a finite state machine. The correctness of the simple gas burner is expressed by

$$((\lceil leak \rceil \wedge \ell \le 1)^\frown(\lceil nonleak \rceil \wedge \ell \ge 30))^* \Rightarrow$$
$$\Box(\ell \ge 60 \Rightarrow \smallint leak \le (1/20)\ell).$$

With recursion and iteration operators, it has been shown that DC can be used to define semantics for real-time programming languages like Verilog, OC-CAM and WHILE like languages ([32, 48, 23]).

Apart from the fact that it makes the calculus more powerful and more comfortable to specify loops and recursive procedures in programs, proof systems have been developed for the calculus which are complete for a class of formulas that are good enough in most of applications encountered in practice. Readers are referred to [25, 15] for these proof systems. The proof system developed in [25] for Duration Calculus with iterations is complete for a class of formulas that is as expressive as the class of timed automata. Proof systems are a basis for the formal verification of designs. A formal proof of the validity of the above formula for the correctness of the simple gas burner is given in [25].

2.4   Probabilistic Duration Calculus

Reasoning about the probability of the satisfaction of a requirement written in DC by a system (a kind of timed automata) plays an important role in verifying the dependability of real-time systems. In the project, we have proposed a probabilistic model for analysing system dependability as finite probabilistic automata with stochastic delays of state transitions.

A continuous time probabilistic automaton is a tuple $M = (S, A, s_0)$, where S is a finite set of states, $s_0 \in S$ is the initial state of M, and A is a finite set of transitions, $A \subseteq (S \times S) \setminus \{(s, s) \mid s \in S\}$ (here we reject idle transitions, and therefore assume $(s, s) \notin A$ for all $s \in S$). Each transition $a \in A$ is associated with a probability density function $p_a(t)$ and a probability q_a. Let $a = (s, s') \in A$ and $A_s = \{(s, s') \in A | s' \in S\}$. Our intention of introducing $p_a(t)$ is to specify that if M enters the state s at an instant τ of time, then the probability density that the transition a occurs at $\tau + t$ (delay-time of a is t) and causes M to change to the state s' is $p_a(t)$ independent of τ, given that this transition is chosen to occur in the case that there is more than one transition enabled in s.

The probability that a is chosen to occur when M is in s is given by q_a. Thus, we require that $\sum_{a \in A_s} q_a = 1$ for $s \in S$ which satisfies $A_s \neq \emptyset$.

Each behaviour of M corresponds to an interpretation of the DC language over the set of state variables S in the obvious way. Given a DC formula D over the set of state variables S, we can partition the set of timed behaviours of the automaton into a finite number of subsets, for which the probability that D is satisfied in an interval $[0, t]$ can be defined. Hence, the probability that D is satisfied in an interval $[0, t]$ by all the behaviours of M is just the sum of the probabilities that D is satisfied in the interval $[0, t]$ by the behaviours in the partitions i. In this way, we can compute the probability $\mu_t(D)$ that the automaton M satisfies a DC formulas D in an interval of time $[0, t]$ according to the classical probability calculus. The computation is very complicated and is not necessary in many applications. Therefore, we need a technique for reasoning about this probability in a comfortable way. We have developed a set of rules towards this aim. The rules capture the properties of the $\mu_t(D)$s including the forward equation in the classical theory of stochastic processes. For example, consider a simple gas burner in the previous section. Assume that the rate of becoming $leak$ in one second is $\lambda = (10 \times 24 \times 3600)^{-1}$ (meaning that on average, once in every 10 days), and that stopping $leak$ has a normal probability distribution with mean value 0.5 and deviation δ. By using our rules, we can prove that the requirement is satisfied by the gas burner in one day with the probability at least 0.99 if the deviation δ is less than 0.0142. This value characterises the necessary precision of the components of the system.

The readers are referred to [24, 55] for the detail of the technique. This technique and idea has been generalised into a probabilistic neighbourhood logic recently by Guelev in [16].

3   Model Checking Techniques for Duration Calculus

In general, DC is highly undecidable. Only the class of DC formulas built from $\lceil P \rceil$ using Boolean connectives and the modality $\frown$ is decidable [9]. Note that the behaviour of a timed automaton can be represented by a DC formula, and hence, checking a timed automaton for a DC requirement can be converted to checking the validity of a DC formula by using the deduction theorem of DC. As a result, we cannot expect a universal model checking technique for DC formulas. In order to achieve relatively efficient model checking techniques, we have to restrict ourselves to a restricted class of system models and restricted class of DC requirements.

3.1   Checking Timed Regular Expression for Duration Invariants

In [12], a class of DC formulas is introduced to express the behaviour of real-time systems. The formulas in this class are said to be simple and are generated by the following grammar:

$$\varphi \mathrel{\hat{=}} \lceil S \rceil \mid a \le \ell \mid \ell \le a \mid (\varphi \vee \varphi) \mid (\varphi \wedge \varphi) \mid (\varphi^\frown \varphi) \mid \varphi^*$$

The primitive formulas in this class are either a phase of a state, or a simple constraint on time.

From the work of Asarin, Caspi and Maler [1], the expressive power of this class is equivalent to the class of timed automata with possible renaming of states. So, given a timed automaton A we can easily construct a formula $D(A)$ in this class to express the behaviour of A in the sense that any observation of A in an interval corresponds intuitively to a model of $D(A)$ and vice-versa. If the Büchi acceptance condition is used for A then $D(A)$ will be a conjunction of a simple DC formula and a formula in Neighbourhood Calculus to express the fairness of acceptance states. For simplicity, we do not apply the Büchi acceptance conditions here. The class of real-time properties to be checked is of the form of *linear duration invariants* [8]:

$$\Box(a \le \ell \le b \Rightarrow \textstyle\sum_{k=1}^{n} c_k \int s_k \le M)$$

The requirement of the simple gas burner and the performance requirement of the double tank systems mentioned earlier in this paper are of this form. The model checking techniques developed by us are to decide automatically whether $D(A) \Rightarrow R$, where R is a linear duration invariant expressing the safety requirement of a real-time system. The fact $D(A) \Rightarrow R$ says that any observation of A in an interval of time corresponds to a model of R. So, R is satisfied by A.

The results presented in [8, 12, 13] can be summarised as follows: If there is no conjunction occurring in $D(A)$ then we can construct a finite set $\mathcal{P}$ of linear programming problems such that $A \models R$ if and only if the maximal value of any problem in $\mathcal{P}$ does not exceed M.

When conjunction is allowed in $D(A)$, checking $A \models R$ involves some mixed integer linear programming problems. It has been shown in [40] that in most cases, we can avoid mixed integer linear programs.

Even if the linear programming techniques are acceptable in practice, the above method could result in a huge number of programming problems in which some problems have very big size (with a large number of variables). To reduce further the complexity, we have to restrict ourselves to a more specific class of real-time properties. In [28, 53], we propose two other classes for the requirement R:

$$\Box \lceil S \rceil^\frown \lceil \neg S \rceil^\frown \lceil S \rceil \Rightarrow \textstyle\sum_{k=1}^{n} c_k \int s_k \le M, \text{ and}$$
$$\Box \lceil s_1 \rceil^\frown \lceil s_2 \rceil^\frown \ldots {}^\frown \lceil s_m \rceil \Rightarrow \textstyle\sum_{k=1}^{m} c_k \int s_k \le M$$

An interesting property of this class is that $D(A) \Rightarrow R$ is satisfied by all the timed behaviours of A if and only if it is satisfied by all integer behaviours of A (corresponding to the DC models in which any state can only change its value at an integer). Hence, we can use exhaustive depth-first search in the region graph of the timed automaton A to decide on the problem. The complexity of the algorithm is in the same class as for the reachability problem of timed automata. For the second case of the requirement R, we can convert the problem of checking the validity of $D(A) \Rightarrow R$ to a finite set of integer problems, and because of the above results, they can be solved with linear programming techniques. One should notice here that the size of the linear programming problems to be solved in this case is bounded by m, and the number of the problems is the same as the number of the paths in the region graph that matches $\lceil s_1 \rceil ^\frown \lceil s_2 \rceil ^\frown \ldots ^\frown \lceil s_m \rceil$.

3.2   Model-Checking Discrete DC

As it was mentioned earlier, the model checking problem we are concerned with can be converted into the validity checking problem. Although DC is highly undecidable for continuous time, it is mostly decidable for discrete time. In [18], a set of algorithms has been developed for checking the validity of a wide class of DC formulas for discrete time. Paritosh Pandya, in a long term cooperation with UNU/IIST staff and fellows, has developed a DC validity checker called DC-Valid to check the validity of discrete time DC formulas. This tool has been used to formally verify the correctness of a multimedia protocol [29]. We also developed some algorithms (different from and more comprehensive than that of Martin Frankzle's works [36]) to check if a DC formula is satisfied by all integer models (called synchronous models) [46].

4   Designing Real-Time Systems with Duration Calculus

In parallel with the development of the formal calculi to satisfy the need in specification and reasoning, we have developed some techniques for designing real-time embedded systems, and apply them to some practical case studies. We have also developed some techniques for integrating Duration Calculus with other formalisms like Timed CSP [34], Phase Transition Systems [44], hardware description languages like Verilog [33, 31] and RAISE [14, 35]. In the work [26, 48, 47], we have developed a technique for discretisation of time, and for deriving a real-time program from a specification in Duration Calculus. The work [30] presents a technique to refine a formula for continuous time into a formula in discrete time. Due to the limitation of space, we show here only a case study on our discretisation technique.

4.1   Specification and Verification of Biphase Mark Protocols in DC

We present in this subsection a case study on the specification and verification of the Biphase Mark Protocol (BMP) described in [21]. There have been several papers presenting methods for formal specification and verification of BMP, e.g. [37]. However, the model in that paper is too abstract, and does not give the concrete relations on parameters. We need a natural way to specify the Biphase Mark Protocol with more detailed physical assumptions and higher accuracy.

The BMP protocol encodes a bit as a cell consisting of a mark subcell and a code subcell. If the signal in the mark subcell is the same as the one in the code subcell then the information carried by that cell is 0. Otherwise, the information carried is 1. There is a phase reverse between two consecutive cells, i.e. the signal at the beginning of the following cell is held as the negation of the signal at the end of the previous cell. The receiver detects the beginning of a cell by recognising a change of the signals received, which is called an *edge*. The receiver, after having detected the beginning of a cell, skips some cycles called sampling distance and samples the signal. If the sampled signal is the same as the signal at the beginning of the cell, it decodes the cell as 0; otherwise it decodes the cell as 1. Let b be the length in time of a mark subcell, a the length in time of a code subcell and d the sample distance. We model the sender's signals by the state variable X and receiver's signals by the state variable Y. Since we use the sender's clock as the reference for time, the state X is *discrete*. Suppose that the signals sent are unreliable for r cycles ($r < a$ and $r < b$) after a change. Without loss of generality, we assume that the delay between the sender and the receiver is 0.

Suppose the time length between two consecutive ticks of the receiver's clock is Δ. The parameters b, a, r and Δ must satisfy certain constraints to guarantee conditions: (1) the receiver recognises the edges, and (2) the receiver samples the belief codes. We suggest the following constraints: (C1) $b - r \geq 2\Delta$, $a - r \geq 2\Delta$, and (C2) $d \geq \lceil (b+r)\theta \rceil + 1$, $d \leq \lceil (b + a - r)\theta \rceil - 3$, where $\theta = \Delta^{-1}$ and $\lceil x \rceil$ is the least integer greater than or equal to x.

Our discretisation technique is essentially a formalisation of the relationship between the discrete state X and the continuous state Y in DC:

$$(\mathcal{A}1) \;\; \square(\lceil X \rceil \wedge \ell > r + \delta \Rightarrow (\ell \leq r + \Delta)\frown\lceil Y \rceil)$$
$$(\mathcal{A}2) \;\; \square(\lceil \neg X \rceil \wedge \ell > r + \delta \Rightarrow (\ell \leq r + \Delta)\frown\lceil \neg Y \rceil)$$

Let $\mathcal{L}_{DC}$ be the language of DC. For each $\omega \in \{0,1\}^+$, let the DC formula $f(\omega)$ represent the coding of ω by BMP as a DC formula to characterise the behaviour of the state X in the time interval for sending ω. Let $g(\omega)$ be a DC formula representing the behaviour of the state Y for the received signals that results in ω after decoding by BMP. It is not difficult to give a definition of the encoding functions f and g to formalise the BPM protocol. Readers are referred to [26, 39] for the details of the definition.

The protocol will be correct if for all $\omega \in \{0,1\}^+$, $f(\omega)$ implies $g(\omega)$ in DC, and for all $\omega, \omega' \in \{0,1\}^+$ such that $\omega \neq \omega'$, we have $\neg(g(\omega) \wedge g(\omega'))$ holds.

A formal proof of the correctness of BMP with the PVS based Duration Calculus proof checker has been carried out in [22] on the assumption ($C1$) and ($C2$). The constraints ($C1$) and ($C2$) are a basis for reasoning about the values of parameters in the design of BMP. For example, let $b = 5$, $a = 13$ and $r = 1$. If we choose $d = 10$, the allowed ratio of clock rates is within 33%. If the ratio of clock rates is given to be within $\alpha = 10\%$, the allowed value of d is in between 8 and 13.

4.2   Some Other Case Studies

Besides the modelling and mechanical verification of the Biphase Mark Protocol mentioned above, Zheng Yuhua and Zhou Chaochen have given the first formal verification of the Earliest Deadline Driven Scheduler [54]. Later on, the techniques have been generalised for more general kinds of schedulers by Philip Chan and Dang Van Hung [3], and by Xu Qiwen and Zhan Naijun [45]. Some other case studies about the development of hybrid systems have been also carried out in the project. In [52], Zhou Chaochen and He Weidong have shown that DC can be used to specify and prove the correctness for the optimal controller TMC (time minimal controller). In [50] Hong and Dang have shown how DC can be used together with control theory for the formal development of hybrid systems. We have tried to use DC for some other kinds of real-time systems like real-time databases [43]. This research is still going on.

5   Research on DC in Other Institutions and Conclusion

To our knowledge, DC has been used and developed further in some other universities such as the Technical University of Denmark, the University of Oldenburg, Germany and the Tata Institute for Fundamental Research. Some UNU/IIST ex-fellows and visitors also carry out projects in their home institutions to continue their works at UNU/IIST such as Li Xuandong, Wang Hanpin, Victor A. Braberman. Some works on DC carried out in the University of Oldenburg are summarised as follows.

In [11] Henning Dierks et al. have considered Programmable Logic Controller (PLC) Automata as an implementable model for design. This model is widely used for hardware design. A PLC automaton is an I/O automaton working in cycles. On entering a state, the automaton starts the polling phase. In this phase, it waits for inputs and then decides a polled input. Depending on the polled input, it moves to the next state after broadcasting its output. There is a time bound for the polling phase. He has given a DC semantics and a timed automata semantics for the PLC automata as their denotational and operational semantics. A tool has been developed [49] to design a PLC automaton from a DC specification and to verify it against some DC properties.

We have given a brief description of the main achievements of UNU/IIST in the project "Design Techniques for Real-Time Systems" using Duration Calculus. Our techniques seem to be simple and cover all important aspects of the development of the real-time systems. In dealing with some special aspects of systems such as discretisation, synchrony hypothesis, and recursion, some small extensions to the calculus have been developed and these seem to be inevitable. However, these extensions are conservative and intuitive which make them easily acceptable by the developers. From many case studies, we strongly believe that our techniques for the formal development of real-time systems are not only powerful but also promising in practice. We understand that in order to put our techniques into practice, more effort has to be paid to develop some efficient tools to support design and verification, and to develop a language, methods and rules that are intuitive and easy enough to be accepted by engineers and programmers.

Because of the limitation of the space, we cannot describe here all of our achievements. We refer the readers to the web page of the UNU/IIST reports www.iist.unu.edu/newrh/III/1/page.html for the materials that detail our work.

References

1. E. Asarin, P. Caspi, and O. Maler. A Kleene Theorem for Timed Automata. In G. Winskel, editor, *International Symposium on Logics in Computer Science LICS'97*, pages 160–171. IEEE computer Society Press, 1997.
2. Rana Barua and Zhou Chaochen. Neighbourhood Logics : NL and NL^2. Presented at ComBaS Group, Technical University of Denmark, 4–7 September, 1997.
3. Philip Chan and Dang Van Hung. Duration Calculus Specification of Scheduling for Tasks with Shared Resources. LNCS 1023, Springer-Verlag 1995, pp. 365–380.
4. Zhou Chaochen, Dimitar P. Guelev, and Zhan Naijun. A Higher-Order Duration Calculus. Published in: the proceedings of the Symposium in Celebration of the Work of C.A.R. Hoare, Oxford, 13-15 September, 1999.
5. Zhou Chaochen and Michael R. Hansen. An Adequate First Order Interval Logic. *International Symposium, Compositionality – The Significant Difference*, Hans Langmaack et al. (eds), Springer–Verlag, 1998.
6. Zhou Chaochen, C.A.R. Hoare, and Anders P. Ravn. A calculus of durations. *Information Processing Letters*, 40(5):269–276, 1991.
7. Zhou Chaochen, Dang Van Hung, and Li Xiaoshan. A Duration Calculus with Infinite Intervals. *Fundamentals of Computation Theory*, Horst Reichel (ed.), pp. 16–41, LNCS 965, Springer-Verlag, 1995.
8. Zhou Chaochen, Zhang Jingzhong, Yang Lu, and Li Xiaoshan. Linear Duration Invariants. LNCS 863, Springer-Verlag, 1994.
9. Zhou Chaochen, Hansen Michael R., and Sestoft P. Decidability and Undecidability Results in Duration Calculus. LNCS 665. Springer-Verlag, 1993.
10. Zhou Chaochen and Li Xiaoshan. A Mean Value Duration Calculus. *A Classical Mind*, Festschrift for C.A.R. Hoare, Prentice-Hall International, 1994, pp. 432–451.
11. Henning Dierks, Ansgar Fehnker, Angelika Mader, and Frits Vaandrager. Operational and Logical Semantics for Polling Real-Time Systems. *LNCS* 1486, pages 29–40, Springer-Verlag, 1998.
12. Li Xuan Dong and Dang Van Hung. Checking Linear Duration Invariants by Linear Programming. LNCS 1179, Springer-Verlag, Dec 1996, pp. 321–332.
13. Li Xuan Dong, Dang Van Hung, and Zheng Tao. Checking Hybrid Automata for Linear Duration Invariants. LNCS 1345, Springer-Verlag, 1997, pp. 166–180.
14. Chris George and Xia Yong. An Operational Semantics for Timed RAISE. LNCS 1709, Springer-Verlag, 1999, pp. 1008–1027.
15. Dimitar P. Guelev. A Complete Fragment of Higher-Order Duration μ-Calculus. LNCS 1974, Springer-Verlag, 2000, pp. 264–276.
16. Dimitar P. Guelev. Probabilistic Neighbourhood Logic. LNCS 1926, Springer-Verlag, 2000, pp. 264–275.
17. Dimitar P. Guelev and Dang Van Hung. Prefix and Projection onto State in Duration Calculus. *Electronic Notes in Theoretical Computer Science*, Volume 65, Issue 6, Elsevier Science 2002
18. Michael R. Hansen. Model-checking Discrete Duration Culculus. *Formal Aspects of Computing*, 6(6A): 826–845, 1994.
19. Michael R. Hansen and Zhou Chaochen. Chopping a point. In *BCS-FACS 7th refinement workshop*, Electronics Workshops in Computing. Spriger-Verlag, 1996.
20. Michael R. Hansen and Zhou Chaochen. Duration calculus: Logical foundations. *Formal Aspects of Computing*, 9:283–330, 1997.
21. Zhu Huibiao and He Jifeng. A DC-based Semantics for Verilog. Published in the proceedings of the ICS2000, Yulin Feng, David Notkin and Marie-Claude Gaudel (eds), Beijing, August 21-24, 2000, pp. 421–432.

22. Dang Van Hung. Modelling and Verification of Biphase Mark Protocols in Duration Calculus Using PVS/DC$^-$. The proceedings of CSD'98, 23-26 March 1998, Aizu-wakamatsu, Fukushima, Japan, IEEE Computer Society Press, 1998, pp. 88 - 98.

23. Dang Van Hung. Projections: A Technique for Verifying Real-Time Programs in Duration Calculus. Technical Report 178, UNU/IIST, Macau, November 1999.

24. Dang Van Hung and Zhou Chaochen. Probabilistic Duration calculus for Continuous Time. Formal Aspects of Computing (1999) 11: 21–44.

25. Dang Van Hung and Dimitar P. Guelev. Completeness and Decidability of a Fragment of Duration Calculus with Iteration. LNCS 1742, Springer-Verlag, 1999, pp. 139–150.

26. Dang Van Hung and Ko Kwang Il. Verification via Digitized Model of Real-Time Systems. Published in the proceedings of Asia-Pacific Software Engineering Conference 1996 (APSEC'96), IEEE Computer Society Press, 1996, pp. 4–15.

27. Dang Van Hung and Wang Ji. On The Design of Hybrid Control Systems Using Automata Model. LNCS 1180, Springer-Verlag, Dec 1996, pp. 156–167.

28. Zhao Jianhua and Dang Van Hung. Checking Timed Automata for Some Discretisable Duration Properties. Journal of Computer Science and Technology, Vol. 15, No. 5, September 2000, pp. 423–429.

29. Wang Jianzhong, Xu Qiwen, and Ma Huadong. Modelling and Verification of Network Player System with DCValid. The proceedings of the First Asia-Pacific Conference on Quality Software, Hong Kong, October 2000, IEEE Computer Society Press, pp. 44–49.

30. He Jifeng. A behavioural Model for Co-design. LNCS 1709, Springer-Verlag, 1999, pp. 1420–1439.

31. He Jifeng. An Integrated Approach to Hardware/Software Co-design. Published in the proceedings of the ICS2000, Yulin Feng, David Notkin and Marie-Claude Gaudel (eds), Beijing, August 21-24, 2000.

32. He Jifeng and Xu Qiwen. Advanced Features of DC and Their Applications. The proceedings of the Symposium in Celebration of the Work of C.A.R. Hoare, Oxford, 13-15 September, 1999.

33. He Jifeng and Xu Qiwen. An Operational Semantics of a Simulator Algorithm. The proceedings of the PDPTA'2000, Las Vegas, Nevada, USA, June 26-29, 2000.

34. He Jifeng and Viktor Verbovskiy. Integrating CSP and DC. Published in the proceedings of the 8th IEEE International Conference on Engineering of Complex Computer Systems, Maryland, USA, 2–4 December 2002.

35. Li Li and He Jifeng. Towards a Denotational Semantics of Timed RSL using Duration Calculus. Chinese Journal of Advanced Software Research, 2000.

36. Franzle Martin. Synthesizing Controllers of Duration Calculus. LNCS 1135, pages 168–187, Springer-Verlag, 1996.

37. J S. Moore. A Formal Model of Asynchronous Communication and Its Use in Mechanically Verifying a Biphase Mark Protocol. FAC, 6:60–91, 1994.

38. Zhan Naijun. Completeness of Higher-Order Duration Calculus. The proceedings of CSL2000, Fischbachau, Munich, Germany, 22–27 August, 2000.

39. Do Van Nhon and Dang Van Hung. A Systematic Design of Real-time Systems Using Duration Calculus. Published in the proceedings of the conference SCI 2001, Orlando, USA, July 22-25, 2001, IEEE Computer Society Press, pp. 241–246.

40. Paritosh K. Pandya and Dang Van Hung. Duration Calculus with Weakly Monotonic Time. LNCS 1486, pp. 55–64, Springer-Verlag, 1998.

41. Paritosh K. Pandya and Y Ramakrishna. A Recursive Duration Calculus. Technical Report CS-95/3, TIFR, Mumbai, 1995.

42. P.K. Pandya, Wang Hanpin, and Xu Qiwen. Towards a Theory of Sequential Hybrid Programs. The proceedings of PROCOMET'98, 8-12 June 1998, Shelter Island, New York, USA, David Gries and Willem-Paul de Roever (eds), Chapman & Hall, 1998, pp. 366–384.

43. Ekaterina Pavlova and Dang Van Hung. A Formal Specification of the Concurrency Control in Real-Time Databases. In the proceedings of APSEC'99, December 7-10, Takamatsu, Japan. IEEE Computer Society Press, 1999, pp. 94–101.

44. Xu Qiwen. Semantics and Verification of the Extended Phase Transition Systems in the Duration Calculus. LNCS 1201, Springer-Verlag, 1997, pp. 301–315.

45. Xu Qiwen and Zhan Naijun. Formalising Scheduling Theories in Duration Calculus. Technical Report 243, UNU/IIST, P.O. Box 3058, Macau, October 2001.

46. Manoranjan Satpathy, Dang Van Hung, and Paritosh K. Pandya. Some Results on The Decidability of Duration Calculus under Synchronous Interpretation. LNCS 1486, pp. 186–197, Springer-Verlag, 1998.

47. François Siewe and Dang Van Hung. From Continuous Specification to Discrete Design. Published in the proceedings of the ICS2000, Yulin Feng, David Notkin and Marie-Claude Gaudel (eds), Beijing, August 21-24, 2000, pp. 407–414.

48. François Siewe and Dang Van Hung. Deriving Real-Time Programs from Duration Calculus Specifications. LNSC 2144, Springer-Verlag, 2001, pp. 92–97.

49. Josef Tapken and Henning Dierks. MOBY/PLC - Graphical Development of PLC-Automata. LNCS 1486, pages 311–314, Springer-Verlag, 1998.

50. Hong Ki Thae and Dang Van Hung. Formal Design of Hybrid Control Systems: Duration Calculus Approach. The proceedings of COMPSAC 2001, October 8–12, Chicago, USA, IEEE Computer Society Press, 2001, pp. 423–428.

51. Yde Venema. A modal logic for chopping intervals. *Journal of Logic Computation*, 1(4):453–476, 1991.

52. He Weidong and Zhou Chaochen. A Case Study of Optimization. *The Computer Journal*, Vol. 38, No. 9, British Computer Society, pp. 734–746, 1995.

53. Li Yong and Dang Van Hung. Checking Temporal Duration Properties of Timed Automata. *Journal of Computer Science and Technology*, 17(6):689-698, 2002.

54. Zheng Yuhua and Zhou Chaochen. A Formal Proof of a Deadline Driven Scheduler. LNCS 863, 1994, pp. 756–775.

55. Liu Zhiming, Sørensen E. V., Ravn P. Anders, and Zhou Chaochen. Towards a calculus of systems dependability. *Journal of High Integrity Systems*, 1(1):49–65, 1994. Oxford Press.

56. Chen Zongji, Wang Ji, and Zhou Chaochen. An Abstraction of Hybrid Control Systems. Research Report 26, UNU/IIST, Macau, June 1994.

X2Rel: An XML Relation Language
with Formal Semantics

Tomasz Janowski*

The United Nations University
International Institute for Software Technology
P.O. Box 3058, Macau

Abstract. X2Rel is a new language to express binary relations between XML documents. A wide range of relations can be expressed: between different versions of the same document, between an instance and a schema document, between documents before and after a transformation, and others. The syntax of X2Rel is given in XML and its semantics is defined formally. The language relies on the well-established XML technologies of XML Schema and XSL Transformations. The paper presents the ongoing development of the language.

1   Introduction

Since its appearance in 1998, Extensible Markup Language (XML) [7] has become the data description meta-language of the choice for a lot of industrial data processing. This is clearly demonstrated by more than a thousand industrial data formats currently listed by the XML Industry Portal at www.xml.org as well as the fast-growing family of notations, processors, tools, interfaces, browsers, etc. to support writing, checking, printing, displaying, transforming, sending and receiving XML documents.

XML continues to evolve. One major trend is shifting the bulk of document processing from browsers to stand-alone applications. Browsers typically rely on so-called data islands to carry XML inside HTML documents, and use languages like JavaScript to process such data. Stand-alone applications perform transformations from XML to itself or other data formats using: SAX (Simple API for XML) to respond to the events issued by an XML parser [2], DOM (Document Object Model) to traverse parser-created document trees [5], or XSLT (Extensible Stylesheet Language Transformations) to carry out transformation rules [4]. Another trend is departure from native non-XML formats to describe various aspects of XML, and relying instead on the power of XML for self-description. The prominent example of this is how XML Schemas [6], themselves XML documents, are used to define classes of XML documents.

Continuing this trend, the paper introduces a new language X2Rel to express binary relations between XML documents. There are many situations when such relations arise in practice: comparing two versions of the same document if they do not deviate "too much" from each other, comparing an instance and a schema document if the former satisfies the rules imposed by the latter, comparing two schema documents if one is

---

* Current affiliation: Department of Computer Science, Institute of Mathematics, University of Gdańsk, ul. Wita Stwosza 57, 80-952 Gdańsk, Poland, tj@math.univ.gda.pl.

B.K. Aichernig and T. Maibaum (Eds.): Formal Methods ..., LNCS 2757, pp. 97–114, 2003.

more permissive – permits more instance documents than another one, comparing two documents describing document transformations if one refines – performs at least all modifications prescribed by another one, comparing the documents before and after the transformation if they share certain properties, and many others. There is currently little support to describe and process such relations explicitly. Instead, we have to rely on the dedicated XML processors, implemented on a case-by-case basis, and include the definition of the relation as part of the processor's code. This makes it rather difficult to: compare different relations (e.g. compare the strength of different schema definition languages), make modifications to the relation without intrusive changes to the processor's code (e.g. using one validating processor for different versions of a schema language), maintain consistent definitions of the relation across different programming languages (e.g. one version of the processor in Java and another one in Perl), verify if the code correctly implements the relation, and in general – approach the definition of relations in a systematic way. X2Rel has been designed to partly overcome such difficulties.

The syntax of X2Rel is based on XML – every X2Rel document is also an XML document, and its semantics is defined formally – every X2Rel document represents a binary relation on XML documents. Given a pair of XML documents and an X2Rel document, an X2Rel processor verifies if the former documents satisfy the relation described by the latter. The processor also generates a report (another XML document) to explain the outcome; we do not explain the generation of reports. The semantics of X2Rel is defined in the notation of RSL - the RAISE Specification Language [10], but the formal machinery used is simple set theory. RSL has been chosen to offer support for developing valid X2Rel processors. The definition of the language comprises two documents: `x2rel.xsd` (XML Schema) to constrain the class of valid X2Rel documents and `x2rel.rsl` (RSL) to constrain the behavior of any valid X2Rel processor.

The design of the language is based on several ideas. The main syntactic entity is `relation`. It consists of a sequence of logical steps. Such steps are evaluated one-by-one, the result depends on the evaluation mode: conjunctive, disjunctive and others. The evaluation takes place in the context of a pair of documents and a pair of nodes in each of them (initially the root nodes). The context also selects one of the documents as the current one. There are seven kinds of steps: `switch` to change the current document; `select` to select new context nodes; `assert` to check whether a given assertion holds on them; `apply` to check if a given relation holds on the context nodes; `associate` to arrange two sets of nodes in the first and in the second document into pairs, so that a given assertion holds on every pair; `transform` to transform the context nodes according to a given XSLT template; `typeCheck` to check whether the context nodes are valid with respect to a given XML Schema type. Each of the steps above can be customized to modify their behavior. For instance, `associate` has the attribute `type` whose value is one of nine association types: `x2y` in all combinations of `x` and `y` equal to `one`, `many` or `all`. A relation may also contain declarations of: nested X2Rel relations, XSLT templates, and XML Schema types, all assigned unique names. In order to allow for different languages to co-exist within the same document, we apply different namespaces: `x2r` for X2Rel elements, `xsl` for XSLT templates, and `xsd` for XML Schema types, but any other prefixes can in fact be declared and used. A relation also decides what kind of report (another XML document) is generated by the X2Rel processor. Later, this report could be processed by an external application.

In the rest of the paper, Section 2 explains by example the XML syntax and supporting technologies. Section 3 defines a formal model to represent XML documents in RSL. Section 4 introduces the syntax and semantics of the datatypes used by X2Rel, and Section 5 describes the evaluation steps and relations. Both sections use the example in Section 2 to illustrate the syntax of X2Rel, and the model in Section 3 to define its semantics. The final Section 6 presents some conclusions.

2   XML by Example

Consider an invoice document described using the XML syntax [7]. The invoice is issued by the travel agent `Travelog` (supplier) in the name of `Kevin White` (buyer). The document contains the root element `invoice` that starts with the opening tag `<invoice>` and ends with `</invoice>`. The element has two attributes, `currency` whose value is `USD` and `next` whose value is `10-22-12`, and four children, one each of "type" `buyer` and `supplier`, and two of "type" `item`. The first item has four and the second two children. They are assigned unique identifiers via the `id` attribute, and are arranged into a cyclic list using the reference attribute `next`. So the document defines two kinds of relations between its elements: one imposed by the syntactic nesting of elements within each other, and another one using explicit references.

```
<invoice currency="USD" next="10-22-12">
  <buyer email="kw@yahoo.com"> Kevin White </buyer>
  <supplier email="info@travelog.com"> Travelog </supplier>
  <item id="10-22-12" next="15-23-12">
    <desc> room charges </desc>
    <quantity> 3 </quantity>
    <unitprice> 60.5 </unitprice>
    <subtotal> 181.5 </subtotal>
  </item>
  <item id="15-23-12" next="10-22-12">
    <desc> long distance call </desc>
    <subtotal> 20.75 </subtotal>
  </item>
</invoice>
```

Now, consider the XML Schema document that describes the structure and content of all legal invoice documents. The root element, `schema`, contains four children: one `element`, two `complexType` and one `simpleType`. According to this schema, a valid instance document must contain the root element `invoice` with the children `buyer` and `supplier` of type `Party`, one or more children `item` of the type `Item`, and the attributes `currency` of type `string` and `first` of type `IDREF`. `Party` and `Item` are complex types and `positiveDecimal` is a simple type, all defined in the rest of the document, while `string` and `IDREF` are the built-in types of the XML schema language. We use the `xsd` namespace to distinguish between the elements that belong to the vocabulary of XML Schema and other elements.

```
<xsd:schema xmlns:xsd="XMLSchema">
  <xsd:element name="invoice">
    <xsd:complexType>
      <sequence>
        <xsd:element name="buyer" type="Party"/>
        <xsd:element name="supplier" type="Party"/>
        <xsd:element name="item" type="Item" maxOccurs=.../>
      </sequence>
      <xsd:attribute name="currency" type="xsd:string"/>
      <xsd:attribute name="first" type="xsd:IDREF"/>
    </xsd:complexType>
  </xsd:element>
  <xsd:complexType name="Party"> ... </xsd:complexType>
  <xsd:complexType name="Item"> ... </xsd:complexType>
  <xsd:simpleType name="positiveDecimal"> ... </xsd:simpleType>
</xsd:schema>
```

Suppose we would like to generate an email, given an invoice document, to inform the buyer about the items purchased and the total amount due. Below is a fragment of the XSLT document [4] that describes this transformation. The root element, stylesheet contains two templates to produce the output document when matched against the input document. The first template is matched against the invoice element, recursively applies the templates for buyer and supplier, and generates the content of the output document using a mixture of plain text and XSLT elements: value-of displays the value of the selected element, if controls conditional execution, and for-each controls iteration. XSLT relies on XPath [3] to select the nodes: @email selects the email attribute, buyer|supplier selects both buyer and supplier children, /invoice/item selects all item children of invoice, relative to the root, and //subtotal selects all subtotal nodes. Here is the document:

```
<xsl:stylesheet xmlns:xsl="XSL/Transform">
  <xsl:template match="invoice">
    <email>
      <xsl:apply-templates select="buyer|supplier"/>
      <body>
        Dear <xsl:value-of select="buyer"/>,
        Your hotel charges include
        <xsl:for-each select="/invoice/item">
          ... <item> <xsl:value-of select="desc"/> </item> ...
        </xsl:for-each>.
        The total is
        <total currency="@currency">
          <xsl:value-of select="sum(//subtotal)"/>
        </total> Sincerely, <xsl:value-of select="supplier"/>
      </body>
    </email>
  </xsl:template>
  <xsl:template match= "buyer"> ... </xsl:template> ...
</xsl:stylesheet>
```

Using `xerces` from Apache [9] or any other validating processor, we can check that the invoice document is a valid instance of the schema. Using Apache `xalan` [8] or any other XSLT processor, we can transform this document into an email document.

```
<email>
  <to> kw@yahoo.com </to>
  <from> info@travelog.com </from>
  <body>
    Dear Kevin White,
    Your hotel charges include
    <item> long distance call </item>
    and <item> room charges </item>.
    The total is <total currency="USD"> 202.25 </total>
    Sincerely, Travelog
  </body>
</email>
```

There are various kinds of properties one may like to formulate between the email and invoice documents. For instance: the receiver of the email should be the invoicee, the sender should be the invoicer, the list of items in the email should be exactly the items in the invoice, and so on. X2Rel allows us to capture such properties explicitly.

3   A Model for XML

A large number of languages have their syntax defined using XML. The meaning of the documents written with such languages is expressed informally with the concepts from the corresponding application domains. For instance, the meaning of the documents conforming to the VISA Invoice format [15] is expressed in terms of taxes, discounts, currencies, payments, unit prices, net and gross values, etc. The meaning of the documents in the broad domain of XML technologies (XML Schemas, X2Rel, etc.) refer to the technical concepts like elements, attributes, names, children and parents, etc. The purpose of this section is to define such concepts formally, preparing for the formal definition of X2Rel. We also briefly explain the notation of RSL.

We use three kinds of RSL entities: values, types and axioms. A type is a collection of values with some operations on them. We have pre-defined types like **Text** to represent character strings, and user-defined types like Name to represent well-formed XML names. Name is a subtype of **Text**, whose values are restricted by the function isName from **Text** to **Bool**. Another method to build a type is a record – a set of values of various types. Element′ is a record type with four fields: name of type Name – the tag name of an element; id of type Id – the attribute name that contains this element's identifier, if one exists; refs of type Name-**set** – a set of attribute names that contain references to other elements; and attrib of type Name $\overrightarrow{m}$ **Text** – a map from names to strings. We use the name of the field to extract its value, e.g. id(e) for a record e. Id is a type created by enumerating its elements: none and put(n) for every n of type Name. put is a constructor – it creates the value put(n) given a name n, while get is a destructor – it returns the name get(i) given i $\neq$none. Finally, we declare Element as a subtype of Element′ to rule out, via the function iswf, those records that refer to non-existing attributes. The function `iswf` makes use of the destructors (`id`, `refs`, `attrib`, `get`), logical connectives ($\land$, $\Rightarrow$), relations ($\neq$), operators on sets ($\subseteq$, $\in$) and maps (**dom**). Here are the declarations:

type
    Name $= \{| \ n: \textbf{Text} \bullet \text{isName}(n) \ |\}$,
    Id $==$ none $|$ put(get : Name),
    Element$'$ ::
        name : Name
        id : Id
        refs : Name-**set**
        attrib : Name $\overrightarrow{m}$ **Text**

type
    Element $= \{| \ e:\text{Element}' \bullet \text{iswf}(e) \ |\}$
value
    iswf: Element$'$ $\rightarrow$ **Bool**
    iswf(e) $\equiv$
        refs(e) $\subseteq$ **dom** attrib(e) $\land$
        (id(e) $\neq$ none $\Rightarrow$ get(id(e))
                $\in$ **dom** attrib(e))

Two comments are in order. First, we often say in RSL that the values in `Element` are well-formed. This should not be confused with well-formedness of XML documents, which is the basic assumption we make in this paper about all XML documents. Second, we took the freedom to describe in the model some aspects of XML documents that are part of this document's DTD: identifiers and references. This was to make explicit the reference structure of a document, in addition to its nesting structure.

Continuing the definition of the model, `Node` represents two kinds of nodes: element nodes and text nodes. It is a subtype of `Node'`, which is a record type with the fields: `data` – the content of the node, `up` – the parent node, if one exists, and `down` – the list of the children nodes. `Data` is a variant type that contains an element or text, depending on the type of the node. The subtype `Node` of `Node'` is subject to the following five constraints: every text node has a parent but no children, the parent of any node (if one exists) is an element node, every child of an element node has this node as its parent (`isParent`), and no node can be a descendant of itself (`isDesc(n,n)`).

type
    Data $==$
        text(getText: **Text**) $|$
        elem(getElem: Element),
    Node$'$::
        data: Data
        up: NodeOrNone
        down: Node*

type
    Node $= \{| \ n: \text{Node}' \bullet \text{isNode}(n) \ |\}$,
    NodeOrNone $==$ none $|$ put(get: Node)
value
    isNode: Node$'$ $\rightarrow$ **Bool**
    isNode(n) $\equiv$
        (up(n) $\neq$ none $\Rightarrow$ isElem(get(up(n)))) $\land$
        (isText(n) $\Rightarrow$ up(n) $\neq$ none $\land$ down(n) $= \langle\rangle$) $\land$
        (isElem(n) $\Rightarrow$ isParent(n) $\land \sim$isDesc(n, n))

`Document` is a subtype of `Node` such that: the document is an element node, it has no parent, the identifiers assigned in the document to element nodes are unique (`hasUniqueIds`), and it is closed with respect to references (`hasClosedRefs`).

type
    Document $=$
        $\{| \ n : \text{Node} \bullet \text{isDoc}(n) \ |\}$

value
    isDoc : Node $\rightarrow$ **Bool**
    isDoc(n) $\equiv$ isElem(n) $\land$ up(n) $=$ none $\land$
        hasUniqueIds(n) $\land$ hasClosedRefs(n)

4   X2Rel Datatypes

We define six datatypes used by X2Rel: `content`, `selection`, `collection`, `string`, `number` and `assertion`. They are applied to build value expressions over the context documents, and support the definition of evaluation steps in Section 5.

Before we consider the datatypes, let us fix the context for their evaluation. This context includes: a pair of documents, a pair of nodes in each of them, and selection which of the documents is the current one. Here is the corresponding declaration of the type `Context` – a subtype of the record type with the five fields, and the functions `currentNode`, `currentDoc`, `changeNode` and `changeCurrent`:

type
  Context$'$::
    doc1: Document
    doc2: Document
    node1: Node $\leftrightarrow$ reNode1
    node2: Node $\leftrightarrow$ reNode2
    current: **Nat** $\leftrightarrow$ reCurrent,
  Context=$\{|$x: Context$'$ • iswf(x) $|\}$

value
  iswf: Context$'$ $\rightarrow$ **Bool**
  iswf(x) $\equiv$ current(x) $\in \{1, 2\}$ $\wedge$
    isDesc(node1(x), doc1(x)) $\wedge$
    isDesc(node2(x), doc2(x)),
  currentNode: Context $\rightarrow$ Node,
  currentDoc: Context $\rightarrow$ Document,
  changeNode: Node $\times$ Context $\rightarrow$ Context,
  changeCurrent: **Nat** $\times$ Context $\rightarrow$ Context

4.1   `x2r:content`

The `content` element helps to extract various kinds of information from the context documents, like: the text content of the current node, the tag name of this node, the value of an attribute given by a string expression, the value of a content expression applied (recursively) to another document, and so on. The result is always a string of characters.

Semantically, we define the type `Content` as a variant type with values `text`, `name`, `attrib(s)` where s is a string expression, `doc(n,c)` where n is a number and c a content expression, and others. The function `eval` evaluates such expressions in a given context, returning a string of characters. For instance, for `attrib(s)` it returns the value of the attribute of the current element whose name is the value of the string expression s. If the current node is not an element or the attribute does not exist, it returns the empty string. `String` and `Number` are defined later in this section.

type
  Content ==
    text $|$
    name $|$
    attrib(String) $|$
    doc(Number, Content) $|$
    ...
value
  eval: Content $\times$ Context
    $\rightarrow$ **Text**
  eval(c, x) $\equiv$

case c **of**
  attrib(s) $\rightarrow$
    if $\sim$isElem(currentNode(x)) **then** $''''$ **else**
      let e = getElem(data(currentNode(x))) **in**
        if eval(s, x) $\notin$ **dom** attrib(e)
        then $''''$ **else** attrib(e)(eval(s, x)) **end**
      end
  end,
  doc(n, c) $\rightarrow$
    if eval(n, x) $\notin \{1, 2\}$ **then** eval(c, x)
    else eval(c, changeCurrent(eval(n, x), x)) **end** ...
end

The following X2Rel element extracts the value of the `currency` attribute of the current node. The element contains the `op` attribute whose value describes the operator to be applied, and the children, if any, describe the arguments. This exemplifies a typical way to build expressions in X2Rel. Here the operator is `attrib` and the argument is the element `string`, created with the operator `literal` applied to `currency`.

```
<content op="attrib">
  <string op="literal"> currency </string>
</content>
```

4.2 x2r:selection

This element selects the nodes in the context documents, such as: the current node, the node selected recursively from the root, the node selected from the child of the current node whose index is given by a number expression, the node selected from a given collection expression, and so on. If a node does not exist, the evaluation returns `none`.

The type `Selection` describes the syntax of such expressions, including the values: `self` – the current node, `root(1)` – the node determined by the selection expression `1` starting from the root of the current document, `parent(1)` – the node selected by `1` starting from the parent of the current node, `child(n,1)` – the node selected by `1` starting from the n-th child (a number expression) of the current node, `elem(n,o)` – the n-th node in the list of nodes returned by the collection `o`, and so on. The function `eval` evaluates such expressions in a given context, returning a node or `none`.

type
    Selection ==
       self |
       root(Selection) |
       parent(Selection) |
       child(Number,Selection)|
       elem(Number,Collection)|
       ...

value
    eval: Selection $\times$ Context
       $\rightarrow$ NodeOrNone
    eval(l, x) $\equiv$

case l **of**
    self $\rightarrow$ put(currentNode(x)),
    child(n, l) $\rightarrow$
      let c = currentNode(x), i = eval(n, x) **in**
      if i $\notin$ **inds** down(c) **then** none
      else eval(l,changeNode(down(c)(i), x))**end**
      end,
    elem(n, o) $\rightarrow$
      let nl = eval(o, x), i = eval(n, x) **in**
      if i $\notin$ **inds** nl **then** none **else** put(nl(i)) **end**
      end ...
    end

For example, the following element returns the third child of the root node in the current document, if one exists. The element applies the `root` operator and contains another `selection` as an argument. This `selection` applies the `child` operator to the pair of arguments: `number` whose value is the constant 3, and `selection` whose op value is `self`; as a convenience, this element can be omitted.

```
<selection op="root">
  <selection op="child">
    <number op="literal"> 3 </number> <selection op="self"/>
  </selection>
</selection>
```

4.3 `x2r:collection`

The `collection` element returns a list of nodes from the context documents, such as: the list created for a given selection, the children of the selected node, the list of nodes in a given collection that satisfy an assertion, concatenation of two collections, etc.

Formally, the type `Collection` represents collection expressions, it includes the values like: `empty`, `one(l)`, `children(l)`, `partOf(o,a)`, `add(o1,o2)` and others, where `l` is a selection expression, `a` is an assertion, and `o`, `o1` and `o2` are collections. The function `eval` returns a list of nodes given a collection and a context.

type
    Collection ==
        empty |
        one(Selection) |
        children(Selection) |
        partOf(Collection, Assertion) |
        add(Collection, Collection) | ...
value
    eval: Collection $\times$ Context $\to$ Node*
    eval(o, x) $\equiv$

case o **of**
    one(l) $\to$
        if eval(l, x) = none **then** $\langle \rangle$
        else $\langle$ get(eval(l, x)) $\rangle$ **end**,
    children(l) $\to$
        if eval(l, x) = none **then** $\langle\rangle$
        else down(get(eval(l, x))) **end**,
    partOf(o, a) $\to$
        $\langle$ n | n **in** eval(o,x) • eval(a,x) $\rangle$...
end

The following `collection` element defines the list of children of the current node that are element nodes. It applies the `partOf` operator given: a collection to generate the list of children of the current node and an assertion to check if a node is an element.

```
<collection op="partOf">
  <collection op="children"/> <assertion op="isElem"/>
</collection>
```

4.4 `x2r:string`

This element defines expressions to represent strings of characters. The operators are: `literal` to include a given text literally, `content` to include the content of the selected node, `concat` to concatenate two strings, `substr` to calculate a substring from a given string, and others. Formally, the type `String` includes the values such as: `literal(t)`, `content(c,l)`, `concat(s1,s2)`, `substr(n1,n2,s)` and others. The `eval` function returns a string of characters given a string expression and a context, as usual. If the value cannot be calculated, it returns the empty string.

type
    String ==
        literal(**Text**)|
        content(Content, Selection)|
        substr(Number,Number,String)|
        concat(String, String)| ...
value
    eval: String $\times$ Context $\to$ **Text**
    eval(s, x) $\equiv$

case s **of**
    content(c, l) $\to$
        if eval(l, x) = none **then** $''''$ **else**
        eval(c,changeNode(get(eval(l,x)),x))
        end,
    substr(n1, n2, s) $\to$
        $\langle$ eval(s, x)(i) | i **in**
            $\langle$ eval(n1, x) .. eval(n2, x) $\rangle$ $\rangle$ ...
end

The following element calculates a substring, from the index 3 until 7, created from the name of the current node. If the current node were `invoice`, the expression would evaluate to `voice`. The element is as follows:

```
<string op="substr">
  <number op="literal"> 3 </number>
  <number op="literal"> 7 </number>
  <string op="content"> <content op="name"/> </string>
</string>
```

4.5 x2r:number

The `number` element represents numerical expressions. The operators are: `literal` to return a given integer, `children` to return the number of children of a selected node, `number` to convert a string into a number, `random` to select randomly a number less than or equal to the value of a given numerical expression, `add` to add the values of two expressions, and so on. If the expression cannot be calculated, `eval` returns zero.

type
    Number ==
        literal(**Int**) |
        children(Selection) |
        number(String) |
        random(Number) |
        add(Number, Number) | ...
value
    eval: Number $\times$ Context $\to$ **Int**
    eval(n, x) $\equiv$

case n **of**
    children(l) $\to$
        if eval(l, x) = none **then** 0
        else len down(get(eval(l, x))) **end**,
    number(s) $\to$
        if elems eval(s, x) $\subseteq \{'0' .. '9'\}$
        then stringToNumber(eval(s, x)) **else** 0 **end**,
    random(n) $\to$ **let** i: **Nat** $\bullet$ i$\leq$ eval(n, x) **in** i **end**,
    ...
end

The following expression calculates the number of children of the current node whose name is `item`. If this node were `invoice`, the expression would evaluate to 2.

```
<number op="member">
  <collection op="partOf"> <collection op="children"/>
    <assertion op="equal">
      <content op="name"/> <string op="literal"> item </string>
    </assertion>
  </collection>
</number>
```

4.6 x2r:assertion

This element is used to build properties about the context documents. The operators are: `isElem` – if the current node is an element, `hasChild` – if the element has a child whose index is the value of a given number expression, etc. There are also operators about collections (`allSat` – all nodes in the collection satisfy an assertion), strings (`isSubStr`), numbers (`isGreater`) and the operators for negation, conjunction, etc.

Formally, the type `Assertion` describes assertion expressions. Their semantics is determined by the function `eval` that given an assertion and a context returns a boolean value. For instance, `eval(allSat(o,a),x)` is true provided every node in the list of nodes obtained for the collection o satisfies the assertion a.

type
  Assertion ==
    literal(**Bool**) |
    isElem(Selection) |
    hasChild(Number, Selection) |
    allSat(Collection, Assertion) |
    isSubStr(String, String) |
    and(Assertion, Assertion) | ...
value
  eval: Assertion × Context → **Bool**
  eval(a, x) ≡

case a of
  isElem(l) → eval(l, x) ≠ none ∧
    let n = get(eval(l, x)) **in** isElem(n) **end**,
  hasChild(i, l) → eval(l, x) ≠ none ∧
    let n = get(eval(l, x))
    in eval(i, x) ∈ **inds** down(n) **end**,
  allSat(o, a) →
    (∀ n: Node • n ∈ **elems** eval(o, x) ∧
      eval(a, changeNode(n, x))
) ...
end

The following assertion represents the property that all children of the root node of the current document have the `id` attribute:

```
<assertion op="allSat">
  <collection op="children"> <selection op="root"/> </collection>
  <assertion op="hasId"/>
</assertion>
```

5   X2Rel Steps and Relations

The aim of this section is to present both syntax and semantics of the main elements of X2Rel: evaluation steps and relations. The presentation relies on the example described in Section 2, the model in Section 3, and the datatypes introduced in Section 4.

5.1 `x2r:relation`

`relation` is the root element of any X2Rel document. The attribute `xmlns` declares the default namespace, referring to the X2Rel syntax definition document `x2rel.xsd`. Here is the general form of `relation`:

```
<relation xmlns="x2rel.xsd" ...>
   ...
</relation>
```

Inside `relation`, there is a sequence of evaluation steps. There are seven kinds of evaluation steps: `switch`, `select`, `assert`, `associate`, `apply`, `transform` and `typeCheck`. They are evaluated one-by-one, the `mode` attribute decides how to calculate the result. For instance, `mode=impl` means the evaluation continues until the first step returning **true** and subsequent one returning **false** (the result is then **false**) or until the end of the list (the result is then **true**). Here is the sketch of an example to check equality between the values of the buyer/receiver and supplier/sender elements:

```
<relation xmlns="x2rel.xsd" mode="con">
  <select> buyer ... to </select>
  <assert> ... </assert>
  <select> supplier ... from </select>
  <assert> ...</assert>
</relation>
```

Semantically, relation corresponds to the RSL type Relation and the function eval that returns **Bool** given a relation and a pair of documents ($Document^2$). Relation is a record of: mode – an evaluation mode, steps – a list of evaluation steps, and rels – a named map of relations, types – schema types and temps – transformation templates. Given the input documents, eval creates the evaluation context initializing the current nodes as roots of both documents, and applies the auxiliary function evalAll. evalAll takes as arguments a list of steps, a relation, and a context record. It evaluates one-by-one the evaluation steps, taking into account the result returned by each step and how it modifies the context, and produces the result in **Bool** depending on the evaluation mode. evalOne is responsible for evaluating individual steps, returning a result – res(**true**), res(**false**) or none, and a new context.

type

    Mode ==

        con | dis | impl,

    Step == ...

    Relation::

        mode: Mode

        steps: Step*

        rels: Relations

        types: Types

        tems: Templates,

    Result ==

        none | res(**Bool**)

value

eval: Relation × $Document^2$ → **Bool**

eval(r, d1, d2) ≡

    let x = mk_Context′(d1, d2, d1, d2, 1)

    in evalAll(steps(r), r, x) **end**,

evalAll: Step* × Relation × Context → **Bool**

evalAll(ss, r, x) ≡

    case mode(r) **of**

        con → ss = ⟨ ⟩ ∨

            let (r, x′) = evalOne(**hd** ss, r, x)

            in r ≠ res(**false**) ∧ evalAll(**tl** ss, r, x′) **end**,

        dis → ss ≠ ⟨ ⟩ ∧

            let (r, x′) = evalOne(**hd** ss, r, x)

            in r = res(**true**) ∨ evalAll(**tl** ss, r, x′) **end** ...

    end,

evalOne: Step × Relation × Context → Result × Context

5.2 x2r:switch

The purpose of switch is to change the current document according to the value of a given number expression. If the value is different than one or two, the context remains unchanged. Formally, switch(n) (n is a number expression) is one of the values of the type Step. Given a context x, evalOne evaluates this value to return none and the new context x′ where the current document is given by eval(n, x) (a number).

type

    Step ==

        switch(Number) |

        ...

axiom

    ∀ n: Number, r: Relation, x: Context •

        evalOne(switch(n), r, x) =

        (none, changeCurrent(eval(n, x), x))

Here is an example of a relation with two occurrences of `assert` and a `switch` element whose `number` argument contains the value 2. The effect of `switch` is to change the evaluation context so that the second document becomes the current one.

```
<relation mode="con">
  <assert>...</assert>
  <switch> <number op="literal"> 2 </number> </switch>
  <assert>...</assert>
</relation>
```

5.3 x2r:select

The purpose of `select` is to change the context node in the current document to the value of a given `selection` expression, or leave the current node unchanged if this expression returns none. Formally, `select(l)` (`l` is a selection expression) is one of the values of `Step`. Given `select(l)` and the context `x`, `evalOne` first evaluates the expression `l`. If `eval(l,x)` fails to produce a node then `evalOne` returns none and leaves the context `x` unchanged. Otherwise, it returns none and the context `x` such as the node returned by `eval(l,x)` is the new current node.

type	axiom
Step ==	∀ l: Selection, r: Relation, x: Context •
select(Selection) |	evalOne(select(l), r, x) =
...	**if** eval(l, x) = none **then** (none, x)
	else (none, changeNode(get(eval(l, x)), x)) **end**

The following relation moves the current node to the third child of the root of the current document, then performs `assert` on the new context.

```
<relation mode="con">
  <select> <selection op="root">
      <selection op="oneChild">
        <number op="literal"> 3 </number>
      </selection>
  </selection> </select> <assert> ... </assert>
</relation>
```

5.4 x2r:assert

This step is used to evaluate logical properties about the input documents, relative to the current evaluation context. Formally, `assert(a)` (`a` is an assertion) is a value of the type `Step`. Given a context `x`, `evalOne` evaluates `assert(a)` by first evaluating the expression `a` in `x`. It returns the result obtained from `a` and the context `x` unchanged.

type	axiom
Step ==	∀ a: Assertion, r: Relation, x: Context •
assert(Assertion) | ...	evalOne(assert(a), r, x) = (res(eval(a, x)), x)

As an example, the relation below consists of two steps. The first selects the root of the current document as the new current node. The second asserts the property about this new context, that all children of the current node have the `id` attribute.

```
<relation mode="con">
  <select> <selection op="root"/> </select>
  <assert> <assertion op="allSat">
     <collection op="children"/> <assertion op="hasId"/>
  </assertion> </assert>
</relation>
```

5.5 x2r:apply

The element `relation` is always the root element of any X2Rel document. But `relation` can be also declared locally, inside the root element. Such local relations are subject to the same rules of formation, but they have to contain the attribute `name`, whose value has to be unique among all local relations. The step `apply` takes such a name as an argument and evaluates the corresponding relation in a given evaluation context. Then it returns the result obtained from this local relation, and leaves the context unchanged. If there is no relation for a given name then `apply` returns **false**.

Formally, `apply(n)` (n is a name) is one of the values of the type `Step`. To evaluate such a step, `evalOne` first checks if n is the name of an existing relation. It takes a relation r as an argument, and checks if n is in the domain of `rels(r)` – a map from names to relations. If not, `evalOne` returns **false**. Otherwise, it applies `evalAll` to `rels(r)(n)` in a given context x, and returns the result obtained and the context x unchanged. The declarations are as follows:

type	**axiom**
Relation::	$\forall$ n: Name, r: Relation, x: Context •
rels: Relations ...	evalOne(apply(n), r, x) =
Relations = Name $\xrightarrow{m}$ Relation,	**if** n $\notin$ **dom** rels(r)
Step == apply(Name) | ...	**then** (res(**false**), x) **else**
	let r$'$ = rels(r)(n) **in**
	(res(evalAll(steps(r$'$), r$'$, x)), x)
	end
	end

The following relation contains the local relation `allHaveId` to check if all children of the current node have the `id` attribute. The relation decides if all children of the root nodes in both context documents contain the `id` attribute. To this end, it applies the local relation twice: once when the first document is the current one (by default), then it switches to the second document and applies the relation again.

```
<relation mode="con">
  <apply name="allHaveId"/>
  <switch> <number op="literal"> 2 </number> </switch>
  <apply name="allHaveId"/>
  <relation name="allHaveId">
```

```
  <assert> <assertion op="allSat">
      <collection op="children"/> <assertion op="hasId"/>
  </assertion> </assert>
  </relation>
</relation>
```

5.6 x2r:associate

The aim of this step is to arrange two collections of nodes, in the first and in the second document into pairs, then compare such pairs further using assertions. We have nine association types, in all combinations of x2y where x and y can be one, many or all. They "roughly" correspond to the implicit quantification over the two sets: there exists one (one), there are many (many), and for all (all). For instance, suppose ns_1 and ns_2 are collections of nodes selected in the first and in the second document, and a is an assertion expression. Then all2one means that for all n_1 in ns_1 there exists n_2 in ns_2 such that a holds on n_1 and n_2. Formally, the type Step contains the values like one2all(o1,o2,a), all2one(o1,o2,a) and others, and evalOne evaluates such values given a relation r and a context x. First, it calculates the collections o1 and o2 for the first and the second document, then checks that a holds on all pairs of nodes quantified according to the association type. The declarations are as follows:

type
    Step ==
        one2all(Collection^2, Assertion) |
        all2one(Collection^2, Assertion) |
        ...

axiom
    $\forall$ o1, o2: Collection, a: Assertion,
        r: Relation, x: Context •
        evalOne(all2one(o1,o2,a),r,x)=

let
    ns1 = eval(o1, changeCurrent(1, x)),
    ns2 = eval(o2, changeCurrent(2, x))
in
    (res($\forall$ n1: Node • n1 $\in$ **elems** ns1 $\Rightarrow$
        ($\exists$ n2: Node • n2 $\in$ **elems** ns2 $\wedge$
          eval(a,reNode1(n1,reNode2(n2,x)))
)
    ), x)
end

The following relation associates every child of the context node in the first document with an equally-named child of the context node in the second document.

```
<relation mode="con">
  <associate type="all2one">
    <collection op="children"/> <collection op="children"/>
    <assertion op="equal">
      <content op="name"/>
      <content op="doc">
        <number op="literal"> 2 </number> <content op="name"/>
      </content>
    </assertion>
  </associate>
</relation>
```

5.7 x2r:transform

X2Rel provides the mechanism to transform (parts of) the documents before comparing them, relying on the syntax of XSLT [4] to define such transformations and the element transform to invoke them. The example below illustrates the use of transformations to check if the total element of the email is correct. Instead of checking separately the currency and the total values, the transformation creates the element based on the invoice, and compares with one inside the email. Afterwards, the current node of the invoice is the root of the created element (i.e. total), while the current node of the email is unchanged (also total). The assertion checks if they are the same.

```
<relation xmlns:xsl="XSL/Transform">
  <transform name="makeTotal"/>
  <switch> <number op="literal"> 2 </number> </switch>
  <select> ... 3 ... 6 ... </select>
  <assert> <assertion op="equal"/> </assert>
  <xsl:template name="makeTotal">
    <total currency="@currency">
      <xsl:value-of select="sum(//subtotal)"/>
    </total>
  </xsl:template>
</relation>
```

Note the use of the namespace xsl for XSLT elements. The syntax of XSLT templates allows parameters, so we can define a transformation that depends on one document (via the template parameter) and affects another (via the template invocation).

5.8 x2r:typeCheck

The last evaluation step is typeCheck. It brings to power of XML Schemas to X2Rel, in particular the large number of datatypes to describe the contents of XML documents. We allow simple and complex type definitions of the XML Schema language as children of relation. Via its name attribute, typeCheck decides if the current node complies with the restrictions of the corresponding type. The value of name can be the name of the built-in schema type (e.g. xsd:date) or of the user-defined type (e.g. Currencies below). Unfortunately, XML Schemas do not provide type definitions with parameters, so we cannot customize a type definition depending on the content of one document and apply the result to type-check another document.

```
<relation xmlns:xsd="XMLSchema">
  <typeCheck name="Currencies"/>
  <xsd:simpleType name="Currencies">
    <xsd:restriction base="xsd:string">
      <xsd:enumeration value="USD"/> ...
      <xsd:enumeration value="PLZ"/> ...
    </xsd:restriction>
  </xsd:simpleType>
</relation>
```

6   Conclusions

The paper describes the on-going development of a language X2Rel to describe and evaluate binary relations between XML documents. The syntax of X2Rel is entirely based on XML: every X2Rel documents is a well-formed XML document. The XML Schema document `x2rel.xsd` defines precisely what is the X2Rel syntax. The semantics of X2Rel is also defined formally, to capture what the expressions are supposed to represent. The document `x2rel.rsl`, written using RSL [10] contains the formal definition of X2Rel semantics. We only use a small subset of RSL. `x2rel.rsl` defines what it means to evaluate a given relation on a pair of XML documents: how to obtain the result (true or false) and how to generate the report (an XML document) to explain it. Together, `x2rel.xsd` and `x2rel.rsl` comprise the formal definition of the language: `x2rel.xsd` defines what is a valid X2Rel document, and `x2rel.rsl` constrains the behavior of any valid X2Rel processor.

In this work we relied on the recommendations issued by the World Wide Web Consortium concerning XML and related technologies. In fact, X2Rel explicitly relies on two major technologies: XSL Transformations [4] and XML Schemas [6]. We do not know any other attempts to define a language to capture binary relations between XML documents. However, there is a number of schema languages for XML, notably DSD (Document Structure Description) [13] is a schema language defined with formal semantics, where every DSD document describes a regular tree language. [14] describes a taxonomy of XML schema languages on the grounds of formal language theory, considering the time complexity of the schema validation algorithms. [11] propose to use a certain kind of regular expressions, with a notion of subtyping, as a foundation to define XML processing languages, and [12] applies such types to define XDuce, a statically typed programming language for XML processing. [16] describes the formal semantics of patters and pattern-matching in XSLT.

The main direction of our future work is to reach a stable definition of the language, with complete definitions of its syntax and semantics. There are several language features that we had no place to describe here, e.g. generating evaluation reports, arranging associations into groups, selecting the nodes simultaneously in the two documents, etc. others still require investigation. One of them is creating a more convenient syntax of the language, with shorthand notations for the frequently used constructions. Schema validation provides the main benchmark application, so we want to make sure the language is expressive enough for this purpose, but we plan to validate the language with other real-life examples. In order to implement the X2Rel processor, we consider using the RSL-to-C++ generator [1] to generate the code from the definition of X2Rel semantics. The two language definition documents – `x2rel.xsd` and `x2rel.rsl` – currently appear disconnected, but it is quite possible to obtain `x2rel.xsd` from `x2rel.rsl` in a systematic process involving gradually replacing RSL type definitions with the corresponding type definitions of the XML Schema language. We could formalize this process relying on the function `syntax: Relation` $\rightarrow$ `Doc` that maps X2Rel relations into XML documents.

Acknowledgments

The author wishes to thank the anonymous referee for useful comments about the content and presentation of this paper.

References

1. Univan Ahn and Chris George. C++ Translator for RAISE Specification Language. Technical Report 220, UNU/IIST, 2000.
2. David Brownell. *SAX2*. O'Reilly, 2002.
3. James Clark and Steve DeRose, editors. *XML Path Language (XPath), W3C Recommendation*. 1999. http://www.w3.org/TR/xpath.
4. James Clark, editor. *XSL Transformations (XSLT), W3C Recommendation*. 1999. http://www.w3.org/TR/xslt.
5. Arnaud Le Hors et. al., editor. *Document Object Model (DOM) Level 2 Core Specification, W3C Recommendation*. 2000. http://www.w3.org/TR/DOM-Level-2-Core.
6. Henry S. Thompson et. al., editor. *XML Scheme Part 1 (Structures), W3C Recommendation*. 2001. http://www.w3.org/TR/xmlschema-1/.
7. Tim Bray et. al., editor. *Extensible Markup Language (XML) 1.0, W3C Recommendation*. 2000. http://www.w3.org/TR/REC-xml.
8. The Apache Software Foundation. Xalan Java 2.3.1. http://xml.apache.org/xalan-j.
9. The Apache Software Foundation. Xerces Java Parser 2.0.0. http://xml.apache.org/xerces2-j.
10. The RAISE Language Group. *The RAISE Specification Language*. Prentice Hall, 1992.
11. Haruo Hosoya, Jérôme Vouillon, and Benjamin C. Pierce. Regular expression types for XML. *ACM SIGPLAN Notices*, 35(9):11–22, 2000.
12. H. Hosoya and B. C. Pierce. XDuce: A Typed XML Processing Language. In *Int'l Workshop on the Web and Databases (WebDB)*, Dallas, TX, 2000.
13. N. Klarlund, A. Moller, and M. I. Schwatzbach. DSD: A Schema Language for XML. In *ACM SIGSOFT Workshop on Formal Methods in Software Practice*, Portland, OR, 2000.
14. M. Murata, D. Lee, and M. Mani. Taxonomy of XML Schema Languages using Formal Language Theory. In *Extreme Markup Languages*, Montreal, Canada, 2001.
15. Visa International. *General XML Invoice*, 2000. http://international.visa.com.
16. P. Wadler. A Formal Model of Pattern Matching in XSL, 1999. citeseer.nj.nec.com.

Where, Exactly, Is Software Development?

Michael Jackson

101 Hamilton Terrace, London NW8 9QY, England
jacksonma@acm.org

Abstract. Viewed narrowly, software development is concerned only with formal computations; viewed more broadly, it is concerned also with the problem world outside the computer. The broader view compels us to deal with the physical and human world by formalisations that bring it within the scope of formal reasoning, allowing us to deal effectively with the causal chain that relates the customer's requirements to the formally described external behaviour of the computer. It offers not only a sparsely explored field of application for formal techniques, but also fresh challenges that can contribute to shaping and extending those techniques. The primary challenge centres on the impossibility of exact true description of the problem world: any description is only an approximation to the reality. Appropriate specification and design structures can achieve the reliability and extensibility necessary for each particular system. The study of such structures merits an important place in computer science.

1   Introduction

The theme of this colloquium is "Formal Methods at the Crossroads: from Panacea to Foundational Support", and one of its original purposes was "to discuss the underpinnings of software engineering based on formal methods." We are concerned, then, with the relationship between the practical activity of software development and the more theoretical foundational subjects commonly associated with the discipline of computer science.

To many computer scientists the relationship is transparently obvious. The essence of software development, they say, is the application of computer science to programming. To the extent, therefore, that practitioners fail to master and exploit the results obtained and offered by computer science they are failing in the most immediate and elementary obligation of their profession. The responsibility for determining the scope and content of computer science belongs, of course, to the computer scientists.

To some practising software developers the relationship is no less compelling, but has an almost contrary sense. Computer science, they say, addresses chiefly those aspects of software development that cause them little or no difficulty in their daily practice; it ignores many aspects that present serious development challenges and thus have a large impact on the quality and value of the system finally produced. Computer science, they believe, is largely irrelevant to their practical needs.

B.K. Aichernig and T. Maibaum (Eds.): Formal Methods ..., LNCS 2757, pp. 115–131, 2003.

This disagreement arises partly from the uncertain scope of *software engineering*. For some practitioners software engineering comprises not only software construction but also the business justification of the proposed system, the political activities necessary to obtain the required investment, the human problems of managing the development team, the negotiation of conflicting demands from different groups of potential users and other stakeholders, ethnographic studies to discover unobvious properties of the system's human environment, and other similar tasks. Evidently computer science has little or nothing to contribute in these areas, and to computer scientists, *qua* computer scientists, they are of little or no interest.

But even when we restrict the scope of software engineering to exclude these 'soft' concerns – for example, by defining it as "the development of software to meet a clearly identified need", there is still a large unresolved issue about what that restricted scope actually is[1]. This paper cites a narrower and a broader view of the restricted scope and sets them in context; it argues that we should take the broader view; and it presents some topics and concerns that the broader view would embrace.

2   The Scope of Software Development

The narrower of the two views holds that software development is concerned only with the software product itself and the computations it evokes in the machine. This view has been most eloquently advocated by Dijkstra. In an article[3] in Communications of the ACM he wrote:

> "When all is said and done, the only thing computers can do for us is to manipulate symbols and produce results of such manipulations ... .
> "The programmer's main task is to give a formal proof that the program he proposes meets the equally formal functional specification ... .
> "And now the circle is closed: we construct our mechanical symbol manipulators by means of human symbol manipulation."

Of the formal functional specification he wrote:

> "The choice of functional specifications – and of the notation to write them down in – may be far from obvious, but their role is clear: it is to act as a logical 'firewall' between two different concerns. The one is the 'pleasantness problem,' ie the question of whether an engine meeting the specification is the engine we would like to have; the other one is the 'correctness problem,' ie the question of how to design an engine meeting the specification. ... the two problems are most effectively tackled by ... psychology and experimentation for the pleasantness problem and symbol manipulation for the correctness problem."

---

[1] To reflect this restricted scope we will use the term 'software development' in preference to 'software engineering'.

Dijkstra always described himself, proudly, as a programmer[2]. His view is relevant to our concerns here because he advocates with perfect clarity the restriction of his discipline to the construction of programs to satisfy given formal specifications. A specification describes the computer's externally visible behaviour, perhaps in the form of an input-output relation. The choice of specification is a matter of 'pleasantness', for which the software developer or programmer is not responsible. The programmer's concern is simply to produce a program whose executions will satisfy the specification. Programming correctly is programming to a given specification of machine behaviour.

Dijkstra's article evoked several invited responses. One response, by Scherlis, clearly expressed a broader view of the scope of software development [17]:

> "... one of the greatest difficulties in software development is formalization – capturing in symbolic representation a worldly computational problem so that the statements obtained by following rules of symbolic manipulation are useful statements once translated back into the language of the world. The formalization problem is the essence of requirements engineering ..."

In this broader view, the concerns and difficulties of software development extend more widely into the world, to where the customer for the software will look to evaluate the success of the system.

3   The Context of Software Development

Dijkstra speaks of the computing 'engine', and Scherlis of the 'world'. These are the fundamental notions in understanding the context of software development. For consistency with some earlier accounts [7, 8] the term 'machine' will be used here for 'engine', and 'problem world' or 'problem domain' for 'world'.

3.1   The Machine, the World and the Requirement

In software development, the machine is what must be constructed by programming: it is realised by a general-purpose computer executing the software we develop. The problem domain is that part of the world in which our customer requires the machine to have its effect. For example, in a lift control system the problem domain contains the lift shafts, the cars, the doors, the winding gear, the motor, the buttons, the indicator lights and the passengers. In a library administration system the problem domain contains the members, the books, the membership cards, the library staff, the library building, and so on. For us, as software developers, the problem world is *given*: our task does not include designing or constructing the lift mechanism, but only exploiting its properties to achieve the effects our customer demands.

The machine and the problem world interact at an interface of *shared phenomena*. Their interaction, along with the customer's requirement, is shown in the simple diagram of Figure 1.

---

[2] He eschewed the term 'software engineer', which he despised.

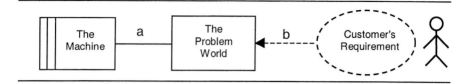

Fig. 1. The Machine, the Problem World and the Requirement

The shared phenomena at interface a are typically shared physical events and states. For example, in the lift control system the machine can turn the motor on by setting a certain line to high; we may then regard this interaction phenomenon as a shared event *MotorOn*, controlled by the machine, in which both machine and problem domain participate. Other such shared events may be *MotorOff*, *MotorPos* and *MotorNeg*, the last two setting the motor polarity and hence its direction of rotation. Similarly, when the lift arrives at a floor it closes an electrical switch, and the machine can sense the state of this switch; we may regard this phenomenon as a shared state *SensorOn[f]*, controlled by the problem domain. Another shared state may be *UpButton[f]*, allowing the machine to detect that the Up button at floor f is depressed. These phenomena at the interface a are the *specification phenomena*, because they are the phenomena in terms of which the specification of the machine's external behaviour must be expressed[3].

The customer appears in the diagram connected to the problem world by the dashed arrow marked b. This arrow indicates the customer's interest in a set of physical phenomena b, that in general are distinct from the set at the interface a. For example, the customer's requirement is that in certain circumstances the lift should rise and eventually arrive at a certain floor. These phenomena – *rise* and *arrive* – are not shared by the machine at interface a: they are distinct from the specification phenomena *MotorOn* and *SensorOn[f]*. The phenomena at b are the *requirement* phenomena, because they are the phenomena in terms of which the customer's requirement is expressed. The requirement phenomena are related to the specification phenomena by causal properties of the lift mechanism – for example, that if the motor polarity is set positive and a *MotorOn* event occurs, then the lift car will start to rise. It is these causal properties that the machine exploits in order to satisfy the customer's requirement by sensing and controlling the phenomena at its interface with the problem world.

---

[3] Shared phenomena present two faces. From a vantage point in the problem world they may be called *MotorOn* etc; but in a formal specification of machine behaviour they would more properly be named as they are seen from the machine side of the interface, as 'line X31FF high' etc.

3.2   Solution in the World and in the Machine

A solution of the problem must be based on at least the following descriptions:

- **requirement** $\mathcal{R}$: a statement of the customer's requirement;
- **domain properties** $\mathcal{W}$: a description of the given properties of the problem world;
- **specification** $\mathcal{S}$: a specification of the machine's behaviour at its interface with the problem world; and
- **program** $\mathcal{P}$: a program describing the machine's internal and external behaviour in a language that the general-purpose computer can interpret.

To show that the problem is solved we must discharge a proof obligation whose form is, roughly:

$$(\mathcal{P} \Rightarrow \mathcal{S}) \wedge ((\mathcal{S} \wedge \mathcal{W}) \Rightarrow \mathcal{R})$$

Each implication must be separately proved. We must show that a machine satisfying the specification, installed in a problem world satisfying the domain properties, will ensure satisfaction of the requirement[4]. The task of identifying, capturing and analysing the domain properties, and developing the specification, may be characterised as *solving the problem in the world*. The task of developing a program to satisfy the specification may be characterised as *solving the problem in the machine*. Dijkstra's 'logical firewall' marks the boundary between the two tasks.

There is an obvious analogy between the two tasks. A requirement referring to phenomena that are not in the machine interface is analogous to a machine specification that refers to specification constructs that are not in the programming language. Immediate and direct implementation is impossible, and some kind of refinement is needed to obtain a version, equivalent to the original, from which unimplementable constructs have been eliminated. In refinement aimed at program development we rely on the semantics of the programming language to justify each refinement step. In developing the program specification from the requirement we must rely on the domain properties, which alone can bridge the gap between the requirement phenomena and the specification phenomena.

But the analogy must not be carried too far. The two implications in the proof obligation have slightly different forms: the domain properties are explicitly mentioned in the second implication, but the programming language semantics are not mentioned in the first. This difference reflects the formality and relative simplicity of the programming language semantics: by writing the program text in a well-known language we bring in the semantics implicitly. For a good language, the programming constructs are few and their semantics are regular and certain: the programmer is not expected to choose some small subset of the semantics in preference to the rest. But the domain properties are not like this. Although we regard them as given, in the sense that they are not a part of what must be constructed, exploring the domain and choosing which properties are useful for the purpose in hand is often a major development concern.

---

[4] A more substantial (but imperfect) discussion of this proof obligation is given in [5].

In general, a problem domain exhibits an unbounded set of causal and other relevant properties. It is therefore not trivial to identify the 'semantics of the specification' – that is, all the consequences of the machine's actions at its interface with the domain. Further, the analogue of linguistic meta-properties like *referential transparency*, that contribute to the regularity of programming language semantics, are rarely found in the physical world. As a result, the task of choosing, describing and analysing the domain properties needed to allow the worldly problem to be solved is far from straightforward. The developer must record exactly which properties have been chosen, and assert them explicitly in discharging the proof obligation.

3.3   The Broader and the Narrower View

In the context of this relationship between the machine and the problem world we can characterise the narrower and broader view of software development by the different subject matters that they encompass. The narrower view is concerned only with $\mathcal{P}$ and $\mathcal{S}$ and the first implication: with the machine and its specified behaviour at its interface a to the problem world. Because the shared phenomena at interface a are phenomena of the machine no less than phenomena of the problem world, the narrower view can be properly said to be concerned only with the machine. The broader view encompasses not only the machine but also $\mathcal{W}$ and $\mathcal{R}$ and the second implication: that is, it is concerned with the problem world itself and the customer's requirement expressed in terms of the requirement phenomena at b. In short: the narrower view holds that software development is solely in the machine, while the broader view holds that it is both in the machine and in the problem world.

At first sight it may seem that the broader view is just a simple extension of the narrower view: it merely enlarges our notion of the machine. In the narrower view the machine was just the computer and the software; now it includes the lift mechanisms and the passengers, or the library books and the membership cards. The customer's requirement has taken the place of the functional specification in the narrower view; once again, we are not responsible, as software developers, for its choice.

But the effect of the extension runs deep. The problem world is not just a simple extension of the machine, because it is – in general – informal where the machine is formal. Important consequences flow from this informality.

4   Formal and Informal Domains

The general-purpose computer has been carefully engineered so that, for most practical purposes, it can be regarded as a *formal domain*: that is, as the physical embodiment of a formal system. This is why programming, in the narrow sense of creating a program $\mathcal{P}$ to satisfy a given formal specification $\mathcal{S}$ can fruitfully be regarded as an entirely formal discipline. A formal system, physically embodied, has two fundamental properties:

1. Occurrences of the phenomena that are significant for the purpose in hand can be recognised with perfect reliability. For example, a bit in store is either 1 or 0: there are no doubtful cases. (More precisely, the doubtful cases, in which a bit is in course of changing from one state to the other, are hidden from view by clocking and other synchronisation mechanisms.)
2. Universally quantified assertions can be made that are useful for the purpose in hand and are true without exception. The assertions that constitute the description of the computer's order code are of this kind.

These fundamental properties underpin reliable formal reasoning. True statements about the programmed behaviour of the computer, symbolically manipulated according to appropriate formal rules, are guaranteed to result in further true statements[5].

In an informal domain we can rely on neither of these two fundamental properties. The denotation of any term we introduce, and the correctness of any universally quantified assertion we make, may be beset by a multitude of hard cases. We say what we mean by a vehicle, and we are immediately confronted by the difficult question: Is a skateboard a vehicle? We assert confidently that every human being has a human mother, and we are immediately pressed to consider the very first *homo sapiens*. We calculate and exploit the properties of certain aircraft components; but we soon find that they cease to hold in the presence of metal fatigue, a phenomenon that we had previously ignored. The source and symptom of this multitude of hard cases is the unbounded nature of an informal domain. We can never say with perfect confidence, as we can in a formal mathematical domain, that all relevant considerations have been taken into account.

5   The Meeting of Formal and Informal

In some computer applications the problem world too can be regarded as a formal domain. It may be abstract rather than physical, as in the problem of factorising a large integer. It may be itself a part of the same or another computer, as in the problem of recording and analysing the usage of CPU cycles. It may be a domain already formalised for a specific purpose, as in the problem of playing a game of chess.

But formal problem domains are the exception, not the rule. Most useful applications deal with an informal world, in which distinctions between phenomena are fuzzy and no universally quantified assertion is unconditionally true. These applications present the 'worldly computational problems' to which Scherlis alludes. In discharging the proof obligation $(\mathcal{P} \Rightarrow \mathcal{S}) \wedge ((\mathcal{S} \wedge \mathcal{W}) \Rightarrow \mathcal{R})$ we are confronted by the uncomfortable fact that $\mathcal{P}$ and $\mathcal{S}$ are formal descriptions of a

---

[5] Of course, this guarantee depends on correct design and implementation of the computer and fault-free execution of the program. But in most practical circumstances these conditions are satisfied. Computer failure need be considered only for the most critical systems of all.

formal domain, but $\mathcal{W}$ and $\mathcal{R}$ are formal descriptions of an informal domain – with all that this implies. We must, somehow, construct a convincing proof that relates the formal and the informal.

Of course, we will not succeed by abandoning formality in our descriptions and arguments. On the contrary, we must deal with the informal problem world in a formal way that is effective for the particular problem in hand. We will still use formal terms, and their denotations will be inescapably fuzzy; we will use universally quantified formulae, and they will not be unconditionally true. The challenge is to ensure nonetheless that, in Scherlis's words, 'the statements obtained by following rules of symbolic manipulation are useful statements once translated back into the language of the world'. We aim at sufficient usefulness, not at unconditional truth.

6   Problem World Complexity

Introducing a computer into a system can hugely increase the system's discrete behavioural complexity. Consider, for example, a central locking system for a typical four-door car. The customer's requirements are about the opening and closing of the doors and the boot. These requirements include security against theft, protection – so far as possible – against locking oneself out of the car, accessibility for employees in a parking garage while keeping the boot locked, protection against carjacking, convenient locking and unlocking, protecting children against unintended opening of doors while the car is in motion, automatic unlocking in the event of a crash, and so on. The problem domain encompasses the contexts in which these requirements have meaning (including their human actors), and also the equipment of the car, including at least:

- four exterior door handles;
- an exterior lock on the driver's door;
- an exterior boot lock;
- four interior door handles with individual locking buttons;
- a central locking switch;
- an ignition switch sensor;
- a boot release lever;
- two child-locking activation levers on the rear doors; and
- a crash sensor.

The possible states and usage scenarios of this equipment give rise to a very large state space and great behavioural complexity. Certainly there is much more complexity than was possible in an old-fashioned car in which the locks are operated mechanically: it was difficult to construct practicable direct mechanical or electro-mechanical linkages between locks on different doors, and a typical system would not go far beyond locking and unlocking all four doors when the driver's door is locked or unlocked from the inside.

The need to master this kind of complexity is not new: it is central to software engineering techniques. However, because the broader view of the scope of software development takes in the customer requirements and the relevant aspects of the problem world, it becomes necessary to consider the requirement phenomena and their causal connections to the handles, switches and sensors that participate in the specification phenomena. This is where the informality of the problem world can introduce new difficulties. For example, one well-known and much admired make of car provided automatic unlocking in the event of a crash by unlocking all the doors unconditionally whenever a sensor located in the front bumper detected an impact. This scheme, unfortunately, frustrated the requirement of security against theft: an intelligent thief realised that he could open a locked car by simply kicking the front bumper in the right place.

This kind of anomaly in a complex problem world system is not new. Very complex legal, business and administrative systems existed in the Roman empire and in some earlier civilisations. Anomalies arise because of the informal nature of the problem world: it is always possible for a consideration to arise that the system has not previously encountered and is not designed to handle. Traditionally, such anomalies are handled by an *ad hoc* overriding of the system's rules by human intervention. In an automated system no such overriding is possible. There is therefore an obligation to build a system that is – so far as practicable – robust against such eventualities. Formal methods are needed for analysing the vulnerabilities of the descriptions S, W and R to unexpected considerations, and the implications of those vulnerabilities for the demonstration that the system satisfies its requirements.

7   Problem World Unreliability

Conviction that a system built to a certain behavioural specification S at the machine interface will guarantee satisfaction of the customer's requirement depends on a proof that $(S \wedge W) \Rightarrow R$. The description W describes those properties of the problem world that we rely on to ensure satisfaction of the requirement R. For example, in the lift problem we rely on such properties as these:

– If a *MotorPos* event occurs, followed by a *MotorOn* event, then the lift car will start to rise in the lift shaft;
– *SensorOn[f]* holds if and only if the lift car is within $6in$ of the home position at floor f;
– the concrete lift shaft constrains the lift car not to move from floor n to floor $n+2$ without passing floor $n+1$.

These properties allow the machine to provide the required lift service, in terms of lifts moving to floors in response to requests, by a suitably designed behaviour in terms of the specification phenomena.

Unfortunately, because the problem world of the lift's mechanical and electrical equipment is not a formal domain like the domain of the integers, no properties W can be guaranteed to hold unconditionally. The motor may fail to rotate when a *MotorOn* event occurs, because an electrical connection may have been severed, or the motor windings have burned out. Even if the motor rotates, the lift car may fail to rise, because the gearbox connecting the motor to the winding drum has failed, or because the cable has snapped. A floor sensor may be stuck at closed. The lift shaft may collapse in an earthquake. This unreliability of the problem world itself is a major barrier to improving the reliablity [9] of the systems we build.

At first sight it may seem that the description W should be elaborated to take account of as many of these failures as are considered likely enough to merit explicit treatment. But this is not really an attractive approach. The resulting description W would be tremendously complicated, and its complications would lead to many errors in development of the system. More importantly, the properties on which we rely for normal correct operation of the system would be obscured by epicycles of possible but improbable failures.

A more attractive approach is to separate the normal operation of the system in the absence of failure from its operation in the presence of various failures. Failure operation may be structured as a set of fallback modes. For example, if a slight overheating of the motor is detected it may be appropriate to return the lift car slowly to the ground floor and keep it there; but if the lift car reaches floor $n - 1$ from floor n in less than a preset minimum time, suggesting some failure or impending failure of the winding gear, it may be appropriate to apply the emergency braking system to prevent a catastrophic fall.

Such a separation gives rise to a problem decomposition into several subproblems: one corresponding to each operation mode, and one or more corresponding to the choice of execution mode at each point in time. Each subproblem, of course, has its own set of descriptions – specification, problem world properties and requirement – and its own proof obligation. The relationship among the subproblems of this set raises some non-trivial concerns:

- The different subproblems have, in general, different but possibly intersecting sets of requirement and specification phenomena. For example, the event in which the machine applies the emergency brake appears in the specification phenomena of one failure-mode subproblem but not in the specification phenomena of the normal operation subproblem.
- The different requirements Ri are, in general, mutually contradictory. For example, the requirement to return the lift car to the ground floor if the motor overheats contradicts the requirement to provide service in response to requests.
- The different problem world properties Wi fit into some structure of approximations to the reality. If this structure is sufficient for the reality actually encountered by the system, then at every stage in execution at least one of the descriptions Wi describes problem world properties that hold at that stage.
- The different specifications Si represent different machine behaviours that are, in general, mutually incompatible. Correct switching from one operation mode to another must respect certain conditions of atomicity and of state inclusion, both in the software machine and in the problem domain.

These concerns have been addressed by a number of researchers and practitioners in the field of software engineering[6]. Their significance for computer science is that they may be susceptible to a more general treatment than they have so far received.

8   Feature Interactions

Some systems (particularly, but not only, telephone systems and telecommunication systems more generally) evolve over a long period by successive addition of new features. For example, one telephone feature is OCS (Originating Call Screening), which allows a subscriber to enter into the system a list of directory numbers calls to which are banned at the subscriber's phone. Another feature is SD (Speed Dialling), which allows a subscriber to specify abbreviations for frequently called numbers, the system expanding the abbreviations into the corresponding numbers. A third feature is CFB (Call Forwarding on Busy), which allows a subscriber to enter into the system a directory number to which incoming calls will be automatically forwarded when the subscriber's phone is busy. A fourth is VMB (VoiceMail on Busy), which invites a caller to leave a recorded message if the subscriber's phone is busy. New features are motivated by market demand, and must be provided by any supplier who hopes to continue in business. The system may have a very large installed base of hardware, software, attached devices, and users; so redesigning the whole system to accommodate a new feature is not a feasible option. Instead, new features must be added to the existing system with the minimum disruption of software structure and functionality and of users' expectations.

Such a system inevitably suffers from the *feature interaction* problem. Two features interact if the presence of one frustrates or modifies the operation of the other. The interaction may be desirable or undesirable, but the problem is always to manage it appropriately both for the users and for the software. To take a simple example, Call Forwarding on Busy and VoiceMail on Busy are competitive 'busy treatments'; if one of them is applied to a particular incoming call the other is bypassed. This competition between these features can be resolved by a fixed or variable priority scheme in the requirements structure. In the software structure it is desirable that each feature should be implementable by an independent module[6, 18] from which all reference to the other feature is rigorously excluded.

A more interesting interaction arises between Originating Call Screening (OCS) and Call Forwarding on Busy (CFB). A subscriber who enters the number of a chat line into the OCS list, to prevent a teenage child from calling the chat line, can be frustrated by the teenager and a cooperative friend. The friend first configures CFB at the friend's phone, specifying the chat line as the forward number, and then ensures that the friend's phone is busy when the teenager wants to call the chat line. The teenager calls the friend's number, and the call is forwarded to the chat line.

This second, more interesting, interaction raises some interesting concerns about requirements and specifications, and about the relationship between them

---

[6] Contradictory requirements, for example, have been treated in [13].

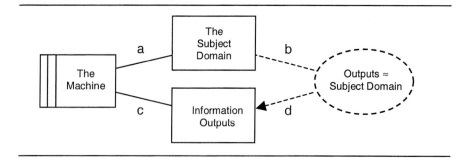

Fig. 2. An Information Problem

and an implementation. The OCS feature may originally have been conceived in terms of directory numbers *dialled* at the subscriber's phone: in this original form it acts to bar any call initiated by dialling a forbidden number. Then, perhaps, the addition of the SD (Speed Dialling) feature causes an immediate interaction: if an abbreviation is used the barred number is not actually dialled at the subscriber's phone, but is retrieved by the system from the subscriber's SD dictionary to place the call. With hindsight it can then be seen that the OCS feature should rather have been conceived in terms of numbers *initiated* at the subscriber's phone, whether directly by dialling or indirectly by abbreviation. But the interaction with CFB then shows that even this change is insufficient. The chat line number is never initiated at the subscriber's phone; it is only entered at the friend's phone when Call Forwarding is set up.

Essentially the difficulty is that adding new features changes the problem world in ways that were not foreseen. In the specific context of telecommunication system the difficulty can be addressed by special-purpose architecture[6, 18]. The full challenge is to find a sound general basis for incremental feature-based development that minimises, or at least mitigates, the effects of this difficulty. Certainly, standard notions of refinement can not meet this challenge, and other approaches – for example, retrenchment[2] – merit energetic exploration. The goal is to identify or develop formal structures that will be more resilient under the impact of this particular class of changes to the requirements.

9   Building and Using Analogic Models

A simple information problem may have the form shown in Figure 2.

The problem world has been structured as two domains: the Subject Domain, about whose state and behaviour information is required; and the Information Outputs domain, to which the required information is to be delivered by the machine. For example, the Subject Domain might be a chemical process plant, and the Information Outputs domain a display panel used by the plant operating staff. The requirement is that a certain correspondence should be maintained between some phenomena b of the Subject Domain and some phenomena d of the Information Outputs domain. For example, the value of a certain field shown in the display must correspond to the current level of liquid in a certain vessel;

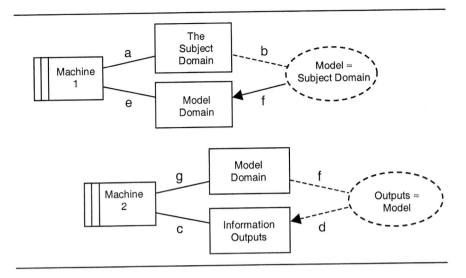

Fig. 3. Decomposition of an Information Problem

the value of another field must correspond to the cumulative flow through a certain valve; and so on[7]. The machine has access to the phenomena a, which it shares with the Subject Domain; from these phenomena it must determine the values of the requirement phenomena b. It also has access to the phenomena c, which it shares with the Information Outputs domain; it uses these phenomena to set the values in the display.

In general, the values to be set in the display fields will not simply be representations of states immediately available at interface a. Calculation of the field values will need the use of local variables internal to the machine; some of these variables correspond to phenomena of b that can not be directly observed but must be computed by inference from the Subject Domain properties; others correspond to phenomena that may be directly observed but must be remembered, or perhaps integrated over time, or otherwise summarised. These local variables of the machine constitute an *analogic model*[1] of the Subject Domain.

Where a non-trivial analogic model of this kind is necessary, it is appropriate to separate the problem into two subproblems: one of maintaining the model, and the other of using it to furnish the required information. This decomposition is shown in Figure 3.

The decomposition makes explicit the role of the model domain as an intermediary between the Subject Domain and the Information Outputs. Clearly, it is desired that the original requirement should be equivalent to the composition of the two subproblem requirements. That is:

$$(Model \approx SubjectDomain \wedge Outputs \approx Model) \Leftrightarrow Outputs \approx SubjectDomain$$

---

[7] The presence of an arrowhead on one dashed line and not the other indicates that the correspondence must be achieved by constraining the Information Outputs, not the Subject Domain.

However, there are many reasons why this goal can be achieved only imperfectly. These reasons may include:

- approximation of continuous by discrete phenomena;
- unreliability of the tranmission of phenomena a across the interface;
- unreliability of the feasible inferences of phenomena b from phenomena a;
- loss of information due to lack of storage for an unbounded history of the Subject Domain;
- imperfect synchronisation of the Model with the Subject Domain; and
- delays due to avoidance of interference between $Machine1$ and $Machine2$ in accessing the Model.

The study of these difficulties, both individually and in combination, is important. Many system failures are at least partly attributable to unanalysed deviation of a model from its subject domain. The topic may, perhaps, be regarded as analogous to the study of error terms in numerical analysis.

10   Dependable Systems

A dependable system is one for which reliance may justifiably be placed on certain aspects of its conformity to requirements and quality of service. If the term 'dependable' is to mean something significantly different from 'good' it must surely mean that some of these aspects are more dependable than others. For example, in a system to control a radiotherapy machine one might distinguish two requirements: that each patient receive the dose prescribed for his case; and that no patient receive a lethal dose. A thoroughly successful system will conform dependably to both of these requirements; but the dependability of conformance to the second requirement is clearly more important.

An example of this kind of priority of requirements appeared in Section 7, where the requirement that the lift must not crash in the event of motor failure takes precedence over the requirement for servicing requests. In that example, and in the whole discussion in Section 7, the root source of the difficulty was problem domain unreliability: any property on which satisfaction of the requirement depends may fail to hold. In a dependable system it is necessary also to handle difficulties whose source is unreliability in the software components that we ourselves have developed. We must be able to be sure that the subprogram precluding a lethal dose will have priority over the less critical subprogram guaranteeing delivery of the prescribed dose – even if the latter is incorrectly programmed. This is a different concern from our earlier concern with unreliability of the problem world.

In physical systems priority may be straightforwardly achieved by exploiting quantitative physical properties that allow one component to be made *stronger* than another, ensuring that the weaker component will break before the stronger. The most obvious example of explicit design on this basis is a fuse in an electrical circuit: if the circuit is overloaded the fuse blows before any damage can be done to the other parts of the circuit. Implicit illustrations are found everywhere, especially in mechanical structures. Repainting a suspension bridge does not risk causing immediate collapse, because the weight and other physical attributes of the paint are quantitatively negligible compared to the corresponding attributes of the piers, chains, roadway and other major components.

In the software technologies in common use there is, unfortunately, no obvious sysematic analogue of strength and other quantitative physical properties: in a certain sense every software component is equally strong. As the Ariane-5 and Therac-25 catastrophes showed, failure in a relatively unimportant component can result in disastrous malfunction of a component critical to the whole operation of the system. As is well known, the Therac-25 replaced some hardware safety interlocks present in the predecessor Therac-20 design with new software safety interlocks[10]. An important factor contributing to the catastrophe was the vulnerability of these software interlocks to failures in other, relatively unimportant, software components. What was needed was provided by the discarded hardware interlocks but was not, apparently, achievable in software: that is, that the interlocks should be *stronger* than the other components, and so invulnerable to their failures.

In safety-critical systems it is acknowledged that the most critical components must be identified. Their correctness, and provision of a protected environment for their execution, must take priority and should receive an appropriately large share of the development resources. Identifying the most critical components, and enabling this preferential treatment, are central goals of software design. In effect, the emphasis in such developments moves from a simplistic goal of uniform correctness of every part of a system to a more sophisticated goal of appropriate relative strengths of different components in a software structure. Software faults can be tolerated, just as the inevitability of physical failure can be tolerated.

A substantial body of work on software fault tolerance goes back at least to the ideas of recovery blocks[14]. It seems desirable that more general formal foundations should be established, on which a systematic discipline of design in the presence of potential software failure can become the norm, as design in the presence of physical component failure is the norm in traditional engineering disciplines.

11   Conclusion

There is nothing new in this paper except, perhaps, the emphasis of its central argument. For every topic proposed here as a worthy subject for the attention of computer scientists it is possible to point to computer scientists who have already produced important work on that topic[8]. It is also true that formal calculi and notations are often strongly influenced by the problems thrown up by technological developments – the π-calculus being a notable example[11]. And yet the centre of gravity of computer science today seems to lie elsewhere.

---

[8] For an excellent review of work on dependable systems, for example, see[15, 16].

The argument of this paper is that the scope of computer science – more precisely, the active interests of typical computer scientists – could fruitfully be broadened to take in more of the problem world and with it a more direct understanding of the consequences of its complexity, untidiness and unreliability. It is not enough to look on the problem world from afar, hoping that distance will lend perspective and will help to make the largest and most important difficulties stand out from a mass of trivia. Nor is it enough to listen carefully to practitioners, trusting that they have already winnowed out the important concerns and can be relied on to express their essence in a compact form and bring them to computer scientists for solution. As Newton wrote in a letter to Nathaniel Hawes[12]:

> "If, instead of sending the observations of able seamen to able mathematicians on land, the land would send able mathematicians to sea, it would signify much more to the improvement of navigation and the safety of men's lives and estates on that element."

Such a broadening of computer science would surely lead to a greater emphasis on topics that are close to some core difficulties of software development. One goal of computer science is to provide sound scientific and mathematical foundations for the practice of software development. Those foundations will be deeper and better placed if they grow out of a wholehearted engagement with the whole range of what Eugene Ferguson[4] calls 'the incalculable complexity of engineering practice in the real world'.

Acknowledgements

Thanks are due to a reviewer who raised a number of interesting questions leading to clarifications and improvements.

References

1. Ackoff, R; Scientific Method: Optimizing Applied Research Decisions. With the collaboration of S. K. Gupta and J. S. Minas; Wiley, 1962
2. Banach R. and Poppleton M.; Retrenchment, Refinement and Simulation. In Proceedings of ZB-00, Bowen, Dunne, Galloway, King (eds.), LNCS 1878, Springer, pp304–323
3. E W Dijkstra; On the Cruelty of Really Teaching Computer Science; CACM 32,12, December 1989, pp1398–1404
4. Eugene S Ferguson; Engineering and the Mind's Eye; MIT 1992, p168
5. Carl A Gunter, Elsa L Gunter, Michael Jackson and Pamela Zave; A Reference Model for Requirements and Specifications; Proceedings of ICRE 2000, Chicago Ill, USA; reprinted in IEEE Software 17, 3, May/June 2000, pp37–43
6. Michael Jackson and and Pamela Zave; Distributed Feature Composition: A Virtual Architecture For Telecommunications Services; IEEE Transactions on Software Engineering 24,10, Special Issue on Feature Interaction, October 1998, pp831-847

7. Michael Jackson; Problem Analysis and Structure; in Engineering Theories of Software Construction, Tony Hoare, Manfred Broy and Ralf Steinbruggen eds; Proceedings of NATO Summer School, Marktoberdorf; IOS Press, Amsterdam, Netherlands, August 2000

8. Michael Jackson; Problem Frames: Analysing and Structuring Software Development Problems; Addison-Wesley, 2000

9. Laprie J C ed. Dependability: Basic Concepts and Associated Terminology; Dependable Computing and Fault-Tolerant Systems 5; Springer Verlag, 1992

10. Nancy G Leveson and Clark S Turner; An Investigation of the Therac-25 Accidents; IEEE Computer 26,7, July 1993, pp18–41

11. Robin Milner; Communicating and Mobile Systems: the π-Calculus; Cambridge University Press, 1999

12. Isaac Newton; letter to Nathaniel Hawes, quoted in R V Jones, Most Secret War; Wordsworth Editions 1998, p377

13. B. Nuseibeh and A. Russo; Using Abduction to Evolve Inconsistent Requirements Specifications, Austrialian Journal of Information Systems 7(1), Special Issue on Requirements Engineering, 1999, ISSN: 1039-7841.

14. B. Randell. System structure for software fault tolerance. IEEE Trans-actions on Software Engineering, SE-1(2), June 1975, pp220–232

15. John Rushby; Critical System Properties: Survey and Taxonomy; Reliability Engineering and System Safety 43,2, 1994, pp189–219

16. John Rushby. Formal Methods and Their Role in the Certification of Critical Systems; in Roger Shaw ed, Safety and Reliability of Software Based Systems: Twelfth Annual CSR Workshop; Springer Verlag, 1997

17. W Scherlis; responding to E W Dijkstra's *On the Cruelty of Really Teaching Computer Science*; CACM 32,12, December 1989, p1407

18. Pamela Zave; Feature-Oriented Description, Formal Methods, and DFC; in Proceedings of the FIREWORKS Workshop on Language Constructs for Describing Features; Springer Verlag, 2000

From Formal Techniques to Well-Founded Software Development Methods*

Egidio Astesiano, Gianna Reggio, and Maura Cerioli

DISI, Università di Genova - Italy

Abstract. We look at the main issue of the Colloquium "Formal Methods at the Crossroads from Panacea to Foundational Support" reflecting on our rather long experience of active engagement in the development and use of formal techniques. In the years, we have become convinced of the necessity of an approach more concerned with the real needs of the software development practice. Consequently, we have shifted our work to include methodological aspects, learning a lot from the software engineering practices and principles.

After motivating our current position, mainly reflecting on our own experience, we suggest a *Virtuous Cycle* for the formal techniques having the chance of a real impact on the software development practices. Then, to provide some concrete illustration of the suggested principles, we propose and advocate a strategy that we call *Well-Founded Software Development Methods*, of which we outline two instantiations.

1 Introduction

The concern reflected in the title of the Colloquium[1] and explained in its motivation came as a no surprise to us. We have been involved in the development and experimental use of formal techniques since more than twenty years and we have witnessed and experienced dramatic changes. The changes, positive and negative, refer to many aspects of the research in the field: quality, amount, scope, relevance and acceptance. In our community of formal techniques there is no need to push for more research in theoretical work in general, since the advocates of the merits and value of such research abound, as much as the good papers in the field (see, e.g., the over 8000 pages of the 2001 issues of a prestigious journal such as TCS). Thus, here we concentrate more on some critical issues, mainly concerning our personal experience from which we try to learn some lessons.

The first uncontroversial fact is the large gap between theory and practice and the increasing awareness, starting in the middle 90's, that the many hopes for a

---

* Work supported by the Italian National Project SAHARA (Architetture Software per infrastrutture di rete ad accesso eterogeneo).

[1] The 10th Anniversary Colloquium of the United Nations University International Institute for Software Technology (UNU/IIST): Formal Methods at the Crossroads from Panacea to Foundational Support. Lisbon - Portugal, March 18-21, 2002.

B.K. Aichernig and T. Maibaum (Eds.): Formal Methods ..., LNCS 2757, pp. 132–150, 2003.
© Springer-Verlag Berlin Heidelberg 2003

prominent role of formal techniques in software development were fading away, as recognized even by some of the pioneers and more convinced supporters (see [12]). Things have not changed much since, but in a sense they have worsened for what concerns academic research on software engineering in general, as noticed by B. Meyer in [20]:

"When considering the evolution of the field over the last decades, we cannot escape the possibly unpleasant observation that if much of the innovation in the '60s and 70's came from academic institutions, contributions from small entrepreneurial companies and the research labs of large companies dominated the '80s and '90s."

The reactions to the existence of such gap between theory and practice have been mixed and sometimes diverging. In his invited lecture at Formal Methods Europe '96 in Oxford [14] T. Hoare was suggesting

"We must aim our future theoretical research on goals which are as far ahead of the current state of the art as the current state of industrial practice lags behind the research we did in the past. Twenty years perhaps?"

History shows that such remark may well be applied to few fundamental pioneering concepts and insights, but cannot be taken as a rule for research in formal techniques. For example, more than twenty years ago, the foundations have been laid down for a neat formal treatment of requirement and design specifications, including clean semantics. Consider e.g., the enormous effort in the techniques for algebraic specification, as summarized in an IFIP State-of-the-art Report jointly produced by the members of the IFIP WG 1.3. [2], not to mention the wealth of results on denotational and operational semantic, for almost any kind of languages.

Now, after so many years of work in formal techniques, what do we have on the table of the current practice in the corresponding area? The most evident phenomenon is the Unified Modeling Language UML (see, e.g., [29]), not only a standard of the Object Management Group (OMG[2]), but a de facto industry standard for modelling/specifying systems at different levels of abstraction and from different viewpoints. The UML intends to *"provide a formal basis for un-derstanding the modeling language"* and indeed it tries to incorporate not only many lessons from the software engineering side, but also some good ideas about abstraction, encapsulation, and dynamic behavior developed by researchers in formal techniques in the years before. Nevertheless, the result for most of us is frustrating: not even the static/syntactic semantics is clear, and as for the semantics in general *"UML expresses the operational meaning of most constructs in precise natural language"*[3]. Still the UML represents a significant advance over current industry practices, for what concerns, e.g., the use of an appropriate level of abstraction and the separation between modelling/specification and implementation, an issue emphasized very recently by the adoption of the Model

---

[2] http://www.omg.org/.

[3] By the way, in this regard we can even find in the reference manual [29] a pearl statement such as *"The fully formal approach taken to specify languages such as ALGOL 68 was not approachable enough for most practical usage"*.

Driven Architecture (MDA) [18] by the OMG, as a separate step from the building of a Platform Driven Architecture. Moreover, to be fair, one has to say more generally that, if on one side the figures related to failures in software projects are appalling, on the other side one can be amazed that the existing software is quite often satisfactory enough. Significantly, indeed, the cited talk by T. Hoare at Formal Methods Europe '96 [14] had the curious title *"How did software get so reliable without proof?"*. I must however mention that the software consumer view may be different and not so positive, as explained in a very interesting book *The software Conspiracy* by M. Minasi [21].

All the above to say that, apart from some very few remarkable exceptions, there is little chance for theory in isolation to filter in the practice in a sensible way. We need to look ourselves at what is going on in the practice of software development. We are encouraged in this belief by the following two remarks, always by T. Hoare in [14], *"personal involvement in current practices ... may lead to quite rapid benefits, both to the practitioner and to the theorist"* and *"the influence of practice on the development of theory is more beneficial and actually quicker than the other way round."* Indeed, the last two remarks may sound surprising w.r.t. the previous statement on the quest for theories looking twenty years ahead. We are instead inclined to believe that the three remarks complement each other to give a correct perspective. Here, obviously we restrict our attention to the interplay between research in formal techniques and its impact on software development practices. That restriction relies on an assumption better phrased, and with the authority of a pioneer of formal methods, by our good friend C. Jones in his invited talk at the first ETAPS-FASE'98 [17] *"I assume that the purpose of developing formal methods is to influence practical engineering of computer systems (whether hardware or software)."* Such assumption should sound trivial, but it must not be so, since he adds immediately: *"It is a measure of my unease with some research in the area of computer science that I feel necessary to state this fact"*. That quotation leads us to introduce the main general thesis of our contribution and position, as an answer to the debate raised by this colloquium.

Let us assume that our concern is software development and then let us try to define a suitable role for formalization. Here we are soon faced with an ill-defined dichotomy that has to be dismissed, as pointed out by B. Meyer in [19]:

"For some scientists, software development is a branch of mathematics; for some engineering it is branch of applied technology. In reality, it is both."

Thus, inevitably the *Great General Challenge* of the work in formal techniques is to address in a recognized way the relevant issues in software development, paying more attention at the engineering needs. We are well aware that the above statement sounds like preaching and needs to be made concrete. So, in the following we try to motivate and articulate our thesis. First we reflect on our own experience to draw some lessons (Sect. 2); then, to illustrate more concretely our view, we outline some of our current directions of research towards a viable strategy that we call *Well-Founded Software Development Methods* (Sect. 3).

Recall that in the conclusions we try to summarize and make an assessment of the proposed strategy.

2 Shifting the Focus and the Attitude of Our Research in Formal Techniques

The following reflections are certainly biased by our experience and thus we think it is better to present them mainly as reflections on the work our group has done in the years on the subject.

2.1 On the Formalist Side

For what matters in this context, the work of our group on the use of formal techniques in the specification of systems has started at the beginning of the '80 when we have been engaged in a very ambitious national project on the prototypical design and implementation of a local area network, the Cnet project. Our task was the formal specification of the rather sophisticated software architecture, in two levels: the intra-node with Ada-like tasks and the inter-node with both point-to-point and broadcast communication. After some serious attempt at using CCS and CSP, we soon became aware that higher-level specification techniques, also able to manipulate complex structures, data and processes as data, were required. That led us to develop in the years an approach to the specification of possibly concurrent/reactive systems (see [4] and [6] for a later comprehensive outline), which, with some further improvement [3], was then used successfully and adopted as the technical basis in the EEC project (lead by D. Björner) for the full Formal Definition of Ada ('85/'87).

In those years, and during those projects, we have experienced the value of our formal setting to make precise any aspect of the modelled systems in an unambiguous way. First, in the Cnet project there was an endless feedback with the designers of the architecture and always the formalization was proved helpful. Then, in the Ada project the people in the board for the language standard were forced to accept some of our proposed modifications to make the language consistent. The presentation of the full definition, in a 13 hours seminar (by the first author and by J. Størbark Pedersen, then at DDC, DK) at Triangle Park-USA, to the people of the Ada Joint Program Office, and later at an international school, was received with enthusiastic comments, which were then forwarded to the EEC officers.

That was a time when we were convinced that the formal techniques were the real solution to put software development on a firm basis. That atmosphere was reflected in the title of another EEC initiative, lasting altogether seven years, the Esprit BR WG COMPASS (COMPrehensive Algebraic Approach to Software Specification) '89-96. It is within that project that was conceived the idea of publishing a comprehensive book on the algebraic specification of systems leading to the mentioned IFIP State-of-the-art Report sponsored by IFIP WG 1.3. [2]. Moreover, just before the end of the COMPASS initiative, we contributed

to start the CoFI initiative (Common Framework Initiative for algebraic specification and development of software) [22], whose first aim was to define, within
a future family of related extension and restriction languages, CASL, the Common Algebraic Specification Language, approved by the IFIP WG1.3, see [1]. Of
course CASL, which encompasses all previously designed algebraic specification
languages, has a clean, perfectly defined semantics. Within CoFI, some extensions of CASL have been provided to deal, e.g., with concurrency and reactivity;
our LTL [6] can be seen as one of these extensions. Still the target of the work
within CoFI was and is the research community and not industry practice.

2.2   Some Lessons from the Practice
and the Software Engineering Sides

While contributing to the development and improvement of formal techniques
we have been involved in some projects with industry to apply our techniques
to real-size case studies. It was soon evident that our (us and our community)
work had not taken into consideration some aspects of paramount importance in
software development, generally qualifiable as methodological aspects. That has
led us first to take care in some way of those aspects in the application of our
techniques, and then to reflect on our approach. The results of our reflections
were presented at the last TAPSOFT in Lille in '97 (for a journal version, see
[5]). The main findings of that investigation, significantly titled *Formalism and
Method*, were

- the distinction between formalism and method,
- the inclusion of a formalism, if any, as a part of a method,
- the essential relevance of *modelling rationale* as the link between the end
  product (system, item) and the formal structures (models) representing it,
- the role of pragmatics.

In Fig. 1 we outline those distinctions for the case when our aim is to provide
a rigorous specification of a system, at some level of abstraction. In that paper
we have also suggested the use of some systematic way of presenting a method,
with the use of method patterns. The target of that study was essentially the
formalist community. We were arguing that the impact of formalisms would
much benefit from the habit of systematically and carefully relating formalisms
to methods and to the engineering context. In addition, we were opposing the
widespread attitude of conflating formalism and method, with the inevitable
consequence, within a community of formalists, of emphasizing the formalism
or even just neglecting the methodological aspects. Curiously enough, we discovered that in a sense the abused phrase *formal method* is somewhat strange
etymologically, since the word *method* comes from Greek and means *way through*
and its Latin translation (both *ratio et via* and *via et ratio*) was making explicit
that that word was conveying the meaning of *something rational with the purpose
of achieving something, together with the way of achieving it*. Later it was very
illuminating and encouraging to discover that more or less the same remarks,

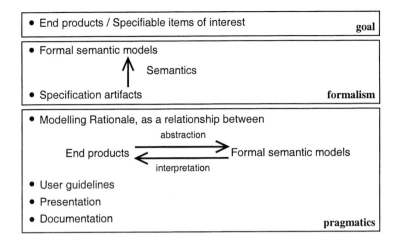

Fig. 1. Formalism and Method

but from a methodological viewpoint relating software development to the usual other engineering practices, were made by D. Parnas, who at about the same time was writing in [23] *"the phrase "formal methods" is strange and the issue of technology transfer of such methods even stranger"*.

Since then, we were always trying to look at the lessons from the Software Engineering side. For example, the work of M. Jackson [15, 16] with his careful analysis of the method and modelling aspects was and is very inspiring. More generally, we have personally learnt how much it is advisable for people working in the area of the formal techniques to try to put the work into the perspective of what is considered essential for the development of software. To be short, we can, for example, look at the notions that A.I. Wassermann in his '96 Stevens lecture [30] considers fundamental in software engineering, which are Abstraction, Analysis and Design Methods and Notations, Prototyping, Software Architecture, Software Process, Reuse, Measurement, Tools and Integrated Environment. Definitely, the area of formal techniques has contributed enormously to provide tools for Abstraction, and a wealth of Notations; but how many of those are really linked to, or exploitable by, Methods of Analysis and Design? Then, it would be quite interesting to make a serious assessment of the contributions to the other six notions.

Another useful lesson and challenge comes from the continuous evolution in today's applications. In the words of C. Jones [17]

"Much has happened in computing since the stack *and the problem of* Dining Philosophers *were first taken as important paradigms on which to test formal approaches. Whatever the disadvantage of modern software (and I know many of them), significant systems are now constructed on top of flexible and general interfaces to packages which handle much of the detail of - for example - the precise presentation on the screen."*

We do not believe that we formalists have coped with the evolution fast enough. Let us just mention one paradigmatic example. We have available plenty of formal techniques for explaining the principles of programming languages (not to say of the multitude of researchers still working on the minimal details even of languages sometimes quite dated). But when, early this year, we have tried to set up a university course providing viable clean principles for building software in a component-based way, using open systems, and the like, we could not find any rigorous setting allowing us to teach the basic techniques without having to come out just with teaching the Java/SUN or the Microsoft/DCOM/.Net way. We are still looking around . . . .

2.3   The UML Case

We single out the emergence of the UML as a de facto standard (it is anyway an OMG standard) because it is for us a paradigmatic example of an avoidable mismatch between formal techniques and practical software engineering. In a bit more ideal world we would speak of a lost opportunity for good formalisms to meet best practices.

Indeed, the UML and the related work is trying to provide an answer to reasonable requests from the software developers. It is visual, multiview, offering notations for different phases of the development from requirements to document management, supportable and supported by tools. Moreover, in principle it incorporates a number of concepts and techniques provided in the years by various streams of research: object orientation; abstraction in a number of ways, starting with the central concept of model/specification; behaviour description by means of statemachines (borrowed from D. Harel's work) and activity diagrams (from Petri Nets); though not mandatory, OCL, the Object Constraint Language, which is a variant of first order logic for expressing properties on parts of the models. Altogether, the UML, used in a sensible way, is far better than the majority of notations and techniques used in the current industry practice.

Still, strictly measured as support to rigorous development, it is a nightmare. Not only it lacks a comprehensive formal semantic foundation (that could apply to Java too), but the semantics is at its best based on common understanding. Differently from Java, even the informal semantics has still to be defined for some aspects and the one provided is a source of many ambiguities. Being the UML built following a typical notation-aggregation approach, even the attempts in the literature to provide a semantics by many researchers are limited to isolated subsets, usually with restrictive constraints w.r.t. their usage. Furthermore, there is another problem, how to assembly the different formal semantics of the various sub-notations to get a consistent semantics of the complete UML[4]. And of course it has the usual limitation of a purely object-oriented approach, namely the lack of direct support for concurrency, cooperation, distribution, mobility, and the like. Moreover, according to some studies by well-known software architecture

---

[4] This task is far from trivial and needs skills that our community developed and proved, for instance, in the definition of the CASL. Indeed, the Common Algebraic Specification Language includes features and aspects developed and studied in isolation in several other specification languages having non-obvious intersection.

experts, its support to define software architectures is definitely non-explicit and somewhat controversial. There are different possible ways for representing software architectures and none without some mismatch, at least as they are seen in that community.

Thus, why do we speak, ideally, of lost opportunity? Because we are convinced that at the same time of the birth of the UML, it was the mid-nineties, there was in our research community all the knowledge and the ability for coming out with a much better proposal encompassing by far the current UML. Our conviction is grounded on the studies we have performed both on many semantic issues of the UML (see [26, 27]) and on possible reformulation of some of its aspects in a cleaner way (see part of the following section). Admittedly, that ideal proposal could have happened in a different world, both because the market is following different routes than research, and because our research community is neither cooperative nor much sensible to the real needs of software development. Still we notice that it was not the case of a good substitute for the UML swept away by a market move; simply there was not such a substitute.

2.4   A Virtuous Cycle for the Research in Formal Techniques

There has been a clear lesson for us from the above and has been a different attitude in the way we devise, use and advocate formal techniques. We summarize our position in what may be called a *Virtuous Cycle*:

- Inspect and learn from software engineering practices and problems
- Look for/provide formal foundations when needed
- Experiment near-to practice but well-founded methods, hiding formalities
- Anticipate needs providing sound engineering concepts and methods

Clearly the above four directions are in a somewhat increasing order of difficulty and ingenuity. We have already done some work along the first three (the fourth being quite ambitious and to be judged by history and success). To be concrete, in the following section we will outline two experiments in what we call *Well-Founded Software Development Methods*; by that we roughly mean a revisitation or possibly a proactive proposal of engineering best practice methods, but with the guarantee that the notation is amenable to a rigorous formal foundation, though such formalization is not apparent to the user.

3   Some Strategies and Experiments in the Search for *Well-Founded Software Development Methods*

3.1   An Experimental Java Targeted Notation

Our oldest line of research in *Well-Founded Software Development Methods* (see [10]) stemmed directly from our work in the specification of concurrent systems with algebraic techniques and is aimed at providing a notation for the specifications, at design level, of concurrent/distributed/reactive systems. That notation is Java targeted, in the sense that the specified systems should be ideally implemented in Java, and has three special features: it is

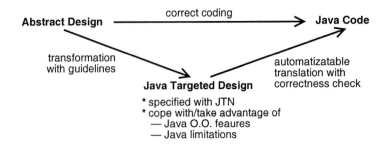

Fig. 2. The JTN approach

- graphical, i.e., given by diagrams,
- completely formal, i.e., amenable to a formal description with algebraic techniques (but hidden from the user),
- endowed with an easily automatized (correct) translation into Java.

In Fig. 2 we provide a graphical view of the approach supported by JTN.

By *Abstract Design* we mean a specification given in the graphical notation of [28]. Essentially, it consists of a visual representation of an algebraic specification of a concurrent system at design level, following the LTL approach [6]. The syntactic form of such specifications guarantees that it corresponds to a positive conditional algebraic specification, which admits the existence of a unique (modulo isomorphism) well-defined labelled transition system matching the specification. Notably, a similar approach has been recently adopted within the MDA (Model Driven Architecture) OMG Proposal [18]. Using the MDA terminology, the abstract design specification is a platform independent model (PIM), in the sense that it does not depend on a particular implementation platform (Java), whereas the Java Targeted Design specification is a (Java) Platform Specific Model (PSM), and the transformation from the Abstract to the Java Targeted design corresponds to the mapping into the Java implementation platform.

The JTN aims to mimic some nice diagrammatic features of UML, but, together with possessing a completely formal basis, that is totally absent in UML, it favours some technical distinctions that we consider methodologically useful.

For example, the elements building the systems are typed by means of classes, but classes are of three kinds: *datatype*, whose instances are just values, *passive*, whose instances are standard imperative objects, and *active*, whose instances are processes. Indeed, in the underlying formal semantics the three kinds of classes have completely different formal models. Moreover, classes, of any kind, are strictly encapsulated, that is they have an interface, describing in a precise way how their instances can interact with the outside entities, and a fully private body describing their behaviour. More details about the different kinds of classes are in Fig. 4. Moreover, each specification (model) has a precise structure, described in Fig. 3.

A specification (model) consists of
Class diagram
- datatype/passive/active class interfaces
- dependency - specialization relationships among them

Body diagrams for all classes in the class diagram, different for each kind of class

Architecture diagram (system structure) a graph where
- nodes: system constituents (passive/active objects)
- arcs: connectors (synchronous/asynchronous one-way channels, method calls)

Sequence diagrams (auxiliary, showing sample system executions)

Fig. 3. JTN: Specification/Model Structure

Notice, that JTN provides an *architecture diagram* for depicting the overall structure of the system. The lack of this kind of diagram in the UML has been criticized by many authors who have then provided various alternatives; on the other hand, that kind of diagram reminds of diagrams found so useful in the so-called Modern (and Postmodern) Structured Analysis (see[31]). Another distinction w.r.t. UMLis that in JTN the use of sequence diagrams is only complementary to the one of behaviour diagrams, to provide an insight of possible scenarios. It is instead well-known that the use of sequence diagrams in UML as a basic tool is the source of ambiguities for users (see in this respect the illuminating paper on a nice substitute, the live sequence charts of [13]).

Another novelty is the way the body of an active class, and then the behaviour of its instances is described. To this aim we have introduced what we call *a behaviour diagram*, just a diagrammatic form for representing some labelled transition system also expressible algebraically in LTL, but that, differently from UML statecharts, allow to visually depict also non-reactive behaviour (see [25] for a proposal of an integration within the UML). Finally, it is almost obvious that, because of its formal basis in JTN, there is a precise framework for defining and dealing with static semantics consistency problems, what is instead a problem in the UML, as witnessed by the many papers and different tools addressing that issue [8].

3.2   Reformulating Current Practice Development Methods

Another line of our research consists in looking at current development practices, noticing problems and attempting at a reformulation based upon, and inspired by, related work in formal techniques.

As we have already discussed, one of the foremost contributions coming from the software engineering side is the concept and use of development process models to guide the software development. We can take as a paradigmatic example, among the best well-known process models, the Rational Unified Process (RUP), proposed by the same authors of the UML (see [24]) and incorporating many insights coming from the software engineering best practices. The problems that

DATATYPE CLASS
    instances values
    characterized by
        − Constructors
        − Operations
    interface visible constructors and operations
    body private constructors and operations + definitions of all the operations by (ordered) lists of conditional rules of the form (pt_i patterns built with the constructors)

$$\text{Op}(pt_1,....,pt_n) \begin{bmatrix} \text{Cond}_1 \text{ -> exp}_1 \\ .... \\ \text{Cond}_m \text{ -> exp}_m \end{bmatrix}$$

PASSIVE CLASS
    instances standard objects
    characterized by
        − Attributes
        − Methods
    interface visible methods
    body attributes + private methods + definitions of all the methods by (ordered) lists of conditional statements of the form (pt_i patterns built with the constructors, $stat_i$ imperative statements acting on the object local state)

$$\text{M}(pt_1,....,pt_n) \begin{bmatrix} \text{Cond}_1 \text{ -> stat}_1 \\ .... \\ \text{Cond}_m \text{ -> stat}_m \end{bmatrix}$$

ACTIVE CLASS
    instances processes
    characterized by
        − Attributes
        − Interactions (with the external world)
            • Write/Read on one way typed synchronous channels
            • Write/Read on one way typed asynchronous channels
            • Call of methods of passive objects
    interface
        − Used synchronous channels
        − Used asynchronous channels
    body attributes + behaviour definition by a BEHAVIOUR DIAGRAM, i.e., a graph s.t.
        − nodes are characterized by a name (just usual control states)
        − arcs have the form

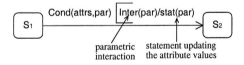

                          parametric   statement updating
                          interaction   the attribute values

Fig. 4. JTN: CLASSES

we have encountered with RUP are twofold. On one side it relies on the UML as a supporting notation, which admittedly does not have a rigorous (neither static nor dynamic) semantics. On the other, to be liberal and accommodate, at least nominally, a number of variants, subcases and personal tastes, RUP gives so much freedom that a non-experienced user is often disconcerted among the possible modelling choices. These two kinds of problems have as a consequence that the resulting artifacts are much more prone to ambiguities, inconsistencies and the like. We have undertaken some work attempting at proposing a more stringent method, which we are in part experimenting in course projects. For example, in [7, 9] we have presented a new way of structuring the Requirement Specification, within an overall RUP-compatible approach, with the aim of guiding the developer to

- use only semantically sound constructs,
- have better means for making the modelling decisions,
- produce as a result a set of artifacts under tighter constraints and as an overall result, to make the process faster, cutting sometimes endless discussions, and to better support consistency both in the construction and in the checking phase.

Though we have expressed our approach in a rigorous multiview, use-case driven and UML-based way, its essence is UML-independent and it could be even given a formal algebraic dress.

Before giving some technical highlights, let us mention the inspiring sources and the technical basis. First, the choice of a restricted subset of the UML constructs has been guided by a formal semantic analysis of those constructs. The general approach to address the semantic problems of UML, together with references to our work on more specific aspects, can be found in [27]. Essentially, it shows how the (generalized) labelled transition systems of our LTL approach [6] can be taken as a basis for defining what we call UML-systems as formal semantic models for all UML. Notably, that work has been pursued within the CoFI initiative[5] [22]. Second, we have incorporated some ideas from well-known methods, such as Structured Analysis [32] and the work of some pioneer methodologists such as M. Jackson [15, 16]. From the latter in particular we have taken the total separation of the domain from the system, a distinction somewhat blurred in many object-oriented approaches; while the distinction between the system and the environment especially comes from the Structured Analysis. Finally, from the overall formal (algebraic) approach, together with the strong typing as a must, we have also borrowed the idea of the black box abstraction of a system and of its minimal white box structure to express the requirements about its interaction with the environment. To that end we have introduced the notion of "abstract state" for the system, without providing an object-oriented structuring at a stage when such a structure is not required.

We now give a short technical outline to get the flavour of the approach.

---

[5] http://www.brics.dk/Projects/CoFI/.

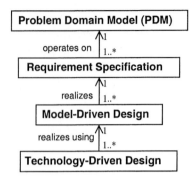

Fig. 5. Artifacts

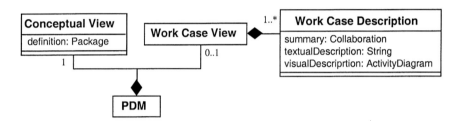

Fig. 6. PDM Structure

The context of our work is sketchily represented in Fig. 5, where we present some essential steps (artifacts to be produced) in a modern software development process. We intend the Requirement Specification activity built over the Problem Domain Modelling and preliminary to Model-Driven Design, followed by Technology-Driven design. As currently widely advocated, by Model-Driven Design we intend the activity of providing a solution of the problem in terms of Model-Driven Architecture (see, e.g., [18]), namely an architecture based on the abstract modelling and independent of the implementation platform, to which is targeted the Technology-Driven Design. Notice, that a PDM artifact may be used as a starting point for many different systems, as well as a Requirement Specification may be used for many different Model-Driven Designs, which in turn may be used to get many different Technology-Driven Designs. We cannot deal here with all those activities; however, we intend to stress that in our approach Requirement Specification is the first activity in which the (Software) System is taken into consideration.

The Requirement Specification activity we propose assumes that the Problem Domain Modelling produces as an artifact, PDM, a UML object-oriented description of the part of the real world that concerns the System, but without any reference to the System itself nor to the problem to which the System provides a solution.

The structure of a PDM in our proposal is shown in Fig. 6. We propose to model the various entities present in the domain by the Conceptual View, a UML

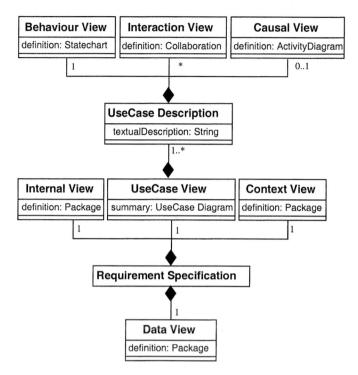

Fig. 7. Requirement Specification Structure

package including a class diagram, where the classes may be also active, thus with a dynamic behaviour, also autonomous, and not just purely reactive. Then, the most relevant cooperation among such entities may be modelled in the Work Case View part, which consists of a special kind of workflows named *work cases*.

Our proposal, centered on two views, the Conceptual View and the Work Case View, in a structural sense encompasses the two most popular current approaches to domain modelling, namely conceptual modelling and business modelling, and can be reduced as a specialization to each of those.

Then we propose a "system placement" activity, to relate the System to the domain and, by that, to locate the System boundary.

In our approach, the Requirement Specification artifacts consist of different views of the System, plus a part, Data View, which lists and makes precise all data appearing in the various views of the System to help guarantee the consistency of the concepts used in such views. Its structure is shown in Fig. 7 by a UML class diagram.

Context View describes the context of the System, that is which entities (*context entities*) and of which kinds may interact with the System, and in which way they can do that. Such entities may appear int he PDM or to be external entities needed by the particular problem/solution under consideration. That explicit splitting between the System and the context entities should help avoid confusions between what exists and needs just to be precisely described (context entities) and what instead has to be developed (System) and on which we have to find (capture) the requirements The context entities are further classified into those taking advantage of the System (*service users*), and into those cooperating to accomplish the System aims (*service providers*). This further splitting between users and providers should help distinguish which context entities cannot be modified by the developer (providers), and those which may be partly tuned by the developer (users), e.g., by fixing their interface towards the System, since it is sensible to require that they adapt themselves to use the System.

Internal View describes abstractly the internal structure of the System, which is essentially its Abstract State. It will help precisely describe the behaviour of the use cases, by allowing to express how they read and update it. UML allows a single use case to have a proper state, but we prefer to have a unique state for all the use cases, to help model their mutual relationships.

Use Case View, as it is now standard, shows the main ways to use the System (*use cases*), making clear which actors take parts in them.

The Use Case View consists of a UML "Use Case Diagram" and of a Use Case Description for each use case appearing in it. The actors appearing in the Use Case diagram are possible *roles (generic instances)* for the entities outside the System interacting with it (context entities) defined in the Context View. Thus, each actor will be denoted by a name, expressing the played role, and by a class, appearing in the Context View, showing which kind of context entities may play such role.

A Use Case Description consists of a textual presentation and of one or more views, of different kinds, of the use case.

Any Use Case Description must include a Behaviour View, which is a statechart describing the complete behaviour of the System with respect to such use case. Such statechart has particular features. Its events may be only call of the operations of the interfaces of the class corresponding to System, its conditions may test only the System Abstract State and the event parameters, and its actions may only be calls of the operations of the actors, as defined by their interfaces, or actions updating the System Abstract State.

A Use Case Description may include any number of Interaction View, which are sequence (or collaboration) diagrams representing the interactions happening in a scenario of the use case among the context entities and the System. Any Interaction View must be coherent with the Behaviour View (that is, it must represent a particular execution of the complete behaviour of System described by such view). We think that the Interaction View are really important, showing visually who does what, but they are complementary to the Behaviour View because they cannot show under which conditions the various messages may be exchanged and their effects on the System Abstract State.

A Use Case Description may include also a Causal View, which is an activity diagram describing all the relevant facts happening during the use case and their causal relationships. The relevant facts (technically represented by action-states of the activity diagram) can be only calls of the interface operations of System by the actors, calls of the operations of the actors by System, UML actions producing side effects on the System Abstract State. Also the Causal View must be coherent with the Behaviour View, in the sense that the causal relationships among "facts" that it depicts may happen in the behaviour depicted by the state chart.

Some of the above views (e.g., Internal View and Context View) are new w.r.t. the current methods for the OO UML-based specification of requirements. In our approach, they play a fundamental role to help ensure the consistency among the various use cases and of the whole specification.

4   Conclusions

Reflecting on our own experience, we have advocated a shift of the research in formal techniques toward a stronger engagement in issues immediately relevant for the software development practice. That is not in opposition to providing the necessary formal foundations when needed, nor to proposing new fundamental ideas, as long as they have a clear potential applicative target. Our emphasis was especially in the direction of the care for the methodological aspects. We have singled out the case of UML as paradigmatic, in our view, of what could have been achieved by our community and was not.

The illustration here of some of our current research had no ambition of showing "The way", but only the meaning of a sincere effort in trying to lighten some suffered isolation; moreover, it is an effort to exploit a significant and mature background in formal techniques, whose value we never underestimate. In that sense, we are convinced that the strategy of *Well-Founded Software Development Methods* has a lot of potential value.

We summarize the (meta)guidelines constituting the essence of that strategy and what we can gain by that.

There is a not so obvious preliminary assumption that the issues addressed are potentially relevant to software engineering practice and that, addressing them, we look at, and borrow as much as we can, from the best practices in the field and from the methodology side, avoiding what we have called the formalism (not so) splendid isolation; this is a kind of first imperative.

A second imperative is the rigorous discipline coming from the area of formal techniques, that imposes both the use of semantically well-defined structures and of rigorously justified methods.

A third and last imperative is that the formal aspects should be not forced on the end-users, who in principle are not experts, but used in the background to achieve the second imperative.

To clarify by an example the three points and their benefits, in our sample activity presented in the previous sections

- we have only used those UML constructs and in such restricted way that their semantics is clear, in the sense that a formal semantics exists (that is the case of statecharts) or need only to be worked out in detail (that is the case of active classes); from that we can precisely answer in the natural language any relevant question for clarifying ambiguities, without exposing the formal definitions;

- the method for structuring, e.g., the requirements leads to a collection of artifacts that have passed a number of consistency constraints, and, thus, they are much less prone to faults and moreover define an unambiguous body of requirements.

There is another aspect that can be seen as an aside benefit. It may happen that the disciplined rigour that we borrow from the formal techniques habit, shows the inadequacy of some proposed construct or techniques and stimulates the introduction of new ones. That has been the case of the inadequacy of sequence diagrams and the proposal by D. Harel and W. Damm of Live Sequence Charts (see [11]) and by us of behaviour diagrams [25] and of Context diagrams, as we have seen in the paper.

On the sociological side, it is a constant finding that formal techniques are liked and accepted only by people extremely well-trained in formal techniques, that is not the case of the vast majority of software engineers. Moreover, there is a reported tension, if not a contrast, between formalism and productivity/efficiency. Hiding formalities, but keeping their disciplined rigour in the methods they use, is a strategy that can overcome both disadvantages. In support of this belief, we have made some experiments in the last two years with undergraduate students without any formal background, with the exception of an elementary short course in mathematical logic. The results have been very encouraging, especially comparing with previous experiments, some using explicitly formal techniques with students better skilled in formalities and, on the opposite side, some using visual techniques (UML) and related methods as they usually are, namely without any underpinning rigour. In conclusion we believe that *Well-Founded Software Development Methods* should be explored seriously and improved, of course, with the help of appropriate tools exploiting their hidden formal basis, as much as it happens with other engineering professions and practices (for this point see the interesting remarks in [23]).

Because of the fast and somewhat wild evolution in information technology in general and in software applications in particular, it is difficult to assess the situation and look at the right new directions of research. Still, we see some *fundamental challenges* ahead. We mention two.

The first comes from our research interests and can be summarized in the slogan *Beyond UML*. Though the UML (and the OMG initiatives) has tried to touch many important issues and satisfy some real needs, from abstract modelling (MDA) to multiview and to support for tools, we need to go beyond UML in a number of directions. The object oriented technology underpinning the UML is inadequate, as it is now recognized by many, for a real quality leap; the notation is shaking and not cleanly defined, endangering consistency; the semantic foundations are missing; also due to the lack in semantic foundations, the development of powerful semantic tool is difficult (look at a comprehensive view of the problem by D. Harel in [13]); the support for evolution is left to the user.

The second challenge we see is in the lack of foundations and principles for some current trends in software development and applications characterized by components, open systems, web services, middleware stratifications and variety, mobile and heterogeneous access, comprehensive proprietary platforms (.Net, Java/SUN,...). Though some of those issues are nominally addressed by some current formal research, it seems to us that, as most often in the past, the way those issues are addressed, more with the obsession of mathematical elegance and sophistication than with applicability in mind, shows a little chance of making an impact on software development practices.

References

1. E. Astesiano, M. Bidoit, H. Kirchner, B. Krieg-Brückner, P. D. Mosses, D. Sannella, and A. Tarlecki. CASL: the Common Algebraic Specification Language. *T.C.S.*, 286(2):153–196, 2002.
2. E. Astesiano, B. Krieg-Brückner, and H.-J. Kreowski, editors. *IFIP WG 1.3 Book on Algebraic Foundations of System Specification*. Springer Verlag, 1999.
3. E. Astesiano and G. Reggio. Direct Semantics of Concurrent Languages in the SMoLCS Approach. *IBM Journal of Research and Development*, 31(5):512–534, 1987.
4. E. Astesiano and G. Reggio. SMoLCS-Driven Concurrent Calculi. In H. Ehrig, R. Kowalski, G. Levi, and U. Montanari, editors, *Proc. TAPSOFT'87, Vol. 1*, number 249 in Lecture Notes in Computer Science, pages 169–201. Springer Verlag, Berlin, 1987.
5. E. Astesiano and G. Reggio. Formalism and Method. *T.C.S.*, 236(1,2):3–34, 2000.
6. E. Astesiano and G. Reggio. Labelled Transition Logic: An Outline. *Acta Informatica*, 37(11-12):831–879, 2001.
7. E. Astesiano and G. Reggio. Knowledge Structuring and Representation in Requirement Specification. In *Proc. SEKE 2002*. ACM Press, 2002. Available at `ftp://ftp.disi.unige.it/person/ReggioG/AstesianoReggio02a.pdf`.
8. E. Astesiano and G. Reggio. Consistency Issues in Multiview Modelling Techniques. Technical Report DISI–TR–03–05, DISI, Università di Genova, Italy, 2003. To appear in Proc. WADT 2002.
9. E. Astesiano and G. Reggio. Tight Structuring for Precise UML-based Requirement Specifications: Complete Version. Technical Report DISI–TR–03–06, DISI, Università di Genova, Italy, 2003. Available at `ftp://ftp.disi.unige.it/person/ReggioG/ReggioEtAll03c.pdf`.
10. E. Coscia and G. Reggio. JTN: A Java-targeted Graphic Formal Notation for Reactive and Concurrent Systems. In Finance J.-P., editor, *Proc. FASE 99*, number 1577 in Lecture Notes in Computer Science. Springer Verlag, Berlin, 1999.
11. W. Damm and D. Harel. LSCs: Breathing Life into Message Sequence Charts. *Formal Methods in System Design*, 19(1):45–80, 2001.
12. H. Ehrig and B. Mahr. A Decade of TAPSOFT: Aspects of Progress and Prospects in Theory and Practice of Software Development. In P.D. Mosses, M. Nielsen, and M.I. Schwartzbach, editors, *Proc. of TAPSOFT '95*, number 915 in Lecture Notes in Computer Science, pages 3–24. Springer Verlag, Berlin, 1995.
13. D. Harel. From Play-In Scenarios to Code: An Achievable Dream. *IEEE Computer*, 34(1):53–60, 2001.
14. C.A.R. Hoare. How did Software Get so Reliable Without Proof? In M.-C. Gaudel and J. Woodcock, editors, *FME'96: Industrial Benefit and Advances in Formal Methods*, number 1051 in Lecture Notes in Computer Science, pages 1–17. Springer Verlag, Berlin, 1996.

15. M. Jackson. *Software Requirements & Specifications: a Lexicon of Practice, Principles and Prejudices*. Addison-Wesley, 1995.

16. M. Jackson. *Problem Frames: Analyzing and Structuring Software Development Problems*. Addison-Wesley, 2001.

17. C. Jones. Some Mistakes I Have Made and What I Have Learned FromThem. In E. Astesiano, editor, *Proc. FASE'98*, number 1382 in Lecture Notes in Computer Science. Springer Verlag, Berlin, 1998.

18. OMG Architecture Board MDA Drafting Team. Model Driven Architecture (MDA). Available at http://cgi.omg.org/docs/ormsc/01-07-01.pdf, 2001.

19. B. Meyer. *Object-Oriented Software Construction*. Prentice-Hall, 1997.

20. B. Meyer. Software Engineering in the Academy. *Computer*, 34(5):28–35, 2001.

21. M. Minasi. *The Software Conspiracy*. Mc Graw Hill, 2000.

22. P.D. Mosses. CoFI: The Common Framework Initiative for Algebraic Specification and Development. In M. Bidoit and M. Dauchet, editors, *Proc. TAPSOFT '97*, number 1214 in Lecture Notes in Computer Science, pages 115–137. Springer Verlag, Berlin, 1997.

23. D.L. Parnas. "Formal Methods" Technology Transfer Will Fail. *J. Systems Software*, 40(3):195 – 198, 1998.

24. Rational. Rational Unified Process© for System Engineering SE 1.0. 2001.

25. G. Reggio and E. Astesiano. An Extension of UML for Modelling the non Purely-Reactive Behaviour of Active Objects. Technical Report DISI–TR–00–28, DISI, Università di Genova, Italy, 2000. Available at ftp://ftp.disi.unige.it/person/ReggioG/ReggioAstesiano00b.pdf.

26. G. Reggio, E. Astesiano, C. Choppy, and H. Hussmann. Analysing UML Active Classes and Associated State Machines – A Lightweight Formal Approach. In T. Maibaum, editor, *Proc. FASE 2000*, number 1783 in Lecture Notes in Computer Science. Springer Verlag, Berlin, 2000.

27. G. Reggio, M. Cerioli, and E. Astesiano. Towards a Rigorous Semantics of UML Supporting its Multiview Approach. In H. Hussmann, editor, *Proc. FASE 2001*, number 2029 in Lecture Notes in Computer Science. Springer Verlag, Berlin, 2001.

28. G. Reggio and M. Larosa. A Graphic Notation for Formal Specifications of Dynamic Systems. In J. Fitzgerald and C.B. Jones, editors, *Proc. FME 97 - Industrial Applications and Strengthened Foundations of Formal Methods*, number 1313 in Lecture Notes in Computer Science. Springer Verlag, Berlin, 1997.

29. UML Revision Task Force. *OMG UML Specification 1.3*, 1999. Available at http://www.rational.com/media/uml/post.pdf.

30. A.I. Wasserman. Toward a Discipline of Software Engineering. *IEEE Software*, 13(6):23–31, 1996.

31. R.J. Wieringa. *Requirements Engineering: Frameworks for Understanding*. John Wiley, 1996.

32. E. Yourdon. *Modern Structured Analysis*. Prentice-Hall, 1989.

Towards the Verifying Compiler

Tony Hoare

Microsoft Research Ltd., Cambridge, UK

Abstract. A verifying compiler is one that proves automatically that a program is correct before allowing it to be run. Correctness of a program is defined by placing assertions at strategic points in the program text, particularly at the interfaces between its components. From recent enquiries among software developers at Microsoft, I have discovered that assertions are widely used in program development practice. Their main role is as test oracles, to detect programming errors as close as possible to their place of occurrence. Further progress in reliable software engineering is supported by programmer productivity tools that exploit assertions of various kinds in various ways at all stages in program development. The construction and exploitation of a fully verifying compiler remains as a long-term challenge for twenty-first century Computing Science. The results of this research will be of intermediate benefit long before the eventual ideal is reached.

1 Introduction

An understanding of the role of assertions in Checking a Large Routine goes back to Alan Turing in 1950. The idea of a verifying compiler, which uses automatic theorem proving to guarantee the correctness of the assertions, goes back to a 1967 article by Bob Floyd on Assigning Meanings to Programs. And the idea of writing the assertions even before writing the program was propounded in 1968 by Edsger Dijkstra in an article on a Constructive Approach to the Problem of Program Correctness. Dijkstra's insight has been the inspiration of much of the research in formal methods of software engineering conducted in University Computing Departments over the last thirty years.

An assertion in its most familiar form is a Boolean expression that is written as an executable statement at any point in the program text. It can in principle or in practice be evaluated by the computer, whenever control reaches that point in the program. If an assertion ever evaluates to false, the program is by definition incorrect. But if all assertions always evaluate to true, then at least no program defect has ever been detected. But best of all, if it can be proved that the assertion will always evaluate to true on every possible execution, then the program is certainly correct, at least insofar as correctness has been captured by the assertions embedded in it. The construction and validation of such proofs are the goal of the verifying compiler.

Early attempts to implement a verifying compiler were frustrated by the inherent difficulties of mechanical theorem proving. These difficulties have inspired productive research on a number of projects, and with the aid of massive increases in computer power and capacity considerable progress has been made. I suggest that an

B.K. Aichernig and T. Maibaum (Eds.): Formal Methods ..., LNCS 2757, pp. 151–160, 2003.

intensification of co-operative research efforts will result in the emergence of a workable verifying compiler some time in the current century.

A second problem is that meaningful assertions are notoriously difficult to write. This means that work on a verifying compiler must be matched by a systematic attempt to attach assertions to the great body of existing software libraries and services. The ultimate goal is that all the major interfaces in freely available software should be fully documented by assertions approaching in expressive power to a full specification of its intended functionality. Such a major long-term challenge accords well with the ideals of the proponents of open software, whose quality is assured by contributions from many sources.

But would the results of these related research projects ever be exploited in the production of software products used throughout the world? That depends on the answer to three further questions. Firstly, will programmers use assertions? The answer is yes, but they will use them for many other purposes besides verification; in particular, they are already widely used to detect errors in program test, as I shall describe in the next section. The second question is: will they ever be used for verification of program correctness? Here, the answer is conditional: it depends on wider and deeper education in the principles and practice of programming, and on integration of verification and analysis tools in the standard software development process. And finally, the sixty-four billion dollar question: is there a market demand for the extra assurances of reliability that can be offered by a verifying compiler?

For many years, my friends in the software industry have told me that in all surveys of customer requirements the top two priorities have always been firstly an increase in features, and secondly an increase in performance. Reliability takes only the third place. But now it seems that widely available software already provides enough features to satisfy nearly all demands, and widely available hardware already satisfies most demands for performance and capacity. The main remaining obstacle to the integration of computers into the life of society is a wide-spread and well-justified reluctance to trust the software. A recent email by Bill Gates to Microsoft and all its subsidiaries has put trustworthy computing at the head of the agenda. This policy statement has already been put into force by devoting the efforts of the entire Microsoft Windows team during the whole month of February to a security drive. Expensive it is, but not as expensive as some recent viruses like Code Red, which have led to world-wide losses estimated at over a billion dollars.

2   Assertions in Program Testing

In my thirty years as an academic scientist, I pursued the traditional academic ideals of rigour and precision in scientific research. I sought to enlarge our understanding of the theory of programming to show that large-scale programs can be fully specified and proved to be correct with absolute mathematical certainty. I hoped that increased rigour in top-down program development would significantly reduce if not eliminate the burden of program testing and debugging. I would quote with approval the famous dictum of Dijkstra, that program testing can prove the existence of program bugs, but never their absence.

A very similar remark was made by the famous philosopher Karl Popper. His Philosophy of Science is based on the principle of falsification, namely that a scientific theory can never be verified by scientific experiment; it can only be falsified. I accept his view that a scientific advance starts with a theory that has some a priori grounds for credibility, for example, by deduction from the principle that a force has an effect that is inversely proportional to the square of the distance at which it acts. A new theory that applies such a principle to a new phenomenon is subjected to a battery of tests that have been specifically designed, not to support the theory but to refute it. If the theory passes all the tests, it is accepted and used with high confidence. A well tested theory will be used with confidence to help in the formulation and test of further and more advanced theories, and in the design of experiments to refute them.

Extending this analogy to computer software, we can see clearly why program testing is in practice such a good assurance of the reliability of software. A competent programmer always has a prior understanding, perhaps quite intuitive, of the reasons why the program is going to work. If this hypothesis survives rigorous testing regime, the software has proved itself worthy of delivery to a customer. If a few small changes are needed in the program, they are quickly made – unfortunate perhaps, but that happens to scientific theories too. In Microsoft, every project has assigned to it a team of testers, recruited specially for their skill as experimental scientists; they constitute about a half of the entire program development staff on each project.

This account of the vital role of testing in the progress of science is reinforced by consideration of the role of test in engineering. In all branches of engineering, rigorous product test is an essential prerequisite before shipping a new or improved product to the customer. For example, in the development of a new aero jet engine, an early working model is installed on an engineering test bench for exhaustive trials. This model engine will first be thoroughly instrumented by insertion of test probes at every accessible internal and external interface. A rigorous test schedule is designed to exercise the engine at all the extremes of its intended operating range. By continuously checking tolerances at all the crucial internal interfaces, the engineer detects incipient errors immediately, and never needs to test the assembly as a whole to destruction. By continuously striving to improve the set points and tighten the tolerances at each interface, the quality of the whole product can be gradually raised. That is the essence of the six sigma quality improvement philosophy, which has been widely applied in manufacturing industry to increase profits at the same time as customer satisfaction.

In the engineering of software, assertions at the interfaces between modules of the program play the same role as test probes in engine design. The analogy suggests that programmers should increase in the number and strength of assertions in their code. This will make their system more likely to fail under test; but the reward is that it is subsequently much less likely to fail in the field.

In the three years since I retired from academic life, I have been working in the software industry. This has enabled me to balance the idealism that inspires academic research with the practical compromises that are essential to industrial engineering. In particular, I have radically changed my attitude towards program testing which I now understand to be entirely complementary to scientific design and verification methods, and makes an equal contribution to the development of reliable software on an industrial scale. It is no accident that program testing exploits the same kind of specifications by assertions that form the basis of program verification.

3 Assertions in Current Microsoft Development Practice

The defining characteristic of an engineering test probe is that it is removed from the engine before manufacture and delivery to the customer. In computer programs, this effect is achieved by means of a conditionally defined macro. The macro is resolved at compile time in one of two ways, depending on a compile-time switch called DEBUG, set for a debugging run, and unset when compiling retail code that will be shipped to the retail customer. An assertion may be placed anywhere in the middle of executable code by means of this ASSERT macro.

```
#ifdef DEBUG
#define ASSERT(b,str) {
        if (b) { }
        else {report (str);
              assert (false)}     }
#else #define ASSERT(b,str)
#endif
```

In addition to their role in product test, assertions are widely recommended as a form of program documentation. This is of vital concern to major software suppliers today, because their main development activity is the continuous evolution and improvement of old code to meet new market needs. Even quite trivial assertions, like the following, give added value when changing the code.

```
{if (a >= b){ .. a++ ; .. };
         .. ..
    ASSERT(a != b, 'a has just been incremented to
              avoid equality') ;
    x = c/(a - b)
```

One Development Manager in Microsoft recommends that for every bug corrected in test, an assertion should be added to the code which will fire if that bug ever occurs again. Ideally, there should be enough assertions in a program that nearly all bugs are caught by assertion failure, because that is much easier to diagnose than other forms of failure, for example, a crash. Some developers are willing to spend a whole day to design precautions that will avoid a week's work tracing an error that may be introduced later, when the code is modified by a less experienced programmer. Success in such documentation by assertions depends on long experience and careful judgment in predicting the most likely errors a year or more from now. Not everyone can spare the time to do this under pressure of tight delivery schedules. But it is likely that a liberal sprinkling of assertions in the code would increase the accumulated value of legacy, when the time comes to develop a new release of the software.

In the early testing of a prototype program, the developer wants to check out the main paths in the code before dealing with all the exceptional conditions that may occur in practice. In order to document such a development plan, some developers have introduced a variety of assertion which is called a simplifying assumption.

```
SIMPLIFYING_ASSUMPTION
(strlen(input) < MAX_PATH, 'not yet checking for over-
flow')
```

The quoted assumption documents exactly the cases which the developer is not yet ready to treat, and it also serves as a reminder of what remains to do later. Violation of such assumptions in test will simply cause a test case to be ignored, and should not be treated as an error. Of course, in compiling retail code for delivery to the customer, the debug flag is not set; and then the macro will give rise to a compile-time error; it will not just be ignored like an ordinary assertion. This gives a guarantee against the risk incurred by more informal comments and messages about known bugs and work that is still TO DO; such comments occasionally and embarrassingly find their way into code shipped by Microsoft.

All the best fault diagnoses are those given at compile time, since that is much cheaper than diagnosis of errors by test. In one product team in Microsoft, a special class of assertion has been implemented called a compile-time check, because its value, true or false, can be computed at compile time.

```
COMPILE_TIME_CHECK   (sizeof(x)==sizeof(y),   'addition   is
undefined for arrays of different sizes')
```

The compile time error message is generated by a macro that compiles to an invalid declaration (negative array bound) in C; of course, the assertion must be restricted to use only values and functions computable by the compiler. (The compiler will still complain if not). The example above shows a test of conformity of the size of two array parameters for a method. Of course, as we make progress towards a verifying compiler, the aim will be to increase the proportion of assertions whose violation will be detected at compile time.

Assertions can help a compiler produce better code. For example, in a C-style case statement, a default clause that cannot be reached can be marked with an UNREACHABLE assertion, and a compiler (for example Visual C) avoids emission of unnecessary code for this case. In future, perhaps assertions will give further help in optimisation, for example by asserting that pointers or references do not point to the same location. Of course, if such an assertion were false, the effect of the optimisation could be awful. But fortunately assertions which have been frequently tested are remarkably reliable; indeed, they are widely believed to be the only believable form of program documentation. When assertions are automatically proved by a verifying compiler, they will be even more believable.

```
switch (condition) {
case 0:   .. ..   ; break;
case 1:   .. ..   ;break;
default: UNREACHABLE('condition is really a boolean');}
```

A global program analysis tool called PREfix is now widely used by Microsoft development teams. Like PCLint and Purify, its role is to detect program defects at the earliest possible stage, even before the program is compiled. Typical defects are a NULL pointer reference, an array subscript out of bound, a variable not initialised. PREfix works by analysing all paths through each method body, and it gives a report for each path on which there may be a defect. The trouble is that most of the paths can never in fact be activated. The resulting false positive messages are called noise, and they still require considerable human effort to analyse and reject; and the rejection of noise is itself highly prone to error. It is rumoured that the recent Code Red virus gained access through a loophole that had been detected by PREfix and deliberately ignored.

Assertions can help the PREfix anomaly checker to avoid unnecessary noise. If something has only just three lines ago been inserted in a table, it is annoying to be told that it might not be there. A special ASSUME macro allows the programmer to tell PREfix relevant information about the program that cannot at present be automatically deduced.

```
pointer = find (something);
PREFIX_ASSUME ( pointer != NULL,
        "see the insertion three lines back");
...    pointer ->mumble = blat   ...
```

Assertions feature strongly in the code for Microsoft Office – around a quarter of a million of them. They are automatically given unique tags, so that they can be tracked in successive tests, builds and releases of the product, even though their line-number changes with the program code. Assertion violations are recorded in RAID, the standard data base of unresolved issues. When the same fault is detected by two different test cases, it is twice as easy to diagnose, and twice as valuable to correct. This kind of fault classification defines an important part of the team's programming process.

In Microsoft, over half the effort devoted to program development is attributed to test. For legacy code, there is an accumulation of regression tests that are run for many weeks before each new release. It is therefore very important to select tests that are exceptionally rigorous, so as to increase the chance of catching bugs before delivery. Obviously, tests that have in the past violated assertions are the most important to run again. Violation of a simplifying assumption is a particular reason for increasing the priority of a test, because it is likely to exercise a rare and difficult case.

The original purpose of assertions was to ensure that program defects are detected as early as possible in test, rather than after delivery. But the power of the customer's processor is constantly increasing, and the frequency of delivery of software upgrades is also increasing. It is therefore more and more cost-effective to leave a certain proportion of the assertions in shipped code; when they fire they generate an exception, and the choice is offered to the customer of sending a bug report to Microsoft. The report includes a dump of the stack of the running program. About a million such reports arrive in Redmond every day for diagnosis and correction. A controlled dump is much better than a crash, which is a likely result of entry into a region of code that has never been encountered in test. A common idiom is to give the programmer control over such a range of options by means of different ASSERT macros.

4   Assertions in Programming Languages

The examples of the previous section have all been implemented as macro definitions by various teams in Microsoft, and each of them is used only by the team which implemented them. In the code for Microsoft Windows, we have found over a thousand different assertion macros. This is a serious impediment to the deployment of programming analysis tools to exploit assertions. The best way of solving this problem in the long term is to include an adequate range of assertions into the basic programming language. A standard notation is likely to be more widely accepted, more widely taught, and more widely used than a macro devised by an individual programmer or programming team. Furthermore, as I suggested when I first started research on assertions, provision of support for sound reasoning about program correctness is a suitable objective criterion for judging the quality of a programming language design.

Significant progress towards this goal has been made by Bertrand Meyer in his design of the Eiffel programming language. Assertions are recommended as a sort of contract between the implementers and the users of a library of classes; each side undertakes certain obligations in return for corresponding guarantees from the other. The same ideas are incorporated in draft proposals for assertion conventions adapted for specifying Java programs. Two examples are the Java modelling language JML (Leavens, Baker and Ruby) and the Extended Static Checker ESC for Modula 3 and Java (Nelson, Leino and Saxe). ESC is already an educational prototype of a verifying compiler.

Assertions at interfaces presented by a library give exceptionally good value. Firstly, they are exploited at least twice, once by the implementer of the interface and possibly many times by all its users. Secondly, interfaces are usually more stable than code, so the assertions that define an interface are used repeatedly whenever library code is enhanced for a later release. Interface assertions permit unit testing of each module separately from the programs that use it; and they give guidance in the design of rigorous test cases. Finally, they enable the analysis and proof of a large system to be split into smaller parts, devised and checked separately for each module. This is absolutely critical. Even with fully modular checking, the first application of PREfix to a twenty million line product took three weeks of machine time to complete the analysis; and even after a series of optimisations and compromises, it still takes three days.

Three useful kinds of assertions at interfaces are preconditions, postconditions and invariants. A precondition is defined as an assertion made at the beginning of a method body. It is the caller of the method rather than the implementer who is responsible for the validity of the precondition on entry; the implementer of the body of the method can just take it as an assumption. Recognition of this division of responsibility protects the virtuous writer of a precondition from having to inspect faults which have been caused by a careless caller of the method. In the design of test cases for unit test, each case must be generated or designed to satisfy the precondition, preferably at the edges of its range of validity.

A post-condition is an assertion which describes (at least partially) the purpose of a method call. The caller of a method is allowed to assume its validity. The obligation is on the writer of the method to ensure that the post-condition is always satisfied. Test cases for unit test must be generated or designed with the best possible chance of falsifying the postcondition. In fact, postconditions and other assertions should be so strong that they are almost certain to find any defect in the program. As with a scientific theory, it should be almost inconceivable that an incorrect program will escape detection by one of the tests.

In object oriented programs, preconditions and post-conditions document the contract between the implementer and the user of the methods of a class. The interface between successive calls of different methods of an object of the the class is specified by means of an invariant. An invariant is defined as an assertion that is intended to be true of every object of a class at all times except while the code of the class is executing. It can be specified as a suitably named boolean method of the same class. An invariant does not usually feature as part of the external specification of a class; but rather describes the strategy of the implementation of the individual methods. For example, in a class that maintains a private list of objects, the invariant could state the implementer's intention that the list should always be circular. While the program is under test, the invariant can be retested after each method call, or even before as well.

Invariants are widely used today in software engineering practice, though not under the same name. For example, every time a PC is switched on, or a new application is launched, invariants are used to check the integrity of the current environment and of the stored data base. In the Microsoft Office project, invariants on the structure of the heap are used to help diagnose storage leaks. In the telephone industry, they are used by a software auditing process, which runs concurrently with the switching software in an electronic exchange. Any call records that are found to violate the invariant are just re-initialised or deleted. It is rumoured that this technique once raised the reliability of a newly developed system from undeliverable to irreproachable.

In Microsoft, I see a future role for invariants in post-mortem dump-cracking, to check whether a failure was caused perhaps by some incident long ago that corrupted data on the heap. This test has to be made on the customer machine, because the heap is too voluminous to communicate the whole of it to a central server. There is a prospect that the code to conduct the tests will be injected into the customer's software as the occasion demands. The scale of the current problem of dumps is easy to calculate. With the target Microsoft customer base, it is not long before the number of dumps arising from anomalies at the customer site could exceed one million dumps per day.

5 Summary and Conclusion

The primary use of assertions today is for program instrumentation; they are inserted as probes in program testing, and they serve as a test oracle to give early warning of program defects, close to the place that they occur. They are also used for program documentation, to assist later developers to evolve the product to meet new market needs. In particular, they specify interfaces between major software components, such as libraries and application programs. Assertions are just beginning to be used by the C compiler in code optimisation. They are used to classify and track defects between customer sites, between test cases, and between code changes. Assertions are being introduced into program analysis tools like PREfix, to raise the precision of analysis and reduce the noise of false positives. Increasingly, assertions are shipped to the customer to make a program more rugged, by forestalling errors that might otherwise lead to a crash.

At present, Microsoft programmers have achieved each of these benefits separately. This gives rise to an attractive opportunity to all the benefits together, by reusing the same assertion again and again for different purposes, one after the other. In this way, they will be encouraged to introduce assertions as early as possible into the development process. They can then play a guiding role in a top-down process of program design, as suggested in Dijkstra's original constructive approach to correctness.

I expect that assertions will bring even greater benefits in the future, when they are fully supported by a range of programmer productivity tools. They will help in deep diagnosis of post-mortem dumps. They will serve as a guide in test case generation and prioritisation. They will help to make code concurrency-safe, and to reduce security loop-holes. In dealing with concurrency and security, there is still plenty of scope for fundamental research in the theory of programming.

In conclusion, I would like to re-iterate the research goal which I put forward when (in 1968) I first embarked on research into program correctness based on assertions. It was to enable future programming languages and features to be designed from the beginning to support reasoning about the correctness of programs, in the hope that this would provide an objective criterion for evaluating the quality of the design. I believe that modern language designers, including the designers of Java and C#, are beginning to recognise this as a valuable goal, though they have not yet had the brilliant idea of using assertions to help them achieve it. As a result, these languages still include a plethora of fashionable features, and low-level constructions which are supposed to contribute to efficiency. These make it difficult or impossible to use local reasoning about the correctness of a component, in the assurance that correctness will be preserved when the components are assembled into a large system.

Fortunately, these problems are soluble even without a switch to a more disciplined programming language. Program analysis tools like PREfix show the way. By conducting an analysis of the source code for the entire system, it is possible to identify the use of the more dangerous features of a programming language, identified as those which violate modularity and invalidate normal correctness reasoning. A notorious example is the introduction of aliasing by passing the same (or overlapping) parameter more than once by reference to the same procedure call. Such violations are flagged by a warning message. Of course, the warnings can be ignored. But in Microsoft, at least, there is a growing reluctance to ignore warning messages. It is a brave programmer who has the confidence to guarantee program correctness in the face of such a warning, when the penalty for incorrectness is the introduction of a virus that causes a billion dollars of damage. And when all programmers rewrite their code to eliminate all such warnings, they are effectively already using a much improved programming language.

These are the reasons for optimism that professional programmers in the software industry will be ready to accept and use a verifying compiler, when it becomes available. In industry, work towards the evolution of a verifying compiler will progress gradually by increasing the sophistication of program analysis tools. But there is a splendid opportunity for academic research to lead the way towards the longer term future. I have already mentioned the verifying compiler as one of the major challenges of Computing Science in the twenty first century. To meet the challenge we will need to draw on contributions from all the different technologies relevant to mechanised proof. Like the Human Genome project, or the launch of a new scientific satellite, or the design of a sub-atomic particle accelerator, progress on such a vast project will depend on a degree of collaboration among scientists that is so far unprecedented in Computer Science.

There is now a great mass of legacy software available as test material for evaluating progress. Work can start by annotating and improving the quality of the interfaces to the base class libraries, which come with the major object oriented languages. The work will be meticulous, exhausting and like most of scientific research, it will include a large element of routine. It will require deep commitment, and wide collaboration, and certainly the occasional breakthrough. Fortunately, the goal of the project is closely aligned with the ideals of the open source movement, which seeks to improve quality by contributions from many workers in the field.

We will also need to recognise the complementary role of rigorous program testing; we must integrate verification with all the other productivity tools that are aimed at facilitating the program development process, including the maintenance and enhancement of legacy code. I expect that the use of full program verification will always be expensive; and the experienced software engineer will always have to use good engineering judgement in selecting a combination of verification and validation techniques to achieve confidence in correctness, reliability and serviceability of software. For safety critical software, the case for full verification is very strong. For operating system kernels and security protocols, it is already known that there is no viable alternative. For assurance of the structural integrity of a large software system, proof of avoidance of overflows and interference is extremely valuable. There will also be many cases where even a partial verification will permit a significant reduction in the volume and the cost of testing, which at present accounts for more than half the cost of software development. Reduction in the high cost of testing and reduction in the interval to delivery of new releases will be major commercial incentives for the expansion of the role of verification; they will be just as persuasive as the pursuit of an ideal of absolute correctness, which has been the inspiration of scientific endeavour. In this respect, software engineering is no different from other branches of engineering, where well-judged compromises in the light of costs and timescales are just as important as an understanding of the relevant scientific principles.

The fact that formal software verification will not by itself solve all the problems of software reliability should not discourage the scientific community from taking up the challenge. Like other major scientific challenges, the appeal of the project must be actually increased by its inherent difficulty, as well as its contribution to the old academic ideals of purity and integrity, based on the enlargement of understanding and the discovery and exploitation of scientific truth.

Acknowledgements

My thanks to all my new colleagues in Microsoft Research and Development, who have told me about their current use of assertions in programming and testing. Their names include Rick Andrews, Chris Antos, Tom Ball, Pete Collins, Terry Crowley, Mike Daly, Robert Deline, John Douceur, Sean Edmison, Kirk Glerum, David Greenspoon, Yuri Gurevich, Martyn Lovell, Bertrand Meyer, Jon Pincus, Harry Robinson, Hannes Ruescher, Marc Shapiro, Kevin Schofield, Wolfram Schulte, David Schwartz, Amitabh Srivastava, David Stutz, James Tierney.

Acknowledgments also to all my colleagues in Oxford and many other Universities, who have explored with me the theory of programming and the practice of software engineering. In my present role as Senior Researcher in Microsoft Research, I have the extraordinary privilege of witnessing and maybe even slightly contributing to the convergence of academic and industrial developments, and I have good hope of seeing results that contribute back to the development of the theory and also to the practice of programming.

A Grand Challenge Proposal
for Formal Methods:
A Verified Stack

J. Strother Moore

Department of Computer Sciences
University of Texas at Austin
Taylor Hall 2.124, Austin, Texas 78712
`moore@cs.utexas.edu`

Abstract. We propose a grand challenge for the formal methods community: build and mechanically verify a practical computing system, from transistors to software. The challenge is both competitive and collaborative. It is collaborative because practical systems are too large for any one group or tool to handle in isolation: groups will have to team together. Furthermore, the vertical integration of systems at different levels of abstractions – from transistors to software – will encourage the team to adopt different tools for different levels and connect them. It is competitive because there are many systems from which to choose and different teams may form around different target systems.

Keywords: hardware verification, software verification, simulation, modeling, theorem proving, model checking

1 Definition

The challenge is: mechanically verify a practical computing system, from transistors to software.

Even if one focuses on small computing systems, the number of choices is enormous: smartcards, hundreds of embedded controllers, cryptographic processors, pagers and other "simple" personal devices.

The challenge may be more precisely described as follows.

- The project should produce an artifact, e.g., a chip.
- The artifact's behavior should be of interest to people not in formal methods.
- The artifact should come with a "warranty" expressed as a mathematical theorem.
- The warranty should be certified mechanically; user input and interaction are allowed but mechanical checkers must be responsible for the soundness of the claim.
- The checkers used to certify the warranty should be available for others, at least, to use and test, if not inspect.

B.K. Aichernig and T. Maibaum (Eds.): Formal Methods ..., LNCS 2757, pp. 161–172, 2003.

An initial attempt at a verified system was the so-called "CLI stack" of the late 1980s and early 1990s. In the next section we discuss the CLI stack and why it does not meet the challenge. In subsequent sections we address ourselves to basic questions concerning grand challenges, e.g., scientific significance, impact on practice, etc., and answer those questions for this particular challenge.

2   Why the CLI Stack Is Not Enough

In the late 1980s, Computational Logic, Inc. (CLI), with support from DARPA and others, built and verified the "CLI stack" [4] using the Boyer-Moore theorem prover, Nqthm [6]. The author was one of the principle architects of the stack. The major layers in the stack were:

- a register transfer level (RTL) design for a microprocessor,
- an operational semantics for a machine code instruction set architecture (ISA),
- an operational semantics for a relocatable, stack-based assembly language,
- operational semantics for two simple high-level languages, one based on Gypsy (a derivative of Pascal) and one based on Lisp,
- some application programs, including a program to play winning Nim, and
- a simple operating system.

Connecting these layers were various functions. The "downward" functions were

- compilers that map from the high-level language states to the assembly language states,
- an assembler, linker and loader that, when composed, map from the assembly language states to ISA states, and
- a function that maps from ISA states to RTL states.

In addition, partial "upward" maps were also defined, allowing us to speak of the high-level data represented by a region of a low-level state. The obvious theorems relating these layers and maps were all proved mechanically. Finally, pre- and post-conditions for the applications programs were defined and the programs were proved correct with respect to the high-level language semantics.

These theorems were then composed into a main theorem that may be paraphrased informally as follows:

Warranty Theorem.
Suppose one has a high-level language state satisfying the pre-condition of a given application program (e.g., the Nim application). Construct the RTL state obtained from the high-level state by successively compiling, assembling, linking, and loading. Run the RTL machine on the constructed state. Map certain data regions up, using the partial inverse functions, producing some high-level data objects. Then the post-condition holds of that high-level data.

This theorem was formalized in the Nqthm logic and mechanically proved. It glued together all of the lemmas describing the various interfaces in the stack.

In the 1989 description of the stack, the microprocessor at the base was the FM8502 (a 32-bit version of the 16-bit FM8501 [22]), whose ISA was designed, implemented at the gate-level, and verified by Warren Hunt. The assembly language was named Piton [34] and the assembler, linker, and loader were designed, implemented and verified by the author, with help from Matt Kaufmann. The two high-level languages, micro-Gypsy[48] and a subset of the Nqthm Pure Lisp[15] and their compilers were implemented and verified by Bill Young and Art Flatau, respectively. The operating system, KIT [3], was designed, implemented, and verified by Bill Bevier. The NIM application [47] was implemented and verified by Matt Wilding.

In 1992, Bishop Brock and Warren Hunt formalized the Netlist Description Language (NDL) of LSI Logic, Inc. They used this formal NDL to describe a new microprocessor, the FM9001, and verified that the new design implemented the new ISA. Unlike the FM8501 and FM8502, the FM9001 was fabricated (by LSI Logic, Inc.) [23]. The author then ported the Piton assembly language to the FM9001 ISA, by changing and reverifying the code generators. The rest of the stack was then ported painlessly and automatically. The porting process is described in some detail in [34]. Thus, by 1992, a functioning verified stack existed.

This description makes it seem as though the challenge was met a decade ago. How did the CLI stack fall short? There are many reasons.

- The FM9001 was modeled at the gate level, not the transistor level. But many hardware design flaws occur below the gate level.
- The FM9001 had memory-mapped io and a crude interrupt facility because one of the sponsors did not want a useful trusted microprocessor competing with the product of a much larger project.
- The FM9001 was fabricated on a gate-array.
- None of the programming languages described had io facilities, for obvious reasons.
- The high-level languages were too simple to be of practical use. For example, the micro-Gypsy language had very few primitives and no dynamically allocated data types (e.g., records). The Pure Lisp had automatic storage allocation (e.g., cons) but no verified garbage collector.
- The assemblers and compilers were "cross-platform" transformers: they did not run on the FM9001 but on commercial machines. For example, using a Sun workstation running Nqthm (written in Common Lisp) it was possible to produce, from a high-level micro-Gypsy state, a binary image for the FM9001. But it was not possible to produce this image using only an FM9001, much less was it possible to produce it *in situ*. In addition to implementing the full Nqthm programming language and a verified garbage collector, one would have to implement and verify the parsers and a file system.
- No useful applications programs were verified.

– The operating system was not ported to the FM9001 (because it was not actually implemented for the FM8501 but for a different, concurrently developed machine).

In short, the stack was too simple. Thus it fails our criteria that the artifact's behavior be of interest to people outside the formal methods community.

One reason the stack was so simple was the difficulty of vertical integration between successive layers of abstraction. This problem was perhaps the major reason that the Software Implemented Fault Tolerance project (SIFT) [17] failed to achieve its stated aims. In SIFT, many individual properties were checked, some mechanically, but there was no overriding coherent logical framework in which all the results could be combined. A mechanically checked "warranty theorem" requires such a framework. In the CLI stack work it was convenient to adopt a single general-purpose mechanized tool (Nqthm) and do all of the mechanically checked reasoning with it. That allowed the different layers to be related formally within a single logical framework. But it also meant the tool was not perfectly suited for any layer. To manage the complexity, we kept the artifact simple.

3   Scientific Significance

In this and subsequent sections we explore basic questions that might be asked of any purported "grand challenge."

Is it driven by curiosity about foundations, applications, or limits of basic science? Yes. Computing science is essentially about abstraction: how is one layer of abstraction implemented on top of others? Foundational questions are (a) how do we know that the intended abstraction meets the requirements and (b) how do we know the intended abstraction is correctly implemented? A "stack" of verified systems forces question (a) to be addressed, at least for all the layers but the top-most, by providing as assumptions to higher layers only what was proved about lower layers. Mechanical checking forces clear answers to (b).

Is there a clear criteria for success? Yes. The project will produce an artifact.

Does it promise a revolutionary shift in the accepted paradigm of thinking or practice? Yes. There are two mechanisms here. First, the production of a useful artifact with formally specified interfaces will encourage the construction of additional abstractions on top of it or its components. Second, project will so challenge the formal methods community that useful new tools will be built and these will open up new applications and drastically reduce the cost of applying formal methods.

The CLI stack was a *technology driver* for the Boyer-Moore community. Two important products came from the stack work.

The first was the formalized operational semantics methodology. This methodology is characterized by a certain style of definition for state machines, a certain collection of lemmas to control the symbolic simplification of successive state transitions, the use of clock functions to specify how long the paths of interest are, the formalization of commuting diagrams and how to "stack" them, and the understanding of the role of successive refinement as formalized by subtly different operational models [5]. While most of these ideas pre-date the Boyer-Moore community, their formal expression and careful orchestration came to fruition in that community, and the CLI stack was the ultimate crucible in which those techniques were refined. Since then these methods have been used repeatedly in industry to verify microcode, microprocessor models, and Java byte code.

For example, shortly after the CLI stack was completed, Yuan Yu used these techniques to model of the Motorola 68020 and he used Nqthm to verify 21 of the 22 Berkeley C String Library subroutines [7]. Yu verified these subroutines by verifying the binary machine code produced by gcc -o.

The second product of the CLI stack research was an industrial strength version of the Nqthm theorem prover, ACL2 [25]. ACL2 was started in 1989 and was ready for its first industrial trials by 1992. The design of ACL2 was directly influenced by the inadequacies of Nqthm as highlighted by challenges in the CLI stack. These challenges included automation, execution efficiency, abstraction, name and rule scoping, finer-grained control, incremental library development, and simply dealing with "industrial strength" models.

After the stack work was completed and ACL2 was operational, it began being used to verify designs and components of industrial interest.

- The Motorola CAP digital signal processor was modeled at the pipelined architecture level and the sequential microcode ISA level, with bit- and cycle-accurate models. The second model executed several times faster than Motorola's own simulator. These ACL2 models were proved equivalent under the hypothesis that no pipeline hazards were present in the code sequence being executed. The hazard predicate was defined as an executable ACL2 function on the microcode ROM. Hazards not identified by the architects were identified during the equivalence proof. In addition, the ROM was found to contain programs with hazards, despite the fact that the Motorola microcode programmers had been forewarned of some of the hazard conditions. Two microcode programs were proved correct. See [10, 9].
- The pseudo-code representing the microcode of the kernel of the FDIV floating-point divide operation on the Advanced Micro Devices K5 was verified to implement the IEEE 754 floating point standard. See [35].
- The register-transfer level (RTL) circuit descriptions for all the elementary floating-point arithmetic on the AMD Athlon have been proved to implement the IEEE 754 floating point standard. The ACL2 functions modeling the RTL circuits – functions produced by a mechanical translator – were executed on over 80 million floating point test vectors from AMD's standard test suite and found to produce exactly the same output as AMD's RTL simulator; thus ACL2's executability was crucial to corroborating the translation scheme against AMD's accepted, if informal, RTL "semantics," its C simulator. Upon attempting to prove that the ACL2 functions implemented floating point arithmetic correctly, bugs were found. This is important since the RTL had been extensively tested. The bugs were fixed by modifying the

RTL. The modified models were verified mechanically. All of this happened at AMD and before the Athlon was first fabricated. See [40, 41].
- The Java Virtual Machine was modeled and fabricated by Rockwell Collins and manufactured by aJile Systems, Inc. The ACL2 model executed at 90% of the speed of Rockwell Collin's previously written C simulator for the design and became the standard test bench for the chip design. See [21, 20].
- Theorems were proved relating code sequences running on different members of a family of Rockwell Collins microprocessors. See [19].
- An academic microprocessor, the FM9801, with speculative execution, exceptions and interrupts was verified to implement an ISA. See [43, 42].
- A security model for the IBM 4758 secure co-processor was produced and analyzed to obtain FIPS-140 Level 4 certification. See [44].
- A safety-critical compiler-checker was verified for train-borne real-time control software written by Union Switch and Signal. See [2].
- A checker for the Ivy theorem prover from Argonne National Labs was verified to be sound. Ivy proofs are thus generated by unverified code but confirmed to be proofs by a verified ACL2 function. See [32].
- Proof methods have been developed whereby ACL2 can be used to verify that one state machine is a stuttering bisimulation of another. After so verifying the appropriateness of a finite-state abstraction of an infinite-state system, for example, it is sometimes possible to use a model checker to verify the correctness of the finite-state machine and then infer the correctness of the infinite-state system. A verified ACL2 model checker [29] has been produced. See [28, 30]
- A BDD package was verified to be sound and complete with ACL2. This package uses ACL2's single-threaded objects to achieve runtime speeds of about 60% those of the CUDD package. However, unlike CUDD, the verified package does not support dynamic variable reordering and is thus more limited in scope. See [46].
- A operational JVM thread model was produced and Java code was verified by verifying the bytecode produced by the javac compiler of Sun Microsystems, Inc. The particular Java application creates an unbounded number of threads in contention for a single object in the heap. The correctness proof required establishing mutual exclusion. See [36, 37].
- In addition, the CLI stack has had impact on other verification groups. In particular, the ProCos project [26] was directly inspired by the CLI stack and focused the work of many European verification groups. One in particular, the VERIFIX group [16] centered in Kiel and Karlsruhe, Germany, has focused extensively on the compiler verification problem. Thanks to that work we now understand much better how to host the verified stack on the verified microprocessor.

Had CLI not embarked on the CLI stack project in the mid-1980s, had it confined its attention to the niche in which Nqthm was most suited (number theory, meta-mathematics, algorithms), it is doubtful that ACL2 would have been created or that such a large number of commercial projects would have exploited formal methods in the 1990s.

This new grand challenge, which is significantly larger than the CLI stack, can be expected to produce a comparably larger number of major paradigm shifts.

Does it avoid duplicating evolutionary development of commercial products? Yes. Industry is too market- and feature-driven to devote time and resources to tool development. At the same time, industry recognizes the enormous cost and drawbacks of traditional hardware/software testing and the enormous cost of bugs. They simply cannot get off the treadmill and it will take an effort like this to show that there is another way.

4   Impact on Practice

Will its promotion as grand challenge contribute to the progress of science? Yes. Essentially this project will demonstrate that computer science is a *science* and not merely an art, by developing and demonstrating the efficacy of mechanically checked mathematical verification techniques.

Does it have enthusiastic support of the established scientific community? Yes. The formal methods community is thriving and is developing a wide variety of tools.

- decision procedures, such as BDD packages [11, 45], SAT solvers [49], and arithmetic procedures [39],
- model checkers [33] or model checking techniques [14, 12]
- special purpose analysis tools such as ESC/Java [27], Java PathFinder [8], and SLAM [1], and
- general-purpose theorem provers such as as ACL2 [25], Coq [13], HOL [18], and PVS [38].

What is lacking is sufficient motivation to integrate these tools.

Does it appeal to the imagination of other scientists and the general public? Scientists are intrigued by the idea of machines reasoning about machines and inevitably ask the question "who checks the checkers?" Firm answers depend upon the production of verified hardware platforms via bootstrapping. Absolute certainty is illusory. But the systematic use of mathematics and mechanical checkers can reduce the "trusted core" to something that can be checked by the scientific community's standard "social process." The public understands both the need for reliable (and secure and private) computing platforms.

What kind of benefits to science, industry, or society may be expected from the project, even if only partially successful? If the project produces a verified artifact, it and key components in it are likely to find additional uses because of their trustworthiness. The tools created from this project will significantly reduce the cost of the development of trusted hardware and software. The resulting benefits to industry and society are enormous, including more reliability and more security in our computing infrastructure.

5   Scale and Distribution

Does it have international scope? Yes. Formal methods is being investigated world wide. There are significant groups in the United States, eastern and western Europe, Australia, India, China and Japan.

How does it split into sub-tasks or sub-phases with identifiable goals and criteria, say at 5-year intervals? An artifact of general utility and interest is sufficiently large that no single group can design and mechanically verify one. Furthermore, only general-purpose tools (e.g., theorem provers) are sufficiently flexible to deal with the vertical integration between layers of abstraction, but theorem provers are cumbersome at dealing with the specifics of any one layer. Additional tools and interfaces will have to be identified and built.

The first task is to assemble a team capable of spanning the entire spectrum of abstractions: from transistors to software. There are so many artifacts of interest that it is likely many teams will be formed, each focusing on some particular category of artifact. Thus there will be both collaboration and competition.

The second task, for a given team, is to choose an artifact and factor its design into modules with clearly but informally specified interfaces. It would be best if the entire team then refined each of the models at least one level, to expose problems likely to change the interfaces and to bring to bear the mixed skills of the team on the entire project.

The third task is then to specify the interfaces so precisely that they can be formalized without requiring much creativity or imagination. This task will likely identify serious deficiencies in the tools that the team members might individually advocate. It is at this point that tool designers and advocates can begin to explore extensions of and connections between their tools.

The fourth task is for individual team members to begin working on the design and verification of each module. Even this will likely involve teams expert in several layers of abstraction. Members working on higher-level modules will assume only the "contracted" interfaces of lower-level ones. It is likely this effort will cause much communication as additional requirements are discovered passed down and new functionality is verified and passed up.

The fifth task, which must go on concurrently with the fourth, is the formal "gluing together" of the guarantees produced by the various tools. For example, a special-purpose static analysis tool might be used to determine that no object of a certain class leaks out of a given thread. But if this fact is to be exploited by a theorem prover being used to verify the functional correctness of the thread, the special-purpose analysis tool must "export" its findings in the form of theorems "guaranteed" by its computation. By formally outputing the theorem guaranteed by such a special-purpose tool, the authors of the tool advertise clearly what they claim to insure and permit others to integrate the tool and to check its claims and the care with which they are made.

But these five tasks will likely be iterated several times as new requirements are discovered and interfaces are changed. This is the very phenomenon the project is meant to study. If no "mistakes" are made the entire project could probably be carried out in 5 years by a distributed academic team. But "mistakes" will be made and previously verified components will be changed and have to be "re-verified." These components will be sufficiently large that tools will have to be built to make incremental re-verification convenient.

A proposed 10 year timeline might be: Team assembly, identification of the artifact and informal specification: 2 years. First cut at formal proofs and gluing of most modules: 3 years. Enlargement of the team, tool building and support for iteration: 3 years. Redesign and "re-verification" of major components with new tools: 2 years. It is likely that the artifact finally built will be very different than the one initially driving the development.

What calls does it make for collaboration of research teams with diverse skills? See above.

How can it be promoted by competition between teams with diverse approaches? Despite the fact that there are many different artifacts from which to choose, most share many common features, e.g., microprocessor models, machine code models, higher level language models, io device models. It is likely that progress made by one team on one artifact will inform and aid progress made by another team on a different artifact.

6 Timelines

When was it first proposed as a challenge? Why has it been so difficult? Mechanized program verification was first proposed by McCarthy [31] in the early 1960s and explored extensively. It basically failed for lack of theorem proving power, which in turn was due, in part, to lack of computing power and effective decision procedures for key fragments. Looked at more generally, the problem is hard because it involves mechanized reasoning about algorithms and abstractions of such size and complexity that they challenge the best human minds.

Why is it now expected to be feasible in 10-15 years? The intervening forty years of advances in computing, decision procedures, and automatic theorem proving, together with the engineering work necessary to integrate these advances, suggests that it is now possible. The fact that formal methods are being applied in industry to verify commercially designed components supports this conclusion.

What are the first steps? The self-assembly of teams of interested researchers spanning several layers of abstraction and discussion of the problems presented by some particular artifact.

What are the most likely reasons for failure? One likely reason for failure is that a team will put "all of its eggs in one basket," i.e., will attempt to do everything with one tool rather than reach out for the special-purpose tools developed by academic/scientific competitors. Another likely reason for failure is that team members will underestimate the difficulty of "gluing tools together" and work too long in isolation. The result is likely to be the verification of a large number of local properties without mechanized enforcement or checking that the properties are sufficient to guarantee the ultimate "warranty theorem."

7   Conclusion and Acknowledgements

This challenge is plausible only because of the work of many scientists over the past 40 years. I am especially appreciative of the formal, mechanized work by my students and by the Nqthm and ACL2 user communities. We have come so far and can do so many different parts of the problem that, surely, combination with others, we can put it all together into a single formal warranty for an interesting artifact.

I would like to thank Tony Hoare for helping me think about the criteria defining a grand challenge.

References

1. T. Ball and S. K. Rajamani. The SLAM project: debugging system software via static analysis. *SIGPLAN Notices: Conference Record of POPL 2002*, 37(1):1–3, January 2002.
2. P. Bertoli and P. Traverso. Design verification of a safety-critical embedded verifier. In Kaufmann et al. [24], pages 233–246.
3. W. R. Bevier. A verified operating system kernel. Ph.d. dissertation, University of Texas at Austin, 1987.
4. W.R. Bevier, W.A. Hunt, J S. Moore, and W.D. Young. Special issue on system verification. *Journal of Automated Reasoning*, 5(4):409–530, 1989.
5. R. S. Boyer and J S. Moore. Mechanized formal reasoning about programs and computing machines. In R. Veroff, editor, *Automated Reasoning and Its Applications: Essays in Honor of Larry Wos*, pages 147–176, Cambridge, MA, 1996. MIT Press.
6. R. S. Boyer and J S. Moore. *A Computational Logic Handbook, Second Edition*. Academic Press, New York, 1997.
7. R. S. Boyer and Y. Yu. Automated proofs of object code for a widely used microprocessor. *Journal of the ACM*, 43(1):166–192, January 1996.
8. G. Brat, K. Havelund, S. Park, and W. Visser. Java PathFinder - a second generation of a Java model checker. In *post-CAV 2000 Workshop on Advances in Verification, Chicago, IL.*, Moffett Field, CA., July 2000.
   `http://ase.arc.nasa.gov/jpf/wave00.ps.gz`.
9. B. Brock and J S. Moore. A mechanically checked proof of a comparator sort algorithm, 1999.
   `http://www.cs.utexas.edu/users/moore/publications/csort/main.ps.Z`.
10. B. Brock and W. A. Hunt, Jr. Formal analysis of the motorola CAP DSP. In *Industrial-Strength Formal Methods*. Springer-Verlag, 1999.
11. R. E. Bryant. Symbolic Boolean manipulation with ordered binary decision diagrams. *ACM Computing Surveys*, 1992.
12. E. M. Clarke, S. Campos, and O. Grumberg. Selective quantitative analysis and interval model checking: Verifying different facets of a system. *Formal Methods in System Design*, 17(2), October 2000.
13. G. Dowek, A. Felty, H. Herbelin, G. Huet, C. Paulin, and B. Werner. The Coq proof assistant user's guide, Version 5.6. Technical Report TR 134, INRIA, December 1991.

14. E. A. Emerson and R. J. Trefler. From asymmetry to full symmetry: New techniques for symmetry reduction in model checking. In *CHARME 1999*, pages 142–156, 1999.
15. A. D. Flatau. A verified implementation of an applicative language with dynamic storage allocation. Phd thesis, University of Texas at Austin, 1992.
16. W. Goerigk and U. Hoffmann. Rigorous Compiler Implementation Correctness: How to Prove the Real Thing Correct. In *Proceedings FM-TRENDS'98 International Workshop on Current Trends in Applied Formal Methods*, LNCS, Boppard, 1998.
17. J. Goldberg, W. Kautz, P. M. Mellear-Smith, M. Green, K. Levitt, R. Schwartz, and C. Weinstock. Development and analysis of the software implemented fault-tolerance (sift) computer. Technical Report NASA Contractor Report 172146, NASA Langley Research Center, Hampton, VA, 1984.
18. M. Gordon and T. Melham. *Introduction to HOL: A Theorem Proving Environment for Higher Order Logic.* Cambridge University Press, 1993.
19. D. Greve and M. Wilding. Evaluatable, high-assurance microprocessors. In *NSA High-Confidence Systems and Software Conference (HCSS)*, Linthicum, MD, March 2002. http://hokiepokie.org/docs/hcss02/proceedings.pdf.
20. D. Greve, M. Wilding, and D. Hardin. High-speed, analyzable simulators. In Kaufmann et al. [24], pages 113–136.
21. David A. Greve. Symbolic simulation of the JEM1 microprocessor. In G. Gopalakrishnan and P. Windley, editors, *Formal Methods in Computer-Aided Design – FM-CAD*, LNCS 1522, Heidelberg, 1998. Springer-Verlag.
22. W. A. Hunt. *FM8501: A Verified Microprocessor.* Springer-Verlag LNAI 795, Heidelberg, 1994.
23. W.A. Hunt and B. Brock. A formal HDL and its use in the FM9001 verification. *Proceedings of the Royal Society*, April 1992.
24. M. Kaufmann, P. Manolios, and J S. Moore, editors. *Computer-Aided Reasoning: ACL2 Case Studies.* Kluwer Academic Press, Boston, MA., 2000.
25. M. Kaufmann, P. Manolios, and J S. Moore. *Computer-Aided Reasoning: An Approach.* Kluwer Academic Press, Boston, MA., 2000.
26. H. Langmaack. The ProCoS Approach to Correct Systems. *Real Time Systems*, 13:253–275, 1997.
27. K. R. M. Leino, G. Nelson, and J. B. Saxe. Esc/java user's manual. Technical Report Technical Note 2000-002, Compaq Systems Research Center, October 2000.
28. P. Manolios. Correctness of pipelined machines. In *Formal Methods in Computer-Aided Design, FMCAD 2000*, pages 161–178, Heidelberg, 2000. Springer-Verlag LNCS 1954.
29. P. Manolios. Mu-calculus model-checking. In Kaufmann et al. [24], pages 93–112.
30. P. Manolios, K. Namjoshi, and R. Sumners. Linking theorem proving and model-checking with well-founded bisimulation. In *Computed Aided Verification, CAV '99*, pages 369–379, Heidelberg, 1999. Springer-Verlag LNCS 1633.
31. J. McCarthy. A basis for a mathematical theory of computation. In *Computer Programming and Formal Systems*. North-Holland Publishing Company, Amsterdam, The Netherlands, 1963.
32. W. McCune and O. Shumsky. Ivy: A preprocessor and proof checker for first-order logic. In Kaufmann et al. [24], pages 265–282.
33. K. L. McMillan. *Symbolic Model Checking.* Kluwer Academic Publishers, 1993.
34. J S. Moore. *Piton: A Mechanically Verified Assembly-Level Language.* Automated Reasoning Series, Kluwer Academic Publishers, 1996.

35. J S. Moore, T. Lynch, and M. Kaufmann. A mechanically checked proof of the correctness of the kernel of the AMD5K86 floating point division algorithm. *IEEE Transactions on Computers*, 47(9):913–926, September 1998.

36. J S. Moore and G. Porter. An executable formal JVM thread model. In *Java Virtual Machine Research and Technology Symposium (JVM '01)*, Berkeley, CA., April 2001. USENIX.
http://www.cs.utexas.edu/users/moore/publications/m4/model.ps.gz.

37. J S. Moore and G. Porter. The apprentice challenge. *TOPLAS*, (accepted for publication, 2002).
http://www.cs.utexas.edu/users/moore/publications/m5/index.html.

38. S. Owre, J. Rushby, and N. Shankar. PVS: A prototype verification system. In D. Kapur, editor, *11th International Conference on Automated Deduction (CADE)*, pages 748–752, Heidelberg, June 1992. Lecture Notes in Artificial Intelligence, Vol 607, Springer-Verlag.

39. H. Ruess and N. Shankar. Deconstructing shostak. In *16th Annual IEEE Symposium on Logic in Computer Science*, Lecture Notes in Computer Science, pages 19–28. IEEE Computer Society, 2001.

40. D. Russinoff. A mechanically checked proof of IEEE compliance of a register-transfer-level specification of the AMD-K7 floating-point multiplication, division, and square root instructions. *London Mathematical Society Journal of Computation and Mathematics*, 1:148–200, December 1998.
http://www.onr.com/user/russ/david/k7-div-sqrt.html.

41. D. M. Russinoff and A. Flatau. Rtl verification: A floating-point multiplier. In Kaufmann et al. [24], pages 201–232.

42. J. Sawada. Verification of a simple pipelined machine model. In Kaufmann et al. [24], pages 137–150.

43. J. Sawada and W. Hunt. Processor verification with precise exceptions and speculative execution. In *Computed Aided Verification, CAV '98*, pages 135–146, Heidelberg, 1998. Springer-Verlag LNCS 1427.

44. S. W. Smith and V. Austel. Trusting trusted hardware: Towards a formal model for programmable secure coprocessors. In *The Third USENIX Workshop on Electronic Commerce*, September 1998.

45. F. Somenzi. CUDD: CU decision diagram package, 1997. public software, Colorado University, Boulder, CO.

46. R. Sumners. Correctness proof of a BDD manager in the context of satisfiability checking. In *Proceedings of ACL2 Workshop 2000*. Department of Computer Sciences, Technical Report TR-00-29, November 2000.
http://www.cs.utexas.edu/users/moore/acl2/workshop-2000/final/sumners2/paper.ps.

47. M. Wilding. A mechanically verified application for a mechanically verified environment. In Costas Courcoubetis, editor, *Computer-Aided Verification – CAV '93*, volume 697 of *Lecture Notes in Computer Science*, Heidelberg, 1993. Springer-Verlag. See URL ftp://ftp.cs.utexas.edu/pub/boyer/nqthm/wilding-cav93.ps.

48. W. D. Young. A verified code generator for a subset of Gypsy. Technical Report 33, Comp. Logic. Inc., Austin, Texas, 1988.

49. L. Zhang and S. Malik. The quest for efficience boolean satisfiablity solvers. In Andrei Voronkov, editor, *Automated Deduction - CADE-18, 18th International Conference on Automated Deduction, Copenhagen, Denmark, July 27-30, 2002, Proceedings*, volume 2392 of *Lecture Notes in Computer Science*, pages 295–313. Springer, 2002.

"What Is an Infrastructure?" Towards an Informatics Answer

Dines Bjørner

Department of Computing Science and Engineering
Institute of Informatics and Mathematical Modelling
Technical University of Denmark
Bldg.322, Richard Petersens Place
DK–2800 Kgs.Lyngby, Denmark
db@imm.dtu.dk
http://www.imm.dtu.dk/~db

Abstract. We briefly discuss the dogmas of a domain engineering oriented and a formal techniques based approach to software engineering. Then we try delineate the concepts of infrastructure and infrastructure components. Finally we hint at an abstract example work flow domain model: transaction script work flows. It is claimed that such are one of the core informatics characteristics of infrastructure components. The paper ends with some reflections on 10 years of UNU/IIST.

1 Some Software Engineering Dogmas

1.1 From Science via Engineering to Technology

The "ST" in UNU/IIST stands for software technology. But UNU/IIST seems, in the last 10 years, to have stood for an engineering basis for construction of software. The engineering basis was scientific, and was based on computer science. The approach to the construction of software was based on computing science — programming methodology. We saw it, and I believe UNU/IIST still sees it, this way: The engineer as "walking the bridge" between science and technology: Creating technology based on scientific insight; and, vice–versa, analysing technological artifacts with a view towards understanding their possible scientific contents. Both science and technology; both synthesis and analysis.

1.2 CS ⊕ CS ⊕ SE

Computer science, to me, is the study and knowledge of the artifacts that can "exist" inside computers: Their mathematical properties: Models of computation, and the underlying mathematics itself. Computing science, to me, is the study and knowledge of how to construct those artifacts: programming languages, their pragmatics, their semantics, including proof systems, their syntax; and the principles and techniques of use. The difference is, somehow, dramatic.

B.K. Aichernig and T. Maibaum (Eds.): Formal Methods ..., LNCS 2757, pp. 173–190, 2003.

Software engineering is the art, discipline, craft, science and logic of conceiving, constructing, and maintaining software. The sciences are those of applied mathematics and computing. I consider myself both a computing scientist and a software engineer.

1.3   Informatics

Informatics, such as I saw it in the early 1990s, at UNU/IIST, was a combination of mathematics, computer & computing science, software engineering, and applications. Perhaps this is a way still to see it? Some "sobering" observation: Informatics relates to information technology (IT) as biology does to bio—technology; $\mathcal{E}$tcetera! The political (UN, Macau, PRC, &c.) world is, forever (?) caught by the syntax of "gadgets". UNU/IIST was steadfast in its focus on pragmatics and semantics.

1.4   A Triptych Software Engineering

The Dogma. The *Triptych Dogma:* Before software can be designed, we must understand the requirements. Before requirements can be expressed we must understand the domain. This then was a dogma — is it still? Software engineering consists of the engineering of domains, engineering of requirements, and the design of software. In summary, and ideally speaking: We first *describe* the domain: $\mathcal{D}$, from which we *define* the domain requirements; from these and interface and machine requirements, ie. from $\mathcal{R}$, we *specify* the software design: $\mathcal{S}$. In a suitable reality we secure that all these are properly documented and related: $\mathcal{D}, \mathcal{S} \models \mathcal{R}$, when all is done!

In proofs of correctness of software ($\mathcal{S}$) wrt. requirements ($\mathcal{R}$) assumptions are often stated about the domain ($\mathcal{D}$). But, by domain descriptions, $\mathcal{D}$, we mean "much more" than just expressing such assumptions.

Some Issues of Domain Engineering

The Facets: To understand the application domain we must describe it. We must, I believe, describe it, informally (ie. narrate), and formally, as it is, the very *basics*, ie. the *intrinsics*; the *technologies* that *support* the domain; the *management & organisation* structures of the domain; the *rules & regulations* that should guide human behaviour in the domain; those *human behaviours:* the correct, diligent, loyal and competent work; the absent–minded, "casual", sloppy routines; and the near, or outright criminal, neglect. &c.

In [2] we go into more details on domain facets while our lecture notes (cum planned book [3]) brings the "full story".

The Evidence: How are we describing the domain? We are *rough sketching* it, and *analysing* these sketches to arrive at *concepts*. We establish a *terminology* for the domain. We *narrate* the domain: A concise professional language description of the domain using only (otherwise precisely defined) terms of the domain. And

we *formalise* the *narrative*. We then *analyse* the *narrative* and the *formalisation*
with the aims of *validating* the *domain description* "against" domain stakeholders, and of *verifying* properties of the *domain description*.

On Documentation in General: In general there will be many documents for
each phase[1], stage[2] and step[3] of development: Informative documents: Needs and
concepts, development briefs, contracts, *&c.* Descriptive/prescriptive documents:
Informal (rough sketches, terminologies, and narratives) and (formal models)
analytic documents: Concept formation, validation, and verification. These sets
of documents are related, and occur and re–occur for all phases. See for example
our distinction, below, between what is elsewhere called: User requirements, vs.
system requirements.

Some Issues of Requirements Engineering. How are we otherwise to formulate requirements? We see requirements definitions as composed from three
viewpoints: Domain, interface and machine requirements. We survey these.

Requirements are about the machine: The hardware and software to be designed.

Domain Requirements: Requirements that can be expressed solely with reference
to, ie. using terms of, the domain, are called *domain requirements*. They are, in
a sense, "derived" from the *domain understanding*. Thus whatever vagueness,
non–determinism and undesired behaviour in the domain, as expressed by the
respective parts of the domain *intrinsics, support technologies, management &
organisation, rules & regulations,* and *human behaviour,* can now be constrained,
if need be, by becoming requirements to a desirably performing computing system.

The development of domain requirements can be supported by a number of
principles and techniques. *Projection:* Not all of the domain need be supported
by computing — hence we project only part of the domain description onto
potential requirements; *Determination:* Usually the domain description is described abstractly, loosely as well as non–deterministically — and we may wish
to remove some of this loosenes and non–determinism. *Instantiation:* Typically
domain rules & regulations are different from instance to instance of a domain. In
domain descriptions they are abstracted as functions. In requirements prescrip-
tions we typically design a script language to enable stake–holders to "program",
ie., to express, in an easily computerisable form, the specific rules & regulations.
Extension: Entities, operations over these, events possible in connection with

---

[1] Domain, requirements and software design are three main phases of software development.

[2] Phases may be composed of stages, such as for example the domain requirements,
the interface requirements and the machine requirements stages of the requirements
phase, or, as another example, the software architecture and the program organisation stages of the software design phase.

[3] Stages may then consist of one or more steps of development, typically data type
reification and operation transformation — also known as refinements.

these, and behaviours on some kinds of such entities may now be feasibly "realisable" — where before they were not, hence some forms of domain requirements extend the domain. *Initialisation:* Phenomena in the world need be represented inside the computer — and initialising computing systems, notably the software "state", is often a main computing task in itself, as is the ongoing monitoring of the "state" of the 'outside' world for the purpose of possible internal state (ie. database) updates. There are other specialised principles and techniques that support the development of requirements.

Interface Requirements: Requirements that deal with the phenomena shared between external users (human or other machines) and the machine (hardware and software) to be designed, such requirements are called *interface requirements.* Examples of areas of concern for interface requirements are: Human computer interfaces (HCI, CHI), including graphical user interfaces (GUIs), dialogues, etc., and general input and output (examples are: Process control data sampling (input sensors) and controller activation (output actuator)). Some interface requirements can be formalised, others not so easily, and yet others are such for which we today do not know how to formalise them.

Machine Requirements: Requirements that deal with the phenomena which reside in the machine are referred to as *machine requirements.* Examples of machine requirements are: performance (resource [storage, time, etc.] utilisation), maintainability (adaptive, perfective, preventive, corrective and legacy–oriented), platform constraints (hardware and base software system platform: development, operational and maintenance), business process re–engineering, training and use manuals, and documentation (development, installation, and maintenance manuals, etc.).

Some Issues of Software Design. Once the requirements are reasonably well established software design can start. We see software design as a potentially multiple stage, and, within stages, multiple step process. Concerning stages one can identify two "abstract" stages: The software architecture design stage in which the domain requirements find an computable form, albeit still abstract. Some interface requirements are normally also, abstract design–wise "absolved", and the programme organisation design stage in which the machine requirements find a computable form. Since machine requirements are usually rather operational in nature, the programme organisation design is less abstract than the software architecture design. Any remaining interface requirements are also, abstract design–wise "absolved".

This finishes our overview of the triptych phases of software development.

1.5   Formal Techniques

A significant characteristics in our approach is that of the use of formal techniques: formal specification, and verification by proofs and by model checking.

The area as such is usually — colloquially — referred to as "formal methods". By a method we understand a set of principles of analysis and for selecting techniques and tools in order efficiently to achieve the construction of an efficient artifact. By formal specification we mean description by means of a formal language: One having a formal semantics, a formal proof system and a formal syntax. In this paper we shall rather one–sidedly be illustrating just the specification side and not at all show any verification issues. And in this paper we shall rather one–sidedly also be using only one tool: The Raise Specification Language: RSL [11, 10].

2   On Infrastructures and Their Components

UNU/IIST was placed in a UN + World Bank environment[4]. In that environment such terms as: infrastructure, self–reliance, and sustainable development, were part of the daily parlance. How was UNU/IIST to respond to this. It had to!

2.1   The World Bank Concept of Infrastructure — A 1st Answer

One may speak of a country's or a region's infrastructure[5]. But what does one mean by that?

A Socio–Economic Characterisation. According to the World Bank[6], 'infrastructure' is an umbrella term for many activities referred to as 'social overhead capital' by some development economists, and encompasses activities that share technical and economic features (such as economies of scale and spill-overs from users to non-users).

Our interpretation of the 'infrastructure' concept, see below, albeit different, is, however, commensurate.

Concretisations. Examples of infrastructure components are typically: The transportation infrastructure sub–components (road, rail, air and water [shipping]); the financial services industry (banks, insurance companies, securities trading, etc.); health–care; utilities (electricity, natural gas, telecommunications, water supply, sewage disposal, etc.), etc.?

---

[4] Also known as the Bretton Woods Institutions.

[5] Winston Churchill is quoted to have said, during a debate in the House of Commons, in 1946: ... *The young Labourite speaker that we have just listened to, clearly wishes to impress upon his constituency the fact that he has gone to Eton and Oxford since he now uses such fashionable terms a 'infra–structure'* ...

[6] Dr. Jan Goossenarts, an early UNU/IIST Fellow, is to be credited with having found this characterisation.

Discussion. There are thus areas of human enterprises which are definitely included, and others areas that seem definitely excluded from being categorised as being infrastructure components. The production (ie. the manufacturing) — of for example consumer goods — is not included. Fisheries, agriculture, mining, and the like likewise are excluded. Such industries rely on the infrastructure to be in place — and functioning. What about the media: TV, radio and newspapers? It seems they also are not part of the infrastructure. But what about advertising and marketing. There seems to be some grey zones between the service and the manufacturing industries.

2.2 The mid 1990's UNU/IIST Concept of Infrastructure — A 2nd Answer

UNU/IIST took[7] a more technical, and, perhaps more general, view, and saw infrastructures as concerned with supporting other systems or activities.

Software for infrastructures is likely to be distributed and concerned in particular with supporting communication of information, people and/or materials. Hence issues of (for example) openness, timeliness, security, lack of corruption, and resilience are often important[8].

2.3 "What Is an Infrastructure?" — A 3rd Answer

We shall try answer this question in stages: First before we bring somewhat substantial examples; then, also partially, while bringing those examples; and, finally, in a concluding section, Section 4.2 of this paper. The answer parts will not sum up to a definitive answer!

An Analysis of the Characterisations. The World Bank characterisation, naturally, is "steeped" in socio–economics. It implies, I claim, that what is characterised is well–functioning. It could, possibly, be criticised for not giving a characterisation that allowed one to speak of well-functioning, and of not so well--functioning infrastructures. It cannot be used as a test: Is something presented an infrastructure, or is it not? And it begs the question: Can one decompose an infrastructure into parts, or as we shall call them, components?

The UNU/IIST characterisation, naturally, is "steeped" in systems engineering. It seems we were more defining requirements to the business process engineering of an infrastructure (component), than the domain — which, as for the World Bank characterisation, assumes a concept of "good functionality".

We shall, despite these caveats, accept the two characterisations in the following spirit: For a socio–economically well–functioning infrastructure (component) to be so, the characterisations of the intrinsics, the support technologies, the management & organisation, the rules & regulations, and the human behaviour, must, already in the domain, meet certain "good functionality" conditions.

---

[7] I write "mid 1990's" since that is what I can vouch for.

[8] The above wording is due, I believe, to Chris George, UNU/IIST.

That is: We bring the two characterisations together, letting the latter "feed" the former. Doing so expresses a conjecture: One answer, to the question" *"What is an infrastructure"*, is, seen from the viewpoint of systems engineering, that it is a system that can be characterised using the technical terms typical of computing systems.

The Question and Its Background. The question and its first, partial answer, only makes sense, from the point of view of the computer & computing sciences if we pose that question on the background of some of the achievements of those sciences. We mention a few analysis approaches. They are the denotational, the concurrency, the modal (incl. temporal) logic, the type/value, and the knowledge engineering approaches.

An important aspect of my answer, in addition to be flavoured by the above, derives from the *semiotics* distinctions between: *pragmatics, semantics,* and *syntax.* So we will also discuss this aspect below.

A Third Attempt at an Answer. A first concern of the socio–economics of infrastructures seems to be one of pragmatics: For society, through state or local government intervention, either by means of publicly owned, or by means of licensed semi–private enterprises, to provide infrastructure component means for "the rest of society": Private people and private (or other public) enterprises, to function properly. Depending on "the politics of the day" provision of such means may, or may not be state subsidised. So efficiency and profitability of such infrastructure components were sometimes not a main concern. The above observations certainly seems to have applied in the past.

With the advent of *informatics,* the confluence of computing science, mathematics (incl. mathematical modelling), and applications, the business process re–engineering of infrastructure components forces as well as enables a new way of looking at infrastructure components. We therefore recapitulate the UNU/IIST view of infrastructures.

Computing systems for infrastructures are distributed and concurrent, and are concerned with the flow of information, people, materials,and control, and the manipulation of the "flowed items".

Concepts like denotations, concurrency, types, logics (including modal logics), agents and speech acts, computational models, and semiotics (pragmatics, semantics and syntax) seems to offer a mind set associated with a vocabulary that "lifts" daily, short-range, and hence often short–sighted reasoning, and thus a framework for long–range thinking about necessary infrastructure process re–engineering.

So our "third try" at an answer to the question: *"What is an Infrastructure?"*, is a rather unconventional one: An infrastructure, as seen from the point of view of informatics (mathematics $\oplus$ computing science $\oplus$ applications), is a challenge: A class of systems that we need characterise both from the point of view of socio––economics, and from the point of view of computing science, and to relate the two answers.

3   Work Flow Domains

We first motivate these seeming digressions: From, in Section 1, overviewing a software enineering paradigm, via, in Section 2, discussing the socio–economic as well as other meanings of the term 'infrastructure', to now, in Section 3, bringing an example of a domain description. It may puzzle some readers.

At UNU/IIST we had to be, and were glad to be involved with providing research and methods for the development of software for the support of infrastructure components.

Firstly it was natural for us, then, to ask such questions as: "What is a Railway?", mathematically, that is, formally speaking. What is a "Financial Service System?", etc. And we found ways of answering these questions, well, to tolerably well! So it was obvious that we had to ask, and try answer the more general question: "What is an, or 'the' Infrastructure?". Since answers to such questions as: "What is a computer progam" can be given in denotational, or other computer science terminology, we should, naturally think of railways and infrastructures also having such computer science attributes.

Secondly, to provide such answers we had to delve deep into the modelling, such as we knew how to do it, of example such domains. It seems that work flow systems, of various kinds, are at the core of infrastructure component systems. And it seems, when abstracting several rather different kinds of work flow systems, that transaction processing systems are at the core of either of these infrastructure component systems.

So the first and the second section now finds its first "reunion" — in this section — in trying to apply just a tiny fragment of software engineering (and then again it is only a tiny fragment of domain engineering) to provide the basis for subsequent answers. The larger setting of software engineering: With domains, requirements and software design, is necessary, we believe, in order not to loose sight of the larger picture, namely that, eventually, after answering esoteric, abstract questions, of providing software!

3.1   Work Flows and Transactions

We would have liked to exemplify three kinds of concrete work flow systems: (1) Electronic business: Buyers and sellers in the form of consumers, retailers, wholesalers, and producers. Agents and brokers acting on behalf of one side (buyer or seller), respectively both sides of these. Transactions like inquiry, quotation, order placement, order confirmation, delivery, acceptance, invoicing, payment, etc. &c. (See [1].) (2) Health–care system: Citizens visiting medical doctors, pharmacies, clinical test laboratories, hospitals, etc. Medicine flowing from doctor to patient, from pharmacy to patient, etc. Patient medical journals flowing between the above "layers". &c. (3) Freight transport logistics. People sending and receiving fraight. Logistics firms arranging for the transport of freight. Transport companies: Railways, trucking firms, shipping companies, air cargo lines. Their vehicles: Trains, trucks, boats and air crafts. Transport networks: rail lines, road nets, shipping lanes and air corridors. Transport hubs: Train stations, truck depots, harbours and airports. The traffics: Trains, trucks, ships, air crafts. &c. All exemplify the movement of information, materials and control.

But we refrain — for lack of space!

Instead we illustrate some of the facets of a transaction script work flow example. You can interpret the transaction script work flow as an abstract E–business, an abstract health–care, or an abstract logistics system!

3.2 Transaction Scripts

The Problem. In domains 1–2–3 (see the previous section) tasks were carried out by a distributed set of activities either on potential or real trade (as for the electronic business example), or on patients (as for the health–care system), or on freight (as for the logistics example), The distributed set of operations were somehow effected by there being an actual or a virtual (a tacitly understood) protocol. We will now examine this notion of "protocol" further.

There are two issues at stake: To find a common abstraction, a general concept, by means of which we can (perhaps better) understand an essence of what goes on in each of the previously illustrated examples; and thus to provide a "common denominator" for a concept of work flow systems, a concept claimed to be a necessary (but not sufficient) component of "being an infrastructure"[9]. We could now proceed to a slightly extended *discussion & analysis* of various issues that are exemplified by the previous three examples; but we omit such a *discussion & analysis* here — leaving it to a more vivid "class–room" interaction to do so. Instead we delve right into one outcome of, ie. one solution to, this *discussion & analysis*, respectively search for a *common abstraction, a general concept*.

Clients, Work Stations (Servers), Scripts and Directives. There are *clients* and there are *work stations* (servers). Clients initialise and *interpret scripts*. A script is a set of *time–interval* stamped collection of *directives*. Interpretation of a script may lead a client to *visit* (ie. to *go to*) a work station. A client can at most visit one work station at a time. Thus clients are either *idle*, or *on their way* to or from a work station: Between being idle or visiting a previous work station. At a work station a client is being *handled* by the work station. Thus work stations handle clients, one at a time. That is, a client and a work station enter into a *"rendez vous"*, ie. some form of *co–operation*. Client/work station co–operation exhibits the following possible *behaviours*: A directive is *fetched* (thus *removed*) from the script. It is then being *interpreted* by the client and work station in unison. A directive may either be one which prescribes one, or another, of a small set of *operations* to take place — with the possible effect that, at operation completion, one or more directives have been added to the

---

[9] Railway systems, as are indeed all forms of transportation systems, are thought of as being infrastructure components, yet, in our past models of railway systems the work flow nature was somewhat hidden, somewhat less obvious.

client script; or a directive prescribes that the client *goes on to* visit another work station; or a directive prescribes that the client be *released*. Release of a client sets the client free to leave the work station. Having left a work station as the result of a release directive "puts" the client in the idle state. In the idle state a client is free either to fetch only *go to* work station directives, or to add a *go to work station w* directive to its script, or to remain idle.

A Simple Model of Scripts

Formalisation of Syntax:

type
    T, Δ
axiom
    $\forall$ t,t':T, $\exists$ δ:Δ • t'>t $\Rightarrow$ δ = t'−t
type
    C, Cn, W, Wn
    S' = (T × T) $\overrightarrow{m}$ D-set
    S = {| s:S' • wf_S(s) |}
    D == g(w:Wn) | p(w:W,f:F) | release
    F' = (C × W) → (W × C)
    F = {| f:F • wf_F(f) |}
value
    obs_Cn: C → Cn
    obs_S: C → S
    obs_Wn: W → Wn
    wf_S: S → **Bool**
    wf_S(s) ≡ $\forall$ (t,t'):(T×T) • (t,t')∈ **dom** s • t≤t'
    wf_F: F → **Bool**
    wf_F(c,w) **as** (c',w')
    post obs_Cn(c)=obs_Cn(c') ∧ obs_Wn(w)=obs_Wn(w')

Annotations I: There are notions of (absolute) time (T) and time intervals (Δ). And there are notions of named (Cn, Wn) clients (C) and work stations (W). Clients possess scripts, one each. A script associates to (positively directed) intervals over (absolute) times zero, one or more directives. A directive is either a *go to*, or a *perform*, or a *release* directive. *Perform* directives specify a function to be performed on a pair of clients and work stations, leaving these in a new state, however constrained by not changing their names.

A Simple Model of Work Flow

Formalisation of Semantics — The Work Flow System:

type
    Cn, Wn
    CΣ, WΣ

$C\Omega = Cn \underset{m}{\overrightarrow{}} C\Sigma$
$W\Omega = Wn \underset{m}{\overrightarrow{}} W\Sigma$

value
  obs_S: $C\Sigma \to S$
  remove: $(T \times T) \times D \to S \to S$
  add: $(T \times T) \times D \to S \to S$
  merge: $S \times C\Sigma \to C\Sigma$
  obs_$C\Sigma$: $C \to C\Sigma$
  obs_$W\Sigma$: $W \to W\Sigma$

  $c\omega:C\Omega$, $w\omega:W\Omega$, $t_0:T$, $\delta:\Delta$

  sys: **Unit** $\to$ **Unit**
  sys() $\equiv \|\{$client(cn)$(t_0)(c\omega(cn))|cn:Cn\}$ $\|$
        $(\|\{$ work_station(wn)$(t_0)(w\omega(wn))|wn:Wn\})$

Annotations II: Clients and work stations have (ie. possess) states. From a client state one can observe its script. From a script one can remove or add a time interval stamped directive. From the previous notions of clients and work stations one can observe their states[10] $c\omega$, $w\omega$ t_0, and δ represent initial values of respective types — needed when intialising the system of behaviours. A work flow system is now the parallel combination of a number (# Cn) of clients and a number (# Wn) of work stations, the latter all occurring concurrently.

Formalisation of Semantics — Clients:

channel
  $\{$ cw[cn,wn] $|$ cn:Cn, wn:Wn $\}$ M

value
  client: cn:Cn $\to$ T $\to$ $C\Sigma$ $\to$ **in,out** $\{$ cw[cn,wn] $|$ wn:Wn $\}$ **Unit**
  client(cn)(t)$(c\sigma)$ $\equiv$ c_idle(cn)(t)$(c\sigma)$ $\lceil\rceil$ c_step(cn)(t)$(c\sigma)$

  c_idle: Cn $\to$ T $\to$ $C\Sigma$ $\to$ **Unit**
  c_idle(cn)(t)$(c\sigma)$ $\equiv$ **let** t':T•t'>t **in** client(cn)(t')$(c\sigma)$ **end**

  c_step: cn:Cn $\to$ T $\to$ $C\Sigma$ $\to$ **in,out** $\{$ cw[cn,wn] $|$ wn:Wn $\}$ **Unit**

Annotations III: Any client can, in principle, visit any work station. Channels model this ability. A client is either idle or potentially visiting a work station (making one or more transaction steps). The client makes the (ie. a non–deterministic internal) choice, whether idle or potential action steps. To "perform" an idle "action" is to non–deterministically advance the clock.

---

[10] The two notions may eventually, in requirements be the same. In the domain it may be useful to make a distinction.

Formalisation of Semantics — Clients Continued:

> c_step(cn)(t)(cσ) ≡
>   **let** s = obs_S(cσ) **in**
>   **if** ∃ (t′,t″):(T×T),g(wn):D • (t′,t″) ∈ **dom** s ∧ t′≤t≤t″ ∧ g(wn) ∈ s(t′,t″)
>   **then**
>   **let** (t′,t″):(T×T),g(wn):D •
>   (t′,t″) ∈ **dom** s ∧ t′≤t≤t″ ∧ g(w) ∈ s(t′,t″) **in**
>   **let** cσ′ = remove((t′,t″),g(wn))(cσ) **in**
>   **let** (t‴,cσ″) = c2ws_visit(t′,t″)(cn,wn)(t)(cσ′) **in**
>   client(cn)(t‴)(cσ″) **end end end**
>   **else**
>   **let** t‴:T • t‴ = t + δ **in**
>   client(cn)(t‴)(cσ) **end**
>   **end end**

> c2ws_visit: (T×T×cn:Cn×wn:Wn)→T→CΣ→
>   **in,out** {cw[cn,wn′]|wn′:Wn} (T×CΣ)
> c2ws_visit(t′,t″)(cn,wn)(t)(cσ) ≡
>   cw[cn,wn]!((t′,t″),cn,t,cσ);[]{cw[cn,wn′]?|wn′:Wn}

Annotations IV: From a client state we observe the script. If there is a time interval recorded in the script for which there is a goto directive then such a time interval and goto directive is chosen: removed from the script, and then a visit is made, by the client to the designated work station, with this visit resulting in a new client state — at some "later" time. Otherwise no such visit can be made, but the clock is advanced. A work station visit starts with a rendez--vous initiated by the client, and ends with a rendez–vous initiated by the work station.

Formalisation of Semantics — Work Stations:

> work_station: wn:Wn → WΣ → **in,out** { cw[cn,wn] | cn:Cn } **Unit**
> work_station(wn)(wσ) ≡
>   **let** ((t′,t″),cn,t‴,cσ) = []{cw[cn,wn]?|cn:Cn} **in**
>   **let** (t⁗,(sσ′,wσ′)) = w_step((t′,t″),cn,t‴,(cσ,wσ)) **in**
>   cw[cn,wn]!(t⁗,sσ′) ;
>   work_station(wn)(wσ′) **end end**

> w_step: (T×T) → wn:Wn → (CΣ×WΣ) →
>   **in,out** { cw[cn,wn] | cn:Cn } **Unit**
> w_step((t′,t″),(cn,wn),t‴,(cσ,wσ)) ≡
>   **let** s = obs_S(cσ) **in**
>   **if** s={} **then** (t‴,(cσ,wσ))
>   **else assert:** (t′,t″) ∈ **dom** s
>   **let** d:D • d ∈ s(t′,t″) **in**

case d **of**

    p(wn,f) →

        let (t''''',(sσ',wσ')) = act(f,t'''',(sσ',wσ')) **in**

        let sσ'' = remove((t',t''),p(wn,f))(sσ') **in**

        w_step((t',t''),(cn,wn),t''''',(sσ'',wσ')) **end end**

    release →

        let sσ' = remove((t',t''),p(wn,f))(sσ) **in**

        (t''',(cσ',wσ)) **end**,

       _ → (t''',(cσ,wσ))

  end end end end

Annotations V: Each work station is willing to engage in co–operation with any client. Once such a client has been identified (cn, cσ), a work station step can be made. If the client script is empty no step action can be performed. A work station step action is either a function performing action, or a release action. Both lead to the removal of the causing directive. Script *go to* directives are ignored (by work station steps). They can be dispensed by client steps. Function performing actions may lead to further work station steps.

Discussion. We have sketched a semi–abstract notion of transaction flow. A syntactic notion of directives and scripts have been defined. And the behavioural semantics of scripts as interpreted by clients and work stations. We emphasize that the model given so far is one of the domain. This is reflected in the many non–deterministic choices expressed in the model, and hence in the seemingly "erratic", unsystematic and not necessarily "exhaustive" behaviours made possible by the model. We shall comment on a number of these. See the client behaviour: Whether or not a client is step is possible, the client may choose to remain idle. See the client idle behaviour: The client may choose to remain idle for any time interval, that is "across" time points at which the script may contain directives "timed" for action. Now we turn to the client step behaviour. The purpose of the client step behaviour is to lead up to a client to (2) work station visit: Several 'goto work station' directives may be prescribed to occur sometime during a time interval "surrounding" the "current" time t of the client: $t' \leq t \leq t''$. Which one is chosen is not specified. In fact, one could argue that we are over–specifying the domain. A client may choose to go to a work station ahead of time: $t < t' \leq t''$. or late: $t' \leq t'' < t$. We leave such a domain "relaxation" as an exercises to the reader. If there are no selectable 'goto work station' directive, time (t) is stepped up by a fixed amount, but, again, one could choose any positive increment, but that would make no difference as it would just "reduce" (correspond) to the client idle behaviour. The client to (2) work station visit (c2ws_visit) behaviour models the interface between *clients* and *work stations* as seen from the *client* side. That "same" interface as seen from the side of *work stations* is modelled by the two formula lines surrounding the formula line in which the 'work station step' behaviour is invoked. We now turn to work station step behaviour. This is the behaviour "where things get done!". The behaviours described above effected the flow. Now we describe the work. And the work is done by performing functions. Here it should be recalled that when a client interacts with a work station both their states are "present". This is amply illustrated in the work station step behaviour. The functions to be performed apply to both client and work station states, and may affect both.

If the script is empty nothing more can be done — so we are finished. If the script is not empty then we can assert that the work station step time interval argument is one for which an entry can be, and is, selected from the script — non–deterministically. That entry can (thus) be either of several: It can be a perform directive aimed at the present work station — in which case the designated function is acted upon, the directive is removed from the script, and another step is encouraged. It can be a release directive — in which case the client is released, becoming an unengaged client again after the release directive has been removed. Or it can be any other directive (other perform directives, aimed at other work stations, or go to directives) — in which case the client is likewise "released", but the directive is not removed. Observe the looseness of description. Besides including all the possibly desirable behaviours, the full model above also allows for such behaviours as could be described as being sloppy, delinquent, or even outright criminal. This concludes our sketch model of transaction scripts and their intended work flow.

4   Conclusion

4.1   Summary and Discussion

We have tried to conjure an image of a notion of infrastructure components. We have brought forward both a question and a number of fragments of concurrency and type/value models of such infrastructure components. And we have tried encircle the problem: Namely trying to answer the question "*What is an infrastructure?*" by mentioning claimed engineering disciplines of software development: Denotational semantics, process algebras (concurrency), type/value systems, logics, including modal logics, agents and linguistics.

Our attempt at "decomposing" development of software into "featuring" denotational, concurrency, type/value, knowledge and other engineering considerations is, somehow, orthogonal (read: Complementary to) to Michael Jackson's work on *Problem Frames* [12].

An Apology: It is lamentable that my examples did not illustrate uses of other than RSL [10]. It ought also have contained examples of uses of one or another Duration Calculus [5, 14, 8, 4, 9, 7, 6]. Especially since I brought an example which excudes temporalities. I really apologise.

Infrastructure Models and Abstract Specification. UNU/IIST, had to address issues of developing countries, and newly industrialised countries, and thus had to address issues of (i) infrastructures, (ii) self–sufficiency and (iii) self–reliance. We found that we could do so, believably, with respect to all three facets mentioned above (i–ii–iii), by applying the dogmas of: domain engineering, and abstract (hence: Formal) specification. And we found that our Fellows had little problem in learning and practising this! Myths about so–called "Formal Methods" were — I should say — decisively dispelled.

4.2 "What Is an Infrastructure?"

Perhaps the question is an ill–posed question? One that does not make sense! Are the infrastructure components so complex, anyway, as to escape simple characterisations? Perhaps! Do they not, these components, encompass the whole spectrum of all the applications to which we put computers? Perhaps! &c. We shall, persist, however, and try a fourth attempt at an answer. One that seems "a cop out", an "escape from under the rug!"

A Fourth Answer. An infrastructure is a collection of infrastructure components. There is synchronisation and communication between and within the components. The transaction script example is claimed to illustrate some facets of this.

An infrastructure component is a language: The professional, specialised jargon language spoken by professionals and users of the infrastructure component. We have, in Section 3.1, mentioned several such languages: The language of "the market"; the language of logistics; the language of health–care, and the language of transaction scripts and directives; &c.

Through the transaction script abstraction of work flow systems we have modelled verbs of these languages in terms of behaviours over states and events. So infrastructure components are seen as "computing systems" although they are not necessarily computable!

A Possible Impact of Computing Science upon Infrastructures. If, what we are saying above, has any relevance, then it is perhaps this: That in future business process re–engineering (BPR) of infrastructure components the BPR engineer may be well served in being fluent in — and in using — the kind of informatics and computing science concepts exemplified by this paper.

It is all a matter of language!

4.3 10 Years of UNU/IIST

Having "founded" UNU/IIST, of course, makes my next statements rather biased. I believe that UNU/IIST — exactly in spanning computer and computing science with software engineering (along the lines of denotational, concurrency, temporal and type/value engineering) was able to contribute (i) socio–economically, helping its "client" countries in easening their way towards software reliance and self–sufficiency, (ii) "informatically" to better understanding problems of infrastructure component computing systems development, (iii) programming methodologically by researching and developing principles and techniques for development of software for infrastructure components, and (iv) scientifically in providing firmer theoretical bases for the development of real–time, embedded, safety critical systems. Macau, in the 1990s, was not like Florence of the Renaissance. For that to have been the case we needed even more generous support from our sponsors   and Mr. Stanley Ho and others are not the Medicis of our day — and Macau was not exactly at the science cross–roads. But I think we did rather well in comparison.

When I started in Macau, my dear friends, at the Academy and at universities in China, asked: *"How big will the Institute be; how many staff?"*. When I answered, casually, and truthfully: *"Oh, I guess, some 6–8 scientists, some 6 administrative staff and some 12–24 Fellows!"*, they rather immediately lost interest. Big was important. When I left after five years we had been far more productive in science and, to some extent in advanced engineering, than most of their departments. I believe there is no secret here: We were, and they still are, two well–fitted, harmonious groups, both understanding the didactics of one anothers' fields and disciplines; both supporting each other; and in a well-defined area. We did not, as do usual departments, have to cover "the world". Small, if not 'important' in the eyes of politicians, can be beautiful.

Let us wish that UNU/IIST can continue along its course: improving here and there, adjusting here and there, diversifying just a bit, not too much. *"If it works, don't fix it,"* the saying goes. It works.

Acknowledgements

UNU/IIST, in my days, owed its successes to several groups of people.

To my colleagues at the IBM Vienna Laboratory of the early 1970s, when VDM was first conceived: To the late Hans Bekič, to Peter Lucas, Kurt Walk, Cliff Jones and others, and to the visitors at IBM: Dana Scott, John Reynolds, and many others.

To the Board Members of UNU/IIST with whose much appreciated support we were able to "fight" some myths. Perhaps that Board did not know it, but they were really of immense help. A delight to work for.

More generally, to the computing scientists who have inspired us in what we had propagated: The members of IFIP WG 2.1, WG 2.2 and WG 2.3 — Manfred Broy, Sir Tony Hoare, Michael Jackson, Cliff Jones, Jayadev Misra, Carroll Morgan, David Parnas, Amir Pnueli, Natarajan Shankar, Douglas R. Smith, and several of whom came to visit us at Macau (Egidio Astesiano, Hans Langmaack, J S. Moore, Wlad Turski, etc.). As well as to many others.

To the devoted and loyal staff and Fellows of UNU/IIST:

To the lovely ladies of the administrative staff who now for many, many years have endured these strange scientists and their fellows, who have ensured our daily, smooth operations, and who have stood by, in physical as well as mental typhoons; to the 77 Fellows who had visited UNU/IIST by June 1997; and to the professional staff: To Mrs. Margaret Stewart, my Financial & Administrative officer, and to such wonderful scientists as: Zhou Chaochen, Søren Prehn, Chris George, Dang Van Hung, Xu Qi Wen, Tomasz Janowski, Richard Moore, and Kees Middelburg — while I was in charge. What more can one want?

My most emotional thanks, perhaps, goes to Zhou Chao Chen: Thanks for your readiness to take charge, thanks for all the loyal support during the "mental typhoons", and thanks for your wise and wonderful way of continuing UNU/IIST. Like me, You will be very proud of what has been achieved here. Thanks.

I also think it appropriate here to commemorate the memory of the late Dr. António Rodrigues Juniór, the Macau Foundation President, who, on behalf of the Macau Government, helped UNU/IIST through many, many years, but whose untimely passing away saddened us all deeply. *God Bless his Soul.*

Bibliographical Notes

A book has just been published: *Specification Studies in RAISE.* It is edited by Chris George, Tomasz Janowski, Richard Moore, and Dan Van Hung. It is published, early 2002, in the Springer–Verlag UK FACT series [13]. It contains so many relevant papers and references that the below should suffice.

References

1. Dines Bjørner. Domain Models of "The Market" — in Preparation for E–Transaction Systems. In *Practical Foundations of Business and System Specifications (Eds.: Haim Kilov and Ken Baclawski),* page 34 pages, The Netherlands, December 2002. Kluwer Academic Press.
2. Dines Bjørner. *"What is a Method?"* — *An Essay of Some Aspects of Software Engineering,* chapter 9, pages 175–203. Monographs in Computer Science. IFIP: International Federation for Information Processing. Springer Verlag, New York, N.Y., USA, 2003. Programming Methodology: Recent Work by Members of IFIP Working Group 2.3. Eds.: Annabelle McIver and Carrol Morgan. .
3. Dines Bjørner. *The SE Book: Principles and Techniques of Software Engineering,* volume I: Abstraction & Modelling (750 pages), II: Descriptions and Domains (est.: 500 pages), III: Requirements, Software Design and Management (est. 450 pages). [Publisher currently (June 2003) being negotiated], 2003–2004.
4. Zhou Chaochen. Duration Calculi: An Overview. In *Proceedings of Formal Methods in Programming and Their Applications, D. Bjørner, M Broy, and I.V. Pottosin (Eds.),* pages 256–266. LNCS 735, Springer-Verlag, 1993.
5. Zhou Chaochen, C.A.R. Hoare, and A.P. Ravn. A Calculus of Durations. *Information Processing Letters,* 40(5):269–276, 1991.
6. Zhou Chaochen, Dang Van Hung, and Li Xiaoshan. A duration calculus with infinite intervals. In *Fundamentals of Computation Theory, Horst Reichel (Ed.),* pages 16–41. LNCS 965, Springer-Verlag, 1995.
7. Zhou Chaochen, Zhang Jingzhong, Yang Lu, and Li Xiaoshan. Linear duration invariants. In *Formal Techniques in Real-Time and Fault-Tolerant Systems, H. Langmack, W.-P. de Roever, and J. Vytopil (Eds.),* pages 86–109. LNCS 863, Springer-Verlag, 1994.

8. Zhou Chaochen, A.P. Ravn, and M.R. Hansen. An extended duration calculus for hybrid systems. In R.L. Grossman, A. Nerode, A.P. Ravn, and H. Rischel, editors, *Hybrid Systems*, volume 736 of *Lecture Notes in Computer Science*, pages 36–59. Springer-Verlag, 1993.

9. Zhou Chaochen and Li Xiaoshan. A mean value calculus of durations. In A.W. Roscoe, editor, *A Classical Mind: Essays in Honour of C.A.R. Hoare*, pages 431–451. Prentice Hall International, 1994.

10. Chris George, Peter Haff, Klaus Havelund, Anne Haxthausen, Robert Milne, Claus Bendix Nielsen, Søren Prehn, and Kim Ritter Wagner. *The RAISE Specification Language*. The BCS Practitioner Series. Prentice-Hall, Hemel Hampstead, England, 1992.

11. Chris George, Anne Haxthausen, Steven Hughes, Robert Milne, Søren Prehn, and Jan Storbank Pedersen. *The RAISE Method*. The BCS Practitioner Series. Prentice-Hall, Hemel Hampstead, England, 1995.

12. Michael A. Jackson. *Problem Frames — Analysing and structuring software development problems*. ACM Press, Pearson Education. Addison–Wesley, Edinburgh Gate, Harlow CM20 2JE, England, 2001.

13. Hung Dang Van, Chris George, Tomasz Janowski, and Richard Moore, editors. *Specification Case Studies in RAISE*. FACIT: Formal Approaches to Computing and Information Technology. Springer–Verlag, April 2002. ISBN 1-85233-359-6.

14. Liu Zhiming, A.P. Ravn, E.V. Sørensen, and Zhou Chaochen. A probabilistic duration calculus. In H. Kopetz and Y. Kakuda, editors, *Responsive Computer Systems*, volume 7 of *Dependable Computing and Fault-Tolerant Systems*, pages 30–52. Springer Verlag Wien New York, 1993.

A Formal Basis
for Some Dependability Notions

Cliff B. Jones

School of Computing Science,
University of Newcastle
NE1 7RU, UK
`cliff.jones@ncl.ac.uk`

Abstract. This paper shows how formal methods ideas can be used to clarify basic notions used in the field of dependability. Central to this endeavour is fixing a notion of system. Relationships between systems are also considered: in particular, the importance of the situation where one system is generated by another (possibly human) system is explored. The formalisation is used as a basis for definitions of the notions of *fault, error* and *failure*. Some applications to examples from the dependability literature and extensions of the basic model of system are also sketched.

1   Introduction

This paper is written by a researcher from the "formal methods" community who has been trying to understand notions used in work on "Dependability". The term *dependability* is used broadly to cover many aspects such as reliability, integrity, correctness (with respect to a specification), availability, security and privacy. To begin to understand such a range of concepts, this paper starts at the bottom: the notions of *fault, error, failure* in [Lap92,Ran00]) appear to be both useful and widely accepted. The idea here is to offer definitions of these terms with respect to a particular notion of what constitutes a *system*. This choice is discussed in Section 2 and an initial formalisation is outlined in Section 3. More realistic notions of system are discussed in Section 5.

The intention here is not to offer formalism for its own sake. In fact, the details of the particular notation etc. are unimportant. The hope is that understanding can be increased by building on a firm foundation. The first fruits of the formalisation are given in Section 4 where, among other things, some relationships between systems are explored: the propagation of *fault, error, failure* chains where one system is *built on* another system is well understood; many of the failure propagation situations of interest in socio-technical systems arise where one system is *created by* another. Lastly, the idea of one system being *deployed with* another system is considered.

A concluding section lists some topics for further work including how the system notion can be enriched.

B.K. Aichernig and T. Maibaum (Eds.): Formal Methods ..., LNCS 2757, pp. 191–206, 2003.

2   Systems

There are many, rather different, things that can be loosely viewed as "systems". Few would decline to use the term for an airline seat reservation system. In such a system it is easy to see an interface and the effect of using this interface. For example, requests can be made and information displayed that reflects the contents of a "database"; other interactions change the database of reservations so that (as well as reserving a seat for a passenger) similar requests for information at two points in time give different results. Other computer systems are linked to processes that evolve autonomously. In, say, an automatic braking system (ABS) for a car, the speed of rotation of a wheel is influenced by the friction of the road surface which is not under control of the ABS[1]. Less conventionally, the "system" notion here includes those where humans play an essential role. The adjective "socio-technical" is often used for such systems. The term *computer-based system* is used here to indicate that, while a computer is involved, a study of the system which ignores the human involvement is hopelessly inadequate. The emphasis in the *Interdisciplinary Research Collaboration* (IRC) on the *Dependability of Computer-Based Systems*[2] is on such systems. Although taken for granted here, it is not difficult to argue that a computer-based system can only be made dependable by examining the roles of the people involved. This should not be equated to an attempt to view humans as machines. It can, in fact, be argued that understanding potential human failure is a key step towards designing systems that are safe and pleasant to operate or use.

To indicate the range of things that need to be covered, consider motor cars. At a coarse level, one could distinguish the mechanical car from the human operator or driver. In a modern car, however, the mechanics of the brakes etc. are controlled by computer systems with which the operator actually interacts. A typical linking of three systems (operator, control and (relevant portion of) reality) is pictured in Figure 1[3]. Each of these three classes of system has distinct properties. An operator is likely to make unpredictable errors[4] whose frequency will vary over time; the likelihood of such errors will be influenced by how easy it is to understand the interface of the control system. The control system receives signals from actuators operated by the human and from sensors that are intended to measure aspects of reality. To earn the name "control system", it would have some degree of autonomy in sending signals to the actuators; it would also provide feedback to the operator. The reality is a system itself which will evolve even without inputs: for example, a car will continue to move while the driver tries to decelerate. Each of the components indicated in Figure 1 can be

---

[1] Such systems are called "open" in [Kop02a] in contrast to a "closed" system where all essential interactions are under control of the program. The target formalisation must cover both closed and open systems. See [Kop02b] for more on Real-Time Systems.

[2] *DIRC*: Consult www.dirc.org.uk for information about the Dependability IRC.

[3] The additional concept of an *advisory system*, together with an analysis of its failure modes, is studied in [SO02] .

[4] See [Rea90] for a classification of human errors.

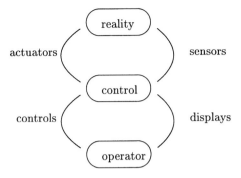

Fig. 1. A controlled system

viewed as a system. The notion is also recursive in that the whole can be usefully viewed as one system for some purposes; it is also easy to see that each of the systems might be further decomposed.

Because there can be several interlinked systems to consider, there is always a danger of confusion over *system boundaries*. A lack of exactness here can give rise to pointless debates about the cause of a problem with a system. The topic of *system boundaries* is picked up in Section 4.2.

For many systems, it is useful to discuss a distinction between their externally observable behaviour (a "black box" view) and their internal design. For example, a "transparent box" view of computer software involves looking at its code. Many interesting properties of a system can be discussed via its "black box" view that concerns *only* the behaviour at its interface. To make these issues precise, it is time to turn to the topic of formalisation.

3   Formalisation

This section initiates the formalisation effort by considering simple systems; this is not the limit of ambition of the paper but even such simple systems suffice to illustrate some benefits of formalisation. The notion of system is enriched in Sections 4.3 and 5. What follows is not claimed to be deep: it is a selection of known concepts from formal development methods. The intention is to show that these ideas make it possible to discuss core dependability notions more precisely than in the absence of a formal foundation.

3.1   Simple Systems

To view something as a system, it is necessary to choose an interface. An interface offers a collection of ways of interacting with a system: here, interaction points are termed "operations". So, for example, a seat reservation system is likely to offer some enquiry operations and others for reserving places. One requirement, then, for pinning down an interface to a system is to list its operations. For a simple (computer) system, each operation is likely to have a name. In addition to the name of each operation, it is likely that there will be information that is either required as input to narrow down the operation (parameters to an enquiry might be starting and finishing locations) or information which is returned as a result of the operation[5]. The parameters and results of software operations are normally recorded by some form of type annotation but, rather than worrying about a specific notation for this, there is a more fundamental concept to be understood.

If systems with even simple databases are to be described, it is necessary to find a way of discussing how operations are affected by –and in turn affect– that database. The notion of *state* can be used to generalise situations from those where a system updates a simple counter to those where a large database is required. Thus the formalisation of the behaviour of an operation will relate, not only its parameters and results, but also state values. Is it true that all systems, have a state? Strictly, no! A pure function like square root could well deliver the same result (for a given parameter) at any time; even a sorting system might behave like a mathematical function whose result does not depend in any way on the history of its use. Be that as it may, it is useful to say that systems do have states and to regard functions as a special case.

So a system will be characterised by its states and its set of operations. To go further, formulae will be used — but remember what is made clear in the introduction: these formulae indicate a possible notation; they are not the main point of the paper[6].

A description[7] of a system comprises a class of states (Σ) and a set of named operations. The states used in a specification will typically be an abstraction of those of any particular implementation. The set of states can be defined, for example, as VDM objects with the possible use of a *data type invariant* which records that subset of the overall set of objects that can arise.

In simple cases, each operation OP_i would be a function from states to states OP_i: $\Sigma \to \Sigma$. More generally, operations are not defined for all possible starting states (or combinations of states and parameters). The fact that operations can be *partial* is recorded in VDM or B by noting a *pre-condition* that defines, what might be called, the "termination set" of an operation. (The notion of a pre-condition is a simple example of an assumption about the deployment of a system; this is key to the discussion in Section 4.4.)

The topic on *non-determinism* is important even for systems which will actually behave deterministically (i.e. always deliver the same final state and result for a given starting state and parameters). It is often convenient in a specifica-

---

[5] One could discuss whether there is a single "reserve" operation or a whole set thereof; for practical purposes it is worth grouping like operations together even though this necessitates separating the idea of parameters and results.

[6] The notation used here is motivated by VDM (cf. [Jon90]) but avoids specific details and could trivially be translated into other notations such as Z (cf. [Hay93]) or B (cf. [Abr96]).

[7] The term *specification* indicates some official status; it is often more useful to discuss "descriptions" of systems. There can be different descriptions for different purposes.

tion or description of a system to leave open the possibility of different results. In order to record this, the effect of an operation is given by a relation over states.

Thus, the termination set for OP_i is a set of states $T_i\colon \mathcal{P}\Sigma$ and the result is a relation over states $M_i\colon \mathcal{P}(\Sigma \times \Sigma)$. It is required for $Op_i = (T_i, M_i)$ that the meaning relation gives possible results for any state in the termination set $T_i \subseteq \mathbf{dom}\, M_i$.

To make this more concrete, consider the following description of a *Stack* of natural numbers ($\mathbb{N}$). A suitable model of the state is a sequence of those numbers that have been *Pushed* onto the *Stack* but not *Popped* off: $\Sigma = \mathbb{N}^*$. A plausible list of operations might be $Ops = \{Init, Push(i), Pop, Top, IsEmpty\}$. The *Pop* operation ($Pop = (T_{Pop}, M_{Pop})$) only works (is defined) for non-empty states and removes the top element of a stack (but returns no result)

$$T_{Pop} = \{l \in \mathbb{N}^* \mid \mathbf{len}\, l \neq 0\}$$

To emphasise that the meaning can be stated as a relation, it is written as

$$M_{Pop} = \{([e] \frown l, l) \mid \ldots\}$$

Notice that $T_{Pop} \subseteq \mathbf{dom}\, M_{Pop}$ but that the meaning relation would not be defined for empty starting states.

In this case, the result is deterministic but the same style could be used to specify an operation that yielded an arbitrary element of the stack

$$M_{Arb} = \{(l, l(i)) \mid 1 \leq i \leq \mathbf{len}\, l\}$$

3.2   Concepts from Development Methods

There are a number of established development methods (e.g. VDM [Jon90] or B [Abr96]) that are built around state-based specifications and which contain useful, thought out, concepts that can be utilised when discussing systems.

The cornerstone of any formal development method is a precise notion of a specification. The desirability of separating a specification from any implementation is one of the tenets of this paper. It could be extremely wasteful if users were forced to understand the detail of an implementation in order to use an artifact. Moreover, denying users a specification is likely to result in them detecting properties that the developer regards as accidental; but any subsequent change of these "irrelevant details" might offend the users. A classic example of this was seen when early computer architectures were simulated on newer, faster, machines: users frequently found that their legacy programs no longer worked because they had relied on undocumented features of the instruction set. Crucially, it is difficult to see how an engineering process can be used to create a system where there is no initial notion of specifying the required properties of the to-be-created artifact. The concept of what is required might evolve (see Section 5) but at any time there ought be something other than the implementation which defines the functionality.

There are different styles of specifications and there was at one time a claimed dichotomy between model-oriented and property-oriented specifications but this is now largely resolved by recognising that *property-oriented* specifications are more conveniently used for basic data types whereas *model-oriented* specifications are better for systems with more complex states.

A *model-oriented* specification (as in VDM, Z or B) is built around a *state* that is an abstraction of internal values retained by a system between uses. The *Stack* example above retains the elements that have been *Pushed* onto (but not yet *Popped* from) the stack; many operating systems store user preferences (and maybe desktops) between invocations; or a database system might contain enormous amounts of data about an enterprise. It is important to remember that a good specification will be built around an *abstract* state and the VDM literature (e.g. [Jon90, pp 216–219]) includes a discussion of specification "bias" and offers a precise test for sufficiently abstract states[8]. For now, it is only necessary to accept that the idea of using an abstract state in a specification does not constrain implementations. What is specified is the behaviour as observed via the operations of a system; the state is a convenience for the description[9].

Methods like VDM offer a precise notion of what it means for a system to *satisfy* a specification. In fact, this question can be addressed at the level of specifications. To say that system B satisfies the specification of system A, is to claim that for each operation of A, there is one in B that respects the specification in A. An operation b respects a if it terminates for at least the required termination set of a and is more deterministic than a (over the termination set of a). Formally OP_i **sat** OP_s where $OP = (T, M)$ iff $T_s \subseteq T_i$ and $T_s \lhd M_i \subseteq M_s$. There are important properties of this relation: it is, for example, reflexive and transitive; furthermore, a reasonable set of programming constructs are monotone in the relation. These mathematically expressed properties make for a useful development method[10].

There are two approaches to such proofs. The most commonly used *data reification* proof obligation in VDM relies on finding a *retrieve function* (homomorphism) from the state of the implementation to that of the specification. This rule suffices for most steps of development but is based on the assump-

---

[8] An unbiased state is one whose equality can be tested by the operations of a system.

[9] Because of the widespread literature on property-oriented specifications, it is worth pausing to repeat comparisons that are elaborated elsewhere (e.g. [Jon89,Jon99]). In the 1980s, model-oriented specification methods were much less written about than so-called "Algebraic Specifications" of data types [AKKB99]. The objective of an *algebraic specification* is to fix the meaning of the operations (or functions) solely in terms of their interrelationships. For example, in an algebraic description of a *Stack*, a key equation is $pop(push(i, s)) = s$. It is actually interesting that such descriptions can ever fix a system and it does work for small systems like a simple stack. In some cases, the implied model (technically, equivalence classes of the word algebra of the functions) is by no means minimal and even –for example– a definition of a *Queue* is far less obvious than that of a *Stack*.

[10] A discussion of "compositionality", its importance, and why it is much harder to achieve for concurrent programs can be found in [Jon00].

tion that development always proceeds by adding detail. Lynn Marshall [Mar86] identified an important case where this was not true and a complete rule that uses a relation between the specification and representation states is described in [Nip86,Nip87].

The topic of concurrency has proved challenging for formalisation. Whereas the appropriate form of specification for sequential systems is uncontroversial, pinning down a suitable specification notion for concurrent systems has led to many experiments. The key challenge (see [Jon00,dR01]) has been to support *compositional* development of concurrent systems. One approach is the use of rely and guarantee-predicates to record assumptions and limits of *interference* for an operation. Although [Jon83,Stø90,Col94] etc. apply the idea to shared-variable concurrent systems, it is not difficult to argue that the notion of interference is at the heart of what is meant by concurrency and that taming it is also essential in communication-based concurrency such as embodied in process algebras. (Stirling describes a related approach in [Sti88].) While the details of such approaches to concurrency are not germane here, it is important for Section 4.4 to observe that concurrent operations can also be described formally including assumptions on the environment in which the operations will be deployed.

For what follows, the single most important point from this section is that there is a precise notion of satisfying a specification.

4   Some Uses of the Formalisation

This section begins to explore what can do done with the formalisation of even simple systems.

4.1   Dependability Notions

The division of what might loosely be called "problems" into faults, errors and failures in [Lap92,Ran00] is a significant contribution to our ability to discuss causes and effects. This section re-examines this basic terminology with reference to the notions in Section 3.

The term *failure* in [Lap92,Ran00] is described as "A system *failure* occurs when the delivered service deviates from fulfilling the system *function*, the latter being what the system is *aimed at*." (all emphasis in the original). Presumably the intention of the phrase "what the system is aimed at" is to acknowledge that a specification could itself be wrong or even not exist. The position taken here is that an implementation can only be judged to fail if there is a specification against which a deviation can be identified. Thus, a failure of an operation is a behaviour that is not in accordance with the specification of that operation. (Questions of missing or erroneous specifications are addressed in Section 4.3.) An appropriate definition might therefore be

> A system *failure* (with respect to a specification) occurs when the delivered service deviates from that specification.

Brian Randell in [Ran00] has made the additional point that failure is a *judgement* that is made by another system. This observation sits nicely with the view here. Clearly, one system can observe the behaviour of another and emit messages that claim to report the detection of erroneous results. But such *Beckmesser*-like systems are potentially just adding confusion unless their complaints are based on a specification of the required behaviour. As the allusion to *Die Meistersinger* indicates, the judging system could well be human. It could also be wrong (in its judgements)! It is illuminating to consider how the notion of one system judging another ties in with law courts. There is a pleasing recursiveness in the way that a higher court can sit in judgement on the decisions of a lower court and that judgement is in turn subject to the review of a yet higher court. It is also known for non-legal institutions (history or –more worryingly– the press) to express opinions on the wisdom of judgements from even the highest courts. Courts do, of course, make their judgements against a codified specification of behaviour: the law. They rely on evidence of deviations from the law. It is thus possible to have a system in which error reports from some sub-systems are "ignored" or overridden in a larger system.

To return to the domain of computer (based) systems, the main point being made here is that the notion of a failure can only be judged against a specification and such a judgement can only be made by another system. As indicated in Section 3.2, a specification is anyway required in order for any plausible development process to deliver a product that has a chance of satisfying its specification[11].

The description of *errors* in [Ran00] is worded in terms of a state ("An *error* is that part of the system state which is *liable* to lead to subsequent failure; an error affecting the service is an indication that a failure occurs or has occurred.") which fits well with the state and system notions of Section 3. It is quite reasonable to say that an underlying cause (fault) can give rise to erroneous values in a state (the question of whether this is the abstract state is considered below). The qualification "liable to lead to subsequent failure" can be taken to indicate that erroneous values in a state might never be detected. This situation can arise if particular sequences of operations are avoided (e.g. recording a wrong salary in a database might not be detected if the employee leaves the organisation). Erroneous values in a state *can* result in failure – but whether or not they do depends on the operations used.

One might question whether the wording "that part of the system state" precisely accords with the definition given here but this question can only be judged by the original authors. The definition suggested here is

> An *error* is present when the state of a system is inconsistent with that required by the specification.

There are actually two sorts of inconsistencies to be considered. The implementation state is likely to be a reification of that in the specification (a set might

---

[11] Thus far, only logical failure of a single invocation of an operation has been considered; in order to discuss stochastic properties it is obviously necessary to define requirements on (or measure) multiple observations.

be represented by, say, a doubly-linked list). If the retrieved state is not that required by a specification, then subsequent operations can expose a wrong result. When this happens an error has occurred and a subsequent failure may follow. But it is also possible that the representation state is internally inconsistent (e.g. forward and backward list pointers do not agree): in this case an implementation can malfunction in ways which are not easy to predict from the specification. There is here a subtle question about the level of abstraction of the notion of state in the definition of "error". It is certainly desirable to be able to describe behaviour in terms of abstractions of particular state representations chosen in implementations. Unfortunately faults can manifest themselves at a low level of abstraction. This is a serious obstacle and is one that is likely to need some layering idea in the implementation to contain errors of this kind.

It is a corollary of the definition of fault given here that

> Whether or not a failure occurs depends on operations invoked subsequently

The notion that something causes the erroneous state which has been taken to be the internal manifestation of an error is useful. But the notion of *fault* is described in [Ran00], "The *adjudged or hypothesised cause* of an error is a *fault*." Invoking judgement here could be argued to confound a cause and the process of determining that cause. It might be preferable to be more definite about the link with errors — here, the definition

> The cause of an error is a *fault*

is suggested. It is of course true that attributing the cause is a judgement (which can be erroneous). But as with failure, this is the task of a separate system. It is interesting to observe that any judgement of what fault caused an error is likely to need access to the internals ("transparent box" view) of a system.

In the definitions offered here, there is a clear separation between what might be thought of as absolute truth and the judgements which are made about failures and their causes. The notion of probability has also been avoided so far by focusing on single failures; the separation of logical and stochastic properties is maintained until some other issues are clear.

4.2   System Boundaries

A source of significant confusion in trying to attribute faults/errors/failures is the question of which system is being discussed at any point in time. Behind the whole of this section so far is the assumption that the boundary of a system is agreed. While this will not always be the case, it must be clear that little consensus or understanding can follow from a discussion where the boundary of a system is itself a matter of dispute. For example, a discussion of a rail disaster between someone who observes the effect of a broken rail on a high speed train and someone who is claiming that long term financing is the cause of all ills is unlikely to be edifying. An agreement on the nesting of systems might help the discussants understand each others' viewpoint.

It is not always true that the boundary of a system is a clear and static concept. Even before coming to socio-technical systems below, there are difficulties to be considered. The topic of multiple interfaces is considered in Section 5. It is also true that interfaces can change over time: on the micro-level, the topic of *rendez-vous* is also considered in Section 5. But the question of interfaces which actually evolve is a whole avenue of research which is recently receiving attention (e.g. [JRW02]).

4.3   Systems That Create Systems

A significant contribution of the separation of faults/errors/failures is that the terms can be used to explain causal chains with the failure of one system giving rise to a fault in another. This is easy to see in the case where system B is *built on* system A. An example is where software runs on some hardware in which an (uncorrected) hardware memory problem gives rise to a failure of the hardware to meet its specification; this is seen as a fault for the software (that is likely to result in an erroneous value in the state of the running program). The purpose of this section is to explore another relationship between systems.

The fact that a failure in one system can cause a fault in another is particularly interesting in the case where one system *creates* another. A simple case of this is a manufacturing system that creates products: many sorts of failure in manufacturing can result in faulty products. A specific example with computer software is that a failure in a compiler can introduce faults into a program which would have otherwise fulfilled its specification.

Thus a failure of the creating system A can give rise to a fault in the created system B. The interest in DIRC extends to systems in which humans play a role both by interacting with a final system and by their involvement in creating such a system. In the former case, the concern might be with the way a system embeds in a group of people; in the latter case, the consequences of the fact that humans design or implement a system are considered.

One can view –as a system– the organisation that creates another system. Thus the development organisation which designs and develops a program can be thought of as a system that creates programs. These programs can, in turn, be seen as systems which create computations[12].

In an example like the Therac-25 [LT93], it is clear that failures in the development organisation created a system that contained potentially fatal faults. The deployed system included a faulty program and physical apparatus without

---

[12] It is worth saying a word in defence of the much maligned programmer: there is an inherent difficulty in writing a program which will be mindlessly executed by a computer. When constructing instructions for humans, there is the chance that a stupid instruction will be questioned. One only need look at the chaos created by the "work to rule" form of industrial action to see that humans rarely follow rules as mindlessly as computers. Computers derive their power and their weakness from the fact that they always work to rule!

a secondary hardware guard. One can go further and analyse faults in the development process and how they might have been caused by management failures but that is not the objective here.

Good software development processes use some form of review or inspection. This is a place where the program text (i.e. the "transparent box" view) is necessary; this would also be true if one were trying to make the judgement – without testing– whether a program was "fit for purpose". This is a form of fault-tolerance applied within the development process. As in most human processes, inspections etc. apply some form of (human) diversity to increase the chance of catching errors.

It is now easy to deal with the issue –alluded to in Section 4.1– of missing or erroneous specifications. The position taken above is that the judgement that a system fails can only be made against a specification. What if the "specification is wrong"? Presumably, this means that the specification is in some sense inappropriate; the specification might be precise, but it can be seen to result in faults and failures in a bigger system. For example, a specification might state that a developer can assume that the user will respond in one micro-second — but failing to so do can result is fatal consequences. The developer writes a program which "times out" after one micro-second and an accident occurs. It is surely not right to say that the software system (which meets its specification) is failing. Nor, of course, is it reasonable to blame "operator error" with such an unreasonable assumption. The only reasonable conclusion is that it is an earlier system which exhibited erroneous behaviour: the act of producing the silly specification itself is the failure that causes a fault in the combined system of software and operator. The judgement that a specification is "silly" must of course be made by another (external) system. A similar argument can be made for missing specifications: an engineering process requires a reference point.

There is one more relationship between systems that is interesting to consider: the idea of *deploying* one system with another has already been hinted at and is discussed in more detail in the next section.

4.4   Deploying Systems

A system A can be deployed with another B [13] and they may, or may not, live happily ever after. Even with the simplest of systems discussed above, operations were specified with pre-conditions. For an artificially created system, the assumptions (pre-conditions) are an invitation to the developer to ignore certain possibilities. It is clear that robust systems should avoid unnecessary assumptions but almost no useful system can be created without some assumptions. It is also this author's experience that specifiers are much more likely to overlook assumptions (pre or rely-conditions) than to fail to describe the intended function.

It is a mistake to deploy two systems which do not respect each others assumptions. Thus, a deployment of the *Stack* in a situation where more *Pop* than

---

[13] It is tempting to think of this relationship between systems as embedding one system in another; here a more symmetrical view like a cross-product is preferred.

Push operations can be used is a faulty deployment and is likely to result in a failure of the combined system.

Section 3.2 refers to work on concurrency that enriches the notion of assumptions and commitments by using rely and guarantee predicates. These can be used to discuss the appropriate deployment of systems whose behaviour is influenced by concurrent processes.

Nothing in the idea of recording assumptions makes, in itself, deployment safer. It is like recording warnings on the box of an electrical product: if the warnings are ignored, the customer might still be electrocuted. But the recording of assumptions does, like the commitment part of a specification, at least make it possible for the deployment process to be undertaken circumspectly.

The discussion in this section also links to hazard analysis in that there is now a prompt to distinguish between hazards which can result from components failing to satisfy their specifications and deployment errors where (assumptions of) specifications do not match.

4.5   Error Recovery

There is an extensive literature on "fault tolerance" and "error recovery". Given the definitions chosen in Section 4.1, it should be clear why the latter term is preferred here. Space does not permit a full analysis of concepts like forward and backward error recovery or exception handling here but some simple points are worth making.

It is well understood that simple replication redundancy (as in "Triple Modular Redundancy") can be used to guard against random faults or decay. Software can deploy *redundancy* in a way which prevents single faults coming from data corruptions resulting in failures with respect to the specification of the software system. It should also be clear that some form of diversity is required to make any impact on guarding against design failure[14]. Given that the scope of DIRC is computer-*based* systems, the ambition is to be able to describe tolerance of human failures. In this area, the distinctions in [Rea90] between "slips", "rule-based mistakes" and "knowledge-based mistakes" is interesting. It might be possible to record assumptions about certain classes of operator error.

One more topic which is worth addressing is the view that there are often "multiple causes" of a failure. This is commonly discussed in accident postmortems. The point made in Reason's graphic "Swiss Cheese" picture in [Rea97] is that any layer of fault-tolerance will have residual holes (thus the slice of cheese) and that an accident occurs when circumstances are such that the holes coincide. The position here is that *each* of the nested systems has failed. It might also be true that (as in the Therac-25 case) the human system which created the physical system deployed too few layers of protection or that the layers were insufficiently diverse.

---

[14] There is evidence (a joint paper with Ian Hayes and Michael Jackson is making slow progress) that forms of rely-conditions can be used to describe fault tolerance.

4.6   Further Stimuli

It would be profitable to reconsider many of the points made in [Per99] in the light of the formalisation above. To cite just one example, designing the architecture of a system so that user can both understand and predict its behaviour is key to the dependability of computer-based systems.

A related source is the recent research of John Rushby on "pilot errors". Rushy [Rus99] uses finite state diagrams to describe systems. The notion of system description in Section 3 of this paper is more general but would not serve Rushby's aim of automatic analysis. More controversially, Rushby requires a finite state description of the pilot's perception of the control system (in order to perform state exploration and locate inconsistencies). The difficulty of getting users to couch their understanding of a system in this way is conceded in [Rus99]. It would be interesting to explore other approaches (such as rely-conditions) and to question whether the user's view is actually of the control system or of the reality which is ultimately being controlled (see Figure 1).

5   Further Work

This paper makes only a beginning and clearly much more needs to be done with a cooperation between formalists and dependability researchers. Some of these topics require further research but the direction of the work to be done is relatively clear.

The notion of system in Section 3.1 is deliberately simple and there are many ways in which enrichment is desirable. Principal among these is for systems that interface with the physical world where states evolve autonomously.

Many systems deployed in safety-critical applications involve sensors which link to physical phenomena like temperatures. This is of course the distinction referred to above "closed versus open" systems (cf. [Kop02a]). One problem to be faced here is that values are time-indexed quantities. This issue has been faced by several researchers (e.g. Duration calculus, Mahony/Hayes[MH91]).

It is also imperative to recognise that systems themselves evolve. In the DSoS project (Dependable Systems of Systems), building systems from components which are not under the control of a central organisation is a major concern. The interfaces of such components can change without consultation. Rather than just say that such systems will never work, the approach being researched in DSoS is to understand to what extent such interface evolution can be brought under the control of an exception handling view (see [JRW02]).

Another issue which is being considered in the DSoS project is the fact that it is frequently convenient to view a system as having multiple interfaces. Hermann Kopetz talks of service, diagnostic and configuration interfaces. This idea might usefully be generalised because something like evolving the topology of a system is likely to have different behaviour than the basic operation interface. But it does not appear that any new conceptual problems are introduced by splitting the view of a system's interface in this way.

The simple model of Section 3.1 assumes that any operation is executed atomically (without interruption) and also that all operations are available at any time. It is often argued that this is a reason for rejecting this model and moving to a process algebra which can express the fact that the changes in which operations are available can be expressed. In fact, it is not difficult to express interfaces with such a *rendez-vous* behaviour. Several object-oriented languages such as POOL [Ame89] offer, in addition to the methods of a class, a process per class which executes in each object of that class to say which methods are "available" at any time.

There is also the question of the meaning of the notation for describing systems. If development methods are to be based on particular notations for describing systems, there must be a firm semantic foundation in terms of which the correctness of results like the monotonicity of refinement can be argued. For VDM, (sets and) relations suffice (see [Jon87]) to prove, for example, that the satisfaction relation is transitive and that it is monotone in standard program combinators. For the sort of concurrent object-based language mentioned above, the π-calculus (see [MPW92,SW01]) has proved ideal (see [Wal91,Jon94,San99]). For systems that create systems, some form of higher-order π-calculus might be required.

Acknowledgements

This paper owes its inception to the EU-funded project known as "DSoS" (IST-1999-11585) and the author is grateful to colleagues on that project for many useful discussions and patient hearings of early versions of the ideas presented here. The work has also been supported by the EPSRC-funded "Interdisciplinary Research Collaboration" on "Dependability of Computer-Based Systems". Here again members of that project have made many useful comments. The author would like to thank in particular Denis Besnard, Sadie Creese, John Dobson, Ian Hayes, Michael Jackson, Michael Jones, Tony Lawrie, Nick Moffat, Brian Randell, Carles Sala-Oliveras, Ian Sommerville and an anonymous referee for their sustained interest in –and stimulating criticisms of– drafts of the material.

References

[Abr96]   J.-R. Abrial. *The B-Book: Assigning programs to meanings*. Cambridge University Press, 1996.

[AKKB99] Egidio Astesiano, Hans-Jorg Kreowski, and Bernd Krieg-Bruckner, editors. *Algebraic Foundations of Systems Specification*. Springer-Verlag, 1999.

[Ame89]   Pierre America. Issues in the design of a parallel object-oriented language. *Formal Aspects of Computing*, 1(4), 1989.

[Col94]   Pierre Collette. *Design of Compositional Proof Systems Based on Assumption-Commitment Specifications – Application to UNITY*. PhD thesis, Louvain-la-Neuve, June 1994.

[dR01]   W. P. de Roever. *Concurrency Verification: Introduction to Compositional and Noncompositional Methods*. Cambridge University Press, 2001.

[Hay93]   Ian Hayes, editor. *Specification Case Studies*. Prentice Hall International, second edition, 1993.

[Jon83]   C. B. Jones. Specification and design of (parallel) programs. In *Proceedings of IFIP'83*, pages 321–332. North-Holland, 1983.

[Jon87]   C. B. Jones. Program specification and verification in VDM. In M. Broy, editor, *Logic of Programming and Calculi of Discrete Design*, volume 36 of *NATO ASI Series F: Computer and Systems Sciences*, pages 149–184. Springer-Verlag, 1987.

[Jon89]   C. B. Jones. Data reification. In J. A. McDermid, editor, *The Theory and Practice of Refinement*, pages 79–89. Butterworths, 1989.

[Jon90]   C. B. Jones. *Systematic Software Development using VDM*. Prentice Hall International, second edition, 1990. ISBN 0-13-880733-7.

[Jon94]   C. B. Jones. Process algebra arguments about an object-based design notation. In A. W. Roscoe, editor, *A Classical Mind*, chapter 14, pages 231–246. Prentice-Hall, 1994.

[Jon99]   C. B. Jones. Scientific decisions which characterise VDM. In *FM'99 – Formal Methods*, volume 1708 of *Lecture Notes in Computer Science*, pages 28–47. Springer-Verlag, 1999.

[Jon00]   C. B. Jones. Compositionality, interference and concurrency. In Jim Davies, Bill Roscoe, and Jim Woodcock, editors, *Milennial Perspectives in Computer Science*, pages 175–186. Macmillian Press, 2000.

[JRW02]   Cliff Jones, Alexander Romanovsky, and Ian Welch. A structured approach to handling on-line interface upgrades. In *(to appear in) proceedings of COMPSAC*, 2002.

[Kop02a]   Hermann Kopetz. On the specification of linking interfaces in distributed real-time systems. Technical Report 2002/8, Institut fuer Technische Informatik, TU Vienna, 2002.

[Kop02b]   Hermann Kopetz. *Real-Time Systems*. Kluwer, 2002.

[Lap92]   Jean-Claude Laprie. *Dependability: basic concepts and terminology—in English, French, German, Italian and Japanese*. Springer-Verlag, 1992.

[LT93]   N. G. Levenson and C. S. Turner. An investigation of the Therac-25 accidents. *Computer*, pages 18–41, July 1993.

[Mar86]   L.S. Marshall. *A Formal Description Method for User Interfaces*. PhD thesis, University of Manchester, 1986.

[MH91]   B Mahony and I Hayes. Using continuous real functions to model timed histories. In P. Bailes, editor, *Engineering Safe Software*, pages 257–270. Australian Computer Society, 1991.

[MPW92]   R. Milner, J. Parrow, and D. Walker. A calculus of mobile processes. *Information and Computation*, 100:1–77, 1992.

[Nip86]   T. Nipkow. Non-deterministic data types: Models and implementations. *Acta Informatica*, 22:629–661, 1986.

[Nip87]   T. Nipkow. *Behavioural Implementation Concepts for Nondeterministic Data Types*. PhD thesis, University of Manchester, May 1987.

[Per99]   Charles Perrow. *Normal Accidents*. Princeton University Press, 1999.

[Ran00]   B. Randell. Facing up to faults. *The Computer Journal*, 43(2):95–106, 2000.

[Rea90]   James Reason. *Human Error*. Cambridge University Press, 1990.

[Rea97]   James Reason. *Managing the Risks of Organisational Accidents*. Ashgate Publishing Limited, 1997.

[Rus99]   John Rushby. Using model checking to help discover mode confusions and other automation surprises. In *Proceedings of 3rd Workshop on Human Error*, pages 1–18. HESSD'99, 1999.

[San99]   Davide Sangiorgi. Typed π-calculus at work: a correctness proof of Jones's parallelisation transformation on concurrent objects. *Theory and Practice of Object Systems*, 5(1):25–34, 1999.

[SO02]   Carles Sala-Oliveras. Systems, advisory systems and safety, 2002. Private communication.

[Sti88]   C. Stirling. A generalisation of Owicki-Gries's Hoare logic for a concurrent while language. *TCS*, 58:347–359, 1988.

[Stø90]   K. Stølen. *Development of Parallel Programs on Shared Data-Structures*. PhD thesis, Manchester University, 1990. available as UMCS-91-1-1.

[SW01]   Davide Sangiorgi and David Walker. *The π-calculus: A Theory of Mobile Processes*. Cambrisge University Press, 2001.

[Wal91]   D. Walker. π-calculus semantics for object-oriented programming languages. In T. Ito and A. R. Meyer, editors, *TACS'91*, volume 526 of *Lecture Notes in Computer Science*, pages 532–547. Springer-Verlag, 1991.

Multi-view Modeling of Software Systems

Manfred Broy

Institut für Informatik, Technische Universität München, D-80290 München Germany
broy@in.tum.de
http://wwwbroy.informatik.tu-muenchen.de

Abstract. Software construction is essentially a modeling task. The most important decisions in software development are decisions that deal with modeling. The better, the more adequate and more powerful the available modeling paradigms are, the easier the program development task is and the better its results are. However, a large complex software system can hardly be described and understood by providing one huge model. Instead a number of partial models are used that describe certain aspects of software systems in so-called views and that are in certain mutual relationships such as in levels of abstraction. In the following we describe the role of models and views in program development and show how closely the issue of modeling is related to the so-called formal methods in program development. Moreover, we give a comprehensive family of models of aspects of software systems and show how to relate and integrate them.

1 Motivation

Software development is still one of the most complex and powerful tasks in engineering. Just by formulating the right programs we obtain engineering artifacts that can control systems, calculate results, communicate messages, and illustrate and animate all kinds of information. Since programs are - implicitly or explicitly - based on models and since well-chosen models are the best way to understand software, modeling is an essential and crucial step in software construction.

In all disciplines, models play a prominent role. In physics, mathematics has provided lots of models. The same holds for many engineering disciplines. Economy works with models; biology works more and more with models, chemistry works with models. Constructing models is at the heart of science.

In Informatics modeling is even more crucial. Developing software is more or less nothing than developing the right models finally represented in the right notation such that they can be executed on computing machinery.

In the development of large complex software system it is simply impossible to provide one huge model for the system in one step. Rather we

- provide a sequence of models on different levels of abstraction,
- give at each level of abstraction several views,
- decompose the system into components,
- add stepwise details – refinement.

B.K. Aichernig and T. Maibaum (Eds.): Formal Methods ..., LNCS 2757, pp. 207–225, 2003.

Each step in these activities introduces models, refines them, or integrates them. Concentrating on the modeling issues we have to manage the following tasks:

- selection of the appropriate model concept for an aspect,
- identifying and documenting all the details for a model,
- integrating several view into a overall model,
- decomposing a model into components.

Also programming is a modeling activity, which constructs operational models in terms of the canonical models of the used programming language.

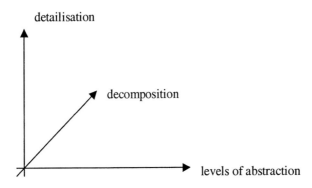

Fig. 1. The Dimensions of Software Development

Fig. 1 shows three dimensions of modeling in software development. These will be explained in more detail throughout the paper.

2   Nature of Software Development

Still we have the ongoing discussion in our community what the essence of software development really is. Is it an engineering task? Is it an art, a science, a handicraft or just a simple profession? Of course, there are many viewpoints onto program development, more scientific ones or more pragmatic ones. We study and discuss two extreme viewpoints in the following:

- Academic viewpoint: Software development always means the construction of a formal/mathematical/logical model - therefore it is a formal activity. Software is a mathematical object, formally specifiable and verifiable.
- Pragmatic viewpoint: Software development is an art and a craft; it proceeds by esoteric lore, by stepwise improvement, by trial and error. Software needs to be changed and redesigned as well as tested over and over again. It is unreliable and hard to predict.

Thus, software is a complex, unreliable and unpredictable artifact.

Of course, both viewpoints are extreme and therefore hardly fully correct. But both viewpoints provide relevant aspects and valuable insights into the nature of software development. In fact, the two views (academic and pragmatic) are the essence of any engineering discipline, not only software engineering. We claim that we have to integrate both viewpoints to obtain a realistic and respectable discipline of software engineering. Only if we manage to have a compromise between that both viewpoints in a smart way, software development can be improved into a scientifically well founded, practically relevant engineering discipline.

2.1 Models, Their Structure and Views

In this section we define the concept of a model, the structure of models and define what a model view is.

In software engineering the word "model" used in many different contexts with many quite different meanings. Examples are terms like "metamodel", "process model", or "system model". We are interested in the following two variations and meanings of the usage of the word model.

Definition. Conceptual Model
A conceptual model is a presentation of certain aspects of a software system. In essence, it provides an abstraction.   ❏

To find a good conceptual model is perhaps the most critical modeling task. We have to keep in mind that one builds a model for a certain purpose. For example, to be able to establish a certain property of the system before building the system. A model is good or bad depending on scope for which the model is built.

Definition. Mathematical Model
A mathematical model is a mathematical structure, often an algebra, that consists of sets, functions, graphs, relations, or logical predicates. It represents a conceptual model in mathematical terms.   ❏

A good mathematical model has a number of properties such as modularity, flexibility (in the sense of the ability to incorporate changes) and thus fulfils a number of essential logical and mathematical properties.

Definition. Description Technique
A description technique is a set of syntactic concepts (text, formula, graphs, or tables) for the description of a conceptual model. Mathematics provide the semantic theory for description techniques.   ❏

In general, we use description techniques (syntax) to represent a mathematical model (semantics) that is the conceptual model (abstraction and intention) for a particular development aspect. In fact, we are at the same time interested in conceptual modeling, in mathematical models and description techniques.

The description techniques should be *hierarchical* to support the hierarchical decomposition and a hierarchical top down design of systems and their description. This requirement induces a requirement on the system model: there we need a composition operator. In addition we are interested in an abstraction concept. Given a description of a system building block, we are interested in an abstraction function that maps the description on its black box behavior, such that we can calculate the black box behavior of the composed system from the abstractions of the subsystems.

Often description techniques do not describe an entire system, but rather views and properties of a system.

Definition. View
A view is - like a model – an abstraction that concentrates on a particular aspect of a software system.   ❑

Being interested in software engineering and its foundations we consider all three issues of conceptual and mathematical modeling and description techniques as interesting scientific fields of research.

2.2 Formal Methods, Models, Software Engineering

Our scientific community has invested lots of time and efforts into so called formal methods. In formal methods the idea is that the task of software development including specification, its incremental design, its implementation and its verification can be done completely within a logical and mathematical theory. This is a striking idea, full of interesting scientific issues and insights. However, practitioners often consider formal methods inadequate, insufficient, too expensive, too difficult, and "not at all practical".

On the other side the state of the art in pragmatics and practical software development is still far from being satisfactory. Practical software development is often considered being "ad hoc", "immature", uncontrollable, and "not an engineering discipline".

Therefore a very interesting question is how we can find a good compromise between the rigorous scientific approach to programming and the pragmatic practical approach. One idea of course is the use of well-chosen, sufficiently formal models. Programming means in any case using explicitly or implicitly models. We claim that it is important to identify the used model very explicitly and that this is of great practical advantage since finally formal methods provide a rich tool kit of methods.

2.3 Conceptual Modeling in Software Engineering

Systematic development of distributed mutually communicating software systems needs basic system models. To reduce the complexity and to be able to concentrate on particular aspects we need simplifying abstractions. Description techniques are to provide specific views and abstractions of systems such as:

- the data view,
- the interface view,
- the architecture, logical structure and distribution view,
- the process view,
- the interaction view,
- the deployment view,
- the state transition view.

All these views have to be captured by carefully chosen description methods leading to helpful conceptual models. The development of systems concentrates on working out these views that lead step by step to an implementation.

In fact, the collection of views mentioned above is somewhat narrow. It concentrates on structural and behavioral aspects. There are further aspects and corresponding views the often crosscut the entire systems structure. Examples are security aspects, global error handling, or functionalities distributed over the system. Such views are captured by what is often called aspect oriented program development.

We give a mathematical model setting for the following abstract views onto a system. A system is based on an algebra A that describes its basic data types and its characteristic operations. A system has an *interface view (black box view)* which describes its behavior for the users of the system (It can even have more than one interface, since there can be several kinds of "users". Just as an example, a class interface can be different for classes that use the exported resources and for classes that extend its behavior. This is an example of a concept that depends on the viewpoint. For simplicity we only consider one monolithic interface which nevertheless can be further structured). Each system has an implementation in terms of a monolithic *state machine* or an *architecture* defining a *distributed system*. A system always has a *state space* and can be viewed as a *state machine*. Systems can be *refined* and described at several *levels of abstraction*. A systems has a set of *traces* (processes, system runs) as its histories. Each view defines a mathematical model. An overview over these sorts, functions, and relations is given in Fig. 2.

This metamodel defines the most relevant sorts and their relationships.

Each model in software development serves a purpose. We concentrate very much on models for the structure and the behaviors of software systems. In fact, there are many other models in software engineering for different purposes such as performance models, reliability models, cost models and many others.

2.4 Software Development as Modeling Tasks

Software development can be seen and understood as a sequence of modeling tasks. From the very beginning, when analyzing and understanding a problem domain we start to work towards finding the right models. This goes on and on when we analyze the use cases and their specifications, the software architecture, the modularization of the system and its implementation. Software development includes the modeling and description of various aspects, such as:

- application domains, their data structures, laws, and processes,
- software requirements, based on data models, functions, and processes,
- software architectures, their structure and principles,
- software components, their roles, interfaces, states, and behaviors,
- programs and modules, their internal structure, their implementations and execution traces,
- test cases.
- If models are so important in software and systems engineering, a central question of course is, what is a model in software engineering?

- An annotated graph or diagram?
- A collection of class names, attributes, and method names?

In engineering, a model is always given by a collection of formulas, diagrams, and tables as well as text expressed in some notation with a well-understood mathematical theory. In analogy, software engineering needs mathematical modeling theories of digital systems – algebra, logic, model theory. Logic provides a unifying frame for that.

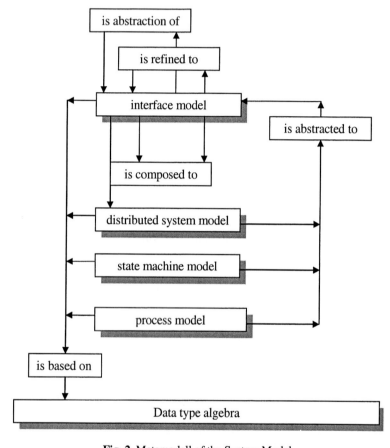

Fig. 2. Metamodell of the System Model

2.5 Scientific Foundations of Modeling in Software Development

As explained above in software development we work out step by step models and views at different levels of abstraction. They are represented with the help description techniques. Therefore we have to be able to answer the following question:

- What exactly does a view address?
- What is the meaning of a description technique?

- When are several views complementary and consistent?
- Which views are helpful?
- In which order should the views be worked out?
- How are views related?
- How can we integrate several views into one comprehensive model?
- What are useful levels of abstraction?
- How are different levels of abstraction related?

These questions touch deep methodological and foundational issues. We concentrate on foundational topics. Our main concern in the following is a comprehensive setting of mathematical models and their integration and their relationships.

2.6 Criteria for Foundations of Modeling

For a scientifically and practically useful approach to modeling in software engineering we list in the following as number of criteria and essential ingredients. First of all we need a system model, a mathematical model of a system, that is powerful enough to incorporate all envisaged views, supports the concept of levels of abstraction, hierarchical decomposition and modularity.

Second we need concepts to integrate the views in terms of syntactic consistency and a comprehensive system model. In the following we identify and define these requirements more precisely.

3 The Role of Diagrams

Practical software engineers often prefer the use of diagrams to textual notation using formulas and programming languages. The reason is quite obvious. They assume that diagrams are more telling, easier to understand and better to grasp. Whether this holds actually true leads into a long, controversial discussion.

Nevertheless in some applications certainly diagrams are helpful. However, on the long run diagrams are only helpful if they are based on a proper theory of understanding. Well-chosen models can provide such an understanding. Then the question whether to work with text, formula, table, or diagram boils down to the mere question of syntactic presentation.

3.1 Practice Today: Diagrams

In practice, today we find many diagrammatic methods for modeling and specification (SA, SADT, SSADM, SDL, OMT, UML, ROOM, ..., see [UML 97], [Jacobson 92], [Room 94], [Booch 91], [Rumbaugh 91]) in software and systems engineering. Especially UML has gained much attention. The idea of universal modeling languages is certainly a great one - but a closer look shows, however, how ad hoc most of these "methods" especially as found in UML are. At best, they reflect essential insights into the engineering of software applications. Never have practical diagrammatic modeling been justified on the basis of a comprehensive mathematical foundation. In contrast, only after the languages where published scientists work hard to define and explain the ad hoc constructs of modeling language post mortem.

3.2 Limitations of Diagrams with Unspecified Menaning

By a look at the state of the art today we see that a lot of diagrams are used without a proper theory and without a good support of understanding. To underline this remark we mention three bad examples (see also [Zave, Jackson 97]):

- UML and its statecharts dialect with its endless discussions about its semantics.
- Behavior specification of interfaces of classes and components in object oriented modeling techniques in the presence of callbacks.
- Concurrency and co-operation: Most of the practical methods especially in object orientation seem to live in the good old days of sequential programming and do not properly address the needs of highly distributed, mobile, asynchronously co-operating software systems.

We need proper theories and methodological insights (see [Rumpe 96]) to overcome these shortcomings.

3.3 From Logic to UML Back to Logic

It is a disaster for academic informatics that it did not manage to design a modeling language that is used as widely as UML. The vision, however, remains – an academic, scientific view on modeling! How can we achieve that? We start from foundations: A tractable scientific basis, understanding, and theory for modeling, specifying, and refining in programs, software and system. On that basis we identify powerful models supporting levels of abstractions, multi-view modeling, domain modeling. This leads to comprehensive description techniques based on these foundations. Thus we gain a family of justified engineering methods based on these foundations and finally a flexible process model combining these methods.

All this is the necessary prerequisite for a comprehensive tool support in software development including validation, consistency checks, verification, and code generation by algorithms and methods justified by the theories. Finally we arrive at modeling and its theory as an integral part of software construction as an engineering discipline.

We do not think that it is the right direction to give a precise meaning to UML. We need a radically different approach to modeling languages firmly based on modeling theory.

4 The System Model

In this section we introduce an example of a system model which illustrates all the requirements.

4.1 Types of Models for Mutually Communicating Systems

We identify three basic concepts of communication in distributed systems that interact by message exchange:

- *Asynchronous communication* (message asynchrony): a message is sent as soon as
  the sender is ready, independently of the fact whether a receiver is ready to receive
  it. Sent messages are buffered (by the communication mechanism) and can be received by the receiver at any later time; if a receiver wants to receive a message
  but no message was sent it has to wait. However, senders never have to wait (see
  [Kahn 74], [SDL 88]) until receivers are ready since messages may be buffered.
- *Synchronous communication* (message synchrony, rendezvous, handshake communication): a message can be sent only if both the sender and the receiver are simultaneously ready to communicate; if only one of them (receiver or sender) is
  ready for communication, it has to wait until a communication partner gets ready
  (see [CSP 85], [CCS 80]).
- *Time synchronous communication* (perfect synchrony): several interaction steps
  (signals or atomic events) are conceptually gathered into one time slot; this way
  systems are modeled with the help of sequences of sets of events (see [Esterel 88]
  as a well-known example).

In the following, we work with asynchronous message passing since for this model
view integration seems to be most simple. We follow the system model of [Broy 96]
and base our approach on a concept of a component that communicates messages
asynchronously in a synchronous time frame with its environment via named channels.

4.2 Selected System Model

We think of a system as being composed of a number of subsystems that we call its
components. In fact, a composed system itself is and can be used as a component
again as part of a larger system. A component is a unit with a precisely specified
interface. When instantiated it encapsulates a state. Via its interface it is connected to
and communicates with its environment. In this section, we shortly introduce a simple, very abstract mathematical notion of a system component.

4.2.1 The Data Model: Algebras

From a mathematical point of view, a data model consists of a *heterogeneous algebra*. Such an algebra is given by a family of *carrier sets* and a family of *functions*
(including predicates and thus relations). More technically, we assume a set T of
types (often also called sorts or modes). We believe, like many others, that data types
(typing) are a very helpful concept in a structured modeling of application domains
and software structures. With types we consider a set F of function symbols with a
predefined functionality (T^* stands for the set of finite sequences over T)

$$\mathbf{fct} : F \to (T^* \times T)$$

The function **fct** associates with every function symbol in F its domain types and its range type. Both the sets T and F provide only names for sets and functions. The pair (T, F) together with the type assignment **fct** is often called the *signature* of the algebra. The signature is the *static* (also called *syntactic*) *part* of a data model.

4.2.2   The Interface Model: Components

A (system) component is an active information processing unit that communicates asynchronously with its environment through a set of input and output channels. This communication takes place within a global (discrete) time frame. Channels are static and we do not consider any form of subtyping here.

Let I be the set of input channels and O be the set of output channels of the component f. With every channel in the channel set $I \cup O$ we associate a data type indicating the type of messages sent along that channel. Then by $(I \blacktriangleright O)$ the *syntactic interface* of a system component is described. A graphical representation of a component with its syntactic interface and individual channel types is shown in Fig. 3.

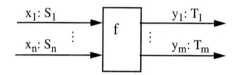

Fig. 3. Graphical Representation of a Component as a Data Flow Node with Input Channels x_1, ..., x_n and Output Channels y_1, ... , y_m and their Respective Types

By $M^\omega = M^* \cup M^\infty$ we denote the set of streams of elements from the set M which are finite or infinite sequences of elements from M. A stream represents the sequence of messages sent over a channel during the lifetime of a system. Of course, in concrete systems this communication takes place in a time frame. In fact, it is often convenient to be able to refer to this time. Therefore we work with *timed streams*. Since we do not always want to care about time we use mechanism to abstract from time when appropriate.

Our model of time is extremely simple. We assume that time is represented by an infinite sequence of time intervals of equal length. In each interval on each channel a finite, possibly empty sequence of messages is transmitted. By $(M^*)^\infty$ we denote the set of infinite streams of sequences of elements of set M. Mathematically, a timed stream in $(M^*)^\infty$ can also be understood as a function $\mathbb{N} \backslash \{0\} \to M^*$.

The system class that we consider are distributed, reactive systems. First we have to select a model for such systems. Let C be a set of channels with types assigned by the function

$$\text{type: } C \to T$$

Here T is a set of types $\tau \in T$ which are carrier sets of data elements. Let M be the universe of all messages. This means

$$M = \bigcup \{\tau : \tau \in T\}$$

We define the valuations of the set C of channels by functions

$$x: C \rightarrow (M^*)^{\infty}$$

where for each channel $c \in C$ with type(c) = Stream τ the elements of the stream x.c are of the type τ (throughout the paper we denote the application of a function f to an argument b not only by f(b) but also by f.b to save parenthesis):

$$x.c \in (\tau^*)^{\infty}$$

The set of valuations of the channels in C is denoted by $\vec{C}$. Let in the following I and O be sets of typed channels.

By Com[I ▶ O] we denote the set of all I/O-functions with input channels I and output channels O. By Com we denote the set of all I/O-functions for arbitrary channel sets I and O. For any $f \in$ Com we denote by In(f) its set of input channels and by Out(f) its set of output channels.

4.2.3 The Distributed System Model: Composed Systems

An mutually communicating distributed system consists of a family of interacting components (in some approaches also called *agents* or *objects*). These components interact by exchanging messages on their channels by which they are connected. A *structural system view*, also called a *system architecture*, consists of a network of communicating components. Its nodes represent components and its arcs communication lines (channels) on which streams of messages are sent.

We model distributed systems by data flow nets. Let K be a set of identifiers for components and I and O be sets of input and output channels, respectively. A distributed system (v, O) with syntactic interface (I ▶ O) is represented by the mapping

$$v: K \rightarrow Com$$

that associates with every node a component behavior in the form of a black box view, formally, an interface behavior given by an I/O-function. O denotes the output channels of the system.

4.3 System States

One way to model a system and its behavior is to describe its *state space* and its *state transitions*. Each state of a system consists the states of its internal and external channels and the states of its components. This leads to a state view of the system.

4.3.1 State Machine Model: State Transitions

By Σ we denote the set of all states.

A state machine with input and output is given by a set $\Lambda \subseteq \Sigma \times (O \rightarrow M^*)$ of pairs (σ_0, y_0) of initial states $\sigma_0 \in \Sigma$ and initial output sequences $y_0 \in (O \rightarrow M^*)$ as well as a state transition function

$$\Delta: (\Sigma \times (I \rightarrow M^*)) \rightarrow \wp(\Sigma \times (O \rightarrow M^*))$$

For each state $\sigma \in \Sigma$ and each valuation u: $I \rightarrow M^*$ of the input channels in I by sequences we obtain by every pair $(\sigma', r) \in \Delta(\sigma, u)$ a successor state σ' and a valuation
r: $O \rightarrow M^*$ of the output channels consisting of the sequences produced by the state
transition.

4.3.2 States of State Transition Systems: State Attributes
Often a component can be described in a well-understandable way by a state transition machine with input and output. We describe the data state of a transition machine
by a set of typed attributes V that can be seen as *program variables*. A data state is
given by the mapping

$$\eta: V \rightarrow \bigcup_{v \in V} \text{type}(v)$$

It is a valuation of the attributes in the set V by values of the corresponding type. By
$\vec{V}$ we denote the set of valuations of the attributes in V. By Σ we denote the set of
all states.
A system that is modeled by a state machine has a *local* data state. Each local data
state is an element in the set $\vec{V}$ which is the set of valuations for its attributes. In
addition to the channel attributes, we use the attributes of the local states of the systems to refer to the data and control state of a system.

4.3.3 States of Channels
The term channel is used with two different roles. A channel is a synonym for a component's input or output port. Here it is used as the connector between a component's
output port and input port. For simplicity we assume that an output port be connected
to only one input port (no multicasting) and an input port must not be connected to
several output ports. Moreover, is there an assumption that data are not lost by the
channel.
  In this section we show that a channel has a state. It is represented by the stream of
messages sent over it (its communication history) and the stream of messages which
have been sent but not received so far and therefore stored in its buffer. The content
of the buffer of a channel is a stream, which is of course a postfix of the communication history of the channel. To take care of pending (buffered) messages in state assertions, we associate with each channel c the following three derived variables:

  c^+ denotes the sequence of messages sent but not received yet on the channel c,
         called the *channel buffer*,

  c   denotes the sequence of messages sent on the channel c, called the *channel
         history*.

c^+ denotes the content of the buffer. The identifiers c and c^+ are called the *channel
attributes*.

4.3.4 Distributed System States
The variables and derived variables for the channels and the attributes of the systems
form the alphabet of a system. Each system state is represented by a valuation of the

system alphabet. Thus a system state provides values for all the pasts, buffers, and histories of its channels as well as for all the local data and control states of its components.

Given a set B of typed attributes, a set C of typed channels the system state space Σ is defined by the direct product of their sets of valuations:

$$\Sigma = \vec{V} \times \vec{C} \times \vec{C}^+$$

For states $\sigma \in \Sigma$ and state or channel attributes x, we write $\sigma.x$ to denote the value associated with x in the state σ.

4.4 The Process Model

In this section we give several process models. To keep the approach simple we consider only sequential processes.

4.4.1 The Basic Process Model

For simplicity we consider only a simple version of sequential processes. We work with sets of snapshots that provide observations at specific points of the system. Given a snapshot set H a process over H is a finite or infinite sequence of snapshots, with other words, a stream

$$H^{\omega}$$

Dependent on the choice of the snapshot set, we get processes for different system views.

4.4.2 The Process Model: Interface Processes

Given a syntactic interface (I $\blacktriangleright$ O) with the set $C = I \cup O$ of typed channels the snapshot set HI for the processes is given by the evaluation of the channels by finite streams

$$HI = C \rightarrow M^*$$

A process is a finite or infinite stream of valuations of the channels by finite sequences of messages. The set of processes over the channels set C is denoted by PRC[C]. We easily recalculate the interface for a process by a simple limit construction. We get a function:

$$\Pi: IF(I \blacktriangleright O) \rightarrow PRC[I \cup O]$$

The function Π maps an interface on an interface process

4.4.3 The Process Model: State Machine Processes

For a state machine (Δ, Λ) where Λ is a set Λ of pairs (σ_0, y_0) and Δ state transition function

$$\Delta: (\Sigma \times (I \rightarrow M^*)) \rightarrow \wp(\Sigma \times (O \rightarrow M^*))$$

we define the snapshot set HS by

$$HS = \Sigma \times (C \rightarrow M^{*})$$

The set of processes $p \subseteq HS^{\omega}$ for the state machine is defined by

$$\{(\sigma.t, z.t): t \in \mathbb{N}\backslash\{0\}\} \in p \Leftrightarrow$$

$$\forall t \in \mathbb{N}\backslash\{0\}: (\sigma.t+1, (z.t+1)|_O) \in \Delta((\sigma.t, (z.t)|_I) \wedge (\sigma.1, (z.1)|_O) \in \Lambda$$

If we add components and a state for each component a process is a finite or infinite stream of valuations of the channels by finite sequences of messages and of the components by component states.

4.4.4 The Process Model: Distributed System Processes

The state machines model the behavior of systems by state transitions. State machines generate executions also called *system histories* which are finite or infinite sequences of system states. An abstraction of this view leads to *communication histories*, which consist of the streams of messages exchanged over the channels of a system.

Given a set K of components and a state machine (Δ_k, Λ_k) for each component k $\in$ K where Λ_k is a set Λ_k of pairs (σ_o, y_o) and Δ_k state transition function

$$\Delta: (\Sigma_k \times (I_k \rightarrow M^{*})) \rightarrow \wp(\Sigma_k \times (O_k \rightarrow M^{*}))$$

we define the snapshot set HC by (let STATES be the set of all state spaces)

$$HC = (K \rightarrow STATES) \times (C \rightarrow M^{*})$$

The set of processes $p \subseteq HC^{\omega}$ for the state machine is defined by

$$\{(\pi.t, z.t): t \in \mathbb{N}\backslash\{0\}\} \in p \Leftrightarrow$$

$$\forall t \in \mathbb{N}\backslash\{0\}, k \in K: \quad ((\pi.k).t+1, (z.t+1)|_O) \in \Delta(((\pi.k).t, (z.t)|_I)$$

$$\wedge \quad ((\pi.k).1, (z.1)|_O) \in \Lambda_k$$

If we add components and a state for each component a process is a finite or infinite stream of valuations of the channels by finite sequences of messages and of the components by component states.

4.4.5 Communication Histories

Data flow networks composed of data flow components represent distributed communicating systems. Data flow components communicate via channels. The history of a channel is the stream of messages sent along it. The communication history of a system consists of the histories of its input and output channels. The communication history of a composed system consists of the communication histories of its components and thus of the histories of its channels. In a state assertion each channel occurs formally as an identifier of type stream. Given a system with the set C of channels by $\vec{C}$ we denote the set of system communication histories.

Since in a state trace $s \in \Sigma^{\omega}$ the streams associated with each channels are monotonically increasing, for each system state trace there exists a uniquely defined communication history which is the least upper bound of all the streams associated with a channel. Hence, according to the requirements above for a state traces the set

$$\{(s.k).c: k \in \mathbb{N} \}$$

forms a chain. Since the set of streams forms a cpo this chain has a least upper bound. For each state trace $s \in \Sigma^\omega$ we denote by

$$\uparrow s \in \vec{C}$$

the channel valuation specified by the equation

$$(\uparrow s).c = \text{lub } \{(s.k).c: k \in \mathbb{N} \}$$

This way we associate a unique system communication history with every system state trace. This communication history $\uparrow s$ defines an abstraction for the state trace s.

4.5 Composition

In this section we study forms of composition. Composition should always be hierarchical. We distinguish vertical composition and horizontal composition

4.5.1 Horizontal Composition of Interfaces
In our interface model a system is a set-valued function. As a consequence all operations on sets are available. The interface model forms a complete lattice. This way we can form the union and the disjunction of interfaces.

4.5.2 Vertical Composition of Interfaces
Each data flow net describes an I/O-function. This I/O-function is called the *black box view* of the distributed system described by the data flow net. We get an abstraction of a distributed system to its black box view by mapping it to a component behavior in Com[I ▶ O] where I denotes the set of input channels and O denotes the set of output channels of the data flow net. This black box view is represented by the component behavior $f \in$ Com[I ▶ O] specified by the following formula (note that y $\in \vec{C}$ where $C \equiv \text{Chan}((v, O))$ as defined above):

$$f_{(v, O)}(x) = \{y|_O: y|_I = x \wedge \forall\, k \in K: y|_{\text{Out}(v(k))} \in v(k)(y|_{\text{In}(v(k))}) \}$$

Here, we use the notation of function restriction. For a function g: D → R and a set T $\subseteq$ D we denote by g|$_T$: T → R the restriction of the function g to the domain T. The formula essentially expresses that the output history of a data flow net is the restriction of a fixpoint for all the net-equations for the output channels.

4.5.3 Composition of State Machines
Given a distributed system (v, O) with a set K of components with state machines

$$\Delta_k: (\Sigma_k \times (I_k \to M^*)) \to \wp(\Sigma_k \times (O_k \to M^*))$$

for each component $k \in K$ we define a state machine

$$\Delta: (\Sigma \times (I \to M^*)) \to \wp(\Sigma \times (O \to M^*))$$

of the composed system by

$$\Sigma = (\times \{\Sigma_k : k \in K \}) \times (Intern((v, O)) \to M^*)$$

for $(\sigma, z) \in \Sigma$ we define by σ_k the substate of σ in Σ_k. The state transition function is defined by:

$$\Delta((\sigma, z), x) = \{(\sigma', y|_O): \forall k \in K: \ (\sigma'_k, y|_{Out(v(k))}) \in \Delta_k(\sigma_k, y|_{In(v(k))})$$

$$\wedge \ y|_I = x \wedge y|_{Intern(v, O)} = z \}$$

This way we associate a large state machine with a distributed system of state machines. Its initial state is the product of all the initial states of the individual components.

4.5.4 Composition of Processes
Also processes can be defined along these lines. Given a process for every component k in K we get a process of the composed system in a straightforward way both in the case of state based processes and history based processes putting together the system snapshots of the individual components.

4.6 Refinement

In requirements engineering and in the design phase of system development many issues have to be addressed such as requirements elicitation, conflict identification and resolution, information management as well as the selection of a favorable software architecture. These activities are connected with development steps. Refinement relations are the medium to formalize development steps and in this way the development process.

There are many useful relations in software development. We concentrate on refinement and formalize the following basic ideas of refinement:

- *property refinement* - enhancing requirements - allows us to add properties to a specification,
- *glass box refinement* - designing implementations - allows us to decompose a component into a distributed system or to give a state transition description for a component specification,
- *interaction refinement* - relating levels of abstraction - allows us to change the representation of the communication histories, in particular, the granularity of the interaction as well as the number and types of the channels of a component.

In fact, these notions of refinement describe the steps needed in an idealistic view of a strictly hierarchical top down system development. The three refinement concepts mentioned above are formally defined and explained in detail in the following.

5 Summary and Outlook

Why did we present this setting of mathematical models? First of all, we wanted to show how rich and flexible the tool kit of mathematical model is and how far we are in integrating and relating them. Perhaps, it should emphasized that the we get two first of all a integrated system models very close to practical approaches by SDL or UML where a system is a set or hierarchy of components. In this tree of components the leaves are state machines. In our case the usage of streams and stream processing function is the reason for the remarkable flexibility of a model toolkit and the simplicity of the integration task.

Software development is a difficult and complex engineering task. It would be very surprising if such a task could be carried out properly without a proper theoretical framework. It would at the same time be quite surprising if a purely scientifically theoretical framework would be the right approach for the practical engineer. The result has to be a compromise as we have argued between formal techniques and theory on one side and intuitive notations based on diagrams. Work is needed along those lines including experiments and feedback from practical applications. But as already our example shows a lot is to be gained that way.

Theory and practical understanding are the key to mature software development. To achieve that we need a much deeper and more intensive interaction between researchers working on the foundations, the designers of practical engineering methods and tools, the programmers and engineers in charge of practical solutions, and application experts modeling application domains.

Successful work does not only require the interaction between these types of people - it also needs *hybrid* people that have a deep understanding in all three of these areas.

Acknowledgements

It is a pleasure to thank Ingolf Krüger and Radu Grosu for stimulating discussions and helpful remarks on draft versions of the manuscript. It is a pleasure for me to acknowledge valuable remarks by Carlo Ghezzi who refereed the paper.

References

[Baeten, Bergstra 92] J.C.M. Baeten, J. Bergstra: Process Algebras with Signals and Conditions. In: M. Broy (ed.): Programming and Mathematical Method. Springer NATO ASI Series, Series F: Computer and System Sciences, Vol. 88, 1992, 273-324

[Ben-Abdallah, Leue 97] H. Ben-Abdallah, S. Leue: Timing Constraints in Message Sequence Charts Specifictions. In: Proceeding of the FORTE/PSTV'97

[Booch 91] G. Booch: Object Oriented Design with Applications. Benjamin Cummings, Redwood City, CA, 1991

[Broy 91] M. Broy: Towards a formal foundation of the specification and description language SDL. Formal Aspects of Computing 3, 1991, 21-57

[Broy 98] M. Broy: Compositional Refinement of Interactive Systems Modelled by Relations. Malente 1997

[Broy et al. 97] M. Broy, C. Hofmann, I. Krüger, M Schmidt: A Graphical Description Technique for Communication in Software Architectures. Technische Universität München, Institut für Informatik, TUM-I9705, Februar 1997 URL: http://www4.informatik.tu-muenchen.de/reports/TUM-I9705, 1997. Also in: Joint 1997 Asia Pacific Software Engineering Conference and International Computer Science Conference (APSEC'97/ICSC'97)

[Broy, Stoelen 01] M. Broy, K. Stølen: Specification and Development of Interactive Systems: FOCUS Focus on Streams, Interfaces, and Refinement. Springer 2001

[CSP 85] C.A.R. Hoare: Communicating Sequential Processes. Prentice Hall, 1985

[CCS 80] R. Milner: A Calculus of Communicating Systems. Lecture Notes in Computer Science 92, Springer 1980

[Damm, Harel 98] W. Damm, D. Harel: Breathing Life into Message Sequence Charts. Weismann Insitute Tech. Report CS98-09, April 1998, revised July 1998, to appear in: FMOODS'99, IFIP TC6/WG6.1 Third International Conference on, Formal Methods for Open Object-Based Distributed Systems, Florence, Italy, February 15-18, 1999

[Esterel 88] G. Berry, G. Gonthier: The ESTEREL Synchronous Programming Language: Design, Semantics, Implementation. INRIA, Research Report 842, 1988

[Hettler 94] R. Hettler: Zur Übersetzung von E/R-Schemata nach SPECTRUM. Technischer Bericht TUM-I9409, TU München, 1994

[Hinkel 98] U. Hinkel: Formale, semantische Fundierung und ein darauf abgestützte Verifikationsmethode für SDL. Dissertation, Fakultät für Informatik, Technische Universität München 1998

[Hoare et al. 81] C.A.R. Hoare, S.D. Brookes, A.W. Roscoe: A theory of communicating sequential processes. Oxford University Computing Laboratory Programming Research Group, Technical Monograph PRG-21, Oxford 1981

[Jacobson 92] I. Jacobsen: Object-Oriented Software Engineering. Addison-Wesley, ACM Press 1992

[Kahn 74] G. Kahn: The Semantics of a Simple Language for Parallel Processing. In: J.L. Rosenfeld(ed.): Information Processing 74. Proc. of the IFIP Congress 74, Amsterdam: North Holland 1974, 471-475.

[Klein 98] C. Klein: Anforderungsspezifikation durch Transitionssysteme und Szenarien. Promotion, Fakultät für Informatik, Technische Universität München, Dezember 1997

[Krüger et al. 99] I. Krüger, R. Grosu, P. Scholz, M. Broy: From MSCs to statecharts. In: Proceedings of DIPES'98, Kluwer, 1999

[MSC 93] ITU-T (previously CCITT) (March 1993) Criteria for the Use and Applicability of Formal Description Techniques. Recommendation Z. 120, Message Sequence Chart (MSC), 35pgs.

[MSC 95] ITU-T. Recommendation Z.120, Annex B: Algebraic Semantics of Message Sequence Charts. ITU-Telecommunication Standardization Sector, Geneva, Switzerland, 1995.

[Ladkin, Leue 95] P.B. Ladkin, S. Leue. Interpreting Message Flow Graphs. Formal Aspects of Computing, 7(5): 473-509, 1995.

[Room 94] B. Selic, G. Gullekson. P.T. Ward: Real-time Objectoriented Modeling. Wiley, New York 1994

[Rumbaugh 91] J. Rumbaugh: Object-Oriented Modelling and Design. Prentice Hall, Englewood Cliffs: New Jersey 1991

[Rumpe 96] B. Rumpe: Formale Methodik des Entwurfs verteilter objektorientierter Systeme. Ph.D. Thesis Technische Universität München, Fakultät für Informatik 1996. Published by Herbert Utz Verlag

[SDL 88] Specification and Description Language (SDL), Recommendation Z.100. Technical report, CCITT, 1988

[SPECTRUM 93] M. Broy, C. Facchi, R. Hettler, H. Hußmann, D. Nazareth, F. Regensburger, O. Slotosch, K. Stølen: The Requirement and Design Specification Language SPECTRUM. An Informal Introduction. Version 1.0. Part I/II Technische Universität München, Institut für Informatik, TUM-I9311 / TUM-I9312, May 1993

[UML 97] G. Booch, J. Rumbaugh, I. Jacobson: The Unified Modeling Language for Object-Oriented Development, Version 1.0, RATIONAL Software Cooperation

[Zave, Jackson 97] P. Zave, M. Jackson: Four dark corners of requirements engineering. ACM Transactions on Software Engineering and Methodology, January 1997

An Executable Specification Language Based on Message Sequence Charts

Abhik Roychoudhury and P.S. Thiagarajan

School of Computing, National University of Singapore
3 Science Drive 2, Singapore 117543
{abhik,thiagu}@comp.nus.edu.sg

Abstract. Message Sequence Charts (MSCs) are an appealing visual formalism that play a useful role in the early design stages of reactive systems such as telecommunication protocols. They also constitute one of the behavioral diagram types in the UML framework [4]. MSCs are usually intended to capture system requirements. However there is no standard relationship between such requirements and an executable specification . Here we deploy MSCs instead as refinements of actions at the executable level by formulating a state-based model called Cyclic Transaction Processes. We provide a transition system semantics for the CTP model as also a detailed example to illustrate its modeling and behavioral features.

1   Introduction

Message Sequence Charts (MSCs) are an appealing visual formalism that play a useful role in the early design stages of reactive systems [22]. They also constitute one of the behavioral diagram types in the UML framework [7]. MSCs are usually deployed to capture system requirements. A variety of choices exist as to what ought to be the relationship between such requirements and an executable specification of the system, say, in the form of a statechart [8]. Two extreme possibilities are:

- The requirements constitute a *necessarily incomplete* testbench that the executable specification must satisfy.
- The requirements constitute a complete behavioral description and hence the executable specification must exhibit *exactly* the set of scenarios (MSCs) captured as requirements.

In the first case, the MSCs play a rather weak role and in the second instance one has to usually synthesize an executable specification from the requirements which is a difficult problem even in abstract settings [16, 15, 10, 13]. An alternative approach that has been advocated -and which we follow here- by Harel and his co-workers [6, 9, 12, 11] is to develop executable specification mechanisms called Live Sequence Charts (LSCs) that are *directly* based on MSCs. The key idea here is that LSCs can be used to describe scenario-based liveness and safety properties : for instance, interactions which *must* occur provided

B.K. Aichernig and T. Maibaum (Eds.): Formal Methods ..., LNCS 2757, pp. 226–241, 2003.

some pre-condition holds and such charts are referred to as universal charts. An executable specification would then consist of a collection of universal charts (and existential charts), namely, all possible executions that do not violate the specification. This is the so-called Play-in/Play-out approach developed in the papers cited above. Even though such a description is complete and executable, it does not contain explicit control flow information. This raises questions about the efficiency of the execution engine, lack of concurrency and the ease of code synthesis from the executable specification. Our specification formalism aims to address these problems.

We illustrate the main features of our MSC based executable specification by formulating the model called Cyclic Transaction Processes (CTP). The CTP model consists of a set of processes where each process represents a system component. Each process p repeatedly executes a *cyclic* pattern of transaction schemes in each of which p is a participating process. A *transaction scheme* is the unit of interaction between the processes. Naturally, different transaction schemes along the cycle could involve different sets of other processes and more than two processes may be involved in a transaction scheme. The restriction that the control flow of a single process must be cyclic makes the analysis of the model tractable. It also suffices to capture the illustrative example discussed in section 2. In our subsequent work, we have weakened this cyclicity restriction to allow for more generous control flow for the component processes [21]. In the present paper we have not included features to model the interactions with the environment but they can be easily added as shown in [21].

A transaction scheme consists of a collection of *transactions* where a transaction is modeled as an MSC. An execution of a transaction scheme will choose one of its transactions depending on the current values of the local variables of the participating processes. For instance, consider a co-processor P_m trying to transfer data to a co-processor P_s via a bus B. In addition to the three processes corresponding to these components, assume there is a master interface process I_m to mediate between P_m and the bus B and a slave interface process I_s to mediate between the bus and P_s. One possible transaction scheme in this setting would model an interaction where P_m queries I_m as to whether it can buffer data for eventual transfer to P_s via the bus. This transaction scheme will consist of (at least) two transactions ; one in which P_m requests and receives a positive response from I_m to transfer data to the buffer of I_m. This will be followed by a series of data transfer operations. In the second transaction, the response from I_m is negative because its buffer is currently full. This will terminate the transaction and there will be no data transfer.

Related Work. Turning now to related work, as mentioned above, the notion of Live Sequence Charts (LSCs) [6] has been an important source of inspiration for the present work. As pointed out in [6], a variety of MSC-based mechanisms for capturing requirements are rather weak. Loosely speaking, using these mechanisms, one can merely say that a scenario *may* arise during a system execution. However as the design moves closer to an implementation, one would also like to specify that under a given condition a particular scenario *must* arise. The

LSC formalism is designed to fill this gap. Using LSC terminology, a transaction scheme may be viewed as consisting of a set of *universal* charts guarded by a total set of mutually exclusive predicates. However our model differs from LSCs in that we explicitly fix the *distributed* control flow. As a result our operational semantics -even though given in terms of conventional transition systems here- can capture concurrency whereas in the play-in play-out approach of [12], the play engine has to monitor against the violation of any universal chart in every step and hence is inherently sequential. We however envision the key logical aspects of LSCs to play a role in the formal verification of executable CTP specifications. There is a wealth of literature available concerning MSCs as evidenced in [2, 13, 14, 17–20]. Here we shall only be using the the basic definition of MSCs. We do however expect parts of the rich theory cited above to play a useful role in the analysis of CTPs.

Organization. In section 2, we provide a detailed example specification capturing the data communication between two co-processors via a bus running the AMBA protocol (which is widely used in System-On-Chip designs). In the section 3, we formally describe the CTP model and provide the operational semantics for a restricted class of CTPs called *anchored* CTPs. Finally, in section 4, we sketch the issues in formal verification of CTP specifications using a CTL-like logic that can incorporate important aspects of the LSC formalism.

2   An Interface Example

Our Cyclic Transaction Processes (CTP) model consists of a finite family of cyclic processes that interact via *transaction schemes*. Each process (agent) repeatedly executes a fixed cycle of transaction schemes. A transaction scheme consists of a guarded choice between a set of *transactions* where a transaction is modeled as an MSC. The choice of a transaction in a particular execution of any transaction scheme, is a distributed choice in general.

In this section, we present an example to show the use of the CTP as a specification language. In particular, we model the data communication between two components via a bus. We call the originator of the data communication the *master* and the receiver of the communication the *slave*. Our model consists of five processes executing in parallel: the master component (called P_m), interface of the master component (called I_m), the bus controller (called BC), interface of the slave component (called I_s) and the slave component (called P_s). The master and slave components (P_m and P_s) are often processors or co-processors. The architecture of interaction between the components is shown in Figure 1. The Petri net representation shown in this figure is used here mainly for illustrative purposes. The circles stand for the local control states of the processes and the boxes represent the transaction schemes. In the diagram, the constituent guarded transactions of the various transaction schemes have not been shown.

To develop our example, we fix: (1) a specific bus protocol, (2) storage capabilities of the interfaces, I_m and I_s (3) interaction between the components and

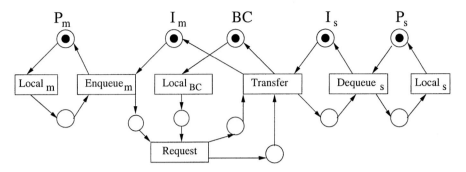

Fig. 1. CTP model of interfaces between two embedded co-processors.

interfaces. We choose the popular AMBA bus protocol used in ARM system-on-chip designs [3]. We assume that each interface contains a bounded queue to hold data in transit. The interaction between a component and its interface then involves enqueueing and dequeuing these queues. In particular, our choice of the component-interface protocol is drawn from the interface modules developed in the European COSY project [5].

We now proceed to model each of the processes. Each process is *cyclic*, and repeats a sequence of *transaction schemes*. A sequence of two transaction schemes T and T' is denoted as $T \circ T'$. The five processes in our example can be described by simple recursive equations as follows. An equivalent visual description of these processes appears in Figure 1.

$$P_m = Local_m \circ Enqueue_m \circ P_m$$
$$I_m = Enqueue_m \circ Request \circ Transfer \circ I_m$$
$$BC = Local_{BC} \circ Request \circ Transfer \circ BC$$
$$I_s = Transfer \circ Dequeue_s \circ I_s$$
$$P_s = Dequeue_s \circ Local_s \circ P_s$$

The transaction schemes $Local_m$, $Local_{BC}$ and $Local_s$ have only one participating process: namely P_m, BC and P_s respectively. They represent internal computations of these processes and we do not describe them here. $Enqueue_m$ involves enqueueing of data by the master process P_m into the queue of the master interface I_m. Similarly, $Dequeue_s$ denotes the dequeuing of data from the queue of the slave interface I_s by slave processor P_s. The scheme $Request$ denotes request for bus access by the master to the bus controller, and subsequent granting of bus access (if any). Finally, the scheme $Transfer$ denotes the transfer of data from master interface I_m into slave interface I_s over the bus.

We now describe the transaction scheme $Transfer$. Due to space limitations, the descriptions of the other transaction schemes, which are simpler, are not presented. Note that $agents(Transfer) = \{I_m, I_s, BC\}$. Conditions on the local variables of each of these processes are used to decide which chart of $Transfer$ is executed in a particular execution. We will freely use values of these local variables in our charts. The events in the charts pass these values between variables of different processes, thereby modeling data transfer.

Local Variables. We present the local variables of the processes I_m, I_s and BC in Figure 2. We wish to note that *maxwait* denotes a predefined fixed positive constant, and $\mathcal{D}$ denotes the data type of the data being transmitted from master component P_m to slave component P_s. Furthermore, *Addr* denotes the range of addresses manipulated by I_m and I_s.

Process	Local Variables
I_m	mq : Queue of $(Addr, \mathcal{D})$
	$data\_sent, wait\_data$: $\mathcal{D}$
	$wait\_addr$: $Addr$
	$grant_m$: boolean
I_s	sq : Queue of $(Addr, \mathcal{D})$
	$addr\_rcvd$: $Addr$
	$waitcnt$: $0 \ldots maxwait$
BC	$gnt_m, split_m$: boolean

Fig. 2. Local Variables in the Interface Example.

The master and slave interfaces I_m and I_s each contain a queue mq and sq. The master queue mq receives data from P_m and passes it to the slave interface I_s. The slave queue sq receives data from master interface I_m and passes it to the slave component P_s. The transfer of data between the master and slave interfaces is over a bus, and is thus dictated by the bus protocol. In this case, we consider the AMBA bus protocol which has the following features. This will clarify the need for the various local variables.

Bus Access Protocol. Each transfer is preceded by a grant of bus access by the bus controller to a master. This information is stored by the bus controller BC in the boolean variable gnt_m. Its value is communicated to I_m in the *Request* transaction scheme (not shown here) when I_m requests for bus access. I_m stores this information in $grant_m$. Thus there is clear relationship between $I_m.grant_m$ and $BC.gnt_m$. Similar relationships exist between other local variables of different processes owing to the flow of values via messages.

Pipelined Transfer. Multiple transfers from I_m to I_s are *pipelined*. For example suppose I_m wants to transfer $(a_1, d_1), (a_2, d_2), (a_3, d_3)$ to I_s. This is a request to write d_1 to address a_1, d_2 to address a_2 and d_3 to address a_3. The transfer over the address and data lines proceeds as follows:

$$\begin{array}{ll} \text{Clock cycle:} & 1\ \ 2\ \ 3\ \ 4 \\ \text{Address :} & a_1\ a_2\ a_3\ - \\ \text{Data :} & -\ \ d_1\ d_2\ d_3 \end{array}$$

Since in every cycle, the data of the previous cycle's address is transmitted, this needs to be remembered. This information is stored in the local variable *data_sent* of I_m. Similarly, on the slave interface side, the address received in previous cycle is stored in the variable *addr_rcvd* of process I_s.

Transfer with Wait Cycles. The slave interface I_s may not be ready to write data in every cycle *e.g.* the slave queue sq may be full. This results in insertion of "*wait cycles*". The number of such wait cycles is stored in the local variable *waitcnt*. In the presence of wait cycles, the transfer can be as follows:

$$\begin{array}{lllllll} \text{Clock cycle:} & 1 & 2 & 3 & 4 & 5 & 6 \\ \text{Address :} & a_1 & a_2 & a_2 & a_2 & a_3 & - \\ \text{Data :} & - & d_1 & d_1 & d_1 & d_2 & d_3 \end{array}$$

Here, d_1 is transfered after two wait cycles. During these wait cycles, the master interface needs to keep on transmitting a_2 as address and d_1 as data; otherwise the correspondence between address and data is lost. Hence the need for the local variables *wait_addr* and *wait_data* in process I_m.

Split Transfer. If the number of wait cycles equals a threshold *maxwait*, the slave interface I_s informs the bus controller BC that it is currently unable to service the master interface I_m. The bus controller BC then records that I_m is suspended by setting $split_m$ (which is reset later when I_s is able to serve I_m).

Sequence Charts. The transaction scheme $Transfer$ is collection of MSCs, one for each of the following mutually exclusive conditions.[1].

1. $\neg grant_m \lor (empty(mq) \land waitcnt = 0) \lor (split_m \land full(sq))$
2. $grant_m \land \neg split_m \land \neg empty(mq) \land \neg full(sq) \land waitcnt = 0$
3. $grant_m \land \neg split_m \land \neg empty(mq) \land full(sq) \land waitcnt = 0$
4. $grant_m \land \neg split_m \land \neg full(sq) \land waitcnt > 0$
5. $grant_m \land \neg split_m \land full(sq) \land waitcnt > 0 \land waitcnt < maxwait$
6. $grant_m \land \neg split_m \land full(sq) \land waitcnt = maxwait$
7. $grant_m \land split_m \land \neg full(sq) \land waitcnt = maxwait$

In case 1, either the bus is busy ($\neg grant_m$ holds) or the master queue mq is empty and $waitcnt = 0$ (*i.e.* new data needs to be dequeued from mq which is empty), or the data transfer from I_m has been split, but I_s is still not ready to input data (sq is full). In these cases, no data is transmitted, no control signals are exchanged and the chart is a no-op.

In case 2 (shown in Figure 3), the master is granted access to the bus, data is dequeued from the master queue mq, and enqueued into the slave queue sq. This corresponds to "normal" data transfer without wait cycles and split transfer. Each message is of the form Signal_name(Value), such as ADDR(a). Access to mq and sq are through the *Enqueue* and *Dequeue* methods.

The chart for case 3 is shown in Figure 4. This corresponds to the scenario where wait cycles are initiated (note that $waitcnt = 0$) for some transfer, since the queue at I_s is full. Note that the first three actions by I_m in this chart are the same as Figure 3. This illustrates the distributed decision-making performed by agents of a transaction scheme in deciding which chart is to be executed. As long as the slave interfáce I_s does not execute its internal actions, we cannot decide whether chart for case 2 or case 3 is being executed.

---

[1] These guards are also total, when the relationships between the local variables of various processes are taken into account.

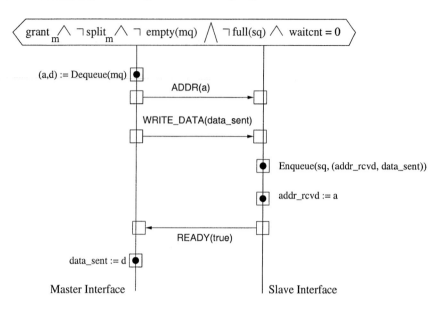

Fig. 3. Normal data transfer between master and slave interface.

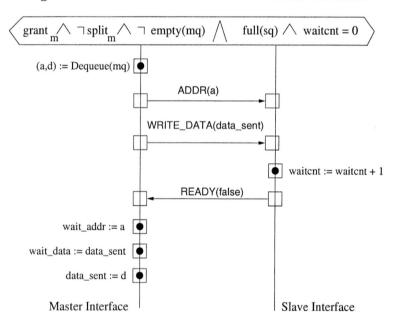

Fig. 4. Initiation of wait cycles.

Case 4 corresponds to $grant_m \wedge \neg split_m \wedge \neg full(sq) \wedge waitcnt > 0$. Thus, the master has been granted bus access (since $grant_m$ holds) and is currently going through a wait cycle (since $waitcnt > 0$). The slave is however ready to

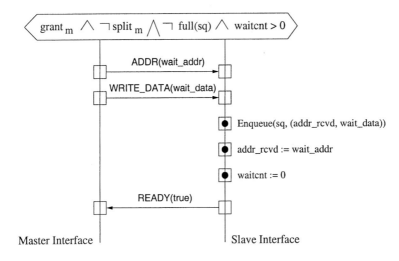

Fig. 5. The last wait cycle.

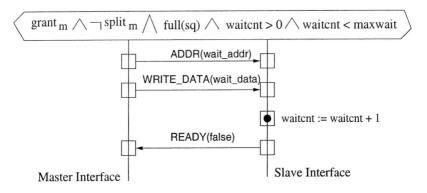

Fig. 6. A wait cycle which is not the last.

input data (since $\neg full(sq)$), that is, the master need not wait any more. Thus, this scenario corresponds to the last wait cycle. The chart is shown in Figure 5.

Case 5 corresponds to $grant_m \wedge \neg split_m \wedge full(sq) \wedge waitcnt > 0 \wedge waitcnt < maxwait$. Here again the master has been granted bus access (since $grant_m$ holds) and is currently going through a wait cycle (since $waitcnt > 0$). The slave is still not ready to input data (since $full(sq)$). This scenario corresponds to a wait cycle which is not the last. The chart appears in Figure 6.

Case 6 corresponds to $grant_m \wedge \neg split_m \wedge full(sq) \wedge waitcnt = maxwait$. Here the master is going through a wait cycle, but the number of wait cycles has reached the pre-defined threshold $maxwait$. Thus, this requires the slave to initiate *split transfer* by interacting with the bus controller. The chart appears in Figure 7.

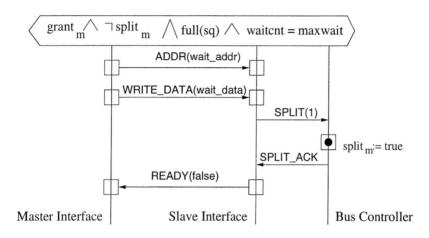

Fig. 7. Initiation of split transfer.

Case 7 corresponds to $grant_m \wedge split_m \wedge waitcnt = maxwait \wedge \neg full(sq)$. This means that the transfer from I_m to I_s was previously split, thus $split_m$ holds. However, the slave is currently ready to input data (since $\neg full(sq)$), thereby terminating the split transfer. Thus, this chart will involve exchange of SPLIT and SPLIT_ACK signals along the lines of Figure 7, and the resetting of $waitcnt$ to zero.

As a matter of fact, the AMBA bus protocol is intended for interaction between multiple masters and multiple slaves. Here we have modeled only one master and one slave. However, all the features for multi-component interaction have been, in principle, captured. For example, the suspension of bus access to a master (split transfers) is to allow another master to take over bus access. In our case, even with one master we have modeled this feature via the variable $split_m$. In future, we plan to explicitly model interaction among multiple masters and slaves, that is, multiple instances of P_m and P_s.

3   Cyclic Transaction Processes

We shall build up our model, starting with the transactions. Through the rest of this section we fix a finite set of processes $\mathcal{P}$ and let p, q range over $\mathcal{P}$. We also fix a finite message alphabet M and let m, m' range over M. In our model each process will have a set of local variables whose values will be updated (and sometimes transmitted) during an execution. The values of these variables will also determine the truth-values of the predicates guarding the individual events as well the transactions. In order to simplify the formal model, we will abstract the role of these variables with the help of propositional variables. In concrete models however, as in the previous section, we will feel free to use local variables explicitly. We now fix a pair-wise disjoint family $\{Prop_p\}_{p \in \mathcal{P}}$ where each $Prop_p$ is a finite set of propositions on the local variables of process p. We also fix a finite set of internal actions Act with a, b ranging over Act.

We use Σ_p to denote the set of actions executed by p; it consists of actions of the form $(g, p!q, m, A)$, $(g, p?q, m, A)$ and (g, p, a, A). In each case, g is called the guard of the action and it is a propositional formula built out of $Prop_p$ (we identify propositionally equivalent formulae). We also require $A \subseteq Prop_p$. The communication action $(g, p!q, m, A)$ stands for p sending the message m to q when the guard g holds. As a result of this action, the set of propositions in A begin to hold. In a similar way, the communication action $(g, p?q, m, A)$ represents p receiving the message m from q with g and A interpreted as before. Finally (g, p, a, A) is an internal action of p with a being the member of Act being executed and g and A interpreted as before. We set $\Sigma = \bigcup_{p \in \mathcal{P}} \Sigma_p$ and let α, β range over Σ.

A *transaction* is finite MSC over Σ. We shall view a transaction (MSC) as a Σ-labeled poset $t = (E, \leq, \lambda)$ with $\lambda : E \to \Sigma$ satisfying the restrictions required by an MSC. We shall assume the usual formalization of MSCs (say, as in [1, 13]). We assume a simple setting where message passing via point-to-point (unbounded) FIFOs is the communication mechanism. Again, in concrete examples, as in the previous section, it is convenient to assume that the messages have an internal structure using which values can be passed between processes. In the formal model however, this will be captured with the help of the truth values of the propositional variables.

Let $t = (E, \leq, \lambda)$ be a transaction. Then $E_p = \{e \mid e \in E$ and $\lambda(e) \in \Sigma_p\}$. Further, $agents(t) = \{p \mid E_p \neq \emptyset\}$. We shall assume without loss of generality that $E \neq \emptyset$ so that $agents(t) \neq \emptyset$. Next suppose $X \subseteq E$. Then $\downarrow X = \{y \mid \exists x \in X$ with $y \leq x\}$. We shall say that X is *down-closed* in case $\downarrow X = X$. Next let $\emptyset \neq P \subseteq agents(t)$. Then the *P-fragment* of t is denoted as $t \upharpoonright P$ and it is the Σ-labeled poset $(E^P, \leq_P, \lambda_P)$ where E^P is the largest down-closed subset of E satisfying : if $e \in E^P$ and $e' \leq e$ then $e' \in E_p$ for some $p \in P$. Further, $\leq_P (\lambda_P)$ is $\leq (\lambda)$ restricted to $E^P \times E^P (E^P)$.

Definition 1 (Transaction Scheme) A *transaction scheme* is a finite family $T = \{G_i : t_i\}_{i=1}^k$ where :

- Each $t_i = (E_i, \leq_i, \lambda_i)$ is a transaction.
- each G_i is of the form $\bigwedge_{p \in agents(t_i)} g_i^p$ where g_i^p is a guard built out of $Prop_p$.
- If $i \neq j$ then t_i and t_j are not isomorphic.
- $\{G_i\}_{i=1}^k$ are mutually exclusive, deterministic and total in the sense :
  - Suppose $\emptyset \neq P \subseteq agents(t_i) \cap agents(t_j)$ and $\bigwedge_{p \in P}(g_i^p \wedge g_j^p)$ is satisfiable. Then the P-fragments of t_i and t_j are isomorphic.
  - $G_1 \vee G_2 \vee \ldots \vee G_k$ is a tautology.

Thus G_i is a global guard which determines when t_i is to be executed. This choice will however be made in a distributed fashion during a computation. It could be the case that at some stage during an execution of the transaction scheme T, for some $\emptyset \neq P \subseteq agents(t_i) \cap agents(t_j)$, the truth values of $\bigcup_{p \in P} Prop_p$ are such that $\bigwedge_{p \in P}(g_i^p \wedge g_j^p)$ is satisfiable. Hence at this stage we still will not know whether t_i or t_j (or some other t_l) will eventually run to completion. In any case, we require that the partial executions relative to t_i and

t_j must be indistinguishable. In this sense the transactions are executed in a deterministic fashion. The above definition captures the intuition that *any particular execution of a transaction scheme $T = \{G_i : t_i\}_{i=1}^k$ must execute one of the constituent transactions of T, that is, one of $t_1, \ldots, t_k$.*

It is worth remarking here that a transaction scheme involving just one agent and only internal actions can be used to model interactions with the environment. These special transaction schemes can be allowed to execute non-deterministically so as to capture the lack of control over the inputs supplied by the environment.

In the following, we shall denote by $agents(T)$ the set of processes given by $agents(T) = \bigcup_{1 \leq i \leq k} agents(t_i)$ where $T = \{G_i : t_i\}_{i=1}^k$ is a transaction scheme. We now define the CTP model:

Definition 2 (CTP) A CTP is a structure $\mathcal{S} = (\{S_p\}_{p \in \mathcal{P}}, \mathcal{T}, \theta, s_{in}, V_{in})$ where:

- Each S_p is a finite set of p-local states, the local control states of p.
- $\mathcal{T}$ is a finite set of transactions schemes.
- θ is a distribution function which assigns to each $T \in \mathcal{T}$ a pair $(pre_T, post_T)$ with $pre_T, post_T : agents(T) \to \bigcup_{p \in \mathcal{P}} S_p$ such that $pre_T(p), post_T(p) \in S_p$ for each $p \in agents(T)$.
- $s_{in} \in \prod_{p \in \mathcal{P}} S_p$ is the global initial control state.
- V_{in} is the initial valuation function which assigns to each p a subset of $Prop_p$.
- To capture the cyclicity property, we let $\mathcal{T}_p = \{T \mid p \in agents(T)\}$ for each p. We also define $R_p = \{(s, T, s') \mid T \in \mathcal{T}_p \text{ and } s = pre_T(p) \text{ and } s' = post_T(p)\}$. We now require that, for each p, the sets S_p and $\mathcal{T}_p$ can be indexed as $S_p = \{s_1, s_2, \ldots, s_{n_p}\}$ and $\mathcal{T}_p = \{T_1, T_2, \ldots, T_{n_p}\}$ so that $R_p = \{(s_i, T_i, s_{i+1}) \mid 1 \leq i < n_p\} \cup \{(s_{n_p}, T_{n_p}, s_1)\}$.

It is the cyclicity requirement which makes the CTP model tractable. Under this regime, each agent p will repeatedly (attempt to) execute $T_1.T_2. \ldots .T_{n_p}$ with the corresponding element in S_p signaling in which portion of the cycle p is currently residing. The function pre_T specifies the local control state that each $p \in agents(T)$ must be in (given by $pre_T(p)$) for it to execute actions belonging to Σ_p within the transactions appearing in T. Similarly $post_T$ specifies the resulting control state for each $p \in agents(T)$ when p has completed all its actions relative to T. In our model, this initiating and terminating of a transaction scheme will in general be *asynchronously* carried out by the participating agents. In other words, we shall consider an interleaved asynchronous semantics here. We can however, use it to model synchronously executing systems; a set of actions being executed in a single step will be then captured by all possible interleavings of this set of actions in the present setting.

Operational Semantics. We now turn to the operational semantics of the CTP model. In order to bring out the main ideas clearly we shall define the semantics only for a restricted subclass called *anchored* CTPs. The example treated in the previous section is an example of anchored CTP. To define anchored CTPs, let $t = (E, \leq, \lambda)$ be a transaction. Then $p \in agents(t)$ is called the *master process* of t if there exist e_{in} and e_{fin} in E_p such that e_{in} is the smallest event and e_{fin} is the greatest event in E under $\leq$. Thus the master process initiates and terminates the whole transaction. The transaction scheme $T = \{G_i : t_i\}_{i=1}^k$ is said to be *anchored* in case there exists $p \in agents(T)$ such that p is the master process of t_i for every $i \in \{1, 2, \ldots, k\}$. Finally the CTP $\mathcal{S}$ is said to be anchored in case all its transactions schemes are anchored. An important consequence of this restriction is that at most one instance of a transaction scheme will be active during an execution and as a result, the state space turn out to be finite.

We now fix an anchored CTP $\mathcal{S} = (\{S_p\}_{p \in \mathcal{P}}, \mathcal{T}, \theta, s_{in}, V_{in})$. Our operational semantics associates a labeled transition system with $\mathcal{S}$ whose label set is $\mathcal{T} \times \Sigma$. The states of this transition system are called configurations. Each configuration consists of four components : a global control state, a valuation function, the states of the communication channels attached to the transaction schemes and a progress table. This last component keeps track of the currently active transaction schemes. Within a scheme, the progress table keeps track of the potential transactions being executed where the final identity of the transaction will be determined only when the truth values of the relevant guards become available in the vicinity of the transaction scheme.

Let $T = \{G_i : t_i\}_{i=1}^k$ be a transaction scheme with $t_i = (E_i, \leq_i, \lambda_i)$. A *progress function* for T assigns to each i the symbol $\#$ or a *down-closed* subset of E_i such that the following conditions are satisfied :

- $f_T(i) \neq \#$ for some i.
- If $f_T(i) \neq \#$ then $f_T(i) \subset E_i$.
- Suppose $f_T(i) \neq \#$, $f_T(j) \neq \#$ and $\preceq_i$ ($\preceq_j$) is $\leq_i$ ($\leq_j$) restricted to $f_T(i) \times f_T(i)$ ($f_T(j) \times f_T(j)$). Further, ν_i (ν_j) is λ_i (λ_j) restricted to $f_T(i)$ ($f_T(j)$). Then $(f_T(i), \preceq_i, \nu_i)$ and $(f_T(j), \preceq_j, \nu_j)$ are isomorphic.

$f_T(i) = \#$ denotes that t_i is ruled out for the current execution. If both t_i and t_j are considered to be currently active then we cannot distinguish between t_i and t_j in terms of the actions that have been executed so far. If $f_T(i) \neq \#$ and $f_T(i) \neq \emptyset$ for some i, we will say that T is active under f.

A *progress table* for $\mathcal{T}$ is a family $\{f_T\}_{T \in \mathcal{T}}$ where each f_T is a progress function for T. The active transaction under a progress table are the transactions that are active under the corresponding progress functions.

Channel states will capture the contents of the communication channels. Let $T \in \mathcal{T}$. Then $Ch_T = \{(p, q) \mid p \neq q \text{ and } p, q \in agents(T)\}$. A T-channel state is a function $\xi_T : Ch_T \to M^\star$.

We define a *configuration* of $\mathcal{S}$ as a quadruple $(s, V, \{\xi_T\}_{T \in \mathcal{T}}, \{f_T\}_{T \in \mathcal{T}})$ s.t.

- $s \in \prod_{p \in \mathcal{P}} S_p$ is a global control state.
- V is a valuation that assigns a subset of $Prop_p$ to each p.
- ξ_T is a T-channel state for each T.
- $\{f_T\}_{T \in \mathcal{T}}$ is a progress table for $\mathcal{T}$.

The initial configuration is $c_{in} = (s_{in}, V_{in}, \{\xi_T^{in}\}_{T \in \mathcal{T}}, \{f_T^{in}\}_{T \in \mathcal{T}})$ whose first two components are as in $\mathcal{S}$. Further, $\xi_T^{in}(ch) = \epsilon$ for every T and every $ch \in$

Ch_T. Finally, for each $T \in \mathcal{T}$ with $T = \{G_i : t_i\}_{i=1}^{k}$, $f_T^{in}(i) = \#$ if there exists $p \in agents(T)$ such that $s_{in}(p) = pre_T(p)$ and $V_{in}(p)$ does not satisfy g_i^p; otherwise $f_T(i) = \emptyset$ (recall that $G_i = \bigwedge_{p \in P} g_i^p$).

We define the notion of a transition label being enabled. The set of transition labels is $L = \mathcal{T} \times \Sigma$. Let $c = (s, V, \{\xi_{\widehat{T}}\}_{\widehat{T} \in \mathcal{T}}, \{f_{\widehat{T}}\}_{\widehat{T} \in \mathcal{T}})$ be a configuration and $(T, \alpha) \in L$. To define the notion of (T, α) being *enabled* at c, consider $T = \{G_i : t_i\}_{i=1}^{k}$ with $t_i = (E_i, \leq_i, \lambda_i)$ for each i. We first construct $J \subseteq \{1, 2, \dots, k\}$ and the family of events $\{e_j\}_{j \in J}$ via : $j \in J$ iff $f_T(j) \neq \#$ and there exists $e_j \in E_j - f_T(j)$ such that $f_T(j) \cup \{e_j\}$ is down-closed and $\lambda_j(e_j) = \alpha$. Now (T, α) is enabled at c iff the following are satisfied (we assume $\alpha \in \Sigma_p$):

- $J \neq \emptyset$ (events which must precede α have completed in a transaction of T)
- $V(p)$ satisfies g where g is the guard of α (the first component of α).
- $s(p) = pre_T(p)$ ((T, α) could be the first action to be executed by T).
- If α is of the form $(g, p?q, m, A)$ then $\xi_T((p, q))$ is of the form $\sigma.m$ with $\sigma \in M^*$ (message m is at the head of the FIFO (p, q)).

We define $\longrightarrow$, the *transition relation*. Consider transition label $(T, \alpha) \in L$ and configuration $c = (s, V, \{\xi_{\widehat{T}}\}_{\widehat{T} \in \mathcal{T}}, \{f_{\widehat{T}}\}_{\widehat{T} \in \mathcal{T}})$. Then $c \xrightarrow{(T, \alpha)} c'$ iff (T, α) is enabled at c and $c' = (s', V', \{\xi'_{\widehat{T}}\}_{\widehat{T} \in \mathcal{T}}, \{f'_{\widehat{T}}\}_{\widehat{T} \in \mathcal{T}})$ satisfies (we assume $\alpha \in \Sigma_p$):

- Let $q \in agents(T)$. Suppose $s(q) = pre_T(q)$ and $(f_T(j) \cup \{e_j\}) \cap E_j^q = E_j^q$ for every $j \in J$ (recall the index set J computed in the definition of the enabledness of (T, α) at c). Then $s'(q) = post_T(q)$. Otherwise $s'(q) = s(q)$. If $q \notin agents(T)$ then $s'(q) = s(q)$ [2].
- $V'(p) = A$ where A is the last component of α. If $q \neq p$ then $V'(q) = V(q)$.
- $\xi'_T((p, q)) = m.\xi_T((p, q))$ when α is of the form $(g, p!q, m, A)$. If α is of the form $(g, p?q, m, A)$ then $\xi'_T((p, q)) = \sigma$ where $\xi_T((p, q)) = \sigma.m$; finally if α is an internal action then $\xi'_T = \xi_T$. For all other transaction schemes $\widehat{T} \neq T$ we set $\xi'_{\widehat{T}} = \xi_{\widehat{T}}$.
- To define f'_T, it is convenient to first define the predicate (PR) as follows.

(PR) $J = \{j\}$ is a singleton and $f_T(j) \cup \{e_j\} = E_j$ [3]

Now suppose (PR) is satisfied. Then $f'_T(i) = \#$ if there exists q such that $s'(q) = pre_T(q)$ and $V'(q)$ does not satisfy g_i^q (as before $T = \{G_i : t_i\}_{i=1}^{k}$ and $G_i = \bigwedge_{q \in P} g_i^q$). Otherwise $f'_T(i) = \emptyset$ [4]. In case (PR) is not satisfied, $f'_T(j) = \#$ if $j \notin J$ and $f'_T(j) = f_T(j) \cup \{e_j\}$ if $j \in J$.

---

[2] Once the transactions t_j with $j \in J$ are updated, it could turn out that some process $q \neq p$ has no more events to execute whereas, before the occurrence of (T, α) there may have been an active transaction t_l in which q still had some events to execute.

[3] This signifies that t_j is the final identity of the transaction that has been chosen for execution and it has just finished.

[4] We need to prepare T for the next possible execution. Some of the transactions in T may already be ruled out by the updated valuation V' (in case $pre_T(q) = post_T(q)$). For those that are not ruled out, we reset the progress function via $f'_T(i) = \emptyset$.

For all other transaction schemes $\widehat{T} \neq T$, we define $f'_{\widehat{T}}$ as follows. Suppose $\widehat{T} \neq T$ with $\widehat{T} = \{\widehat{G}_i : \widehat{t}_i\}_{i=1}^{\widehat{k}}$. Then $f'_{\widehat{T}}(i) = \#$ if there exists q such that $pre_{\widehat{T}}(q) = s'(q)$ and $V'(q)$ does not satisfy $\widehat{g}_i^q$ (we are assuming here that $\widehat{G}_i = \bigwedge_{q \in \mathcal{P}} \widehat{g}_i^q$). Otherwise $f'_{\widehat{T}}(i) = f_{\widehat{T}}(i)$.

Finally, the *transition system* associated with $\mathcal{S}$ is $TS_{\mathcal{S}} = (C_{\mathcal{S}}, L, \Longrightarrow, c_{in})$ where $C_{\mathcal{S}}$ and $\Longrightarrow \subseteq C_{\mathcal{S}} \times L \times C_{\mathcal{S}}$ are the least sets satisfying *(i)* $c_{in} \in C_{\mathcal{S}}$, and *(ii)* if $c \in C_{\mathcal{S}} \wedge c \xrightarrow{(T,\alpha)} c'$ then $c' \in C_{\mathcal{S}}$ and $c \xRightarrow{(T,\alpha)} c'$. It is easy to see that $TS_{\mathcal{S}}$ is a *finite state* transition system. Consequently, interfaces specified with the help of anchored CTPs can be realized as finite state devices.

4 Analysis and Verification Issues

In section 3, we provided the operational semantics for anchored CTPs. This semantics can however be extended to handle all CTPs [21]. The main complication is that, in general, more than one instance of a transaction scheme can be active at a configuration. The number of such instances can be unbounded. The major change in the operational semantics, to handle such CTPs is in the definition of the progress table and the manner in which the table is updated during a transition. The main idea is that the entry in the table corresponding to a transaction scheme T will consist of an ordered set of progress functions $\{f_T^1, f_T^2, \ldots, f_T^m\}$ where m can grow unboundedly. The indexing will reflect the "age" of the various instances with the earlier entries deleted (upon completion) before the later ones. A CTP is *bounded* iff the associated transition system is finite under the full semantics. Anchored CTPs (presented in the last section) will be bounded under the full semantics.

It is not difficult to associate a Petri net with a CTP and hence determining if a CTP is bounded is effectively decidable. A Petri net based operational semantics of the full CTP model appears in [21]. In fact, in this work we show that even the cyclicity restriction of CTP can be weakened.

We can reason about bounded CTPs using standard temporal logics. In fact, we can even use features of the LSC specification language to describe properties of bounded CTPs. To sketch the main ideas, let $\mathcal{S}$ be a bounded CTP and $TS_{\mathcal{S}}$ over be its associated transition system. We can view $TS_{\mathcal{S}}$ as a Kripke structure with $Prop = \bigcup_{p \in \mathcal{P}} Prop_p$ as the set of atomic propositions. We can interpret formulas of the following variant of CTL over this Kripke structure with x ranging over $Prop$ and α ranging over the set of actions Σ.

$$CTPL(\mathcal{P}, Prop) ::= x \mid \sim \varphi \mid \varphi \vee \varphi' \mid \langle \alpha \rangle \varphi \mid EU(\varphi, \varphi') \mid AU(\varphi, \varphi')$$

Thus the only variation from CTL is the next (EX) operator which is now indexed by an action. The assertion $\langle \alpha \rangle \varphi$ holds at a configuration c if there exists a configuration c' and a transaction T such that $c \xRightarrow{(T,\alpha)} c'$ and φ holds at c'. The remaining operators are interpreted in the usual way.

We now encode the existential and universal charts of LSC into this logic along the lines suggested in [10]. Let $t = (E, \leq, \lambda)$ be a transaction, $lin(t)$ be the set of linearizations of the poset $(E, \leq)$ and $Lin(t) = \{\lambda(\tau) \mid \tau \in lin(t)\}$ where λ also denotes the natural extension of λ to $E^\star$. We will say that an existential chart $\langle\langle t \rangle\rangle$ is satisfied at a configuration c if there *exists* a path $c_0 \overset{(T_0, \alpha_0)}{\Longrightarrow} c_1 \overset{(T_1, \alpha_1)}{\Longrightarrow}$ $c_2 \ldots c_n \overset{(T_n, \alpha_n)}{\Longrightarrow} c_{n+1}$ with $c = c_0$ (i.e finite path from c) such that:

- $\sigma \upharpoonright \Sigma_t \in Lin(t)$ where $\sigma = \alpha_0.\alpha_1.\ldots.\alpha_n$, $\Sigma_t = \{\lambda(e) \mid e \in E\}$ and $\sigma \upharpoonright \Sigma_t$ is obtained from σ by deleting all appearances of letters not in Σ_t.

Similarly we will say that a universal chart $[[t]]$ is satisfied at a configuration c if *every* path from c has a prefix whose Σ_t-projection is in $Lin(t)$. Both these assertions (existential and universal charts) can be expressed in CTPL. We can also encode in CTPL existential and universal charts with pre-charts or activation messages (as presented in [6, 10]). Furthermore, one can devise linear time temporal logics in a standard way for bounded CTPs.

Acknowledgments

Luciano Lavagno suggested using MSCs to model component interfaces in embedded systems and this led to the formulation of the CTP model. He also provided a concrete example and valuable insights during discussions with the second author. This work was partially supported by a National University of Singapore Research Grant R-252-000-103-112.

References

1. R. Alur, G.J. Holzmann, and D.A. Peled. An analyzer for message sequence charts. In *International Conference on Tools and Algorithms for Construction and Analysis of Systems (TACAS), LNCS 1055*, 1996.
2. R. Alur and M. Yannakakis. Model checking of message sequence charts. In *International Conference on Concurrency Theory (CONCUR), LNCS 1664*, 1999.
3. ARM Limited. *AMBA On-chip Bus Specification*, 1999.
4. G. Booch, I. Jacobsen, and J. Rumbaugh. *Unified Modeling Language for Object-oriented development*. Rational Software Corporation, 1996.
5. Codesign, Simulation and Synthesis (COSY) project. *Generic Interface Modules for PI-Bus*, 2001.
6. W. Damm and D. Harel. LSCs: Breathing life into message sequence charts. *Formal Methods in System Design*, 19(1), 2001.
7. B.P. Douglass. *Doing Hard Time: Developing Real-time Systems using UML, Objects, Frameworks and Patterns*. Addison-Wesley, 1999.
8. D. Harel. Statecharts: A visual formalism for complex ystems. *Science of Computer Programming*, 8, 1987.
9. D. Harel and H. Kugler. From play-in scenarios to code: An achievable dream. In *Fundamental Approaches to Software Engineering (FASE), LNCS 1783*, 2000.

10. D. Harel and H. Kugler. Synthesizing state-based object systems from LSC specifications. In *International Conference on Implementation and Applications of Automata (CIAA), LNCS 2088*, 2001.
11. D. Harel, H. Kugler, R. Marelly, and A. Pnueli. Smart play-out of behavioral requirements. Technical report, Weizmann Institute of Science, 2002.
12. D. Harel and R. Marelly. Specifying and executing behavioral requirements: The play-in/play-out apprroach. Technical report, Weizmann Institute of Science, 2001.
13. J.G. Hendriksen, M. Mukund, K.N. Kumar, and P.S. Thiagarajan. Message sequence graphs and finitely generated regular MSC languages. In *International Colloquium on Automata, Languages and Programming (ICALP), LNCS 1853*, 2000.
14. J.G. Hendriksen, M. Mukund, K.N. Kumar, and P.S. Thiagarajan. Regular collections of message sequence charts. In *Mathematical Foundations of Computer Science (MFCS), LNCS 1893*, 2000.
15. I. Krueger, R. Grosu, P. Scholz, and M. Broy. From MSCs to statecharts. In *International Workshop on Distributed and Parallel Embedded Systesms (DIPES)*, 1998.
16. S. Leue, L. Mehrmann, and M. Ressi. Synthesizing ROOM models from message sequence chart specifications. Technical report, University of Waterloo, Tech Report 98-06, 1998.
17. P. Madhusudan. Reasoning about sequential and branching behaviours of message sequence graphs. In *International Colloquium on Automata, Languages and Programming (ICALP), LNCS 2076*, 2001.
18. A. Muscholl and D.A. Peled. Deciding properties of message sequence charts. In *Foundations of Software Science and Computation Structures(FoSSaCS)*, 1998.
19. A. Muscholl and D.A. Peled. Message sequence graphs and decision problems on Mazurkiewicz traces. In *Mathematical Foundations of Computer Science(MFCS), LNCS 1672*, 1999.
20. A. Muscholl and D.A. Peled. From finite state communication protocols to high-level message sequence charts. In *International Colloquium on Automata, Languages and Programming (ICALP), LNCS 2076*, 2001.
21. A. Roychoudhury and P.S. Thiagarajan. Communicating transaction processes. Technical report, National University of Singapore, 2002.
22. Z.120. Message Sequence Charts (MSC'96), 1996.

Graph-Based Models
of Internetworking Systems*

Gianluigi Ferrari, Ugo Montanari, and Emilio Tuosto

Dipartimento di Informatica, Università di Pisa
{giangi,ugo,etuosto}@di.unipi.it

Abstract. Graphical notations have been widely accepted as an expressive and intuitive working tool for system specification and design. This paper outlines a declarative approach based on (hyper-)graphs and graph synchronization to deal with the modeling of Wide Area Network applications. This paper aims at contributing to the understanding of crucial issues involved in the specification and design of Wide Area Network systems, as a first step toward the development of software engineering techniques and tools for designing and certificating internetworking systems.

1   Introduction

The problem of supporting the development of highly decentralized applications (from requirement and design to implementation and maintenance) is at the edge of research in software engineering. Several commercial systems (e.g. *Napster*, *Gnutella*) have led to an increasing demand of innovative techniques to model, document and certify the development of applications. On the one hand, the traditional software engineering technologies (e.g. client–server architecture) emphasize an interaction model which is rather different from the interaction model of truly distributed applications. For instance, users of traditional distributed applications can invoke a service regardless of whether the service is local, remote or under the control of a different network authority. Instead, in the context of Wide Area Network applications the *awareness* of network information is crucial for choosing the best services that match user's requirements. Indeed, network awareness can be exploited to provide as much information about the network facilities as possible to designers, aiming at specifying and implementing robust modules. On the other hand, in the next few years evolutionary *middlewares* based on SOAP-XML-UDDI-WSDL will become the standard in software industry. It is interesting to note, however, that some innovative applications (e.g. peer-to-peer) are developed largely "ad hoc", exploiting the traditional client-server interaction model.

Hence, independently from the underlying technology, we argue that requirement engineering technologies must support the shift from the client-server in-

---

* Research supported by European IST FET-GC project AGILE, by MSR Cambridge project NAPI, and by Italian MIUR projects COMETA and NAPOLI.

B.K. Aichernig and T. Maibaum (Eds.): Formal Methods ..., LNCS 2757, pp. 242–266, 2003.

teraction model to other interaction models which better accommodate the constraints posed by the new applications. The present paper intends to address this issue.

The Unified Modeling Language (UML) [6, 40] has been widely accepted throughout the software industries and has become the *de facto* standard for specifying the development of software systems. In fact, UML provides a graphical notation to describe both structural and behavioral aspects of systems. In particular class and state diagrams are the fundamental units which allow the designer to specify the behaviour of object-based systems. However, class and state diagrams provide the abstraction to understand method invocation independently from the location of the object. However, as pointed out by Waldo et al. [47], method invocation in a truly distributed application is inherently different from method invocation in a traditional distributed application. A specification technique which ignores such a difference will not support at the right level of abstraction software design pointing out the possible architectural choices in the system under development.

Previous work on the formalization of UML has produced a semantic framework based on *graph transformations* (see [20, 29, 35] and the references therein). The evolution of a UML specification may be understood as a graph transformation. This paper describes a variation of graph transformation semantics which directly supports network awareness. Hence, what is missing in the UML specification can be actually found at the semantic level.

Our approach is based on (hyper-)graphs and local graph synchronization and extends the graphical calculus for mobility introduced in [33]. Hyper-graphs naturally provide the capabilities to describe internetworking systems: edges are used to represent components and nodes model the network environment of components. The sharing of nodes by some edges means that the corresponding components may interact by exploiting network communication infrastructure. Graph synchronization is purely local and it is obtained by the combination of graph rewriting with constraint solving. The intuitive idea is that properties of components are specified as constraints over their local resources. Hence, the local evolutions of components depend on the outcome of a (possibly distributed) constraint satisfaction algorithm.

In other words, graphs and graph synchronization foster a declarative approach by identifying the points where satisfaction of certain properties has a strong impact on behaviours. The key issue of the approach is that components see the network environment as a set of constraints. Then, the declarative specification of service requests to the network yields various kinds of constraints for the graphical calculus. Thus the actual behaviour is the result of a distributed constraint solving algorithm [39, 50].

This paper aims at providing an understanding of some crucial issues of Wide Area Network computing, as a step toward the development of software engineering techniques and tools for the design and certification of such systems. We first discuss some of the difficult issues involved in building Wide Area Network applications, thus delineating the corresponding requirements for software engineering techniques. To present the basic ideas underlying our graphical calculus, we outline an operational framework for the Ambient calculus [11] in terms hypergraphs and hypergraph synchronization. Finally, we delineate a formal methodology that builds over graph synchronization to equip UML with semantic mechanisms to deal with the modelling of Wide Area Network applications.

2   WAN Computing: A Roadmap

Wide-Area Network (WAN) applications have become one of the most important applications in current distributed computing. Indeed, Internet and the World Wide Web are now the primary environment for designing, developing and distributing applications. Network services have now evolved into self-contained components which inter-operate easily with each other by supporting WEB-based access protocols [34]. In addition, network services may adapt themselves to match the particular capabilities of a variety of devices ranging from traditional PCs to Personal Digital Assistants and Mobile Phones having intermittent connectivity to the network. In other words, WAN applications are highly decentralized and dynamically reconfigurable (e.g. network services are assumed to be *linked* to other services to achieve the required functionalities). This section outlines our perspective on the current status of the research on WAN computing by identifying the fundamental concepts and the proper abstractions which are useful in specifying, designing and implementing WAN applications.

Network Awareness

Current software technologies emphasize the notion of WEB SERVICE as a key idiom to control design and development of applications. Conceptually, WEB SERVICEs are stand-alone components that reside over the nodes of the network. Each WEB SERVICE has an interface which is network accessible through standard network protocols and describes the interaction capabilities of the service (e.g., the message format). Wide Area Network applications are developed by combining and integrating together WEB SERVICEs, which do not have pre-existing knowledge of how they will interact with each other.

The exploitation of components in a WAN setting raises a number of issues. First, given the heterogeneity of the network environment, components should be highly portable: they should be usable everywhere, provided that certain services actually behave properly (i.e. services are used to adapt components to a variety of infrastructures). Second, security should be ensured in any environment: since components downloaded from different authorities have different security requirements, they should be executed within different run-time environments. Third, dynamic adaptability should be ensured: WAN applications have highly dynamic requirements and they should be able to reconfigure their structure and their components at run-time to respond to dynamic changes of the network environment.

Summing up, a WAN application does not appear as a single integrated computer facility to its users as it is the case of traditional distributed applications. For instance, users of traditional distributed applications can invoke a service regardless of whether the service is local, remote or under the control of a different network authority. Instead, in the WAN setting the *awareness* of network information is crucial for choosing the best services that match user requirements. For instance, users can react to phenomena like network congestion by binding their network devices to different available resources. Similarly, network awareness is exploited by WAN application designers to control resource usages and resource accesses in order to ensure and maintain certain security levels. Finally, network awareness can be exploited to provide as much information about the sources of network exceptions as possible, in order to allow the designer to specify robust exception handlers.

Network awareness is thus the distinguished and novel issue of WAN applications and refers to the explicit ability of dealing with the unpredictable Quality of Service (QoS) properties of the network environment. Here, QoS is meant as a measure of the *non functional* properties of services along multiple dimensions. For instance, *network bandwidth* is a QoS measure for multimedia services. *Timely response* and *security* are other examples of (higher level) QoS measures. In general, the perceived QoS of computations is no longer given by the performance of the WEB servers but rather by the availability of certain resources, by the security level provided, by the flow of network traffic, and so on.

Current distributed technologies allow applications to control network connectivity and resource accesses. A paradigmatic example is provided by the Java programming language through the SOCKET and the SECURITY APIs. Similarly, the Microsoft .NET architecture supplies a programming technology embodying general facilities for handling heterogeneity. As far as security is concerned, *cryptographic* techniques have been exploited to solve several problems related to security of data communications (authentication, secrecy and integrity). Finally, *firewalls* are barriers that administrative domains build to disable the access to some critical services. In this new scenario both final users and WAN application designers put special emphasis on QoS issues.

In general, QoS attributes are special parameters of network services. *Awareness* of these information is crucial for choosing network services to match user requirements. For instance, final users can react to network congestion by binding their network devices to different sites where the requested services are available. Similarly, QoS awareness is exploited by WAN application designers to control resource usage and resource access in order to guarantee and maintain certain security levels and to provide users with differentiated QoS.

The advances in network technologies and the growth of commercial WEB services have prompted questions about suitable mechanisms for providing QoS guarantees. In the last few years, several models have been proposed to meet the demands of QoS. We mention the *Resource Reservation Protocol* (RSVP) [7], *Differentiated Services* [5], *Constraint-based Routing* [45], and we refer to [49] for a detailed discussion of this topic. This stream of research is basically *system-oriented*: it focuses on the lower layers of the Internet protocol stack.

Another significant line of research has dealt with enhancing existing distributed programming middlewares to support QoS features. QoS-aware middlewares allow clients to express their QoS requirements at a higher level of abstraction. In this way the application has good degree of control over QoS without having to deal with low-level details. Examples of QoS-aware middleware are Agilos [36], Mobiware [3], and Globus [25].

At a foundational level, most models exhibit explicit localities to reflect the idea of network awareness, e.g. Ambient calculus [11], KLAIM [19], and Mobile-Unity [38] to cite a few. Roughly speaking, locations fully identify the network environment of a component. The aforementioned approaches have improved the formal understanding of the complex mechanisms underlying network awareness. For instance, the problem of modeling resource access control of highly distributed and autonomous components has been faced by exploiting suitable notions of type [18, 30, 9, 13]. The growing demands on security have led to the development of formal models that allow specification and verification of cryptographic protocols (see [1, 46, 24, 37, 16] to cite a few). Indeed, the real challenge is to formally understand which are the features of an integrated security model for WAN applications. Wide Area Network applications integrate different computing environments having different security requirements. Moreover, the application security policy maker cannot decide with full knowledge of the current state of the application. Any realistic approach will have to identify which portion of the state of the WAN application is potentially relevant and may affect or be affected by security policy decisions. Interestingly, the notion of QoS briefly outlined above may help to investigate the proper trade-off between expressiveness and security concerns (some preliminary results can be found in [17]). However, a foundational model dealing with all these facets of network awareness is still missing.

Mobility

Mobility provides a suitable abstraction to design and implement WAN applications. The main breakthrough is that WAN applications may exchange active units of behavior and not just raw data. The usefulness of mobility emerges when developing both applications for nomadic devices with intermittent access to the network (*physical mobility*), and network services having different access policies (*logical mobility*).

Mobility has produced new design patterns [27] other than the traditional client-server paradigm:

- *Remote Evaluation*: the code is sent for execution to a remote host;
- *Code On-Demand*: the code is downloaded from a remote host to be executed locally;
- *Mobile Agents*: processes can suspend their execution and migrate to new hosts, where they can resume it.

Among these design paradigms, Code On-Demand is probably the most widely used (e.g. Java Applets). The mobile agent paradigm is, instead, the most challenging since:

- an agent, in order to run, needs an *execution environment*, i.e. a server that supplies resources for execution;
- an agent is *autonomous*: it executes independently of the user who created it (*goal driven*);
- an agent is able to detect changes in its operational environment and to act accordingly (*reactivity* and *adaptivity*).

Another interesting feature of mobile agents is the possibility of executing *disconnected operations* [42]: an agent may be remotely executed even if the user (its owner) is not connected; if this is the case, the agent may decide to "sleep" and then periodically try to reestablish the connection with its owner. Conversely, the user, when reconnected, may try to *retract* the agent back home (i.e. instruct the remote agent to return its home site).

In addition to this scenario, *ad hoc networks* [15] allow connection of nomadic devices without a fixed network structure. Finally, the shift from client-server to peer-to-peer architectures (e.g. Napster and Gnutella) has introduced a new pattern for internet interaction where information is shared among distributed components and changes dynamically.

Clearly, a formal characterization of the key concepts involved in the development of mobile applications (e.g. QoS, adaptability, resource discovery) is a major concern from a software engineering perspective.

Programming languages and systems provide basic facilities for mobility. A well known example is the Java programming language. Another interesting example is provided by Oracle [41], which supports access to a database from a mobile device by exploiting a mobile agent paradigm. However, current technologies provide only limited solutions to the general treatment of mobility.

At a foundational level, several process calculi have been developed to gain a more precise understanding of distribution and mobility. We mention the Distributed Join-calculus [26], Klaim [19], the Distributed π-calculus [31], the Ambient calculus [11], the Seal calculus [14], and Nomadic Pict [48]. Other foundational models adopt a logical style toward the analysis of mobility. *MobileUnity* [38] and *MobAdtl* [22] are program logics specifically designed to specify and reason about mobile systems exploiting a Unity-like proof system. Spatial logic [12, 10] allows one to specify properties on both the spatial dimension and the temporal dimension of WAN applications.

Coordination

Wide Area Network applications are highly decentralized and dynamically reconfigurable. Hence, they should be easily scalable in order to manage addition/removal of services, subnetworks and users without requiring to be reconfigured. Coordination is a key concept for modeling and designing WAN applications. Coordination principles separate the computational components from composition modules called *coordinators* which glue together components. Coordinators are therefore the basic mechanism to adapt components to network environment changes, to discover resources, to synchronize activities, and so on. For instance, coordinators are in charge of supporting and monitoring the execution of dynamically loaded modules. Moreover, coordinators are able to observe evolutions, and therefore they may react to an action by modifying themselves. Finally, coordination policies must be programmable to meet the evolving composition demands and to accommodate the design and the implementation of open systems. Two recent examples of coordination middlewares for WAN programming are represented by Jini and .NET Orchestration, proposed by Sun and Microsoft, respectively. The distinction between computation and coordination is also at the basis of the research on software architectures [44].

Many approaches to coordination are based on the Linda model [28] which proposes the structure of *tuple space* as the mechanism to represent the environment of applications. Experimental programming languages and middlewares have been designed following this metaphor [4, 43]. Some preliminary results on defining a discipline for orchestrating WEB SERVICEs are outlined in [2]. The approach is based on the idea of separating WEB SERVICE providers from *contract* mechanisms (also known under the name of *connectors*), which regulate WEB SERVICE coordination. Coordination laws which characterize *transactional* mechanisms in the context of distributed middleware have been presented in [8].

Research about coordination languages and models has improved the formal understanding of dynamically adaptable mobile components. However, the definition of the right level of abstraction coordination and the choice of suitable constructs to program crucial policies such as adaptation, loading and security require further research.

3   Hypergraph Synchronization

This section briefly reviews the notion of *hypergraph* as presented in [33]. First the definition of hypergraph is given, then *hypergraph rewriting systems, transitions* and *productions* are introduced. Finally, we give an informal description of how productions are applied to hypergraphs in order to rewrite them.

We assume that $\mathcal{N}$ is an ordered set of nodes. A *hypergraph* has a set of nodes and a set of *hyperedges* connected to the nodes.

In a traditional graph, an edge connects two nodes; instead, a *hyperedge* connects a set of nodes. Intuitively, an edge can be thought of as representing a binary relation between two nodes, while a hyperedge represents a relationships among many nodes. We write $L(x_1, ..., x_n)$ to indicate an edge labeled L connecting nodes $x_1, ..., x_n$. The *rank* of an hyperedge is the number of nodes that it connects, hence we say that the L above has rank n (written as $L : n$) and that L has a tentacle for each x_i; nodes $x_1, ..., x_n$ are the *attachment nodes* (or *attachment points*) of L.

Hypergraphs are described as *syntactic judgments* of the form $\Gamma \vdash G$. In a syntactic judgment, $\Gamma \subseteq \mathcal{N}$ is a set of nodes representing the external interface of the graph, namely the attachment nodes toward the environment. We shall call *external nodes of the graph* the nodes in Γ. Term G is generated by the following grammar

$$G ::= nil \mid L(\boldsymbol{x}) \mid G|G \mid \nu\, y.G.$$

The above productions permits generating the empty graph (represented by nil), single edges (using $L(\boldsymbol{x})$) composing terms in parallel (via $G \mid G$) and hiding nodes (through $\nu\, y.G$). The nodes in G which are in the scope of ν operator are called *bound* nodes; let $bn(G)$ and $fn(G)$ respectively denote the set of the bound and *free* nodes of G (the nodes of G which are not bound). A judgment $\Gamma \vdash G$ is *legal* if $fn(G) \subseteq \Gamma$.

Hereafter, hypergraphs, hyperedges or hyperarcs will be simply called graphs, edges, respectively.

A *graph rewriting system*, $\mathcal{G} = \langle \Gamma_0 \vdash G_0, \mathcal{P} \rangle$, consists of a graph and special *transitions* which we call *productions*. A transition is a logical sequent

$$\Gamma_1 \vdash G_1 \xrightarrow{\Lambda, \pi} \Gamma_2 \vdash G_2. \tag{1}$$

where $\Lambda \subseteq \Gamma_1 \times Act \times \mathcal{N}^*$ is a *set of constraints* and $\pi : \Gamma_1 \to \Gamma_1$ is a *fusion substitution*[1]; both Λ and π are detailed below. The set of actions Act is used to model synchronized rewriting. We associate actions to (some of) the nodes of $\Gamma_1 \vdash G_1$, via Λ. In this way, each rewrite of an edge must synchronize its actions with one or more of its adjacent edges; thus, in general, more that one participants will move: the number depends on the synchronization policy.

Transition (1) above rewrites $\Gamma_1 \vdash G_1$ into $\Gamma_2 \vdash G_2$ whenever the set of constraints Λ is satisfied and the fusion substitution π is applied.

If $(x, a, \boldsymbol{y}) \in \Lambda$ then all edges in G_1 that have a tentacle connected to x participate to the synchronization. They must satisfy condition a that will depend on the chosen synchronization algebra. The nodes in $\boldsymbol{y}$ are the nodes of the constraint; we let $n(\Lambda)$ denote the union of all such nodes in Λ.

Let us now consider the structure of the right hand side of sequent (1). $\Gamma_2 = \pi(\Gamma_1) \cup n(\Lambda)$; it consists of the free nodes of G_1 as transformed by π and the new nodes used in the synchronization. In general, G_2 may be any graph whose free nodes are in Γ_2.

We impose two further conditions on transitions, namely we require:

1. $\forall x, y \in \Gamma_1.\pi(x) = y \Rightarrow \pi(y) = y$, so that π induce a partition on Γ_1, where all nodes in an equivalence class are mapped to a representative element of the class.
2. $n(\Lambda) \cap \Gamma_1 \subseteq \pi(\Gamma_1)$, i.e. the nodes in $fn(G_1)$ used in the synchronization have to be representative elements induced by π.

A *production* is a transition of the form

$$set(\boldsymbol{x}) \vdash L(\boldsymbol{x}) \xrightarrow{\Lambda, \pi} \Gamma \vdash G$$

---

[1] We often omit the fusion substitution in transitions when it is the identity.

where L is an edge label of rank n and $\boldsymbol{x}$ is a n-tuple of nodes with $set(\boldsymbol{x})$ the set of nodes appearing in $\boldsymbol{x}$.

Synchronized edge replacement is obtained using graph rewriting combined with constraint solving. More specifically, we use *context-free* productions labeled with actions for coordinating the simultaneous application of two or more productions. Coordinated rewriting allows the propagation of synchronization all over the graph where productions are applied. Determining the productions to be synchronized at a given stage corresponds to solving a distributed constraint satisfaction problem [39]. In [32, 33, 21] synchronized graph rewriting has been employed to model mobility. There constraint satisfaction amounts to unification. In the present paper (see Section 4.5) an example is given where the constraints represent shortest path requirements for the routers.

A production rewrites a single edge into an arbitrary graph. A production $p = (L \rightarrow R)$ can be applied to a graph G yielding H if there is an occurrence of an edge labeled by L in G. Graph H is obtained from G by removing the previously matched edge and by embedding a fresh copy of R in G by coalescing its external nodes with the corresponding attachment nodes of the replaced edge.

A derivation is obtained by starting from the initial graph and by executing a sequence of transitions, each obtained by synchronizing possibly several productions. The synchronization of a rewriting rule requires matching of the actions and unification of the third components of the constraints Λ. After productions are applied, the unification function is used to obtain the final graph by merging the corresponding nodes.

Given a graph rewriting system $\langle \Gamma_0 \vdash G_0, \mathcal{P} \rangle$, the set $T(\mathcal{P})$ of possible transitions is obtained from the productions $\mathcal{P}$ using four inference rules. We refer to [21] for a complete presentation of our graph rewriting system.

4   The Ambient Calculus

This section outlines the application of the graph synchronization framework to the Ambient calculus. We will not consider the whole calculus, but only a simple fragment since we aim at presenting the key ideas of the approach. The interested reader if referred to [21] for a detailed presentation.

4.1   The Calculus

The Ambient calculus relies on the notion of *ambient* that can be thought of as a bounded environment where processes interact. The syntax of Ambient is[2]

$$P ::= a[P] \mid P \mid Q \mid M.P$$
$$M ::= in\ a \mid out\ a \mid open\ a \mid M.M$$

An *ambient process* is written as $a[P]$ and represents a "place", called a, containing a process P. P is made of the parallel composition of processes

---

[2] We consider a fragment of Ambient without communication and restriction.

and subambients or it is prefixed with a sequence of capabilities M. An example of ambient together with an intuitive graphical representation are given below

$$a[in\ c.P \mid b[Q]] \mid c[R]$$

Processes exploit *capabilities* to control ambient interactions.

For instance, the in-capability in the previous example, allows the (pilot) process to drive a inside c in accordance with the following reduction

$$a[in\ c.P \mid b[Q]] \mid c[R] \rightarrow c[R \mid a[P \mid b[Q]]]$$

Dually, the out-capability makes a process to drive its surrounding ambient a outside the ambient containing a:

$$b[a[out\ b.P \mid Q] \mid R] \rightarrow b[R] \mid a[P \mid Q].$$

The semantics of the *open* prefix is defined by the following reduction:

$$open\ a.P \mid a[Q] \rightarrow P \mid Q.$$

4.2   Graph Representation of Ambient Calculus

The Ambient calculus can be casted in our graphical framework preserving the semantics of processes. We do not entirely report the translation which is detailed in [21] and limit our attention to the following translation:

$$
\begin{aligned}
[\![\ \mathbf{0}\ ]\!]_x &= x \vdash nil \\
[\![\ a[P]\ ]\!]_x &= x \vdash \nu\ y.(G \mid n(y,x)), && \text{if } y \neq x \wedge [\![\ P\ ]\!]_y = y \vdash G \\
[\![\ in\ a.P\ ]\!]_x &= x \vdash L_{in\ a.P}(x) \\
[\![\ P_1 | P_2\ ]\!]_x &= x \vdash G_1 \mid G_2, && \text{if } [\![\ P_i\ ]\!]_x = x \vdash G_i, \text{where } i = 1, 2.
\end{aligned}
$$

(We have ignored translation of out- and open-capabilities.) The above equations introduce the mapping $[\![\ P\ ]\!]_x$ that returns a graph whose (only) free node x corresponds to the root of the ambient process P.

The first equation defines the translation of the deadlocked process $\mathbf{0}$; its corresponding graph has an isolated node. The graph of $a[P]$ with free node x is obtained by constructing the graph of P on node y, attaching it to the edge $a(y,x)$ and restricting y; note that the ambient name a is interpreted as an edge from y to x labeled a. The capability $in\ a.P$ is directly represented by edges labeled by $in\ a.P$. The parallel composition $P_1 \mid P_2$ is obtained by making the graph of P_1 and P_2 to share their root node x.

4.3   Graph Semantics of Ambient Calculus

There are two kinds of productions: *activity productions*, and *coordination productions*. The activity productions describe the evolution of sequential processes
of the form $M.P$, which, in our approach, become edge labels: when an action is
performed, an edge labeled by $M.P$ is rewritten as the graph corresponding to P.
For each production, we give both the sequent and its graphical representation.
When $(x, \mu, \langle y \rangle) \in \Lambda$, node x in the right member is labeled by $\mu, \langle y \rangle$.

The activity production of an *in* capability has the form

$$\boxed{L_{in\ a.P}} \xrightarrow{\quad} \overset{\overline{in\ a}}{\underset{x}{\circ}} \implies [\![P]\!]_x \qquad x \vdash L_{in\ a.P}(x) \xrightarrow{\{(x,\overline{in\ a},\langle\rangle)\}} [\![P]\!]_x.$$

Coordination productions describe ambient interactions. In particular, coordination productions define which are the complementary actions that ambients
must perform in order to fire the required synchronization. For instance, the
coordination productions for the *in* capability are given as follows.

$(input1)$

$$x, y \vdash b(x, y) \xrightarrow{\{(x,in\ a,\langle\rangle),(y,\overline{input\ a},\langle z\rangle)\}} x, y, z \vdash b(x, z)$$

$(input2)$

$$x, y \vdash a(x, y) \xrightarrow{\{(y,input\ a,\langle x\rangle)\}} x, y \vdash a(x, y)$$

Production $(input1)$ asserts that when a process inside b wants to drive b in
an ambient a, then the destination of b will become the new node z. Production $(input2)$ controls the entrance of an external process inside ambient a: this
production simply passes the source x of a to the entering process.

4.4   Example

We now show the correspondence between reductions in the Ambient calculus
and the corresponding graph transitions. Let us consider the ambient reduction

$$b[in\ a.P \mid Q] \mid a[0] \rightarrow a[b[P \mid Q]]$$

where P and Q are sequential processes. Intuitively, a system evolution should
be of the form (we represent the restricted nodes with $\bullet$ and the free nodes with

o)

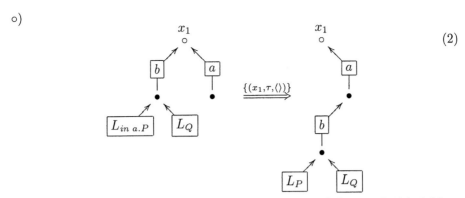

(2)

The picture on the left is the graphical representation of $[\![\, b[in\ a.P \mid Q] \mid a[0]\,]\!]_{x_1}$, while the rightmost picture is $[\![\, a[b[P \mid Q]]\,]\!]_{x_1}$.

Transition 2 will indeed be the result of a two-stages procedure:

1. the initial graph is decomposed into its constituent edges; for each edge, the productions of the edge are considered,
2. external nodes of each component are fused together in order to obtain the initial graph again; however, in this phase the productions determined in the previous step are synchronized.

First we decompose the graph in its elementary edges and determine the productions that correspond to the elementary components of the transition.

$$x_1, y_1 \vdash b(y_1, x_1) \xrightarrow{\left\{\begin{array}{l}(x_1,\ \overline{input\ a},\ \langle z_1\rangle),\\(y_1,\ in\ a,\ \langle\rangle)\end{array}\right\},\mathrm{id}} x_1, y_1, z_1 \vdash b(y_1, z_1) \tag{3}$$

$$y_2 \vdash L_{in\ a.P}(y_2) \xrightarrow{\{(y_2,\overline{in\ a},\langle\rangle)\},\mathrm{id}} y_2 \vdash L_P(y_2) \tag{4}$$

$$x_2, z \vdash a(z, x_2) \xrightarrow{\{(x_2,input\ a,\langle z\rangle)\},\mathrm{id}} x_2, z \vdash a(z, x_2) \tag{5}$$

$$y_3 \vdash L_Q(y_3) \xrightarrow{\emptyset,\mathrm{id}} y_3 \vdash L_Q(y_3) \tag{6}$$

Transitions (3) and (5) are instances of the coordination productions ($input1$) and ($input2$), respectively; transition (4) is the activity production of $in\ a.P$ and transition (6) is the identity transition that leaves L_Q idle.

Graphically, we have:

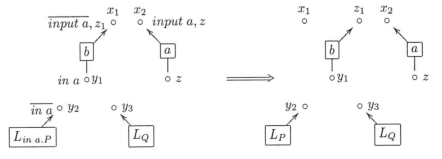

The previous graph represents the transition obtained by collecting the productions (3), (4), (5) and (6). Let

$$G_1 = b(y_1, x_1) \mid a(z, x_2) \mid L_{in\ a.P}(y_2) \mid L_Q(y_3)$$
$$G_2 = b(y_1, z_1) \mid a(z, x_2) \mid L_P(y_2) \mid L_Q(y_3)$$
$$\Gamma = \{x_1, x_2, y_1, y_2, y_3, z\}$$

then, in terms of sequents we have:

$$\Gamma \vdash G_1 \xrightarrow{\left\{\begin{array}{l}(x_1, \overline{input\ a}, \langle z_1 \rangle), \\ (x_2, input\ a, \langle z \rangle) \\ (y_1, in\ a, \langle \rangle) \\ (y_2, \overline{in\ a}, \langle \rangle)\end{array}\right\}, id} \Gamma, z_1 \vdash G_2 \tag{7}$$

The synchronization of these productions provides the fusion of the nodes in order to obtain a graph of the same shape of the ambient process. Let σ be the function that behaves as the identity on all nodes different from x_2, y_2 and y_3 and

$$\sigma : \begin{cases} x_2 \mapsto x_1 \\ y_2 \mapsto y_1 \\ y_3 \mapsto y_1 \end{cases}$$

that determines $\Lambda' = \{(x_1, \tau, \langle \rangle), (y_1, \tau, \langle \rangle)\}$ and $\rho : z_1 \mapsto z$ and the transition

$$x_1, y_1, z \vdash \sigma(G_1) \xrightarrow{\left\{\begin{array}{l}(x_1, \tau, \langle \rangle), \\ (y_1, \tau, \langle \rangle)\end{array}\right\}, id} x_1, y_1, z \vdash \rho(\sigma(G_2))$$

that is graphically represented as

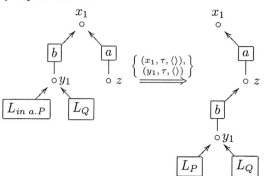

We remark that the above transition requires a synchronization involving three edges and two nodes: the edges corresponding to $in\ a.P$ and b (that synchronize on node y_1), and the edges of ambients b and a (that synchronize on node x_1). This makes clear that the in capability of ambients requires the synchronization of three components. Finally, transition 2 is obtained by applying a rule which restricts nodes on the left and the right hand side whenever no visible action occurs on them.

We want to emphasize that the steps of the example above (decomposition-synchronization) constitute a standard proof technique of our framework. Indeed, in [21] they have been used to prove a correspondence theorem between the Ambient reduction semantics and the graph semantics.

4.5   Remote Actions and Optimal Routing

In this Section we underpin the features of our graph-based model which allows us to describe and reason about non-functional aspects of WAN programming. We specify the productions of an extended *in a* capability that permits an ambient *b* to enter a *remote* ambient *a*. Furthermore, we sketch how it is possible to compute and "select" the optimal route to an ambient *a* by augmenting name unification with the solution of Bellman-Ford shortest path equations. In [17] a similar approach has been adopted for a calculus based on KLAIM [19] using the Floyd-Warshall algorithm [23].

Remote Actions. Productions for *in a* prefix requires that the moving ambient has a sibling ambient called *a*. This "neighborhood" condition reflects the reduction rule of the ambient calculus. However, we can relax such requirement and consider the possibility of having "remote" *in a* in the sense that the moving ambient can enter an ambient *a* that is a sub-ambient of one of its sibling ambients.

The idea is to add a production (*input3*) that may forward *input* signals to its inner ambients

(*input3*)
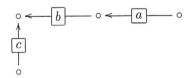

$$x, y \vdash b(x, y) \xrightarrow{\{(x,\overline{input\ a},\langle z\rangle),(y,input\ a,\langle z\rangle)\}} x, y, z \vdash b(x, y)$$

Let us consider the ambient graph

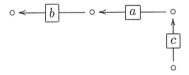

Production (*input3*) and the productions in the previous section allow the evolution whose graph representation is

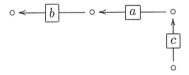

Note that *c* enters a non-sibling ambient *a*. A similar production would allow to forward input signals also to outer ambients. Exploiting both productions, an ambient with an in-capability could enter an ambient labeled *a* anywhere in the network.

Optimal Routing. We consider *weighted link edges* and *router edges*; link edges represent the connections between sites. Each link edge is labeled with a cost c. We assume that c is not null. The production schema for a link edge $c(u,v)$ is

$$u, v \vdash c(u,v) \xrightarrow{\{(u,c+\kappa'\,a,x),(v,\overline{\kappa'\,a},x)\}} u, v, x \vdash c(u,v)$$

When a link edge $c(u,v)$ finds on v the minimal cost κ' of a path to an ambient a, then it "backward" propagates to node u the cost obtained by summing c and κ'.

A router edge selects the minimal cost between two paths:

$$u, v, w \vdash \mu(u,v,w) \xrightarrow{\begin{cases} (u,\overline{\kappa_1\,a},\langle x_1\rangle) \\ (v,\overline{\kappa_2\,a},\langle x_2\rangle) \\ (w,\kappa_1\,a,\langle x_1\rangle) \end{cases}} u, v, w \vdash \mu(u,v,w), \quad \kappa_1 \le \kappa_2$$

The edge $\mu(u,v,w)$ propagates to w cost κ_1 and node x_1, where κ_1 is the minimal cost between the costs κ_1 and κ_2 of u and v.

Ambient coordination productions are extended with two new productions. The first production allows an ambient to communicate its name to a router edge, at zero cost.

$$x, z \vdash a(x,z) \xrightarrow{\{(z,0\,a,\langle x\rangle)\}} x, z \vdash a(x,z)$$

The production below states that, when an ambient b is asked to enter an ambient a from one of its internal processes and the router of b communicates the continuation x with the minimal cost κ, then b detaches from v and re-connects itself to x.

$$u, v \vdash b(u,v) \xrightarrow{\{(u,in\,a,\langle\rangle),(v,\overline{\kappa\,a},\langle x\rangle)\}} u, v, x \vdash b(u,x)$$

It can be proved (similarly to what done in Section 4.4) that the following graph transition can be obtained.

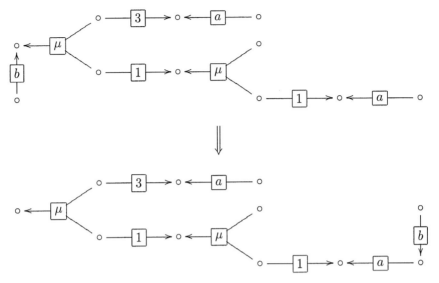

Note that the upper-most a is not entered because the path leading to it costs 3, while the bottom-most a has a path cost 2 and has been selected.

5   System Development

In this Section we show how synchronized edge rewriting can be exploited in the earlier phases of software development. In particular, we will consider UML [40] specifications and their graph transformation semantics as given in [35]. We first outline the main ideas of the methodology introduced in [35].

The Drive-Through Example. A drive-through can be visited by an ordered set of clients. Each client has a running number which indicates his/her turn. A client may submit an order to the drive-through that later will be served. The service order is established by the running number assigned at visit time.

A UML *class diagram* describing the main relations among the component (i.e. the classes) of the system may be depicted as in Figure 1. Other features of systems are expressed in UML by means of *object diagrams* that may be thought of as diagrams describing the state of the system at a given moment. Figure 2 displays an object diagram of a possible evolution of the system described in Figure 1; a drive-through and three clients have been instantiated. Two of the clients visit the drive-through and one of them has issued an order. The operations listed in the class diagram may affect the relations among the objects in a given state of the system's evolution. This is captured by transformation rules related to class diagrams. These rules transforms object diagrams in object diagrams. In general, a set of graph transformations is associated to each specified

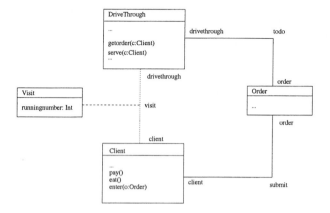

Fig. 1. UML class diagram

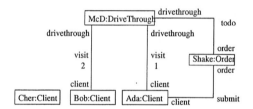

Fig. 2. UML object diagram

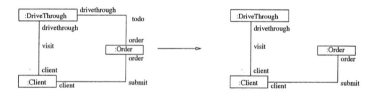

Fig. 3. Serve operation

operation. Figure 3 illustrates the rule of the serve operation for drive-through objects. The serve rule expresses that the link between the instance of an order and the instance of the drive-through that processes it is removed when the serve action is executed.

Dynamic behaviour of the system's components is described in terms of *state diagrams*. State diagrams are associated to classes and describe the state changes of their objects. They are finite state automata whose transitions are labeled with an event, a guard and an action. Labels are written as $e[g]/o'.e'$, where e is the event that triggers the transition, g is a logic formula specified in OCL [40] and represents a pre-condition to the firing of the transition. Finally, $o'.e'$ is the invocation of the method e' of object o'.

Figure 4 describes the state diagrams of classes DriveThrough and Client. The Client diagram details the activity of a client as a cyclic sequence of entering

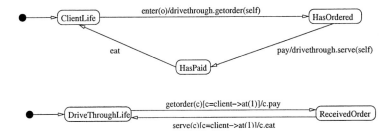

Fig. 4. UML state diagram

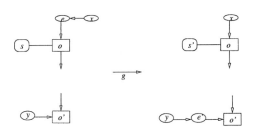

Fig. 5. Graph Transformation of a Transition

an order/asking for the order to be executed, paying/waiting for being served and eating. When a drive-through must process an order, it checks that the order has been issued by the client on the top of the stack. In this case, the client is asked to pay for it and eventually the client is served and can start eating provided that payment has been performed.

Given a state diagram, it is possible to associate a graph transformation to each transition of the diagram. For this purpose, we assume that event stacks are associated to objects. Let us consider a transition $t = s \xrightarrow{e[g]/o'.e'} s'$ of a state diagram of class C. We may interpret t as the evolution of each object o in C whose first event in its event stack is e and the guard $[g]$ is evaluated to true; transition t also dispatches the event e' to the event stack of object o'. This interpretation may naturally be formalized with the graph transformation in Figure 5 while Figure 6 is an instance of the schema detailed above and describes the rule corresponding to the serve transition of the drive-through state diagram.

Roughly, the object transformations represent the global evolution of the system caused by the activity of its components, while transitions of state diagrams represent the local state changes. The graph transformation rules corresponding to those different facets of system evolution must be mixed together in order to obtain the so called *integrated rules*. In the case of the serve rules, we have Figure 7.

Notice that the rule above do not specify some crucial aspects of the specification. For instance, the integrated rule of Figure 7 does not describe how the eat event is pushed on the event stack of the client. In other words, the inter-

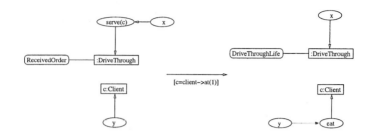

Fig. 6. Transition rule for serve

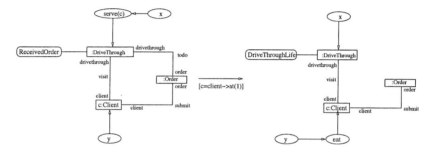

Fig. 7. Integrated rule for serve

actions between the client and the drive-through remain at the abstract level of method invocation, without being "network aware".

5.1 Formal Specification with Edge Replacement

In this section we describe how it is possible to associate productions of our calculus to the graph transformation rules given previously. We aim at showing the use of edge synchronization to formalize the issues that in the above specification have not been considered.

We consider three different forms of edges; events, controls and objects. They are graphically represented as

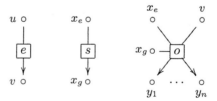

We assume that an edge label e does exist for each event e, and that a control edge exists for each state in a state diagram. Similarly, an object edge exists for each class in the UML specification. Edge e has two nodes such that a stack may be formed by merging node u of an edge labeled by e with a node v of another event edge. However, v nodes may also be fused with v of object edges.

A control edge has two nodes. Node x_e is used to acquire the actual event from the object edge, while node x_g is used for checking guard satisfaction. These nodes are fused with the corresponding nodes of an object edge. An object edge has nodes for synchronizing with its control and event edges but also nodes $y_1, ..., y_n$ for connections with other objects according to the UML class diagram of the system.

Event edges must be popped when they synchronize with objects, and they must be pushed on the existing stack when they are created. Thus event edges have two productions; the first synchronizes with objects sending to them the event name. After the transition, the edge disappears and reconnects the rest of the stack with the v node of the corresponding object by fusing u and v. The second reacts to a "push" message:

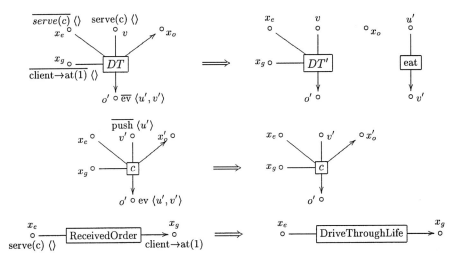

Note that the event that receives a push synchronization shifts back and fuses the v' node with the v node of the relative object edge. We remark that the previous productions are obtained by considering the intended semantics of event stacks in the UML specification. Moreover, productions for control and object edges may be derived from the UML class, object and state diagrams in a uniform way.

Let us consider the rules for serve in Figure 3 and 6. The following productions describe the evolution of each component of the system in terms of hypergraphs.

The first production states that an object edge DT that receives an event 'serve(c)' on the node corresponding to the event stack, evaluates the guard 'client→at(1)' and forwards the signal together with the evaluated guard to its control edge. It also sends the new event 'eat' on the node o' connected to the client; this is obtained by passing to the client object the nodes of the 'eat' event. As stated before, guards are expressed as OCL formulas; however, we do not model how they can be mapped into graphs and how they can be evaluated using edge replacement. The second production is the complementary rule of the previous production: when the client object receives the 'eat' event, it pushes the event and its stack. The last production states that the control edge 'ReceivedOrder' changes its label to 'DriveThroughLife' when the 'DriveThrough' object signals the 'serve(c)' event and the verification of the corresponding guard 'client→at(1)'.

The productions introduced above guarantee that it is possible to obtain a transition which is equivalent to the integrated graph transformation in Figure 7.

In order to make the stack of events properly work, it is necessary to have an edge that manages the empty stack and allows an object edge to synchronize on push action only.

$$\boxed{void} \xrightarrow[push\ \langle u',v'\rangle]{v} \circ \quad \Longrightarrow \quad \boxed{void} \xrightarrow{u'} \circ \quad \overset{v}{\circ}$$

The edge behaves as an event edge that receives a push signal and, after the transition, it is connected to the node u' that is the last node of the stack of events.

The synchronization rules ensure that the following transition can be derived

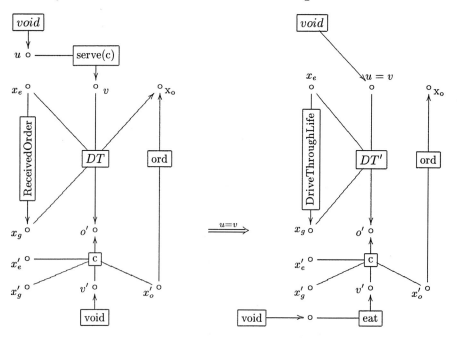

Note also that the proof technique used to obtain it is as described in Section 4.4.

6   Conclusions

This paper has introduced a formal model for specifying and designing Wide Area Network applications. The novelty of our proposal is given as the combination of the following ingredients:

- the graphical notation is designed to deal with distribution;
- mobility is obtained via local synchronization constraints and their solution using unification;
- the declarative approach based on constraints can be extended to quantitative QoS requirements, e.g. to Bellman-Ford equations for optimal routing.

We showed the applicability of the approach by considering two illustrative case studies. Indeed, we gave an interactive distributed semantics for the Ambient calculus. Moreover, our framework permits extending the Ambient calculus with capabilities for remote interaction in a straightforward manner. Finally, we outlined a technique to refine UML specifications to include explicit synchronization among components which have to reconfigure their connections to accomplish a state change.

References

1. M. Abadi and A. Gordon. A calculus for cryptographic protocols: The spi calculus. *Information and Computation*, 148(1):1–70, 1999.
2. L. Andrade and J.L. Fiadeiro. Coordination for orchestration. In *COORDINATION 2002*. LNCS, 2002.
3. O. Angin, A. Campbell, M. Kounavis, and R. Liao. The Mobiware Toolkit: Programmable Support for Adaptive Mobile Networking. *IEEE Personal Communications Magazine*, August 1998.
4. L. Bettini, R. De Nicola, G. Ferrari, and R. Pugliese. Interactive Mobile Agents in X-KLAIM. In *Proc. of the 7th Int. IEEE Workshops on Enabling Technologies: Infrastructure for Collaborative Enterprises (WETICE)*, pages 110–115, 1998.
5. S. Blake, D. Black, M. Carlson, E. Davies, Z. Wand, and W. Weiss. An architecture for differentiated services. Technical Report RFC 2475, 1998.
6. G. Booch, J. Rumbaugh, and I. Jacobson. *The Unified Modeling Language User Guide*. Addison-Wesley, 1998.
7. R. Braden, L. Zhang, S. Berson, S. Herzog, and S. Jamin. Resource reservation protocol (rsvp) - version 1 functional specification.
8. R. Bruni, C. Laneve, and U. Montanari. Orchestrating Transactions in Join Calculus. In L. Brim, P. Jancar, and M. Kretinsky, editors, *Proceedings of CONCUR 2002, 13th International Conference on Concurrency Theory*, volume 2421 of *Lecture Notes in Computer Science*, 2002.
9. M. Bugliesi, G. Castagna, and S. Crafa. Reasoning about Security in Mobile Ambients. In *Concur 2001*, number 2154 in Lecture Notes in Computer Science, pages 102–120. Springer, 2001.
10. L. Caires and L. Cardelli. A spatial logic for concurrency (part II). In *CONCUR'02*, volume 2421 of *Lecture Notes in Computer Science*. Springer, 2002.

11. L. Cardelli and A.D. Gordon. Mobile Ambients. *Theoretical Computer Science*, 240(1):177–213, 2000. An extended abstract appeared in *Proceedings of FoSSaCS '98*, number 1378 of LNCS, pages 140-155, Springer, 1998.
12. L. Cardelli and A. Gordon. Anytime, anywhere — modal logics for mobile ambients. In *Proceedings of POPL '00*, pages 365–377. ACM, 2000.
13. G. Castagna, G. Ghelli, and F. Zappa Nardelli. Typing mobility in the seal calculus. In *Concur 2001*, number 2154 in Lecture Notes in Computer Science, pages 82–101. Springer, 2001.
14. G. Castagna and J. Vitek. Seal: A Framework for Secure Mobile Computations. In H. Bal, B. Belkhouche, and L. Cardelli, editors, *Internet Programming Languages*, number 1686 in Lecture Notes in Computer Science, pages 47–77. Springer, 1999.
15. G. Cinciarone, M. Corson, and J. Macker. Internet-based mobile ad hoc networking. *Internet Computing*, 3(4), 1999.
16. E.M. Clarke, S. Jha, and W. Marrero. Using state space exploration and a natural deduction style message derivation engine to verify security protocols. In *IFIP Working Conference on Programming Concepts and Methods (PROCOMET)*, 1998.
17. R. De Nicola, G. Ferrari, U. Montanari, R. Pugliese, and E. Tuosto. A formal basis for reasoning on programmable qos, verification–theory and practice. Proceedings of an International Symposium in Honor of Zohar Manna's 64th Birthday, Springer LNCS, submitted for publication.
18. R. De Nicola, G. Ferrari, R. Pugliese, and B. Venneri. Types for Access Control. *Theoretical Computer Science*, 240(1):215–254, 2000.
19. R. De Nicola, G. Ferrari, and R. Pugliese. KLAIM: A kernel language for agents interaction and mobility. *IEEE Transactions on Software Engineering*, 24(5):315–330, May 1998. Special Issue: Mobility and Network Aware Computing.
20. G. Engels, J.H. Hausmann, R. Heckel, and S. Sauer. Dynamic meta modeling: A graphical approach to the operational semantics of behavioural diagrams in UML. In *UML 2000*, number 1939 in Lecture Notes in Computer Science, pages 323–337. Springer, 2000.
21. G. Ferrari, U. Montanari, and E. Tuosto. A lts semantics of ambients via graph synchronization with mobility. In *7th Italian Conference on Theoretical Computer Science – ICTCS'01*, volume 2202 of *Lecture Notes in Computer Science*. Springer, 2001.
22. G. Ferrari, C. Montangero, L. Semini, and S. Semprini. Mark: A reasoning kit for mobility. *Automated Software Engineering*, 9(2):137–150, 2002.
23. Robert, W. Floyd. Algorithm97 (shortestpath). *Communication of the ACM*, 5(6):345, 1962.
24. R. Focardi and R. Gorrieri. The Compositional Security Checker: A tool for the verification of information flow security properties. *IEEE Transaction on Software Engineering*, 23(9):550–571, 1997.
25. I. Foster, C. Kesselman, C. Lee, R. Lindell, K. Nahrstedt, and A. Roy. A distributed resource management architecture that supports advance reservations and co-allocation. In *Proceedings of the International Workshop on Quality of Service*, 1999.
26. C. Fournet, G. Gonthier, J. J. Levy, L. Maranget, and D. Remy. A Calculus of Mobile Agents. In U. Montanari and V. Sassone, editors, *Proc. of 7th Int. Conf. on Concurrency Theory (CONCUR'96)*, volume 1119 of *LNCS*, pages 406–421. Springer, 1996.
27. A. Fuggetta, G. Picco, and G. Vigna. Understanging Code Mobility. *IEEE Transactions on Software Engineering*, 24(5), 1998.

28. D. Gelernter. Generative Communication in Linda. *ACM Transactions on Programming Languages and Systems*, 7(1):80–112, 1985.

29. M. Gogolla. Graph transformations on the UML Metamodel. In *ICALP Workshop on Graph Transformations and Visual Modeling Techniques*, pages 359–371. Carleton Scientific, 2000.

30. M. Hennessy and J. Riely. Resource Access Control in Systems of Mobile Agents. In Uwe Nestmann and Benjamin C. Pierce, editors, *Proc. of HLCL '98: High-Level Concurrent Languages*, volume 16.3 of *ENTCS*, pages 3–17. Elsevier, 1998. To appear in Information and Computation.

31. M. Hennessy and J. Riely. Distributed Processes and Location Failures. *Theoretical Computer Science*, 266, 2001.

32. D. Hirsch, P. Inverardi, and U. Montanari. Reconfiguration of Software Architecture Styles with Name Mobility. In Antonio Porto and Gruia-Catalin Roman, editors, *Coordination 2000*, volume 1906 of *LNCS*, pages 148–163. Springer, 2000.

33. D. Hirsch and U. Montanari. Synchronized hyperedge replacement with name mobility. In *CONCUR 01*, number 2154 in Lecture Notes in Computer Science, pages 121–135. Springer, 2001.

34. IBM Software Group. Web services conceptual architecture. In *IBM White Papers*, 2000.

35. S. Kuske, M. Gogolla, R. Kollmann, and H.J. Kreowski. An Integrated Semantics for UML Class, Object, and State Diagrams based on Graph Transformation. In Michael Butler and Kaisa Sere, editors, *3rd Int. Conf. Integrated Formal Methods (IFM'02)*. Springer, Berlin, LNCS, 2002.

36. B. Li. *Agilos: A Middleware Control Architecture for Application-Aware Quality of Service Adaptations*. PhD thesis, University of Illinois, 2000.

37. G. Lowe. An attack on the needham-schroeder public-key authentication protocol. *Information Processing Letter*, 56(3):131–133, 1995.

38. P.J. McCann and G. Catalin-Roman. Compositional programming abstraction for mobile computing. *IEEE Transactions on Software Engineering*, 24(2):97–110, 1998.

39. U. Montanari and F. Rossi. Graph Rewriting and Constraint Solving for Modelling Distributed Systems with Synchronization. In P. Ciancarini and C. Hankin, editors, *Proceedings of the First International Conference COORDINATION '96, Cesena, Italy*, volume 1061 of *LNCS*. Springer, April 1996.

40. OMG. Unified modelling language specification. Available at http://www.omg.org, 2001.

41. Oracle. Oracle 8*i* lite web page. In *http://www.oracle.com/*, 1999.

42. A.S. Park and P. Reichl. Personal Disconnected Operations with Mobile Agents. In *Proc. of 3rd Workshop on Personal Wireless Communications, PWC'98*, 1998.

43. G. Picco, A.L. Murphy, and G.C. Roman. LIME: Linda meets mobility. In *International Conference on Software Engineering*, pages 368–377, 1999.

44. M. Shaw and D. Garlan. *Software Architecture: Perspective on an Emerging Discipline*. Prentice Hall, 1996.

45. J.L. Sobrinho. Algebra and algotithms for qos path computation and hop-by-hop routing in the internet. *IEEE Transactions on Networking*, 10(4):541–550, August 2002.

46. U. Ster and M. Mitchell, J.C.and Mitchell. Automated analysis of cryptographic protocols using murϕ. In *10th IEEE Computer Security Foundations Workshop*, pages 141–151. IEEE Press, 1997.

47. J. Waldo, G. Wyant, A. Wollrath, and S. Kendall. A note on distributed computing. Technical Report SMLI TR-94-29, Sun Microsystems Laboratories, Inc., November 1994.

48. P.T. Wojciechowski and P. Sewell. Nomadic Pict: Language and infrastructure design for mobile agents. *IEEE Concurrency*, 8(2):42–52, 2000.

49. X. Xiao and L. M. Ni. Internet qos: A big picture. *IEEE Network*, 13(2):8–18, Mar 1999.

50. M. Yokoo and K. Hirayama. Algorithms for Distributed Constraint Satisfaction: A Review. *Autonomous Agents and Multi-Agent Systems*, 3(2):185–207, 2000.

Software Development by Refinement

Dusko Pavlovic and Douglas R. Smith

Kestrel Institute, 3260 Hillview Avenue
Palo Alto, California 94304 USA

Abstract. This paper presents an overview of the technical foundations
and current directions of Kestrel's approach to mechanizing software development. The approach emphasizes machine-supported refinement of
property-oriented specifications to code, based on a category of higher-
order specifications. A key idea is representing knowledge about programming concepts, such as algorithm design, and datatype refinement
by means of taxonomies of abstract design theories and refinements. Concrete refinements are generated by composing library refinements with a
specification.

The framework is partially implemented in the research systems
Specware, Designware, Epoxi, and Planware. Specware provides basic
support for composing specifications and refinements via colimit, and
for generating code via logic morphisms. Specware is intended to be
general-purpose and has found use in industrial settings. Designware extends Specware with taxonomies of software design theories and support
for constructing refinements from them. Epoxi builds on Designware to
support the specification and refinement of systems. Planware transforms
behavioral models of tasks and resources into high-performance scheduling algorithms. A few applications of these systems are presented.

1 Overview

A software system can be viewed as a composition of information from a variety
of sources, including

- the application domain,
- the requirements on the system's behavior,
- software design knowledge about system architectures, algorithms, data
  structures, code optimization techniques, and
- the run-time hardware/software/physical environment in which the software
  will execute.

This paper presents a mechanizable framework for representing these various
sources of information, and for composing them in the context of a refinement
process. The framework is founded on a category of specifications. Morphisms are
used to structure and parameterize specifications, and to refine them. Colimits
are used to compose specifications. Diagrams are used to express the structure of
large specifications, the refinement of specifications to code, and the application
of design knowledge to a specification.

B.K. Aichernig and T. Maibaum (Eds.): Formal Methods ..., LNCS 2757, pp. 267–286, 2003.

The framework features a collection of techniques for constructing refinements based on formal representations of programming knowledge. Abstract algorithmic concepts, datatype refinements, program optimization rules, software architectures, abstract user interfaces, and so on, are represented as diagrams of specifications and morphisms. We arrange these diagrams into taxonomies, which allow incremental access to and construction of refinements for particular requirement specifications. For example, a user may specify a scheduling problem and select a theory of global search algorithms from an algorithm library. The global search theory is used to construct a refinement of the scheduling problem specification into a specification containing a global search algorithm for the particular scheduling problem.

The framework is partially implemented in the research systems Specware, Designware, Epoxi and Planware. Specware provides basic support for composing specifications and refinements, and generating code. Code generation in Specware is supported by inter-logic morphisms that translate between the specification language/logic and the logic of a particular programming language (e.g. CommonLisp or C++). Specware is intended to be general-purpose and has found use in industrial settings. Designware extends Specware with taxonomies of software design theories and support for constructing refinements from them. Epoxi extends Specware to support the specification and refinement of behavior and the generation of imperative code. Planware transforms behavioral models of tasks and resources into high-performance scheduling algorithms.

The remainder of this paper presents an overview of the technical foundations and current directions of Kestrel's approach to mechanizing software development. A few applications of these techniques are described in Section 6.

2   Basic Concepts

2.1   Specifications

A specification is a finite presentation of a theory. The signature of a specification provides the vocabulary for describing objects, operations, and properties in some domain of interest, and the axioms constrain the meaning of the symbols. The theory of the domain is the closure of the axioms under the rules of inference.

Example: Here is a specification for partial orders, using notation adapted from Specware [18]. It introduces a sort E and an infix binary predicate on E, called *le*, which is constrained by the usual axioms. Although Specware allows higher-order specifications, first-order formulations are sufficient in this paper.

```
spec Partial-Order is
    sort E
    op _le_ : E, E → Boolean
    axiom reflexivity is x le x
    axiom transitivity is x le y ∧ y le z ⟹ x le z
    axiom antisymmetry is x le y ∧ y le x ⟹ x = y
end-spec
```

The generic term *expression* will be used to refer to a term, formula, or sentence.

A model of a specification is a structure of sets and total functions that satisfy the axioms. However, for software development purposes we have a less well-defined notion of semantics in mind: each specification denotes a set of possible implementations in some computational model.

2.2   Morphisms

A specification morphism translates the language of one specification into the language of another specification while preserving the property of provability, so that any theorem in the source specification remains a theorem under translation.

A *specification morphism* $m : T \to T'$ is given by a map from the sort and operator symbols of the *domain* spec T to the symbols of the *codomain* spec T'. To be a specification morphism it is also required that every axiom of T translates to a theorem of T'. It then follows that a specification morphism translates theorems of the domain specification to theorems of the codomain. An *interpretation* (between theories) is a slightly generalized morphism that translates symbols to expressions.

Example: A specification morphism from *Partial-Order* to *Integer* is:

> morphism *Partial-Order-to-Integer* is
> $\{E \mapsto Integer, \; le \mapsto \leq\}$

Translation of an expression by a morphism is by straightforward application of the symbol map, so, for example, the *Partial-Order* axiom $x \; le \; x$ translates to $x \leq x$. The three axioms of a partial order remain provable in *Integer* theory after translation.

Morphisms come in a variety of flavors; here we only use two. An *extension* or *import* is an inclusion between specs.

Example: We can build up the theory of partial orders by importing the theory of preorders. The import morphism is $\{E \mapsto E, \; le \mapsto le\}$.

> spec *PreOrder*
>   sort E
>   op $\_le\_ : E, E \to Boolean$
>   axiom *reflexivity* is $x \; le \; x$
>   axiom *transitivity* is $x \; le \; y \; \wedge \; y \; le \; z \implies x \; le \; z$
> end-spec

> spec *Partial-Order*
>   import *PreOrder*
>   axiom *antisymmetry* is $x \; le \; y \; \wedge \; y \; le \; x \implies x = y$
> end-spec

A *definitional extension*, written $A \xrightarrow{d} B$, is an import morphism in which any new symbol in B also has an axiom that defines it. Definitions have implicit axioms for existence and uniqueness. Semantically, a definitional extension has the property that each model of the domain has a unique expansion to a model of the codomain.

A parameterized specification can be treated syntactically as a morphism. A functorial semantics for first-order parameterized specifications via coherent functors is given by Pavlović [10].

2.3   The Category of Specs

Specification morphisms compose in a straightforward way as the composition of finite maps. It is easily checked that specifications and specification morphisms form a category SPEC. Colimits exist in SPEC and are easily computed. Suppose that we want to compute the colimit of $B \xleftarrow{\ i\ } A \xrightarrow{\ j\ } C$. First, form the disjoint union of all sort and operator symbols of A, B, and C, then define an equivalence relation on those symbols:

$$s \approx t \ \textit{iff} \ (i(s) = t \ \lor \ i(t) = s \ \lor \ j(s) = t \ \lor \ j(t) = s).$$

The signature of the colimit (also known as pushout in this case) is the collection of equivalence classes wrt $\approx$. The cocone morphisms take each symbol into its equivalence class. The axioms of the colimit are obtained by translating and collecting each axiom of A, B, and C.

Example: Suppose that we want to build up the theory of partial orders by composing simpler theories.

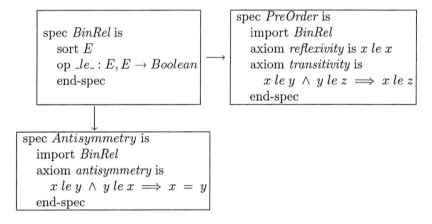

The pushout of *Antisymmetry* ← *BinRel* → *PreOrder* is isomorphic to the specification for *Partial-Order* in Section 2.1. In detail: the morphisms are $\{E \mapsto E,\ le \mapsto le\}$ from *BinRel* to both *PreOrder* and *Antisymmetry*. The equivalence classes are then $\{\{E, E, E\},\ \{le, le, le\}\}$, so the colimit spec has one sort (which we rename E), and one operator (which we rename le). Furthermore, the axioms of *BinRel*, *Antisymmetry*, and *PreOrder* are each translated to become the axioms of the colimit. Thus we have *Partial-Order*.

Example: The pushout operation is also used to instantiate the parameter in a parameterized specification [3]. The binding of argument to parameter is represented by a morphism. To form a specification for Containers of integers, we compute the pushout of *Container* ← *Triv* → *Integer*, where *Container* ← *Triv* is {$E \mapsto E$}, and *Triv* → *Integer* is {$E \mapsto Integer$}.

Example: A specification for sequences can be built up from *Container*, also via pushouts. We can regard *Container* as parameterized on a binary operator

>   spec *BinOp* is
>   sort E
>   op $\_bop\_ : E, E \rightarrow E$
>   end-spec

>   morphism *Container-Parameterization* : *BinOp* → *Container* is
>   {$E \mapsto E,\ bop \mapsto join$}

and we can define a refinement arrow that extends a binary operator to a semigroup:

>   spec *Associativity* is
>   import *BinOp*
>   axiom *Associativity* is $((x\ join\ y)\ join\ z)\ =\ (x\ join\ (y\ join\ z))$
>   end-spec

The pushout of *Associativity* ← *BinOp* → *Container*, produces a collection specification with an associative join operator, which is *Proto-Seq*, the core of a sequence theory (See Appendix in [16]). By further extending *Proto-Seq* with a commutativity axiom, we obtain *Proto-Bag* theory, the core of a bag (multiset) theory.

2.4   Diagrams

Roughly, a *diagram* is a graph morphism to a category, usually the category of specifications in this paper. For example, the pushout described above started with a diagram comprised of two arrows:

$$BinRel \longrightarrow PreOrder$$
$$\downarrow$$
$$Antisymmetry$$

and computing the pushout of that diagram produces another diagram:

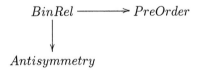

A diagram *commutes* if the composition of arrows along two paths with the same start and finish node yields equal arrows.

The Structuring of Specifications. Colimits can be used to construct a large specification from a diagram of specs and morphisms. The morphisms express various relationships between specifications, including sharing of structure, inclusion of structure, and parametric structure. Several examples will appear later.

Example: The finest-grain way to compose *Partial-Order* is via the colimit of

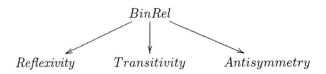

Refinement and Diagrams. As described above, specification morphisms can be used to help *structure* a specification, but they can also be used to *refine* a specification. When a morphism is used as a refinement, the intended effect is to reduce the number of possible implementations when passing from the domain spec to the codomain. In this sense, a refinement can be viewed as embodying a particular design decision or property that corresponds to the subset of possible implementations of the domain spec which are also possible implementations of the codomain.

Often in software refinement we want to preserve and extend the structure of a structured specification (versus flattening it out via colimit). When a specification is structured as a diagram, then the corresponding notion of structured refinement is a diagram morphism. A *diagram morphism M* from diagram *D* to diagram *E* consists of a set of specification morphisms, one from each node/spec in *D* to a node in *E* such that certain squares commute (a functor underlies each diagram and a natural transformation underlies each diagram morphism). We use the notation $D \implies E$ for diagram morphisms.

Example: A datatype refinement that refines bags to sequences can be presented as the diagram morphism *BtoS* : *BAG* $\implies$ *BAG-AS-SEQ*:

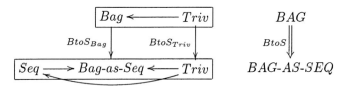

where the domain and codomain of *BtoS* are shown in boxes, and the (one) square commutes. Here *Bag-as-Seq* is a definitional extension of *Seq* that provides an image for *Bag* theory. Specs for *Bag*, *Seq* and *Bag-as-Seq* and details of the refinement can be found in Appendix A of [16]. The interesting content is in spec morphism $BtoS_{Bag}$:

morphism $BtoS_{Bag}$: *Bag* → *Bag-as-Seq* is
  {*Bag* $\mapsto$ *Bag-as-Seq,*
   empty-bag $\mapsto$ *bag-empty,*

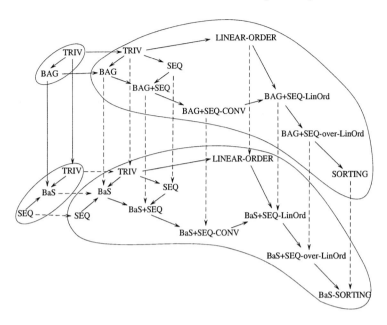

Fig. 1. Refining Bags to Seqs in Sorting.

$$
\begin{array}{rcl}
empty\text{-}bag? & \mapsto & bag\text{-}empty?, \\
nonempty? & \mapsto & bag\text{-}nonempty?, \\
singleton\text{-}bag & \mapsto & bag\text{-}singleton, \\
singleton\text{-}bag? & \mapsto & bag\text{-}singleton?, \\
nonsingleton\text{-}bag? & \mapsto & bag\text{-}nonsingleton?, \\
in & \mapsto & bag\text{-}in, \\
bag\text{-}union & \mapsto & bag\text{-}union, \\
bag\text{-}wfgt & \mapsto & bag\text{-}wfgt, \\
size & \mapsto & bag\text{-}size\}
\end{array}
$$

Diagram morphisms compose in a straightforward way based on spec morphism composition. It is easily checked that diagrams and diagram morphisms form a category. In the sequel we will generally use the term refinement to mean a diagram morphism.

Colimits in this category can be computed using left Kan extensions and colimits in SPEC. Figure 1 shows the pushout of the diagram morphism *BtoS* and a structured specification (diagram) for the problem of sorting a bag over linearly ordered sets (see [16] for details). Intuitively, the universality of the colimit asserts that the resulting diagram is the simplest diagram that refines the sorting diagram and incorporates the refinement information of *BtoS*.

The fact that the colimit calculation constructs a refinement of a given diagram (here the sorting specification) with respect to an abstract refinement (here *BtoS*) is a key tool in our approach to mechanizing the development process.

2.5   Logic Morphisms and Code Generation

Inter-logic morphisms [9] are used to translate specifications from the specification logic to the logic of a programming language. See [18] for more details. They are also useful for translating between the specification logic and the logic supported by various theorem-provers and analysis tools. They are also useful for translating between the theory libraries of various systems.

3   Software Development by Refinement

The development of correct-by-construction code via a formal refinement process is shown to the left. The refinement process starts with a specification S_0 of the requirements on a desired software artifact. Each S_i, $i = 0, 1, ..., n$ represents a structured specification (diagram) and the arrows $\Downarrow$ are refinements (represented as diagram morphisms). The refinement from S_i to S_{i+1} embodies a design decision which cuts down the number of possible implementations. Finally an inter-logic morphism translates a low-level specification S_n to code in a programming language. Semantically the effect is to narrow down the set of possible implementations of S_n to just one, so specification refinement can be viewed as a constructive process for proving the existence of an implementation of specification S_0 (and proving its consistency).

Clearly, two key issues in supporting software development by refinement are: (1) how to construct specifications, and (2) how to construct refinements. Section 4 describes mechanizable techniques for constructing refinements.

3.1   Constructing Specifications

A specification-based development environment supplies tools for creating new specifications and morphisms, for structuring specs into diagrams, and for composing specifications via importation, parameterization, and colimit. In addition, a software development environment needs to support a large library of reusable specifications, typically including specs for (1) common datatypes, such as integer, sequences, finite sets, etc. and (2) common mathematical structures, such as partial orders, monoids, vector spaces, etc. In addition to these generic operations and libraries, the system may support specialized construction tools and libraries of domain-specific theories, such as resource theories, or generic theories about domains such as satellite control or transportation.

3.2   Constructing Refinements

A refinement-based development environment supplies tools for creating new refinements. One of our innovations is showing how a library of abstract refinements can be applied to produce refinements for a given specification. In this paper we focus mainly on refinements that embody design knowledge about (1) algorithm design, (2) datatype refinement, and (3) expression optimization. We believe that other types of design knowledge can be similarly expressed and exploited, including interface design, software architectures, domain-specific requirements capture, and others. In addition to these generic operations and libraries, the system may support specialized construction tools and libraries of domain-specific refinements.

The key concept of this work is the following: abstract design knowledge about datatype refinement, algorithm design, software architectures, program optimization rules, visualization displays, and so on, can be expressed as refinements (i.e. diagram morphisms). The domain of one such refinement represents the abstract structure that is required in a user's specification in order to apply the embodied design knowledge. The refinement itself embodies a design constraint – the effect is a reduction in the set of possible implementations. The codomain of the refinement contains new structures and definitions that are composed with the user's requirement specification.

The figure to the left shows the application of a library refinement $A \Longrightarrow B$ to a given (structured) specification S_0. First the library refinement is selected. The applicability of the refinement to S_0 is shown by constructing a *classification arrow* from A to S_0 which classifies S_0 as having A-structure by making explicit how S_0 has at least the structure of A. Finally the refinement is applied by computing the pushout in the category of diagrams. The creative work lies in constructing the classification arrow [14, 15].

4   Scaling Up

The process of refining specification S_0 described above has three basic steps:

1. select a refinement $A \Longrightarrow B$ from a library,
2. construct a classification arrow $A \Longrightarrow S_0$, and
3. compute the pushout S_1 of $B \Longleftarrow A \Longrightarrow S_0$.

The resulting refinement is the cocone arrow $S_0 \Longrightarrow S_1$. This basic refinement process is repeated until the relevant sorts and operators of the spec have sufficiently explicit definitions that they can be easily translated to a programming language, and then compiled.

In this section we address the issue of how this basic process can be further developed in order to scale up as the size and complexity of the library of specs and refinements grows. The first key idea is to organize libraries of specs and refinements into *taxonomies*. The second key idea is to support *tactics* at two levels: theory-specific tactics for constructing classification arrows, and task-specific tactics that compose common sequences of the basic refinement process into a larger refinement step.

4.1   Design by Classification: Taxonomies of Refinements

A productive software development environment will have a large library of reusable refinements, letting the user (or a tactic) select refinements and decide where to apply them. The need arises for a way to organize such a library, to support access, and to support efficient construction of classification arrows. A library of refinements can be organized into *taxonomies* where refinements are indexed on the nodes of the taxonomies, and the nodes include the domains of various refinements in the library. The taxonomic links are refinements, indicating how one refinement applies in a stronger setting than another.

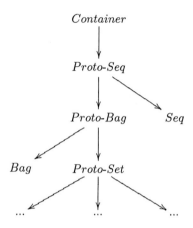

Fig. 2. Taxonomy of Container Datatypes.

Figure 2 sketches a taxonomy of abstract datatypes for collections. The arrows between nodes express the refinement relationship; e.g. the morphism from *Proto-Seq* to *Proto-Bag* is an extension with the axiom of commutativity applied to the join constructor of *Proto-Seqs*. Datatype refinements are indexed by the specifications in the taxonomy; e.g. a refinement from (finite) bags to (finite) sequences is indexed at the node specifying (finite) bag theory.

Figure 3 shows a taxonomy of algorithm design theories. The refinements indexed at each node correspond to (families of) program schemes. The algorithm theory associated with a scheme is sufficient to prove the consistency of any instance of the scheme. Nodes that are deeper in a taxonomy correspond to specifications that have more structure than those at shallower levels. Generally, we wish to select refinements that are indexed as deeply in the taxonomy as possible, since the maximal amount of structure in the requirement specification will be exploited. In the algorithm taxonomy, the deeper the node, the more structure that can be exploited in the problem, and the more problem-solving power that can be brought to bear. Roughly speaking, narrowly scoped but faster algorithms are deeper in the taxonomy, whereas widely applicable general algorithms are at shallower nodes.

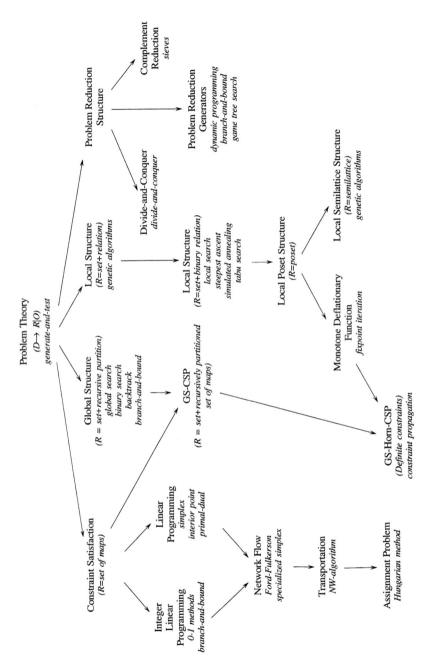

Fig. 3. Taxonomy of Algorithm Theories.

Two problems arise in using a library of refinements: (1) selecting an appropriate refinement, and (2) constructing a classification arrow. If we organize a library of refinements into a taxonomy, then the following *ladder construction* process provides incremental access to applicable refinements, and simultaneously, incremental construction of classification arrows.

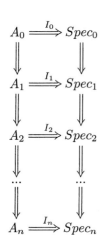

The process of incrementally constructing a refinement is illustrated in the *ladder construction* diagram to the left. The left side of the ladder is a path in a taxonomy starting at the root. The ladder is constructed a rung at a time from the top down. The initial interpretation from A_0 to $Spec_0$ is often simple to construct. The rungs of the ladder are constructed by a constraint solving process that involves user choices, the propagation of consistency constraints, calculation of colimits, and constructive theorem proving [14, 15]. Generally, the rung construction is stronger than a colimit – even though a cocone is being constructed. The intent in constructing $I_i : A_i \Longrightarrow Spec_i$ is that $Spec_i$ has sufficient *defined* symbols to serve as the codomain. In other words, the *implicitly* defined symbols in A_i are translated to *explicitly* defined symbols in $Spec_i$.

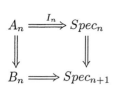

Once we have constructed a classification arrow $A_n \Longrightarrow Spec_n$ and selected a refinement $A_n \Longrightarrow B_n$ that is indexed at node A_n in the taxonomy, then constructing a refinement of $Spec_0$ is straightforward: compute the pushout, yielding $Spec_{n+1}$, then compose arrows down the right side of the ladder and the pushout square to obtain $Spec_0 \Longrightarrow Spec_{n+1}$ as the final constructed refinement.

Again, rung construction is *not* simply a matter of computing a colimit. For example, there are at least two distinct arrows from *Divide-and-Conquer* to *Sorting*, corresponding to a mergesort and a quicksort – these are distinct cocones and there is no universal sorting algorithm corresponding to the colimit. However, applying the refinement that we select at a node in the taxonomy *is* a simple matter of computing the pushout. For algorithm design the pushout simply instantiates some definition schemes and other axiom schemes.

It is unlikely that a general automated method exists for constructing rungs of the ladder, since it is here that creative decisions can be made. For general-purpose design it seems that users must be involved in guiding the rung construction process. However in domain-specific settings and under certain conditions it will possible to automate rung construction (as discussed in the next section). Our goal in Designware is to build an interface providing the user with various general automated operations and libraries of standard components. The user applies various operators with the goal of filling out partial morphisms and specifications until the rung is complete. After each user-directed operation, constraint propagation rules are automatically invoked to perform sound extensions to the partial morphisms and specifications in the rung diagram. Constructive theorem-proving provides the basis for several important techniques for constructing classification arrows [14, 15].

4.2   Tactics

The design process described so far uses primitive operations such as (1) selecting a spec or refinement from a library, (2) computing the pushout/colimit of (a diagram of) diagram morphisms, and (3) unskolemizing and translating a formula along a morphism, (4) witness-finding to derive symbol translations during the construction of classification arrows, and so on. These and other operations can be made accessible through a GUI, but inevitably, users will notice certain patterns of such operations arising, and will wish to have macros or parameterized procedures for them, which we call *tactics*. They provide higher level (semiautomatic) operations for the user.

The need for at least two kinds of tactics can be discerned.

1. *Classification tactics* control operations for constructing classification arrows. The divide-and-conquer theory admits at least two common tactics for constructing a classification arrow. One tactic can be procedurally described as follows: (1) the user selects a operator symbol with a DRO requirement spec, (2) the system analyzes the spec to obtain the translations of the DRO symbols, (3) the user is prompted to supply a standard set of constructors on the input domain D, (4) the tactic performs unskolemization on the composition relation in each Soundness axiom to derive a translations for O_{Ci}, and so on. This tactic was followed in the mergesort derivation.

   The other tactic is similar except that the tactic selects constructors for the composition relations on R (versus D) in step (3), and then uses unskolemization to solve for decomposition relations in step (4). This tactic was followed in the quicksort derivation.

   A classification tactic for context-dependent simplification provides another example. Procedurally: (1) user selects an expression *expr* to simplify, (2) type analysis is used to infer translations for the input and output sorts of *expr*, (3) a context analysis routine is called to obtain contextual properties of *expr* (yielding the translation for C), (4) unskolemization and witness-finding are used to derive a translation for *new-expr*.

2. *Refinement tactics* control the application of a collection of refinements; they may compose a common sequence of refinements into a larger refinement step. Planware [2] has a code-generation tactic for automatically applying spec-to-code interlogic morphisms. Another example is a refinement tactic for context-dependent simplification; procedurally, (1) use the classification tactic to construct the classification arrow, (2) compute the pushout, (3) apply a substitution operation on the spec to replace *expr* with its simplified form and to create an isomorphism. Finite Differencing requires a more

complex tactic that applies the tactic for context-dependent simplification repeatedly in order to make incremental the expressions set up by applying the *Expression-and-Function* → *Abstracted-Op* refinement.

We can also envision the possibility of metatactics that can construct tactics for a given class of tasks. For example, given an algorithm theory, there may be ways to analyze the sorts, ops and axioms to determine various orders in constructing the translations of classification arrows. The two tactics for divide-and-conquer mentioned above are an example.

5   Specifying Behavior

The results described above most naturally support the development of *functional* programs. To support the specification and development of *concurrent* systems, we felt the need to specify behaviors via some notion of state machine [11].

We are developing an extension of the framework, called *evolving specifications* (or simply *especs*), that supports the specification and development of complex systems. Especs provide the means for explicitly modeling the logical structure and behavior of systems. The framework supports precise, automatable operations for the composition of especs and their refinement. The espec framework is partially implemented in the Epoxi system.

Especs can be seen as a way to naturally extend the Specware/Designware foundation (the category of diagrams of higher-order algebraic specifications) with a combination of the evolving algebras of Gurevich (aka abstract state machines) [6], with the classical axiomatic semantics of Floyd/Hoare/Dijkstra. As in Specware/Designware, especs use morphisms and colimits to support the composition of systems and their refinement to code, but in addition especs provide a natural and novel way to combine logical structure and behavior.

There are four key ideas underlying our representation of state machines as evolving specifications (especs). Together they reveal an intimate connection between behavior and the category of logical specifications. The first three are due to Gurevich [6].

1. *A state is a model* – A state of computation can be viewed as a snapshot of the abstract computer performing the computation. The state has a set of named stores with values that have certain properties.
2. *A state transition is a finite model change* – A transition rewrites the stored values in the state.
3. *An abstract state is a theory* – Not all properties of a state are relevant, and it is common to group states into abstract states that are models of a theory. The theory presents the structure (sorts, variables, operations), plus the axioms that describe common properties (i.e. invariants). We can treat states as static, mathematical models of a global theory thy_A, and then all transitions correspond to model morphisms. Extensions of the global theory thy_A provide local theories for more refined abstract states, introducing local variables and local properties/invariants.

4. *An abstract transition is an interpretation between theories* – Just as we abstractly describe a class of states/models as a theory, we abstractly describe a class of transitions as an interpretation between theories [8, 11]. To see this, consider the correctness of an assignment statement relative to a precondition P and a postcondition Q; i.e. a Hoare triple $P \{x := e\} Q$. If we consider the initial and final states as characterized by theories thy_{pre} and thy_{post} with theorems P and Q respectively, then the triple is valid iff $Q[e/x]$ is a theorem in thy_{pre}. That is, the triple is valid iff the symbol map $\{x \mapsto e\}$ is an interpretation from thy_{post} to thy_{pre}. Note that interpretation goes in the *opposite* direction from the state transition.

The basic idea of especs is to use specifications as state descriptions, and to use interpretations to represent transitions between state descriptions.

The idea that abstract states and abstract transitions correspond to specs and interpretations suggests that state machines are diagrams over Spec^{op}. Furthermore, state machines are composed via colimits, and state machines are refined via diagram morphisms [11]. These concepts are implemented in the Epoxi extension of Specware. Epoxi includes a translator from especs to C code.

Especs support an architectural approach to system design [13]. Components and connectors are represented by parameterized especs where the parameters are the interfaces for components and connectors (ports and roles respectively). The interconnection of components and connectors, forming the architecture, is presented by a diagram in the category of especs (cf.[5, 7]). The colimit of the diagram serves to glue the interfaces together and to form the parallel composition of the constituent behaviors.

In [12], we present a detailed example of a simple system comprised of a radar unit and a mission controller connected by a synchronous communication channel. Especs for the components and the connector specify the structure, behavior, and roles/ports. They are interconnected by means of a diagram and composed via a colimit of especs. A glue-code generator is used to refine the connector, serving to reconcile the data structure mismatches between the two components [4].

6   Applications

We briefly describe several application projects underway at Kestrel that exploit the refinement technology discussed above.

Mission Planning System (MPS). The planning of large-scale cargo transportation missions is one of the most complex scheduling problems in the world. It involves simultaneously scheduling a variety of resources including aircraft, crews, and port facilities as well as supporting resources such as fuel. Other complexities such as routing and diplomatic clearances further complicate any model. Commercial airlines face a related problem, but they are able to separate aircraft and crew scheduling because of the regularities of their service. Kestrel and BBN Technologies have developed a prototype mission planning system for the US Air Force satisfying most requirements for operation. The main algorithm has been entirely developed and evolved by modifying requirement specifications (stated as pre/post-conditions on the input/output data types), and applying algorithm design, datatype refinement, and optimization tactics. To our knowledge there is no more complex algorithm that has been developed formally from a property-oriented specification and with such as high degree of automation.

Planware. The Planware system is a domain-specific generator of high-performance schedulers [1]. It provides an answer to the question of how to help automate the acquisition of requirements from the user and to assemble a formal requirement specification for the user. The key idea is to focus on a narrow well-defined class of problems and programs and to build a precise, abstract domain-specific specification formalism that covers the class. Interaction with the user is only required in order to obtain the refinement from the abstract spec to a specification of the requirements of the user's particular problem.

To allow users to specify complex multi-resource problems, Planware uses especs to model the behavior of tasks and resources, and uses a service matching theory to handle the interactions of multi-resource problems. For example, a transportation organization might want a scheduler to simultaneously handle its aircraft, crews, fuel, and airport load/unload facilities. Each resource has its own internal required patterns of behavior and may have dependencies on other resources.

The semantics of a resource is the set of possible behaviors that it can exhibit. We treat these behaviors as (temporal) sequences of activities which are modeled as espec modes (abstract states). Each activity has mode variables (e.g. start-time and duration) and any services that it offers (e.g. the flying mode of an aircraft offers transportation service) and services that it requires (e.g. the flying mode of an aircraft requires the services of a crew). A formal theory of a resource should have as models exactly the physically feasible behaviors of the resource. The axioms serve to constrain the values that mode variables can take on in states (e.g. the weight of cargo cannot exceed a maximum bound during the flying mode of an aircraft). The transitions serve to constrain the evolution of the mode variables (e.g. the finish time of one activity must occur no later than the start time of the next activity).

A task is also expressed formally as an espec. The main difference between a task and a resource is that a task offers no service - it only requires services of resources. For example, a cargo container requires transportation service.

We believe that Planware's modeling language is general for expressing scheduling and resource allocation problems. However, the design process currently focuses on the generation of centralized, offline algorithms. The Planware design process has the following steps:

1. Requirement Acquisition – The user supplies a model of a scheduling problem in terms of especs for the kinds of tasks and resources that are of concern. The problem model is formalized into a specification that can be read abstractly as follows: given a collection of task instances (that accord with the task especs) and a collection of resource instances, find a schedule that ac-

complishes as many of the tasks as possible (or (approximately) optimizes the given cost function), subject to all the constraints of the resource models and using only the given resources.

The required and offered services of a resource express the dependencies between resource classes. Planware analyzes the task and resource models to determine a hierarchy of service matches (service required matched with service offered) that is rooted in a task model.

2. Algorithm Design – The problem specification is used to automatically instantiate program schemes that embody abstract algorithmic knowledge about global search and constraint propagation. The algorithm generation process follows the structure of the service hierarchy, resulting in a nested structure of instantiated search schemes.

3. Datatype Refinement and Optimization – Abstract datatypes are refined to concrete programming-language types, and other optimizations are applied.

4. Code generation – Finally code in a programming language (currently CommonLisp) is generated. In one recent example, we developed formal models for air cargo packages, cargo aircraft, air crews, and port facilities (i.e. four espec models). In about one second Planware generates 6560 LOC in our local MetaSlang language, and then translates it to 19088 LOC in Commonlisp comprising over 1780 definitions.

JBV/Applet Generation. Another Kestrel project uses refinement techniques to automate the correct-by-construction generation of secure Java applets from specifications. Previous work developed a formal specification of a Java ByteCode Verifier, and generated correct code from it.

AIM Chip. Motorola Corporation used the Specware tool to produce a successful commercial chip, called the Advanced InfoSec (Information Security) Machine, a VLSI programmable cryptographic processor that was released in 1998. Specware was used to generate and certify the secure kernel of the operating system.

Formal Methods versus CMM Level 4 Process Management. The US Department of Defense sponsored one relatively carefully controlled experimental comparison of two competing development methodologies. One company used the Specware tool and another company used the SEI CMM level 4 process management on the same task and with the same budget. The requirements were expressed in natural language, and the parties were given the same access to domain experts regarding the specification. The formal Specware-based approach was found to result in significantly fewer errors in the final design. Details may be found in [19].

7   Toward Embedded System Design

Current work is extending the modeling capability of especs to the domain of hybrid embedded systems [17]. The ultimate objective is to produce a software development environment that provides extensive tool support for the development of high-assurance real-time embedded systems from specifications.

The foundation of the development process is a module/interface specification formalism that is abstract, semantically precise, expressive, and provides machine support for key design operations, such as composition (via colimit), refinement (by applying libraries of design knowledge), and reasoning (via general-purpose and specialized inference procedures).

We have attempted to combine in one formalism the ability to precisely specify a module in terms of both the functionality/behavior of its services (based on especs), and their resource constraints (based on the Planware use of especs). Moreover, services are categorized along several dimensions: required versus offered services, and pull services (functions and procedures) versus push services (disseminating state and event information). To our knowledge, there is no other specification formalism that supports compositional reasoning of embedded systems at all levels of abstraction.

Based on this module/interface specification formalism, the framework emphasizes a compositional and refinement-oriented approach to design. The user assembles a high-level model of the physical environment, monitored/controlled system, and the embedded software. Refinements that introduce structure and implementation detail are applied. A key idea is to represent knowledge about embedded system design concepts, and to semiautomatically use those representations to generate refinements. Finally, there is a partitioning process that groups components and connectors that will be mapped to the same target component. The use of specialized resource allocation algorithms can help search for (near)-optimal partitions and maps.

8   Summary

This paper summarizes Kestrel's ongoing efforts to provide practical support for the development of efficient, high-assurance software. The main features of these efforts are:

- *A comprehensive and uniform mathematical foundation* that encompasses requirements (both property-oriented and behavioral), composition, refinement, and code generation, as well as the representation of program/system design knowledge. Building on the category of higher-order specifications, we are developing natural extensions into behavioral specification including features of concurrency, resource constraints, continuity, and stochastic processes.
- *Tool Support* - a practical development formalism must be amenable to extensive automated support, hence our emphasis on a category of syntactic objects (specs) versus semantic objects (structures). The examples and most concepts described are working in the Specware, Designware, Epoxi, and Planware systems. Inference tools such as theorem-provers, constraint propagation, and other analysis tools are critical to providing assurance during refinement.

- *Design Theories* - although it is not emphasized here, a key to practical support for software development from specifications is the reuse of abstract design knowledge. If the ultimate language for communication with computers is a requirements language, then the means must exist to supply the design information that allows the generated system to carry out those requirements (e.g. architectures, algorithms, data structures). Current interest in design patterns, O-O frameworks, and various approaches to generic programming begin to get at this capture of reusable design knowledge, but typically in a way that doesn't relate requirements to code.

Acknowledgments

The work reported here is the result of extended collaboration with our colleagues at Kestrel Institute. We would particularly like to acknowledge the contributions of Matthias Anlauff, Marcel Becker, LiMei Gilham, and Stephen Westfold. This research has been supported by the Office of Naval Research, the US Air Force Research Lab, Rome NY, and by the Defense Advanced Research Projects Agency.

References

1. BECKER, M., AND SMITH, D. R. Planware: Synthesis of resource allocation algorithms. Tech. rep., Kestrel Institute, 2002.
2. BLAINE, L., GILHAM, L., LIU, J., SMITH, D., AND WESTFOLD, S. Planware – domain-specific synthesis of high-performance schedulers. In *Proceedings of the Thirteenth Automated Software Engineering Conference* (October 1998), IEEE Computer Society Press, pp. 270–280.
3. BURSTALL, R. M., AND GOGUEN, J. A. The semantics of clear, a specification langue. In *Proceedings, 1979 Copenhagen Winter School on Abstract Software Specification*, D. Bjorner, Ed. Springer LNCS 86, 1980.
4. BURSTEIN, M., McDERMOTT, D., SMITH, D., AND WESTFOLD, S. Formal derivation of agent interoperation code. *Journal of Autonomous Agents and Multi-Agent Systems* (2001). (earlier version in Proceedings of the Agents 2000 Conference, Barcelona, Spain, 2000).
5. GOGUEN, J. A. Categorical foundations for general systems theory. In *Advances in Cybernetics and Systems Research*, F. Pichler and R. Trappl, Eds. Transcripta Books, 1973, pp. 121–130.
6. GUREVICH, Y. Evolving algebra 1993: Lipari guide. In *Specification and Validation Methods*, E. Boerger, Ed. Oxford University Press, 1995, pp. 9–36.
7. J.L.FIADEIRO, LOPES, A., AND T.MAIBAUM. Synthesising interconnections. In *Algorithmic Languages and Calculi* (London, 1997), R. Bird and L. Meertens, Eds., Chapman & Hall, pp. 240–264.
8. KUTTER, P. W. State transitions modeled as refinements. Tech. Rep. KES.U.96.6, Kestrel Institute, August 1996.
9. MESEGUER, J. General logics. In *Logic Colloquium 87*, H. Ebbinghaus, Ed. North Holland, Amsterdam, 1989, pp. 275–329.

10. PAVLOVIC, D. Semantics of first order parametric specifications. In *Formal Methods '99* (1999), J. Woodcock and J. Wing, Eds., vol. 1708 of *Lecture Notes in Computer Science*, Springer Verlag, pp. 155–172.

11. PAVLOVIC, D., AND SMITH, D. R. Composition and refinement of behavioral specifications. In *Proceedings of Sixteenth International Conference on Automated Software Engineering* (2001), IEEE Computer Society Press, pp. 157–165.

12. PAVLOVIC, D., AND SMITH, D. R. System construction via evolving specifications. In *Complex and Dynamic Systems Architectures (CDSA 2001)* (2001).

13. SHAW, M., AND GARLAN, D. *Software Architecture: Perspectives on an Emerging Discipline*. Prentice-Hall, NJ, 1996.

14. SMITH, D. R. Constructing specification morphisms. *Journal of Symbolic Computation, Special Issue on Automatic Programming 15*, 5-6 (May-June 1993), 571–606.

15. SMITH, D. R. Toward a classification approach to design. In *Proceedings of the Fifth International Conference on Algebraic Methodology and Software Technology, AMAST'96* (1996), vol. LNCS 1101, Springer-Verlag, pp. 62–84.

16. SMITH, D. R. Mechanizing the development of software. In *Calculational System Design, Proceedings of the NATO Advanced Study Institute*, M. Broy and R. Steinbrueggen, Eds. IOS Press, Amsterdam, 1999, pp. 251–292.

17. SMITH, D. R. Harbinger: Formal development of embedded systems. Tech. rep., Kestrel Institute, 2002.

18. SRINIVAS, Y. V., AND JÜLLIG, R. Specware: Formal support for composing software. In *Proceedings of the Conference on Mathematics of Program Construction*, B. Moeller, Ed. LNCS 947, Springer-Verlag, Berlin, 1995, pp. 399–422.

19. WIDMAIER, J., SCHMIDTS, C., AND HUANG, X. Producing more reliable software: Mature software engineering process vs. state-of-the-art technology? In *Proceedings of the International Conference on Software Engineering 2000* (Limerick, Ireland, 2000), ACM, pp. 87–92.

Formal Methods within a Totally Functional Approach to Programming

Paul A. Bailes and Colin J.M. Kemp

School of Information Technology and Electrical Engineering
The University of Queensland QLD 4072 AUSTRALIA
{paul,ck}@itee.uq.edu.au

Abstract. Taking functional programming to its extremities in search of simplicity still requires integration with other development (e.g. formal) methods. Induction is the key to deriving and verifying functional programs, but can be simplified through packaging proofs with functions, particularly "folds", on data (structures). "Totally Functional Programming" avoids the complexities of interpretation by directly representing data (structures) as "platonic combinators" - the functions characteristic to the data. The link between the two simplifications is that platonic combinators are a kind of partially-applied fold, which means that platonic combinators inherit fold-theoretic properties, but with some apparent simplifications due to the platonic combinator representation. However, despite observable behaviour within functional programming that suggests that TFP is widely-applicable, significant work remains before TFP as such could be widely adopted.

1 Programming Is Too Hard

There can be little doubt that "programming" (both as metaphor for and essence of the entirety of software development activity), after a half-century of unceasing research, remains too complex. The plethora of complaints about:

- performance of software systems;
- inefficiency of software development; and
- the proposed remedies that have failed to accomplish dramatic change

all encourage the search for a new view that will yield significant improvement.

Our ultimate goal accordingly is to discover a radical simplification of software development. Our starting point in the achievement of this goal is functional programming, but with an important difference from previous treatments. Whereas functional programming has hitherto combined applicative behaviours (functions) and inert symbols (data), our approach is through replacement to the greatest extent possible of non-functional components, i.e. data and data structures, by appropriate applicative alternatives, i.e. functions. In other words, what distinguishes our approach is that it explores the functional paradigm to its limits (hence "Totally Functional" programming). This will be done by discovering functions that implement the essential applicative behaviour that is hypothesised to exist when processing each data (structure) type. The choice of functional programming as a basis is no mere accident or preference, but is rather objectively suggested for this purpose in formal terms because it inherently supplies most *convenient* access to the richest range of computable

B.K. Aichernig and T. Maibaum (Eds.): Formal Methods ..., LNCS 2757, pp. 287–307, 2003.

functions compared to other paradigms (see discussion of "expressive completeness" in section 7.5 below).

However, radical as the new proposal may ultimately be proven to be, there is an obligation to demonstrate its integration with existing development methods, especially formal methods (which is the subject of this paper) for at least two reasons. First, a feature of our proposal is that it can co-exist with existing (functional programming) technologies. Thus, it's important to coexist with other methods that use these technologies. Secondly, and more objectively, the our motivation for the new proposal does not contain any conflict in principle with formal methods, so a demonstration of formal-methods compatibility indicates the soundness of the derivation of the detail of our proposal from its motivation (in addition to enjoying the actual benefits of formal methods).

Finally, we would expect that if our proposal promises simplification in general, then some of this simplification should be observable from a formal methods point of view.

2   Formal Methods and Functional Programming

One of the major claims for functional programming is that the paradigm (strictly its pure applicative superset) supports formal methods in a more accessible, simple way than compared with imperative programming [1, 2]. Referential transparency permits equational reasoning on the texts of programs, using in which programmer-defined functions are accommodated naturally. Program branching is reflected by case analysis in derivations/proofs, and iteration/recursion is reflected by induction. An implicit requirement, that any new exploitation of functional programming such as we propose, should preserve the accessibility of formal methods, is met by exploiting the technique of "fusion", which takes it place in the formal methods landscape of functional programming as follows.

2.1   Recursion and Induction

For example (following Bird [3]), given the definition of a function to reverse a list[1] (equations numbered for reference)
1. *reverse [ ] = [ ]*
2. *reverse (x:xs) = reverse xs ++ [x]*

we prove that "reverse (reverse Xs) = Xs" for all finite lists Xs.

Case [ ]:
　　　　reverse (reverse [ ])
　　　　= reverse.1
　　　　reverse [ ]
　　　　= reverse.1
　　　　[ ]

---

[1] Generally, example code fragments will be rendered in Haskell [4] notation, which has become the *lingua franca* of the functional programming community.

Case X:Xs

> *reverse (reverse (X:Xs))*
> = reverse.2
> *reverse (reverse Xs ++ [X])*
> = assuming "reverse (Ys ++ [Y])" = "Y : reverse Ys"
> *X : reverse (reverse Xs)*
> = induction hypothesis
> *X : Xs*

The assumption is a typical example of a necessary lemma or "auxiliary result", and can be proved similarly.

Because:

- the same techniques are used in proving the equivalence of non-executable definitions with executable definitions of functions as are used in proving the equivalence of executable with executable definitions;
- the techniques for deriving equivalent definitions are the same as for proving equivalence of definitions

the notion of proof of equivalence of executable function definitions serves as a metaphor as well for

- proof of correctness against specifications
- synthesis of programs from proofs
- optimization of implementations.

2.2 Packaging List Recursion & Induction with "Fold"

However, it's arguable that recursion, case analysis and induction place too-great demands upon programmers' intellectual resources:

- an over-emphasis on "unnatural" recursion is sometimes raised as an obstacle the wider adoption of applicative/functional programming even in contexts (such as learning introductory programming), even when the relative familiarity of functional programming's equational style of definition and rewriting model of evaluation would appear to be the solution to the complexity of imperative programming;
- in any case, programmers have better things to do (i.e. developing applications-oriented solutions) if the basic processes of program derivation and verification can be further simplified.

However, it's possible to package sub-proofs as general laws, and thereby obviate the need for repeated consideration of inductive proofs. Thus, the simplification of program structures that results from packaging code fragments into a hierarchy of components (e.g. procedures, functions, types, etc.) is paralleled by a simplification of the processes of program derivation and verification that result from the availability of packaged laws/theorems about these components. The above auxiliary result for "reverse" is an example, albeit with limited application.

A particular advantage of functional (as opposed to mere applicative) programming is that this process is applicable not just to first-order operations on data, but also to the higher-order constructs that combine and produce functional program components. That is, programmers may define their own control constructs, and derived laws about the behaviours of these constructs can be used in deriving and verifying programs that use them.

An outstanding example of this approach is how laws about the "fold" function can be used to derive and verify functional programs that operate on list structures, and indeed this approach is immediately extendable to all regular recursive datatypes, for which analogies to the list "fold" exist.

For example, the list "fold" function (earlier known as "reduce" in APL):

1. *fold op b [ ] = b*
2. *fold op b (x:xs) = op x (fold op b xs)*

is well-known (e.g. [3]) to simplify derivation or verification of functions on lists. Also for example, the definitions:

> *sum = fold (+) 0*
> *map f = fold (\ x xs -> f x : xs) [ ]*
> *reverse = fold append [ ] **where** append x xs = xs ++ [x]*

(n.b. '\' is Haskell for 'λ') respectively define the functions:

- to sum elements of a list (of numbers);
- to apply a function f to each element of a list
- "reverse" but more elegantly than before.

The explicit recursion that would otherwise be required is encapsulated within "fold".

Consequently, formal proofs of list-processing functions need not depend upon induction, but rather depend upon (ultimately inductively-defined) laws about "fold".

Universal Property of Fold. The universal property of fold [5] is that

> *G = fold F V*
> iff
> *G [ ] = V and G (X : Xs) = F X (G Xs)*

This property follows from the definition of "fold", and can be used in proofs about functions defined using "fold" without recourse to explicit induction. For example, using universality we reconsider the proof of "reverse (reverse Xs) = Xs" for all finite lists Xs. First, express reverse in terms of a self-inverse:

> *reverse . reverse = id*

where "id" is identity, for lists Xs thus "id Xs = Xs". Then, expand

> *reverse . reverse = reverse . fold append [ ]*

Second, observe that application of "fold" to the list constructors simply reconstructs the list, i.e.

> *id = fold (:) [ ]*

Thus, we require that

> *reverse . fold append [ ] = fold (:) [ ]*

To do so by universality, prove

1. *(reverse . fold append [ ]) = [ ]*
   iff (.)
   reverse (fold append [ ] [ ]) = [ ]
   iff (fold.1)
   reverse [ ] = [ ]
   etc. by "reverse"
2. *(reverse . fold append [ ]) (X:Xs) = X : ((reverse . fold append [ ]) Xs)*
   iff (.)
   reverse (fold append [ ] (X:Xs)) = X : reverse (fold append [ ] Xs)

iff (fold.2)

reverse (append X (fold append [ ] Xs)) = X : reverse (fold append [ ] Xs)

iff (append)

reverse (fold append [ ] Xs ++ [X]) = X : reverse (fold append [ ] Xs)

which is true by the auxiliary result "reverse (Ys ++ [Y])" = "Y : reverse Ys"

Fusion Property of Fold. Another, which is simpler to use than the universal property when applicable, is the "fusion" property [5]:

$\qquad$ *H . fold G W = fold F V*

or equivalently

$\qquad$ *H (fold G W Xs) = fold F V Xs*

provided that

$\qquad$ *H W = V*

$\qquad$ ***and***

$\qquad$ *H (G Y Ys) = F Y (H Ys)*

Thus, to prove "reverse . reverse = id" as above, proceed first to

$\qquad$ *reverse . fold append [ ] = fold (:) [ ]*

Then proceed by fusion, which proves the above equation provided that

1. *reverse [ ] = [ ]*

    trivially

2. *reverse (append Y Ys) = Y : (reverse Ys)*

    iff (expanding "append")

    reverse (Ys ++ [Y]) = Y : (reverse Ys)

    which is the auxiliary result assumed true earlier, and which is subject to proof via the fusion law.

Fusion demonstrably makes for simpler proofs, but furthermore its connection to "fold" makes it particularly useful in our new approach to functional programming.

3 Interpretation vs Definition in Programming

The relatively greater expressiveness of functional languages is used to differentiate between two styles of programming: "interpretational" vs "definitional". The former corresponds to typical imperative programming in which algorithmic and data components play complementary roles; the latter depends upon programmer-definable function-valued functions in order to represent data by functions. This "definitional" style is exactly the new approach we seek to elaborate. (Again, "Totally Functional Programming" (TFP) refers to this subset of functional programming in which *total* dependence upon functions exclusive of data to the greatest extent is the goal.)

The key components of the defintional/TFP style are of course the functions that replace data and thus the need to interpret these applicative behaviours from data. We call these "platonic combinators", of two kinds "pure" and "impure", conceived of as follows.

3.1 Pervasivess of Interpretation of Data

Consider the elementary "Boolean" datatype:

$\qquad$ *data Bool = True | False*

Operations on booleans are programmable by cases:

> *not True = False*
> *not False = True*
> *and True x = x*
> *and False x = False*
> *etc.*

This example, though simplest, is also signal: the various operations individually repeat the same essential role at each stage, of selecting one of two result paths depending upon the value of an operand True vs False. We contend that this exemplifies the essential characteristics of the "interpretational" style:

- a common essential operation is performed when processing a data type, in this case selection between two alternatives;
- the operation is not explicit, but is animated from the inert data by case analysis on the symbols/data type constructors;
- the common operation has to be replicated consistently across the different operations on the type.

The same appears to apply to other types. For example, consider the implementations of some basic operations on natural numbers:

> *add 0 n = n*
> *add (m+1) n = (add m n) + 1*
> *mul 0 n = 0*
> *mul (m+1) n = add n (mul m n)*

The characteristics of interpretation are present once again:

- an essential operation, this time of iteration, is applied (to some other operation that is in turn characteristic of the specific arithmetic operator – successor "+ 1" of 0 in the case of "add", addition of "n" to 0 in the case of "mul");
- the iteration is not explicit but is implicit in the (in this example, recursive) pattern of cases;
- the same general pattern of cases is used for each different specific operation ("add", "mul", etc.)

We use the term "interpretational" because this kind of animation of inert data to generate a computation is also characteristic of how an interpreter (for all kinds of programming language) induces a computation on the representation of a program. See further below ("Basis in language extensibility") for more on the relationship with general programming language design and implementation.

3.2 "Platonic Combinators" - Definition without Data

We define functions to represent the entities hitherto represented by symbolic data, and accordingly the functions on data are lifted to higher-order functions. We coin the phrase "platonic combinator" to refer to the functional representations of data, in that these functions (a.k.a. "combinators") purport to embody the "essence" (following Plato) of data in terms of the inevitable characteristic applicative behaviour that is animated from the data.

The simplest of these functional representations unsurprisingly correspond to those invented for Church's untyped lambda-calculus [6], where the unavailability of data necessitates such representations.

"Church Booleans". Rather than interpreting symbols "True" and "False", the computation inherent in Boolean values may be defined directly in the following terms:

$$true = \backslash x\, y \rightarrow x$$
$$false = \backslash x\, y \rightarrow y$$

That is, either Boolean value represents one of the possible choices form among two operands, and to make the choice is simply to apply the Boolean. Thus, instead of

$$if\ C\ then\ E1\ else\ E2$$

which interpretationally tests C for equality to the symbols "True" or "False", we can write simply the direct application

$$C\ E1\ E2$$

Higher Boolean operations are redefinable accordingly:

$$not\ x = x\ False\ True$$
$$and\ x\ y = x\ y\ False$$

To summarise, the purpose of type Boolean is to make a choice, which these functional representations for truth values directly express.

"Church Numerals". Similarly, rather than interpreting symbols "0", "+ 1" to induce the iteration inherent in natural numbers, instead directly define the naturals as iterators:

$$zero = \backslash f\, x \rightarrow x$$
$$succ\ n = \backslash f\, x \rightarrow f\, (n\, f\, x)$$
$$one = succ\ zero$$
$$etc...$$

so that for any function F and any X

$$succ\ zero\ F\ X = F\ X$$
$$succ\ one\ F\ X = F\ (F\ X)$$
$$etc.$$

Arithmetic operations are redefinable in the direct definitional style e.g. as

$$add\ m\ n = m\ succ\ n$$
$$mul\ m\ n = m\ (add\ n)\ zero$$

To summarise, the purpose of type Natural is to iterate, which these functional representations for truth values directly express. Any other behaviour for Naturals represents a misuse, for which another type should be used. (NB this corresponds with good programming practice e.g. enumerated types should be used to represent types such as error codes, colurs, etc., rather than misleading numerical representations.)

3.3 Pure vs Impure Platonic Combinators

The platonic combinators themselves can be distinguished on the basis of whether they are "pure" i.e. eschew, or are "impure" i.e. necessarily retain, some degree of interpretation. The above examples of Church booleans and numerals are evidently pure (though their operands may be interpretational).

As an example of a necessarily-impure platonic combinator consider the representation of sets by characteristic predicates, constructed and manipulated by operations as follows:

emptyP = \ *y* -> *False*
singleP x = \ *y* -> *x*==*y*
unionP s1 s2 =\ *y* -> *memberP s1 y* or *memberP s2 y*
memberP s y = *s y*

The "memberP" is of course superfluous, the whole point of platonic combinators being that they are directly applicable in their essential behaviour as functions.

Characteristic predicates are platonic combinators because they represent sets as their essential computations, i.e. the essence of a set is the membership test, which the characteristic predicate implements. They are impure, because the characteristic predicate for a singleton set "single e" involves interpretation: testing that the element 'e' is equal to the putative element 'x'; and because equality testing is ultimately definable only in terms of symbols or symbolic structures. That is, sets (as defined here in terms of empty, singleton and union of sets) only have meaning in terms of a domain of elements that is interpretational. As such, sets serve as a model for all kinds of structure where, while the interpretational nature of the elements enjoys no improvement, the structure itself can be improved to become definitional.

Superficially, there is little apparent difference between pure platonic combinators (PPCs) and impure platonic combinators (IPCs), but formal derivations of the latter are somewhat more involved than the former.

3.4 Practicality of Platonic Combinators

Examples of platonic combinators, especially of the impure variety, abound. Indeed, we speculate that much of the appeal of impressive examples of higher-order functional programming derives from how they replace symbolic data with functional representations, exactly in as platonic combinators. Consider the following examples.

Combinator Parsers. Typically, a parser is realised in terms of a representation of a metalanguage or grammar (often in optimised terms, e.g. LR parse table) animated by a parsing engine [7], which is rather obviously a case of interpretation. However, the alternative TFP-compatible approach is to represent grammar components (terminal & nonterminal symbols) by their parsers, and to implement context-free compositions of concatenation and alternation by higher-order functions that operate on parsers to produce "larger" parsers. The independent existence of such so-called "combinator" parsers [8] seems to provide powerful independent support for TFP.

Exact Real Arithmetic. Boehm & Cartwright [9] identify a class of impure platonic combinators for exact real arithmetic. Basically, a real number is represented by a function which computes a real to any required rational precision.

Programmed Graph Reduction. Just as combinator parsers replace a static structure (the grammar) and its interpreter (parsing engine) with a single applicative entity, so does programmed graph reduction of lambda-expressions [14]. It would seem that this is a further instance of the platonic combinator idea, perhaps requiring further investigation of the links in detail.

4 "Fold" and Pure Platonic Combinators

PPCs emerge exactly as partial applications of folds to data, which enables very simple formal derivations.

4.1 Generalising "Fold"

Analogies to "fold" exist for all "regular" datatypes [10], as do corresponding analogies for laws such as fusion. Consider an ADT T with constructors C1 ... Cn where each Ci has arity m and the jth operand is of type Tj (without loss of generality, this also applies for polymorphic T):

$$data\ T = ...\ |\ Ci\ Ti1\ ...\ Tm\ |\ ...$$

Generally then, the definition of foldT consists of a set of equations, one for each different pattern of construction (i.e. depending on each different constructor Ci) in T:

$$foldT\ c1\ ...\ cn\ (Ci\ a1\ ...\ am) = ci\ A1\ ...\ Am$$

where

- each equation includes formal parameters ci corresponding to constructors Ci
- the body of the equation for Ci applies corresponding parameter ci to operands Aj, each in turn corresponding to the operands of Ci
- each operand Aj of ci is derived from operands aj of the prevailing Ci: if aj corresponds to a nested element of T, then Aj is aj "folded", i.e. of the form "foldT c1 ... cn aj"; otherwise Aj is just aj

This pattern can be observed for "fold" as defined on lists above. Other simple folds are for "Cons"-pairs:

$$foldP\ m\ (Cons\ a\ b) = m\ a\ b$$

for Booleans:

$$foldB\ t\ f\ True = t$$
$$foldB\ t\ f\ False = f$$

(formal parameters named 't' and 'f' are suggestive of their function i.e. of what is to be returned when the other operand is either "True" or "False") and for Naturals, with constructors 0, and successor denoted (+1):

$$foldN\ s\ z\ 0 = z$$
$$foldN\ s\ z\ (m+1) = s\ (foldN\ s\ z\ m)$$

(formal parameters named 's' and 'z' are suggestive of their function i.e. of what to do when the other operand is either an application of the successor function or zero).

Corresponding generalisations of the fusion (and thus universality law) suggest themselves, but we will defer treatment to their context in terms of PPCs below.

4.2 From Folds to PPCs

As generalised above, it emerges that folds are somewhat more than packaged recursion: they are a means of representing data structures that is abstract in terms of constructors, as effected by the general schema above. The "recursion packaging" capability exists precisely because the constructors are replaced by the operands of the fold.

Things become clearer in this regard if we invert the order of the parameters to fold in order to place the data (structure) over which the fold operates first. Thus the schema above becomes

ifoldT (Ci a1 ... ain) c1 ... cn = ci A1 ... Ain

with applications of fold to ak inside Ai rewritten accordingly. For example

ifold [ ] op b = [ ]

ifold (x:xs) op b = op x (ifold xs op b)

It may be observed now that our PPCs (Church booleans and naturals) are simply the results of the partial application of these inverted folds to the corresponding data:

ifoldB True = \t f -> t = true

ifoldB False = \t f -> f = false

$ifoldN\ 0 = \backslash s\ z \to z = \forall x \to x = zero$

ifoldN (m+1)

$= \backslash s\ z \to s\ (ifoldN\ m\ s\ z)$

$= ...$

$= \backslash s\ z \to s^{m+1}\ z$

$= \forall x > f^{m+1}x$

$= succ^{m+1}\ zero$

Likewise, we can synthesise what we might call "Church lists":

$ifold\ [\ ] = \backslash op\ b \to b$

ifold [X1...Xn]

$= \backslash op\ b \to op\ X1\ (ifold\ [X2:...:Xn]\ op\ b)$

$= ...$

$= \backslash op\ b \to op\ X1\ (op\ X2\ ...\ (op\ Xn\ b)...)$

In this example, note how Church lists are the computational embodiment of the essence of lists: the order of operands to "op" embodies the ordering of elements in a list, and the role of 'b' signifies the list's finiteness.

It's thus clear as claimed above that PPCs are data structures from which the constructors have been abstracted. The relationships between "ifoldT" for some type T, PPCs corresponding to T, data D of type T and the constructors C1 ... Cn that generate values of T, can be summarised as follows:

ifoldT D = PPC

PPC C1 ... Cn = D

A fixed-point property is more apparent when presented in terms the "original" fold:

foldT C1 ... Cn D = D

4.3   Generating PPCs from Specifications

The above generation of PPCs by folding over data (structures) is of course satisfactory to a limited degree – to achieve totally functional programming's goal of "datalessness", it's essential to generate PPCs directly. In other words, how to synthesise the functions creating PPCs (e.g. "succ" on Church numerals), and even the "atomic" PPCs (e.g. "zero"), directly from specifications?

Consider the difference between the generation of PPCs, e.g. of Church numerals by "succ" and "zero", and the corresponding partial applications of "ifoldN":

$$zero = \backslash f\, x \rightarrow x$$
$$succ\ n = \backslash f\, x \rightarrow f\,(n\, f\, x)$$

vs

$$ifoldN\ 0 = \backslash s\ z \rightarrow\ z$$
$$ifoldN\ (M+1)= \backslash s\ z \rightarrow s\ (ifoldN\ M\ s\ z)$$

The differences with PPCs are that

- the "fold" and the data constructor are absorbed together into the PPC generator
- the PPC generator is directly applicable to the data to which the constructor was applicable
- PPCs themselves (e.g. as represented by parameter 'n' to "succ") are applicable to the remaining operand of the (inverted) fold.

Consequently, the derivation of PPCs, or more specifically the derivation of generators that yield PPCs, mirrors the derivation of the fold-function for the ADT but accounting for these differences. Thus in general, consider again the above ADT T with constructors $C1 \ldots Cn$ where each Ci has arity m and the jth operand is of type Tj:

$$data\ T = \ldots\ |\ Ci\ Ti1\ \ldots\ Tm\ |\ \ldots$$

Thus, the generator functions Gi of PPCs for T are defined by a set of equations, one for each different pattern of construction (i.e. depending on each different constructor Ci) in T:

$$Gi\ a1\ldots\ am = \backslash c1\ \ldots\ cn \rightarrow ci\ A1\ \ldots\ Am$$

where :

- the construction pattern "$(Ci\ a1\ \ldots\ am)$" formerly present in the definition for the various folds is replaced by direct citation of the aj as formal parameters to Gi, since the discriminating role of Ci is discharged through its absorption with the folds to form distinct PPC generators Gi;
- each equation still includes formal parameters ci corresponding to constructors Ci
- as before, the body of the equation for Gi (corresponding to constructor Ci) applies corresponding parameter ci to operands Aj, each in turn corresponding to the operands of Ci
- as before, each operand Aj of ci is derived from operands aj of the prevailing Ci but slightly differently in order to account for the absorption of "fold" into the PPC at the same time as the aj are PPCs, not data (structures): if aj corresponds to a nested element of T, then Aj is aj "folded", but now of the form "$aj\ ci\ \ldots\ cn$"; otherwise Aj is just aj

As a further example, consider binary trees:

$$data\ Tree\ t = Null\ |\ Leaf\ t\ |\ Branch\ (Tree\ t)\ (Tree\ t)$$

"Church tree" generators are therefore

$$null = \backslash n\ l\ b \rightarrow n$$
$$leaf\ e = \backslash n\ l\ b \rightarrow l\ e$$
$$branch\ b1\ b2 = \backslash n\ l\ b \rightarrow b\ (b1\ n\ l\ b)\ (b2\ n\ l\ b)$$

Continuing/elaborating the summary at the end of the last section, expressing data D as a construction of constructor Ci of arity m applied to operands Xj, and introducing Gi as the PPC generator corresponding to the absorption of "ifoldT" and Ci, gives:

$$ifoldT\ (Ci\ X1\ \ldots\ Xm) = PPC$$
$$Gi\ X1\ \ldots\ Xm = PPC$$

There is a further property:
$$PPC\ G1 \ldots Gn = PPC$$
which can be expressed as a fixed-point
$$(\backslash p \to p\ G1 \ldots Gn)\ PPC = PPC$$
and which can be expressed "old style" as
$$ifoldT\ D\ G1 \ldots Gn = ifoldT\ D = PPC$$

4.4 Generalised Fusion for PPCs

A fusion law for PPCs would seem to be able to be generalised and adapted from that presented for list fold above. In general, for the usual ADT T
$$data\ T = \ldots \mid Ci\ Ti1 \ldots Tm \mid \ldots$$
we envisage that (for any applicable Gi, Fi, not necessarily restricted to the specific Gi from which the PPC was generated)
$$H\ (PPC\ G1 \ldots Gn) = PPC\ F1 \ldots Fn$$
provided that
$$H\ (Gi\ A1 \ldots Am) = Fi\ A1' \ldots Am'$$
where
$Aj' = H\ Aj$ when the jth operand of Ci/Gi is a nested occurrence of T
$Aj' = Aj$ otherwise
  For example, the fusion law for "Church trees" CT above would be
$$H\ (CT\ G1\ G2\ G3) = CT\ F1\ F2\ F3$$
provided that
$$H\ G1 = F1$$
$$H\ (G2\ X) = F2\ X$$
$$H\ (G3\ X1\ X2) = F3\ (H\ X1)\ (H\ X2)$$
  An example application of generalised fusion is presented in the context of IPCs further below.

5 Formal Derivation of Impure Platonic Combinators

While derivation of PPCs from folds follows the derivation of folds from ADT signature in a straightforward fashion, derivation of the IPCs that account for other ADT operations is a little more challenging. However, as with PPCs, "fold" functions play a key role.

  Recall that the idea of an IPC (compared to a PPC) is that the IPC corresponds to a function that extracts data from a structure and processes it interpretively, whereas a PPC (from the above laws) is a partially-applied fold that further applies to contructors/generators. Application of a PPC to the generators regenerates the PPC; however application of the PPC to other functions yields different behaviours. "Normally" these behaviours are instances of the essential computation for the PPC, e.g. applying a church numeral N to some F and some X executes N-fold composition of F over X. However, with care the operands to a PPC (derived from an ADT signature) can be chosen to generate the IPC corresponding to the ADT signature along with the behavioural specification for the extractor function that the IPC models.

  The essence of our technique is as follows:

1. IPCs can result from applying PPCs to IPC generators
2. by definition, an IPC is the function resulting from (partial) application of an ADT extractor to the data structure (e.g. the characteristic predicate for a set is the partial application of "member" to the set)
3. 1. above can be expressed as a fold
4. 2. above can be expressed as an operation on a fold
5. 3. and 4. above can be related by fusion, allowing the IPC generators to be solved for.

This technique is exemplified below by the "set" ADT for which the IPC was exposed above.

5.1 "Set" ADT Specification

The algebraic specification for this version of sets is as follows.

    Empty :: Set t
    Single :: t -> Set t
    Union :: Set t -> Set t -> Set t

    member :: Set t -> t -> Bool
    member Empty y = False
    member (Single x) y = x==y
    member (Union s1 s2) y = member s1 y or member s2 y

The PPC generators for this ADT are thus

    empty = \e s u -> e
    single x = \e s u -> s x
    union s1 s2 = \e s u -> u (foldS s1 e s u) (foldS s2 e s u)

Naturally, the PPC ignores "member", which will be accounted for in the IPC to follow. In view of the isomorphism between Sets and Church trees above, isomorphism of PPCs follows. Likewise, the above fusion law for Church trees also holds for Sets.

5.2 "Set" IPC Derivation

Notation:
- ADT constructors have an initial capital, the corresponding IPC generators are all in lower case but with a capital 'I' suffix
- other ADT operations are all in lower case, the corresponding IPC operations likewise but with a capital 'I' suffix
- variables denoting members of the ADT are all in lower case, the corresponding IPC/PPC instances likewise but with a capital 'I'/'P' suffix.

We require that
- the IPC for a set is the set's characteristic predicate; in terms of the above specification:

    sI = member s

- sI be derived from the PPC corresponding to 's' by application to IPC generators:

    sI = sP emptyI singleI unionI

- that is,

    member s = sP emptyI singleI unionI

Now, recall a set 's' can be expressed as the inverted fold for Sets "ifoldS" applied to 's' then applied to the set constructors (just as a PPC applied to generators regenerates the PPC). At the same time, PPC "sP" is similarly "ifoldS" applied to "s", by definition of PPCs.

Thus rewriting each side of the above:

$\quad$ *member ((ifoldS s) Empty Single Union) = (ifoldS s) emptyI singleI unionI*

Now, according to the fusion law for Sets, this equation holds provided that

1. *emptyI = member Empty*
2. *singleI x = member (Single x)*
3. *unionI (member s1) (member s2) = member (Union s1 s2)*

In each case, we derive

1. *emptyI = member Empty = \y -> False*
2. *singleI x = member (Single x) = \y -> x==y*

(recalling that member si = siI)

3. *unionI s1I s2I = member (Union s1 s2)*
$\qquad\qquad\qquad\quad$ *= \y -> member s1 y or member s2 y*
$\qquad\qquad\qquad\quad$ *= \y -> (s1I y) or (s2I y)*

6   Proving with Platonic Combinators

We show how the platonic combinator representation can simplify proofs as well as derivations above.

6.1   Exploiting PPCs as Folds

To prove (associativity of +):

$\quad$ *add A (add B C) = add (add A B) C*

iff (expanding all occurrences of "add")

$\quad$ *A succ (B succ C) = (A succ B) succ C*

i.e.

$\quad$ *A succ (B succ C) = (\x -> x succ C) (A succ B)*

Now the fusion law for Church numerals applies:

$\quad$ *N F' X' = H (N F X)*

provided that

$\quad$ *H X = X'*

$\quad$ *H (F N) = F' (H N)*

Thus, we proceed

1. *(\x -> x succ C) B = B succ C*
$\quad$ trivially
2. *(\x -> x succ C) (succ A) = succ ((\x -> x succ C) A)*
$\quad$ iff (expanding anonymous function applications)
$\quad$ *((succ A) succ C) = succ (A succ C)*
$\quad$ iff (expanding "succ n = \f x -> f (n f x)")
$\quad$ *succ (A succ C) = succ (A succ C)*

To conclude, when all data is represented by the results of folds, then some operations on data are more apparently subject to analysis by fold laws.

6.2 Exploiting Specifics of Platonic Combinators

Finally, specific properties of representations of platonic combinators or of operations can be exploited.

For example, further simplification of the above associativity of "add" is possible if an alternate representations for the operation is used. The equivalent definition of "add" (which can be derived by fusion)

$$add\ m\ n = \bigvee x \to m\,f\,(n\,f\,x)$$

results in the trivialisation of the above proof:

$$add\ A\ (add\ B\ C)$$
$$= \text{expanding "add"}$$
$$\bigvee x \to A\,f\,(add\ B\ C\,f\,x)$$
$$= \text{expanding "add"}$$
$$\bigvee x \to A\,f\,(B\,f\,(C\,f\,x))$$
$$= \text{recognising "add"}$$
$$\bigvee x \to add\ A\ B\,f\,(C\,f\,x)$$
$$= \text{recognising "add"}$$
$$add\ (add\ A\ B)\ C$$

For an IPC example, consider how trivially we may prove that set union is associative.

$$unionI\ A\ (unionI\ B\ C)$$
$$= \text{expand union}$$
$$\backslash y \to A\ y\ or\ (B\ y\ or\ C\ y)$$
$$= \text{associativity of 'or' - trivial}$$
$$\backslash y \to (A\ y\ or\ B\ y)\ or\ C\ y$$
$$= \text{recognise union}$$
$$unionI\ (unionI\ A\ B)\ C$$

7 Related Technical Issues

While the focus of this paper is on the relationship between formal methods and TFP, a number of other issues are of interest, either of necessity for practical development of this field (i.e. types for TFP) or because they indicate the greater potential of TFP in a wider context of computer science and related fields.

7.1 Types for TFP

The inadequacy of Hindley-Milner-based typing [11] (as implemented in current functional languages, e.g. Haskell) for TFP is apparent: for example, reconsider operations on Church numerals

$$add\ m\ n = m\ succ\ n$$
$$mul\ m\ n = m\ (add\ n)\ zero$$

The complementary rendition of exponentiation is

$$exp\ m\ n = n\ (mul\ m)\ (succ\ zero)$$

which however leads to a type error: given further definitions

$$one = succ\ zero$$
$$two = succ\ one$$

then for the application

$$exp\ one\ two$$

the HUGS implementation of Haskell gives the daunting response

```
ERROR: Type error in application
*** Expression    : exp one two
*** Term          : one
*** Type          : ((d -> e -> e) -> (((a -> b) -> c -> a) ->
(a -> b) -> c -> b) -> ((a -> b) -> c -> a) -> (a -> b) -> c ->
b) -> (d -> e -> e) -> (((a -> b) -> c -> a) -> (a -> b) -> c ->
b) -> ((a -> b) -> c -> a) -> (a -> b) -> c -> b
*** Does not match : (((a -> b) -> c -> a) -> (a -> b) -> c ->
b) -> (d -> e -> e) -> (((a -> b) -> c -> a) -> (a -> b) -> c ->
b) -> ((a -> b) -> c -> a) -> (a -> b) -> c -> b
*** Because       : unification would give infinite type
```

Other "surprises" are only to be expected as more complex platonic combinators are discovered in the course of development of TFP.

This situation can be recovered from in different ways. First, we can re-express our definitions. For example, redefining either as

$$exp\ m\ n = n\ m$$

or

$$mul\ m\ n = m \cdot n$$

will allow "exp one two" to type-check. The new "mul" and "exp" can be derived (in turn) from the originals, but it seems doubtful that programmers could reasonably be expected to perform these derivations (but there is scope for this to be automated).

Second (and arguably preferably in that it lets us express what we want!), is to adopt a more powerful type system. Second-order polymorphic typed-lambda-calculus [12] is much more expressive, and seems to be able to type the above "erroneous" application, but has the drawback of not enjoying the convenience of type inference, unlike Hindley-Milner. A compromise by which polymorphic values are represented as datatype components [13] allows for a combination of greater type-expressiveness and effective type inference. However, this representation conflicts with the anti-interpretational goal of TFP. Clearly, more research is needed before a pure outcome for TFP is available.

7.2 Efficiency?

While the goal of TFP is to provide simplicity for programmers, it appears there may be some opportunity to observe performance *improvement*. This is despite TFP's extreme dependence upon functions and higher-order functions in particular, which are the essential source of the celebrated inefficiency of functional languages [14]. In particular, some of the functional representations appear extraordinarily inefficient, e.g. Church numerals are in effect a unary representation.

However, definitional TFP has an advantage over interpretational programming (functional or imperative) in that the costly process of interpreting/animating inert data into a computation is avoided. Moreover, the inevitable functional representations for various platonic combinators reflect the computation that will take place. For example, natural numbers give rise to a sequence of operations as the inherent iteration executes, which is essentially a unary representation of the number. In other words, unary representation is not always inconvenient, especially in a pure TFP setting.

Of course, when integrating TFP in impure contexts, it may be necessary to provide efficient built-in representations for key platonic combinators, such as naturals. We envisage possibly that an implementation could represent them in traditional binary form (and basic operations accordingly), but this representation could be recognised by the implementation as an iteration operator as well.

7.3 Integration with OOP?

By their nature, pure/impure platonic combinators can be thought of as objects with just one method (other than generators) – the PPC/IPC. This varies with universal object-oriented practice. However, our restriction is not necessarily nonsense: surely a well-designed component (function) should have a single cohesive behaviour, so why should multiple behaviours be permitted?

Of course, we entertain an apparent counter-example of our own policy: different kinds of IPC can be generated from the one PPC by supplying different seeds, so we do seem to permit multiple behaviours. However, it is the relationship of these behaviours though a common "mother behaviour" in the PPC that makes our approach different and supports our claim of "one object, one method". It will however be necessary to demonstrate a "mother" for apparently different operations on the one class. We are currently working on a demonstration that the multiple behaviours that can be associated with a context-free grammar (recognise, parse, unparse) all stem from a common platonic combinator.

7.4 Subrecursive Programming and TFP?

A by-product of eschewing interpretation is that the full expressive power needed to write interpreters, and associated complications (i.e. possibility of nontermination), is not necessary. While a feature of TFP is that it integrates smoothly into contexts where at least a residue of essential data/interpretation prevails, at least some TFP components would be able to be written in a subrecursive functional language subset.

It's surprising, but questionable, as to why Turing-completeness, and the language constructs the enable it such as recursion, should be an essential desideratum for programming language expressiveness. Without it, it becomes impossible to write an interpreter for a universal Turing machine, or any other universal interpreter, but what else that is moreover pragmatically useful is unavailable? Indeed, within second-order polymorphic typed lambda-calculus which lacks recursion, it is possible to express any function that is provably terminating in second-order arithmetic. An implication of this is that Ackerman's function is expressible! Is the only point of having the expressive power of a Turing Machine so that a Universal Turing Machine can be programmed? Our TFP can be thought of as an hybrid version of second-order polymorphic typed lambda-calculus, hence the "total" in TFP also refers to this subrecursive component.

Besides, there has been a long history of other research-cum-speculation about the theory and pragmatics of "subrecursive" programming [15]. Of most apparent relevance to TFP is Turner's proposal [16] for "elementary strong functional programming", which restricts functional programming to total functions.

Turner's approach has the following salient points:

- the simplicity of equational reasoning for functional programs is not quite as attractive as promoted, in view of the need to handle nonterminating computations;
- type-theoretic approaches to the problem (e.g. constructive type theory) have poor pragmatics;
- essentially syntactic restrictions on a pragmatic functional language give a computationally-equivalent result;
- even operating systems can be programmed in this style;
- in the context of all the above, the inability of the language to program its own interpreter is no loss, especially as compilers can still be programmed;
- the appearance at least of data is retained (in contradistinction to TFP).

We might also recall that Backus' seminal Turing Award paper [17] promoted a language that eschewed programmer-defined recursion/iteration, relying instead upon a fixed set of specific iterators (including a version of fold).

The import of these observations is that the subrecursive aspect of TFP, far from being an eccentricity, locates it in a significant stream of programming language development. Likewise, TFP's links to the mainstream of functional programming may offer the Subrecursion theme fulfilment.

7.5 Basis in Language Extensibility

The origins of this project lie in the vision of projecting the idea of language extensibility into mainstream software development. It's demonstrable that programming is a language design/extension activity: pragmatically, standard criteria for program quality assessment parallel those for assessing language designs [18]; formally, a straightforward reordering of the parameters to the denotational semantic meaning function exposes declarations as explicit language-extending constructs [19].

At the same time however, language design/extension is a programming activity, and language extension should eschew undesirable programming practices. We consider that recourse to writing an interpreter (anew, or by modification to the host language's existing interpreter), whereby the syntax identifying some new semantic entity is provided with those semantics through a comprehensive translation of the extended language into the original base language, is the hallmark of bad language extension practice:

- writing of interpreters requires particular skills;
- there is no guarantee that the semantics of the base language will be preserved in the extension, unless proven so;
- in all, interpretation is a complex undertaking which does little to simplify things.

The complexity of interpretation can also be thought of in terms of the impossibility of providing a simple, localized translation of the extension's terms into base language semantics. Far simpler and thus preferable is direct definition, whereby the association of new syntax with new semantics is provided by a local replacement rule, such as macro expansion or identifier declaration. Thus, language extension should be carried out on an expressively-complete [20] base language, in which all conceivable semantic entities can be expressed/defined directly without interpretation of symbolic representations.

Reverting to programming as language extension, it follows that undesirable language extension practices, especially interpretation, should be eliminated or at least minimised in programming. How then is interpretation manifested in "normal programming", and how may it be avoided? We contend that the need to animate inert symbolic data by a combination of branching and iterative processing is what mirrors the complexities of interpretation. Programming could be greatly simplified if data could be replaced by the functions that these interpretations eventually achieve, which proposition leads directly into TFP as presented above.

7.6 Beyond Programming?

TFP appears to have applications beyond mere software development, some of which are identified here.

Canonical Software Design Representation. One of the drawbacks of Interpretational programming is that it allows the characteristics of a software system to be disguised in varying degrees in the data, while the program is correspondingly more or less generic. This poses dual problems in a software reverse engineering/design recovery context [21], where (i) the data-disguised design needs to be uncovered, and (ii) it's essential that the recovered design itself retain no data-disguised design information. The more a software system depends upon data for its behaviour, the less the program structure indicates what's really happening. It would appear that TFP, which by eschewing Interpretation minimises the possibility for such disguises, is an ideal candidate for a canonical representation for software designs, in reverse- as well as forward-engineering.

Analog Systems Specifications and Prototyping. There appears to be an interesting connection between analog computing, where computations are composed from physical components whose behaviours model the domains being computed with, and TFP where data are represented by (the behaviours of) platonic combinators. Indeed, the existence of TFP suggests that the hitherto one-dimensional division of computation into the poles Analog vs. Digital should be replaced by a two-dimensional structure: (Interpretational vs Definitional, Discrete/Symbolic vs Continuous). Conventional "digital" computing is identified by the (Interpretational, Discrete/Symbolic) point, analog by (Definitional, Continuous), and TFP by (Interpretational, Discrete/Symbolic), as in the following diagram:

	Discrete/Symbolic	Continuous
Interpretational	Digital	???
Definitional	TFP	Analog

TFP would seem to have potential as a design/specification/prototyping language for analog systems: functionality can be developed in the relatively relaxed Discrete/Symbolic domain before being built in the exacting electronic manifestation of the Continuous domain.

Systems Engineering. The TFP-analog computing connection seems capable of further generalisation to any system composed in terms of the behaviours of its components. The tools and techniques envisaged above for analog design could therefore be applicable to systems engineering in general.

8   Conclusions

We have covered related issues as follows.

First, we provided the reader with an introduction to "Totally Functional Programming", and referred to its varied roots in language extensibility, formal methods and type theory. TFP is an approach to functional programming that eschews data (inert symbolic representations) for functions (dynamic applicative representations) that empody what we hypothesise to be the distinctive applicative behaviour inherent in every datum.

Second, and as the essence of this paper, we have shown how TFP is compatible with advanced formal methods for functional programming, in particular formal derivation of platonic combinators using laws about "fold", as well as examples of how reasoning is sometimes simpler in "dataless" TFP than in usual "dataful" functional programming.

Finally, we indicated some aspects of the research agenda to be followed in order to make TFP practicable.

Acknowledgements

We are grateful to our numerous students/colleagues whom have contributed to the work reported above over the years and to its presentation in this form, notably Trevor Chorvat, Simeon Cran, Ming Gong, Ian Peake and Sean Seefried.

References

1. Turner, D.A., "Miranda - a non-strict functional language with polymorphic types", in Jouannaud (ed.), Conference of Functional Programming Languages and Computer Architecture, Lecture Notes in Computer Science, vol. 201, Springer, Berlin (1985) 1-16
2. Hughes, J., "Why Functional Programming Matters", The Computer Journal, vol. 32, no. 2 (1989) 98-107
3. Bird, R., "Introduction to Functional Programming", Prentice-Hall (2000)
4. http://www.haskell.org
5. Hutton, G., "A Tutorial on the Universality and Expressiveness of Fold", Journal of Functional Programming", vol. 9, no. 4 (1999) 355-372
6. Barendregt, H.P., "The Lambda Calculus - Its Syntax and Semantics", North-Holland, Amsterdam (1984)
7. Aho, A.V. and Ullman, J.D., "The Theory of Parsing, Translation and Compiling", Prentice-Hall (1972)
8. Hutton, G., "Parsing Using Combinators", Proc. Glasgow Workshop on Functional Programming, Springer (1989)

9. Boehm, H. and Cartwright, R., "Exact Real Arithmetic: Formulating Real Numbers as, Functions", in Turner, D.A. (ed.), Research Topics in Functional Programming, Addison-Wesley (1990) 43-64

10. Sheard, T. and Fougaras, L., "A fold for all seasons", Proc. ACM Conference on Functional Programming and Computer Architecture, Springer (1993)

11. Milner, R., "A Theory of Type Polymorphism in Programming", J. Comp. Syst. Scs., vol. 17 (1977) 348-375

12. Reynolds, J.C. "Three approaches to type structure", in Mathematical Foundations of Software Development, LNCS Vol 185, Springer-Verlag (1985)

13. Jones, Mark P., "First-class Polymorphism with Type Inference", Proc. 24th ACM Symposium on Principles of Programming Languages (1997)

14. Peyton Jones, S., "The Implementation of Functional Programming Languages", Prentice-Hall International, Hemel Hempstead (1987)

15. Royer, J.S., & J.Case, J., "Subrecursive Programming Systems: Complexity & Succintness", Birkhauser (1994)

16. Turner, D.A., "Elementary Strong Functional Programming", Proceedings of the first international symposium on Functional Programming Languages in Education, Springer LNCS vol. 1022 (1995) 1-13

17. Backus, J., "Can programming be liberated from the von Neumann style? A functional style and its algebra of programs", Comm. ACM, vol. 21, no. 8 (1978) 613-641

18. Bailes, P.A., "The Programmer as Language Designer (Towards a Unified Theory of Programming and Language Design)", Proceedings of the 1986 Australian Software Engineering Conference, Canberra (1986) 14-18

19. Bailes, P.A., Chorvat, T. and Peake, I., "A Formal Basis for the Perception of Programming as a Language Design Activity", Proc. 1994 International Conference on Computing and Information, Peterborough (1994)

20. Plotkin, G.D., "PCF Considered as a Programming Language", Theoretical Computer Science, vol. 5 (1977) 223-255

21. Chikofsky, E. and Cross, J.H.II, "Reverse engineering and design recovery: a taxonomy", IEEE Software, January (1990) 13-17

Coordination Technologies for Just-in-Time Integration

José Luiz Fiadeiro

Department of Mathematics and Computer Science
University of Leicester
University Road, Leicester LE1 7RH, UK
jose@fiadeiro.org

Abstract. Whereas the emphasis of research in "Formal Methods" has been mainly directed to help developers in taming the complexity of constructing new systems, the challenge today is on evolution, namely on endowing system components with agility in responding to change and dynamically procuring collaborations from which global properties of the system can emerge. As a result, we are running the risk of building a new generation of legacy systems: systems in which interactions are too tightly coupled and rigid to operate in application environments that are "time critical", for instance those that make use of Web Services, B2B, P2P or operate in what is known as "internet-time". We suggest, and demonstrate, that support for "agility" can be found in what we call "coordination technologies" – a set of analysis techniques, modelling primitives, design principles and patterns that we have been developing for externalising interactions into explicit, first-class entities that can be dynamically superposed, "just-in-time", over system components to coordinate their joint behaviour.

1   Introduction

The fierce competition that the evolution of the Internet is inducing on the way companies do business, the growing dependency of vital functions of our modern society (telecommunications, financial services, transports, energy supplies, etc) on information-intensive systems too often built over unreliable networks of heterogeneous, fragile platforms, and the pace at which acquisitions and mergers happen in the enterprise world, are only three examples of the pressures that are now put on systems to be flexible and agile in the way they can respond to change. As put in [12], "... the ability to change is now more important than the ability to create [e-commerce] systems in the first place. Change becomes a first-class design goal and requires business and technology architectures whose components can be added, modified, replaced and reconfigured".

As a result, building applications is becoming a dynamic process that consists in locating services that provide required basic functionalities, and "orchestrating" them, i.e. establishing collaborations between them, so that the global properties required of the application, at *that* time, can emerge from their joint behaviour. This translates

B.K. Aichernig and T. Maibaum (Eds.): Formal Methods ..., LNCS 2757, pp. 308–321, 2003.
© Springer-Verlag Berlin Heidelberg 2003

directly to the familiar characterisation of Web Services as "late binding" or, better, "just-in-time binding", showing that flexible architectures are required for making the resulting systems amenable to a continuous process of reconfiguration. For this purpose, interactions cannot be hardwired in the code that implements the services. If collaborations are not modelled explicitly as first-class entities that can be manipulated by a process of dynamic reconfiguration, the overhead that just-in-time integration and other operational aspects of this new architecture represent will not lead to the levels of agility that are required for the paradigm to impose itself.

If the complexity of constructing software-based systems has been challenging enough, the ability to make them evolve is clearly growing beyond the reach of Formal Description Techniques as we know them today. Design mechanisms, making use of event publishing/subscription through brokers and other well-known patterns [14], have already found their way into commercially available products that support various forms of agility. However, solutions based on the use of design patterns are not at the level of abstraction in which the need for change arises and needs to be managed. Being mechanisms that operate at the design level, there is a wide gap that separates them from the application modelling levels at which change is better perceived and managed. This conceptual gap is not easily bridged, and the process that leads from the business requirements to the identification and instantiation of the relevant design patterns is not easily documented or made otherwise explicit in a way that facilitates changes to be operated. Once instantiated, design patterns code up interactions in ways that, typically, requires evolution to be intrusive because they were not conceived to be evolvable. Hence, most of the times, the pattern will dissolve as the system evolves. Therefore, we need semantic primitives, founded on first-principles, through which interconnections can be externalised, modelled explicitly, and evolved directly.

Our purpose in this paper is to show that support for "just-in-time" integration as required by "service-oriented" development can be found in what we have been calling "coordination technologies": a set of analysis techniques, modelling primitives, design principles and patterns that we have been developing for externalising interactions into explicit, first-class entities that can be dynamically superposed over system components to coordinate their joint behaviour. The key to the move is in the separation between "computation" and "coordination", i.e. the ability to address the computations that need to take place locally within components to implement the functionalities that they advertise through their interfaces, separately from the coordination mechanisms that need to be superposed on these computations to enable the properties that are required of the global behaviour of the system to emerge.

In order to address the challenge of the colloquium "Formal Methods at the Crossroads from Panacea to Foundational Support", we start by addressing the fundamental principles of the approach and their formal underpinnings, after which we focus on the means through which these principles can be put in effective use and the architectures that support their application.

2 Component Design in CommUnity

The model we propose is based on concepts and mechanisms that have been made available for Parallel Program Design, namely those that support the Unity language [8] such as the notion of superposition (also available in Action Systems [5] and Interacting Processes [13]), and also on contributions from the area of "Coordination Languages and Models" [15], "Software Architectures" [6] and Reconfigurable Distributed Systems" [21]. All these different contributions are integrated over a common mathematical framework that builds on Goguen's categorical approach to General Systems Theory [e.g. 16] and is best explained through a "canonical" language that we call CommUnity,

CommUnity, introduced in [9], is a parallel program design language that is similar to Unity [8] in its computational model but adopts a different coordination model. More concretely, whereas, in Unity, the interaction between a program and its environment relies on the sharing of memory, CommUnity relies on the sharing (synchronisation) of actions and exchange of data through input and output channels. Furthermore, CommUnity requires interactions between components to be made explicit whereas, in Unity, these are defined implicitly by relying on the use of the same variables names in different programs. As a consequence, CommUnity takes to an extreme the separation between "computation" and "coordination" in the sense that the definition of the individual components of a system is completely separated from the interconnections through which these components interact, making it an ideal vehicle for illustrating and formalising the approach that we wish to put forward.

CommUnity is independent of the actual data types that can be used for modelling the exchange of data and, hence, we take them in the general form of a first-order algebraic specification. We assume a data signature $<S,\Omega>$, where S is a set (of sorts) and Ω is a $S^{*}\times S$-indexed family of sets (of operations), to be given together with a collection Φ of first-order sentences specifying the functionality of the operations.

The version of CommUnity that we will be using is not the original one [9], but an extension that we have been developing for supporting the architectural approach to software development and evolution that we motivated in the introduction. What we call a CommUnity design is a structure of the following form:

```
design  P is
out     O
in      I
prv     V
do      [ ,
          gsh(Γ)   g[D(g)]: L(g), U(g)  →  R(g)

        [ ,
          gprv(Γ)  g[D(g)]: L(g), U(g)  →  R(g)
```

- I and O are the sets of input and output channels of design P, respectively, and V is the set of channels that model internal communication. Input channels are used for reading data from the environment of the component. The component has no control on the values that are made available in such channels. Moreover, reading a value from an input channel does not "consume" it: the value remains available until the environment decides to replace it.

- Output and private channels are controlled locally by the component, i.e. the values that, at any given moment, are available on these channels cannot be modified by the environment. Output channels allow the environment to read data produced by the component. Private channels support internal activity that does not involve the environment in any way. We use X to denote the union $I \cup O \cup V$ and $local(X)$ to denote the union $V \cup O$ of *local* channels. Each channel v is typed with a sort $sort(v) \in S$.
- Γ is the set of *action names*. The named actions can be declared either as *private* or *shared*. Private actions represent internal computations in the sense that their execution is uniquely under the control of the component. Shared actions represent possible interactions between the component and the environment, meaning that their execution is also under the control of the environment. The significance of naming actions will become obvious below; the idea is to provide points of *rendezvous* at which components can synchronise.

Guarded commands are associated with actions as follows:
- $D(g)$ is a subset of $local(X)$ consisting of the local channels into which executions of the action can place values. This is what is sometimes called the *write frame* of g. For simplicity, we will often omit the explicit reference to the write frame when $D(g)$ can be inferred from the assignments. Given a private or output channel v, we will also denote by $D(v)$ the set of actions g such that $v \in D(g)$.
- $L(g)$ and $U(g)$ are two conditions such that $U(g) \supset L(g)$. These conditions establish an interval in which the enabling condition of any guarded command that implements g must lie. The condition $L(g)$ is a lower bound for enabledness in the sense that it is implied by the enabling condition. Therefore, its negation establishes a *blocking* condition. On the other hand, $U(g)$ is an upper bound in the sense that it implies the enabling condition, therefore establishing a *progress* condition. Hence, the enabling condition is fully determined only if $L(g)$ and $U(g)$ are equivalent, in which case we write only one condition.
- $R(g)$ is a condition on V and $D(g)'$ where by $D(g)'$ we denote the set of primed local channels from the write frame of g. As usual, these primed names account for references to the values that the channels offer after the execution of the action. $R(g)$ is a specification of the effects of the action g. These conditions are usually a conjunction of implications of the form $pre \supset pos$ where pre does not involve primed names. They correspond to pre/post-condition specifications in the sense of Hoare. When $R(g)$ is such that the value displayed at each local channel in the write frame of g is fully determined, we obtain what corresponds to a conditional multiple assignment, in which case we use the notation that is normally found in programming languages. When the write frame $D(g)$ is empty, $R(g)$ is tautological, which we denote by *skip*.

Although we have acquired experience in a number of business domains – including banking [3], stock-trading [20] and telecommunications [19] – the example we chose to illustrate our approach is closer to what can be typically found in Software Architectures and Coordination Languages. It consists of a typical airport luggage delivery system in which carts move along a track and stop at designated locations for handling luggage. Locations in the track are modelled through natural numbers modulo the length of the circuit. Pieces of luggage are also modelled through natural numbers, zero being reserved to model the situation in which a cart is empty. Given this, a CommUnity design (actually, a program in the sense that it is fully deterministic) that models the behaviour of a cart can be given as follows:

```
design cart is
out bag, loc: nat
in  nbag, ndest: nat
prv  dest: nat
do  move: [loc•dest → loc:=loc+1]
    [] load: [loc=dest∧bag=0 → bag:=nbag || dest:=Dest(nbag)]
    [] unload: [loc=dest∧bag•0 → bag:=0 || dest:=ndest]
```

That is to say, a cart is able to move, load and unload. It moves by incrementing *loc* while it has not reached its destination. The current destination is available locally in *dest* and is computed from the bag each time the cart stops to load, using a function *Dest* that we assume is provided in the data type (eg abstracting the scanning of a bar code on the luggage), or from the environment, when unloading, using the input channel *ndest*. Loading and unloading take place only when the cart has reached its destination. The fact that *dest* is private means that the environment cannot change the destination of the cart until it reaches the pre-assigned one. There, the environment can control where the cart will go next because *ndest* is an input channel.

The behaviour of a program (i.e. a design that is fully deterministic) such as this one is as follows. At each execution step, any of the actions whose enabling condition holds of the current state can be selected, in which case its assignments are executed atomically as a transaction. Furthermore, it is guaranteed that private actions that are infinitely often enabled are selected infinitely often.

3   Coordination in CommUnity

Consider now a typical situation of evolution. Assume that we need to monitor the behaviour of given carts by observing how many times they visit a given location in the circuit. The typical way of doing so would be to extend the program as follows:

```
design monitored_cart is
out bag, loc: nat; count:nat
in   nbag, ndest: nat; cpoint:nat
prv  dest: nat
do  j&move: [loc•dest ∧ loc•cpoint → loc:=loc+1]
    [] c&move: [loc•dest ∧ loc=cpoint → loc:=loc+1 || count:=count+1]
    [] load: [loc=dest∧bag=0 → bag:=nbag || dest:=Dest(nbag)]
    [] unload: [loc=dest∧bag•0 → bag:=0 || dest:=ndest]
```

The extension (highlighted in **bold**) of the original program includes a new output channel that makes available the number of times the cart has gone through the control point. The control point itself is read from an input channel and, hence, can be dynamically changed by the environment. The *move* action is now split in two: *j&mov* accounts for movements that do not go through the control point, and *c&move* for those that do (thus incrementing *count*).

This sort of extension is supported in languages for parallel program design like Unity through the notion of superposition. The program *monitored_cart* was obtained from *cart* by superposing additional behaviour accounting for the required monitoring activity. Extension by superposition follows certain rules that make sure that the original program is "protected" in a very precise sense that can be captured through the following notion of morphism:

A superposition morphism of designs $\sigma\colon P_1 \to P_2$ *consists of a total function* $\sigma_{ch}\colon V_1 \to V_2$ *and a partial mapping* $\sigma_{ac}\colon \Gamma_2 \to \Gamma_1$ *s.t.:*

1. *for every* $v \in V_1, i \in in{\cdot}V_1), o \in {\cdots}V_1), x \in {\cdots}{\cdot}V_1)$

    $sort_2(\sigma_{ch}(v)) = sort_1(v)$

    $\sigma_{ch}(o) \in {\cdots}V_2)$

    $\sigma_{ch}(i) \in {\cdots}V_2) \cup in{\cdot}V_2)$

    $\sigma_{ch}(x) \in prv(V_2)$

2. *for every* $g \in \Gamma_2$ *s.t.* $\sigma_{ac}(g)$ *is defined*

    if $g \in sh(\Gamma_2)$ *then* $\sigma_{ac}(g) \in sh(\Gamma_2)$

    if $g \in prv(\Gamma_2)$ *then* $\sigma_{ac}(g) \in prv(\Gamma_2)$

3. *for every* $v \in loc(V_1{\cdot}$

    σ_{ac} *is total on* $D_2(\sigma_{ch}(v))$

    $\sigma_{ac}(D_2(\sigma_{ch}(v))) \supseteq D_1(v)$

4. *for every* $g \in \Gamma_2$ *s.t.* $\sigma_{ac}(g)$ *is defined*

    $\sigma_{ch}(D_1(\sigma_{ac}(g))) \supseteq D_2(g)$

    $\Phi \therefore (R_2(g) \supset \underline{\sigma}(R_1(\sigma_{ac}(g))))$

    $\Phi \therefore (L_2(g) \supset \underline{\sigma}(L_1(\sigma_{ac}(g))))$

    $\Phi \therefore (U_2(g) \supset \underline{\sigma}(U_1(\sigma_{ac}(g))))$

where $\underline{\sigma}$ *is the extension of* σ *to the language of expressions and conditions and* $\therefore$ *means entailment in the first-order sense. As already mentioned,* Φ *stands for some axiomatisation of the underlying data types. Designs and superposition morphisms define a category that we name* **DSGN**.

A morphism $\sigma\colon P_1 \to P_2$ identifies a way in which P_1 is "augmented" to become P_2 so that it can be considered as havings been obtained from P_1 through the superposition of additional behaviour, namely the interconnection of one or more components. In other words, σ identifies P_1 as a component of P_2 (what we normally call "the system").

The map σ_{ch} identifies for every channel of the component the corresponding channel of the system. The first group of constraints also establishes that the data sorts associated with channels have to be preserved. Notice, however, that an input channel of a component can become an output channel of the system. This is because the result of interconnecting an input channel of a component with an output channel of another component is an output channel of the overall system. Mechanisms for hiding communication, i.e. making it private, can be applied, but they are not the default in a configuration.

The partial mapping σ_{ac} identifies the action of the component that is involved in each action of the system, if ever. The second group of constraints states that the type of actions (shared or private) is preserved. The last groups of conditions establishes that change within a component is completely encapsulated in the structure of actions defined for the component and that the computations performed by the system reflect the interconnections established between its components. The conditions on write frames imply that actions of the system in which a component is not involved cannot have local channels of the component in their write frame. The second condition of the fourth group reflects the fact that the effects of the actions of the components can only be preserved or made more deterministic in the system. The last two conditions allow the bounds that the design specifies for the enabling of the action to be strengthened but not weakened. Strengthening of these bounds reflects the fact that all the components that participate in the execution of a joint action have to give their permission for the action to occur.

Superposition morphisms do not correspond to the mathematical pattern that we wish to provide for supporting the approach to evolution through "just-in-time" integration that we outlined in the introduction. This is because extensions performed in this way require changes to be carried out on the way components have been implemented, e.g. changing the guards of given actions. The way we want to support the evolution of the system is by interconnecting an explicit, external, component to the original program in a way that ensures the required monitoring activity. The component that is required for monitoring the cart can be given by the following program:

```
design monitor is
out   count:nat
in    loc,cpoint:nat
do    inc: [loc=cpoint → count:=count+1]
      ◻ skip: [loc•cpoint →]
```

This is a component that is able to read two values from its environment (through the channels *loc* and *cpoint*) and perform two actions: one that increments a counter *count* when the two input channels hold the same value, and another that just "skips" (does "nothing", computationally speaking) when these values are different.

In order for this component to monitor the behaviour of the cart as intended, we need to interconnect it with *cart* as follows:

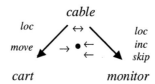

where

```
design cable is
in    a
do g: [ → ]
```

This "cable", defined as a program itself, does not perform any computation. It provides a pure coordination function by establishing the means for the two components to communicate, just like an ideal, neutral "cable". In the case of the example above, we need a complex cable with two "wires": one for the monitor to read the location of the cart, and another for synchronising the move action of the cart with those of the monitor.

The interconnection itself is established through the arrows. The left arrow maps *a* to *loc* and *move* to *g*, and the right arrow maps *a* to *loc* and both *inc* and *skip* to *g*. Because there are no computations involved in the cable, the arrows are, in fact, trivial superposition morphisms. Hence, the diagram is a categorical entity i.e. a mathematical object which, in this case, expresses a given system configuration. Such a configuration diagram establishes input/output relations, as in the case of *loc*, as well as synchronisation sets as in the cases of *{move,inc}* and *{move,skip}*. This semantics of the configuration is the one that corresponds to taking the colimit of the diagram. The colimit returns a program whose behaviour corresponds to the joint behaviour of the components thus interconnected. In the case above, it is easy to prove that the colimit returns, up to isomorphism, the program *monitored_cart*.

It is not possible to provide herein the full explanation of how colimits in the category of programs work. In the case of interconnections such as the one above, and besides establishing these input/output relations and synchronisation sets as illustrated, the colimit assigns to each synchronisation set an action whose guard is the conjunction of the guards of the actions in the set, and whose assignments are given, for every output channel, by the conjunction of the assignments performed locally by the actions in the set. This operation captures what in IP [13] is actually called superposition – a generalised parallel composition operator based on a *rendez-vous* synchronisation mechanism. In this case, cables can be seen to provide the places in which the *rendez-vous* take place, which in IP is handled implicitly through global naming.

It is this pattern of extension that we wish for supportting the method of evolution through "just-in-time" integration: components are not extended in the sense that we rewrite whatever features we want to change (even if subject to certain rules), but superposed with other components that regulate their behaviour. In the general case, the superposition may be performed over more than one component using what in Software Architectures are called *connectors* [1]. Such connectors coordinate the behaviour of the given components (roles or partners) via a mediator (the glue). See [10] for a semantics of architectural connectors using Category Theory as above and [2] for their application to OO modelling through coordination contracts.

There is, however, one further ingredient in our approach to evolution that needs to be accounted for, precisely the one that corresponds to *coordination*. How can we capture the fact that, through the interconnections expressed above, we do not have to change the way the components are programmed? That is to say, how can we express that computation has actually been separated from coordination?

In CommUnity, this separation is captured by distinguishing two different parts of designs: signatures, or interfaces, and bodies. Signatures consist of the features that are used to perform the interconnections – the input and output channels, and the action names, together with their types. Hence, they provide the model of coordination that is built into the design language. The bodies consist of the features through which each program ensures a given functionality – the guards and assignments per-formed by the actions.

Superposition morphisms, once their effects on the computational aspects are ig-nored, endow signatures with the structure of a category as well, which we denote by **INTF** (for interfaces). Designs and their interfaces are related through a (forgetful) functor **intf:DSGN→INTF**. The fact that the computational side does not play any role in the interconnections is captured by the following properties of this functor:

- **intf** is faithful;
- **intf** lifts colimits;
- **intf** has discrete structures.

The fact that **intf** is faithful (injective over each hom-set), means that morphisms of designs cannot induce more relationships between designs than between their un-derlying signatures (interfaces). That is to say, by taking into consideration the com-putational part, we may not get additional observational power over the external be-haviour of designs.

The second property means that, given any configuration diagram **dia:I→DSGN** over designs and colimit $(intf(S_i) \rightarrow C)_{i:I}$ of **(dia;intf)**, there exists a colimit $(S_i \rightarrow S)_{i:I}$ of **dia** such that $intf(S_i \rightarrow S) = (intf(S_i) \rightarrow C)$. In other words, if we interconnect system components through a diagram, then any colimit of the underlying diagram of inter-faces establishes a signature for which a computational part exists that captures the joint behaviour of the interconnected designs. This is a "correctness" result in the sense that it states that, by interconnecting the signatures of designs, we are intercon-necting the designs themselves.

The corresponding "completeness" result – that all interconnections can be estab-lished via signatures – is given by the third property. The fact that **intf** has discrete structures means that, for every interface **C:INTF** there exists a design **s(C):DSGN** such that, for every signature morphism $f:C \rightarrow intf(S)$, there is a design morphism $g:s(C) \rightarrow S$ such that $intf(g)=f$. That is to say, every signature C has a "realisation" (a discrete lift) as a design **s(C)** in the sense that, using C to interconnect a component S, which is achieved through a morphism $f:C \rightarrow intf(S)$, is tantamount to using s(C) through any $g:s(C) \rightarrow S$ such that $intf(g)=f$. In CommUnity, the discrete lift of a sig-nature is the "empty program" over that signature: every action has a true guard and performs a completely underdetermined assignment. This is exactly how the cable in the example above looked like, which justifies that cables are, essentially, just inter-faces. Hence, the interconnections are established via interfaces, independently of the computations performed locally by the components.

These three properties constitute the definitional characteristics of what in [11] we called a *coordinated functor* or, equivalently, for a given category of systems to be coordinated over a category of interfaces. In [11], we provided more examples of coordinated functors, including concurrency models, specification logics, and coordi-nation languages like Linda, which supports the view that this is, indeed, an abstrac-tion of typical properties of coordination that hold across a range of formalisms (and not just CommUnity). Therein, we further show how a number of properties hold of coordinated formalisms that are useful for software development, including the ability of synthesising interconnections between programs from interconnections established at the level of their specifications.

4   From Theory to Practice

The degree of flexibility of just-in-time integration can be achieved in coordinated languages like CommUnity because the mechanisms through which interactions between system components are coordinated can be completely externalised from the code that implements them and modelled explicitly as first-class citizens. The categorical semantics that we outlined in the previous section serves the purpose of providing a formal characterisation of the frameworks in which this separation can be carried through from first principles.

Indeed, not every language supports this separation. Object-oriented languages are a typical example of frameworks in which interactions are "hard-wired": by relying on feature calling as the main mechanism for establishing interconnections (inheritance and composition being even more intrusive), it is very hard to understand, let alone change, the way objects collaborate without having to search in the code for the chains of method calling [22]. As a consequence, object-oriented systems are too rigid when it comes to change, thus generating "legacy" in what concerns evolution. This does not mean that object-oriented environments cannot be used for just-in-time integration. It just means that a layer of adaptation needs to be introduced in which the separation of interfaces is carried out. This is precisely what we have provided in [17] through a micro-architecture that makes use of well-known design patterns for enforcing superposition [4], a propotype of which is available for Java-based development environments [24].

CommUnity was developed precisely to illustrate how this separation can be supported by Formal Description Techniques. It is not itself a language that we use for the day-to-day analysis and design activities. For this purpose, we have developed a set of modelling primitives that build on the separation between Computation and Coordination, which can be used to extend languages like the UML [7].

The centrepiece of this modelling kernel is the notion of *coordination contract* [2]. A coordination contract makes available the expressive power of a *connector* in the terminology of Software Architectures [1]. It consists of a prescription of *coordination effects* (the *glue* of the connector) that are superposed on a collection of partners (system components) when the occurrence of given *triggers* is detected in the system. For instance, the monitor that we discussed above is an example of a coordination contract: as a connector, it has a single role (formal parameter). This role identifies the abstract properties that the components that can be monitored have to exhibit: basically that, in their public interfaces, they make available a trigger that allows for the monitor to detect the passage of the cart through the control point. The glue of the monitor as a connector consists of the counting process that we described above. This glue exhibits a public interface through which the counter is made available.

Space is too scarce for a proper definition and explanation of the language, methodology and pragmatics associated with the coordination modelling primitives that we have developed. There are several publications available on their application to business information systems [e.g. 3].

5 A Layered Architecture for Evolution

As already motivated, our approach to system development is based on a methodological and technological separation between the computations performed by system components and the mechanisms that coordinate their interaction. Components encapsulate collections of services that determine specific system functionalities that are made available through computations performed on local states. Components correspond to "core", "stable" entities (even if mobile) in the sense that evolution should not be intrusive on their implementation but, instead, make different uses of the services that they provide or adapt them to new circumstances through the superposition of coordination mechanisms. These are modelled explicitly and outside the components in the form of what we have named "coordination contracts", leading to a two-tiered architecture for distributed and networked systems in which basic components and coordination contracts reside in different layers:

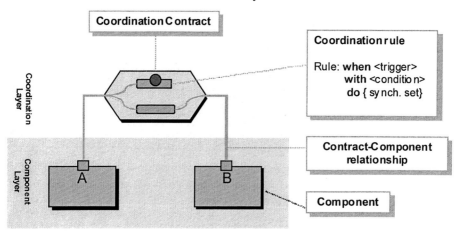

Coordination contracts ensure that given global properties of the system will emerge from the functionalities of the components and the interaction established between them through the contracts. They are the means through which we propose that evolution be conceived in the sense that, in order to be adapted to new requirements, the system should be reconfigured by removing existing contracts and plugging in new contracts from which different behaviour can emerge.

Hence, it is important that we make it possible for the system to be reconfigured in terms of revising which contracts apply to which components without interfering in the way components are implemented. The micro-architecture that we developed for implementing coordination contracts in platforms for component-based development [17] supports, precisely, this degree of dynamic, non-intrusive reconfiguration.

Having mechanisms for evolving systems is not the same as prescribing when and how these mechanisms should be applied. Evolution is a process that needs to be subject to rules that aim at enforcing given global properties for systems that should be evolution invariant. For this purpose, we have developed a modelling primitive – coordination contexts – through which the reconfiguration capabilities of the system can be automated, both in terms of ad-hoc services that can be invoked by authorised users, and programmed reconfigurations that allow systems to react to well identified triggers and, hence, adapt themselves to changes brought about on their state or configuration.

For instance, in order to avoid collisions between carts moving along the same track, we may superpose binary coordination contracts on pairs of carts to synchronise their movements: a cart that is just behind another one should not move until the front one has moved. The glue of the contract can be designed as follows:

```
design  subsume is
do      sync: [true → skip]
    []  free: [true → skip]
```

The idea is to synchronise the move action of the cart behind with *sync* and that of the cart in front with both *sync* and *free* so that the cart in front can move freely but the cart just behind just moves synchronised with the one in front.

Because this coordination mechanism only needs to be in place when there is a risk of collision, it makes no sense to have it superposed on permanence. What we would like to do is to program the configuration of the system in a way that the contract is superposed whenever the risk of collision arises. This is what coordination contexts are for: they consist of sets of trigger/reaction rules that can react to changes occurring in the state of the system by reconfiguring it, such as:

when front.loc+1<behind.loc

do   superpose subsume(sync↔{front.move,behind.move},free↔front.move)

This also shows how we can build self-adaptable systems.

Coordination contexts reside on a third-layer of the architecture above the computation and coordination layers: it uses components and contracts for reconfiguring the system but components and contracts are developed without knowing in which contexts they will be used.

In the mathematical setting that we outlined in the previous section, configurations are (labelled) graphs, which enables configuration operations to be over basic graph-rewriting techniques. That is to say, the basic reconfiguration actions like creation and deletion of component and contract instances can be formalised directly in an algebraic graph-rewriting setting, for instance using the double pushout approach. More details on the graph-rewriting based operational semantics can be found in [23].

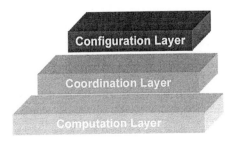

Ad-hoc and programmed reconfiguration operations that support evolution, including auto-adaptation

Coordination units that can be plugged and removed dynamically without interfering with the computation layer.

Stable computational components offering core functionalities.

6 Concluding Remarks

In this paper, we presented a set of technologies that, in our opinion,, backed up by experience in concrete applications, can supplement the shortcomings of current Formal Methods in endowing systems with the levels of agility required for operating in "internet-time" and support the next generation of the e-world – Web Services, B2B, P2P... Basically, we argued that the move from an "identity" to a "service"-oriented approach, replacing the tight coupling that mechanisms like explicit feature calling – the object-oriented basic mechanism of computation – imposes on system, in favour of external interconnections that can be established "just-in-time", can be supported by clearly separating computation and coordination concerns [15] and relying on superposition mechanisms [18] for establishing interconnections between components that are otherwise completely unaware of one another. Reconfiguration techniques as known from Distributed Systems [21] can then be used for addressing system evolution, namely the process of dynamically interconnecting components according to the business rules that determine how the system should behave at each time.

Our approach is well supported (1) at the foundational level through a mathematical characterisation of the notions of coordination, superposition and reconfiguration [e.g. 11], (2) at the implementation level through micro-architectures that show how coordination technologies can be deployed in existing environments for component-based development [e.g. 17], and (3) at the methodological level through a set of semantic primitives – coordination contracts, laws and contexts – that have been tested in a series of case studies in typical areas where agility is a key concern [e.g. 19,20].

Acknowledgements

The work that we reported in this paper has been developed within a mixed research team of academics and developers that includes L. Andrade, J. Gouveia, G. Koutsoukos, A. Lopes and M. Wermelinger. Much useful feedback has also been received from L. Barroca, K. Lano and A. Moreira. We would like to thank all of them for the opportunity to discuss ideas and be challenged by their critical minds!

References

1. R.Allen and D.Garlan, "A Formal Basis for Architectural Connectors", *ACM TOSEM,* 6(3), 1997, 213-249.
2. L.F.Andrade and J.L.Fiadeiro, "Interconnecting Objects via Contracts", in *UML'99 – Beyond the Standard*, R.France and B.Rumpe (eds), LNCS 1723, Springer Verlag 1999, 566-583.
3. L.F.Andrade and J.L.Fiadeiro, "Agility through Coordination", *Information Systems* 27, 2002, 411-424.

4. L.F.Andrade, J.L.Fiadeiro, A.Lopes and M.Wermelinger, "Patterns for Coordination", in *Proc. COORDINATION'00*, G.Catalin-Roman and A.Porto (eds), LNCS 1906, Springer-Verlag 2000, 317-322.
5. R.Back and R.Kurki-Suonio, "Distributed Cooperation with Action Systems", *ACM TOPLAS* 10(4), 1988, 513-554.
6. L. Bass, P.Clements and R.Kasman, *Software Architecture in Practice*, Addison Wesley 1998.
7. G.Booch, J.Rumbaugh and I.Jacobson, *The Unified Modeling Language User Guide*, Addison-Wesley 1998.
8. K.Chandy and J.Misra, *Parallel Program Design - A Foundation*, Addison-Wesley 1988.
9. J.L.Fiadeiro and T.Maibaum, "Categorical Semantics of Parallel Program Design", *Science of Computer Programming* 28, 1997, 111-138.
10. J.L.Fiadeiro and A.Lopes, "Semantics of Architectural Connectors", in *TAPSOFT'97*, LNCS 1214, Springer-Verlag 1997, 505-519.
11. J.L.Fiadeiro and A.Lopes, "Algebraic Semantics of Coordination, or what is in a signature?", in *AMAST'98*, A.Haeberer (ed), Springer-Verlag 1999.
12. P.Finger, "Componend-Based Frameworks for E-Commerce", *Communications of the ACM* 43(10), 2000, 61-66.
13. N.Francez and I.Forman, *Interacting Processes*, Addison-Wesley 1996.
14. E.Gamma, R.Helm R.Johnson and J.Vlissides, *Design Patterns: Elements of Reusable Object Oriented Software*, Addison-Wesley 1995.
15. D.Gelernter and N.Carriero, "Coordination Languages and their Significance", *Communications ACM* 35, 2, pp. 97-107, 1992.
16. J.Goguen, "Categorical Foundations for General Systems Theory", in F.Pichler and R.Trappl (eds), *Advances in Cybernetics and Systems Research*, Transcripta Books 1973, 121-130.
17. J.Gouveia, G.Koutsoukos, L.Andrade and J.L.Fiadeiro, "Tool Support for Coordination-Based Software Evolution", in *Technology of Object-Oriented Languages and Systems – TOOLS 38*, W.Pree (ed), IEEE Computer Society Press 2001, 184-196.
18. S.Katz, "A Superimposition Control Construct for Distributed Systems", *ACM TOPLAS* 15(2), 1993, 337-356.
19. G.Koutsoukos, J.Gouveia, L.Andrade and J.L.Fiadeiro. "Managing evolution in Telecommunications Systems", in *New Developments on Distributed Applications and Interoperable Systems*, K.Zielinski, K.Geihs and A.Laurentowski (eds), Kluwer Academic Publishers 2001, 133--139.
20. G.Koutsoukos, T.Kotridis, L.Andrade, J.L.Fiadeiro, J.Gouveia and M.Wermelinger, "Coordination technologies for business strategy support: a case study in stock-trading", in *Proceedings ECOOP 2001 Workshop on Object Oriented Business Solutions (WOOBS'01)*, 2001, 41-52.
21. J.Magee and J.Kramer, "Dynamic Structure in Software Architectures", in *4th Symp. on Foundations of Software Engineering*, ACM Press 1996, 3-14.
22. M.Shaw, "Procedure Calls are the Assembly Language of Software Interconnection: Connectors Deserve First-Class Status", in D.A. Lamb (Ed.), *Studies of Software Design*, LNCS 1078, Springer-Verlag 1996.
23. M.Wermelinger and J.L.Fiadeiro, "Algebraic Software Architecture Reconfiguration" in *ESEC/FSE'99*, LNCS 1687, Springer-Verlag 1999, 393-409.
24. www.atxsoftware.com/CDE

Real-Time Process Algebra and Its Applications

Yingxu Wang

Theoretical and Empirical Software Engineering Research Centre
Department of Electrical and Computer Engineering
University of Calgary
2500 University Drive NW, Calgary, AB., Canada T2N 1N4
wangyx@enel.ucalgary.ca
Tel: (403) 220 6141, Fax: (403) 282 6855

Abstract. It is recognized that human and system behaviors may be modeled by a 3-D process comprising actions, time, and space. Software behaviors, similarly, can be modeled in the three dimensions known as the mathematical operations, event/process timing, and memory manipulation. This paper introduces Real-Time Process Algebra (RTPA) as a coherent software engineering notation system. RTPA is used to address the 3-D problem in software system description and specification in terms of architecture, static and dynamic behaviors. Case studies on applications of RTPA in real-time system modeling and specification are provided in this paper with real-world examples.

Keywords: Software engineering, descriptive mathematics, formal methods, real-time systems, algebraic specification, 3-D problems, architecture specification, static/dynamic behaviors specification

1 Introduction

Although there are various ways to express actions and behaviors in natural languages, it is found in cognitive informatics [14] that human and system behaviors may be classified into three basic categories: to *be*, to *have*, and to *do*. All mathematical means and forms, in general, are an abstract description of these three categories of system behaviors and their common rules. Taking this view, mathematical logic may be perceived as the abstract means for describing 'to be,' set theory for describing 'to have,' and algebras, particularly the process algebra, for describing 'to do.' This is a fundamental view toward the formal description and modeling of human and system behaviors in general, and software behaviors in particular, because a software system can be perceived as a virtual agent of human beings, and it is created to do something repeatable, to extend human capability, reachability, and/or memory capacity.

Rigorous and formal techniques are required for describing architectures and behaviors of software systems in component-based software engineering (CBSE). Conventional formal methods are based on logic and set theories [3, 10]. They are not adopted in CBSE because they lack the capability to describe component and system architectures and dynamic behaviors. A number of algebra-based formal methods were developed in the 1990's [1-2, 4-9, 11-13], which are considered suitable to describe component dynamic behaviors but they are still weak in describing component

B.K. Aichernig and T. Maibaum (Eds.): Formal Methods ..., LNCS 2757, pp. 322–336, 2003.

architectures. This paper introduces the real-time process algebra (RTPA) [14-18] to describe and specify component-based software systems, particularly real-time systems.

Algebra is a form of mathematics that enables complicated problems to be expressed and investigated in a formal and rigorous way. Hoare [7], Milner [11], and others developed various algebraic approaches to represent communicating and concurrent systems, known as process algebra. A *process algebra* is a set of formal notations and rules for describing algebraic relations of software engineering processes. RTPA [15, 16] is a real-time process algebra that can be used to formally and precisely describe and specify architectures and behaviors of large-scale software systems.

A *process* in RTPA is a computational operation that transforms a system from a state to another by changing its inputs, outputs, and/or internal variables. A process can be a single meta-process or a complex process formed by using the process combination rules of RTPA known as process relations. A software system can be perceived and described mathematically as a set of coherent and interacting processes.

In a well-designed formal method, complicated system specification should be carried out via a number of programmatic refinements in a top-down approach by using a set of coherent notations. Three essential aspects of a software system can be described and specified by a coherent set of mathematical notations in RTPA, i.e.:

$$§(SysIDS) ≙ SysIDS.Architecture$$
$$\| SysIDS.StaticBehaviors$$
$$\| SysIDS.DynamicBehaviors \tag{1}$$

The specification of each of the above subsystems, in terms of system architecture, system static behaviors, and system dynamic behaviors, can be implemented by a three-level refinement process at the system, class, and detailed levels as shown in Figure 1.

Figure 1 provides a strategic scheme of system specification and refinement in RTPA. Figure 1 also shows the defined work products of each specification subsystem at different refinement levels. In the RTPA specification and refinement scheme, a new concept, the *component logical model* (CLM), is introduced, which is a special architectural component for describing the abstract logical models of system hardware and system control mechanisms.

A *component logical model (CLM)* is defined as an abstract model of a system architectural component that represents a hardware interface, an internal logic model, and/or a common control structure of a system.

The three refinement steps for system architecture specification (S1 in Figure 1) are: system architecture, CLM schemata, and CLM objects. Similarly, the refinement strategy for system static behavior specification (S2) is: system static behaviors, process schemata, and process implementations. System dynamic behaviors (S3) can be specified by: system dynamic process relations, process deployment, and process dispatch, in a three-level refinement.

This paper introduces RTPA as a comprehensive and expressive mathematical notation system for component-based software engineering. Section 2 describes the structure of the RTPA notation system, and the RTPA method for the specification and refinement of system *architectural components* and *operational components* via three-level refinements. Section 3 demonstrates how static behaviours of software systems are described in RTPA. Section 4 describes the modelling and specification of system dynamic behaviours at run-time. Case studies and examples are provided throughout the paper to explain the applications of RTPA in real-world environment.

Refinement → ↓ Specification	R1. System-Level Specification	R2. Class-Level Specification	R3. Detailed-Level Specification

S1. System Architecture	**1.1 System architecture**
	SysID$.Architecture ≙
	    CLM₁$ [n₁,₩]
	    ‖ CLM₂$ [n₂,₩]
	    ‖ ...
	    ‖ CLM₄$ [n₄,₩]
		1.2 CLM schemas
		CLMSchema ≙
		    CLM-ID(i₩): (
		    Field₁ : type₁ | constraint₁>,
		    Field₂ : type₂ | constraint₂>,
		    ...
		    Fieldₙ : typeₙ | constraintₙ>)
			1.3 CLM objects
			CLMObject ≙
			    CLMSchema$T
			    ‖ ObjectID$
			    ‖ {InstanceParameters}
			    ‖ {InitialValues}

S2. Static Behaviors	**2.1 System static behaviors**
	SysID$.StaticBehaviors ≙
	    SysInitial
	    ‖ Process₁
	    ‖ Process₂
	    ‖ ...
	    ‖ Processₙ
		2.2 Process schemas
		ProcessSchema ≙
		    PN₩ // process number
		    ‖ ProcessID$ ({I}; {O})
		    ‖ {OperatedCLMs}
		    ‖ {RelatedProcesses}
		    ‖ FunctionDescription$
			2.3 Process implementation
			ProcessImplementation ≙
			    ProcessSchema$T
			    ‖ ProcessInstID$
			    ‖ {DetailedProcesses}

S3. Dynamic Behaviors	**3.1 System dynamic behaviors**
	SysID$.DynamicBehaviors ≙
	    ‖ {Base-level processes}
	    ‖ {High-level processes}
	    ‖ {Low-interrupt-level processes}
	    ‖ {High-interrupt-level processes}
		3.2 Process deployment
		ProcessDeployment ≙ § →
		(BaseTimeEvent ↳ {ProcessSet₁}
		| HighLevelTimeEvent ↳ {Process set₂}
		| LowIntTimeEvent ↳ {Process set₃}
		| HighIntTimeEvent ↳ {Process set₄}
		) → §
			3.3 Process dispatch
			ProcessDispatch ≙ § →
			(Event₁ ↳ {ProcessSet₁}
			| Event₂ ↳ {ProcessSet₂}
			| ...
			| Eventₙ ↳ {ProcessSetₙ}
			)
			→ §

Fig. 1. The Scheme of System Specification and Refinement by RTPA

2   Component Architecture Description by RTPA

As described in Section 1, the requirement for a 3-D formal method is theoretically and practically fundamental in software engineering. RTPA has been developed as a coherent notation system and a formal engineering method for addressing the 3-D problem in software system specification, refinement, and implementation, particularly for real-time and embedded systems.

2.1   The RTPA Notation System

RTPA models 16 meta processes and 16 process relations as shown in Table 1. A *meta-process* of RTPA is an elementary and primary process that serves as a common and basic building block for modeling a software system. Complex processes in RTPA can be derived from meta-processes by a set of *process relations* that serve as process combinatory rules. Detailed semantics of RTPA may be referred to [15].

RTPA can be used to describe both logical and physical models of a system. Therefore, logic views of the architecture of a software system and its operational platform can be described by using the same set of notations. When the system architecture is formally defined, the static and dynamic behaviors associated with the system architectural models, can be specified by a three-level refinement scheme at the system, class, and object levels in a top-down approach.

Table 1. The RTPA Notation System

Meta-Process		Process Relation	
Description	Syntax	Description	Syntax
System	§(SysID**S**)	Sequence	$P \rightarrow Q$
Assignment	y**Type** := x**Type**	Branch	$(?exp\mathbf{BL} = \mathbf{T}) \rightarrow P$ $\mid (?\sim) \rightarrow Q$ where '$\sim$' means 'exp**BL** = **F**
Addressing	Ptr**P^** := x**Type**	Switch	$?exp\mathbf{Type} =$ $\quad 0 \rightarrow P_0$ $\quad \mid 1 \rightarrow P_1$ $\quad \mid \ldots$ $\quad \mid n\text{-}1 \rightarrow P_{n\text{-}1}$ $\quad \mid else \rightarrow \varnothing$ where exp**Type** = {**N, B, S**}
Input	Port(ptr**P^**)**Type** |> x**Type**	For-do	$\overset{n}{\underset{i=1}{R}} (P(i))$
Output	x**Type** |< Port(ptr**P^**)**Type**	Repeat	$expBL \neq T$ $\underset{\geq 1}{R} (P)$
Read	Mem(ptr**P^**)**Type** > x**Type**	While-do	$\overset{15}{\underset{i=0}{R}} (P)$
Write	x**Type** < Mem(ptr**P^**)**Type**	Function call	$P \downarrow F$
Timing	a) @**hh:mm:ss:ms** := §**hh:mm:ss:ms** b) @t**yy:MM:dd** := §t**yy:MM:dd** c) @ t**yy:MM:dd:hh:mm:ss:ms** := §t**yy:MM:dd:hh:mm:ss:ms**	Recursion	$P \cup P$
Duration	@t_n**N** := §t_n**N** + Δn**N**	Parallel	$P \parallel Q$
Memory allocation	AllocateObject (ObjectID**S**, NofElements**N**, ElementType**RT**)	Concurrence	$P \oiint Q$
Memory release	ReleaseObject (ObjectID**S**)	Interleave	$P \parallel\!\parallel Q$
Increase	↑(n**Type**)	Pipeline	$P \gg Q$
Decrease	↓(n**Type**)	Time-driven dispatch	@t_i**hh:mm:ss:ms** ↳ P_i, $i \in \{1..n\}$
Exception detecting	! (@e**S**)	Event-driven dispatch	@e_i**S** ↳ P_i, $i \in \{1..n\}$
Skip	∅	Interrupt	$P \parallel \odot (@e\mathbf{S} \nearrow Q \searrow \odot)$
Stop	⊠	Jump	$P \rightarrowtail Q$

2.2 System Architectural Description in RTPA

In RTPA, component and system architectural descriptions are carried out via a number of programmatic refinements in a top-down manner using the same set of coherent notations.

There are four types of system meta-architectures known as: parallel, serial, pipeline, and nested as shown in Figure 2. Any complex system architecture can be represented by the combination of these four meta-architectures of component relations. It is interesting to note that each of the meta-architecture can be modeled by a certain RTPA process relation as defined in Table 1. Therefore, not only system behaviors, but also system architectures can be expressed by the same set of formal notations in RTPA.

No.	Type of Architecture	Syntax	Examples
1	Parallel	$P \parallel Q$	§(ParallelSys$) ≜ $P_1 \parallel P_2 \parallel ... \parallel P_n$
2	Serial	$P \to Q$	§(SerialSys$) ≜ $P_1 \to P_2 \to ... \to P_n$
3	Pipeline	$P \gg Q$	§(PipelinedSys$) ≜ $P_1 \gg P_2 \gg ... \gg P_n$
4	Nested	$P \leftrightarrow Q$	§(NestedSys$) ≜ $P_1 \leftrightarrow P_2 \leftrightarrow ... \leftrightarrow P_n$

Fig. 2. RTPA meta-architectures

Components of a software system can be classified as *architectural components* and *operational components*. In RTPA, the former is modeled by the *component logical model* (CLM), which is an abstract model of a system architectural component that represents a hardware interface, an internal logic model, and/or a common control structure of a system.

The framework for a component-based system can be described as a set of parallel CLMs in RTPA, i.e.:

$$\text{SysID}\mathbf{S}.\text{Architecture}\mathbf{ST} \triangleq \text{CLM}_1\mathbf{S}[n_1\mathbf{N}]$$
$$\| \text{CLM}_2\mathbf{S}[n_2\mathbf{N}]$$
$$\| \cdots$$
$$\| \text{CLM}_k\mathbf{S}[n_k\mathbf{N}] \tag{2}$$

A generic *CLM schema* in RTPA can be represented as a record-type abstract data structure as shown below:

$$\text{CLMSchema}\mathbf{ST} \triangleq \text{CLM-ID}\mathbf{S}\ (i\mathbf{N}):$$
$$(\ \text{Field}_1 : \text{type}_1\ |\ \text{constraint}_1>,$$
$$\text{Field}_2 : \text{type}_2\ |\ \text{constraint}_2>,$$
$$\cdots$$
$$\text{Field}_n : \text{type}_n\ |\ \text{constraint}_n>$$
$$) \tag{3}$$

The instantiation of a CLM schema is known as a *CLM object* in RTPA. A CLM object, as shown in Expression 4, is a derived instance of a CLM schema that describes detailed implementation and initialisation of a CLM object.

$$\text{CLMObject}\mathbf{ST} \triangleq \text{CLMSchema}\mathbf{ST}$$
$$\| \text{ObjectID}\mathbf{S}$$
$$\| \{\text{InstanceParameters}\}$$
$$\| \{\text{InitialValue} \tag{4}$$

CLM objects are results of the final refinement of the specification of system's architecture. After the three-step refinement, known as system architecture, CLM schemas, and CLM objects, all architectural components, their relations, and implementations are obtained systematically.

For example, the structure of a lift dispatching system (LDS) [17] is shown in Figure 3. The high-level specification of the architecture of LDS in RTPA can be derived as shown in Expression 5, where the number in the square brackets, [n$\mathbf{N}$], specify the required number of instance objects for a CLM in the system architectural configuration.

$$\text{LSD.Architecture} \triangleq\ <\text{Buttons} : \mathbf{ST}\ |\ [30]>$$
$$\| <\text{Lifts}: \mathbf{ST}\ |\ [3]>$$
$$\| <\text{SysClock}: \mathbf{ST}\ |\ [1]>$$
$$\| <\text{RequestEventRecord} : \mathbf{ST}\ |\ [30]>$$
$$\| <\text{LiftStatusRecord} : \mathbf{ST}\ |\ [30]>$$
$$\| <\text{LiftDispatchList} : \mathbf{ST}\ |\ [3]> \tag{5}$$

The RTPA specification of the architectures of request buttons in LDS, **ButtonsST**, is given in Figure 4. Referring to Expression 3, Figure 4 shows there are 30 buttons in LDS that share the same architectural model of 'ButtonsST'.

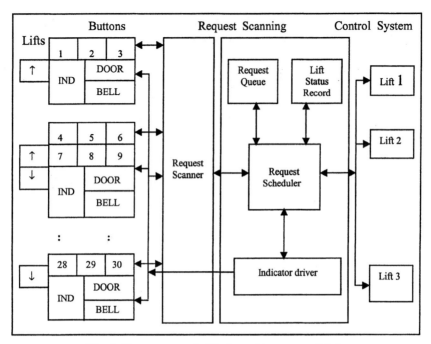

Fig. 3. The structure of a lift dispatching system (LDS)

$$\text{Buttons\textbf{ST}} \triangleq \overset{30}{\underset{i=1}{R}} \, (\text{Key (i\textbf{N}):}$$

<PortAddress : **H** | FF00H ≤ PortAddress**H** ≤ FF09H>,
<KeyInput : **B** | KeyInput**B** = <xxxx xkkk**B**>,
<Direction : **BL** | T = Up ∧ F = Down>,
<KeyPosition : **N** | 1 ≤ KeyPosition**N** ≤ 6>
)

Fig. 4. The architectural schema of request buttons in LDS

In Figure 4, the *big-R notation* of RTPA, $\overset{30}{\underset{i=1}{R}} \text{Key(i\textbf{N})}$, is used to denote the repetition of the button schema for 30 times. This is a new mathematical calculus for iteration specification in RTPA for both architectural and operational components.

Based on the schema of component, e.g. Buttons**ST**, a set of 30 component architectural objects can be derived by further refinement as shown in Figure 5. At this level of refinement, absolute port addresses are assigned within the ranges specified in the schemas. Initial values of control variables are also provided for ensuring the system enters a valid initial state when it is started.

On the basis of the description of component and system architectures by a set of CLMs, the operational components of a system and their behaviours can be easily described as shown in the following sections.

$$\textbf{ButtonsST} \triangleq \overset{30}{\underset{i=1}{R}} \ (\ \text{Key (iN):}$$

<PortAddress : H | FF00H ≤ PortAddressH ≤ FF09H>,
<KeyInput : B | KeyInputB = <xxxx xkkkB>,
<Direction : BL | T = Up ∧ F = Down>,
<KeyPosition : N | 1 ≤ KeyPositionN ≤ 6>
)
= Key(1): <PortAddressH, KeyInputB, DirectionBL, KeyPositionN> := <FF00H, 0000 0001B, T, 1>
|| Key(2): <PortAddressH, KeyInputB, DirectionBL, KeyPositionN> := <FF00H, 0000 0010B, T, 1>
|| ...
|| Key(30):<PortAddressH, KeyInputB, DirectionBL, KeyPositionN>:=<FF09H, 0000 0100B, F, 6>

Fig. 5. The architectural objects of request buttons in LDS

3 System Static Behaviors Description by RTPA

1. *Static behaviors* of a software component are valid operations of system that can
   be determined at compile-time. Component static behaviors describe the high-level
   configuration of processes of a system and their relations. This section describes
   how RTPA can be used to formulate detailed process specifications based on the
   CLM architectures described in Section 2.

3.1 System Static Behaviours

The specification of system static behaviors at the top level can be generally represented by a set of parallel processes as shown in Expression 6.

$$
\begin{aligned}
\text{SysID\textbf{S}.StaticBehaviors} \triangleq \ &\text{SysInitial} \\
&\| \text{Process}_1 \\
&\| \text{Process}_2 \\
&\| \ ... \\
&\| \text{Process}_n
\end{aligned}
\tag{6}
$$

For example, the static behaviors of a telephone switching system (TSS) [14] consist
of six processes as specified below:

$$
\begin{aligned}
\text{TSS.StaticBehaviors} \triangleq \ &\text{SysInitial\textbf{ST}} \\
&\| \text{SysClock\textbf{ST}} \\
&\| \text{LineScanning\textbf{ST}} \\
&\| \text{DigitsReceiving\textbf{ST}} \\
&\| \text{ConnectDrive\textbf{ST}} \\
&\| \text{CallProcessing\textbf{ST}}
\end{aligned}
$$

In the above example, the CallProcessing**ST** process is a complex process of 7 components that can be further refined as follows:

$$CallProcessing\textbf{ST} \triangleq CallOrigination\textbf{ST}$$
$$\| Dialling\textbf{ST}$$
$$\| CheckCalledStatus\textbf{ST}$$
$$\| Connecting\textbf{ST}$$
$$\| Talking\textbf{ST}$$
$$\| CallTermination\textbf{ST}$$
$$\| ExceptionalTermination\textbf{ST}$$

Each of the above processes in TSS can be further extended and refined into a detailed level that is close to method code in a class. The following subsections demonstrate component refinement by process schemas and implementations.

3.2   Component Process Schemas

A process schema of a component is the functional architecture of a component. A process schema consists of the process identifier (ID), I/Os, operated CLMs, other related processes, and brief functional descriptions, as shown in Expression 7.

$$ProcessSchema \triangleq PN\textbf{N} \qquad // \text{ process number}$$
$$\| ProcessID\textbf{S}\ (\{\textbf{I}\}; \{\textbf{O}\})$$
$$\| \{OperatedCLMs\}$$
$$\| \{RelatedProcesses\}$$
$$\| FunctionDescription\textbf{S} \qquad\qquad (7)$$

For example, the component schema of the CallOrigination**ST** process in TSS as specified in Section 3.1 can be refined as shown in Figure 6.

CallOrigination (<I:: LineNum**N**>; <O:: CallProcess**N**>) ≙
{ // **PNN** = 1
// **Operated CLMs ::** {LineScanners**ST**, CallRecords**ST**}
// **Related processes ::** {LineScanning, ConnectDrive}
// **Related processes ::** {
  • Find hook-off subscribers from LineScanners**ST**
  • Record originated calls in CallRecords**ST**}
}

Fig. 6. Description of process schema in RTPA

3.3   Component Process Implementation

The final refinement step of component static behaviours is to extend the process schemas into detailed processes. It is called component process implementation as shown in Expression 8.

$$ProcessImplementation \triangleq ProcessSchema\textbf{ST}$$
$$\| ProcessInstID\textbf{S}$$
$$\| \{DetailedProcesses\} \qquad\qquad (8)$$

For example, the schema of a TSS process, CallOrigination**ST**, has been specified in Figure 6. The implementation refinement of the CallOrigination**ST** process can be carried out as shown in Figure 7.

Based on the detailed process specifications of system components, program code can be derived easily and rigorously, and tests of the code can be generated prior to the coding phase.

4 System Dynamic Behaviors Description by RTPA

Dynamic behaviors of a software component are process relations at run-time, which can be specified by a number of execution priority levels of processes based on their real-time timing requirements.

CallOrigination (<I:: LineNumN>; <O:: CallProcess**N**>) ≙
{ // PN**N** = 1
   // **Operated CLMs ::** {LineScanners**ST**, CallRecords**ST**}
   // **Related processes ::** {LineScanning, ConnectDrive}
   // **Related processes ::** {
      • Find hook-off subscribers from LineScanners**ST**
      • Record originated calls in CallRecords**ST**}

   i**N** := LineNum**N**
   → LineScanner(i**N**).Status**N** := 2   // Show line is busy
   ↳ ConnectDrive (SubscriberLine(i**N**)**N**, SignalDialTone**N**, On**BL**)
   → CallRecord(i**N**).Timer**SS** := 5   // Set no dial timer
   → CallRecord(i**N**).CallStatus**BL** = **T**   // Set call record active
   → CallRecord(i**N**).CallProcess**N** := 2   // To dialling
}

Fig. 7. Detailed specification of TSS call processing behaviours in RTPA

4.1 System Dynamic Behaviors

Generally, component dynamic behaviors or the timing relationships between the static processes provided by a component can be specified at four levels as shown in Expression 9.

$$\text{SysID}\textbf{S}.\text{DynamicBehaviors} \triangleq \{\text{Base-level processes}\}$$
$$\| \{\text{High-level processes}\}$$
$$\| \{\text{Low-interrupt-level processes}\}$$
$$\| \{\text{High-interrupt-level processes}\} \qquad (9)$$

where some of the priority levels may be absent for a specific system.

For example, the dynamic behaviors of TSS, at the high-level refinement, can be specified as shown in Figure 8.

4.2 Dynamic Behaviors Deployment

Process deployment is defined as detailed dynamic process relations at run-time, which refines component dynamic behaviors by specifying precise *time-driven relations* between the system clock, system interrupt sources, and processes at different priority levels as follows:

ProcessDeployment ≙ § →

$$
\begin{array}{lll}
(& \text{BaseTimeEvent\textbf{S}} & \hookrightarrow \ \{\text{ProcessSet}_1\} \\
| & \text{HighLevelTimeEvent\textbf{S}} & \hookrightarrow \ \{\text{ProcessSet}_2\} \\
| & \text{LowIntTimeEvent\textbf{S}} & \hookrightarrow \ \{\text{ProcessSet}_3\} \\
| & \text{HighIntTimeEvent\textbf{S}} & \hookrightarrow \ \{\text{ProcessSet}_4\} \\
) & & \\
& \to \S &
\end{array}
\tag{10}
$$

For example, according to the time-driven process relations in process deployment, the TSS dynamic behaviours specified in Expression 10 can be further refined as shown in Figure 9, where precise timing relationships between different priority levels are specified.

```
TSS.DynamicBahaviors ≙   {Base-level processes}
                    || {High-level processes}       // No high-level process in TSS
                    || {Low-interrupt-level processes}
                    || {High-interrupt-level processes}
                      =    SystemInitial              // Base level
                      || ( CallOrigination            // Call processing
                        | Dialing
                        | CheckCalledStatus
                        | Connecting
                        | Talking
                        | CallTermination
                        | ExceptionalTermination
                      )
                      || LineScanning                 // Low-int level
                      || ( SysClock                    // High-int level
                        || DigitsReceiving
                      )
```

Fig. 8. Specification of TSS dynamic behaviors

Figure 9 shows that according to the system timing priority at run-time, the TSS system deploys the *LineScanning* process into the 100ms low-level interrupt processes, and *SysClock* and *DigitsReceiving* into the 10ms high-level interrupt processes. The rest processes are deployed into the base-level services because there is no strict timing constraint in operation.

```
TSS.ProcessDeployment ≜
{
// Base level processes
  @SystemInitial
   ↳ ( SysInitial
        @SysShutDownS=T
       ↳        R          CallProcessing
                ≥1
       → ⊠
     )
|| // High-interrupt-level processes
  ⊙ @SysClock1msInt
    ↗ (SysClock
     ↳ DigitsReceiving
     )
   ↘ ⊙
|| // Low-interrupt-level processes
  ⊙ @SysClock100msInt
    ↗ LineScanning
   ↘ ⊙
}
```

Fig. 9. Specification of TSS process deployment

4.3 Dynamic Behaviors Dispatch

As that of process deployment, *process dispatch* is another dynamic process relation behaving at run-time. Process dispatch refines dynamic behaviors of components by specifying their *event-driven relationships* in a software system as shown in Expression 11.

$$
\begin{aligned}
\text{ProcessDispatch} \triangleq \S \to \\
(\; \text{Event}_1 \hookrightarrow \{\text{ProcessSet}_1\} \\
| \; \text{Event}_2 \hookrightarrow \{\text{ProcessSet}_2\} \\
| \; \dots \\
| \; \text{Event}_n \hookrightarrow \{\text{ProcessSet}_n\} \\
) \\
\to \S
\end{aligned}
\tag{11}
$$

Process dispatch specifies event-driven relations of components in a system. For instance, the specification of TSS process dispatch is developed in Figure 10.

As specified in Figure 10 and Section 4.2, the CallProcessing**ST** process is a combined process with seven state-transition processes for controlling a call from origination to termination. Since TSS is operating at the millisecond level, while a telephone call may last for a considerably long period, the system cannot serve and wait for the completion of a transition for a specific call for all the time. Therefore, switching functions for an individual call are divided into seven states, corresponding to the 7 dispatching processes as shown in Figure 10.

$$
\begin{aligned}
&\textbf{CallProcessing} \triangleq \\
&\{ \ nN := 15 \\
&\quad \overset{n}{\underset{i=0}{\rightarrow R}} \ (? \ \circledS CallRecord.CallStatus\textbf{BL} = T \qquad\qquad \text{// A calling subscriber} \\
&\qquad\qquad \rightarrow LineNumN := iN \\
&\qquad\qquad \rightarrow (\quad @ \ CallRecord(iN).CallProcessN = 0 \qquad \text{// Idle} \\
&\qquad\qquad\qquad\quad \rightarrow \varnothing \\
&\qquad\qquad \ | \ @ \ CallRecord(iN).CallProcessN = 1 \qquad \text{// Call origination} \\
&\qquad\qquad\qquad\quad \hookrightarrow \ CallOrigination \ (\{I:: \ LineNumN\}; \ \{O:: \ CallProcessN\}) \\
&\qquad\qquad \ | \ @ \ CallRecord(iN).CallProcessN = 2 \qquad \text{// Dialing} \\
&\qquad\qquad\qquad\quad \hookrightarrow \ Dialling \ (\{I:: \ LineNumN\}; \ \{O:: \ CallProcessN\}) \\
&\qquad\qquad \ | \ @ \ CallRecord(iN).CallProcessN = 3 \qquad \text{// Check called status} \\
&\qquad\qquad\qquad\quad \hookrightarrow \ CheckCalledStatus \ (\{I:: \ LineNumN\}; \ \{O:: \ CallProcessN\} \\
&\qquad\qquad \ | \ @ \ CallRecord(iN).CallProcessN = 4 \qquad \text{// Connecting} \\
&\qquad\qquad\qquad\quad \hookrightarrow \ Connecting \ (\{I:: \ LineNumN\}; \ \{O:: \ CallProcessN\}) \\
&\qquad\qquad \ | \ @ \ CallRecord(iN).CallProcessN = 5 \qquad \text{// Talking} \\
&\qquad\qquad\qquad\quad \hookrightarrow \ Talking \ (\{I:: \ LineNumN\}; \ \{O:: \ CallProcessN\}) \\
&\qquad\qquad \ | \ @ \ CallRecord(iN).CallProcessN = 6 \qquad \text{// Call termination} \\
&\qquad\qquad\qquad\quad \hookrightarrow \ CallTermination \ (\{I:: \ LineNumN\}; \ \{O:: \ CallProcessN\}) \\
&\qquad\qquad \ | \ @ \ CallRecord(iN).CallProcessN = 7 \qquad \text{// Exceptional termination} \\
&\qquad\qquad\qquad\quad \hookrightarrow \ ExceptionalTermination \ (\{I:: \ LineNumN\}; \ \{O:: \ CallProcessN\}) \\
&\qquad\qquad \ ) \\
&\qquad \ ) \\
&\}
\end{aligned}
$$

Fig. 10. Specification of TSS process dispatch

The final-level specifications of the above examples provide a set of detailed and precise design blueprints for code implementation, test, and verification. A number of real-world case studies [17-20] demonstrate that RTPA is a practical formal engineering method for component-based system specification and refinement based on a small and coherent set of formal notations.

5 Conclusions

RTPA has been developed as an expressive, easy-to-comprehend, and language-independent notation system, and a specification and refinement method for real-time system description and specification. This paper has described the methodology, features, and applications of RTPA as a comprehensive and expressive mathematical notation system. A set of 16 meta-processes and 16 process relations has been elicited from software engineering practices for software system description and specification.

A stepwise specification and refinement method has been developed for modeling both system architectural and operational components by RTPA.

This paper has demonstrated that a component-based real-time or embedded system, including its architecture, and static and dynamic behaviours, can be essentially and sufficiently described by RTPA. The case studies and examples of RTPA applications provided in this paper have demonstrated the feature and descriptive power of the RTPA notation system and its specification and refinement method. The application results encouragingly demonstrated that RTPA is an expressive and practical software engineering notation system for both academics and practitioners in software engineering.

Acknowledgements

This work is supported by the NSERC research fund. It also related to the author's work in the IEEE Software Notation Planning Group (SNPG) towards the development of a standard software engineering notation system. The author would like to acknowledge the support of NSERC and IEEE SNPG. The author would thank the anonymous reviewers for their constructive comments.

References

1. Baeten, J.C.M. and J. A. Bergstra (1991), Real Time Process Algebra, *Formal Aspects of Computing*, Vol.3, pp.142-188.
2. Cerone A. (2000), Process Algebra versus Axiomatic Specification of a Real-Time Protocol, *LNCS, Vol.1816*, Springer, Berlin, pp.57-67.
3. Derrick, J. and E. Boiten (2001), *Refinement in Z and Object-Z: Foundations and Advanced Applications*, Springer-Verlag, London.
4. Dierks, H. (2000), A Process Algebra for Real-Time Programs, *LNCS, Vol. 1783*, Springer, Berlin, pp. 66-76.
5. Fecher, H. (2001), A Real-Time Process Algebra with Open Intervals and Maximal Progress, *Nordic Journal of Computing*, Vol.8, No.3, pp.346-360.
6. Gerber, R., E. L. Gunter, and I. Lee (1992), Implementing a Real-Time Process Algebra, in Archer, M. et al. eds., *Proceedings of the International Workshop on the Theorem Proving System and its Applications*, IEEE Computer Society Press, Los Alamitos, CA, USA, August, pp.144-154.
7. Hoare, C.A.R. (1985), *Communicating Sequential Processes*, Prentice-Hall Inc., ISBN 0-13-153271-8.
8. Jeffrey, A. (1992), Translating Timed Process Algebra into Prioritized Process Algebra, in J. Vytopil ed., *Proceedings of the 2nd International Symposium on Formal Techniques in Real-Time and Fault-Tolerant Systems*, LNCS Vol. 571, Springer-Verlag, Nijmegen, The Netherlands, pp.493-506.
9. Klusener, A.S. (1992), Abstraction in Real Time Process Algebra, in J. W. de Bakker, C. Huizing, W. P. de Roever, and G. Rozenberg eds., *Proceedings of Real-Time: Theory in Practice*, LNCS, Springer, Berlin, pp. 325-352.
10. Martin-Lof, Per (1975), An Intuitionist Theory of Types: Predicative Part, in H. Rose and J.C. Shepherdson (eds.), *Logic Colloquium 1973*, North-Holland.
11. Milner, R. (1989), *Communication and Concurrency*, Prentice-Hall, Englewood Cliffs, NJ.
12. Nicollin, X. and J. Sifakis (1991), An Overview and Synthesis on Timed Process Algebras, *Proc. 3rd International Computer Aided Verification Conference*, pp. 376-398.

13. Vereijken, J.J. (1995), A Process Algebra for Hybrid Systems, in A. Bouajjani and O. Maler eds., *Proceedings Second European Workshop on Real-Time and Hybrid Systems*, Grenoble, France, June.
14. Wang, Y. (2003), Using Process Algebra to Describe Human and Software Behaviours, *Bran and Mind: A Transdisciplinary Journal of Neuroscience and Neurophilosophy*, Vol.4, No.2.
15. Wang, Y. (2002), The Real-Time Process Algebra (RTPA), *Annals of Software Engineering: An International Journal*, Vol.14, USA, pp. 235-274.
16. Wang, Y. (2002b), A New Math for Software Engineering – The Real-Time Process Algebra (RTPA), *Keynote Speech* at The 2nd ASERC Workshop on Quantitative and Soft Computing Based Software Engineering (QSSE'02), April, Banff, AB., Canada.
17. Wang, Y. and Foinjong, N.C. (2002), Formal Specification of a Real-Time Lift Dispatching System, *Proceedings of the 2002 IEEE Canadian Conference on Electrical and Computer Engineering (CCECE'02)*, Winnipeg, Manitoba, Canada, May, pp.669-674.
18. Wang, Y. and N.C. Foinjong (2003), Formal Specification of Real-Time Operating Systems using RTPA, *Proceedings of the 2003 IEEE Canadian Conference on Electrical and Computer Engineering (CCECE'03)*, Montreal, Canada, May.
19. Wang, Y. (2001), Formal Description of the UML Architecture and Extendibility, *The International Journal of the Object*, Hermes Science Publications, Paris, Vol. 6, No.4, pp.469-488.
20. Wang, Y. and King, G. (2000), *Software Engineering Processes: Principles and Applications*, CRC Press, USA, ISBN: 0-8493-2366-5, 752pp.

Making Timed Automata Communicate⋆

Jing Chen and Huimin Lin

Laboratory for Computer Science
Institute of Software, Chinese Academy of Sciences
P.O. Box 8718, Beijing 100080
{cj,lhm}@ios.ac.cn

Abstract. A computation model is introduced in which real-time constraints as well as data communications can be explicitly expressed. The model is presented in a graphical form. Its semantics is studied and algorithms to compute bisimulation equivalences for such graphs are proposed.

Keywords: real-time, value-passing, timed automata, timed symbolic transition graph

1 Introduction

The last decade had seen various extensions to concurrency models: real-time, probability, value-passing, mobility, ... The purpose of these extensions is to increase the expressive power of the models so that real-life computing phenomenon can be more easily modelled. For instance, using real-time formalisms such as timed process algebras ([Wan91,RR86]) or timed automata ([AD94]) one can specify concurrent computations in which each step is executed within a certain amount of time; an example is a real-time vending machine which, if the customer does not make any choice within one minute after he/she inserted a coin, will automatically abort the transaction by returning the coin and going back to its starting state. In a different direction, value-passing formalisms, an example of which is *symbolic transition graphs* [HL95,Lin96], allow one to specify communicating processes which cooperate with each other by sending/receiving data rather than just synchronising on signals; an example is a flexible vending machine which can accept an arbitrary amount of money, accumulate consumptions and return changes upon finishing.

The extensions proposed so far tend to be "non-interfering" with each other, with little collaboration between them. For instance, it is difficult to specify a flexible *as well as* real-time vending machine, because, on the one hand, real-time models do not have facilities for sending/receiving data and manipulating them; on the other hand value-passing models, which do have features for data communication and manipulation, lack the notion of time. Thus there is a real need to combine different extensions in a uniform framework, and we shall explore in this paper a simple kind of such combination, the combination of real-time and

---

⋆ Supported by grant 69833020 from National Science Foundation of China.

B.K. Aichernig and T. Maibaum (Eds.): Formal Methods ..., LNCS 2757, pp. 337–351, 2003.
© Springer-Verlag Berlin Heidelberg 2003

value-passing mechanisms. More specifically, we shall study a framework that extends timed automata with primitives for data exchange, or equivalently, extends finite symbolic transition graphs, which is an abstract model for value-passing processes, with clocks to express real-time constraints.

Both timed automata and symbolic transition graphs are extensions of finite state machines. Syntactically they appear very much alike, as can be seen from Figure 1 which shows a timed automaton on the left and a symbolic transition graph on the right. The difference lies in semantics. A timed automaton has associated with it a finite number of *clock variables*; and each of its edges of it is labelled with a triple (ϕ, r, a) where ϕ is a clock constraint, a a synchronisation action, and r a clock reset of the form $c := 0$. In a symbolic transition graph each node has a finite set of *data variables*, each edge is also marked with a triple (ψ, θ, α) where ψ is a boolean condition on data variables, α a communication action, and θ an assignment to data variables. A communication action can be an input of the form $c?x$ (c is a communication channel and x a data variable), an output of the form $c!e$ (e a data expression), or τ representing an internal communication.

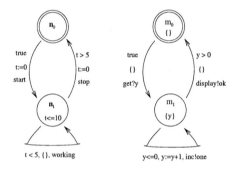

Fig. 1. A Timed Automaton (left) vs. A Symbolic Transition Graph (right).

A timed symbolic transition graph, to be introduced in the next section, has clocks as well as data variables. It can perform communication actions (inputs and outputs) as in symbolic transition graphs; at the same time, it is subject to real-time constraints as in timed automata. Each transition is guarded by a clock constraint as well as a boolean condition (on data variables). When both guards are satisfied then the transition can be fired, with some specified clocks reset to zero and the values of some data variables modified. The aim of this paper is to formalise this intuitive idea by presenting an operational semantics, to advance a semantic equivalence based on bisimulation, and to develop an algorithm to decide such equivalence.

The paper is organised as follows: the notion of timed symbolic transition graphs and its operational semantics are presented in the next section. In Section 3 timed and time abstract bisimulations are introduced. Section 4 is devoted to bisimulation checking algorithms. The paper is concluded with Section 5 where directions for further research are also outlined.

2   Timed Symbolic Transition Graphs

Timed Symbolic Transition Graphs (TSTG) are a hybrid of timed automata and symbolic transition graphs. To present the defintion of TSTG we need to introduce some notations.

The first category of notations concerns data manipulation and communication. Let Var be a countably infinite set of data variables, ranged over by x, y, etc., and Val a set of data values, ranged over by v, v_1, v_2, etc.. Our results will be parameterised on a few general properties of data and boolean expressions, denoted by DExp (ranged over by e, e_1, e_2, etc.) and BExp (ranged over by $\psi_d, \psi_d^1, \psi_d^2$, etc.), respectively. For a data expression e, $fv_d(e)$ denotes the set of free variables of e; Similarly, $fv_d(\psi_d)$ is the set of free variables of ψ_d. If S is a set of expressions then $fv(S) = \bigcup \{fv(e) \mid e \in S\}$. It is assumed that $\mathrm{Var} \cap \mathrm{Val} = \emptyset$ and $\mathrm{Val} \cup \mathrm{Var} \subseteq \mathrm{DExp}$. We also assume a set of communication channels, Chan. There are three kinds of communication actions: an input action $ch?x$, where $ch \in \mathrm{Chan}$ and $x \in \mathrm{Var}$, which can receive a value along channel ch and store it in x; an output action $ch!e$, where $ch \in \mathrm{Chan}$ and $e \in \mathrm{DExp}$, which can send the current value of e via channel ch; and the invisible action τ representing internal communications. The sets of free and bound variables of actions are defined thus: $fv_d(ch!e) = fv_d(e)$, $bv(ch?x) = \{x\}$, and for any other action α, $fv_d(\alpha) = bv(\alpha) = \emptyset$. Assn_d, ranged over by $\theta_d, \theta_d^1, \theta_d^2$, etc., is a set of *assignments*, each of which has the form $\bar{x} := \bar{e}$ where $\bar{x}$ is a vector of distinct variables and is of the same length as $\bar{e}$. If θ_d is an assignment of the form $\bar{x} := \bar{e}$ then we write $e\theta_d$ to denote the outcome of substituting $\bar{e}$ for $\bar{x}$ in e.

A data evaluation ρ_d is a total mapping from Var to Val, and we write $\rho_d(e)$ for the result of evaluating e with respect to ρ_d. This notation generalises to vectors in the expected way. For simplicity we shall assume that $\rho_d(e) \in \mathrm{Val}$ for any $e \in \mathrm{DExp}$, and $\rho_d(\psi_d) \in \{\text{true,false}\}$ for any $\psi_d \in \mathrm{BExp}$; that is we assume evaluation will always terminate with a value.

We write $\rho_d[x \mapsto v]$ to mean the modification of ρ_d at x by v, defined thus:

$$\rho_d[x \mapsto v](y) = \begin{cases} v & y = x \\ \rho_d(y) & y \neq x \end{cases}$$

The notation can also be generalised by using vectors $\bar{x}$ and $\bar{v}$ (instead of x and v) in the point-wise way. For an evaluation ρ_d and an assignment θ_d of the form $\bar{x} := \bar{e}$, we write $\rho_d\theta_d$ for $\rho_d[\bar{x} \mapsto \rho_d(\bar{e})]$ which is the modification of ρ_d at $\bar{x}$ by the resulting values of evaluating $\bar{e}$ with repsect to ρ_d.

The second category of notations concerns the manipulation of time. Let $\mathcal{C}$ be a countably infinite set of clock variables, ranged over by c, c_1, c_2, etc.. We assume $\mathcal{C} \cap \mathrm{Var} = \emptyset$. Clock constraints are given by the following BNF grammar, where e ranges over data expressions whose values are restricted to a finite subrange of integers:

$$\psi_t ::= c \bowtie e \mid c_1 - c_2 \bowtie e \mid \neg \psi_t \mid \psi_t \wedge \psi_t , \qquad \bowtie \in \{\leq, <, =, >, \geq\}$$

The set of clock constraints is denoted by Φ. Compared with the standard model of timed automata [AD94], the form of clock constraints is generalised slightly to allow comparisons between clock variables and finite-valued data expressions rather than just constants. $fv_t(\psi_t)$ is the set of clock variables of ψ_t. Since ψ_t may contain data variables, we use $fv_d(\psi_t)$ to denote the set of free data variables of ψ_t. A clock evaluation ρ_t is a total mapping from $\mathcal{C}$ to $\mathcal{R}^{\geq 0}$, the set of non-negative real numbers. The modification of ρ_t at c by δ will be denoted by $\rho_t[c \mapsto \delta]$. A clock resetting θ_t is of the form $\bar{c} := \bar{0}$, where $\bar{c}$ is a vector of distinct clock variables. The set of clock resettings is denoted by $Assn_t$. Let $Cl(\bar{c} := \bar{0}) = \{\bar{c}\}$, let δ be a non-negative real number, θ_t a clock resetting, we define two useful operations $\rho_t + \delta$ (time increment) and $\rho_t \theta_t$ (clock reset) thus: for all $c \in \mathcal{C}$,

$$(\rho_t + \delta)(c) := \rho_t(c) + \delta$$
$$(\rho_t \theta_t)(c) := \begin{cases} 0 & c \in Cl(\theta_t) \\ \rho_t(c) & c \notin Cl(\theta_t) \end{cases}$$

We also write $\rho \models \psi$ for $\rho(\psi)$ =true. A clock evaluation ψ_t is *downward closed* if $\rho + \delta \models \psi_t$ implies $\rho \models \psi_t$ for any $\delta \in \mathcal{R}^{\geq 0}$.

In the sequel we shall write ρ for the pair (ρ_t, ρ_d), with the understanding that $\rho[x \mapsto v]$ means $(\rho_t, \rho_d[x \mapsto v])$, $\rho + d$ means $(\rho_t + d, \rho_d)$ etc. Similarly, we shall write θ for (θ_t, θ_d), and understand $\rho\theta$ to be an abbreviation for $(\rho_t\theta_t, \rho_d\theta_d)$. $Assn$ will denote the product $Assn_t \times Assn_d$.

Definition 1 (Timed Symbolic Transition Graphs (TSTG)) *A Timed Symbolic Transition Graph is a tuple* $(\mathcal{A}, N, n_0, E, Inv, fv)$ *where*

- $\mathcal{A} = \{ch?x, ch!e, \tau \mid ch \in Chan, x \in Var, e \in DExp\}$ *is the set of abstract actions;*
- N *is a finite set of nodes;*
- $n_0(\in N)$ *is the initial node;*
- $E \subseteq N \times (\Phi \times BExp \times Assn \times \mathcal{A}) \times N$ *is a finite set of edges;*
- $Inv : N \to \Phi$ *associates each node with a constraint (invariant);*
- $fv : N \to 2^{Var} \cup 2^{\mathcal{C}}$ *associates each node n with a pair of sets, one is the set of clocks $fv_t(n)$ and the other the set of free data variables $fv_d(n)$.*

A TSTG is *well-formed* if the invariant of every node is downward closed, and for any edge $n \xrightarrow{\psi_t, \psi_d, \theta, \alpha} n'$ with $\theta \equiv (\bar{c} := 0, \bar{x} := \bar{e})$, it holds that $fv_d(\{\psi_d, \psi_t\} \cup \{\bar{e}\}) \subseteq fv_d(n)$, $fv_d(\alpha) \subseteq \{\bar{x}\}$, $fv_t(\psi_t) \subseteq fv_t(n)$, $fv_d(n') \subseteq \{\bar{x}\} \cup bv(\alpha)$, and $fv_t(n') \subseteq \{\bar{c}\} \cup fv_t(n)$. We shall only consider well-formed TSTGs in this paper.

Note that new clock variables can be introduced and redundant clocks can be removed at each node in the TSTG model.

Given a TSTG $\mathcal{G}$, Let $S = \{ n_\rho \mid n$ is a node of $\mathcal{G}$, ρ is an evaluation$\}$ be the set of *processes* (or *states*) over $\mathcal{G}$. The operational semantics is given by the rules in Figure 2. It induces a labelled transition system on S, where each transition is labelled with one of the following four kinds of actions: the invisible action τ, an output action $ch!v$ with $v \in Val$, an input action $ch?x$, or a *delay action* δ where $\delta \in \mathcal{R}^{\geq 0}$.

Tau $\dfrac{n \xrightarrow{\psi_t, \psi_d, \theta, \tau} n'}{n_\rho \xrightarrow{\tau} n'_{\rho\theta}}$ $\rho \models \psi_t \wedge Inv(n), \ \rho_d \models \psi_d, \ \rho\theta_t \models Inv(n')$

Output $\dfrac{n \xrightarrow{\psi_t, \psi_d, \theta, ch!e} n'}{n_\rho \xrightarrow{ch!\rho_d(e)} n'_{\rho\theta}}$ $\rho \models \psi_t \wedge Inv(n), \ \rho_d \models \psi_d, \ \rho\theta_t \models Inv(n')$

Input $\dfrac{n \xrightarrow{\psi_t, \psi_d, \theta, ch?x} n'}{n_\rho \xrightarrow{ch?x} n'_{\rho\theta}}$ $\rho \models \psi_t \wedge Inv(n), \ \rho_d \models \psi_d, \ \rho\theta_t \models Inv(n')$

Delay $\dfrac{}{n_\rho \xrightarrow{\delta} n_{\rho+\delta}}$ $\forall r \ 0 \leq r \leq \delta, \ \rho + r \models Inv(n)$

Fig. 2. Operational Semantics.

Assume all clock variables at the root node are initialised to 0. According to the operational semantics, the execution of a TSTG is as follows: at each node, if the invariant and guards of an outgoing edge are satisfied, then the action and assignment associated with the edge can be performed and the system moves to the target node; alternatively, the system may choose to stay at the node letting time pass, as long as the invariant is not violated (rule Delay).

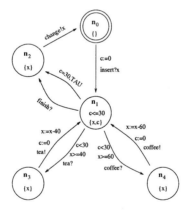

Fig. 3. A Timely and Flexible Vending Machine.

As an example, Figure 3 shows a timed symbolic transition graph for a vending machine which works in a timely manner. It also accumulates consumptions and calculates changes. A user starts interaction with the machine by inserting a certain amount of money. The machine can wait up to thirty seconds for the user to make a choice between coffee and tea. If he/she chooses coffee with no less than 60 cents money left, then the machine will offer coffee, reduce 60 cents from the remaining amount, and wait for further choices; similarly if the user chooses tea. In case the user press the "finish" button, or fails to respond within thirty seconds, the machine will output the change and go back to the starting state, ready for the next customer.

3   Timed and Time Abstract Bisimulations

Bisimulation ([Mil89]) is one of the most popular semantic equivalences for concurrent processes. It has been successfully extended to the timed setting by many authors. Intuitively, two processes are timed bisimilar if they can mimic each other's actions, including delay actions, and arrive at new states which enjoy the same property.

Definition 2 (Timed Bisimulation) *A symmetric relation R between processes is a timed bisimulation if $(n_{\rho_1}, m_{\rho_2}) \in R$ implies*

- *whenever $n_{\rho_1} \xrightarrow{ch?x} n'_{\rho'_1}$ then there exists some $m'_{\rho'_2}$ such that $m_{\rho_2} \xrightarrow{ch?y} m'_{\rho'_2}$ and for all $v \in \text{Val}$, $(n'_{\rho'_1[x \mapsto v]}, m'_{\rho'_2[y \mapsto v]}) \in R$.*
- *for any other actions $a \in \{ch!v, \tau\} \cup \mathcal{R}^{\geq 0}$, whenever $n_{\rho_1} \xrightarrow{a} n'_{\rho'_1}$ then there exists some $m'_{\rho'_2}$ such that $m_{\rho_2} \xrightarrow{a} m'_{\rho'_2}$ and $(n'_{\rho'_1}, m'_{\rho'_2}) \in R$.*

Two processes p, q are timed bisimilar, written $p \sim^t q$, if $(p, q) \in R$ for some timed bisimulation R.

Let $Eval_0 = \{(\rho_t, \rho_d) \mid \forall c \in \mathcal{C}.\rho_t(c) = 0\}$. Given two TSTGs with initial nodes n and m, respectively, if $n_\rho \sim^t m_{\rho'}$ for any $\rho, \rho' \in Eval_0$, then we say that the two graphs are timed bisimilar.

As usual weak bisimulation is defined in terms of a version of transition relation which ignores the invisible τ actions, defined by the following rules:

1. $n_\rho \xLongrightarrow{\tau} n'_{\rho'}$ if $n_\rho(\xrightarrow{\tau})^* n'_{\rho'}$
2. $n_\rho \xLongrightarrow{\alpha} n'_{\rho'}$ if $n_\rho(\xrightarrow{\tau})^* \xrightarrow{\alpha} (\xrightarrow{\tau})^* n'_{\rho'}$
3. $n_\rho \xLongrightarrow{\delta} n'_{\rho'}$ if $n_\rho(\xrightarrow{\tau})^* \xrightarrow{\delta_1} (\xrightarrow{\tau})^* \ldots (\xrightarrow{\tau})^* \xrightarrow{\delta_k} (\xrightarrow{\tau})^* n'_{\rho'}$, where $\delta_i \in \mathcal{R}^{\geq 0}$ and $\Sigma_{i \leq k} \delta_i = \delta$

Definition 3 (Weak Timed Bisimulation) *A symmetric relation R between processes is a weak timed bisimulation if $(n_{\rho_1}, m_{\rho_2}) \in R$ implies*

- *whenever $n_{\rho_1} \xrightarrow{ch?x} n'_{\rho'_1}$ then there exists some $m'_{\rho'_2}$ such that $m_{\rho_2} \xLongrightarrow{ch?y} m'_{\rho'_2}$ and for all $v \in \text{Val}$, $(n'_{\rho'_1[x \mapsto v]}, m'_{\rho'_2[y \mapsto v]}) \in R$.*
- *for any other actions $a \in \{ch!v, \tau\} \cup \mathcal{R}^{\geq 0}$, whenever $n_{\rho_1} \xrightarrow{a} n'_{\rho'_1}$ then there exists some $m'_{\rho'_2}$ such that $m_{\rho_2} \xLongrightarrow{a} m'_{\rho'_2}$ and $(n'_{\rho'_1}, m'_{\rho'_2}) \in R$.*

Two processes p, q are weak timed bisimilar, written $p \approx^t q$, if $(p, q) \in R$ for some weaked timed bisimulation R.

As another variation on the bisimulation theme, one may relax the requirement on exact match of delay actions, to allow a time delay from one process to be mimicked by an arbitrary amount of time from the other. For this purpose we define *time abstract transition* relation as follows:

1. $n_\rho \xrightarrow{\varepsilon} n'_{\rho'}$ if $n_\rho \xrightarrow{\delta_1} \xrightarrow{\delta_2} \cdots \xrightarrow{\delta_k} n'_{\rho'}$, $\delta_i \in \mathcal{R}^{\geq 0}$, $1 \leq i \leq k$.
2. $n_\rho \xrightarrow{\alpha} n'_{\rho'}$ if $n_\rho \xrightarrow{\varepsilon} \xrightarrow{\alpha} \xrightarrow{\varepsilon} n'_{\rho'}$

Definition 4 (Time Abstract Bisimulation) *A symmetric relation R between processes is a time abstract bisimulation if $(n_{\rho_1}, m_{\rho_2}) \in R$ implies*

- *whenever $n_{\rho_1} \xrightarrow{ch?x} n'_{\rho'_1}$ then there exists some $m'_{\rho'_2}$ such that $m_{\rho_2} \xrightarrow{ch?y} m'_{\rho'_2}$ and for all $v \in Val$, $(n'_{\rho'_1[x \mapsto v]}, m'_{\rho'_2[y \mapsto v]}) \in R$*
- *whenever $n_{\rho_1} \xrightarrow{\delta} n'_{\rho'_1}$ then there exists some $m'_{\rho'_2}$ such that $m_{\rho_2} \xrightarrow{\varepsilon} m'_{\rho'_2}$ and $(n_{\rho'_1}, m'_{\rho'_2}) \in R$*
- *For any other action $a \in \{ch!v, \tau\}$, whenever $n_{\rho_1} \xrightarrow{a} n'_{\rho'_1}$ then there exists some $m'_{\rho'_2}$ such that $m_{\rho_2} \xrightarrow{a} m'_{\rho'_2}$ and $(n'_{\rho'_1}, m'_{\rho'_2}) \in R$*

Two processes p, q are time abstract bisimilar, if $(p,q) \in R$ for some time abstract bisimulation R.

The weak version of time abstract bisimulation can be defined by ignoring τ actions, in the same way as Definition 3, and is omitted here.

4   Computing Bisimulations

According to the semantics, a state of a TSTG is a pair n_ρ, where n is a node of the graph and ρ an evaluation. The state space of a TSTG could be infinite, due to the delay actions whose lengths could be any positive real numbers. It is well known that such infinity can be avoided using region technique [AD94,Čer92]. In our setting, we also need to handle data communication between processes, for which we shall employ symbolic bisimulation technique [HL95].

4.1   Region Equivalence

For any $r \in \mathcal{R}^{\geq 0}$, let $fract(r)$ denote the fractional part of r, and $\lfloor r \rfloor$ the integral part of r. Given a TSTG $\mathcal{G}$, $C(\mathcal{G}) \subseteq \mathcal{C}$ is the set of clock variables used in $\mathcal{G}$.

Definition 5 *Given a TSTG $\mathcal{G}$ and a data evaluation ρ_d, for each clock variable $c \in C(\mathcal{G})$, let $M_c^{\rho_d} = max\{\rho_d(e) \mid c \bowtie e \text{ in } \mathcal{G}\}$ (where $max\{\} \stackrel{def}{=} 0$). Furthermore let $M_c = max\{M_c^{\rho_d} | \rho_d \text{ a data evaluation}\}$. Note that M_c is a finite number because Val is assumed finite.*

Definition 6 (Region) *Given a TSTG $\mathcal{G}$, define a binary relation $\simeq$ on evaluations thus: for any $\rho^1 = (\rho_t^1, \rho_d^1)$ and $\rho^2 = (\rho_t^2, \rho_d^2)$, $\rho^1 \simeq \rho^2$ iff the following conditions hold:*
    1. $\rho_d^1 = \rho_d^2$.
    2. For any clock variable $c \in C(\mathcal{G})$, either $\lfloor \rho_t^1(c) \rfloor = \lfloor \rho_t^2(c) \rfloor$, or both $\rho_t^1(c)$ and $\rho_t^2(c)$ are greater than M_c and : $\forall \phi_t \equiv c - c' \bowtie e($ or $\phi_t \equiv c' - c \bowtie e) \in \mathcal{G}$. $\forall \rho_d.\rho_t^1 \models \rho_d(\phi_t)$ iff $\rho_t^2 \models \rho_d(\phi_t)$.

3. *For any clock variables $c_1, c_2 \in C(\mathcal{G})$, $\rho_t^1(c_1) \leq M_{c_1}$ and $\rho_t^1(c_2) \leq M_{c_2}$, $fract(\rho_t^1(c_1)) \leq fract(\rho_t^1(c_2))$ iff $fract(\rho_t^2(c_1)) \leq fract(\rho_t^2(c_2))$.*

4. *For any clock variable c in $\mathcal{G}$ such that $\rho_t^1(c) \leq M_c$: $fract(\rho_t^1(c)) = 0$ iff $fract(\rho_t^2(c)) = 0$.*

Then $\simeq$ is an equivalence relation. A region is an equivalence class of evaluations determined by $\simeq$. We write $[\rho]$ for the region that ρ belongs to. For any regions γ, γ', if $\forall \rho \in \gamma.\exists \delta \in \mathcal{R}^{\geq 0}.\rho + \delta \in \gamma'$, then γ' is called the time successor of γ. As an example, suppose $\mathcal{G}$ contains clock variables c_1 and c_2, data variable x, and data constraints $c_1 < 2, c_2 > 3, c_2 \leq x + 1, c_2 - c_1 \leq x$, a partition of the evaluation space $\{\rho | \rho_d(x) = 3\}$ into regions is shown in Figure 4 where data parts are omitted.

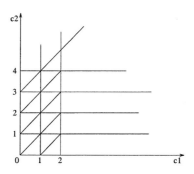

Fig. 4. An example for regions.

In the graph, each line segment (excluding its ends), each grid point and each open area enclosed by line segments are regions. Examples are: a line segment $\{\rho_t | \rho_t \models 1 < c_1 < 2 \wedge 2 < c_2 < 3 \wedge c_2 - c_1 = 1\}$, a point $\{\rho_t | \rho_t \models c_1 = 1 \wedge c_2 = 2\}$ and an area $\{\rho_t | \rho_t \models c_1 > 1 \wedge c_2 < 3 \wedge c_2 - c_1 > 1\}$.

Given a TSTG $\mathcal{G}$ and a data evaluation ρ_d, let $N_c^{\rho_d} = |\{\rho_d(e) \mid c - c' \bowtie e \text{ in } \mathcal{G}\} \cup \{\rho_d(-e) \mid c' - c \bowtie e \text{ in } \mathcal{G}\}|$. We shall restrict data evaluations to the set of data variables appearing in $\mathcal{G}$, and denote the set of such restricted data evaluations as $Eval(\mathcal{G})$. $Eval(\mathcal{G})$ is finite since the set of data values is assumed finite. Let $N_c = \sum_{\rho_d \in Eval(\mathcal{G})} N_c^{\rho_d}$.

Theorem 1 *Given a TSTG $\mathcal{G}$, the number of regions is bounded by $|C(\mathcal{G})|! \cdot 2^{|C(\mathcal{G})|} \cdot \Pi_{c \in C(\mathcal{G})}(2(M_c + N_c) + 2)$.*

Proof: Similar to the proof of lemma 4.5 in [AD94]. □

4.2 Deciding Time Abstract Bisimulations

Based upon the partitioning technique presented above, the problem of deciding time abstract bisimulations can be transformed into a finite form.

Definition 7 (Region Automata) *Given a TSTG $\mathcal{G} = (\mathcal{A}, N, n_0, E, Inv, fv)$, $R(\mathcal{G})$ is the Region Automaton of $\mathcal{G}$, where:*

- the node of $R(\mathcal{G})$ is of the form $\langle n, \gamma \rangle$, where $n \in N$, γ is a region determined by $\mathcal{G}$;
- the initial node is $\langle n_0, [\rho_0] \rangle$, where $\rho_0 \in Eval_0$;
- there is an edge $\langle n, \gamma \rangle \xrightarrow{0} \langle n', \gamma' \rangle$ in $R(\mathcal{G})$ iff there is a transition $n_\rho \xrightarrow{\delta} n'_{\rho+\delta}$ such that $\delta \in \mathcal{R}^{\geq 0}$, $\gamma = [\rho]$ and $\gamma' = [\rho + \delta]$;
- there is an edge $\langle n, \gamma \rangle \xrightarrow{\alpha} \langle n', \gamma' \rangle$ ($\alpha \notin \mathcal{R}^{\geq 0}$) iff there is a transition $n_\rho \xrightarrow{\alpha} n'_{\rho'}$ such that: (1)$[\rho]$ is a time successor of γ, (2)γ' is a time successor of $[\rho']$.

Given a finite TSTG $\mathcal{G}$, as the number of regions is finite by theorem 1, it is easy to see that $R(\mathcal{G})$ is a finite graph. For any region γ, let $\gamma[x \mapsto v] = \{\rho[x \mapsto v] \mid \rho \in \gamma\}$.

Lemma 1 *Given a TSTG, for any region γ, $\gamma[x \mapsto v]$ is also a region.*

Proof: Since for any $\rho, \rho' \in \gamma$, $\rho_d = \rho'_d$, hence $\rho_d[x \mapsto v] = \rho'_d[x \mapsto v]$. $\square$

Theorem 2 *Given two disjoint TSTGs $\mathcal{G}$ and $\mathcal{G}'$ with initial nodes n and m, respectively, and $\rho_0 \in Eval_0$, it can be decided in a finite number of steps whether n_{ρ_0} is time abstract bisimilar to m_{ρ_0}.*

Proof(sketch): Since a region automaton is a finite quotient of a TSTG, its behaviour w.r.t time abstract transition is equivalent to its original TSTG. By constructing region automata for $\mathcal{G}$ and $\mathcal{G}'$ respectively, the problem can be reduced to deciding whether the initial nodes of $R(\mathcal{G})$ and $R(\mathcal{G}')$ are time abstract bisimilar. Because $R(\mathcal{G})$ and $R(\mathcal{G}')$ are finite, their bisimilarity can be decided using the bisimilation algorithm for value-passing processes [Lin98]. $\square$

4.3   Deciding Timed Bisimulations

Timed bisimulation requires delay transitions to be matched exactly, thus the method for time abstract bisimulation in the previous subsection is not applicable. To check timed bisimulation, one needs to build a region graph on the union of clock sets of two TSTGs in question, as proposed in [Čer92,WL97]. Since in our case data variables are also involved, we shall appeal to the symbolic techniques [HL95,Lin98,LW02].

Definition 8 *Given TSTG $\mathcal{G}$, zone is a finite union of regions, of the form $\bigcup\{[\rho^i] \mid i \in I (I$ is a finite set of indexes) where $\forall i, j \in I. \rho^i_d = \rho^j_d\}$.*

Since each region can be represented by a clock constraint, so does a zone. Let $D_{\phi_t} = \{\rho \mid \rho \models \phi_t, \phi_t \in Constr\}$ where ϕ_t is called the characteristic constraint of zone D_{ϕ_t}. In the following the semantics of operations on zones will be presented (except normal operations such as $\cap$ and $\cup$). For any zone D and a finite set of clock variables $T(\subseteq \mathcal{C})$, define

$$D \uparrow \; = \{ \, \rho + \delta \mid \rho \in D, \; \delta \in \mathcal{R}^{\geq 0} \}$$
$$D \downarrow \; = \{ \, \rho \mid \exists \delta \in \mathcal{R}^{\geq 0}, \rho + \delta \in D \}$$
$$D \downarrow_T = \{ \, \rho' \mid \rho \in D, \; \forall c \in \mathcal{C}, \rho'_t(c) := \begin{cases} 0, & c \in T \\ \rho_t(c), & c \notin T \end{cases} \}$$
$$D \uparrow_T = \{ \, \rho[c \mapsto (\delta + k)] \mid \rho \in D, c \in T, \rho(c) = k, \delta \in \mathcal{R}^{\geq 0} \}$$

A zone D_{ϕ_t} can be encoded directly by the formula ϕ_t, or be implemented by data structures like NDD[Aetc97],CDD[Betc99] or RED[Wanf00].

For a finite set $V \subseteq \mathcal{C}$, let $\rho \upharpoonright_V = (\rho_t \upharpoonright_V, \rho_d)$ denote the restriction of ρ on V and $D \upharpoonright_V = \{ \rho \upharpoonright_V \mid \rho \in D \}$. For brevity, n_{ρ_d} is called a parameterized state (an intermediate state obtained by just instantiating n with data evaluations). Given $s \equiv n_{\rho_d}$, let $s[x \mapsto v]$ denote $n_{\rho_d[x \mapsto v]}$, and $s_{\rho_t} = n_{(\rho_t, \rho_d)}$. The transition relation over parameterized states can be generated by the rules shown in Figure 5.

$$\frac{n \xrightarrow{\psi_t, \psi_d, \theta, \tau} n'}{n_{\rho_d} \xrightarrow{\rho_d(\psi_t), \theta_t, \tau} n'_{\rho_d \theta_d}} \quad \rho_d \models \psi_d$$

$$\frac{n \xrightarrow{\psi_t, \psi_d, \theta, ch!e} n'}{n_{\rho_d} \xrightarrow{\rho_d(\psi_t), \theta_t, ch!\rho_d(e\theta_d)} n'_{\rho_d \theta_d}} \quad \rho_d \models \psi_d$$

$$\frac{n \xrightarrow{\psi_t, \psi_d, \theta, ch?x} n'}{n_{\rho_d} \xrightarrow{\rho_d(\psi_t), \theta_t, ch?x} n'_{\rho_d \theta_d}} \quad \rho_d \models \psi_d$$

Fig. 5. Symbolic operational semantics of TSTG.

Given a zone D, a partition of D is a finite set of zones such that their union is equal to D. We will omit the subscript t in symbols ρ_t, ϕ_t, etc. when the context can supply it.

Definition 9 (Symbolic Timed Bisimulation) *A symmetric relation* $S = \{ S^D \mid D \uparrow = D \}$ *indexed by zones (on parameterized states) is a symbolic timed bisimulation if* $(s, t) \in S^D$ *(where* $s \equiv n_{\rho_d}$, $t \equiv m_{\rho_d}$ *and* $\forall (\rho'_t, \rho'_d) \in D.\rho'_d = \rho_d)$ *implies:*

1. $D \subseteq (\overline{D_{Inv(s)}} \cup D_{Inv(t)}) \cap (\overline{D_{Inv(t)}} \cup D_{Inv(s)})$;

2. *For all* $s \xrightarrow{\psi_i, \theta_i, \alpha} s_i$, *there is a partition* $\mathbb{D}$ *of* $D_{\phi_p} = D \cap D_{Inv(s) \wedge \psi_i}$ *such that for each* $D' \in \mathbb{D}$, *there exists* $t \xrightarrow{\psi_j, \theta_j, \alpha} t_j$ *such that* $D' \subseteq D_{Inv(t) \wedge \psi_j}$, *and*

   1) *if* $\alpha = \tau$ *then* $\alpha' = \tau$ *and* $(s_i, t_j) \in S^{D' \downarrow_{Cl(\theta_i) \cup Cl(\theta_j)} \uparrow}$;
   2) *if* $\alpha = ch!v$ *then* $\alpha' = ch!v$ *and* $(s_i, t_j) \in S^{D' \downarrow_{Cl(\theta_i) \cup Cl(\theta_j)} \uparrow}$;
   3) *if* $\alpha = ch?x$ *then* $\alpha' = ch?y$ *and for each* $v \in Val$, $(s_i[x \mapsto v], t_j[y \mapsto v]) \in S^{D' \downarrow_{Cl(\theta_i) \cup Cl(\theta_j)} \uparrow}$.

We write $s \sim^D s'$ iff there is a symbolic timed bisimulation S with $S^D \in S$ such that $(s, s') \in S^D$. Symbolic bisimulations are used to characterize concrete bisimulations : $s \sim^D s'$ iff for any $\rho \in D, s_{\rho_t} \sim^t s'_{\rho_t}$ (proof omitted).

In the following we shall present an algorithm for timed bisimulation using the symbolic technique presented above. The algorithm decides whether two TSTGs with disjoint clock sets are timed bisimilar. It explores the state space consisting of pairs of parameterized states in a depth-first fasion, trying to build the smallest symbolic bisimulation including the pair of initial states of the two TSTGs. At each stage, the elements on the stack are of the form (s,t,D), where s and t are parameterized states and D is a zone. If $s\sim^D t$, then (s, t, D) is called a bis-tuple, otherwise it is a nonbis-tuple. The basic idea of the algorithm is to compute and eliminate those nonbis-tuples so that the remaining are bis-tuples. In the algorithm, three auxiliary sets, Assumed, NotBisim and Visited, are used:

1. $(s, t, D_{AS}) \in$ Assumed *means* it is *assumed* that for any $D \in D_{AS}$, (s, t, D) is a bis-tuple.
2. $(s, t, D_{NB}) \in$ NotBisim *means* for any $D \subseteq D_{NB}$, (s, t, D) is a nonbis-tuple.
3. $(s, t, D_{VS}) \in$ Visited *means* D_{VS} is the union of those D such that (s,t,D) has been visited.

• For each pair (s,t), there is exactly one entry of the form (s,t,D) in each of the above sets.

Each time the algorithm proceeds to compute a (s, t, D), it first eliminates the part $(s, t, D \cap D_{NB})$, and the remaining $(s, t, (D \setminus D_{NB}) \cap D_{VS})$ is assumed to be a bis-tuple. Then $(s, t, (D \setminus D_{NB}) \setminus D_{VS})$ is passed to function $match_\alpha$ to determine whether it is a bis-tuple. Finally $(s, t, D \uparrow)$ is marked as visited.

The cases of those nonbis-tuple (s, t, D'') includes : i) for each $\rho = (\rho_t, \rho_d) \in D''$, t_{ρ_t} can not match some moves (including time delay) of s_{ρ_t} or vice versa; or ii) both after the same length of time delay, t_{ρ_t} can not match some moves of s_{ρ_t} or vice versa. Let D_{Cut} be the union of all those D'', and $D_b = D \setminus D_{Cut}$. If D_b is a proper subset of D, then the old results under the assumption that (s, t, D) is a bis-tuple have to be recomputed, in this case the exception WrongAssumption will be raised to clear Visited and restart computing. Note that NotBisim is kept unchanged since the result of NotBisim is stable. If $D_b = D$ then the assumption is okay and no recomputation is needed.

We define functions $D_{AS}(), D_{NB}(), D_{VS}()$ thus:

$$(s, t, D) \in \textit{Assumed} \ \text{iff} \ D_{AS}(s, t) = D$$
$$(s, t, D) \in \textit{NotBisim} \ \text{iff} \ D_{NB}(s, t) = D$$
$$(s, t, D) \in \textit{Visited} \quad \text{iff} \ D_{VS}(s, t) = D$$

For any S, $S' \in \{\text{Visited,Assumed,NotBisim}\}$,
$$S \setminus S' = \{(s, t, D \setminus D') \mid (s, t, D) \in S, \ (s, t, D') \in S'\}$$
The algorithm is as follows:

$Bisim$(s,t,D_0)=
         NotBisim:={}
         fun bis(s,t,D)={
              Visited:=Assumed:={}
              return($match$(s,t,D))
                        }handle WrongAssumption$\Rightarrow bis$(s,t,D)
         return(bis(s,t,$D_0 \cap D_{Inv(s) \wedge Inv(t)}$))

$match(s,t,D)=$

$$D_{OldVS} := D_{VS}(s,t)$$
$$D_{VS}(s,t) := D_{VS}(s,t) \cup D\!\uparrow$$
$$D_{Upper} := (D\!\uparrow \setminus D_{OldVS}) \cap D_{Inv(s) \wedge Inv(t)}$$
$$D_b := D \cap \bigcap_{a \in \{\tau, ch!v, ch?\}} match_a(s, t, D)$$
$$D_{b\uparrow} := D_{Upper} \cap \bigcap_{a \in \{\tau, ch!v, ch?\}} match_a(s, t, D)$$
$$\text{if } D_b \neq D \text{ then} \{$$
$$\quad D_{NB}(s,t) := D_{NB}(s,t) \cup (D_{Upper} \setminus D_{b\uparrow}\!\uparrow)$$
$$\quad \text{if } D_{AS}(s,t) \cap (D_{Upper} \setminus D_{b\uparrow}\!\uparrow) \neq \emptyset \text{ then}$$
$$\quad\quad \text{raise WrongAssumption } \}$$
$$\text{return}(D_b)$$

$match_{\{a \mid a \in \{\tau, ch!v\}\}}(s,t,D)=$

$$\text{for each } s \xrightarrow{\psi_i, \theta_i, a} s_i, \text{ for each } t \xrightarrow{\psi_j, \theta_j, a} t_j$$
$$D_{Action} := (D\!\uparrow \cap D_{Inv(s) \wedge \psi_i} \cap D_{Inv(t) \wedge \psi_j}) \lceil_{fv_t(s,t) \cup fv_t(s_i, t_j)}$$
$$D_{ij} := close(s_i, t_j, D_{Action} \downarrow_{Cl(\theta_i) \cup Cl(\theta_j)} \cap D_{Inv(s_i) \wedge Inv(t_j)})$$
$$D_{Cut_{ij}} = (\overline{D_{ij}} \uparrow_{Cl(\theta_i) \cup Cl(\theta_j)} \cap D_{Action}) \downarrow \cup (D_{Inv(s) \wedge \psi_i} \cap \overline{D_{Inv(t) \wedge \psi_j}}) \downarrow$$
$$\quad \cup D_{Inv(s) \wedge \neg Inv(t)} \downarrow$$
$$D_{Cut_{ji}} = (\overline{D_{ij}} \uparrow_{Cl(\theta_i) \cup Cl(\theta_j)} \cap D_{Action}) \downarrow \cup (D_{Inv(t) \wedge \psi_j} \cap \overline{D_{Inv(s) \wedge \psi_i}}) \downarrow$$
$$\quad \cup D_{Inv(t) \wedge \neg Inv(s)} \downarrow$$

$$\text{return}(\bigcap_i (\overline{D_{Inv(s)}} \cup \bigcup_j \overline{D_{Cut_{ij}}}) \cap \bigcap_j (\overline{D_{Inv(t)}} \cup \bigcup_i \overline{D_{Cut_{ji}}}))$$

$match_{ch?}(s,t,D)=$

$$\text{for each } s \xrightarrow{\psi_i, \theta_i, ch?x} s_i, \text{ for each } t \xrightarrow{\psi_j, \theta_j, ch?y} t_j$$
$$D_{Action} := (D\!\uparrow \cap D_{Inv(s) \wedge \psi_i} \cap D_{Inv(t) \wedge \psi_j}) \lceil_{fv_t(s,t) \cup fv_t(s_i, t_j)}$$
$$\text{for each } v \in Val$$
$$D_{ij}^v := close(s_i[x \mapsto v], t_j[y \mapsto v], D_{Action} \downarrow_{Cl(\theta_i) \cup Cl(\theta_j)}$$
$$\quad \cap D_{Inv(s_i) \wedge Inv(t_j)})$$
$$D_{Cut_{ij}}^v = (\overline{D_{ij}^v} \uparrow_{Cl(\theta_i) \cup Cl(\theta_j)} \cap D_{Action}) \downarrow \cup (D_{Inv(s) \wedge \psi_i} \cap \overline{D_{Inv(t) \wedge \psi_j}}) \downarrow$$
$$\quad \cup D_{Inv(s) \wedge \neg Inv(t)} \downarrow$$
$$D_{Cut_{ji}}^v = (\overline{D_{ij}^v} \uparrow_{Cl(\theta_i) \cup Cl(\theta_j)} \cap D_{Action}) \downarrow \cup (D_{Inv(t) \wedge \psi_j} \cap \overline{D_{Inv(s) \wedge \psi_i}}) \downarrow$$
$$\quad \cup D_{Inv(t) \wedge \neg Inv(s)} \downarrow$$

$$\text{return}(\bigcap_i (\overline{D_{Inv(s)}} \cup \bigcup_j \bigcap_{v \in Val} \overline{D_{Cut_{ij}}^v}) \cap \bigcap_j (\overline{D_{Inv(t)}} \cup \bigcup_i \bigcap_{v \in Val} \overline{D_{Cut_{ji}}^v}))$$

$close(s,t,D)=$

$$D_{AS}(s,t) := D_{AS}(s,t) \cup ((D\!\uparrow \setminus D_{NB}(s,t)\!\downarrow) \cap D_{VS}(s,t))$$
$$\text{if } (D \setminus D_{NB}(s,t)\!\downarrow \setminus D_{VS}(s,t)) \neq \emptyset \text{ then}$$
$$\quad \text{return}(((D \setminus D_{NB}(s,t)\!\downarrow) \cap D_{VS}(s,t))$$
$$\quad\quad \cup match(s, t, (D \setminus D_{NB}(s,t)\!\downarrow \setminus D_{VS}(s,t))))$$
$$\text{else return}(D \setminus D_{NB}(s,t)\!\downarrow)$$

Theorem 3 (Correctness) *For any (s_0, t_0), the procedure $Bisim(s_0, t_0, D_0)$ will terminate in a finite number of steps, and after it terminates, we have a symbolic timed bisimulation $S = \{S^D \mid D \uparrow = D\}$: $(s, t) \in S^D$ iff $(s, t, D') \in Visited \setminus NotBisim, D \subseteq D'$.*

Proof (Outline). Since a zone is a finite union of regions, and the total number of regions to be compared is finite, so is the number of zones to be computed. It is easy to check that for any (s, t), there is no zone D such that (s, t, D) will be computed more than once. Thus the termination is guaranteed.

For any $(s, t) \in S^{D_I} \in S$, and $(s, t, D_v) \in Visited \setminus NotBisim$, it must be $D_I \subseteq D_v$. Since D_v is accumulated piece by piece, there must be a D_I-Partition where $D_I = \bigcup \mathbb{D}$: for each $D_k \in \mathbb{D}, (s, t) \in S^{D_k}$, and there exists a $D_b = match(\text{s,t,D})$ such that $D_k \subseteq D_b \uparrow \subseteq D$. Then it just need to construct a symbolic bisimulation following the structure of the algorithm.   □

To see the complexity of the algorithm, let **N** be the product of following three numbers: the size of the valule space $|Val|$, the total number of data variables of the two TSTGs, and the number of the nodes in the production graph of the two TSTGs. Let **M** be the maximal number of zones constructed from those time constraints in the two TSTGs. The time required for the first call of $bis()$ is (at most) $O(N \times M)$, while for the second call is $O(N \times (M - k_1))$ where $k_1 \geq 1$ is a natural number,... and the ith call is $O(N \times (M - k_i))$. Hence the worst case complexity of $bisim()$ is $O(N \times (M + (M - k_1) + \cdots + (M - k_n))) = O(N \times M^2)$. Generally, the k_1 (and consequently $k_2, k_3, ...$) is much larger than 1, so the time complexity is much smaller than $O(N \times M^2)$(as in [Lin98]). In the worst case **M** could be the number of regions, however experiences show that it is usually much smaller (as in [WL97]).

5   Conclusion

We have presented a formal model, Timed Symbolic Transition Graphs, in which data communication as well as real-time behaviour of concurrent systems can be described.

Semantic equivalences based on bisimulation have been studied, and algorithms to compute them have also been developed. Our work demonstrates that two different extensions to the traditional concurrency theory, namely timed automata and symbolic transition graphs, can be combined in a consistent manner.

As related work we mention formalisms for real-timed systems [AD94,Wan91, RR86] and study on value-passing processes [Lin96]. However, these efforts so far focus on only either real-time aspect or value-passing aspect. To our knowledge, Timed Symbolic Transition Graph is the first uniform framework for concurrent systems which allow data communication as well as real-time constraints.

In the current paper only bisimulation checking is treated. As future work we would like to investigate model checking for timed symbolic transition graphs. This would involve the introduction of a first-order logic with modalities to express value-passing as well as time constraint, and algorithms for deciding if a system, presented as a timed symbolic transition graph, satisfies a formula in the logic.

The communication primitives of the current model is adopted from value-passing CCS, which allow data values but not communication channels to be transmitted between processes. Another avenue of research would be to consider channel-passing in our framework, leading to "real-time π-calculus".

References

[AD94]   R. Alur and D.L. Dill. A Theory of Timed Automata. *Theoretical Computer Science,* 126:183-235,1994.

[ACH94]   R. Alur, C. Courcoubetis, T.A. Henzinger. The Observational Power of Clocks. *CONCUR'94*, LNCS 836. pp.162-177. 1994.

[Aetc97]   E. Asarin and etc. Data-structures for the verification of timed automata. In: *Proc. HART'97*,1997, LNCS 1201:346-360.

[Betc99]   G. Behrmann and etc. Efficient timed reachability analysis using clock difference diagrams. In: *Proc.CAV'99,* Trento,Italy,July,1999,LNCS 1633,Springer-Verlag.

[BLLPW]   J. Bengtsson, K.G. Larsen, F. Larsson, P. Pettersson, and W. Yi. UPPAAL-a tool suite for the automatic verification of real-time systems.*Hybrid Systems III,*LNCS 1066, pp.232-243,Springer,1996.

[Čer92]   K. Čerāns. Decidability of Bisimulation Equivalences for Parallel Timer Processes. *Proc.CAV'92,* LNCS 663,pp.302-315.1992.

[Dill89]   D.L. Dill. Timing Assumptions and Verification of Finite-state Concurrent Systems. LNCS 407,pp.197-212,Berlin, Springer,1989.

[DKRT]   P.R. D'Argenio, J-P. Katoen, T. Ruys, and J. Tretmans. The Bounded Retransmisson Protocol must be on time!. Report CTIT 97-03, University of Twente,1997.

[HL95]   M. Hennessy and H. Lin. Symbolic Bisimulations. *Theoretical Computer Science,*138:353-389,1995

[HL96]   M. Hennessy and H. Lin. Proof Systems for Message-Passing Process Algebras. *Formal Aspects of Computing,* Vol.8, pp.397-407. Springer-Verlag.1996.

[Holz91]   G.J.Holzmann. *Design and validation of computer protocols.* Prentice Hall,Englewood Cliffs,1991.

[JP92]   B.Jonnson and J.Parrow. Deciding Bisimulation Equivalences for A Class of Non-finite-state Programs. *Information and Computation,*1992.

[Lin96]   H.Lin. Symbolic Transition Graph with Assignment. *CONCUR'96,* LNCS 1119. Springer-Verlag,1996.

[Lin98]   H. Lin. "On-the-fly Instantiation" of Value-passing Processes. *Proc. Joint International Conferences on Formal Description Techniques for Distributed Systems and Communication Protocols and Protocol Specification, Testing and Verification,* Paris, France,November 1998. pp. 215-230. Kluwer Academic Publishers.

[LW02]   Huimin Lin and Wang Yi. Axiomatising Timed Automata. Acta Informatica 38, 277-305, Springer-Verlag 2002.

[Mil89]   R. Milner. *Communication and Concurrency,* Prentice-Hall,1989.

[RR86]   G.M. Reed and A.W. Roscoe, *A Timed Model for Communicating Sequential Processes,* LNCS 226,pp 314-323.Springer-Verlag,1986.

[St94]   W.R. Stevens. *TCP/IP Illustrated Volume 1: The Protocols*. Addison-Wesley, 1994.

[TC96]   S. Tripakis and C. Courcoubetis. Extending PROMELA and SPIN for real time. In T.Margaria and B.Steffen, editors, *Proc. of TACAS'96*, LNCS 1055, pp.329-348.Springer-Verlag,1996.

[Wan91]   Y. Wang. A Calculus of Real Time Systems. PhD thesis, Chalmers University of Technology, Göteborg, Sweden,1991.

[Wanf00] F.Wang. Efficient data structure for fully symbolic verification of real-time software systems. In: *Proc. TACACS 2000 Held as Part of Joint European Conferences on Theory and Practice of Software,ETAPS 2000,*, Berlin,Germany,March/April,2000,LNCS 1784,pp.208-222.Springer-Verlag.

[Wan00]   Y. Wang. Efficient data structure for fully symbolic verification of real-time software systems. In: *Proc. TACACS 2000 Held as Part of Joint European Conferences on Theory and Practice of Software,ETAPS 2000,*, Berlin,Germany,March/April,2000,LNCS 1784,pp.208-222.Springer-Verlag.

[WL97]   C. Weise and D. Lenzkes. Efficient Scaling-Invariant Checking of Timed Bisimulation. *Proc.STACS'97*,1997

A Tool Architecture
for the Next Generation of UPPAAL

Alexandre David[1], Gerd Behrmann[2], Kim G. Larsen[2], and Wang Yi[1]

[1] Department of Information Technology, Uppsala University, Sweden
{adavid,yi}@it.uu.se
[2] Department of Computer Science, Aalborg University, Denmark
behrmann@cs.auc.dk.

Abstract. We present the design of the model-checking engine and internal data structures for the next generation of UPPAAL. The design is based on a pipeline architecture where each stage represents one independent operation in the verification algorithms. The architecture is based on essentially one shared data structure to reduce redundant computations in state exploration, which unifies the so-called passed and waiting lists of the traditional reachability algorithm. In the implementation, instead of using standard memory management functions from general-purpose operating systems, we have developed a special-purpose storage manager to best utilize sharing in physical storage. We present experimental results supporting these design decisions. It is demonstrated that the new design and implementation improves the efficiency of the current distributed version of UPPAAL by about 60% in time and 80% in space.

1 Introduction

Based on the theory of timed automata [1], a number of verification tools have been developed for timed systems in the past years [7, 22]. Various efficient algorithms and data structures, e.g. techniques for approximative analysis[21], state space reduction[18], compact data structures[4], clock reduction [10] and other optimisations, for timed automata are available. However, there has been little information on how these techniques fit together into a common efficient architecture.

This paper provides a view of the architecture and some optimisations of the real time model checker UPPAAL[1]. The goal of UPPAAL has always been to serve as a platform for research in timed automata technology. As such, it is important for the tool to provide a flexible architecture that allows experimentation. It should allow *orthogonal* features to be integrated in an orthogonal manner to evaluate various techniques within a single framework and investigate how they influence each other.

The timed automaton reachability algorithm is basically a graph exploration algorithm where the vertices are *symbolic states* and the graph is unfolded on

---

[1] Visit http://www.uppaal.com for more information.

B.K. Aichernig and T. Maibaum (Eds.): Formal Methods ..., LNCS 2757, pp. 352–366, 2003.

the fly. During exploration, the algorithm maintains two sets of symbolic states: The *waiting list* contains reachable but yet unexplored states, and the *passed list* contains explored states. Maintaining two sets of states does incur some overhead that can be eliminated by unifying them. We show that this results in a significant speedup.

Furthermore states are not generated independently from each other. This means the same sets of locations will be explored several times with different sets of variables. The same holds for the variable and the symbolic representation of time. We show how to take advantage of this in the *storage* layer of the engine.

We present a flexible architecture in the form of a pipeline. We show how this architecture makes it possible to implement various algorithms and data structures in an orthogonal manner making it possible to evaluate these techniques within a common framework. We present results of combining the two main data structures, the waiting list and the passed list, into a single data structure. We show how this improves speed and memory usage. Finally, we show with a storage layer the effect of sharing common data of states, thereby reducing the memory usage by up to 80%. In particular the sharing property holds for the location and variable vectors, and the zones.

Outline. Section 2 summarises the definition of timed automata, the semantics, and the timed automaton reachability algorithm. In section 3 we present the pipeline architecture of UPPAAL and in section 4 we discuss how the passed and waiting list can be combined into a single efficient data structure. The actual representation of the state data is discussed in section 5. We present experimental results in section 6. We conclude the paper with a summary of results and related work.

2   Notations

In this section we summarise the basic definition of a timed automaton, the concrete and symbolic semantics and the reachability algorithm.

Definition 1 (Timed Automaton). *Let C be the set of clocks. Let $B(C)$ be the set of conjunctions over simple conditions on the form $x \bowtie c$ or $x - y \bowtie c$, where $x, y \in C$ and $\bowtie \in \{<, \leq, =, \geq, >\}$. A timed automaton over C is a tuple (L, l_0, E, I), where L is a set of locations, $l_0 \in L$ is the initial location, $E \subseteq L \times (B(C) \times 2^C) \times L$ is a set of edges between locations with guards and clocks to be reset, and $I : L \to B(C)$ assigns invariants to locations.*

Intuitively, a timed automaton is a graph annotated with conditions and resets of non-negative real valued clocks.

Definition 2 (TA Semantics). *A clock valuation is a function $u : C \to \mathbb{R}_{\geq 0}$ from the set of clocks to the non-negative reals. Let $\mathbb{R}^C$ be the set of all clock valuations. Let $u_0(x) = 0$ for all $x \in C$. We will abuse the notation by considering guards and invariants as sets of clock valuations.*

The semantics of a timed automaton (L, l_0, E, I) *over* C *is defined as a transition system* $(S, s_0, \rightarrow)$, *where* $S = L \times \mathbb{R}^C$ *is the set of states,* $s_0 = (l_0, u_0)$ *is the initial state, and* $\rightarrow \subseteq S \times S$ *is the transition relation such that:*

- $(l, u) \rightarrow (l, u + d)$ *if* $u \in I(l)$ *and* $u + d \in I(l)$
- $(l, u) \rightarrow (l', u')$ *if there exists* $e = (l, g, r, l') \in E$ *s.t.* g *holds,* $u' = [r \mapsto 0]u$, *and* $u' \in I(l)$

where for $d \in \mathbb{R}$, $u + d$ *maps each clock* x *in* C *to the value* $u(x) + d$, *and* $[r \mapsto 0]u$ *denotes the clock valuation which maps each clock in* r *to the value* 0 *and agrees with* u *over* $C \setminus r$.

The semantics of timed automata results in an uncountable transition system. It is a well known-fact that there exists an exact finite state abstraction based on convex polyhedra in $\mathbb{R}^C$ called zones (a zone can be represented by a conjunction in $B(C)$). This abstraction leads to the following symbolic semantics.

Definition 3 (Symbolic TA Semantics). *Let* $Z_0 = I(l_0) \wedge \bigwedge_{x,y \in C} x = y = 0$ *be the initial zone. The symbolic semantics of a timed automaton* (L, l_0, E, I) *over* C *is defined as a transition system* $(S, s_0, \Rightarrow)$ *called the simulation graph, where* $S = L \times B(C)$ *is the set of symbolic states,* $s_0 = (l_0, Z_0)$ *is the initial state,* $\Rightarrow = \{(s, s') \in S \times S \mid \exists e = (l_1, g, r, l_2), t : s \overset{e}{\Rightarrow} t \overset{\delta}{\Rightarrow} s'\}$: *is the transition relation, and:*

- $(l, Z) \overset{\delta}{\Rightarrow} (l, norm(M, (Z \wedge I(l))^\uparrow \wedge I(l)))$
- $(l, Z) \overset{e}{\Rightarrow} (l', r(g \wedge Z \wedge I(l)) \wedge I(l'))$ *if* $e = (l, g, r, l') \in E$.

where $Z^\uparrow = \{u + d \mid u \in Z \wedge d \in \mathbb{R}_{\geq 0}\}$ *(the future operation), and* $r(Z) = \{[r \mapsto 0]u \mid u \in Z\}$. *The function* $norm : \mathbf{N} \times B(C) \rightarrow B(C)$ *normalises the clock constraints with respect to the maximum constant* M *of the timed automaton.*

The relation $\overset{\delta}{\Rightarrow}$ contains the delay transitions and $\overset{e}{\Rightarrow}$ the edge transitions. The classical representation of a zone is the Difference Bound Matrix (DBM). For further details on timed automata see for instance [1, 8]. Given the symbolic semantics it is straightforward to construct the reachability algorithm, shown in Fig. 1.

Note that the above definitions can be extended in the standard way to networks of automata (using a location vector), timed automata with finite data variables (using a variable vector) and to hierarchical timed automata [13].

3   Architecture

The seemingly simple algorithm of Fig. 1 turns out to be rather complicated when implemented. It has been extended and optimised to reduce the runtime and memory usage of the tool. Most of these optimisations are optional since they involve a tradeoff between speed and memory usage.

$$waiting = \{(l_0, Z_0 \wedge I(l_0))\}$$
$$passed = \varnothing$$
while $waiting \neq \varnothing$ **do**
$\quad (l, Z) = $ select state from $waiting$
$\quad waiting = waiting \setminus \{(l, Z)\}$
$\quad$ **if** $testProperty(l, Z)$ **then return true**
$\quad$ **if** $\forall (l, Y) \in passed : Z \not\subseteq Y$ **then**
$\quad\quad passed = passed \cup \{(l, Z)\}$
$\quad\quad \forall (l', Z') : (l, Z) \Rightarrow (l', Z')$ **do**
$\quad\quad\quad$ **if** $\forall (l', Y') \in waiting : Z' \not\subseteq Y'$ **then**
$\quad\quad\quad\quad waiting = waiting \cup \{(l', Z')\}$
$\quad\quad\quad$ **endif**
$\quad\quad$ **done**
$\quad$ **endif**
done
return false

Fig. 1. The timed automaton reachability algorithm. The function *testProperty* evaluates the state property that is being checked for satisfiability. The while loop is refered to as the exploration loop.

The architecture of UPPAAL has changed a lot over time. Some years ago UPPAAL was a more or less straightforward implementation of the timed automaton reachability algorithm annotated with conditional tests on features or options. Although it was simple, it had several disadvantages:

- The core reachability algorithm became more and more complicated as new options were added.
- There was an overhead involved in checking if an option was enabled. This might not seem much, but when this is done inside the exploration loop the overhead adds up.
- Some experimental designs and extensions required major changes due to new algorithms.

The architecture of UPPAAL is constantly restructured in order to facilitate new designs and algorithms, see Fig. 2 for the latest incarnation. The main goals of the design are speed and flexibility. The bottom layer providing the system and symbolic state representations has only seen minimal architectural changes over the years. In fact, the code where most options are implemented are in the *state space manipulation* and *state space representation* components.

The idea of our pipeline architecture comes from computer graphics. In pipeline terms our architecture is composed of the connection of the *filters* and *buffers* components. Intuitively a filter has a *put* method to receive data. The result is then sent to the next component. A buffer is a purely passive component that awaits for data with a *put* method and offers data with a *get* method. A pump, ommitted here for simplicity, pumps data from a buffer and sends it to a serie of connected filters ending on the starting buffer. This is a data pipeline

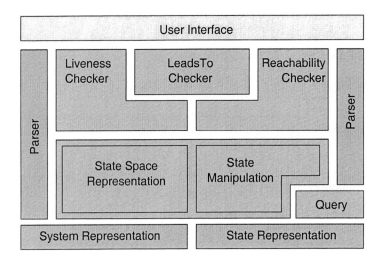

Fig. 2. UPPAAL uses a layered architecture. Components for representing the input model and a symbolic state are placed at the bottom. The state space representations are a set of symbolic states and together with the state operations they form the next layer. The various checkers combine these operations to provide the complex functionality needed. This functionality is made available via either a command line interface or a graphical user interface.

and there is no concurrency involved in contrast with pipeline designs seen in audio and video processing.

The reachability checker is actually a filter that takes the initial state as its input and generates all reachable states satisfying the property. It is implemented by composing a number of other filters into a pipeline, see Fig. 3. The pipeline realises the reachability algorithm of Fig. 1. It consists of filters computing the edge successors (`Transition` and `Successor`), the delay successors (`Delay` and `Normalisation`), and the unified passed and waiting list buffer (`PWList`). Additional components include a filter for generating progress information (e.g. throughput and number of states explored), a filter implementing active clock reduction [10], and a filter storing information needed to generate diagnostic traces. Notice that some of the components are optional. If disabled a filter can be bypassed completely and does not incur any overhead.

Semantically, the `PWList` acts as a buffer that eliminates duplicate states, i.e. if the same state is added to the buffer several times it can only be retrieved once, even when the state was retrieved before the state is inserted a second time. To achieve this effect the `PWList` must keep a record of the states seen and thus it provides the functionality of both the passed list and the waiting list.

Definition 4 (PWList). *Formally, a* `PWList` *can be described as a pair* (P, W) $\in 2^S \times 2^S$, *where* S *is the set of symbolic states, and the two functions put :* $2^S \times 2^S \times S \to 2^S \times 2^S$ *and get :* $2^S \times 2^S \to 2^S \times 2^S \times S$, *such that:*

- $get(P, W) = (P, W \setminus \{(l, Z)\}, (l, Z))$ *for some* $(l, Z) \in W$.

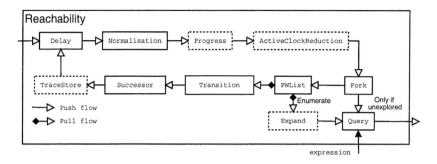

Fig. 3. The reachability checker is actually a compound object consisting of a pipeline of filters. Optional elements are dotted.

$$- \ put(P, W, (l, Z)) = (P \cup \{(l, Z)\}, W') \ where$$

$$W' = \begin{cases} W \cup \{(l, Z)\} & if \ \forall (l, Y) \in P : Z \not\subseteq Y \\ W & otherwise \end{cases}$$

Here P and W play the role of the passed list and waiting list, respectively, but as we will see this definition provides room for alternative implementations. It is possible to loosen the elimination requirement such that some states can be returned several times while still ensuring termination, thus reducing the memory requirements [18]. We will call such states *transient*. Section 4 will describe various implementations of the PWList.

In case multiple properties are verified, it is possible to reuse the previously generated reachable state space by reevaluating the new property on all previously retrieved states. For this purpose, the PWList provides a mechanism for enumerating all recorded states. One side effect of transient states is that when reusing the previously generated reachable states space not all states are actually enumerated. In this case it is necessary to explore some of the states using the Expand filter[2]. Still, this is more effective than starting over.

The number of unnecessary copy operations during exploration has been reduced as much as possible. In fact, a symbolic state is only copied twice during exploration. The first time is when it is inserted into the PWList, since the PWList might use alternative and more compact representations than the rest of the pipeline. The original state is then used for evaluating the state property using the Query filter. This is destructive and the state is discarded after this step. The second is when constructing the successor. In fact, one does not retrieve a state from the PWList directly but rather a reference to a state. The discrete and continous parts of the state can then be copied directly from the internal representation used in the PWList to the memory reserved for the successor. Since handling the discrete part is much cheaper than handling the continous

---

[2] The Expand filter is actually a compound filter containing an instance of the Successor and Transition filters.

part, all integer guards are evaluated first. Only then a copy of the zone is made and the clock guards are evaluated.

The benefits of using a common filter and buffer interface are *flexibility, code reuse,* and *acceptable efficiency.* Any component can be replaced at runtime with an alternate implementation providing different tradeoffs. Stages in the pipeline can be skipped completely with no overhead. The same components can be used and combined for different purposes. For instance, the Successor filter is used by both the reachability checker, the liveness checker, the deadlock checker, the Expand filter, and the trace generator. Since the methods on buffers and filters are declared virtual they do incur a measurable call overhead (approximatively 5%). But this is outweighed by the possibility of skipping stages and similar benefits. In fact, the functionality provided by the Successor filter was previously provided by a function taking a symbolic state as input and generating the set of successors. This function was called from the exploration loop which then added these successors to the waiting list. The function returned the successors as an array of states[3]. The overhead of using this array was much higher than the call overhead caused by the pipeline architecture.

4   Unifying the Passed List and Waiting List

In this section we present the concept of the unified passed and waiting list, and a reference implementation for the structure.

4.1   Unification Concept

The main conceptual difference between the present and previous implementations of the algorithm is the unification of the passed list and waiting list. As described in the previous sections, these lists are the major data structures of the reachability algorithm. The waiting list holds states that have been found to be reachable but not yet been explored whereas the passed list contains the states that have been explored. Thus a state is first inserted into the waiting list where it is kept until it is explored and then moved to the passed list. The main purpose of the passed list is to ensure termination and also to avoid exploring the same state twice. Fig. 1 shows the reachability algorithm based on these lists.

One crucial performance optimisation is to check whether there is already a state in the waiting list being a subset or superset of the state to be added. In this case one of the two states can be discarded [5]. This was implemented by combining the queue or stack structure in the waiting list with a hash table providing a fast method to find duplicate states. Obviously, the same is done for the passed list. This approach has two drawbacks: (i) states are looked up in a hash table twice, and (ii) the waiting list might contain a large number of states that have previously been explored though this is not noticed until the state is moved to the passed list thus wasting memory.

---

[3] It was actually a vector from the C++ *Standard Library.*

```
Q = PW = {(l₀, Z₀ ∧ I(l₀))}
while Q ≠ ∅ do
   (l, Z) = select state from Q
   Q = Q \ {(l, Z)}
   if testProperty(l, Z) then return true
   ∀(l', Z') : (l, Z) ⇒ (l', Z') do
      if ∀(l', Y') ∈ PW : Z' ⊄ Y' then
         PW = PW ∪ {(l', Z')}
         Q.append(l', Z')
      endif
   done
done
return false
```

Fig. 4. Reachability algorithm using the unified PWLISt. In the reference implementation (sub-section 4.2) Q only contains references to the entries in PW.

The present implementation unifies the two hash tables into one. There is still a collection structure representing the waiting list, but it only contains simple references to entries in the hash table. Furthermore pushing a state to the waiting list is a simple append operation.

A number of options are available via different implementations of the PWList to approximate the representation of the state-space such as *bitstate hashing* [15], or choose a particular order for state-space exploration such as *breadth first*, *depth first*, *best first* or *random* [3, 2]. The ordering is orthogonal to the storage structure and can be combined with any data representation.

This unified structure implements the PWList interface defined in the previous section: From the pipeline point of view new states are pushed and waiting states to be explored are popped. Using this structure allows the reachability algorithm to be simplified to the one given in Fig. 4. In this algorithm the states popped from the queue do not need inclusion checking, only the successors need this.

4.2   Reference Implementation

Figure 5 shows the reference implementation of our unified structure. The hash table gives access to the reachable state-space. Every state has a discrete state entry and a union of zones as its symbolic part. The waiting queue is a simple collection of state references (e.g. a linked list).

The first characteristic of this reference implementation is that it builds on top of the storage interface, which allows to change the actual data representation independently of the exploration order. This order depends on the waiting queue that keeps state references.

The second characteristic comes from its state-space representation: the main structure is a hash table giving access to states. The states have a unique entry for a given discrete part, i.e. locations and variables. The symbolic part is a union of

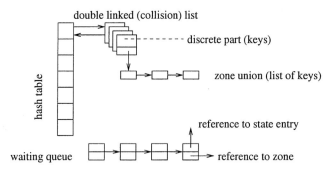

Fig. 5. Reference implementation of PWList.

zones, or more precisely of zone keys handled by the storage structure. As a first implementation this union is a list of keys, but we plan for future experiments a CDD representation that is well-suited for such union of zones [4]. Besides, this representation avoids any discrete state duplicates. The zones share the same discrete parts here. The storage underneath may implement sharing of all data between different discrete states and zones of different unions of zones: this is at a lower level and it is described in section 5.

The third characteristic is the limited use of double-linked lists. The discrete state list (collision list of the hash table) is double-linked because we need to be able to remove transient states when they are popped of the waiting list. The waiting queue is single-linked because its length is rather small and it is efficient to decide on a validity bit if a popped state should be explored or thrown away. In this case we postpone the removal of states. The same applies for the zones in the zone union. Proper removal of states involves a simple flag manipulation. It is an implementation detail, not to be discussed here. At first glance it seems that the unification would not gain anything from a relatively small waiting list compared to the passed list (in most cases). However the costs of look-ups in small or large hash-tables are about the same, and we need one look-up instead of two.

The *put* operation is described as follows: hash the discrete part of the state to get access to the zone union. Check for inclusion, remove included zones, add this new zone, or refuse the zone. Finally add a reference to the waiting queue. The *get* operation consists of popping a state reference and checking for its validity (a simple flag).

4.3   Experiments

To isolate the impact of the unified list, we instrument the reference implementation. We use the same experiments presented in section 6 with the addition of dacapo, a TDMA protocol. We count in the inclusion checking the number of (symbolic) states that are included in the new state and the number of new states rejected because they are already explored. Among these states that are

Table 1. Percentage of waiting states of the inclusion detections. The new states are compared to the waiting states: they may include those (superset result) or may be included in those (subset result).

Model	superset result	subset result
Cups	97%	86%
Bus Coupler	17%	60%
Dacapo	86%	81%

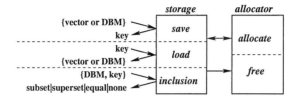

Fig. 6. The interface of the storage with the allocator underneath.

on the passed and the waiting list, we count those that are marked "waiting", i.e. not yet explored. Table 1 shows how often an inclusion is detected with a waiting state. The figures are highly dependent on the model and which states are generated. Compared with the traditional 2-lists approach, we avoid to push states to the passed list or the waiting list. However the exploration is still the same since a waiting state that is going to be explored is guaranteed not to be in the passed or the waiting list in both approaches. In addition to this, if we consider the length of the waiting list compared with the passed list, we expect a performance improvement, but not critical. This is confirmed in the experiments of section 6.

5   Storage Structure

The storage structure is the lower layer whose role is to store simple data. It is in charge of storing location vectors, integer variables, zone data, and other meta variables used for certain algorithms, i.e. guiding [2]. This structure is based on keys: data is sent to the storage that returns a key to be able to retrieve the data later. In addition to this the storage is able to perform simple operations such as equality testing of vectors and inclusion checking of zones to avoid the intermediate step of reading the data first with the associated key. The different storage implementations are built on top of a specialised data allocator. This allocator allocates memory by big chunks and is optimised to deliver many small memory blocks of limited different types. This means that the memory allocation has very little overhead and is very efficient for allocating and deallocating many memory blocks of the same size. This is justified by the nature of the data we are storing: there are few types of vectors and data structures stored but their number is huge. Figure 6 illustrates the main functions of the interface with the allocator underneath.

Table 2. Results from instrumented UPPAAL. The smaller the numbers are, the more copies there are.

Model	Unique locations	Unique variables	Unique DBMs
Audio	52.7%	25.2%	17.2%
Dacapo	4.3%	26.4%	12.7%
Fischer4	9.9%	0.6%	64.4%
Bus coupler	7.2%	8.7%	1.3%

The storage structure is orthogonal to a particular choice of data representation and the PWList structure. We have implemented two variants of this storage, namely one with simple copy and the other one with data sharing. Other particular algorithms aimed at reducing the memory footprint such as *convex hull approximation* [21] or *minimal constraint representation* [18] are possible implementations. These will be ported from the UPPAAL code base.

It is important to notice that UPPAAL implements a minimal constraint representation based on graph reduction. This reduction gives 20-25% gain in memory. It can give even more gain in addition to the shared storage implementation, but it is not implemented here.

5.1   Simple Storage

The simple storage copies data in memory allocated by the allocator and is able to restore original data. This is similar to the default implementation of UPPAAL with the difference that DBM matrices are saved without their diagonal. The diagonal contains the constraints $x_i - x_i \leq 0$ which do not need to be copied[4].

5.2   Shared Storage

To investigate how data might be shared, we instrumented the current implementation of UPPAAL to see how much of the data was shared. We put a printout code at the stage where a state is stored after having tested it for inclusion. The printing was processed through a perl script to analyse it. Table 2 shows consistent results concerning storage of location vectors, integer variables, and DBM data. These results hold through different examples. This can be explained by the way the reachability works: when computing the next state all the possibilities are tried, so for a given location many variable settings exist. The same holds in the other direction: a given variable set will exist in many location configurations. The differences in the results are consistent: *audio* and *dacapo* are middle sized models, *fischer* is the well-known Fischer's protocol for mutual exclusion which behaves badly with respect to timing constraints, and *bus coupler* is a very big example. The bigger the model, the more combinations, and the more sharing we get. The *audio* model is more oriented on control locations. The obtained results justified this shared storage implementation.

---

[4] A DBM representing a non empty zone has always its diagonal set to 0. We store only non empty zones, hence we don't need to copy this diagonal.

Table 3. Experimental results.

	No PWList	PWList - copy	PWList - shared
audio	0.5s 2M	0.5s 2M	0.5s 2M
engine	0.5s 3M	0.5s 4M	0.5s 5M
dacapo	3s 7M	3s 5M	3s 5M
cups	43s 116M	37s 107M	36s 26M
BC	428s 681M	359s 641M	345s 165M
master	306s 616M	277s 558M	267s 153M
slave	440s 735M	377s 645M	359s 151M
plant	19688s > 4G	9207s 2771M	8513s 1084M

The shared storage has a hash table internally to be able to find previously saved data quickly. This requires to compute a hash value for every saved data. However we need to compute hash values anyway to retrieve the discrete part of a state so this is done only once. Another possible overhead is the lookup in collision lists. By a careful choice of the hash function collisions are rare and besides this matches are found in 80% of the cases because of the high sharing property of stored data.

A particular choice has been made concerning the deletion of stored data for this implementation (the interface is free on this point). Only zone data, i.e. DBMs here, are really deallocated. We justify this by the high expected sharing of the discrete part of the states, that is not going to be removed from the passed list. When testing for zone inclusion, we may have to remove zones (this is implemented), but the discrete part is equal. The only case where this does not hold is for transient states because they are stored only in the waiting list and never in the passed list. This will give a set of locations that could be freed from memory. However removing data requires double linked lists, and the locations and variables are saved the same way. For this implementation we adopted this compromise.

6 Experiments

We conduct the experiments on the development version 3.3.24 of UPPAAL without guiding on a Ultra SparcII 400MHz with 4GB of memory. This version incorporates the pipeline and is already twice as fast as the official version due to memory optimization such as reduced number of copies. Here we compare results without and with the PWList structure.

We use an audio protocol [6] (audio), a TDMA protocol [20] (dacapo), an engine gear controller [19] (engine), a combinatorial problem (cups), a field bus communication protocol [14] (different parts BC, master, and slave), and a production plant with three batches [17]. Table 3 shows time and space to generate the whole state space, i.e. the property `A[] true`, except for cups where the reachability property `E<> cups[2] == 4 and y <= 30` is used because the whole state space is too large. Time results under 0.5s are reported as 0.5s in the table. The result $> 4G$ means the verifier crashed because it ran out of memory.

We choose the options -Ca to use DBM representation with active clock reduction. Our implementation does not take full advantage of this because dynamic sized-DBM is not supported in the model-checker. Concerning the four last large examples we used the flag -H273819,273819 to increase manually the size of the hash tables. Default sizes give twice longer verification times.

Depending on the careful chosen options given to UPPAAL our new implementation gives improvements of up to 80% in memory. If we take into account the factor 2 in speed and this improvement we obtain about 60% speed gain. The memory gain is expected due to the showed sharing property of data. The speed gain comes from only having a single hash table and from the zone union structure: the discrete test is done only once and then inclusion checks is done on all the zones in one union. This is showed by the results of the simple copy version. The plant example has 9 clocks and 28 integer variables. The results show the gain in avoiding discrete duplicates. The amount of shared data is less than in other examples. Slight time improvements of the shared version comes from the smaller memory footprint only since there is a computation overhead. We gain on the page and cache faults.

For small examples the results are identical with all versions (results show allocated memory, less memory is used). The results scale with the size of the models, in particular the sharing property of the data holds.

7   Conclusions and Related Work

We have presented a pipeline architecture for the design of a real time model checker based on reachability analysis. The idea of using pipeline is from computer graphics. It is simple, versatile, and easy to maintain. The architechture has been implemented based on a shared data structure unifying the passed and waiting lists adopted in the traditional reachability analysis algorithms for finite state systems. We have also developed a special-purpose memory manager for the architecture to best utilize sharing in physical representation (storage) of logical structures adopted in the verification algorithms.

The work presented in this paper provides a platform for integration of various techniques developed in recent years for efficient analysis of timed systems. It paves the way for a new version of the UPPAAL engine with full support for hierarchical models.

Related Work. The state space storage approach presented in this paper is similar to the one in [11] for hierarhical coloured Petri nets. Both approaches share similarities with BDDs [9] in that common substructures are shared, but avoid the overhead of the fined grained data representation of BDDs. The zone union used in our state representation is a simple list of zones. A more elaborate representation is the CDD [4] that can be used efficiently for analysis. However CDDs pose a number of unresolved problems if we want to use a unified passed and wait structure. Furthermore it is not known how to cope with engine specific data connected to symbolic states. The passed/waiting list unification has been applied to Petri Nets [12] for the purpose of distributed model-checking. Our approach aims at reducing look-ups in the hash table and eliminating waiting states earlier. The particular implementation of the storage that shares data is different from the *state compression* used in Spin [16]. In Spin a *global state descriptor* represents a state and it holds a descriptor for the variables, followed by descriptors for every processes and channels. The user may choose the number of bits for these descriptors, which naturally limits the range of these descriptors. Our representation holds one descriptor for the locations, one for the variables, and one for the zones. The variable sharing is the only similarity. Locations and variables are treated equally as data vectors and are shared as such. It is important to notice that compression is orthogonal and compatible with this representation.

Acknowledgments

As this work was done on the current UPPAAL engine, we are grateful to all its developers. The questions of unification and memory management had been discussed in our group previously. We would like to thank Johan Bengtsson for discussions and his work in implementing the current version of the UPPAAL engine as well as nice scripts to collect statistics.

References

1. R. Alur and D. L. Dill. A theory of timed automata. *Theoretical Computer Science*, 126:183–235, 1994.
2. Gerd Behrmann, Ansgar Fehnker, Thomas S. Hune, Kim Larsen, Paul Petterson, and Judi Romijn. Efficient guiding towards cost-optimality in uppaal. In *Proc. of TACAS'2001*, Lecture Notes in Computer Science. Springer-Verlag, 2001.
3. Gerd Behrmann, Thomas Hune, and Frits Vaandrager. Distributed timed model checking - How the search order matters. In *Proc. of 12th International Conference on Computer Aided Verification*, Lecture Notes in Computer Science, Chicago, Juli 2000. Springer-Verlag.
4. Gerd Behrmann, Kim G. Larsen, Justin Pearson, Carsten Weise, and Wang Yi. Efficient timed reachability analysis using clock difference diagrams. In *Proceedings of the 12th Int. Conf. on Computer Aided Verification*, volume 1633 of *Lecture Notes in Computer Science*. Springer-Verlag, 1999.
5. Johan Bengtsson. Reducing memory usage in symbolic state-space exploration for timed systems. Technical Report 2001-009, Uppsala University, Department of Information Technology, May 2001.
6. Johan Bengtsson, W.O. David Griffioen, Kåre J. Kristoffersen, Kim G. Larsen, Fredrik Larsson, Paul Pettersson, and Wang Yi. Verification of an Audio Protocol with Bus Collision Using UPPAAL. Number 1102 in Lecture Notes in Computer Science, pages 244–256. Springer–Verlag, July 1996.
7. Johan Bengtsson, Kim G. Larsen, Fredrik Larsson, Paul Pettersson, and Wang Yi. UPPAAL — a Tool Suite for Automatic Verification of Real–Time Systems. In *Proc. of Workshop on Verification and Control of Hybrid Systems III*, number 1066 in Lecture Notes in Computer Science, pages 232–243. Springer–Verlag, October 1995.

8. Patricia Bouyer, Catherine Dufourd, Emmanuel Fleury, and Antoine Petit. Are timed automata updatable? In *Proceedings of the 12th Int. Conf. on Computer Aided Verification*, volume 1855 of *Lecture Notes in Computer Science*. Springer-Verlag, 2000.

9. Randal E. Bryant. Graph-based algorithms for boolean function manipulation. In *Transactions on Computers*, volume C-35 no. 8 of *IEEE*, August 1986.

10. C.Daws and S.Yovine. Reducing the number of clock variables of timed automata. In *Proceedings of the 1996 IEEE Real-Time Systems Symposium, RTSS'96*. IEEE Computer Society Press, 1996.

11. S. Christensen and L.M. Kristensen. State space analysis of hierarchical coloured petri nets. In B. Farwer, D.Moldt, and M-O. Stehr, editors, *Proceedings of Workshop on Petri Nets in System Engineering (PNSE'97) Modelling, Verification, and Validation*, number 205, pages 32–43, Hamburg, Germany, 1997.

12. Gianfranco F. Ciardo and David M. Nicol. Automated parallelization of discrete state-space generation. In *Journal of Parallel and Distributed Computing*, volume 47, pages 153–167. ACM, 1997.

13. Alexandre David, Oliver Möller, and Wang Yi. Formal verification uml statecharts with real time extensions. In *Proceedings of FASE 2002 (ETAPS 2002)*, volume 2306 of *Lecture Notes in Computer Science*, pages 218–232. Springer-Verlag, 2002.

14. Alexandre David and Wang Yi. Modeling and analysis of a commercial field bus protocol. In *Proc. of the 12th Euromicro Conference on Real Time Systems*, pages 165–172. IEEE Computer Society, June 2000.

15. Gerard J. Holzmann. On limits and possibilities of automated protocol analysis. In *Proc. 7th IFIP WG 6.1 Int. Workshop on Protocol Specification, Testing, and Verification*, pages 137–161, 1987.

16. Gerard J. Holzmann. The model checker spin. In *IEEE Transactions on Software Engineering*, volume 23, may 1997.

17. Thomas Hune, Kim G. Larsen, and Paul Pettersson. Guided Synthesis of Control Programs Using UPPAAL. In Ten H. Lai, editor, *Proc. of the IEEE ICDCS International Workshop on Distributed Systems Verification and Validation*, pages E15–E22. IEEE Computer Society Press, April 2000.

18. Fredrik Larsson, Kim G. Larsen, Paul Pettersson, and Wang Yi. Efficient Verification of Real-Time Systems: Compact Data Structures and State-Space Reduction. In *Proc. of the 18th IEEE Real-Time Systems Symposium*, pages 14–24. IEEE Computer Society Press, December 1997.

19. Magnus Lindahl, Paul Pettersson, and Wang Yi. Formal Design and Analysis of a Gear-Box Controller. In *Proc. of the 4th Workshop on Tools and Algorithms for the Construction and Analysis of Systems*, number 1384 in Lecture Notes in Computer Science, pages 281–297. Springer–Verlag, March 1998.

20. Henrik Lönn and Paul Pettersson. Formal Verification of a TDMA Protocol Startup Mechanism. In *Proc. of the Pacific Rim Int. Symp. on Fault-Tolerant Systems*, pages 235–242, December 1997.

21. Howard Wong-Toi. *Symbolic Approximations for Verifying Real-Time Systems*. PhD thesis, Standford University, 1995.

22. Sergio Yovine. Kronos: A verification tool for real time systems. In *Int. Journal on Software Tools for Technology Transfer*, pages 134–152, Oct 1997.

Verification by Abstraction[*]

Natarajan Shankar

Computer Science Laboratory
SRI International
Menlo Park CA 94025 USA
shankar@csl.sri.com
http://www.csl.sri.com/~shankar/
Phone: +1 (650) 859-5272   Fax: +1 (650) 859-2844

Abstract. Verification seeks to prove or refute putative properties of a given program. Deductive verification is carried out by constructing a proof that the program satisfies its specification, whereas model checking uses state exploration to find computations where the property fails. Model checking is largely automatic but is effective only for programs defined over small state spaces. Abstraction serves as a bridge between the more general deductive methods for program verification and the restricted but effective state exporation methods used in model checking. In verification by abstraction, deduction is used to construct a finite-state approximation of a program that preserves the property of interest. The resulting abstraction can be explored for offending computations through the use of model checking. We motivate the use of abstraction in verification and survey some of the recent advances.

1   Introduction

The goal of verification is to prove or refute the claim that a given program has a specified property. Deductive methods for imperative programs use program annotations to generate verification conditions that can be discharged using an automated theorem prover [Hoa69]. Model checking [CGP99] is an automatic verification technique based on explicit or symbolic state-space exploration that is applicable to finite-state programs and a limited class of infinite-state programs. The deductive approach requires annotations and manual guidance, whereas model checking does not scale well to large or infinite-state systems. Abstraction can serve as a bridge between these two methods yielding the benefit of generality, scale, and automation. A property-preserving abstraction of a program P and a property B is another program $\hat{P}$ and property $\hat{B}$ such that the verification $P \models B$ follows from $\hat{P} \models \hat{B}$. If the claim $\hat{P} \models \hat{B}$ can be verified by model checking, and $\hat{P}$ and $\hat{B}$ can be automatically constructed from P and B, then we

[*] Funded by NSF Grants CCR-0082560, DARPA/AFRL Contract F33615-00-C-3043, and NASA Contract NAS1-00079. The expert comments of Howard Barringer, Leonardo de Moura, John Rushby, Hassen Saïdi, Maria Sorea, and Tomás Uribe were helpful in the preparation of this article.

B.K. Aichernig and T. Maibaum (Eds.): Formal Methods ..., LNCS 2757, pp. 367–380, 2003.
© Springer-Verlag Berlin Heidelberg 2003

have a powerful verification method that does not depend on manually supplied program annotations.

Deduction can be used to automate the construction of $\hat{P}$ and $\hat{B}$ from P. The proof obligations required to construct property-preserving abstractions can usually be discharged by means of efficient decision procedures. The theorem proving involved in constructing property-preserving abstractions is also *failure tolerant*: the failure to discharge a valid proof obligation might yield a coarser abstraction but does not lead to unsoundness. The power of model checking is also enhanced through the use of abstraction to prune the size of the state space to manageable levels. Since the abstract model loses information, model checking can generate counterexamples that do not correspond to feasible behaviors at the concrete level. The concrete counterparts of abstract counterexamples can be examined using efficient decision procedures and used to refine the abstraction relation. Known properties of the concrete system can be used to sharpen the precision of the abstract model. Amir Pnueli in his invited talk[1] at CAV 2002 identified property-preserving abstraction as one of the cornerstones of a successful verification methodology. The abstraction paradigm brings about a useful synthesis of deduction and model checking where deduction is used *locally* to approximate individual formulas and transition rules, and exploration is used *globally* to calculate, for example, the reachable states on the abstract model. We briefly explain the basic ideas underlying verification by abstraction and summarize some of the recent advances.

2   Abstract Interpretation

The foundations of verification by abstraction go back to the abstract interpretation framework of Cousot and Cousot [CC77, CH78], but practical and general techniques for their use in verification are of more recent vintage. Abstract interpretation operates between a concrete partial order C and an abstract one A related by means of a *Galois connection* which is a pair (α, γ) of maps: α from C to A, and γ from A to C, such that for any $a \in A$ and $c \in C$, $\alpha(c) \leq_A a \Leftrightarrow c \leq_C \gamma(a)$. Intuitively, $\gamma(a)$ is the greatest concretization of a, and $\alpha(c)$ is the least abstraction for c, on the respective partial orders. Note that $c \leq_C \gamma(\alpha(c))$ and $\alpha(\gamma(a)) \leq_A a$ for any $c \in C$ and $a \in A$. The maps α and γ are order-preserving.

If $\langle C, \leq_C \rangle$ and $\langle A, \leq_A \rangle$ are complete lattices, then they admit least and greatest fixpoints of monotone operators. If F_C is a monotone operator on C, then μF_C is the least fixpoint of F in C and can be defined as $\bigcap \{X | F_C(X) \leq_C X\}$. It is possible to derive an abstract operator $\widehat{F_C} = \alpha \circ F_C \circ \gamma$ from a concrete operator F_C. It is easy to see that $\mu F_C \leq_C \gamma(\mu \widehat{F_C})$. Furthermore, if $F(a) \leq_A F'(a)$ for all $a \in A$, $\mu F \leq_A \mu F'$. In particular, if $\widehat{F_C}(a) \leq F_A(a)$ for all $a \in A$, then $\mu F_C \leq \gamma(\mu F_A)$. We write $\mu X : F[X]$ as a shorthand for $\mu(\lambda X : F[X])$.

---

[1] The slides from this talk are available at http://www.wisdom.weizmann.ac.il/~amir/invited-talks.html.

$\hat{+}$	0	+1	−1	T
0	0	+1	−1	T
+1	+1	+1	T	T
−1	−1	T	−1	T
T	T	T	T	T

$\hat{-}$	0	+1	−1	T
0	0	−1	+1	T
+1	+1	T	+1	T
−1	−1	−1	T	T
T	T	T	T	T

Fig. 1. Abstract versions of + and −.

Linear-time and branching-time temporal operators from logics such as CTL, LTL, and CTL* can be expressed in terms of least and greatest fixpoints of monotone predicate transformers on the lattice of predicates or sets of states.

The approximation of concrete fixpoints by abstract fixpoints over a finite space can be used to derive concrete properties. A program over a state space Σ is given by an initialization predicate I and a binary next-state relation N over Σ. The concrete lattice C corresponding to Σ is the boolean algebra of predicates over Σ. Given such a program, the set of reachable states is characterized by $\mu X : I \vee post(N)(X)$, where $post(N)(X) = \{s' \in \Sigma | (\exists (s : \Sigma) : N(s, s')\}$. This is the strongest invariant of the program. Iteration is one way to compute the fixpoint as the limit of $I \vee post(N)(I) \vee post(N)(post(N)(I)) \vee \ldots$, but this computation might not terminate when the state space Σ is infinite.

As a running example, we consider a program π over a state space Σ consisting of an input integer variable x and an output integer variable y. The initialization predicate I_π is given by $y = 0$ and transition relation N_π between the current (unprimed) state and the next (primed) state is given by the formula

$$(x \geq 0 \wedge y' = y + x) \vee (x \leq 0 \wedge y' = y - x).$$

The task is to verify the invariant $y \geq 0$. It can be verified that the postcondition computation $\mu X : I_\pi \vee post(N_\pi)(X)$ on this transition system does not converge. We can use an abstract lattice to compute an approximation $\widehat{post(N_\pi)}$ to $post(N_\pi)$. For this purpose, we use a *sign abstraction* for the integer domain given by an abstract domain $D = \{0, +1, -1, T\}$, where $\gamma(0)$ is the set $\{0\}$, $\gamma(+1)$ is the set of non-negative integers $[0, \infty)$, $\gamma(-1)$ is the set of non-positive integers $(-\infty, 0]$, and $\gamma(T)$ is the set of integers $(-\infty, \infty)$. The operations + and − on integers can be lifted to the corresponding operations $\hat{+}$ and $\hat{-}$ on D as shown in Figure 1. The table of entries in Figure 1 can be precomputed using theorem proving.

The domain D is a finite lattice as is $D \times D$ where the first projection is represented by $\hat{x}$ and the second projection by $\hat{y}$, and $\gamma(\langle \hat{x}, \hat{y} \rangle)$ is just $\langle \gamma(\hat{x}), \gamma(\hat{y}) \rangle$. It is easy to see that the initialization predicate I_π is approximated by $\alpha(I_\pi) = \langle T, 0 \rangle$. With $\sqcap$ and $\sqcup$ as the *meet* and *join* operations on the lattice D, the postcondition operator $post(N_\pi)$ can be approximated by

$$\widehat{post(N_\pi)} = \langle \langle \hat{x}, \hat{y} \rangle \mapsto \langle T, (\hat{y}\hat{+}(+1 \sqcap \hat{x})) \sqcup (\hat{y}\hat{-}(-1 \sqcap \hat{x})) \rangle \rangle.$$

The fixpoint $\mu \hat{X} : \alpha(I_\pi) \sqcup \widehat{post(N_\pi)}(\hat{X})$ can be calculated to yield $\langle \top, +1 \rangle$. The concretization $\gamma(\langle \top, +1 \rangle)$ of the abstract fixpoint yields the concrete invariant $y \geq 0$.

The abstraction can also map to an infinite domain, in which case acceleration techniques like widening and narrowing [CC77, CC92] have to be used to make the fixpoint computations converge. Techniques based on abstract interpretation and fixpoint calculations have been widely used in invariant generation [BBM97, BLS96, GS96, DLNS98, JH98, TRSS01].

3   Property-Preserving Abstraction

In the example above, the sign abstraction allowed us to approximate a fixpoint computation over a concrete lattice by one over an abstract finite lattice. In order to use model checking to explore the abstraction, we need to generate an abstract transition system that preserves the desired property of the concrete transition system. The formal use of abstraction in model checking was considered by Kurshan [Kur93]. Clarke, Grumberg, and Long [CGL92] gave a data abstraction method that preserved ∀CTL* (and hence, LTL) properties by demonstrating a simulation relation between the concrete and abstract systems. Dams, Gerth, and Grumberg [DGG94, Dam96] showed that a bisimulation relation between the abstract and concrete systems preserves CTL* properties. The relationship between abstract interpretation and the familiar simulation and bisimulation relations used to obtain property preservation, has been studied by Loiseaux, Graf, Sifakis, Bensalem, and Bouajjani [LGS+95]. Kesten and Pnueli [KP98] present a data abstraction method for fair transition systems with respect to linear-time temporal logic (LTL) properties. Approximate model checking algorithms based on abstract interpretation for mu-calculus and CTL have been given by Pardo and Hachtel [PH97].

The main challenge in using abstraction in the verification of temporal properties is that of constructing the abstract program $\hat{P}$ and property $\hat{B}$, from the concrete program P and property B. When P is itself a finite-state program given by $\langle I, N \rangle$, and the abstraction between the concrete state space Σ and the abstract state space $\hat{\Sigma}$ is given by a relation ρ, then the abstract initialization $\hat{I}$ can be constructed so that $\hat{I}(\hat{s}) = (\exists s : \rho(s, \hat{s}) \wedge I(s))$ and the transition relation $\hat{N}$ can be computed from the concrete one as $\rho^{-1} \circ N \circ \rho$. Both $\hat{I}$ and $\hat{N}$ can be represented as reduced ordered binary decision diagrams for the purposes of symbolic model checking. Such an abstraction can be shown to preserve ∀CTL* properties.

3.1   Syntactic Data Abstraction

Data abstraction is based on assigning individual abstract values to subsets of a data domain so that a concrete variable over an infinite domain, like x in the program π above, is replaced by an abstract variable, $\hat{x}$, over a finite domain. We have already used data abstraction in the analysis of the example program P above. The Bandera program analysis tool [CDH+00], the Cadence SMV model checker [McM98], and the SCR verification tool [HKL+98] employ precomputed data abstractions to syntactically transform a transition system to a corresponding abstract one. For the case of the program π considered above, we can take the abstract data domain D to be $\{0, +1, -1\}$ where $\gamma(\{0\}) = \{0\}$, $\gamma(\{+1\}) = (0, \infty)$, $\gamma(\{-1\}) = (-\infty, 0)$, and $\gamma(\hat{X} \cup \hat{Y}) = \gamma(\hat{X}) \cup \gamma(\hat{Y})$. The abstract operations $\hat{+}$ and $\hat{-}$ can then be precomputed using theorem proving as shown in Figure 2.

$\hat{+}$	0	+1	-1
0	$\{0\}$	$\{+1\}$	$\{-1\}$
+1	$\{+1\}$	$\{+1\}$	$\{0, -1, +1\}$
-1	$\{-1\}$	$\{0, -1, +1\}$	$\{-1\}$

$\hat{-}$	0	+1	-1
0	$\{0\}$	$\{-1\}$	$\{+1\}$
+1	$\{+1\}$	$\{0, -1, +1\}$	$\{+1\}$
-1	$\{-1\}$	$\{-1\}$	$\{0, -1, +1\}$

Fig. 2. Data Abstraction of $+$ and $-$.

The program $\hat{\pi}$ can then be syntactically computed [Sha02] so that $I_{\hat{\pi}} = (\hat{y} = 0)$ and $N_{\hat{\pi}} = (\hat{x} \in \{0, +1\} \wedge \hat{y}' \in \hat{y}\hat{+}\hat{x}) \vee (\hat{x} \in \{0, -1\} \wedge \hat{y}' \in \hat{y}\hat{-}\hat{x})$. Model checking can be used to compute the set of reachable abstract states as $\mu\hat{X} : I \vee post(\hat{N})(\hat{X})$ to yield the invariant $\hat{y} \in \{0, +1\}$. The concrete counterpart of the abstract invariant is the desired concrete invariant $y \geq 0$.

3.2   Predicate Abstraction

Predicate or *boolean abstraction* is another way of reducing an infinite-state system to a finite-state one by introducing boolean variables that correspond to assertions over the (possibly infinite) state of a program. Predicate abstraction was introduced by Graf and Saïdi [SG97] as a way of computing invariants by abstract interpretation. In this form of abstraction, boolean variables $b_1, \ldots, b_n$ are used to represent concrete predicates $p_1, \ldots, p_n$. The concrete lattice consists of predicates over the concrete state space Σ and the abstract lattice consists of monomials, i.e., conjunctions over literals, b_i or $\neg b_i$, over the abstract boolean variables. The concrete reachability assertion $\mu X : I \vee post(N)(X)$ can be approximated by $\gamma(\mu X : \hat{I} \vee post(\hat{N})(X))$. Here $\gamma(\hat{p})$ for an abstract assertion $\hat{p}$ is the result of substituting the concrete assertion p_i corresponding to the abstract boolean variable b_i. The abstract initialization predicate $\hat{I}$ is computed as $\alpha(I)$, where $\alpha(p) = \bigwedge\{l_i | \vdash p \supset \gamma(l_i)\}$ where each l_i is either b_i or $\neg b_i$. Deduction is used in the construction of the $\alpha(p)$. The strongest invariant is then computed iteratively as $\mu X : \alpha(I) \vee \alpha(post(N)(\gamma(X)))$. In each step of the iteration, the partial invariant X is concretized as $\gamma(X)$, the concrete postcondition $post(N)(\gamma(X))$ is computed, and then abstracted using the definition of α

given above. Since the state space of the abstract program is finite, the abstract reachability computation converges.

For the program π, the abstraction predicates are given by $\gamma(b) = (y \geq 0)$. The abstraction of the initialization predicate, $\alpha(I_\pi)$, is computed to be b. The iteration step $post(N_\pi)(y \geq 0)$ yields $y \geq 0$ and $\alpha(y \geq 0)$ is clearly b. This therefore yields the abstract invariant b as the fixpoint, and $\gamma(b)$ is the desired invariant $y \geq 0$. Graf and Saïdi further noticed that many typical abstraction predicates can be obtained from the initialization, guards, and assignments in the program, and only a few have to be introduced manually. Abstract reachability computation has also been studied by Das, Dill, and Park [DDP99] for the full boolean lattice instead of the monomial lattice.

Graf and Saïdi [SG97] gave a method for calculating the abstract transition relation in terms of monomials. We have already seen how I can be abstracted as $\alpha(I)$. The next state relation N can be abstracted as $\bigvee\{\hat{p} \wedge \hat{q}' | \hat{p} \in \mathcal{M}, \hat{q} = \alpha(post(N)(\gamma(\hat{p})))\}$, where $\mathcal{M}$ is the set of monomials over the abstract boolean variables b_i, $\hat{q}' = \bigwedge_i l_i'$ for $\hat{q} = \bigwedge_i l_i$. The weakest liberal precondition of a transition relation $\widetilde{pre}(N)(p)$ is defined as $\{s : \Sigma | (\forall s' : N(s, s') \wedge p(s'))\}$. Since $post(N)(q) \supset p \iff q \supset \widetilde{pre}(N)(p)$ (a Galois connection), we can compute $\alpha(post(N)(q))$ using $\widetilde{pre}(N)(p)$ which is more easily computed syntactically from the program. Note, however, that the abstract reachability computation $\mu X : \alpha(I) \vee \alpha(post(N)(\gamma(X)))$ can be more precise than $\mu X : \alpha(I) \vee post(\hat{N})(X)$ at the cost of requiring more calls to the theorem prover since the abstraction is computed at each iteration. A variant of the Graf-Saïdi method is used in the SLAM project at Microsoft [BMMR01] for analyzing C programs.

Other methods have been proposed for constructing boolean abstractions. In the InVest system [BLO98], Bensalem, Lakhnech, and Owre use the *elimination method* to construct the abstract transition graph so that a transition $\langle \hat{s}, \hat{s}' \rangle$ is eliminated from the abstract transition relation $\hat{N}$ if $\vdash \gamma(s) \supset \widetilde{pre}(N)(\neg\gamma(s'))$. Each abstract state s is a monomial of the form $\bigwedge_{i \in [0,n)} l_i$. Methods for constructing predicate abstractions based on the full boolean lattice have been explored by Colón and Uribe [CU98], Das, Dill, and Park [DDP99], Saïdi and Shankar [SS99], and Flanagan and Qadeer [FQ02].

The Saïdi–Shankar method has been implemented in an abstractor for PVS 2.4 that integrates both predicate and data abstraction [Sha02]. In this enumeration method, the abstract overapproximation $\alpha(p)$ of a concrete predicate p is computed as the conjunction of clauses c such that $\vdash p \supset \gamma(c)$, where each clause is a disjunction of literals l_i that are *relevant* to p. The criterion of relevance was introduced in InVest [BLO98]. A relation $b_i \sim b_j$ holds between two abstract variables if $vars(\gamma(b_i)) \cap vars(\gamma(b_j)) \neq \emptyset$, where $vars(p)$ is the set of concrete program variables in p. The $\sim$ relation is also closed under transitivity so that it is an equivalence relation. Let $[b_i]$ represent the equivalence class of b_i under $\sim$, and $vars([b_i])$ be the set $\bigcup\{vars(b) | b \in [b_i]\}$. The boolean variable b_i is relevant to p if $vars(p) \cap vars([b_i]) \neq \emptyset$. The clauses c are generated in order of increasing length and tested with the proof goal $p \supset \gamma(c)$. If clause c passes the test, i.e., $p \supset \gamma(c)$ is provable, then any clause that is subsumed by c need not be tested.

If a clause d is such that $c \wedge d$ is equivalent to a proper subclause of c then the test must have failed, and hence d also need not be tested. The transition relation N can also be overapproximated as $\alpha(N)$ over $2n$ boolean variables. Data abstraction where the target of the abstraction is an enumerated type can be smoothly integrated with this method by extending the boolean case analysis in the above enumeration to a multi-valued domain.

On the example program π, we can construct an abstraction where the single abstract variable b represents the concrete predicate $y \geq 0$. The predicate abstraction process yields b for $\alpha(I_\pi)$ and $\neg b \vee b'$ for $\alpha(N_\pi)$. Clearly, b is an invariant for the resulting abstract transition system, and hence the concrete invariant $y \geq 0$ follows. Note that unlike the method shown in Section 3.1, the abstraction here is not syntactic. Since the abstraction is not precomputed, it is possible to construct a more econonomical abstract transition system but with the cost of an exponential number of proof goals. The above enumeration method requires the testing of 3^n proof goals in the worst case, when n abstract boolean variables are introduced.

3.3   Counterexample-Guided Abstraction

Counterexample-guided abstraction is an active current research topic in abstraction. Since the abstraction is only a conservative approximation of the concrete system, the abstract version of a concrete property may fail to hold of the abstracted system. The verification then generates an abstract counterexample. The validity of this counterexample can be examined at the concrete level. If the counterexample is spurious, it is possible to refine the abstraction. Such an idea was investigated by Sipma, Uribe, and Manna [SUM96] in the context of explicit-state LTL model checking. The InVest system [BLO98] examines the failure of the concretized counterexamples to suggest new predicates. Rusu and Singerman [RS99] propose a tight integration of theorem proving and model checking where the deductive proof is used to suggest predicates and identify spurious counterexamples, and model checking on the abstraction generates useful invariants that are fed back to the theorem prover. The verification proceeds until either a proof is successfully completed or a valid counterexample is generated. Clarke, Grumberg, Jha, Lu, and Veith [CGJ+00] have also studied counterexample-guided refinement in the context of the abstraction of finite-state systems as a way of suggesting new abstraction predicates. Saïdi [Saï00] introduces new predicates to eliminate nondeterminism in the abstract model.

Das and Dill [DD01] use a partial abstraction technique that is refined through the elimination of spurious counterexamples. The intuition here is that since transition systems are typically sparse when seen as graphs, the construction of the precise abstract transition system can be wasteful. The Das–Dill method starts with a coarsely abstracted transition system with respect to a given set of abstraction predicates. Such an initial approximation can be obtained by placing some bound on the proof goals used in constructing the abstract transition relation. Model checking is used to construct a possibly spurious counterexample. A decision procedure is used to isolate the abstract transition that is concretely infeasible. The conflict set corresponding to the infeasible transition yields the minimal subset of literals that are sufficient for guaranteeing infeasibility. The negation of conjunction of the literals given by the conflict set is conjoined to the abstract transition relation to yield a more refined abstract transition relation where the spurious counterexample has been eliminated. The next round of the iteration repeats the model checking using the refined abstraction. The lazy abstraction method of Henzinger, Jhala, Majumdar, and Sutre [HJMS02] integrates the refinement and model checking procedures so that the verified parts of the state space are not re-explored in subsequent iterations.

3.4   Abstractions Preserving Liveness

Naïve abstractions are typically not useful for verifying liveness properties since the abstraction can introduce nonterminating loops that do not occur in the corresponding concrete system. Liveness properties are preserved in the sense that they do hold of the concrete system when provable of the abstract system, but the latter situation is largely hypothetical. For example, in the example program P above, we may wish to show that if the input x is infinitely often non-zero, then output y is unbounded. This property fails to hold of the abstract program even when we enrich the abstraction with the predicates $y \leq M$ for a bound M. We add a state variable r to the abstraction ranging over $\{dec, inc, same\}$ such that r is set to dec, inc, or $same$ according to whether the rank $M - y$ has decreased, increased, or remained the same. Since the rank is decreased according to a well-founded order, we can introduce a fairness constraint asserting that r cannot take the value dec infinitely often along a path unless it also takes the value inc infinitely often. Abstraction techniques for progress properties based on the introduction of additional fairness constraints have been studied by Dams [Dam96], Merz [Mer97], Uribe [Uri98], Kesten and Pnueli [KP00], and by Pnueli, Xu, and Zuck [PXZ02]. In this way, abstraction yields a relatively complete verification method [KPV99] for the verification of LTL properties.

3.5   Abstracting Parameterized Systems

The verification of parametric systems consisting of n identical processes through abstraction, has been studied through the *network invariants* method of Wolper and Lovinfosse [WL89] and Kurshan and McMillan [KM89]. Lesens and Saïdi [LS97] combine predicate abstraction with a counting abstraction to verify parameterized networks of processes. A similar 0-1-many abstraction has been studied by Pong and Dubois [PD95] and Pnueli, Xu, and Zuck [PXZ02]. The PAX system [BBLS00] captures parametric systems using the WS1S logic so that finite-state abstractions can be constructed using the MONA tool. The resulting abstractions are model checked using SPIN [Hol91] or SMV [McM93]. The PAX tool has been used to verify safety and liveness properties of examples including algorithms for mutual exclusion and group membership.

3.6   Abstracting Timed and Hybrid Systems

Timed and hybrid systems constitute natural candidates for abstraction. The region graph constructions used in model checking such systems is already a form of abstraction [ACD93]. Colón and Uribe [CU98, Uri98] carried out a verification of a two-process instance of Fischer's real time mutual exclusion protocol using predicate abstraction. Möller, Rueß, and Sorea [MRS02] present a predicate abstraction method for next-free temporal properties of timed systems that uses a restricted semantics for time-flow to ensure non-Zeno behavior in the abstraction. In this restricted semantics, each time increment must ensure that some clock either reaches or crosses an integer boundary. Namjoshi and Kurshan [NK00] give a method for systematically constructing abstraction predicates that is complete for systems with finite bisimulations.

Khanna and Tiwari [TK02] give a *qualitative* abstraction method for hybrid systems where the flows over a vector $(x_1, \ldots, x_n)$ are specified as $\dot{x}_i = f_i(x_1, \ldots, x_n)$, where $f_i(x_1, \ldots, x_n)$ is a polynomial. The initial set Π_0 of polynomials is fixed to contain the flow polynomials $f_i(x_1, \ldots, x_n)$ and the polynomials occurring in the initializations, guards and assignments. The set Π_0 is then enriched to obtain Π by adding the derivative $\dot{p}$ for each polynomial $p \in \Pi$, unless $\dot{p}$ is a constant or a constant multiple of some polynomial q already in Π. The construction of Π can be terminated at any point without affecting the soundness of the abstraction. Then a sign abstraction with respect to these derivatives is computed by introducing a variable sp ranging over $\{-, +, 0\}$ for each $p \in \Pi$. PVS augmented with the QEPCAD decision procedure [CH91] for the first-order theory of real closed fields is used to determine the concrete feasibility of abstract states. There is a transition on the abstract system from state $\hat{s}$ to $\hat{s}'$ only when the signs of the flows are consistent with the transition. For example, if sp goes from $+$ in $\hat{s}$ to 0 in $\hat{s}'$ for a polynomial p, then sq must be $-$ in $\hat{s}$ for $q = \dot{p}$. Discrete transitions are abstracted as shown earlier for transition systems. Alur, Dang and Ivančić [ADI02] present a predicate abstraction technique for linear hybrid automata.

4   Conclusions

In summary, abstraction is a powerful verification paradigm that combines deduction and model checking. The keys to the effectiveness of abstraction are that

1. Guessing useful abstraction maps is easier than identifying program annotations and invariant strengthenings.
2. It makes use of failure-tolerant theorem proving, largely in effectively decidable domains, to deliver possibly approximate results.
3. The refinement of abstractions can be guided by counterexamples.
4. Abstraction interacts effectively with other verification techniques such as invariant generation, progress verification, and refinement.

We have given a basic introduction to verification methods based on abstraction. The practicality of these abstraction techniques has been demonstrated on several large examples. Flanagan and Qadeer [FQ02] have applied predicate abstraction to a large (44KLOC) file system program and automatically derived over 90% of the loop invariants. Predicate abstraction has also been used in the SLAM project [BMMR01] at Microsoft to find bugs in device driver routines.

Abstraction is an effective approach to the verification of both finite and infinite-state systems since it can be applied to large and complex systems with minimal user guidance. The SAL (Symbolic Analysis Laboratory) framework [BGL+00] developed at SRI provides a toolbus and an intermediate description language for tying together a number of verification tools through the use of property-preserving abstractions.

References

[ACD93]   Rajeev Alur, Costas Courcoubetis, and David Dill. Model-checking in dense real-time. *Information and Computation*, 104(1):2–34, May 1993.

[ADI02]   Rajeev Alur, Thao Dang, and Franjo Ivančić. Reachability analysis of hybrid systems via predicate abstraction. In Tomlin and Greenstreet [TG02], pages 35–48.

[AH96]   Rajeev Alur and Thomas A. Henzinger, editors. *Computer-Aided Verification, CAV '96*, volume 1102 of *Lecture Notes in Computer Science*, New Brunswick, NJ, July/August 1996. Springer-Verlag.

[BBLS00] Kai Baukus, Saddek Bensalem, Yassine Lakhnech, and Karsten Stahl. Abstracting WS1S systems to verify parameterized networks. In Susanne Graf and Michael Schwartzbach, editors, *Tools and Algorithms for the Construction and Analysis of Systems (TACAS 2000)*, number 1785 in Lecture Notes in Computer Science, pages 188–203, Berlin, Germany, March 2000. Springer-Verlag.

[BBM97]   Nikolaj Bjørner, I. Anca Browne, and Zohar Manna. Automatic generation of invariants and intermediate assertions. *Theoretical Computer Science*, 173(1):49–87, 1997.

[BGL+00] Saddek Bensalem, Vijay Ganesh, Yassine Lakhnech, César Muñoz, Sam Owre, Harald Rueß, John Rushby, Vlad Rusu, Hassen Saïdi, N. Shankar, Eli Singerman, and Ashish Tiwari. An overview of SAL. In C. Michael Holloway, editor, *LFM 2000: Fifth NASA Langley Formal Methods Workshop*, pages 187–196, Hampton, VA, June 2000. NASA Langley Research Center. Proceedings available at http://shemesh.larc.nasa.gov/fm/Lfm2000/Proc/.

[BLO98]   Saddek Bensalem, Yassine Lakhnech, and Sam Owre. Computing abstractions of infinite state systems compositionally and automatically. In Hu and Vardi [HV98], pages 319–331.

[BLS96]   Saddek Bensalem, Yassine Lakhnech, and Hassen Saïdi. Powerful techniques for the automatic generation of invariants. In Alur and Henzinger [AH96], pages 323–335.

[BMMR01] T. Ball, R. Majumdar, T. Millstein, and S. Rajamani. Automatic predicate abstraction of C programs. In *Proceedings of the SIGPLAN '01 Conference on Programming Language Design and Implementation, 2001*, pages 203–313. ACM Press, 2001.

[CC77]   P. Cousot and R. Cousot. Abstract interpretation: a unified lattice model
            for static analysis. In *4th ACM Symposium on Principles of Programming
            Languages*. Association for Computing Machinery, January 1977.

[CC92]   P. Cousot and R. Cousot. Abstract interpretation and application to logic
            programs. *Journal of Logic Programming*, 13(2-3):103–179, July 1992.

[CDH⁺00]   James Corbett, Matthew Dwyer, John Hatcliff, Corina Pasareanu, Robby,
            Shawn Laubach, and Hongjun Zheng. Bandera: Extracting finite-state
            models from Java source code. In *22nd International Conference on Soft-
            ware Engineering*, pages 439–448, Limerick, Ireland, June 2000. IEEE
            Computer Society.

[CGJ⁺00]   Edmund M. Clarke, Orna Grumberg, Somesh Jha, Yuan Lu, and Helmut
            Veith. Counterexample-guided abstraction refinement. In *Computer Aided
            Verification*, pages 154–169, 2000.

[CGL92]   E. M. Clarke, O. Grumberg, and D. E. Long. Model checking and abstrac-
            tion. In *Nineteenth Annual ACM Symposium on Principles of Program-
            ming Languages*, pages 343–354, 1992.

[CGP99]   E. M. Clarke, Orna Grumberg, and Doron Peled. *Model Checking*. MIT
            Press, 1999.

[CH78]   P. Cousot and N. Halbwachs. Automatic discovery of linear restraints
            among variables. In *5th ACM Symposium on Principles of Programming
            Languages*. Association for Computing Machinery, January 1978.

[CH91]   G. E. Collins and H. Hong. Partial cylindrical algebraic decomposition.
            Journal of Symbolic Computation, 12(3):299–328, 1991.

[CU98]   M. A. Colón and T. E. Uribe. Generating finite-state abstractions of re-
            active systems using decision procedures. In Hu and Vardi [HV98], pages
            293–304.

[Dam96]   Dennis René Dams. *Abstract Interpretation and Partition Refinement for
            Model Checking*. PhD thesis, Eindhoven University of Technology, P.O.
            Box 513, 5600 MB Eindhoven, The Netherlands, July 1996.

[DD01]   Satyaki Das and David L. Dill. Successive approximation of abstract tran-
            sition relations. In *Annual IEEE Symposium on Logic in Computer Sci-
            ence01*, pages 51–60. The Institute of Electrical and Electronics Engineers,
            2001.

[DDP99]   Satyaki Das, David L. Dill, and Seungjoon Park. Experience with predicate
            abstraction. In Halbwachs and Peled [HP99], pages 160–171.

[DGG94]   Dennis Dams, Orna Grumberg, and Rob Gerth. Abstract interpretation
            of reactive systems: Abstractions preserving ∀CTL*, ∃CTL* and CTL*.
            In Ernst-Rüdiger Olderog, editor, *Programming Concepts, Methods and
            Calculi (PROCOMET '94)*, pages 561–581, 1994.

[DLNS98]   David L. Detlefs, K. Rustan M. Leino, Greg Nelson, and James B. Saxe.
            Extended static checking. Technical Report 159, COMPAQ Systems Re-
            search Center, 1998.

[FQ02]   Cormac Flanagan and Shaz Qadeer. Predicate abstraction for software ver-
            ification. In *ACM Symposium on Principles of Programming Languages02*,
            pages 191–202. Association for Computing Machinery, January 2002.

[Gru97]   Orna Grumberg, editor. *Computer-Aided Verification, CAV '97*, volume
            1254 of *Lecture Notes in Computer Science*, Haifa, Israel, June 1997.
            Springer-Verlag.

[GS96]   Susanne Graf and Hassen Saïdi. Verifying invariants using theorem prov-
           ing. In Alur and Henzinger [AH96], pages 196–207.

[HJMS02]   Thomas A. Henzinger, Ranjit Jhala, Rupak Majumdar, and Gregoire
           Sutre. Lazy abstraction. In *ACM Symposium on Principles of Program-
           ming Languages02*, pages 58–70. Association for Computing Machinery,
           January 2002.

[HKL+98]   Constance Heitmeyer, James Kirby, Jr., Bruce Labaw, Myla Archer, and
           Ramesh Bharadwaj. Using abstraction and model checking to detect safety
           violations in requirements specifications. *IEEE Transactions on Software
           Engineering*, 24(11):927–948, November 1998.

[Hoa69]   C. A. R. Hoare. An axiomatic basis for computer programming. *Comm.
           ACM*, 12(10):576–583, 1969.

[Hol91]   G. J. Holzmann. *Design and Validation of Computer Protocols*. Prentice-
           Hall, 1991.

[HP99]   Nicolas Halbwachs and Doron Peled, editors. *Computer-Aided Verification,
           CAV '99*, volume 1633 of *Lecture Notes in Computer Science*, Trento, Italy,
           July 1999. Springer-Verlag.

[HV98]   Alan J. Hu and Moshe Y. Vardi, editors. *Computer-Aided Verification,
           CAV '98*, volume 1427 of *Lecture Notes in Computer Science*, Vancouver,
           Canada, June 1998. Springer-Verlag.

[JH98]   Ralph Jeffords and Constance Heitmeyer. Automatic generation of state
           invariants from requirements specifications. In *Sixth ACM SIGSOFT Sym-
           posium on the Foundations of Software Engineering*, pages 56–69, Lake
           Buena Vista, FL, November 1998. Association for Computing Machinery.

[KM89]   R.P. Kurshan and K. McMillan. A structural induction theorem for pro-
           cesses. In *Eighth ACM Symposium on Principles of Distributed Computing*,
           pages 239–248, Edmonton, Alberta, Canada, August 1989.

[KP98]   Yonit Kesten and Amir Pnueli. Modularization and abstraction: The keys
           to practical formal verification. In *Mathematical Foundations of Computer
           Science*, pages 54–71, 1998.

[KP00]   Yonit Kesten and Amir Pnueli. Verification by augmented finitary abstrac-
           tion. *Information and Computation*, 163(1):203–243, 2000.

[KPV99]   Yonit Kesten, Amir Pnueli, and Moshe Y. Vardi. Verification by aug-
           mented abstraction: The automata-theoretic view. In J. Flum and M. R.
           Artalejo, editors, *CSL: Computer Science Logic*, volume 1683 of *Lecture
           Notes in Computer Science*, pages 141–156. Springer-Verlag, 1999.

[Kur93]   R.P. Kurshan. *Automata-Theoretic Verification of Coordinating Processes*.
           Princeton University Press, Princeton, NJ, 1993.

[LGS+95]   C. Loiseaux, S. Graf, J. Sifakis, A. Bouajjani, and S. Bensalem. Property
           preserving abstractions for the verification of concurrent systems. *Formal
           Methods in System Design*, 6:11–44, 1995.

[LS97]   David Lesens and Hassen Saïdi. Automatic verification of parameterized
           networks of processes by abstraction. In Faron Moller, editor, *2nd Inter-
           national Workshop on Verification of Infinite State Systems: Infinity '97*,
           volume 9 of *Electronic Notes in Theoretical Computer Science*, Bologna,
           Italy, July 1997. Elsevier.

[McM93]   K.L. McMillan. *Symbolic Model Checking*. Kluwer Academic Publishers,
           Boston, 1993.

[McM98]   Ken McMillan. Minimalist proof assistants: Interactions of technology
            and methodology in formal system level verification. In Ganesh Gopalakr-
            ishnan and Phillip Windley, editors, *Formal Methods in Computer-Aided
            Design (FMCAD '98)*, volume 1522 of *Lecture Notes in Computer Science*,
            Palo Alto, CA, November 1998. Springer-Verlag. Invited presentation—
            no paper in proceedings, but slides available at `http://www-cad.eecs.`
            `berkeley.edu/~kenmcmil/`.

[Mer97]   Stephan Merz. Rules for abstraction. In R. K. Shyamasundar and K. Ueda,
            editors, *Advances in Computing Science—ASIAN'97*, volume 1345 of *Lec-
            ture Notes in Computer Science*, pages 32–45, Kathmandu, Nepal, Decem-
            ber 1997. Springer-Verlag.

[MRS02]   M. Oliver Möller, Harald Rueß, and Maria Sorea. Predicate abstraction
            for dense real-time systems. *Electronic Notes in Theoretical Computer
            Science*, 65(6), 2002. Full version available as Technical Report BRICS-RS-
            01-44, Department of Computer Science, University of Aarhus, Denmark.

[NK00]   K. Namjoshi and R. Kurshan. Syntactic program transformations for au-
            tomatic abstraction. In E. A. Emerson and A. P. Sistla, editors, *Computer-
            Aided Verification, CAV '2000*, volume 1855 of *Lecture Notes in Computer
            Science*, pages 435–449, Chicago, IL, July 2000. Springer-Verlag.

[PD95]   Fong Pong and Michel Dubois. A new approach for the verification of
            cache coherence protocols. *IEEE Transactions on Parallel and Distributed
            Systems*, 6(8):773–787, August 1995.

[PH97]   Abelardo Pardo and Gary D. Hachtel. Automatic abstraction techniques
            for propositional mu-calculus model checking. In Grumberg [Gru97], pages
            12–23.

[PXZ02]   Amir Pnueli, Jessie Xu, and Lenore Zuck. Liveness with $(0, 1, \infty)$-counter
            abstraction. In *Computer-Aided Verification, CAV '02*, Lecture Notes in
            Computer Science. Springer-Verlag, July 2002.

[RS99]   Vlad Rusu and Eli Singerman. On proving safety properties by integrating
            static analysis, theorem proving and abstraction. In W. Rance Cleaveland,
            editor, *Tools and Algorithms for the Construction and Analysis of Systems
            (TACAS '99)*, volume 1579 of *Lecture Notes in Computer Science*, pages
            178–192, Amsterdam, The Netherlands, March 1999. Springer-Verlag.

[Saï00]   Hassen Saïdi. Model checking guided abstraction and analysis. In
            Jens Palsberg, editor, *Seventh International Static Analysis Symposium
            (SAS'00)*, volume 1824 of *Lecture Notes in Computer Science*, pages 377–
            396, Santa Barbara CA, June 2000. Springer-Verlag.

[SG97]   Hassen Saïdi and Susanne Graf. Construction of abstract state graphs
            with PVS. In Grumberg [Gru97], pages 72–83.

[Sha02]   Natarajan Shankar. Automated verification using deduction, exploration,
            and abstraction. In *Essays on Programming Methodology*. Springer-Verlag,
            2002. To appear.

[SS99]   Hassen Saïdi and N. Shankar. Abstract and model check while you prove.
            In Halbwachs and Peled [HP99], pages 443–454.

[SUM96]   H. B. Sipma, T. E. Uribe, and Z. Manna. Deductive model checking. In
            Alur and Henzinger [AH96], pages 208–219.

[TG02]   C.J. Tomlin and M.R. Greenstreet, editors. *Hybrid Systems: Computation
            and Control, 5th International Workshop, HSCC 2002*, volume 2289 of
            Lecture Notes in Computer Science, Stanford, CA, March 2002. Springer-
            Verlag.

[TK02]   Ashish Tiwari and Gaurav Khanna. Series of abstractions for hybrid au-
            tomata. In Tomlin and Greenstreet [TG02], pages 465–478.

[TRSS01]   Ashish Tiwari, Harald Rueß, Hassen Saïdi, and N. Shankar. A technique
            for invariant generation. In T. Margaria and W. Yi, editors, *Tools and Al-
            gorithms for the Construction and Analysis of Systems: 7th International
            Conference, TACAS 2001*, volume 2031 of *Lecture Notes in Computer Sci-
            ence*, pages 113–127, Genova, Italy, April 2001. Springer-Verlag.

[Uri98]   Tomás E. Uribe. *Abstraction-Based Deductive-Algorithmic Verification of
            Reactive Systems*. PhD thesis, Stanford University, 1998. Available as
            Stanford University Computer Science Department Technical Report No.
            STAN-CS-TR-99-1618.

[WL89]   P. Wolper and V. Lovinfosse. Verifying properties of large sets of processes
            with network invariants. In *Proceedings of the International Workshop on
            Automatic Verification Methods for Finite State Systems*, number 407 in
            Lecture Notes in Computer Science, pages 68–80, Grenoble, France, 1989.
            Springer-Verlag.

Combining Decision Procedures

Zohar Manna and Calogero G. Zarba

Stanford University
{zm,zarba}@theory.stanford.edu

Abstract. We give a detailed survey of the current state-of-the-art methods for combining decision procedures. We review the Nelson-Oppen combination method, Shostak method, and some very recent results on the combination of theories over non-disjoint signatures.

1 Introduction

Decision procedures are algorithms that can reason about the validity or satisfiability of classes of formulae in a given decidable theory, and always terminate with a positive or negative answer.

Decision procedures are at the heart of virtually every modern program analysis and program verification system. Decision procedures improve the overall efficiency of the verification system and relieve the user from plenty of boring and tedious interaction. In addition, decision procedures are available for many practical domains such as integers [44] and reals [54], as well as for many data structures frequently appearing in programs such as lists [41], arrays [52], sets [8], and multisets [60].

The major advantage of domain-specific decision procedures is efficiency. Fast and efficient decision procedures can be obtained by cleverly exploiting the structure of the domain itself. However, this efficiency comes at the price of specialization. Most verification conditions arising in program analysis and program verification typically involve a complex combination of multiple domains, which means that a decision procedure for a specific domain can be applied only if it is possible to combine it with the decision procedures for the other domains.

The field of combining decision procedures was initiated more than 20 years ago by Nelson and Oppen [35–37, 40] and Shostak [49, 50].

In 1979, Nelson and Oppen [37] proposed a very general approach for combining decision procedures. Given n theories T_1, ..., T_n satisfying certain conditions, their method combines the available decision procedures for T_1, ..., T_n into a single decision procedure for the satisfiability of quantifier-free formulae in the union theory $T_1 \cup \cdots \cup T_n$. The Nelson-Oppen combination method is at the base of the verification systems CVC [51], ESC [16], EVES [12], SDVS [31], and the Stanford Pascal Verifier [32]. A rigorous analysis of the Nelson-Oppen combination method can be found in [2, 45, 56].

In 1984, Shostak [50] proposed a more restricted method based on congruence closure for combining the quantifier-free theory of equality with theories that are what Shostak called *canonizable* and *solvable*. Shostak's method is at the base

B.K. Aichernig and T. Maibaum (Eds.): Formal Methods ..., LNCS 2757, pp. 381–422, 2003.

of the verification systems ICS [21], PVS [42], SVC [3], and STeP [7]. Shostak method is very popular, as witnessed by the impressive amount of research on it [4, 6, 13, 23, 24, 30, 46, 47, 58]. However, Shostak's original paper suffers from the lack of a rigorous correctness proof. Recently, it was discovered that a correct version of Shostak method can be obtained by recasting it as an instance of the more general Nelson-Oppen combination method [4, 47].

Both Shostak and Nelson-Oppen methods are restricted to the combination of theories over disjoint signatures, that is, theories whose signatures do not have any function or predicate symbol in common.

Combining theories over non-disjoint signatures is a much harder problem, as witnessed by the fact that, more than 20 years after its publication, the Nelson-Oppen combination method is still considered state-of-the-art.

Although it seems that it is not possible to obtain general decidability results in the non-disjoint case, recent research [45, 55, 57, 61] shows that it is always possible to combine decision procedures for theories whose signatures need not be disjoint into a semi-decision procedure for the unsatisfiability of formulae in the union theory.

This paper is organized as follow. In Section 2 we give some preliminary concepts and notations, and we briefly introduce some theories of interest in program verification. In Sections 3 and 4 we describe the Nelson-Oppen combination method, and in Section 5 we describe Shostak's method. In Section 6 we address the problem of combining theories over non-disjoint signatures, and in Section 7 we draw final conclusions.

2   Preliminaries

2.1   Syntax

A *signature* Σ consists of a set Σ^{C} of constants, a set Σ^{F} of function symbols, and a set Σ^{P} of predicate symbols.

A Σ-*term* is a first-order term constructed using variables and the symbols in Σ. A Σ-*atom* is either an expression of the form $P(t_1, \ldots, t_n)$, where $P \in \Sigma^{\mathrm{P}}$ and $t_1, \ldots, t_n$ are Σ-terms, or an expression of the form $s = t$, where $=$ is the logical equality symbol and s, t are Σ-terms. Σ-*literals* are Σ-atoms or expressions of the form $\neg A$, where A is a Σ-atom. Σ-*formulae* are constructed by applying in the standard way the binary logical connectives $\wedge$, $\vee$, $\rightarrow$, $\leftrightarrow$ and the quantifiers $\forall, \exists$ to Σ-literals. Σ-*sentences* are Σ-formulae with no free variables.

When Σ is irrelevant or clear from the context, we will simply write atom, literal, formula, and sentence in place of Σ-atom, Σ-literal, Σ-formula, and Σ-sentence.

If t is a term, we denote with $hd(t)$ the top symbol of t, that is, $hd(t) = f$ if t is of the form $f(t_1, \ldots, t_n)$, and $hd(t) = t$ if t is either a constant or a variable. If φ is either a term or a formula, we denote with $vars(\varphi)$ the set of variables occurring free in φ.

A *substitution* is a finite set $\{x_1 \leftarrow t_1, \ldots, x_n \leftarrow t_n\}$ of replacement pairs $x_i \leftarrow t_i$, where the x_i are variables, the t_i are terms, and each x_i is distinct from the corresponding expression t_i and from all the other variables x_j. The empty substitution $\{\ \}$ is denoted with ϵ. If σ is a substitution and t is a term, $t\sigma$ denotes the term obtained by applying the substitution σ to the term t. If σ and τ are substitutions, $\sigma \circ \tau$ denotes their *composition*, that is, $t(\sigma \circ \tau) = (t\sigma)\tau$, for each term t.

In the rest of this paper, we will often identify a finite sets of formulae $\{\varphi_1, \ldots, \varphi_n\}$ with the conjunction $\varphi_1 \wedge \cdots \wedge \varphi_n$.

2.2 Semantics

Definition 1. Let Σ be a signature. A Σ-*interpretation* $\mathcal{A}$ with domain A over a set of variables V is a map which interprets

- each variable $x \in V$ as an element $x^{\mathcal{A}} \in A$;
- each constant $c \in \Sigma^C$ as an element $c^{\mathcal{A}} \in A$;
- each function symbol $f \in \Sigma^F$ of arity n as a function $f^{\mathcal{A}} : A^n \to A$;
- each predicate symbol $P \in \Sigma^P$ of arity n as a subset $P^{\mathcal{A}}$ of A^n. □

In the rest of the paper we will use the convention that the calligraphic letters $\mathcal{A}$, $\mathcal{B}$, ... denote interpretations, and the corresponding Roman letters A, B, ... denote the domains of the interpretations.

For a term t, we denote with $t^{\mathcal{A}}$ the evaluation of t under the interpretation $\mathcal{A}$. Likewise, for a formula φ, we denote with $\varphi^{\mathcal{A}}$ the truth-value of φ under the interpretation $\mathcal{A}$.

Definition 2. A formula φ is

- *valid*, if it evaluates to true under all interpretations;
- *satisfiable*, if it evaluates to true under some interpretation;
- *unsatisfiable*, if it evaluates to false under all interpretations.

A set $\{\varphi_1, \ldots, \varphi_n\}$ of formulae is *valid*, *satisfiable*, *unsatisfiable* if so is the conjunction $\varphi_1 \wedge \cdots \wedge \varphi_n$. □

We say that two formulae φ and ψ are

- *equivalent*, if φ and ψ have the same truth-value under all interpretations;
- *equisatisfiable*, if φ is satisfiable if and only if so is ψ.

If φ is a formula and S is a set of formulae, the notation $S \models \varphi$ means that φ evaluates to true under every interpretation satisfying S.

Let Ω be a signature and let $\mathcal{A}$ be an Ω-interpretation over some set U of variables. For a subset Σ of Ω and a subset V of U, we denote with $\mathcal{A}^{\Sigma,V}$ the Σ-interpretation obtained by restricting $\mathcal{A}$ to interpret only the symbols in Σ and the variables in V. In particular, $\mathcal{A}^{\Sigma}$ stands for $\mathcal{A}^{\Sigma,\emptyset}$.

Definition 3. Let Σ be a signature, and let $\mathcal{A}$ and $\mathcal{B}$ be Σ-interpretations over some set V of variables. A map $h : A \to B$ is an *isomorphism* of $\mathcal{A}$ into $\mathcal{B}$ if the following conditions hold:

- h is bijective;
- $h(u^{\mathcal{A}}) = u^{\mathcal{B}}$ for each variable or constant $u \in V \cup \Sigma^{\mathrm{C}}$;
- $h(f^{\mathcal{A}}(a_1, \ldots, a_n)) = f^{\mathcal{B}}(h(a_1), \ldots, h(a_n))$, for each n-ary function symbol $f \in \Sigma^{\mathrm{F}}$ and $a_1, \ldots, a_n \in A$;
- $(a_1, \ldots, a_n) \in P^{\mathcal{A}}$ if and only if $(h(a_1), \ldots h(a_n)) \in P^{\mathcal{B}}$, for each n-ary predicate symbol $P \in \Sigma^{\mathrm{P}}$ and $a_1, \ldots, a_n \in A$.   □

We write $\mathcal{A} \cong \mathcal{B}$ to indicate that there exists an isomorphism of $\mathcal{A}$ into $\mathcal{B}$.

2.3   First-Order Theories

Definition 4. Let Σ be a signature. A Σ-*theory* is any set of Σ-sentences.
Given a Σ-theory T, a T-*interpretation* is a Σ-interpretation $\mathcal{A}$ such that all Σ-sentences in T evaluate to true under $\mathcal{A}$.   □

We will write theory instead of Σ-theory when Σ is irrelevant or clear from the context.

Definition 5. Given a Σ-theory T, a Σ-formula φ is

- T-*valid*, if φ evaluates to true under all T-interpretations;
- T-*satisfiable*, if φ evaluates to true under some T-interpretation;
- T-*unsatisfiable*, if φ evaluates to false under all T-interpretations.

A set $\{\varphi_1, \ldots, \varphi_n\}$ of formulae is T-*valid*, T-*satisfiable*, T-*unsatisfiable* if so is the conjunction $\varphi_1 \wedge \cdots \wedge \varphi_n$.   □

For a Σ-theory T, we say that two Σ-formulae φ and ψ are

- T-*equivalent*, if φ and ψ have the same truth-value under all T-interpretations;
- T-*equisatisfiable*, if φ is T-satisfiable if and only if so is ψ.

Given a Σ-theory T, we can define several types of *decision problems*. More precisely, if T is a Σ-theory then

- the *validity problem* for T is the problem of deciding, for each Σ-formula φ, whether or not φ is T-valid;
- the *satisfiability problem* for T is the problem of deciding, for each Σ-formula φ, whether or not φ is T-satisfiable;

Similarly, one can define the *quantifier-free validity problem* and the *quantifier-free satisfiability problem* for a Σ-theory T by restricting the formula φ to be tested for the desired property to be a quantifier-free Σ-formula.

We say that a decision problem is *decidable* if there exists a decision procedure for it. For instance, the validity problem for a Σ-theory T is decidable if there exists a decision procedure for the T-validity of every Σ-formula φ.

Sometimes it is convenient to reduce the (quantifier-free) validity problem for a theory T to the (quantifier-free) satisfiability problem for T. Note that this is always possible because every formula φ is T-valid if and only if $\neg\varphi$ is T-unsatisfiable. Thus, in order to test φ for T-validity, one only needs to test $\neg\varphi$ for T-unsatisfiability.

2.4   Special Theories

In this section we briefly introduce some theories of interest in program verification.

2.4.1   The Theory $T_{\mathbb{E}}$ of Equality

The theory $T_{\mathbb{E}}$ of equality is the empty theory with no axioms, that is, $T_{\mathbb{E}} = \emptyset$.

Due to the undecidability of first-order logic [9, 59], the validity problem for $T_{\mathbb{E}}$ is undecidable.

However, the quantifier-free validity problem for $T_{\mathbb{E}}$ is decidable, a result proved by Ackerman [1]. Efficient decision procedures based on congruence closure are due to Kozen [26], Shostak [48], Downey, Sethi and Tarjan [18], and Nelson and Oppen [38].

2.4.2   The Theory $T_{\mathbb{Z}}$ of Integers

Let $\Sigma_{\mathbb{Z}}$ be the signature containing a constant symbol c_n, for each integer n, a binary function symbol $+$, a unary function symbol $-$, and a binary predicate symbol $\leq$. The theory $T_{\mathbb{Z}}$ of integers is defined as the set of $\Sigma_{\mathbb{Z}}$-sentences that are true in the interpretation $\mathcal{A}$ whose domain A is the set $\mathbb{Z} = \{0, \pm 1, \pm 2, \ldots\}$ of integers, and interpreting the symbols in $\Sigma_{\mathbb{Z}}$ according to their standard meaning over $\mathbb{Z}$.

The validity problem for $T_{\mathbb{Z}}$ is decidable, a result proved in 1929 by Presburger [44] using a technique called quantifier elimination. According to this technique, a $\Sigma_{\mathbb{Z}}$-sentence φ is converted into a $T_{\mathbb{Z}}$-equivalent $\Sigma_{\mathbb{Z}}$-sentence ψ without quantifiers. Since ψ is a boolean combination of ground $\Sigma_{\mathbb{Z}}$-atoms, its truth value can be effectively computed.

Other quantifier elimination algorithms for $T_{\mathbb{Z}}$ are described in classic textbooks [19, 27]. The best known quantifier elimination algorithm for $T_{\mathbb{Z}}$ is due to Cooper [11], and has a triple exponential complexity upper bound $2^{2^{2^n}}$, where n is the size of the input formula [39]. Fischer and Rabin [22] proved that *any* quantifier elimination algorithm for $T_{\mathbb{Z}}$ has a nondeterministic doubly exponential lower bound 2^{2^n}.

Better complexity results can be obtained in the quantifier-free case. In fact, the quantifier-free validity problem for $T_{\mathbb{Z}}$ is $\mathcal{NP}$-complete [43].

If we add the multiplication symbol $\times$ to $\Sigma_{\mathbb{Z}}$, and we interpret it as the standard multiplication over $\mathbb{Z}$, then the resulting theory $T_{\mathbb{Z}}^{\times}$ has an undecidable validity problem [9]. In addition, Matiyasevich [33] proved that even the quantifier-free validity problem for $T_{\mathbb{Z}}^{\times}$ is undecidable.

2.4.3   The Theory $T_{\mathbb{R}}$ of Reals

Let $\Sigma_{\mathbb{R}}$ be the signature containing all the symbols in $\Sigma_{\mathbb{Z}}$, plus a constant c_r, for each rational number $r \in \mathbb{Q}$. The theory $T_{\mathbb{R}}$ of real numbers is the set of $\Sigma_{\mathbb{R}}$-sentences that are true in the interpretation $\mathcal{A}$ whose domain A is the set $\mathbb{R}$ of real numbers, and interpreting the symbols in $\Sigma_{\mathbb{R}}$ according to their standard meaning over $\mathbb{R}$.

The validity problem for $T_\mathbb{R}$ can be proved to be decidable using quantifier elimination [27]. The best known quantifier elimination algorithm for $T_\mathbb{R}$ is due to Ferrante and Rackoff [20], and has a double exponential complexity upper bound 2^{2^n}, where n is the size of the input formula. Fischer and Rabin [22] proved that *any* quantifier elimination algorithm for $T_\mathbb{R}$ has a nondeterministic exponential lower bound 2^n.

The problem of deciding the $T_\mathbb{R}$-satisfiability of conjunctions of quantifier-free $\Sigma_\mathbb{R}$-formulae is solvable in polynomial time [25]. Exponential methods like Simplex [35] and Fourier-Motzkin [29] also also commonly used.

In sharp contrast with the theory of integers, if we add the multiplication symbol $\times$ to $\Sigma_\mathbb{R}$, then the validity problem for the resulting theory $T_\mathbb{R}^\times$ is decidable. This result was proved by Tarski [54] using quantifier elimination. Tarski's method is impractical even for very simple formulae, and a more efficient method based on cylindrical algebraic decomposition is due to Collins [10]. The complexity of the quantifier elimination problem for $T_\mathbb{R}^\times$ is doubly exponential [14].

2.4.4   The Theory $T_\mathbb{L}$ of Lists

Let $\Sigma_\mathbb{L}$ be the signature containing a binary function symbol *cons* and two unary function symbols *car* and *cdr*. The theory $T_\mathbb{L}$ of lists is defined by the following axioms:

1. a construction axiom

$$(\forall x)[cons(car(x), cdr(x)) = x]$$

2. two selection axioms

$$(\forall x)(\forall y)[car(cons(x, y)) = x]$$
$$(\forall x)(\forall y)[cdr(cons(x, y)) = y]$$

3. an infinite number of acyclicity axioms

$$(\forall x)[car(x) \neq x]$$
$$(\forall x)[cdr(x) \neq x]$$
$$(\forall x)[car(car(x)) \neq x]$$
$$(\forall x)[car(cdr(x)) \neq x]$$

$$\vdots$$

Oppen [41] showed that the validity problem for $T_\mathbb{L}$ is decidable but not elementary recursive. In other words, for any positive integer k, there is no decision procedure for the $T_\mathbb{L}$-validity of $\Sigma_\mathbb{L}$-formulae that always stops in time $2^{2^{\cdot^{\cdot^{2^n}}}}$, where the height of the stack of 2's is k.

More reasonable complexity results hold for the quantifier-free case. The problem of deciding the $T_\mathbb{L}$-satisfiability of conjunctions of $\Sigma_\mathbb{L}$-literals is solvable in linear time [41].

2.4.5   The Theory $T_{\mathbb{A}}$ of Arrays

The theory $T_{\mathbb{A}}$ of arrays has signature $\Sigma_{\mathbb{A}} = \{read, write\}$. The intended meaning of the function symbols *read* and *write* is as follows:

- given an array a and an index i, $read(a, i)$ is the result of reading the array a at location i;
- given an array a, an index i, and an element e, $write(a, i, e)$ is a new array b which is the same as a, except that $read(b, i) = e$.

Formally, the theory $T_{\mathbb{A}}$ is defined by McCarthy's *read* and *write* axioms [34]:

$$(\forall a)(\forall i)(\forall e)[read(write(a, i, e), i) = e],$$
$$(\forall a)(\forall i)(\forall j)(\forall e)[i \neq j \;\rightarrow\; read(write(a, i, e), j) = read(a, j)],$$

and the following extensionality axiom

$$(\forall a)(\forall b)\left[((\forall i)(read(a, i) = read(b, i))) \;\rightarrow\; a = b\right].$$

The validity problem for $T_{\mathbb{A}}$ is undecidable [53], whereas the quantifier-free validity problem for $T_{\mathbb{A}}$ is decidable [17, 52].

3   Nelson-Oppen (Nondeterministic)

The Nelson-Oppen combination method combines decision procedures for first-order theories satisfying certain conditions into a single decision procedure for the union theory.

More formally, assume that we are given n signatures $\Sigma_1, \ldots, \Sigma_n$, and let T_i be a Σ_i-theory, for $i = 1, \ldots, n$. Also, assume that there exist decision procedures $P_1, \ldots, P_n$ such that, for $i = 1, \ldots, n$, P_i can decide the T_i-satisfiability of any quantifier-free Σ_i-formula. Using as black boxes the decision procedures P_i, the Nelson-Oppen combination method provides a way of deciding the $(T_1 \cup \cdots \cup T_n)$-satisfiability of $(\Sigma_1 \cup \cdots \cup \Sigma_n)$-formulae.

Three basic assumptions are needed for the Nelson-Oppen method to be applicable:

1. the formula φ to be tested for satisfiability must be *quantifier-free*;
2. the signatures $\Sigma_1, \ldots, \Sigma_n$ must be *disjoint*, that is $\Sigma_i \cap \Sigma_j = \emptyset$, for $i \neq j$;
3. the theories $T_1, \ldots, T_n$ must be *stably infinite* (see Section 3.1).

There are two versions of the Nelson-Oppen combination method: a nondeterministic one and a deterministic one. In this section we describe the nondeterministic version, since it is simpler to explain and easier to understand. We will describe the deterministic version in Section 4.

3.1   Stably Infinite Theories

Definition 6. A Σ-theory T is *stably infinite* if for every T-satisfiable quantifier-free Σ-formula φ there exists a T-interpretation $\mathcal{A}$ satisfying φ whose domain A is infinite.   □

Example 1. Let $\Sigma = \{a, b\}$, where a and b are constants. The Σ-theory

$$T = \{(\forall x)(x = a \vee x = b)\}$$

is not stably infinite. In fact, for every quantifier-free formula φ, there cannot exist an infinite T-interpretation satisfying φ, since every T-interpretation must have cardinality no greater than 2. $\qquad\square$

All the theories $T_{\mathbb{E}}, T_{\mathbb{Z}}, T_{\mathbb{R}}, T_{\mathbb{L}}, T_{\mathbb{A}}$ from Section 2.3 are stably infinite. As an example, we show that the theory $T_{\mathbb{E}}$ of equality is stably infinite.

Theorem 1. *The theory $T_{\mathbb{E}}$ of equality is stably infinite.* $\qquad\square$

PROOF. Let φ be a $T_{\mathbb{E}}$-satisfiable quantifier-free formula, and let $\mathcal{A}$ be a $T_{\mathbb{E}}$-interpretation satisfying φ.

We define a $T_{\mathbb{E}}$-interpretation $\mathcal{B}$ as follows. Fix an infinite set A' disjoint from A, and fix an arbitrary element $a_0 \in A \cup A'$. Then, we let

$$B = A \cup A'$$

and

– for variables and constants:
$$u^{\mathcal{B}} = u^{\mathcal{A}}$$

– for function symbols of arity n:

$$f^{\mathcal{B}}(a_1, \ldots, a_n) = \begin{cases} f^{\mathcal{A}}(a_1, \ldots, a_n) & \text{if } a_1, \ldots, a_n \in A \\ a_0 & \text{otherwise} \end{cases}$$

– for predicate symbols of arity n:

$$(a_1, \ldots, a_n) \in P^{\mathcal{B}} \quad \Longleftrightarrow \quad a_1, \ldots, a_n \in A \text{ and } (a_1, \ldots, a_n) \in P^{\mathcal{A}}.$$

Clearly, $\mathcal{B}$ is an infinite $T_{\mathbb{E}}$-interpretation satisfying φ. $\qquad\blacksquare$

3.2 The Procedure

In this section we decribe the nondeterministic version of the Nelson-Oppen combination method.

To simplify the presentation, we restrict ourselves to the satisfiability of conjunctions of literals. Note that this does not cause any loss of generality since every quantifier-free formula φ can be effectively converted into an equisatisfiable formula in disjunctive normal form $\varphi_1 \vee \cdots \vee \varphi_n$, where each φ_i is a conjunction of literals. Then φ is satisfiable if and only if at least one of the disjuncts φ_i is satisfiable.

In addition, without loss of generality we can restrict ourselves to the combination of just two theories. In fact, once we know how to combine two theories, we can combine n theories, for each $n \geq 2$. For instance, suppose that we want to combine decision procedures P_1, P_2, P_3 for three theories T_1, T_2, T_3. Then we can first combine P_1 and P_2 into a decision procedure $P_{1\&2}$ for $T_1 \cup T_2$, and then we combine $P_{1\&2}$ and P_3 into a decision procedure $P_{1\&2\&3}$ for the theory $T_1 \cup T_2 \cup T_3$.

Thus, let T_i be a stably infinite Σ_i-theory, for $i = 1, 2$, and let $\Sigma_1 \cap \Sigma_2 = \emptyset$. Also, let Γ be a conjunction of $(\Sigma_1 \cup \Sigma_2)$-literals.

The nondeterministic version of the Nelson-Oppen combination method consists of two phases: *Variable Abstraction* and *Check*.

3.2.1   First Phase: Variable Abstraction

Let Γ be a conjunction of $(\Sigma_1 \cup \Sigma_2)$-literals. In the first phase of the Nelson-Oppen combination method we convert Γ into a conjunction $\Gamma_1 \cup \Gamma_2$ satisfying the following properties:

(a) each literal in Γ_i is a Σ_i-literal, for $i = 1, 2$;
(b) $\Gamma_1 \cup \Gamma_2$ is $(T_1 \cup T_2)$-satisfiable if and only if so is Γ.

This can be done by repeatedly applying the following transformations, until nothing more can be done[1].

- Replace each term of the form

$$f(t_1, \ldots, t, \ldots, t_n)$$

in Γ, where $f \in \Sigma_i$ and $hd(t) \in \Sigma_{3-i}$, for some $i \in \{1, 2\}$, with the term

$$f(t_1, \ldots, w, \ldots, t_n),$$

where w is a newly introduced variable, and add the equality

$$w = t$$

to Γ.
- Replace each literal of the form

$$P(t_1, \ldots, t, \ldots, t_n)$$

in Γ, where $P \in \Sigma_i$ and $hd(t) \in \Sigma_{3-i}$, for some $i \in \{1, 2\}$, with the literal

$$P(t_1, \ldots, w, \ldots, t_n),$$

where w is a newly introduced variable, and add the equation

$$w = t$$

to Γ. Literals of the form $\neg P(t_1, \ldots, t, \ldots, t_n)$ are treated similarly.

---

[1] In the following, note that when $i \in \{1, 2\}$, then $3 - i$ is the "complement" of i.

– Replace each equality of the form

$$s = t$$

in Γ, where $hd(s) \in \Sigma_i$ and $hd(t) \in \Sigma_{3-i}$, with the equalities

$$w = s, \quad w = t,$$

where w is a newly introduced variable.
– Replace each literal of the form

$$s \neq t$$

in Γ, where $hd(s) \in \Sigma_i$ and $hd(t) \in \Sigma_{3-i}$, with the literals

$$w_1 \neq w_2, \quad w_1 = s, \quad w_2 = t,$$

where w_1 and w_2 are newly introduced variables.

Clearly, the above process must eventually terminate. In addition, the resulting conjunction can be written as $\Gamma_1 \cup \Gamma_2$ where Γ_i contains only Σ_i-literals and $\Gamma_1 \cup \Gamma_2$ is $(T_1 \cup T_2)$-satisfiable if and only if so is Γ^2.

Example 2. Let $\Sigma_1 = \{f\}$ and let $\Sigma_2 = \{g\}$, where f, g are unary function symbols. Let us apply the Variable Abstraction phase to the conjunction of literals

$$\Gamma = \{f(g(x)) \neq g(f(x))\}.$$

First, we "purify" the term $f(g(x))$, by introducing a new variable w_1, and obtaining the new conjunction

$$\left\{ \begin{array}{l} w_1 = g(x), \\ f(w_1) \neq g(f(x)) \end{array} \right\}.$$

We then purify the term $g(f(x))$, obtaining

$$\left\{ \begin{array}{l} w_1 = g(x), \\ w_2 = f(x), \\ f(w_1) \neq g(w_2) \end{array} \right\}.$$

Finally, we purify the disequality, obtaining

$$\left\{ \begin{array}{l} w_1 = g(x), \\ w_2 = f(x), \\ w_3 = f(w_1), \\ w_4 = g(w_2), \\ w_3 \neq w_4 \end{array} \right\}.$$

---

[2] If x, y are variables, a literal of the form $x = y$ or $x \neq y$ is both a Σ_1-literal and a Σ_2-literal. Therefore, such a literal can be arbitrarily placed in either Γ_1 or Γ_2, or both.

We conclude the Variable Abstraction phase by partitioning the literals, obtaining

$$\Gamma_1 = \left\{ \begin{array}{l} w_2 = f(x), \\ w_3 = f(w_1) \end{array} \right\}, \qquad \Gamma_2 = \left\{ \begin{array}{l} w_1 = g(x), \\ w_4 = g(w_2), \\ w_3 \neq w_4 \end{array} \right\}$$

Note that we chose to place the literal $w_3 \neq w_4$ in Γ_2, but it would have been equally correct to place it in Γ_1, as well as to place it in both Γ_1 and Γ_2.   □

We call $\Gamma_1 \cup \Gamma_2$ a conjunction of literals in $\langle \Sigma_1, \Sigma_2 \rangle$-*separate* form. We also denote with $shared(\Gamma_1, \Gamma_2)$ the set of variables occurring in both Γ_1 and Γ_2, that is, $shared(\Gamma_1, \Gamma_2) = vars(\Gamma_1) \cap vars(\Gamma_2)$.

3.2.2 Second Phase: Check

Let $\Gamma_1 \cup \Gamma_2$ be a conjunction of literals in $\langle \Sigma_1, \Sigma_2 \rangle$-separate form generated in the Variable Abstraction phase.

Definition 7. Let E be an equivalence relation over some set V of variables. The *arrangement* of V induced by E is defined as the conjunction:

$$\alpha(V, E) = \{x = y : x, y \in V \text{ and } xEy\} \cup$$
$$\{x \neq y : x, y \in V \text{ and not } xEy\}$$ □

In the second phase of the Nelson-Oppen combination method we perform the following two checks, for every equivalence relation E of $shared(\Gamma_1, \Gamma_2)$.

1. Check whether $\Gamma_1 \cup \alpha(shared(\Gamma_1, \Gamma_2), E)$ is T_1-satisfiable.
2. Check whether $\Gamma_2 \cup \alpha(shared(\Gamma_1, \Gamma_2), E)$ is T_2-satisfiable.

If there exists an equivalence relation E of $shared(\Gamma_1, \Gamma_2)$ for which both check 1 and check 2 succeed, then we declare that $\Gamma_1 \cup \Gamma_2$ is $(T_1 \cup T_2)$-satisfiable. Otherwise, we declare $\Gamma_1 \cup \Gamma_2$ to be $(T_1 \cup T_2)$-unsatisfiable.

We will show the correctness of the method in Section 3.4.

3.3 Examples

To illustrate how the Nelson-Oppen combination method works, let us consider some examples.

Example 3. Let us consider the combination of the theory $T_{\mathbb{Z}}$ of integers with the theory $T_{\mathbb{E}}$ of equality, and note that the conjunction

$$\Gamma = \left\{ \begin{array}{l} 1 \leq x, \\ x \leq 2, \\ f(x) \neq f(1), \\ f(x) \neq f(2) \end{array} \right\}$$

is $(T_\mathbb{Z} \cup T_\mathbb{E})$-unsatisfiable. In fact, the first two literals imply $x = 1 \vee x = 2$. But then $f(x) = f(1) \vee f(x) = f(2)$, which contradicts the last two literals.

We want to show that Γ is $(T_\mathbb{Z} \cup T_\mathbb{E})$-unsatisfiable using the Nelson-Oppen combination method. In the Variable Abstraction phase we introduce two new variables w_1, w_2, and we obtain the conjunctions

$$\Gamma_\mathbb{Z} = \begin{cases} 1 \leq x, \\ x \leq 2, \\ w_1 = 1, \\ w_2 = 2 \end{cases}, \qquad \Gamma_\mathbb{E} = \left\{ \begin{matrix} f(x) \neq f(w_1), \\ f(x) \neq f(w_2) \end{matrix} \right\}.$$

Let $V = shared(\Gamma_\mathbb{Z}, \Gamma_\mathbb{E}) = \{x, w_1, w_2\}$. There are 5 possible equivalence relations E to examine.

Case 1: $x E w_1$, $x E w_2$, $w_1 E w_2$.
Since $T_\mathbb{E} \cup \Gamma_\mathbb{E}$ implies $x \neq w_1$, it follows that $\Gamma_\mathbb{E} \cup \{x = w_1, x = w_2, w_1 = w_2\}$ is $T_\mathbb{E}$-unsatisfiable.

Case 2: $x E w_1$, not $x E w_2$, not $w_1 E w_2$.
Since $T_\mathbb{E} \cup \Gamma_\mathbb{E}$ implies $x \neq w_1$, it follows that $\Gamma_\mathbb{E} \cup \{x = w_1, x \neq w_2, w_1 \neq w_2\}$ is $T_\mathbb{E}$-unsatisfiable.

Case 3: not $x E w_1$, $x E w_2$, not $w_1 E w_2$.
Since $T_\mathbb{E} \cup \Gamma_\mathbb{E}$ implies $x \neq w_2$, it follows that $\Gamma_\mathbb{E} \cup \{x \neq w_1, x = w_2, w_1 \neq w_2\}$ is $T_\mathbb{E}$-unsatisfiable.

Case 4: not $x E w_1$, not $x E w_2$, $w_1 E w_2$.
Since $T_\mathbb{Z} \cup \Gamma_\mathbb{Z}$ implies $w_1 \neq w_2$, it follows that $\Gamma_\mathbb{Z} \cup \{x \neq w_1, x \neq w_2, w_1 = w_2\}$ is $T_\mathbb{Z}$-unsatisfiable.

Case 5: not $x E w_1$, not $x E w_2$, not $w_1 E w_2$.
Since $T_\mathbb{Z} \cup \Gamma_\mathbb{Z}$ implies the disjunction $x = w_1 \vee x = w_2$, it follows that $\Gamma_\mathbb{Z} \cup \{x \neq w_1, x \neq w_2, w_1 \neq w_2\}$ is $T_\mathbb{Z}$-unsatisfiable.

Thus, for every equivalence relation E of V we have that either $\Gamma_\mathbb{Z} \cup \alpha(V, E)$ is $T_\mathbb{Z}$-unsatisfiable or $\Gamma_\mathbb{E} \cup \alpha(V, E)$ is $T_\mathbb{E}$-unsatisfiable. We can therefore conclude that Γ is $(T_\mathbb{Z} \cup T_\mathbb{E})$-unsatisfiable. $\qquad\square$

In the next example we consider a formula that is satisfiable in the union of two stably infinite theories.

Example 4. Let us consider again the theory $T_\mathbb{Z}$ of integers and the theory $T_\mathbb{E}$ of equality, and note that the conjunction

$$\Gamma = \left\{ \begin{matrix} x + y = z, \\ f(x) \neq f(y) \end{matrix} \right\}$$

is $(T_\mathbb{Z} \cup T_\mathbb{E})$-satisfiable. For instance, a satisfying $(T_\mathbb{Z} \cup T_\mathbb{E})$-interpretation $\mathcal{A}$ can be obtained by letting $A = \mathbb{Z}$ and $x^\mathcal{A} = 1$, $y^\mathcal{A} = 2$, $z^\mathcal{A} = 3$, $f^\mathcal{A}(a) = a$ for each $a \in \mathbb{Z}$.

The Variable Abstraction phase does not introduce new variables, and simply returns the pure conjunctions

$$\Gamma_\mathbb{Z} = \{x + y = z\}, \qquad \Gamma_\mathbb{E} = \{f(x) \neq f(y)\}.$$

Since $shared(\Gamma_{\mathbb{Z}}, \Gamma_{\mathbb{E}}) = \{x, y\}$, there are only two equivalence relations to examine: either xEy or not xEy. In the former case $\Gamma_{\mathbb{E}} \cup \{x = y\}$ is $T_{\mathbb{E}}$-unsatisfiable. However, in the latter case we have that $\Gamma_{\mathbb{Z}} \cup \{x \neq y\}$ is $T_{\mathbb{Z}}$-satisfiable and that $\Gamma_{\mathbb{E}} \cup \{x \neq y\}$ is $T_{\mathbb{E}}$-satisfiable. Thus, we correctly conclude that Γ is $(T_{\mathbb{Z}} \cup T_{\mathbb{E}})$-satisfiable. □

In the previous example the conclusion of the Nelson-Oppen method was correct because both theories were stably infinite. The next example shows that when one of the combined theories is not stably infinite the Nelson-Oppen method may not be correct.

Example 5. Let $\Sigma = \{a, b\}$, where a and b are constants, and consider the combination of the theory $T_{\mathbb{E}}$ of equality with the Σ-theory

$$T = \{(\forall x)(x = a \lor x = b)\}.$$

Recall that in Example 1 we saw that T is not stably infinite.

The conjunction

$$\Gamma = \begin{Bmatrix} a = b, \\ f(x) \neq f(y) \end{Bmatrix}$$

is $(T \cup T_{\mathbb{E}})$-unsatisfiable. In fact $T \cup \{a = b\}$ entails $(\forall u, v)(u = v)$, which contradicts the disequality in Γ.

After the Variable Abstraction phase we obtain the conjunctions

$$\Gamma_1 = \{a = b\}, \qquad\qquad \Gamma_{\mathbb{E}} = \{f(x) \neq f(y)\}.$$

Since $shared(\Gamma_1, \Gamma_{\mathbb{E}}) = \emptyset$, we only need to check Γ_1 for T-satisfiability and $\Gamma_{\mathbb{E}}$ for $T_{\mathbb{E}}$-satisfiability.

We have that Γ_1 is T-satisfiable: a satisfying T-interpretation $\mathcal{A}$ is obtained by letting $A = \{\bullet\}$ and $a^{\mathcal{A}} = b^{\mathcal{A}} = \bullet$. In addition, $\Gamma_{\mathbb{E}}$ is also $T_{\mathbb{E}}$-satisfiable: a $T_{\mathbb{E}}$-interpretation $\mathcal{B}$ satisfying $\Gamma_{\mathbb{E}}$ is obtained by letting $B = \{\bullet, \circ\}$ and $x^{\mathcal{B}} = \bullet$, $f^{\mathcal{B}}(\bullet) = \bullet$, $y^{\mathcal{B}} = \circ$, $f^{\mathcal{B}}(\circ) = \circ$.

Since Γ_1 is T-satisfiable and $\Gamma_{\mathbb{E}}$ is $T_{\mathbb{E}}$-satisfiable, the Nelson-Oppen method *incorrectly* concludes that Γ is $(T \cup T_{\mathbb{E}})$-satisfiable. □

3.4   Correctness

The correctness of the Nelson-Oppen combination method is based upon the following fundamental theorem, whose proof can be found in the appendix.

Theorem 2 (Combination Theorem for Disjoint Signatures). *Let Φ_i be a set of Σ_i-formulae, for $i = 1, 2$, and let $\Sigma_1 \cap \Sigma_2 = \emptyset$.*

Then $\Phi_1 \cup \Phi_2$ is satisfiable if and only if there exists an interpretation $\mathcal{A}$ satisfying Φ_1 and an interpretation $\mathcal{B}$ satisfying Φ_2 such that:

(i) $|A| = |B|$,
(ii) $x^{\mathcal{A}} = y^{\mathcal{A}}$ if and only if $x^{\mathcal{B}} = y^{\mathcal{B}}$, for every variable $x, y \in shared(\Phi_1, \Phi_2)$. □

The following theorem shows that the Nelson-Oppen combination method is correct.

Theorem 3. *Let T_i be a stably infinite Σ_i-theory, for $i = 1, 2$, and let $\Sigma_1 \cap \Sigma_2 = \emptyset$. Also, let $\Gamma_1 \cup \Gamma_2$ be a conjunction of literals in $\langle \Sigma_1, \Sigma_2 \rangle$-separate form.*

Then $\Gamma_1 \cup \Gamma_2$ is $(T_1 \cup T_2)$-satisfiable if and only if there exists an equivalence relation E of $V = \text{shared}(\Gamma_1, \Gamma_2)$ such that $\Gamma_i \cup \alpha(V, E)$ is T_i-satisfiable, for $i = 1, 2$. □

PROOF. Let $\mathcal{M}$ be a $(T_1 \cup T_2)$-interpretation satisfying $\Gamma_1 \cup \Gamma_2$. We define an equivalence relation E of V by letting xEy if and only if $x^{\mathcal{M}} = y^{\mathcal{M}}$, for every variable $x, y \in V$. By construction, $\mathcal{M}$ is a T_i-interpretation satisfying $\Gamma_i \cup \alpha(V, E)$, for $i = 1, 2$.

Vice versa, assume that there exists an equivalence relation E of V such that $\Gamma_i \cup \alpha(V, E)$ is T_i-satisfiable, for $i = 1, 2$. Since T_1 is stably infinite, there exists a T_1-interpretation $\mathcal{A}$ satisfying $\Gamma_1 \cup \alpha(V, E)$ such that A is countably infinite. Similarly, there exists a T_2-interpretation $\mathcal{B}$ satisfying $\Gamma_2 \cup \alpha(V, E)$ such that B is countably infinite.

But then $|A| = |B|$, and $x^{\mathcal{A}} = y^{\mathcal{A}}$ if and only if $x^{\mathcal{B}} = y^{\mathcal{B}}$, for every variable $x, y \in V$. We can therefore apply Theorem 2, and obtain the existence of a $(T_1 \cup T_2)$-interpretation satisfying $\Gamma_1 \cup \Gamma_2$. ■

Combining Theorem 3 with the observation that there is only a finite number of equivalence relations of any finite set of variables, we obtain the following decidability result.

Theorem 4. *Let T_i be a stably infinite Σ_i-theory, for $i = 1, 2$, and let $\Sigma_1 \cap \Sigma_2 = \emptyset$. Also, assume that the quantifier-free T_i-satisfiability problem is decidable.*

Then the quantifier-free $(T_1 \cup T_2)$-satisfiability problem is decidable. □

The following theorem generalizes Theorem 4 for any number n of theories, with $n \geq 2$.

Theorem 5. *Let T_i be a stably infinite Σ_i-theory, for $i = 1, \ldots, n$, and let $\Sigma_i \cap \Sigma_j = \emptyset$, for $i \neq j$. Also, assume that the quantifier-free T_i-satisfiability problem is decidable.*

Then the quantifier-free $(T_1 \cup \cdots \cup T_n)$-satisfiability problem is decidable. □

PROOF. By induction on n, we will prove the stronger result that $T_1 \cup \cdots \cup T_n$ is a stably infinite theory with a decidable quantifier-free satisfiability problem.

For the base case ($n = 2$), by Theorem 4 we know that the quantifier-free $(T_1 \cup T_2)$-satisfiability problem is decidable. In addition, as a corollary of the proof of Theorem 3, it follows that $T_1 \cup T_2$ is stably infinite.

For the inductive step ($n > 2$), we can obtain a decision procedure for the quantifier-free $(T_1 \cup \cdots \cup T_n)$-satisfiability problem by applying a Nelson-Oppen combination between the theories $T_1 \cup \cdots \cup T_{n-1}$ and T_n. Note that this is possible because by the inductive hypothesis we have that $T_1 \cup \cdots \cup T_{n-1}$ is a stably infinite theory with a decidable quantifier-free satisfiability problem. Note also that $(T_1 \cup \cdots \cup T_{n-1}) \cup T_n$ is stably infinite (corollary of the proof of Theorem 3). ■

n	B_n
1	1
2	2
3	5
4	15
5	52
6	203
7	877
8	$4,140$
9	$21,147$
10	$115,975$
11	$678,570$
12	$4,213,597$

Fig. 1. Bell numbers.

3.5   Complexity

The main source of complexity of the nondeterministic version of the Nelson-Oppen combination method is given by the Check phase. In this phase, the decision procedures for T_1 and T_2 are called once for each equivalence relation E of the set of shared variables $shared(\Gamma_1, \Gamma_2)$. The number of such equivalence relations, also known as a *Bell number* [5], grows exponentially in the number of variables in $shared(\Gamma_1, \Gamma_2)$ (see [15] for an in-depth asymptotic analysis).

Figure 1 shows the first 12 Bell numbers. Note when $shared(\Gamma_1, \Gamma_2)$ has 12 variables, there are already more than 4 million equivalence relations!

Despite these discouraging numbers, the nondeterministic version of the Nelson-Oppen combination method provides the following $\mathcal{NP}$-completeness result due to Oppen [40].

Theorem 6. *Let T_i be a stably infinite Σ_i-theory, for $i = 1, 2$, and let $\Sigma_1 \cap \Sigma_2 = \emptyset$. Also, assume that the quantifier-free T_i-satisfiability problem is in $\mathcal{NP}$.*
Then the quantifier-free $(T_1 \cup T_2)$-satisfiability problem is in $\mathcal{NP}$.   □

PROOF. It suffices to note that it is possible to guess an equivalence relation of any set of n elements using a number of choices that is polynomial in n.   ■

3.6   More on Stable Infiniteness

In Section 3.4 we proved that the Nelson-Oppen method is correct under the assumption that the theories T_1, T_2 are stably infinite.

It turns out that stable infiniteness is not a necessary condition for the correctness of the method, but only a *sufficient* one. To see this, consider two theories T_1, T_2 over disjoint signatures for which there exists an integer $n > 0$ such that

$$T_k \models (\exists x_1) \cdots (\exists x_n) \left[\left(\bigwedge_{i \neq j} x_i \neq x_j \right) \wedge (\forall y) \left(\bigvee_{i=1}^{n} y = x_i \right) \right], \quad \text{for } k = 1, 2.$$

In other words, all interpretations satisfying T_i have cardinality n.

Despite the fact that T_1 and T_2 are not stably infinite, in this case the Nelson-Oppen combination method can still be applied correctly, as the following theorem shows.

Theorem 7. *Let T_i be a Σ_i theory, for $i = 1, 2$, let $\Sigma_1 \cap \Sigma_2 = \emptyset$, and assume that there exists a positive integer n such that all T_i-interpretations have cardinality n. Also, assume that the quantifier-free T_i-satisfiability problem is decidable.*

Then the quantifier-free $(T_1 \cup T_2)$-satisfiability problem is decidable. □

PROOF. The proof follows, with minor variations, the same pattern of Section 3.4. ∎

4   Nelson-Oppen (Deterministic)

Because the number of equivalence relations of a set grows exponentially in the number of elements of the set (cf. Figure 1), the nondeterministic version of the Nelson-Oppen combination method is not amenable of a practical and efficient implementation.

A more practical approach is given by the deterministic version of the Nelson-Oppen combination method. In this version we do not enumerate all possible equivalence relations among shared variables, but instead we use the given decision procedures for each theory in order to detect all equalities that must necessarily hold given the input conjunction Γ.

4.1   The Procedure

Let T_i be a stably infinite Σ_i-theory, for $i = 1, 2$, and let $\Sigma_1 \cap \Sigma_2 = \emptyset$. Also, let Γ be a conjunction of $(\Sigma_1 \cup \Sigma_2)$-literals.

The deterministic version of the Nelson-Oppen combination method is obtained from the nondeterministic version by replacing the Check phase with an Equality Propagation phase.

Instead of enumerating all possible equivalence relations among shared variables, in the Equality Propagation phase we manipulate *derivations* that take the form of a tree labeled with states. A *state* is either the logical symbol *false*, or a triple of the form

$$\langle \Gamma_1, \Gamma_2, E \rangle$$

where

- Γ_i is a set of Σ_i-literals, for $i = 1, 2$;
- E is a set of equalities among variables.

Contradiction rule

$$\frac{\langle \Gamma_1, \Gamma_2, E \rangle}{false} \qquad \text{if } \Gamma_i \cup E \text{ is } T_i\text{-unsatisfiable, for some } i \in \{1,2\}$$

Equality Propagation rule

$$\frac{\langle \Gamma_1, \Gamma_2, E \rangle}{\langle \Gamma_1, \Gamma_2, E \cup \{x = y\} \rangle} \qquad \begin{array}{l} \text{if } x, y \in shared(\Gamma_1, \Gamma_2) \text{ and } x = y \notin E \text{ and} \\ T_i \cup \Gamma_i \cup E \models x = y, \text{ for some } i \in \{1,2\} \end{array}$$

Case Split rule

$$\frac{\langle \Gamma_1, \Gamma_2, E \rangle}{\langle \Gamma_1, \Gamma_2, E \cup \{x_1 = y_1\} \rangle \quad | \quad \cdots \quad | \quad \langle \Gamma_1, \Gamma_2, E \cup \{x_n = y_n\} \rangle}$$

$$\text{if } x_1, \ldots, x_n, y_1, \ldots, y_n \in shared(\Gamma_1, \Gamma_2) \text{ and}$$
$$\{x_1 = y_1, \ldots, x_n = y_n\} \cap E = \emptyset \text{ and}$$
$$T_i \cup \Gamma_i \cup E \models \bigvee_{j=1}^{n} x_j = y_j, \text{for some } i \in \{1,2\}$$

Fig. 2. Nelson-Oppen rules

For instance, the triple

$$\langle \{1 \leq x, y \leq 2\}, \ \{f(x) \neq f(y)\}, \ \{x = y\} \rangle .$$

is a state.

Given a conjunction $\Gamma_1 \cup \Gamma_2$ of literals in $\langle \Sigma_1, \Sigma_2 \rangle$-separate form, the *initial derivation* D_0 is a tree with only one node labeled with the state

$$\langle \Gamma_1, \Gamma_2, \emptyset \rangle .$$

Then, we use the rules in Figure 2 to construct a succession of derivations $D_0, D_1, \ldots, D_n$. The rules are to be applied as follows. Assume that D_i is a derivation containing one leaf labeled with the premise s of a rule of the form

$$\frac{s}{s_1 \quad | \quad \cdots \quad | \quad s_n}$$

Then we can construct a new derivation D_{i+1} which is the same as D_i, except that the leaf labeled with s has now n children labeled with $s_1, \ldots, s_n$.

Intuitively, the Contradiction rule detects inconsistencies, and the Equality Propagation and Case Split rules increase the set E of equalities in order to incrementally construct the desired equivalence relation.

If during the Equality Propagation phase we obtain a derivation in which all leaves are labeled with *false*, then we declare that the initial conjunction Γ is $(T_1 \cup T_2)$-unsatisfiable. If instead we obtain a derivation containing a branch whose leaf node is not labeled with *false*, and no rule can be applied to it, then we declare that Γ is $(T_1 \cup T_2)$-satisfiable.

We will show the correctness of the method in Section 4.3.

4.2   Examples

Example 6. Let us consider the combination of the theory $T_{\mathbb{R}}$ of reals with the theory $T_{\mathbb{E}}$ of equality. Note that the conjunction[3]

$$\Gamma = \left\{ \begin{array}{l} f(f(x) - f(y)) \neq f(z), \\ x \leq y, \\ y + z \leq x, \\ 0 \leq z \end{array} \right\}$$

is $(T_{\mathbb{R}} \cup T_{\mathbb{E}})$-unsatisfiable. In fact, the last three literals imply $x = y$ and $z = 0$, so that the first literal simplifies to $f(0) \neq f(0)$.

After applying the Variable Abstraction phase, we obtain the pure conjunctions

$$\Gamma_{\mathbb{R}} = \left\{ \begin{array}{l} x \leq y, \\ y + z \leq x, \\ 0 \leq z, \\ w_3 = w_1 - w_2 \end{array} \right\} \qquad \Gamma_{\mathbb{E}} = \left\{ \begin{array}{l} f(w_3) \neq f(z), \\ w_1 = f(x), \\ w_2 = f(y) \end{array} \right\}$$

Since $shared(\Gamma_{\mathbb{R}}, \Gamma_{\mathbb{E}}) = \{x, y, z, w_1, w_2, w_3\}$, Figure 1 tells us that there are 203 possible equivalence relations among the shared variables. Clearly, it is infeasible to enumerate all of them by hand. Nevertheless, we can quickly detect that Γ is $(T_{\mathbb{R}} \cup T_{\mathbb{E}})$-unsatisfiable with the following derivation.

$$s_0 : \langle \Gamma_{\mathbb{R}}, \Gamma_{\mathbb{E}}, \emptyset \rangle$$

$$s_1 : \langle \Gamma_{\mathbb{R}}, \Gamma_{\mathbb{E}}, \{x = y\} \rangle$$

$$s_2 : \langle \Gamma_{\mathbb{R}}, \Gamma_{\mathbb{E}}, \{x = y, w_1 = w_2\} \rangle$$

$$s_3 : \langle \Gamma_{\mathbb{R}}, \Gamma_{\mathbb{E}}, \{x = y, w_1 = w_2, z = w_3\} \rangle$$

$$s_4 : false$$

In the above derivation, the inferences can be justified as follows:

- s_1 follows by the Equality Propagation rule since $T_{\mathbb{R}} \cup \Gamma_{\mathbb{R}} \models x = y$;
- s_2 follows by the Equality Propagation rule since $T_{\mathbb{E}} \cup \Gamma_{\mathbb{E}} \cup \{x = y\} \models w_1 = w_2$;
- s_3 follows by the Equality Propagation rule since $T_{\mathbb{R}} \cup \Gamma_{\mathbb{R}} \cup \{w_1 = w_2\} \models z = w_3$;

---

[3] Taken from [35].

- s_4 follows by the Contradiction rule since $\Gamma_{\mathbb{E}} \cup \{z = w_3\}$ is $T_{\mathbb{E}}$-unsatisfiable.

Hence, we conclude that Γ is $(T_{\mathbb{R}} \cup T_{\mathbb{E}})$-unsatisfiable.   □

Example 7. Consider the theory $T_{\mathbb{Z}}$ of integers and the theory $T_{\mathbb{E}}$ of equality. In Example 3 we showed that the conjunction

$$\Gamma = \begin{cases} 1 \le x, \\ x \le 2, \\ f(x) \ne f(1), \\ f(x) \ne f(2) \end{cases}$$

is $(T_{\mathbb{Z}} \cup T_{\mathbb{E}})$-unsatisfiable using the nondeterministic version of the Nelson-Oppen combination method. Let us now use the deterministic version.

After the Variable Abstraction phase we obtain the pure conjunctions

$$\Gamma_{\mathbb{Z}} = \begin{cases} 1 \le x, \\ x \le 2, \\ w_1 = 1, \\ w_2 = 2 \end{cases}, \qquad \Gamma_{\mathbb{E}} = \begin{cases} f(x) \ne f(w_1), \\ f(x) \ne f(w_2) \end{cases}.$$

We have the following derivation

$$s_0 : \langle \Gamma_{\mathbb{Z}}, \Gamma_{\mathbb{E}}, \emptyset \rangle$$

$$s_1 : \langle \Gamma_{\mathbb{Z}}, \Gamma_{\mathbb{E}}, \{x = w_1\} \rangle \qquad s_2 : \langle \Gamma_{\mathbb{Z}}, \Gamma_{\mathbb{E}}, \{x = w_2\} \rangle$$

$$s_3 : false \qquad\qquad s_4 : false$$

Note that the inferences can be justified as follows:

- s_1 and s_2 follow by the Case Split rule since $T_{\mathbb{Z}} \cup \Gamma_{\mathbb{Z}} \models x = w_1 \vee x = w_2$;
- s_3 follows from s_1 by the Contradiction rule since $\Gamma_{\mathbb{E}} \cup \{x = w_1\}$ is $T_{\mathbb{E}}$-unsatisfiable;
- s_4 follows from s_2 by the Contradiction rule since $\Gamma_{\mathbb{E}} \cup \{x = w_2\}$ is $T_{\mathbb{E}}$-unsatisfiable.

Since all leaves are labeled with *false*, we conclude that Γ is $(T_{\mathbb{Z}} \cup T_{\mathbb{E}})$-unsatisfiable.   □

4.3   Correctness

We now prove that the deterministic version of the Nelson-Oppen combination method is correct.

The following lemma shows that the inference rules are terminating.

Lemma 1. *The inference rules in Figure 2 form a terminating inference system.*   □

PROOF. The claim easily follows by noting that since there is only a finite number of shared variables, the Equality Propagation and Case Split rules can be applied only a finite number of times.   ∎

Next, we show that the inference rules are sound.

Definition 8. We say that a state $\langle \Gamma_1, \Gamma_2, E \rangle$ is $(T_1 \cup T_2)$-*satisfiable* if and only if so is $\Gamma_1 \cup \Gamma_2 \cup E$.   □

Lemma 2. *For each inference rule in Figure 2, the state above the line is $(T_1 \cup T_2)$-satisfiable if and only if at least one state below the line is $(T_1 \cup T_2)$-satisfiable.*   □

PROOF. We only prove the soundness of the Equality Propagation rule (the other rules can be handled similarly).

Thus, assume that $\langle \Gamma_1, \Gamma_2, E \rangle$ is $(T_1 \cup T_2)$-satisfiable, and that $T_i \cup \Gamma_i \cup E \models x = y$. Let $\mathcal{A}$ be a $(T_1 \cup T_2)$-interpretation satisfying $\Gamma_1 \cup \Gamma_2 \cup E$. Since $T_i \cup \Gamma_i \cup E \models x = y$, it follows that $x^{\mathcal{A}} = y^{\mathcal{A}}$, and therefore $\mathcal{A}$ is a $(T_1 \cup T_2)$-interpretation satisfying $\langle \Gamma_1, \Gamma_2, E \cup \{x = y\} \rangle$.

Vice versa, if $\langle \Gamma_1, \Gamma_2, E \cup \{x = y\} \rangle$ is $(T_1 \cup T_2)$-satisfiable then clearly $\langle \Gamma_1, \Gamma_2, E \rangle$ is also $(T_1 \cup T_2)$-satisfiable.   ∎

Lemma 3. *Let $\langle \Gamma_1, \Gamma_2, E \rangle$ be a state such that no rule in Figure 2 can be applied to it. Then $\Gamma_1 \cup \Gamma_2 \cup E$ is $(T_1 \cup T_2)$-satisfiable.*   □

PROOF. Since the Contradiction rule cannot be applied to $\langle \Gamma_1, \Gamma_2, E \rangle$, we have that $\Gamma_i \cup E$ is T_i-satisfiable, for $i = 1, 2$.

We claim that there exists a T_1-interpretation $\mathcal{A}$ satisfying $\Gamma_1 \cup E$ such that $x^{\mathcal{A}} \neq y^{\mathcal{A}}$, for each $x, y \in shared(\Gamma_1, \Gamma_2)$ such that $x = y \notin E$. To see that this is the case, let $S = \{(x, y) : x, y \in shared(\Gamma_1, \Gamma_2) \text{ and } x = y \notin E\}$, and consider the disjunction

$$\psi : \bigvee_{(x,y) \in S} x = y .$$

If $T_1 \cup \Gamma_1 \not\models \psi$ then our claim is verified. If instead $T_1 \cup \Gamma_1 \models \psi$ then, by the Case Split rule, there exists a pair $(x, y) \in S$ such that $x = y \in E$, a contradiction.

Similarly, there exists a T_2-interpretation $\mathcal{B}$ satisfying $\Gamma_2 \cup E$ such that $x^{\mathcal{B}} \neq y^{\mathcal{B}}$, for each $x, y \in shared(\Gamma_1, \Gamma_2)$ such that $x = y \notin E$.

But then $x^{\mathcal{A}} = y^{\mathcal{A}}$ if and only if $x^{\mathcal{B}} = y^{\mathcal{B}}$, for every variable $x, y \in shared(\Gamma_1, \Gamma_2)$. In addition, since T_1 and T_2 are stably infinite, we can assume without loss of generality that both A and B are countably infinite. We can therefore apply Theorem 2, and obtain the existence of a $(T_1 \cup T_2)$-interpretation satisfying $\Gamma_1 \cup \Gamma_2 \cup E$.   ∎

Combining Lemmas 1, 2 and 3, we obtain the correctness of the deterministic version of the Nelson-Oppen combination method.

Theorem 8. *Let T_i be a stably infinite Σ_i-theory, for $i = 1, 2$, and let $\Sigma_1 \cap \Sigma_2 = \emptyset$. Then the inference rules in Figure 2 provide a decision procedure for the quantifier-free $(T_1 \cup T_2)$-satisfiability problem.*   □

4.4   Convexity

There is an interesting difference between the derivation in Example 6 and the one in Example 7. In Example 6 we never used the Case Split rule. In contrast, in Example 7 we *had to* use the Case Split rule, and no proof can be obtained if we use only the Contradiction and Equality Propagation rules.

Clearly, for efficiency reasons it would be desirable to avoid case splits as much as possible. Indeed, the Case Split rule can be avoided altogether when the combined theories are *convex*.

Definition 9. A Σ-theory T is *convex* if for every conjunction Γ of Σ-literals and for every disjunction $\bigvee_{i=1}^{n} x_i = y_i$,

$$T \cup \Gamma \models \bigvee_{i=1}^{n} x_i = y_i \quad \text{iff} \quad T \cup \Gamma \models x_j = y_j, \text{for some } j \in \{1, \ldots, n\}. \quad \square$$

Examples of convex theories include the theory $T_{\mathbb{E}}$ of equality, the theory $T_{\mathbb{R}}$ of reals, and the theory $T_{\mathbb{L}}$ of lists, whereas examples of non-convex theories are the theory $T_{\mathbb{Z}}$ of integers, and the theory $T_{\mathbb{A}}$ of arrays.

We refer to [37] for a proof of the convexity of $T_{\mathbb{R}}$, and to [38] for a proof of the convexity of $T_{\mathbb{E}}$ and $T_{\mathbb{L}}$. To see that $T_{\mathbb{Z}}$ and $T_{\mathbb{A}}$ are not convex, just note that:

- in $T_{\mathbb{Z}}$, the conjunction $\{x = 1, y = 2, 1 \leq z, z \leq 2\}$ entails $x = z \vee y = z$ but does not entail neither $x = z$ nor $y = z$;
- in $T_{\mathbb{A}}$, the conjunction $\{read(write(a, i, e), j) = x, read(a, j) = y\}$ entails $x = e \vee x = y$ but does not entail neither $x = e$ nor $x = y$.

The following theorem states that when both the combined theories are convex, the deterministic version of the Nelson-Oppen combination method remains correct even if we omit the Case Split rule.

Theorem 9. *Let T_i be a stably infinite and convex Σ_i-theory, for $i = 1, 2$, and let $\Sigma_1 \cap \Sigma_2 = \emptyset$. Then the Contradiction and Equality Propagation rules alone provide a decision procedure for the quantifier-free $(T_1 \cup T_2)$-satisfiability problem.* $\square$

PROOF. In the proofs of Section 4.3, the only place where we used the Case Split rule was in Lemma 3. But the proof of Lemma 3 works fine even if instead of the Case Split rule we use the hypothesis of convexity. ∎

A simple complexity analysis of the procedure presented in this section shows the following complexity result.

Theorem 10. *Let T_i be a stably infinite and convex Σ_i-theory, for $i = 1, 2$, and let $\Sigma_1 \cap \Sigma_2 = \emptyset$. Also, assume that the problem of checking the T_i-satisfiability of conjunctions of quantifier-free Σ_i-formulae can be decided in polynomial time, for $i = 1, 2$.*

Then the problem of checking the $(T_1 \cup T_2)$-satisfiability of conjunctions of quantifier-free $(\Sigma_1 \cup \Sigma_2)$-formulae can be decided in polynomial time. $\square$

We conclude this section by mentioning the following result, first proved in [4], relating the notions of convexity and stable infiniteness.

Theorem 11. *If T is a convex theory then $T \cup \{(\exists x)(\exists y)x \neq y\}$ is stably infinite.* $\qquad\square$

PROOF. Let $T' = T \cup \{(\exists x)(\exists y)x \neq y\}$, and assume, for a contradiction, that T' is not stably infinite. Then there exists a conjunction Γ of literals such that $T' \cup \Gamma$ is satisfiable in some finite interpretation but not in an infinite interpretation.

By the compactness theorem, there must be a positive integer n and an interpretation $\mathcal{A}$ such that:

- $|A| = n$;
- $\mathcal{A}$ satisfies $T' \cup \Gamma$;
- all interpretations having cardinality greater than n do not satisfy $T' \cup \Gamma$.

Let $x_1, \ldots, x_n, x_{n+1}, x', y'$ be distinct fresh variables not occurring in Γ, and consider the disjunction

$$\bigvee_{i \neq j} x_i = x_j$$

By the pigeonhole principle, we have that

$$T \cup \{x' \neq y'\} \cup \Gamma \models \bigvee_{i \neq j} x_i = x_j$$

but

$$T \cup \{x' \neq y'\} \cup \Gamma \not\models x_i = x_j, \qquad \text{for all } i, j \text{ such that } i \neq j,$$

which contradicts the fact that T is convex. $\qquad\blacksquare$

5   Shostak

In 1984, Shostak [50] presented a method for combining the theory $T_{\mathbb{E}}$ of equality with theories $T_1, \ldots, T_n$ satisfying certain conditions.

According to Shostak, such theories must admit so called *canonizers* and *solvers*. These canonizers and solvers are first combined into one single canonizer and solver for the union theory $T = T_1 \cup \cdots \cup T_n$. Then, Shostak's actual procedure is called, and the theory T is combined with the theory $T_{\mathbb{E}}$.

Unfortunately, Shostak's original paper contains several mistakes. First, as pointed out in [28, 30], it is not always possible to combine the solvers for the theories $T_1, \ldots, T_n$ into a single solver for the union theory $T = T_1 \cup \cdots \cup T_n$. Secondly, as pointed out in [46], Shostak's procedure combining T with $T_{\mathbb{E}}$ is incomplete and potentially nonterminating.

Nevertheless, all these mistakes can be elegantly fixed if Shostak's method is recast as an instance of the Nelson-Oppen combination method.

To do this, we introduce the notion of a *Shostak theory*, and we show how a solver for a Shostak theory T_i can be used to produce a decision procedure for

T_i. Then, if $T_1, \ldots, T_n$ are Shostak theories, we do not combine their solvers, but instead we use the Nelson-Oppen combination method to combine the decision procedures for $T_1, \ldots, T_n$ with a decision procedure for $T_{\mathbb{E}}$.

In addition, we show how a solver for a Shostak theory can be used to efficiently detect implied equalities when applying the Nelson-Oppen combination method.

5.1   Solvers

Before defining Shostak theories, we need to define what is a *solver*.

Definition 10 (Solver). A *solver* for a Σ-theory T is a computable function solve that takes as input Σ-equalities of the form $s = t$ and

- if $T \models s = t$ then solve$(s = t) = \textit{true}$;
- if $T \models s \neq t$ then solve$(s = t) = \textit{false}$;
- otherwise, solve$(s = t)$ returns a substitution

$$\sigma = \{x_1 \leftarrow t_1, \ldots, x_n \leftarrow t_n\}$$

such that:
- $x_i \in vars(s = t)$, for all i;
- $x_i \notin vars(t_j)$, for all i, j;
- the following equivalence is T-valid:

$$s = t \;\leftrightarrow\; (\exists y_1) \cdots (\exists y_k) \left[\bigwedge_{i=1}^{n} x_i = t_i \right],$$

where $y_1, \ldots, y_k$ are newly introduced variables, that is

$$\{y_1, \ldots, y_k\} = \left(\bigcup_{i=1}^{n} vars(t_i) \right) \setminus vars(s = t).$$

A theory is *solvable* if it has a solver. □

Example 8. Every inconsistent theory is *not* solvable. To see this, let T be an inconsistent Σ-theory, and let solve be a solver for T.

Since T is inconsistent, for every Σ-equality $s = t$, we have both $T \models s = t$ and $T \models s \neq t$. Thus, solve$(s = t) = \textit{true}$ and solve$(s = t) = \textit{false}$ at the same time. This is a contradiction, because solve is a function. □

Example 9. The simplest solvable theory is the trivial theory

$$T = \{(\forall x)(\forall y)(x = y)\}.$$

A solver for T returns *true* on every input. □

Example 10. A more interesting solvable theory is the theory $T_{\mathbb{R}}$ of reals. Given an equality $s = t$, a solver for $T_{\mathbb{R}}$ can be implemented by employing the following steps:

1. rewrite $s = t$ as $s - t = 0$;
2. combining like terms, rewrite $s - t = 0$ as an equality of the form

$$a_0 + a_1 x_1 + \cdots + a_n x_n = 0,$$

where $a_i \neq 0$, for $i = 1, \ldots, n$;

3. return *true*, *false*, or a substitution σ, according to the following:
   - if $n = 0$ and $a_0 = 0$, return *true*;
   - if $n = 0$ and $a_0 \neq 0$, return *false*;
   - if $n > 0$, return the substitution $\sigma = \left\{ x_1 \leftarrow -\frac{a_0}{a_1} - \frac{a_2}{a_1} x_2 - \cdots - \frac{a_n}{a_1} x_n \right\}$.

For instance, the equation

$$2x - y + z = 2y + z - 1$$

is solved by

1. transposing the right-hand side, obtaining the equation

$$2x - y + z - (2y + z - 1) = 0,$$

2. combining like terms, obtaining the equation

$$2x - 3y + 1 = 0,$$

3. returning the substitution

$$\sigma = \left\{ x \leftarrow \frac{3}{2}y - \frac{1}{2} \right\}.$$

Similarly, we have

$$\mathsf{solve}(x + x = 2x) = \mathsf{solve}(x + x - 2x = 0) = \mathsf{solve}(0 = 0) = \mathit{true}$$

and

$$\mathsf{solve}(1 = 2) = \mathsf{solve}(1 - 2 = 0) = \mathsf{solve}(-1 = 0) = \mathit{false}. \qquad \square$$

Example 11. We now show that no solver can exist for the theory $T_{\mathbb{E}}$ of equality. To see this, suppose, for a contradiction, that solve is a solver for $T_{\mathbb{E}}$, and consider the equation

$$f(x) = a,$$

where x is a variable, a is a constant, and f is a function symbol.

Since $T_{\mathbb{E}} \not\models f(x) = a$ and $T_{\mathbb{E}} \not\models f(x) \neq a$, we have that

$$\mathsf{solve}(f(x) = a) = \{x \leftarrow t\},$$

for some term t such that $x \notin \mathit{vars}(t)$. In addition

$$T_{\mathbb{E}} \models f(x) = a \;\leftrightarrow\; (\exists y_1) \cdots (\exists y_k)(x = t),$$

where $\{y_1, \ldots, y_k\} = \mathit{vars}(t)$. But this is a contradiction, since for any term t, the equivalence $f(x) = a \leftrightarrow (\exists y_1) \cdots (\exists y_k)(x = t)$ is not $T_{\mathbb{E}}$-valid. $\qquad \square$

5.2   Shostak Theories

Definition 11. A Σ-theory T is a *Shostak theory* if

- Σ does not contain predicate symbols, that is, $\Sigma^{\mathrm{P}} = \emptyset$;
- T is convex;
- T is solvable.   □

The trivial theory $T = \{(\forall x)(\forall y)(x = y)\}$ is a Shostak Theory. In fact, in Example 9 we saw that T is solvable. In addition, T is also convex, since for every conjunction Γ and every disjunction of equalities $\bigvee_{i=1}^{n} x_i = y_i$, if $T \cup \Gamma \models \bigvee_{i=1}^{n} x_i = y_i$ then $T \models x_i = y_i$, for all $i = 1, \ldots, n$.

The classical example of a Shostak theory is the theory $T_{\mathbb{R}}^{-}$ obtained by restricting the theory $T_{\mathbb{R}}$ of reals to the functional signature $\Sigma_{\mathbb{R}}^{-} = \{0, 1, +, -\}$ (we remove the predicate symbol $\leq$). In example 10 we saw that $T_{\mathbb{R}}$ is solvable, and in Section 4.4 we noted that $T_{\mathbb{R}}$ is convex. Thus $T_{\mathbb{R}}^{-}$ is both solvable and convex.

On the other hand, the theory $T_{\mathbb{E}}$ of equality is *not* a Shostak theory, since it is not solvable (cf. Example 11).

5.3   The Procedure

Let T be a Shostak Σ-theory. We now present a decision procedure that, using the solver for the theory T, decides the T-satisfiability of any quantifier-free Σ-formula. The decision procedure presented here is a rule-based version of the decision procedure in [4].

As usual, we restrict ourselves to conjunctions of Σ-literals. Since Σ does not contain predicate symbols, each conjunction is of the form

$$s_1 = t_2, \ldots, s_m = t_m, s_1' \neq t_1', \ldots, s_n' \neq t_n'. \tag{1}$$

Thus, let Γ be a conjunction of Σ-literals of the form (1). The decision procedure consists of applying the inference rules in Figure 3, until nothing more can be done.

Intuitively, the Contradiction rules detect the inconsistencies, and the Equality Elimination rule is used to remove all the equalities from the conjunction Γ.

If the literal *false* is deduced, then we declare that the initial conjunction Γ is T-unsatisfiable. If instead the literal *false* is not deduced and no rule can be applied, then we declare that Γ is T-satisfiable.

5.4   An Example

Example 12. Consider the Shostak theory $T_{\mathbb{R}}^{-}$. The conjunction

$$\Gamma = \left\{ \begin{array}{l} x + 2y = 3z\,, \\ x - y = 0\,, \\ y \neq z \end{array} \right\}$$

is $T_{\mathbb{R}}^{-}$-unsatisfiable. In fact, subtracting the second equation from the first one yields $3y = 3z$, which contradicts the disequality $y \neq z$.

The following derivation shows that Γ is $T_{\mathbb{R}}^{-}$-unsatisfiable.

Contradiction rule 1

$$\frac{\Gamma \cup \{s \neq t\}}{false} \qquad \text{if } \mathsf{solve}(s = t) = true$$

Contradiction rule 2

$$\frac{\Gamma \cup \{s = t\}}{false} \qquad \text{if } \mathsf{solve}(s = t) = false$$

Equality Elimination rule

$$\frac{\Gamma \cup \{s = t\}}{\Gamma \sigma} \qquad \text{if } \mathsf{solve}(s = t) = \sigma$$

Fig. 3. Shostak rules.

$$\Gamma : \{x + 2y = 3z, \ x - y = 0, \ y \neq z\}$$

$$\mathsf{solve}(x + 2y = 3z) = \{x \leftarrow -2y + 3z\}$$

$$\Gamma_1 : \{-2y + 3z - y = 0, \ y \neq z\}$$

$$\mathsf{solve}(-2y + 3z - y = 0) = \{y \leftarrow z\}$$

$$\Gamma_2 : \{z \neq z\}$$

$$\mathsf{solve}(z = z) = true$$

$$\Gamma_3 : false$$

Note that Γ_1 and Γ_2 follow by the Equality Elimination rule, and that Γ_3 follows by the Contradiction rule 1. □

5.5   Correctness

In this section we show that our Shostak-based decision procedure is correct. Clearly, the procedure must terminate, as the following lemma states.

Lemma 4. *The inference rules in Figure 3 form a terminating inference system.* □

PROOF. It suffices to note that any application of the inference rules in Figure 3 either deduces *false* or decreases the number of literals in the conjunction. ∎

The following lemma shows that the inference rules in Figure 3 are sound.

Lemma 5. *For each inference rule in Figure 3, the conjunction above the line is T-satisfiable if and only if so is the conjunction below the line.*   □

PROOF. The lemma trivially holds for the Contradiction rules.

Concerning the Equality Elimination rule, assume that $\Gamma \cup \{s = t\}$ is T-satisfiable, and let $\mathcal{A}$ be a T-interpretation satisfying $\Gamma \cup \{s = t\}$. Also, let $\sigma = \mathsf{solve}(s = t) = \{x_1 \leftarrow t_1, \ldots, x_n \leftarrow t_n\}$. Since the equivalence

$$ s = t \;\leftrightarrow\; (\exists y_1) \cdots (\exists y_k) \left[\bigwedge_{i=1}^{n} x_i = t_i \right] $$

is T-valid, we can extend $\mathcal{A}$ over the variables $y_1, \ldots, y_k$ in such a way that $x_i^{\mathcal{A}} = t_i^{\mathcal{A}}$, for all i. But then, by basic model-theoretic properties of substitutions, it follows that $\Gamma\sigma$ is true in $\mathcal{A}$.

Vice versa, assume that $\Gamma\sigma$ is T-satisfiable, where $\sigma = \mathsf{solve}(s = t) = \{x_1 \leftarrow t_1, \ldots, x_n \leftarrow t_n\}$, and let $\mathcal{A}$ be a T-interpretation satisfying $\Gamma\sigma$. Since the variables x_i do not occur in $\Gamma\sigma$, we can redefine $\mathcal{A}$ on the x_i by letting $x_i^{\mathcal{A}} = t_i^{\mathcal{A}}$, for all i. But then, by the definition of solver, we have $s^{\mathcal{A}} = t^{\mathcal{A}}$, and by basic model-theoretic properties of substitutions it follows that Γ is true in $\mathcal{A}$.   ■

Lemma 6. *If upon termination of the procedure the final result is not false, then the final conjunction is T-satisfiable.*   □

PROOF. Assume that upon termination the final result is not *false*. Then the final conjunction must be of the form

$$ s_1 \neq t_1, \ldots, s_n \neq t_n , $$

where $\mathsf{solve}(s_i = t_i) \neq true$, for each $i = 1, \ldots, n$. It follows that $s_i \neq t_i$ is T-satisfiable, for $i = 1, \ldots, n$, and by the convexity of T, we have that the final conjunction is T-satisfiable.   ■

Combining Lemmas 4, 5 and 6, we obtain the following decidability result.

Theorem 12. *Let T be Shostak Σ-theory. Then the quantifier-free T-satisfiability problem is decidable.*   □

5.6   Integration in Nelson-Oppen

Let $T_1, \ldots, T_\ell, T_{\ell+1}, \ldots, T_n$ be stably infinite Σ_i-theories such that $\Sigma_i \cap \Sigma_j = \emptyset$, for $i \neq j$. Also, assume that $T_{\ell+1}, \ldots, T_n$ are Shostak theories.

Using the results of Section 5.3, we know how to obtain, for each $i = \ell + 1, \ldots, n$, a decision procedure for the T_i-satisfiability of quantifier-free Σ_i-formulae. Thus, if we assume that we also have, for each $i = 1, \ldots, \ell$, a decision procedure for the T_i-satisfiability of quantifier-free Σ_i-formulae, we can employ the Nelson-Oppen combination method to obtain a decision procedure for the $(T_1 \cup \cdots \cup T_n)$-satisfiability of $(\Sigma_1 \cup \cdots \cup \Sigma_n)$-formulae. This can be summarized in the following theorem.

Theorem 13. *Let $T_1, \ldots, T_\ell, T_{\ell+1}, \ldots, T_n$ be stably infinite Σ_i-theories such that $\Sigma_i \cap \Sigma_j = \emptyset$, for $i \neq j$, and let $T_{\ell+1}, \ldots, T_n$ be Shostak theories. Also, assume that the quantifier-free T_i-satisfiability problem is decidable, for $i = 1, \ldots, \ell$.*
   Then the quantifier-free $(T_1 \cup \cdots \cup T_n)$-satisfiability problem is decidable. □

Note that a special case of the above theorem is the combination of the theory $T_{\mathbb{E}}$ of equality with n Shostak theories.

In addition, it turns out that when we combine the theory $T_{\mathbb{E}}$ of equality with n Shostak theories $T_1, \ldots, T_n$ then we can obtain a decision procedure for the theory $T_{\mathbb{E}} \cup T_1 \cup \cdots \cup T_n$ even if $T_1, \ldots, T_n$ are not stably infinite.

Theorem 14. *Let $T_{\mathbb{E}}$ be the theory of equality, and let $T_1, \ldots, T_n$ be Shostak theories such that $\Sigma_i \cap \Sigma_j = \emptyset$, for $i \neq j$,*
   Then the quantifier-free $(T_{\mathbb{E}} \cup T_1 \cup \cdots \cup T_n)$-satisfiability problem is decidable. □

PROOF. Let $T = T_{\mathbb{E}} \cup T_1 \cup \cdots \cup T_n$.

Observe that every set of formulae is satisfiable if and only if it is either true under an interpretatin $\mathcal{A}$ such that $|A| = 1$, or true under an interpretation $\mathcal{A}$ such that $|A| > 1$. Thus, we can obtain a decision procedure for the quantifier-free T-satisfiability problem if we are able to obtain a decision procedure for the quantifier-free satisfiability problem of $T \cup \{(\forall x)(\forall y)(x = y)\}$, and a decision procedure for the quantifier-free satisfiability problem of $T \cup \{(\exists x)(\exists y)(x \neq y)\}$.

Case 1: $T \cup \{(\exists x)(\exists y)(x \neq y)\}$.

Note that for every conjuction Γ we have that Γ is $(T_i \cup \{(\exists x)(\exists y)(x \neq y)\})$-satisfiable if and only if $\Gamma \cup \{x' \neq y'\}$ is T_i-satisfiable, where x' and y' are fresh variables not occurring in Γ. Since T_i is a Shostak theory, by applying Theorem 12, we obtain that the quantifier-free satisfiability problem for $T_i \cup \{(\exists x)(\exists y)(x \neq y)\}$ is decidable. In addition, by Theorem 11, it follows that $T_i \cup \{(\exists x)(\exists y)(x \neq y)\}$ is a stably infinite theory. We can therefore apply the Nelson-Oppen combination method between the following theories:

- $T_{\mathbb{E}}$;
- $T_i \cup \{(\exists x)(\exists y)(x \neq y)\}$, for all i,

and obtain a decision procedure for the quantifier-free satisfiability problem of $T \cup \{(\exists x)(\exists y)(x \neq y)\}$.

Case 2: $T \cup \{(\forall x)(\forall y)(x = y)\}$.

In this case we apply the Nelson-Oppen combination method between the following theories:

- $T_{\mathbb{E}} \cup \{(\forall x)(\forall y)(x = y)\}$;
- $T_i \cup \{(\forall x)(\forall y)(x = y)\}$, for all i,

even though none of these theories is stably infinite. To see that this is still correct, first note that all the above theories have decidable quantifier-free problems. In addition, the domain of any interpretation satisfying any of the above theories must have cardinality one, and therefore an application of Theorem 7 allows us to obtain a decidion procedure for the quantifier-free satisfiability problem of $T \cup \{(\forall x)(\forall y)(x = y)\}$. ■

5.7 Using a Solver to Detect Implied Equalities

In this section we show how it is possible to use a solver for a Shostak theory to detect implied equalities.

To do this, we need to extend the definition of a solver to operate on conjunctions of equalities.

Definition 12. Let solve be a solver for a Shostak Σ-theory T. We let

$$\mathsf{solve}(\emptyset) = \epsilon$$
$$\mathsf{solve}(\Gamma \cup \{s = t\}) = \sigma \circ \mathsf{solve}(\Gamma\sigma)\,, \qquad \text{where } \sigma = \mathsf{solve}(s = t).\qquad \square$$

Let solve be a solver for a Shostak Σ-theory T, let Γ be a conjunction of equalities, and let Δ be a conjunction of disequalities. Also, let $\lambda = \mathsf{solve}(\Gamma)$, and assume that $\Gamma \cup \Delta$ is T-satisfiable. We claim that

$$T \cup \Gamma \cup \Delta \models x = y \qquad \text{iff} \qquad \mathsf{solve}(x\lambda = y\lambda) = true\,. \qquad (2)$$

Clearly, (2) provides a way to detect implied equalities using the solver for the Shostak theory T.

Example 13. Let us consider the combination of the theory $T_{\mathbb{E}}$ of equality with the Shostak theory $T_{\mathbb{R}}^-$.

Note that the conjunction[4]

$$\Gamma = \left\{ \begin{array}{l} f(x-1) - 1 = x+1\,, \\ f(y) + 1 = y - 1\,, \\ y + 1 = x \end{array} \right\}$$

is $(T_{\mathbb{E}} \cup T_{\mathbb{R}}^-)$-unsatisfiable. In fact, the first and third equalities imply $f(y) = y + 3$, and the second equality implies $f(y) = y - 2$. But then $y + 3 = y - 2$, a contradiction.

We will use the Nelson-Oppen combination method and a solver for $T_{\mathbb{R}}^-$ to show that Γ is $(T_{\mathbb{E}} \cup T_{\mathbb{R}}^-)$-unsatisfiable.

After the Variable Abstraction phase we obtain the conjunctions

$$\Gamma_{\mathbb{E}} = \left\{ \begin{array}{l} w_1 = f(w_2)\,, \\ w_3 = f(y) \end{array} \right\}, \qquad \Gamma_{\mathbb{R}} = \left\{ \begin{array}{l} w_1 - 1 = x+1\,, \\ w_2 = x - 1\,, \\ w_3 + 1 = y - 1\,, \\ y + 1 = x \end{array} \right\}.$$

We have the following derivation.

---

[4] Taken from [46].

$$s_0 : \langle \Gamma_E, \Gamma_R, \emptyset \rangle$$

$$T_{\mathbb{R}}^- \cup \Gamma_{\mathbb{R}} \models y = w_2$$

$$s_1 : \langle \Gamma_E, \Gamma_R, \{y = w_2\} \rangle$$

$$T_E \cup \Gamma_E \cup \{y = w_2\} \models w_1 = w_3$$

$$s_2 : \langle \Gamma_E, \Gamma_R, \{y = w_2, w_1 = w_3\} \rangle$$

$$T_{\mathbb{R}}^- \cup \Gamma_{\mathbb{R}} \cup \{y = w_2, w_1 = w_3\} \models w_1 \neq w_3$$

$$s_3 : false$$

The inference from state s_1 to state s_2 is obvious. To justify the inference from state s_0 to state s_1, let us compute $\lambda = \mathsf{solve}(\Gamma_{\mathbb{R}})$.

$$\mathsf{solve}(\Gamma_{\mathbb{R}}) = \mathsf{solve}(\{w_1 - 1 = x + 1, w_2 = x - 1, w_3 + 1 = y - 1, \underbrace{y + 1 = x}_{\text{solves to } \{x \leftarrow y+1\}} \})$$

$$= \{x \leftarrow y + 1\} \circ \mathsf{solve}(\{w_1 - 1 = y + 2, w_2 = y, \underbrace{w_3 + 1 = y - 1}_{\text{solves to } \{y \leftarrow w_3+2\}} \})$$

$$= \{x \leftarrow w_3 + 3, y \leftarrow w_3 + 2\} \circ \mathsf{solve}(\{w_1 - 1 = w_3 + 4, \underbrace{w_2 = w_3 + 2}_{\text{solves to } \{w_2 \leftarrow w_3+2\}} \})$$

$$= \{x \leftarrow w_3 + 3, y \leftarrow w_3 + 2, w_2 \leftarrow w_3 + 2\} \circ \mathsf{solve}(\{ \underbrace{w_1 - 1 = w_3 + 4}_{\text{solves to } \{w_1 \leftarrow w_3+5\}} \})$$

$$= \{x \leftarrow w_3 + 3, y \leftarrow w_3 + 2, w_2 \leftarrow w_3 + 2, w_1 \leftarrow w_3 + 5\}$$

Clearly, $\mathsf{solve}(y\lambda = w_2\lambda) = true$, and therefore $T_{\mathbb{R}}^- \cup \Gamma_{\mathbb{R}} \models y = w_2$.

To justify the inference from state s_2 to state s_3, note that

$$\mathsf{solve}(w_1\lambda = w_3\lambda) = \mathsf{solve}(w_3 + 5 = w_3) = false .$$

Thus, $T_{\mathbb{R}}^- \cup \Gamma_{\mathbb{R}} \models w_1 \neq w_3$, which implies that $\Gamma_{\mathbb{R}} \cup \{y = w_2, w_1 = w_3\}$ is $T_{\mathbb{R}}^-$-unsatisfiable.   □

Theorem 15 below formally shows that (2) holds. But before proving it, we need two auxiliary lemmas.

Lemma 7. *Let $\sigma = \{x_1 \leftarrow t_1, \ldots, x_n \leftarrow t_n\}$ be a substitution such that $x_i \notin vars(t_j)$, for all i, j.*

Then for any theory T and for any conjunction Γ of literals:

$$T \cup \Gamma \cup \{x_1 = t_1, \ldots, x_n = t_n\} \models x = y \qquad iff \qquad T \cup \Gamma\sigma \models x\sigma = y\sigma .$$ □

PROOF. Let $T \cup \Gamma \cup \{x_1 = t_1, \ldots, x_n = t_n\} \models x = y$ and assume that $\mathcal{A}$ is an interpretation satisfying $T \cup \Gamma\sigma$. Thus $x^{\mathcal{A}} = y^{\mathcal{A}}$. Since the variables x_i do not occur in $\Gamma\sigma$, we can redefine $\mathcal{A}$ on the x_i by letting $x_i^{\mathcal{A}} = t_i^{\mathcal{A}}$, for all i. But then, by basic model-theoretic properties of substitutions, it follows that $x\sigma = y\sigma$ is true under $\mathcal{A}$.

Vice versa, let $T \cup \Gamma\sigma \models x\sigma = y\sigma$, and let $\mathcal{A}$ be an interpretation satisfying $T \cup \Gamma \cup \{x_1 = t_1, \ldots, x_n = t_n\}$. Then $[x\sigma]^{\mathcal{A}} = [y\sigma]^{\mathcal{A}}$. In addition $x_i^{\mathcal{A}} = t_i^{\mathcal{A}}$, for all i, and by basic model-theoretic properties of substitutions, it follows that $x = y$ is true under $\mathcal{A}$. ∎

Lemma 8. *Let T be a convex theory, Γ a conjunction of equalities, and Δ a conjunction of disequalities. Also, assume that $\Gamma \cup \Delta$ is T-satisfiable.*
Then

$$T \cup \Gamma \cup \Delta \models x = y \qquad iff \qquad T \cup \Gamma \models x = y. \qquad \square$$

PROOF. Clearly, if $T \cup \Gamma \models x = y$ then $T \cup \Gamma \cup \Delta \models x = y$.
Vice versa, assume that $T \cup \Gamma \cup \Delta \models x = y$. Then

$$T \cup \Gamma \models \left(\bigvee_{s \neq t \in \Delta} s = t \right) \vee x = y.$$

Since T is convex, either $T \cup \Gamma \models x = y$ or there exists a disequality $s \neq t$ in Δ such that $T \cup \Gamma \models s = t$. In the former case, the lemma is proved. In the latter case, we have that $\Gamma \cup \Delta$ is T-unsatisfiable, a contradiction. ∎

The following theorem proves (2), thus showing how a solver for a Shostak theory can be used to detect implied equalities.

Theorem 15. *Let solve be a solver for a Shostak Σ-theory T, let Γ be a conjunction of equalities, and let Δ be a conjunction of disequalities.*
If $\Gamma \cup \Delta$ is T-satisfiable then

$$T \cup \Gamma \cup \Delta \models x = y \qquad iff \qquad \mathsf{solve}(x\lambda = y\lambda) = true$$

where $\lambda = \mathsf{solve}(\Gamma)$. $\qquad \square$

PROOF. Since $\mathsf{solve}(x\lambda = y\lambda) = true$ if and only if $T \models x\lambda = y\lambda$, we only need to prove that

$$T \cup \Gamma \cup \Delta \models x = y \qquad iff \qquad T \models x\lambda = y\lambda$$

We proceed by induction on the number of literals in Γ. For the base case, if $\Gamma = \emptyset$ then $\lambda = \mathsf{solve}(\Gamma) = \epsilon$ and

$$T \cup \Gamma \cup \Delta \models x = y \quad iff \quad T \cup \Delta \models x = y$$
$$iff \quad T \models x = y \qquad \text{(by Lemma 8)}$$
$$iff \quad \mathsf{solve}(x\epsilon = y\epsilon) = true .$$

For the inductive step, let $\Gamma = \Gamma' \cup \{s = t\}$. Also let

$$\sigma = \mathsf{solve}(s = t) = \{x_1 \leftarrow t_1, \ldots, x_n \leftarrow t_n\}$$
$$\tau = \mathsf{solve}(\Gamma'\sigma)$$
$$\lambda = \mathsf{solve}(\Gamma) = \sigma \circ \tau .$$

Then

$$
\begin{aligned}
T \cup \Gamma \cup \Delta \models x = y \quad &\text{iff} \quad T \cup \Gamma' \cup \{s = t\} \cup \Delta \models x = y \\
&\text{iff} \quad T \cup \Gamma' \cup \{s = t\} \models x = y &&\text{(by Lemma 8)} \\
&\text{iff} \quad T \cup \Gamma' \cup \{x_1 = t_1, \ldots, x_n = t_n\} \models x = y &&\text{(by Definition 10)} \\
&\text{iff} \quad T \cup \Gamma' \sigma \models x\sigma = y\sigma &&\text{(by Lemma 7)} \\
&\text{iff} \quad T \models x\sigma\tau = y\sigma\tau &&\text{(by induction)} \\
&\text{iff} \quad T \models x\lambda = y\lambda. &&\blacksquare
\end{aligned}
$$

6 Non-disjoint Combination

In this section we consider the problem of combining theories over non-disjoint signatures.

More precisely, let Σ_1 and Σ_2 be arbitrary signatures (that is, not necessarily disjoint), and let T_i be a Σ_i-theory, for $i = 1, 2$. Also, assume that there exist decision procedures P_1 and P_2 such that, for $i = 1, 2$, P_i can decide the T_i-satisfiability of quantifier-free Σ_i-formulae.

Using as black boxes the decision procedures P_1 and P_2, we show how to obtain a procedure $P_{1\&2}$ that is sound and complete for the $(T_1 \cup T_2)$-unsatisfiability of quantifier-free $(\Sigma_1 \cup \Sigma_2)$-formulae. In other words, if φ is $(T_1 \cup T_2)$-unsatisfiable, then $P_{1\&2}$ eventually stops, and reports the unsatisfiability. If instead φ is $(T_1 \cup T_2)$-satisfiable, then $P_{1\&2}$ runs forever.

Indeed, Zarba [61] showed that soundness and completeness hold even if φ is not quantifier-free, but in this paper we prefer to restrict our attention to quantifier-free formulae for clarity of presentation.

For technical reasons, we will assume that the theories T_1 and T_2 are *universal*.

Definition 13. A formula is *universal* if it is of the form $(\forall x_1) \cdots (\forall x_n)\psi$, where ψ is quantifier-free.

A theory is *universal* if all its sentences are universal. $\square$

The condition that the theories T_1 and T_2 be universal is necessary for the completeness proof, because only for universal formulae the following Theorem 16 holds, a theorem that can be seen as a positive version of the well-known Herbrand Theorem.

Theorem 16 (Herbrand). *Let Φ be a set of universal Σ-formulae, where $\Sigma^C \neq \emptyset$. Then Φ is satisfiable if and only if there exists an interpretation $\mathcal{A}$ satisfying Φ such that for each element $a \in A$ there exists a Σ-term t such that $vars(t) \subseteq vars(\Phi)$ and $t^{\mathcal{A}} = a$.* $\square$

6.1 The Procedure

Let Σ_1 and Σ_2 be two arbitrary signatures which are non necessarily disjoint, and let T_i be an universal Σ_i-theory, for $i = 1, 2$.

```
┌─────────────────────────────────────────────────────────────────────────┐
│ Contradiction rule                                                        │
│                                                                           │
│        ⟨Γ₁, Γ₂⟩              if Γᵢ is Tᵢ-unsatisfiable, for some i ∈ {1,2} │
│       ─────────                                                           │
│         false                                                             │
│                                                                           │
│ Abstraction rule 1                                                        │
│                                                                           │
│              ⟨Γ₁, Γ₂⟩                    where t is any Σ₁-term and        │
│    ──────────────────────────────        w is a new variable             │
│    ⟨Γ₁ ∪ {t = w}, Γ₂ ∪ {w = w}⟩                                          │
│                                                                           │
│ Abstraction rule 2                                                        │
│                                                                           │
│              ⟨Γ₁, Γ₂⟩                    where t is any Σ₂-term and        │
│    ──────────────────────────────        w is a new variable             │
│    ⟨Γ₁ ∪ {w = w}, Γ₂ ∪ {t = w}⟩                                          │
│                                                                           │
│ Decomposition rule                                                        │
│                                                                           │
│                        ⟨Γ₁, Γ₂⟩                                           │
│    ──────────────────────────────────────────────────                     │
│    ⟨Γ₁ ∪ {ψ}, Γ₂ ∪ {ψ}⟩  |  ⟨Γ₁ ∪ {¬ψ}, Γ₂ ∪ {¬ψ}⟩                       │
│                                                                           │
│    where ψ is an atom either of the form x = y or of the form P(x₁,…,xₙ), │
│    with x, y, x₁, …, xₙ ∈ shared(Γ₁, Γ₂) and P ∈ Σ₁ᴾ ∩ Σ₂ᴾ               │
└─────────────────────────────────────────────────────────────────────────┘
```

Fig. 4. Non-disjoint combination rules

We now present a procedure that is sound and complete for the $(T_1 \cup T_2)$-unsatisfiabilty of quantifier-free $(\Sigma_1 \cup \Sigma_2)$-formulae. As usual, we restict ourselves to conjunctions of $(\Sigma_1 \cup \Sigma_2)$-literals.

Thus, let Γ be a conjunction of $(\Sigma_1 \cup \Sigma_2)$-literals. We first apply the Variable Abstraction phase from Section 3.2, obtaining a conjunction $\Gamma_1 \cup \Gamma_2$ of literals in $\langle \Sigma_1, \Sigma_2 \rangle$-separate form such that $\Gamma_1 \cup \Gamma_2$ is $(T_1 \cup T_2)$-satisfiable if and only if so is Γ. Then, we construct the *initial state*

$$\langle \Gamma_1, \Gamma_2 \rangle,$$

and we repeatedly apply the rules in Figure 4.

As usual, the Contradiction rule is used to detect the inconsistencies. The intuition behind the Abstraction rules is as follows. Suppose that t is a Σ_1-term but not a Σ_2-term. Then the decision procedure for T_1 "knows" about t, but the decision procedure for T_2 does not. After an application of the Abstraction rule 1, the decision procedure for T_2 is aware of the existence of t. Finally, the Decomposition rule is used to let the decision procedures for T_1 and T_2 agree on the truth value of each atom ψ.

If we obtain a derivation in which all leaves are labeled with *false*, we declare that the initial conjunction Γ is $(T_1 \cup T_2)$-unsatisfiable.

6.2   An Example

Example 14. Let us consider the combination of the theory $T_{\mathbb{Z}}$ of integers with the Σ-theory

$$T = \{ (\forall x)(\forall y)(x \le y \rightarrow f(x) \le f(y)) \},$$

where $\Sigma = \{\le, f\}$. Note that $\Sigma_{\mathbb{Z}} \cap \Sigma = \{\le\} \ne \emptyset$.

The conjunction

$$\Gamma = \left\{ \begin{array}{l} x + y = z \,, \\ 0 \le y \,, \\ \neg(f(x) \le f(z)) \end{array} \right\}$$

is $(T_\mathbb{Z} \cup T)$-unsatisfiable. In fact, the first two literals imply $x \le z$, and by the monotonicity of f we have $f(x) \le f(z)$, which contradicts the third literal.

After the Variable Abstraction phase we get the conjunctions

$$\Gamma_\mathbb{Z} = \left\{ \begin{array}{l} x + y = z \,, \\ 0 \le y \end{array} \right\} \,, \qquad\qquad \Gamma_2 = \{\neg(f(x) \le f(z))\} \,.$$

We have the following derivation.

$$s_0 : \langle \Gamma_\mathbb{Z}, \Gamma_2 \rangle$$

$$s_1 : \langle \Gamma_\mathbb{Z} \cup \{x \le z\}, \Gamma_2 \cup \{x \le z\} \rangle \qquad s_2 : \langle \Gamma_\mathbb{Z} \cup \{\neg(x \le z)\}, \Gamma_2 \cup \{\neg(x \le z)\} \rangle$$

$$s_3 : \mathit{false} \qquad\qquad\qquad\qquad s_4 : \mathit{false}$$

The inferences can be justified as follows.

- s_1 and s_2 follow by the Decomposition rule;
- s_3 follows from s_1 by the Contradiction rule since $\Gamma_2 \cup \{x \le z\}$ is T_2-unsatisfiable;
- s_4 follows from s_2 by the Contradiction rule since $\Gamma_\mathbb{Z} \cup \{\neg(x \le z)\}$ is $T_\mathbb{Z}$-unsatisfiable. □

Hence, we conclude that Γ is $(T_\mathbb{Z} \cup T)$-unsatisfiable.

6.3   Soundness and Completeness

We now prove that the rules in Figure 4 form a sound and complete inference system for the $(T_1 \cup T_2)$-unsatisfiability of quantifier-free $(\Sigma_1 \cup \Sigma_2)$-formulae.

Let us start with soundness.

Definition 14. A state $\langle \Gamma_1, \Gamma_2 \rangle$ is $(T_1 \cup T_2)$-*satisfiable* if and only if $\Gamma_1 \cup \Gamma_2$ is $(T_1 \cup T_2)$-satisfiable. □

Lemma 9 (soundness). *For each inference rule in Figure 4, the state above the line is $(T_1 \cup T_2)$-satisfiable if and only if at least one of the states below the line is $(T_1 \cup T_2)$-satisfiable* □

PROOF. We only prove the soundness of the Decomposition rule (the other rules can be handled similarly).

Thus, assume that $\langle \Gamma_1, \Gamma_2 \rangle$ is $(T_1 \cup T_2)$-satisfiable, and let $\mathcal{A}$ be a $(T_1 \cup T_2)$-interpretation satisfying $\Gamma_1 \cup \Gamma_2$. If $\psi^{\mathcal{A}}$ is true then $\langle \Gamma_1 \cup \{\psi\}, \Gamma_2 \cup \{\psi\} \rangle$ is

$(T_1 \cup T_2)$-satisfiable. If instead $\psi^{\mathcal{A}}$ is false then $\langle \Gamma_1 \cup \{\neg\psi\}, \Gamma_2 \cup \{\neg\psi\} \rangle$ is $(T_1 \cup T_2)$-satisfiable.

Vice versa, if either $\langle \Gamma_1 \cup \{\psi\}, \Gamma_2 \cup \{\psi\} \rangle$ or $\langle \Gamma_1 \cup \{\neg\psi\}, \Gamma_2 \cup \{\neg\psi\} \rangle$ is $(T_1 \cup T_2)$-satisfiable, then clearly $\langle \Gamma_1, \Gamma_2 \rangle$ is $(T_1 \cup T_2)$-satisfiable. ∎

The completeness proof is based upon the following Combination Theorem, due independently to Ringeissen [45] and Tinelli and Harandi [56], and whose proof can be found in the appendix.

Theorem 17 (Combination Theorem). *Let Σ_1 and Σ_2 be signatures, let Φ_i be a set of Σ_i-formulae, for $i = 1, 2$, and let $V_i = vars(\Phi_i)$.*

Then $\Phi_1 \cup \Phi_2$ is satisfiable if and only if there exists a Σ_1-interpretation $\mathcal{A}$ satisfying Φ_1 and a Σ_2-interpretation $\mathcal{B}$ satisfying Φ_2 such that

$$\mathcal{A}^{\Sigma_1 \cap \Sigma_2, V_1 \cap V_2} \cong \mathcal{B}^{\Sigma_1 \cap \Sigma_2, V_1 \cap V_2} .$$
□

Lemma 10 (Completeness). *Let $\Gamma_1 \cup \Gamma_2$ be a $(T_1 \cup T_2)$-unsatisfiable conjunction of literals in $\langle \Sigma_1, \Sigma_2 \rangle$-separate form.*

Then there exists a derivation whose initial state is $\langle \Gamma_1, \Gamma_2 \rangle$ and such that all its leaves are labeled with false.
□

PROOF. Assume, for a contradiction, that no such derivation exists. Starting from the initial state $\langle \Gamma_1, \Gamma_2 \rangle$, apply exhaustively the rules in Figure 4, obtaining a "limit" derivation D^{∞}. This derivation must contain some branch B such that none of its nodes is labeled with *false*. Thus

$$\mathsf{B} = \langle \Gamma_1^{(0)}, \Gamma_2^{(0)} \rangle, \langle \Gamma_1^{(1)}, \Gamma_2^{(1)} \rangle, \dots, \langle \Gamma_1^{(n)}, \Gamma_2^{(n)} \rangle, \dots$$

where $\Gamma_1^{(0)} = \Gamma_1$, $\Gamma_2^{(0)} = \Gamma_2$, and for each $n \geq 0$, $i = 1, 2$ we have $\Gamma_i^{(n)} \subseteq \Gamma_i^{(n+1)}$.

Let Γ_1^{∞} and Γ_2^{∞} be the set of literals defined by

$$\Gamma_1^{\infty} = \bigcup_{n=0}^{\infty} \Gamma_1^i, \qquad\qquad \Gamma_2^{\infty} = \bigcup_{n=0}^{\infty} \Gamma_2^i,$$

and let $S = shared(\Gamma_1^{\infty}, \Gamma_2^{\infty})$.

We claim that Γ_i^{∞} is T_i-satisfiable, for $i = 1, 2$. To see this, note that $\Gamma_i^{(n)}$ is T_i-satisfiable, for each $n \geq 0$. It follows that every finite subset of Γ_i^{∞} is T_i-satisfiable, and by the Compactness Theorem, Γ_i^{∞} is T_i-satisfiable.

Let $\mathcal{A}$ be a T_1-interpretation satisfying Γ_1^{∞}. Since T_1 is universal, by the Herbrand Theorem 16 we can assume without loss of generality that $A = [T(\Sigma_1, vars(\Gamma_1^{\infty})]^{\mathcal{A}}$. Thus, by Abstraction rule 1 we have $A = S^{\mathcal{A}}$.

Similarly, there exists a T_2-interpretation $\mathcal{B}$ satisfying Γ_2^{∞} such that $B = S^{\mathcal{B}}$.

The next step of the proof is to merge the interpretations $\mathcal{A}$ and $\mathcal{B}$ into a single $(T_1 \cup T_2)$-interpretation $\mathcal{M}$ satisfying $\Gamma_1^{\infty} \cup \Gamma_2^{\infty}$. Clearly, this goal can be accomplished by an application of the Combination Theorem 17 if we can show that $\mathcal{A}^{\Sigma_1 \cap \Sigma_2, S} \cong \mathcal{B}^{\Sigma_1 \cap \Sigma_2, S}$. Accordingly, we define a function $h : A \to B$ by letting

$$h(a) = [name_A(a)]^{\mathcal{B}}, \qquad\qquad \text{for each } a \in A,$$

where $name_A : A \to S$ is any fixed function such that

$$[name_A(a)]^{\mathcal{A}} = a, \qquad\qquad \text{for each } a \in A.$$

It is easy, albeit tedious, to verify that h is an isomorphism of $\mathcal{A}^{\Sigma_1 \cap \Sigma_2, S}$ into $\mathcal{B}^{\Sigma_1 \cap \Sigma_2, S}$. We can therefore apply the Combination Theorem 17 and obtain a $(T_1 \cup T_2)$-interpretation satisfying $\Gamma_1^\infty \cup \Gamma_2^\infty$. Since $\Gamma_1 \cup \Gamma_2 \subseteq \Gamma_1^\infty \cup \Gamma_2^\infty$, it follows that $\Gamma_1 \cup \Gamma_2$ is $(T_1 \cup T_2)$-satisfiable, a contradiction. ∎

Combining lemmas 9 and 10 we obtain the following result.

Theorem 18. *Let T_i be an universal Σ_i-theory such that, for $i = 1, 2$, there exists a decision procedure for the T_i-satisfiability of quantifier-free Σ-formulae.*
Then the rules in Figure 4 provide a semi-decision procedure for the $(T_1 \cup T_2)$-unsatisfiability of quantifier-free $(\Sigma_1 \cup \Sigma_2)$-formulae. □

6.4   Why Universal Theories?

Theorem 18 proves that the procedure presented in this section is sound and complete under the assumption that the combined theories T_1 and T_2 are universal. As an example of what can go wrong when one of the theories is not universal, consider the following theories

$$T_1 = \{(\exists x)\neg P(x)\}, \qquad\qquad T_2 = \{(\forall x)P(x)\},$$

and the literal $u \neq v$.

Since $T_1 \cup T_2$ is unsatisfiable, it follows that $u \neq v$ is $(T_1 \cup T_2)$-unsatisfiable, but the decision procedure presented in this section is unable to detect the unsatisfiability.

7   Conclusions

The problem of combining decision procedures is important for the development of program analysis and program verification systems. The problem can be stated as follows: Given decision procedures P_1 and P_2 for the quantifier-free validity problem of theories T_1 and T_2, how can we obtain a decision procedure $P_{1\&2}$ for the quantifier-free validity problem of $T_1 \cup T_2$?

We saw that if T_1 and T_2 are stably infinite and the signatures of the theories T_1 and T_2 are disjoint, then we can construct the decision procedure $P_{1\&2}$ using the Nelson-Oppen combination method.

Despite being more than 20 years old, the Nelson-Oppen combination method is the current state of the art solution for the problem of combining decision procedures in the disjiont case. The Nelson-Oppen method is also a generalization of Shostak's method.

The problem of combining decision procedures for theories over non-disjoint signatures is much more difficult, and has only recently been attacked by researchers. We showed that if T_1 and T_2 are universal, then it is always possible to combine the decision procedures P_1 and P_2, although only a semi-decision result is obtained in general. Further research needs to be done in order to find special cases in which decidability holds.

Acknowledgments

We thank the anonymous referee, Clark W. Barrett, Cesar Sanchez, Emilia Katz, Sriram Sankaranarayanan, Henny B. Sipma, and Matteo Slanina for useful comments.

This research was supported in part by NSF grants CCR-01-21403, CCR-02-20134 and CCR-02-09237, by ARO grant DAAD19-01-1-0723, by ARPA/AF contracts F33615-00-C-1693 and F33615-99-C-3014, and by NAVY/ONR contract N00014-03-1-0939.

References

1. W. Ackermann. *Solvable Cases of the Decision Problem*. North-Holland Publishing Company, 1954.
2. F. Baader and K. U. Schulz. Combining constraint solving. In H. Comon, C. Marché, and R. Treinen, editors, *Constraints in Computational Logics*, volume 2002 of *Lecture Notes in Computer Science*, pages 104–158, 2001.
3. C. W. Barrett, D. L. Dill, and J. L. Levitt. Validity checking for combinations of theories with equality. In *Formal Methods in Computer-Aided Design*, volume 1166 of *Lecture Notes in Computer Science*, pages 187–201, 1996.
4. C. W. Barrett, D. L. Dill, and A. Stump. A generalization of Shostak's method for combining decision procedures. In A. Armando, editor, *Frontiers of Combining Systems*, volume 2309 of *Lecture Notes in Computer Science*, pages 132–146. Springer, 2002.
5. E. T. Bell. Exponential numbers. *American Mathematical Monthly*, 41:411–419, 1934.
6. N. S. Bjørner. *Integrating Decision Procedures for Temporal Verification*. PhD thesis, Stanford University, 1998.
7. N. S. Bjørner, A. Browne, M. Colón, B. Finkbeiner, Z. Manna, H. B. Sipma, and T. E. Uribe. Verifying temporal properties of reactive systems: A STeP tutorial. *Formal Methods in System Design*, 16(3):227–270, 2000.
8. D. Cantone and C. G. Zarba. A new fast tableau-based decision procedure for an unquantified fragment of set theory. In R. Caferra and G. Salzer, editors, *Automated Deduction in Classical and Non-Classical Logics*, volume 1761 of *Lecture Notes in Computer Science*, pages 127–137. Springer, 2000.
9. A. Church. A note on the Entscheidungsproblem. *Journal of Symbolic Logic*, 1:101–102, 1936.
10. G. E. Collins. Quantifier elimination for the elementary theory of real closed fields by cylindrical algebraic decomposition. In H. Brakhage, editor, *Automata Theory and Formal Languages*, volume 33 of *Lecture Notes in Computer Science*, pages 134–183. Springer, 1975.

11. D. C. Cooper. Theorem proving in arithmetic without multiplication. In B. Meltzer and D. Michie, editors, *Machine Intelligence*, volume 7, pages 91–99. Edinburgh University Press, 1972.

12. D. Craigen, S. Kromodimoeljo, I. Meisels, B. Pase, and M. Saaltink. EVES: An overview. In S. Prehen and H. Toetenel, editors, *Formal Software Development Methods*, volume 552 of *Lecture Notes in Computer Science*, pages 389–405. Springer, 1991.

13. D. Cyrluk, P. Lincoln, and N. Shankar. On Shostak's decision procedure for combinations of theories. In M. A. McRobbia and J. K. Slaney, editors, *Automated Deduction – CADE-13*, volume 1104 of *Lecture Notes in Computer Science*, pages 463–477. Springer, 1996.

14. J. H. Davenport and J. Heintz. Real quantifier elimination is doubly exponential. *Journal of Symbolic Computation*, 5:29–35, 1988.

15. N. G. de Bruijn. *Asymptotic Methods in Analysis*. North-Holland Publishing Company, 1958.

16. D. L. Detlefs, K. Rustan, M. Leino, G. Nelson, and J. B. Saxe. Extended static checking. Technical Report 159, Compaq System Research Center, 1998.

17. P. Downey and R. Sethi. Assignment commands with array references. *Journal of the Association for Computing Machinery*, 25(4):652–666, 1978.

18. P. J. Downey, R. Sethi, and R. E. Tarjan. Variations on the common subexpression problem. *Journal of the Association for Computing Machinery*, 27(4):758–771, 1980.

19. H. B. Enderton. *A Mathematical Introduction to Logic*. Academic Press, 2nd edition, 2000.

20. J. Ferrante and C. Rackoff. A decision procedure for the first order theory of real addition with order. *SIAM Journal on Computing*, 4(1):69–76, 1975.

21. J.-C. Filliâtre, S. Owre, H. Rueß, and N. Shankar. ICS: Integrated Canonizer and Solver. In G. Berry, H. Comon, and F. Alain, editors, *Computer Aided Verification*, volume 2102 of *Lecture Notes in Computer Science*, pages 246–249, 2001.

22. M. J. Fischer and M. O. Rabin. Super-exponential complexity of Presburger arithmetic. In R. M. Karp, editor, *Complexity of Computation*, volume 7 of *SIAM-AMS proceedings*, pages 27–42. American Mathematical Society, 1974.

23. H. Ganzinger. Shostak light. In A. Voronkov, editor, *Automated Deduction – CADE-18*, volume 2392 of *Lecture Notes in Computer Science*, pages 332–346. Springer, 2002.

24. D. Kapur. A rewrite rule based framework for combining decision procedures. In A. Armando, editor, *Frontiers of Combining System*, volume 2309 of *Lecture Notes in Computer Science*, pages 87–102. Springer, 2002.

25. L. G. Khachiyan. A polynomial algorithm in linear programming. *Soviet Mathematics Doklady*, 20:191–194, 1979.

26. D. Kozen. Complexity of finitely presented algebras. In *Proceedings of the ninth annual ACM symposium on Theory of computing*, pages 164–177, 1977.

27. G. Kreisel and J. L. Krivine. *Elements of Mathematical Logic*. Studies in Logic and the Foundations of Mathematics. North-Holland Publishing Company, 1967.

28. S. Krstić and S. Conchon. Canonization for disjoint union of theories. Technical Report CSE-03-003, Oregon Health and Science University, 2003.

29. J.-L. Lassez and M. J. Mahler. On Fourier's algorithm for linear constraints. *Journal of Automated Reasoning*, 9(3):373–379, 1992.

30. J. L. Levitt. *Formal Verification Techniques for Digital Systems*. PhD thesis, Stanford University, 1998.

31. B. Levy, I. Filippenko, L. Marcus, and T. Menas. Using the state delta verification system (SDVS) for hardware verification. In T. F. Melham, V. Stavridou, and R. T. Boute, editors, *Theorem Prover in Circuit Design: Theory, Practice and Experience*, pages 337–360. Elsevier Science, 1992.

32. D. C. Luckham, S. M. German, F. W. von Henke, R. A. Karp, P. W. Milne, D. C. Oppen, W. Polak, and W. L. Scherlis. Stanford pascal verifier user manual. Technical Report STAN-CS-79-731, Stanford University, 1979.

33. Y. V. Matiyasevich. Diophantine representation of recursively enumerable predicates. In J. E. Fenstad, editor, *Second Scandinavian Logic Symposium*, volume 63 of *Studies in Logic and the Foundations of Mathematics*, pages 171–177. North-Holland Publishing Company, 1971.

34. J. McCarthy. Towards a mathematical science of computation. In *IFIP Congress 62*, 1962.

35. G. Nelson. Techniques for program verification. Technical Report CSL-81-10, Xerox Palo Alto Research Center, 1981.

36. G. Nelson. Combining satisfiability procedures by equality sharing. In W. W. Bledsoe and D. W. Loveland, editors, *Automated Theorem Proving: After 25 Years*, volume 29 of *Contemporary Mathematics*, pages 201–211. American Mathematical Society, 1984.

37. G. Nelson and D. C. Oppen. Simplification by cooperating decision procedures. *ACM Transactions on Programming Languages and Systems*, 1(2):245–257, 1979.

38. G. Nelson and D. C. Oppen. Fast decision procedures based on congruence closure. *Journal of the Association for Computing Machinery*, 27(2):356–364, 1980.

39. D. C. Oppen. A $2^{2^{2^{pn}}}$ upper bound on the complexity of Presburger arithmetic. *Journal of Computer and System Sciences*, 16(3):323–332, 1978.

40. D. C. Oppen. Complexity, convexity and combinations of theories. *Theoretical Computer Science*, 12:291–302, 1980.

41. D. C. Oppen. Reasoning about recursively defined data structures. *Journal of the Association for Computing Machinery*, 27(3):403–411, 1980.

42. S. Owre, S. Rajan, J. M. Rushby, N. Shankar, and M. K. Srivas. PVS: Combining specification, proof checking and model checking. In R. Alur and T. A. Henzinger, editors, *Computer Aided Verification*, volume 1102 of *Lecture Notes in Computer Science*, pages 411–414. Springer, 1996.

43. C. H. Papadimitriou. On the complexity of integer programming. *Journal of the Association for Computing Machinery*, 28(4):765, 768, 1981.

44. M. Presburger. Über die vollständigkeit eines gewissen systems der arithmetik ganzer zahlen, in welchen die addition als einzige operation hervortritt. In *Comptes Rendus du Premier Congrès des Mathématici04nes des Pays Slaves*, pages 92–101, 1929.

45. C. Ringeissen. Cooperation of decision procedures for the satisfiability problem. In F. Baader and K. U. Schulz, editors, *Frontiers of Combining Systems*, volume 3 of *Applied Logic Series*, pages 121–140. Kluwer Academic Publishers, 1996.

46. H. Rueß and N. Shankar. Deconstructing Shostak. In *Sixteenth Annual IEEE Symposium on Logic in Computer Science*, pages 19–28. IEEE Computer Society, 2001.

47. N. Shankar and H. Rueß. Combining Shostak theories. In S. Tison, editor, *Rewriting Techniques and Applications*, volume 2378 of *Lecture Notes in Computer Science*, pages 1–18. Springer, 2002.

48. R. E. Shostak. An algorithm for reasoning about equality. *Communications of the Association for Computing Machinery*, 21(7):583–585, 1978.

49. R. E. Shostak. A practical decision procedure for arithmetic with function symbols. *Journal of the Association for Computing Machinery*, 26(2):351–360, 1979.

50. R. E. Shostak. Deciding combination of theories. *Journal of the Association for Computing Machinery*, 31(1):1–12, 1984.

51. A. Stump, C. W. Barret, and D. L. Dill. CVC: A cooperating validity checker. In E. Brinksma and K. G. Larsen, editors, *Computer Aided Verification*, volume 2404 of *Lecture Notes in Computer Science*, pages 500–504, 2002.

52. A. Stump, C. W. Barret, D. L. Dill, and J. Levitt. A decision procedure for an extensional theory of arrays. In *Sixteenth Annual IEEE Symposium on Logic in Computer Science*, pages 29–37. IEEE Computer Society, 2001.

53. N. Suzuki and D. Jefferson. Verification decidability of Presburger array programs. *Journal of the Association for Computing Machinery*, 27(1):191–205, 1980.

54. A. Tarski. *A Decision Method for Elementary Algebra and Geometry*. University of California Press, 1951.

55. C. Tinelli. Cooperation of background reasoners in theory reasoning by residue sharing. Technical Report 02-03, Department of Computer Science, University of Iowa, 2002.

56. C. Tinelli and M. T. Harandi. A new correctness proof of the Nelson-Oppen combination procedure. In F. Baader and K. U. Schulz, editors, *Frontiers of Combining Systems*, volume 3 of *Applied Logic Series*, pages 103–120. Kluwer Academic Publishers, 1996.

57. C. Tinelli and C. Ringeissen. Unions of non-disjoint theories and combinations of satisfiability procedures. *Theoretical Computer Science*, 290(1):291–353, 2003.

58. A. Tiwari. *Decision Procedures in Automated Deduction*. PhD thesis, State University of New York at Stony Brook, 2000.

59. A. M. Turing. On computable numbers, with an application to the Entscheidungsproblem. *Proceedings of the London Mathematical Society*, 42:230–265, 1936.

60. C. G. Zarba. Combining multisets with integers. In A. Voronkov, editor, *Automated Deduction – CADE-18*, volume 2392 of *Lecture Notes in Computer Science*, pages 363–376. Springer, 2002.

61. C. G. Zarba. A tableau calculus for combining non-disjoint theories. In U. Egly and C. G. Fermüller, editors, *Automated Reasoning with Analytic Tableaux and Related Methods*, volume 2381 of *Lecture Notes in Computer Science*, pages 315–329. Springer, 2002.

Appendix

We prove the Combination Theorem 17, and then we prove the Combination Theorem for Disjoint Theories 2 as a corollary of the Combination Theorem 17.

We will use the following lemma.

Lemma 11. *Let $\mathcal{A}$ and $\mathcal{B}$ be Σ-interpretations over some set V of variables, and assume that $\mathcal{A} \cong \mathcal{B}$. Then $\varphi^{\mathcal{A}} = \varphi^{\mathcal{B}}$, for each Σ-formula φ whose free variables are in V.*   □

Theorem 17 (Combination Theorem). *Let Σ_1 and Σ_2 be signatures, let Φ_i be a set of Σ_i-formulae, for $i = 1, 2$, and let $V_i = vars(\Phi_i)$.*

Then $\Phi_1 \cup \Phi_2$ is satisfiable if and only if there exists a Σ_1-interpretation $\mathcal{A}$ satisfying Φ_1 and a Σ_2-interpretation $\mathcal{B}$ satisfying Φ_2 such that

$$\mathcal{A}^{\Sigma_1 \cap \Sigma_2, V_1 \cap V_2} \cong \mathcal{B}^{\Sigma_1 \cap \Sigma_2, V_1 \cap V_2} .$$

□

PROOF. To make the notation more concise, let $\Sigma = \Sigma_1 \cap \Sigma_2$ and $V = V_1 \cap V_2$.

Next, assume that $\Phi_1 \cup \Phi_2$ is satisfiable, and let $\mathcal{M}$ be an interpretation satisfying $\Phi_1 \cup \Phi_2$. Then, by letting $\mathcal{A} = \mathcal{M}^{\Sigma_1, V_1}$ and $\mathcal{B} = \mathcal{M}^{\Sigma_2, V_2}$, we clearly have that:

- $\mathcal{A}$ satisfies Φ_1;
- $\mathcal{B}$ satisfies Φ_2;
- $\mathcal{A}^{\Sigma, V} \cong \mathcal{B}^{\Sigma, V}$.

Vice versa, assume that there exists an interpretation $\mathcal{A}$ satisfying Φ_1 and an interpretation $\mathcal{B}$ satisfying Φ_2 such that $\mathcal{A}^{\Sigma, V} \cong \mathcal{B}^{\Sigma, V}$, and let $h : A \to B$ be an isomorphism of $\mathcal{A}$ into $\mathcal{B}$. We define an interpretation $\mathcal{M}$ by letting $M = A$ and:

- for variables and constants:

$$u^{\mathcal{M}} = \begin{cases} u^{\mathcal{A}}, & \text{if } u \in (\Sigma_1^{\mathrm{C}} \cup V_1), \\ h^{-1}(u^{\mathcal{B}}), & \text{if } u \in (\Sigma_2^{\mathrm{C}} \cup V_2) \setminus (\Sigma_1^{\mathrm{C}} \cup V_1), \end{cases}$$

- for function symbols of arity n:

$$f^{\mathcal{M}}(a_1, \ldots, a_n) = \begin{cases} f^{\mathcal{A}}(a_1, \ldots, a_n), & \text{if } f \in \Sigma_1^{\mathrm{F}}, \\ h^{-1}(f^{\mathcal{B}}(h(a_1), \ldots, h(a_n))), & \text{if } f \in \Sigma_2^{\mathrm{F}} \setminus \Sigma_1^{\mathrm{F}}, \end{cases}$$

- for predicate symbols of arity n:

$$(a_1, \ldots, a_n) \in P^{\mathcal{M}} \iff (a_1, \ldots, a_n) \in P^{\mathcal{A}}, \qquad \text{if } P \in \Sigma_1^{\mathrm{P}}$$
$$(a_1, \ldots, a_n) \in P^{\mathcal{M}} \iff (h(a_1), \ldots, h(a_n)) \in P^{\mathcal{B}}, \qquad \text{if } P \in \Sigma_2^{\mathrm{P}} \setminus \Sigma_1^{\mathrm{P}}.$$

By construction, $\mathcal{M}^{\Sigma_1, V_1} \cong \mathcal{A}$. In addition, it is easy to verify that h is an isomorphism of $\mathcal{M}^{\Sigma_2, V_2}$ into $\mathcal{B}$. Thus, by Lemma 11, $\mathcal{M}$ satisfies $\Phi_1 \cup \Phi_2$. ∎

Theorem 2 (Combination Theorem for Disjoint Signatures). *Let Φ_i be a set of Σ_i-formulae, for $i = 1, 2$, and let $\Sigma_1 \cap \Sigma_2 = \emptyset$.*

Then $\Phi_1 \cup \Phi_2$ is satisfiable if and only if there exists an interpretation $\mathcal{A}$ satisfying Φ_1 and an interpretation $\mathcal{B}$ satisfying Φ_2 such that:

(i) $|A| = |B|$,
(ii) $x^{\mathcal{A}} = y^{\mathcal{A}}$ if and only if $x^{\mathcal{B}} = y^{\mathcal{B}}$, for every variable $x, y \in shared(\Phi_1, \Phi_2)$.□

PROOF. Clearly, if there exists an interpretation $\mathcal{M}$ satisfying $\Phi_1 \cup \Phi_2$, then the only if direction holds by letting $\mathcal{A} = \mathcal{M}$ and $\mathcal{B} = \mathcal{M}$.

Concerning the if direction, assume that there exists a Σ_1-interpretation $\mathcal{A}$ satisfying Φ_1 and a Σ_2-interpretation $\mathcal{B}$ satisfying Φ_2 such that both (i) and (ii) hold. Also, let $V = shared(\Phi_1, \Phi_2)$.

In order to apply Theorem 17, we define a function $h : V^{\mathcal{A}} \to V^{\mathcal{B}}$ by letting $h(x^{\mathcal{A}}) = x^{\mathcal{B}}$, for every $x \in V^{\mathcal{A}}$. Note that this position is sound because property (ii) holds.

We claim that h is a bijective function. To show that h is injective, let $h(a_1) = h(a_2)$. Then there exist variables $x, y \in V$ such that $a_1 = x^{\mathcal{A}}$, $a_2 = y^{\mathcal{A}}$, and $x^{\mathcal{B}} = y^{\mathcal{B}}$. By property (ii), we have $x^{\mathcal{A}} = y^{\mathcal{A}}$, and therefore $a_1 = a_2$. To show that h is surjective, let $b \in V^{\mathcal{B}}$. Then there exists a variable $x \in V^{\mathcal{B}}$ such that $x^{\mathcal{B}} = b$. But then $h(x^{\mathcal{A}}) = b$, proving that h is surjective.

Since h is a bijective function, we have $|V^{\mathcal{A}}| = |V^{\mathcal{B}}|$, and since $|A| = |B|$, we also have that $|A \setminus V^{\mathcal{A}}| = |B \setminus V^{\mathcal{B}}|$. We can therefore extend h to a bijective function h' from A to B.

Clearly, by construction h' is an isomorphism of $\mathcal{A}^V$ into $\mathcal{B}^V$. Thus, we can apply Theorem 17, and obtain the existence of an interpretation $\mathcal{M}$ satisfying $\Phi_1 \cup \Phi_2$.   ∎

A Theory of Hints in Model Checking*

Markus Kaltenbach[1] and Jayadev Misra[2]

[1] Transmeta Corporation, Santa Clara, CA 95054
markus@transmeta.com
[2] Department of Computer Sciences
The University of Texas at Austin
Austin, TX 78712
misra@cs.utexas.edu

Abstract. Model checking, in particular symbolic model checking, has proved to be extremely successful in establishing properties of finite state programs. In most cases, the proven properties are safety properties stating that the program never executes outside a specified set of states. But another important class of properties, progress (liveness) properties, which state that program execution eventually reaches some specified set of states, has been difficult to model-check as they, typically, involve doubly-nested fixpoint computations. In this paper, we propose that progress properties can be checked more efficiently if they are accompanied by *hints* as to why they hold. We develop a theory in which hints are given as regular expressions over the actions of the program. We derive a number of inference rules and algebraic properties of hints. Empirical evidence suggests that hints can significantly improve the efficiency of model checking.

1 Introduction

Model checking [CE81,CES86] has been one of the most successful recent techniques for automated verifications of finite state systems. Symbolic model checking ([McM93], [BCM91]) has made it possible to analyze systems of very large size, such as those arising in circuit and protocol designs.

The typical property that is checked for a deterministic system, such as a circuit, is that the outputs are the desired ones given the appropriate inputs, i.e., that the circuit outputs are a specified function of its inputs. In many asynchronous systems, such as communication and synchronization protocols, such properties are not adequate to specify the system behavior. Instead, we specify a set of *safety* and *progress* properties to describe the system. Informally, safety properties express that "Something will *not* happen", whereas progress properties state that "something *must* happen" ([Lam77], [AS85]).

Safety properties can often be checked more efficiently than by just performing a state space exploration (which is the essence of the model checking approach), when adding some deductive reasoning by checking certain predicates

---

* Partially supported by NSF grant CCR–9803842.

B.K. Aichernig and T. Maibaum (Eds.): Formal Methods ..., LNCS 2757, pp. 423–438, 2003.

on each state and its successor states, and supplementing this with finding suitably strong invariants. Decision procedures for progress properties have proved to be far less efficient because such properties cannot be characterized by local conditions asserting how pairs of successive states are related to each other (if this were possible then progress properties could be characterized by finite execution prefixes as well). Establishing progress properties in theorem provers requires transfinite induction over well-founded sets, whereas in model checking a doubly-nested fixpoint computation is required to establish most progress properties under any reasonable definition of fairness. Our experience confirms that progress properties are hard to check; in a model checker developed by the first author, straightforward verifications of progress properties were at least two orders of magnitude slower than the safety properties of those systems. Therefore, in practice, only safety aspects of systems are often verified; progress properties are usually dismissed or argued about informally.

In this paper, we show that progress properties can be often be checked efficiently by supplying hints to the checker. Typically, hints have been used in automated verification systems to guide the prover through a search space interactively, or in guiding the automated checking of safety properties ([BRS00]). In our work, a hint is a regular expression over the actions of the program, suggesting how a goal state is achieved. A central theorem asserts that a property established under any hint is a property of the program. We motivate our work using a small example below.

Consider a program consisting of three actions – [up], [down], [set] – that operate on two program variables, an integer n and a boolean b. The actions are as follows.

$$
\begin{array}{lll}
[\text{up}] & \neg b \to & n := n + 1 \\
[\text{down}] & & n := n - 1 \\
[\text{set}] & & b := \text{true}
\end{array}
$$

The action [up] increments n only if $\neg b$ holds, otherwise (if b holds) its execution has no effect. Actions are executed forever in arbitrary order subject to the fairness rule that every action be executed infinitely often. It follows then that eventually $n \leq 0$ holds no matter what the initial state is. If n is restricted to a finite range, a model checker can verify this property. However, even for moderate ranges of n the computation becomes prohibitively expensive.

Our approach is to provide a hint to the checker as to why the property holds. The hint embodies our intuitive understanding of how $n \leq 0$ is achieved. For this example, we realize that eventually action [set] will be executed, thus setting b to true, and from then on neither [up] nor [set] has any effect on the program state; each subsequent execution of [down] decreases n, establishing $n \leq 0$ eventually. We encode this reasoning in the hint [set][down]* which is a regular expression over the actions of the program; i.e., any execution sequence consisting of [set] and a sufficiently large number of [down] actions achieves $n \leq 0$. The key observation is that *every valid execution sequence, under our notion of fairness, includes every sequence described by a regular expression as* *a subsequence.* Thus, a property proven under a hint (i.e., for specific execution sequences) holds for all execution sequences as well. A model checker can use a hint to eliminate some unnecessary fixpoint computations and to simplify others.

The precise operational meaning of progress under a given hint is surprisingly difficult to state succinctly; see Sect. 4.5. A formal definition using predicate transformers is given in Sect. 4.1 and an algebra of hints that is similar to the Kleene algebra of regular expressions is developed in Sect. 4.3. Hints have been incorporated into a model checker developed by the first author, and they seem to deliver significant improvements in performance; see Sect. 5.

We couch our discussion in terms of the UNITY logic [CM88,Mis95b,Mis95a] though the ideas can be applied to other formalisms. We discovered that the definition of the *leads-to* operator of UNITY mirrors the structure of regular expressions: transitivity of *leads-to* corresponds to concatenation, finite disjunctivity to choice, and general disjunctivity (or induction) to Kleene closure. Also, UNITY's notion of unconditional fairness in execution – every action is executed eventually – guarantees that every execution sequence includes any given finite sequence of actions as a subsequence. This observation permits us to prove a progress property for all execution sequences by proving it for a certain class of finite executions.

2 Background

We give a brief overview of the UNITY programming notation and its temporal logic, to the extent necessary for this paper. See [CM88] for the initial work and [Mis01] for some recent developments.

2.1 A Programming Notation

The computational model of UNITY is that of a deterministic, total, labeled state transition system. This model is well suited for describing many common classes of systems (e.g. hardware circuits or protocols).

A program consists of (1) a *declare* section defining the state space of the program, (2) an *initially* section specifying the initial conditions, and (3) an *assign* section specifying the actions of the program (its transition relation) as guarded multiple assignment statements, that are deterministic and terminating.

An execution of a program consists of selecting a start state satisfying the conditions of the *initially* section and then repeatedly selecting statements (from the *assign* section) and executing them (if the guard of a selected statement evaluates to false in the current state, the entire statement is equivalent to a *skip* operation, i.e., it does not change the state). The selection of statements is subject to the unconditional fairness constraint that every statement be selected infinitely often.

2.2 UNITY Logic

The UNITY logic, a fragment of linear temporal logic, has proof rules for reasoning about properties of programs. Different from many state-based computational models that reason about individual executions of programs, the UNITY operators characterize properties of programs, i.e., properties of *all* unconditionally fair execution sequences.

In the following, we introduce the UNITY operators and some rules for reasoning with them to the extent needed for this paper. Proofs of most rules are straightforward and can be found in chapters 5 and 6 of [Mis01]. In our presentation we make use of the following notation: for a program F the predicate $F.I$ denotes the initial states as characterized by the **initially** section of F, and $F.A$ denotes the set of the actions of F. For any state predicate p of F we write $[p]$ to denote the universal quantification of p over the state space of F [DS90]. We write $\mathbf{wp}.\alpha$, where α is any action in $F.A$, for the *weakest precondition* predicate transformer; i.e., for a state predicate p, the predicate $\mathbf{wp}.\alpha.p$ characterizes those states from which the execution of α terminates in a state satisfying p[1].

Safety. The fundamental safety operator of UNITY is *constrains*, or **co** for short. The **co** operator is a binary relation over state predicates and is defined as follows:

$$\frac{\langle \forall \alpha : \alpha \in F.A : [p \Rightarrow \mathbf{wp}.\alpha.q] \rangle, \ [p \Rightarrow q]}{p \ \mathbf{co} \ q}$$

The property p **co** q asserts that in any execution, a state satisfying p is always followed by a state satisfying q. In order to model stuttering steps p is required to imply q. Several other safety operators are expressed in terms of **co** :

$$\frac{p \ \mathbf{co} \ p}{\mathbf{stable} \ p} \qquad\qquad \frac{\langle \forall e :: \mathbf{stable} \ x = e \rangle}{\mathbf{constant} \ x}$$

$$\frac{\mathbf{stable} \ p, \ [F.I \Rightarrow p]}{\mathbf{invariant} \ p} \qquad\qquad \frac{p \wedge \neg q \ \mathbf{co} \ p \vee q}{p \ \mathbf{unless} \ q}$$

A predicate is *stable*, if it remains true once it becomes true. An expression x is *constant* if its value never changes, i.e., if for any possible value e the predicate $x = e$ is stable. A predicate is *invariant* if it is stable and holds in all initial program states. Finally, p **unless** q holds if starting in any state that satisfies p either p continues to hold forever, or holds up to (but not necessarily including) a state satisfying q.

The Substitution Axiom. The operation of a program is over the reachable part of its state space. The UNITY proof rules, however, do not refer to the set of reachable states explicitly. Instead, the following *substitution axiom* is used to restrict attention to the reachable states.

---

[1] Recall that in the UNITY model all actions are terminating.

$$\text{invariant } p$$
$$\overline{[p]}$$

Since an invariant of a program is true over the reachable part of the state space, it is equivalent to true in any program property. Thereby the substitution axiom allows us to replace any invariant predicate of a program F by true (and vice versa) in any proof of a property of F.

Progress. The basic progress property is **transient** ; it is a unary relation on state predicates. A transient predicate is guaranteed to be falsified in any program execution: predicate p is transient in program F if there is an action in F whose execution *in any state* in which p holds establishes $\neg p$:

$$\frac{\langle \exists \alpha : \alpha \in F.A : [p \Rightarrow \mathbf{wp}.\alpha.(\neg p)]\rangle}{\text{transient } p}$$

From the unconditional fairness rule, the given action α is executed eventually, falsifying p if it held before the execution of α.

The other basic progress property is **ensures** , a binary relation on state predicates:

$$\frac{p \textbf{ unless } q, \textbf{ transient } p \wedge \neg q}{p \textbf{ ensures } q}$$

Given p **ensures** q , from the **transient** part of the definition there is an action of F that establishes $\neg p \vee q$ starting in any state in which $p \wedge \neg q$ holds; from the **unless** part, once p holds it continues to hold up to the point at which q is established. Therefore, starting in a state in which p holds, q is established eventually.

Since there is a single rule for establishing an **ensures** property of a program, we can derive from the **ensures** rule and the substitution axiom the following equivalence:

$$p \textbf{ ensures } q \quad \equiv \quad \begin{aligned}&[p \wedge \neg q \Rightarrow \mathbf{wco}.(p \vee q)] \quad \wedge\\ &[\langle \exists \alpha : \alpha \in F.A : p \wedge \neg q \Rightarrow \mathbf{wp}.\alpha.q\rangle]\end{aligned}$$

where the predicate transformer $\mathbf{wco}$ is defined by $[\mathbf{wco}.p \equiv \langle \forall \alpha : \alpha \in F.A : \mathbf{wp}.\alpha.p\rangle]$; in other words, $\mathbf{wco}.p$ denotes the states from which the execution of *any* action of F terminates in a state satisfying p.

In developing our theory we make use of another property, $\textbf{ensures}_\alpha$, which resembles **ensures** but explicitly names the helpful action, α. For an action α in $F.A$ we define:

$$p \textbf{ ensures}_\alpha q \quad \equiv \quad [p \wedge \neg q \Rightarrow \mathbf{wco}.(p \vee q)] \wedge [p \wedge \neg q \Rightarrow \mathbf{wp}.\alpha.q]$$

The fundamental progress property of UNITY is the $\mapsto$ (leads-to) operator, a binary relation on state predicates. It is the transitive, disjunctive closure of the **ensures** relation, i.e., the strongest relation satisfying the following three conditions:

$$\frac{p \text{ ensures } q}{p \mapsto q} \qquad \textbf{(promotion)}$$

$$\frac{p \mapsto q, \ q \mapsto r}{p \mapsto r} \qquad \textbf{(transitivity)}$$

$$\frac{\langle \forall h : h \in H : p.h \mapsto q\rangle}{\langle \exists h : h \in H : p.h\rangle \mapsto q} \quad \text{for any set } H \qquad \textbf{(disjunction)}$$

There are also several derived rules for reasoning about progress properties [CM88,Mis01]. Among them is the *induction principle*: for a well-founded set $(H, \prec)$ and a function M mapping program states to H we have

$$\frac{\langle \forall h : h \in H : p \wedge M = h \mapsto (p \wedge M \prec h) \vee q\rangle}{p \mapsto q} \qquad \textbf{(induction)}$$

The Predicate Transformer wlt. In [Kna90,JKR89] a predicate transformer, **wlt**, *weakest leads-to*, was introduced for reasoning about progress properties. It is related to the $\mapsto$ relation by

$$[p \Rightarrow \textbf{wlt}.q] \quad \equiv \quad p \mapsto q$$

Using this equivalence we can model check a property of the form $p \mapsto q$ for program F by first computing **wlt**$.q$ and then evaluating $(p \Rightarrow \textbf{wlt}.q)$ over the reachable state space of F. A fixpoint characterization suitable for computing **wlt** is given in [JKR89].

3   Hints and Generalized Progress

Progress properties are specified using the *leads-to* operator in UNITY logic, formulae of the form $\mathbf{AG}(p \Rightarrow \mathbf{AF}q)$ in CTL, or formulae like $\mathbf{G}(p \Rightarrow \mathbf{F}q)$ in linear temporal logic. These operators specify the changes to the program state, but not the way the change is effected. Usually a program designer has some (possibly partial) knowledge of how progress is achieved in the program, either as an operational argument, in the form of a high level proof sketch, or simply based on experience with similar programs. We propose to exploit this knowledge by providing a formal foundation for it.

We elaborate on the small example introduced in Sect. 1 to illustrate how progress properties are generalized by including explicit action-based progress information. We then argue how this theory and its associated methodology can be used in program verification.

```
program UpDown
    declare
        var n : integer
        var b : boolean
    assign
        [up]      ¬b →  n := n + 1
        [down]           n := n − 1
        [set]            b := true
    end
```

Fig. 1. Program *UpDown*.

We consider the UNITY program *UpDown* shown in Fig. 1. As we have argued earlier, for any execution of this program n becomes non-positive eventually, which is expressed by the following leads-to property:

$$\text{true} \quad \mapsto \quad n \leq 0.$$

We reproduce the informal argument from Sect. 1 to justify this progress property. From unconditional fairness, action [set] will eventually be executed, thus setting b to true, and from then on neither [up] nor [set] has any effect on the program state; each subsequent execution of [down] decreases n, establishing $n \leq 0$ eventually. This argument suggests that the progress from true to $n \leq 0$ is achieved by the strategy expressed by the regular expression

$$[\text{set}][\text{down}]^*,$$

over the alphabet of actions of *UpDown*, i.e., by one [set] action followed by some finite number of [down] actions (possibly interleaved with other actions). We combine the hint with the progress property:

$$\text{true} \xrightarrow{[\text{set}][\text{down}]^*} n \leq 0.$$

which is a *generalized progress property* of program *UpDown*. We now show that this property is closely related to the structure of the proof of true $\mapsto n \leq 0$ in the UNITY deductive system.

0.	true **ensures** b	; from program text via [set]
1.	true $\mapsto b$	; promotion from 0
2.	$b \wedge n = k$ **ensures** $b \wedge n < k$	; from program text via [down]
3.	$b \wedge n = k \mapsto b \wedge n < k$	; promotion from 2
4.	$b \wedge |n| = k \mapsto (b \wedge |n| < k) \vee n \leq 0$	; case split and disjunction on 3
5.	$b \mapsto n \leq 0$	; leads-to induction on 4 with
		; metric $|n|$ over the naturals
6.	true $\mapsto n \leq 0$	; transitivity with 1 and 5

Steps 0 and 1 of this proof correspond to the [set] action in our proposed hint; similarly steps 2 and 3 correspond to the [down] action. The inductive argument of steps 4 and 5 establishes progress via [down]*; finally, step 6, combines the subproofs through sequencing. We claim that this proof structure corresponds to the regular expression [set][down]*. However, this regular expression is much less detailed than the complete proof; in particular, the state predicates needed to combine different parts of the proof are omitted. Thus, a general idea about the proof structure, or even an operational argument of a progress property can be turned into a hint.

4   Main Results about Generalized Progress

We now define the *generalized leads-to* relation, a relation of the form $p \overset{W}{\longmapsto} q$ for state predicates p and q and regular expression hints W. This definition is given inductively based on the structure of the regular expression W. In Sect. 4.2 we introduce a predicate transformer **wltr** and establish the central theorem that $[p \Rightarrow \textbf{wltr} . W.q] \equiv p \overset{W}{\longmapsto} q$. This result permits us to prove $p \overset{W}{\longmapsto} q$ by a model checker by first computing **wltr**$.W.q$, using a fixpoint characterization of **wltr**$.W$, and then checking for $[p \Rightarrow \textbf{wltr} . W.q]$.

Notational Conventions. Henceforth, F is a program, α is an action in $F.A$, p, p', q, r, and s are state predicates. Let U, V and W be regular expressions over the alphabet in which each symbol names an unique action of A.

4.1   Definition of Generalized Progress

First, we define a *metric* over the reachable state space of a program. In the following we use **Ord** to denote the set of ordinal numbers.

Definition 1. *A metric M for a program F is $\{i : i \in \textbf{Ord} : M.i\}$, a family of state predicates which satisfy the following two conditions:*

$$[\langle \exists i : i \in \textbf{Ord} : M.i \rangle] \qquad\qquad\qquad (\textbf{\textit{MetricExh}})$$
$$\langle \forall i, j : i \in \textbf{Ord} \wedge j \in \textbf{Ord} : i \neq j \Rightarrow [\neg(M.i \wedge M.j)] \rangle \qquad (\textbf{\textit{MetricDis}}).$$

The first condition states that the predicates in M exhaust the reachable state space of F, the second asserts that any two predicates with different indices are disjoint.

The predicates in M are totally ordered by the ordering relation $\preceq$ induced by the total order relation on the ordinals:

$$\langle \forall i, j : i \in \textbf{Ord} \wedge j \in \textbf{Ord} : i \leq j \equiv M.i \preceq M.j \rangle$$

We proceed with the definition of the generalized leads-to relation:

Definition 2. *For a given program F, $p \stackrel{W}{\longmapsto} q$ is defined as follows:*

$$p \stackrel{\varepsilon}{\longmapsto} q \quad \equiv \quad [p \Rightarrow q] \qquad\qquad\qquad\qquad\qquad\qquad \textbf{\textit{(AxEps)}}$$
$$p \stackrel{\alpha}{\longmapsto} q \quad \equiv \quad \langle \exists p' : [p \Rightarrow p'] : p' \textbf{ ensures}_\alpha q \rangle \qquad\quad \textbf{\textit{(AxAct)}}$$
$$p \stackrel{UV}{\longmapsto} q \quad \equiv \quad \langle \exists r :: (p \stackrel{U}{\longmapsto} r) \wedge (r \stackrel{V}{\longmapsto} q) \rangle \qquad \textbf{\textit{(AxSeq)}}$$
$$p \stackrel{U+V}{\longmapsto} q \quad \equiv \quad \langle \exists r, s : [r \vee s \equiv p] : (r \stackrel{U}{\longmapsto} q) \wedge (s \stackrel{V}{\longmapsto} q) \rangle \quad \textbf{\textit{(AxAlt)}}$$
$$p \stackrel{U^*}{\longmapsto} q \quad \equiv \quad \langle \exists p' : [p \Rightarrow p'] : \langle \exists M : M \text{ is a metric} : \qquad \textbf{\textit{(AxStar)}}$$
$$\langle \forall i : i \in \textbf{Ord} :$$
$$p' \wedge M.i \stackrel{U}{\longmapsto} (p' \wedge \langle \exists j : j < i : M.j \rangle) \vee q \rangle \rangle$$

From these equivalences, using structural induction, we can establish that the generalized leads-to relation is well defined; see [Kal96] for a proof.

Theorem 1. *For a program F, (AxEps), (AxAct), (AxSeq), (AxAlt), and (AxStar) define a unique family of relations $\{W :: p \stackrel{W}{\longmapsto} q\}$, for all predicates p and q.*

If $p \stackrel{W}{\longmapsto} q$ holds in a program, this can be shown by a finite number of applications of the above proof rules (due to the finiteness of the structure of W), and, hence, there is a finite proof. In the following, we write $F \vdash p \stackrel{W}{\longmapsto} q$ to denote the fact that such a proof exists for F, W, p, and q.

It is worth mentioning that the use of ordinals is essential in **(AxStar)**; under unconditional fairness it is not possible, in general, to bound the number of steps required to achieve progress from any particular start state. It can only be asserted that a finite number of steps suffices; see, for example, the second program in Sect. 3. Therefore, natural numbers are not sufficient as metric; all ordinals of cardinality less than or equal to the cardinality of the size of the state space have to be considered.

4.2   Predicate Transformers for Generalized Progress

We define a family of predicate transformers **wltr**.W, which is the set of states from which any execution "characterized by W" leads to a state satisfying q.

In the following we use the notation $\langle \mu Z :: f.Z \rangle$ and $\langle \nu Z :: f.Z \rangle$ to denote the least and greatest fixpoint of the predicate transformer f.

Definition 3. *For a given program F, and α an action in F.A,*

$$[\textbf{wltr}.\varepsilon.q \quad \equiv \quad q] \qquad\qquad\qquad\qquad\qquad\qquad \textbf{\textit{(wltrEps)}}$$
$$[\textbf{wltr}.\alpha.q \quad \equiv \quad \langle \nu Z :: (\textbf{wco}.(Z \vee q) \wedge \textbf{wp}.\alpha.q) \vee q \rangle] \quad \textbf{\textit{(wltrAct)}}$$
$$[\textbf{wltr}.(UV).q \quad \equiv \quad \textbf{wltr}.U.(\textbf{wltr}.V.q)] \qquad\qquad \textbf{\textit{(wltrSeq)}}$$
$$[\textbf{wltr}.(U+V).q \quad \equiv \quad \textbf{wltr}.U.q \vee \textbf{wltr}.V.q] \qquad\qquad \textbf{\textit{(wltrAlt)}}$$
$$[\textbf{wltr}.U^*.q \quad \equiv \quad \langle \mu Z :: q \vee \textbf{wltr}.U.Z \rangle] \qquad\qquad \textbf{\textit{(wltrStar)}}$$

Recall that **wlt** and $\longmapsto$ are related by $[p \Rightarrow \textbf{wlt}.q] \quad \equiv \quad p \longmapsto q$, as described in Sect. 2.2. Now, we establish the relationship between **wltr** and **wlt**. This is a result of fundamental importance that permits us to claim that a property proven under any hint is a property of the program.

Theorem 2. *For a state predicate q:*

$$[\textbf{wltr}.W.q \;\Rightarrow\; \textbf{wlt}.q], \text{ for any } W \qquad\qquad (wltrSound)$$
$$\langle \exists W :: [\textbf{wlt}.q \;\equiv\; \textbf{wltr}.W.q] \rangle \qquad\qquad (wltrCompl)$$

The first part of the theorem can be referred to as a *soundness* result since it asserts that the states from which a q state is reached because of W are states from which a q state is reached eventually in the sense of ordinary progress. Conversely, the second part can be seen as a *completeness* result since it shows that any state from which a q state is reached eventually is a state from which a q state is reached because of some regular expression W; see [Kal96] for proofs.

Next, we establish the connection between the generalized leads-to relation and the **wltr** predicate transformers. The result is analogous to the one relating the ordinary leads-to relation to the **wlt** predicate transformer described in Sect. 2.2. The proof of the following theorem appears in [Kal96].

Theorem 3. *For state predicates p and q:*

$$[p \Rightarrow \textbf{wltr}.W.q] \quad\equiv\quad p \xrightarrow{W} q$$

Finally, we state a number of rules that help us in establishing generalized leads-to properties of any program. These rules resemble the corresponding rules in UNITY ([CM88]).

Theorem 4. *For set S and mappings f and g from S to state predicates:*

$$[p \Rightarrow q] \quad\Rightarrow\quad (p \xrightarrow{W} q) \qquad\qquad (Imply)$$
$$[p' \Rightarrow p] \wedge (p \xrightarrow{W} q) \quad\Rightarrow\quad (p' \xrightarrow{W} q) \qquad\qquad (LhsStr)$$
$$(p \xrightarrow{W} q) \wedge [q \Rightarrow q'] \quad\Rightarrow\quad (p \xrightarrow{W} q') \qquad\qquad (RhsWeak)$$
$$\langle \forall m : m \in S : f.m \xrightarrow{W} g.m \rangle \quad\Rightarrow\qquad\qquad (GenDisj)$$
$$\qquad ((\langle \exists m : m \in S : f.m \rangle \xrightarrow{W} \langle \exists m : m \in S : g.m \rangle)$$
$$(p \xrightarrow{W} false) \quad\Rightarrow\quad [\neg p] \qquad\qquad (Impossible)$$
$$(p \xrightarrow{V} q \vee b) \wedge (b \xrightarrow{W} r) \quad\Rightarrow\quad (p \xrightarrow{VW} q \vee r) \qquad\qquad (Cancel)$$

Theorem 5. *For any W,*

$$(p \xrightarrow{W} q) \quad\Rightarrow\quad (p \mapsto q) \qquad\qquad (Sound)$$
$$(p \mapsto q) \quad\Rightarrow\quad \langle \exists W :: p \xrightarrow{W} q \rangle \qquad\qquad (Compl)$$

4.3   Progress Algebras

In this section we define an algebraic structure, *progress algebra*, by presenting a list of equalities and equational implications which define a congruence relation on regular expressions. For a program F we refer to the resulting algebraic structure as $\mathcal{R}_F$ from now on and call it the *progress algebra* for program F. First we define the equational Horn theory for $\mathcal{R}_F$, then show that $\mathcal{R}_F$ bears many similarities to the well known Kleene algebras and to the algebra of regular events. In the following, we use the familiar formalism and terminology of Kleene algebras.

We start with the definition of progress algebra in which the binary relation $\leq$ (pronounced *subsumed by*) is defined by $U \leq V \equiv U + V = V$.

Definition 4. *A progress algebra $\mathcal{K}$ is the free algebra with binary operations $\cdot$ and $+$, unary operation $*$, and constant ε satisfying the following equations and equational implications for all U, V, and W in $\mathcal{K}$:*

$$
\begin{aligned}
U + (V + W) &= (U + V) + W & \text{(PrAlg0)} \\
U + V &= V + U & \text{(PrAlg1)} \\
W + W &= W & \text{(PrAlg2)} \\
U(VW) &= (UV)W & \text{(PrAlg3)} \\
\varepsilon W &= W & \text{(PrAlg4)} \\
W\varepsilon &= W & \text{(PrAlg5)} \\
UV + UW &\leq U(V + W) & \text{(PrAlg6)} \\
(U + V)W &= UW + VW & \text{(PrAlg7)} \\
\varepsilon &\leq W & \text{(PrAlg8)} \\
\varepsilon + WW^* &\leq W^* & \text{(PrAlg9)} \\
\varepsilon + W^*W &\leq W^* & \text{(PrAlg10)} \\
UW \leq W &\Rightarrow U^*W \leq W & \text{(PrAlg11)} \\
WU \leq W &\Rightarrow WU^* \leq W & \text{(PrAlg12)}
\end{aligned}
$$

*A progress algebra satisfying (**PrAlg11**) but not necessarily (**PrAlg12**) is called a* right-handed *progress algebra, and a progress algebra satisfying (**PrAlg12**) but not necessarily (**PrAlg11**) is called a* left-handed *progress algebra.*

There are three major differences between Kleene algebras and progress algebras:

1. Progress algebras lack the equivalent of the $\emptyset$ constant of Kleene algebras. We could introduce such a constant by defining [**wltr**.$\emptyset$.$q \equiv$ false], which would actually satisfy the Kleene axioms referring to $\emptyset$. Since such a regular expression does not have a counterpart in either the operational model or the deductive system, we omit it from further consideration.
2. A progress algebra does not have to satisfy the left distributivity of $\cdot$ over $+$. Only the weaker inequality (**PrAlg6**) is required instead.
3. A progress algebra satisfies (**PrAlg8**) which is not present in Kleene algebras.

4.4 $\mathcal{R}_F$ as Progress Algebra

Next, we show that the **wltr** predicate transformers can be regarded as a progress algebra. To do so, we have to define the equational theory of **wltr**, relate the operators $\cdot$, $+$, *, and the constant ε of $\mathcal{R}_F$ to operations on predicate transformers, and show that the equations and equational implications defining progress algebras are met by **wltr**.

The equational theory and the algebraic structure of **wltr** are defined as expected: any W in $\mathcal{R}_F$ denotes the predicate transformer **wltr**.W over the state predicates of F; the meaning of the constant ε is given by **(wltrEps)** as the identity transformer; the meaning of the operators $\cdot$, $+$, and * is given by **(wltrSeq)**, **(wltrAlt)**, and **(wltrStar)** as functional composition of predicate transformers, disjunction of predicate transformers, and a least fixpoint construction respectively; the meaning of the basic elements α in $F.A$ is given by **(wltrAct)** as the **wltr**.α predicate transformer. Finally, equality of regular expressions over $F.A$ (written as $=_F$) is defined as equivalence of the corresponding predicate transformers, i.e., for all U, V in $\mathcal{R}_F$:

$$U =_F V \quad \equiv \quad [\textbf{wltr}.U \equiv \textbf{wltr}.V] \; .$$

The induced subsumption relation $\leq_F$ on $\mathcal{R}_F$ is then given by

$$U \leq_F V \quad \equiv \quad U + V =_F V \; .$$

It follows that for all U and V in $\mathcal{R}_F$:

$$
\begin{aligned}
& U \leq_F V \\
\equiv \quad & \{\text{definition of } \leq_F\} \\
& U + V =_F V \\
\equiv \quad & \{(\textbf{wltrAlt}), \text{definition of } =_F\} \\
& [\textbf{wltr}.U \vee \textbf{wltr}.V \equiv \textbf{wltr}.V] \\
\equiv \quad & \{\text{predicate calculus}\} \\
& [\textbf{wltr}.U \Rightarrow \textbf{wltr}.V]
\end{aligned}
$$

In other words, the subsumption relation $\leq_F$ on $\mathcal{R}_F$ is exactly the implication of the corresponding predicate transformers. Therefore, the algebraic structure of $\mathcal{R}_F$ is given by the following theorem; for a proof see [Kal96].

Theorem 6. *For program F, the algebra $\mathcal{R}_F$ is a right-handed progress algebra.*

4.5   On the Operational Meaning of Hints

It is natural to expect the following operational meaning of progress under hints. An interpretation of p leads-to q by hint W (which is written as $p \overset{W}{\longmapsto} q$) is: for any state s in which p holds, there exists a finite sequence of actions, w, such that (1) $w \in W$, and (2) any finite segment of an execution that starts in s and includes w as a subsequence achieves q at some point.

But this interpretation is too restrictive. In general, there are states for which no predetermined action sequence can achieve the goal predicate. To see this consider the program *PairReduce* of Fig. 2.

```
program PairReduce
    declare
        var x, y, d : integer
    assign
        [both]  x > 0 → x, y := x − 1, d
        [one]   y > 0 → y := y − 1
        [up-d]          d := d + 1
end
```

Fig. 2. Program *PairReduce*.

For this program we see that $x \geq 0 \wedge y \geq 0 \mapsto (x, y = 0, 0)$ because each of [both] and [one] decreases the pair (x,y) lexicographically, and [up-d] does not affect (x,y). However, for any specific state, say $(x,y,d) = (3,5,2)$, no action sequence can be specified that corresponds to the operational interpretation given above. A more elaborate interpretation based on games is given in [Kal96].

5   Empirical Results

The algorithm for checking generalized progress properties based on Theorem 3 has been implemented as part of the *UNITY Verifier System*(UV system for short), our symbolic model checker for finite state UNITY programs and propositional UNITY properties ([Kal96,Kal94,Kal95]). The UV system can be used to verify automatically whether UNITY programs satisfy the given safety and progress properties, to obtain debugging information in the form of counterexample states that violate asserted conditions in case a verification attempt fails, and to exploit and manage design information in the form of user supplied invariants and progress hints.

The current version of the UV system employs ordered binary decision diagrams ([Bry86,BBR90]) to represent UNITY programs and properties symbolically. The input language used for writing programs and properties is a strongly typed version of the original UNITY notation that is restricted to finite data types. Since the UV system is implemented using the Tcl/Tk package ([Ous94]) it has a customizable graphical user interface as well as a scripting interface. The current version is available for SunOS, Solaris and Linux operating systems and consists of about 35000 lines of C++ code. It has been used to model check a variety of programs, in particular the ones presented in this section.

In this section we present empirical results of applying the UV system to some practical problems. Each example has been chosen with the intention to emphasize a particular aspect of the UV system. All examples were run on a SPARC-20 workstation with about 20 MB of main memory allocated to the model checker.

5.1   A Counter

In Sect. 3 program *UpDown* was used as an illustrative example to introduce the concept of generalized progress properties and was discussed there in detail. A finite state version of the program restricts the counter variable n to the range from 0 to $N-1$ for a positive integer N.

In the following table we summarize performance measurements for different values of N for two progress properties: the ordinary leads-to property true $\mapsto$ $n = 0$ (indicated by $\mapsto$ in the table), and the generalized leads-to property true $\overset{[set][down]*}{\longmapsto}$ $n = 0$ (indicated by r- $\mapsto$). Three measurements are listed: *iterations* states the number of inner fixpoint iterations needed to complete the check, *ops* states the number of OBDD node lookup requests in thousands, and *time* shows the execution time in seconds. All model checker invocations establish the respective properties as correct.

N		10	20	50	100	200	500	1000	10000
itera-	$\mapsto$	107	320	1551	5608	21222	128000	506006	n/a
tions	r- $\mapsto$	41	81	201	401	801	2001	4001	40001
ops	$\mapsto$	2.5	11	100	548	2810	22283	88933	n/a
in 10^3	r- $\mapsto$	0.8	2.1	8.7	18	39	119	243	3844
time	$\mapsto$	0.3	0.3	1.1	4.8	27.3	227.9	1028.4	n/a
in s	r- $\mapsto$	0.2	0.3	0.3	0.4	0.5	1.1	2.2	38.0

It may be verified from this table that the number of iterations for the ordinary leads-to check is quadratic in N, whereas it is only linear for the generalized leads-to check.

5.2   Scheduling: Milner's Cycler

The scheduling problem known as *Milner's Cycler* ([Mil89]) has been used as a benchmark in the literature to compare different verification methods and systems. Here, we merely present the empirical results; consult[Kal96] for details.

The following table compares the ordinary progress check (indicated by $\mapsto$) for the key progress property with the generalized one (indicated by r- $\mapsto$) using a regular expression hint. The measurements listed are the same as in Sect. 5.1, while N denotes the number of processes:

N		4	8	12	16	20
itera-	$\mapsto$	86	174	268	370	480
tions	r- $\mapsto$	12	12	12	12	12
ops	$\mapsto$	22	287	2030	8917	29334
in 10^3	r- $\mapsto$	7	24	52	87	145
time	$\mapsto$	0.4	2.3	16.5	87.7	369.8
in s	r- $\mapsto$	0.3	0.5	0.8	1.3	1.8

5.3   Elevator Control

Our final example, an elevator control for a building with N floors, has been motivated by similar programs in the literature (e.g. , [CWB94]). Again, we merely present the empirical results; consult[Kal96] for details:

N		20	50	100
states		$3.77 \cdot 10^8$	$1.01 \cdot 10^{18}$	$2.28 \cdot 10^{33}$
itera-	$\mapsto$	2264	13248	51576
tions	r- $\mapsto$	658	1798	3698
ops	$\mapsto$	2.25	18.3	659
in 10^6	r- $\mapsto$	1.17	7.6	95
time	$\mapsto$	10.8	280	>10000
in s	r- $\mapsto$	5.3	83	1150

6   Concluding Remarks

The motivation for developing the theory of generalized progress has been three-fold: such a theory should (i) provide a novel way of establishing ordinary progress properties of programs by allowing the user to characterize explicitly how progress is achieved, (ii) make it possible to take advantage of design knowledge in order to verify programs more effectively, and (iii) increase the efficiency of mechanical verification procedures based on the developed theory. We have addressed these goals by treating hints as formal objects (namely as elements of a progress algebra) and by providing a calculus for reasoning about such hints, for relating them to program executions, and for combining them with state-based reasoning methods (such as proving safety properties).

References

[AS85]   B. Alpern and Fred B. Schneider. Defining liveness. *Information Processing Letters*, 21:181–185, 1985.

[BBR90]   K. S. Brace, R. E. Bryant, and R. L. Rudell. Efficient implementation of a BDD package. In *Proceedings of the 27th ACM/IEEE Design Automation Conference*, 1990.

[BCM91]   J. R. Burch, E. M. Clarke, and K. M. McMillan. Representing circuits more efficiently in symbolic model checking. In *Proccedings of the 28th Design Automation Conference 1991*, pages 403–407, 1991.

[BRS00]   R. Bloem, K. Ravi, and F. Somenzi. Symbolic guided search for CTL model checking. In *Proccedings of the 37th Design Automation Conference 2000*, pages 29–34, 2000.

[Bry86]   Randy E. Bryant. Graph-based algorithms for Boolean function manipulation. *IEEE Transactions on Computing*, (6), 1986.

[CE81]   Edmund M. Clarke and Ernest Allen Emerson. Synthesis of synchronization skeletons for branching time temporal logic. In *Logic of Programs: Workshop*, volume 131 of *Lecture Notes in Computer Sience*, May 1981.

[CES86]   Edmund. M. Clarke, Ernest Allen Emerson, and A. P. Sistla. Automatic verification of finite-state concurrent systems using temporal logic specifications. *ACM Transactions on Programming Languages and Systems*, (2), 1986.

[CM88]   K. Mani Chandy and Jayadev Misra. *Parallel Program Design, A Foundation*. Addison Wesley, 1988.

[CWB94]   Jorge Cuellar, Isolde Wildgruber, and Dieter Barnard. The temporal logic of transitions. In *Formal Methods Europe (Barcelona, Spain)*, 1994.

[DS90]   Edsger W. Dijkstra and Carel S. Scholten. *Predicate Calculus and Program Semantics*. Text and Monographs in Computer Science. Springer Verlag, 1990.

[JKR89]   C. S. Jutla, Edgar Knapp, and J. R. Rao. A predicate transformer approach to semantics of parallel programs. In *Proceedings of the 8th ACM Symposium on Principles of Distributed Computing*, 1989.

[Kal94]   Markus Kaltenbach. Model checking for UNITY. Technical Report TR94-31, The University of Texas at Austin, December 1994.

[Kal95]   Markus Kaltenbach. *The UV System, User's Manual*, February 1995. Revision 1.18.

[Kal96]   Markus Kaltenbach. *Interactive Verification Exploiting Program Design Knowledge: A Model-Checker for UNITY*. PhD thesis, The University of Texas at Austin, December 1996.

[Kna90]   Edgar Knapp. A predicate transformer for progress. *Information Processing Letters*, 33:323–330, 1990.

[Lam77]   Leslie Lamport. Proving the correctness of multiprocess programs. *IEEE Transactions of Software Engineering*, 3(2):125–143, 1977.

[McM93]   Ken L. McMillan. *Symbolic Model Checking*. Kluwer, 1993.

[Mil89]   Robin Milner. *Communication and Concurrency*. International Series in Computer Science. Prentice Hall, 1989.

[Mis95a] Jayadev Misra. A logic for concurrent programming: Progress. *Journal of Computer and Software Engineering*, 3(2):273–300, 1995.

[Mis95b] Jayadev Misra. A logic for concurrent programming: Safety. *Journal of Computer and Software Engineering*, 3(2):239–272, 1995.

[Mis01]   Jayadev Misra. *A Discipline of Multiprogramming*. Monographs in Computer Science. Springer-Verlag New York Inc., New York, 2001. The first chapter is available at http://www.cs.utexas.edu/users/psp/discipline.ps.gz.

[Ous94]   John K. Ousterhout. *Tcl and the Tk toolkit*. Professional Computing Series. Addison-Wesley, 1994.

Type Systems for Concurrent Programs

Naoki Kobayashi

Department of Computer Science
Tokyo Institute of Technology
kobayasi@kb.cs.titech.ac.jp

Abstract. Type systems for programming languages help reasoning about program behavior and early finding of bugs. Recent applications of type systems include analysis of various program behaviors such as side effects, resource usage, security properties, and concurrency. This paper is a tutorial of one of such applications: type systems for analyzing behavior of concurrent processes. We start with a simple type system and extend it step by step to obtain more expressive type systems to reason about deadlock-freedom, safe usage of locks, etc.

1 Introduction

Most of modern programming languages are equipped with type systems, which help reasoning about program behavior and early finding of bugs. This paper is a tutorial of type systems for concurrent programs.

Functional programming language ML [20] is one of the most successful applications of a type system that are widely used in practice. The type system of ML automatically infers what type of value each function can take, and checks whether an appropriate argument is supplied to the function. For example, if one defines a function to return the successor of an integer, the type system of ML infers that it should take an integer and return an integer:

```
fun succ x = x+1;
val succ = fn : int -> int
```

Here, the line in the italic style shows the system's output. If one tries to apply the function to a string by mistake, the type system reports an error before executing the program:

```
f "a";
Error: operator and operand don't agree ...
```

Thanks to the type system, most of the bugs are found in the type-checking phase.

Type systems for concurrent programming languages have been, however, less satisfactory. For example, consider the following program in CML [26].

```
fun f(x:int) = let val y=channel() in recv(y)+x end;
```

B.K. Aichernig and T. Maibaum (Eds.): Formal Methods ..., LNCS 2757, pp. 439–453, 2003.
© Springer-Verlag Berlin Heidelberg 2003

Function f takes an integer as an argument. It first creates a new communication channel y (by channel()) and then tries to receive a value from the channel. It is blocked forever since there is no process to send a value on y. This function is, however, type-checked in CML and given a type $int \rightarrow int$.

To improve the situation above, type systems for analyzing usage of concurrency primitives have been extensively studied in the last decade [2, 4–6, 11–14, 21–23, 33]. Given concurrent programs, those type systems analyze whether processes communicate with each other in a disciplined manner, so that a message is received by the intended process, that no deadlock happens, that no race condition occurs, etc.

The aim of this paper is to summarize the essence of type systems for analyzing concurrent programs. Since concurrent programs are harder to debug than sequential programs, we believe that type systems for concurrent programs should be applied more widely and play more important roles in debugging and verification of programs. We hope that this paper serves as a guide for those who are interested in further extending type systems for concurrent programs or incorporating some of the type systems into programming languages and tools.

We use the π-calculus [18, 19, 29] as the target language of type systems in this paper. Since the π-calculus is simple but expressive enough to express various features of real concurrent programming languages, it is not difficult to extend type systems for the π-calculus to those for full-scale programming languages.

Section 2 introduces the syntax and operational semantics of the π-calculus. In Sections 3–8, we first present a simple type system, and extend it step by step to obtain more advanced type systems. Section 9 concludes this paper.

2   Target Language

We use a variant of the π-calculus [18, 19, 29] as the target language. The π-calculus models processes interacting with each other through communication channels. Processes and communication channels can be dynamically created, and references to communication channels can be dynamically exchanged among processes so that the communication topology can change dynamically.

Definition 1 (processes, values). *The sets of* expressions, process expressions, *and* value expressions, *ranged over by A, P, and v respectively, are defined by the following syntax.*

$$A ::= P \mid v$$
$$P ::= \mathbf{0} \mid x![v_1, \ldots, v_n] \mid x?[y_1 : \tau_1, \ldots, y_n : \tau_n].\, P \mid (P \mid Q)$$
$$\mid (\nu x : \tau)\, P \mid *P \mid \textbf{if } v \textbf{ then } P \textbf{ else } Q$$
$$v ::= x \mid \textbf{true} \mid \textbf{false}$$

In the definition above, τ denotes a type introduced in later sections. The type information need not be specified by a programmer (unless the programmer wants to check the type); As in ML [20], it can be automatically inferred in most of the type systems introduced in this paper.

Process **0** does nothing. Process $x![y_1, \ldots, y_n]$ sends a tuple $[v_1, \ldots, v_n]$ of values on channel x. Process $x?[y_1 : \tau_1, \ldots, y_n : \tau_n].\,P$ waits to receive a tuple $[v_1, \ldots, v_n]$ of values, binds $y_1, \ldots, y_n$ to $v_1, \ldots, v_n$, and behaves like P. $P \mid Q$ runs P and Q in parallel. Process $(\nu x)\,P$ creates a fresh communication channel, binds x to it, and behaves like P. Process $*P$ runs infinitely many copies of P in parallel. Process **if** v **then** P **else** Q behaves like P if v is **true** and behaves like Q if v is **false**. For simplicity, we assume that a value expression is either a boolean (**true, false**) or a variable, which is bound to a boolean or a channel by an input prefix ($x?[y_1, \ldots, y_n].$) or a ν-prefix.

We write $P \longrightarrow Q$ if Q is reduced to P in one step (by a communication or reduction of a conditional expression). The formal operational semantics is found in the literature on the π-calculus [18, 29].

We give below simple examples, which we will use later to explain type systems. In some of the examples, we use integers and operations on them.

Example 1 (ping server). The process $*ping?[r].\,r![\,]$ works as a ping server. It waits to receive a message on channel *ping* and sends a null tuple on the received channel. A typical client process is written as: $(\nu reply)\,(ping![reply] \mid reply?[\,].\,P)$. It creates a fresh channel *reply* for receiving a reply, checks whether the ping server is alive by sending the channel, waits to receive a reply, and then executes P. Communications between the server and the client proceed as follows:

$$*ping?[r].\,r![\,] \mid (\nu reply)\,(ping![reply] \mid reply?[\,].\,P)$$
$$\longrightarrow *ping?[r].\,r![\,] \mid (\nu reply)\,(reply![\,] \mid reply?[\,].\,P)$$
$$\longrightarrow *ping?[r].\,r![\,] \mid (\nu reply)\,P$$

In the second line, $(\nu reply)$ denotes the fact that the channel *reply* is a new channel and known by only the processes in the scope.

Example 2 (recursive processes). Recursive processes can be defined using replications $(*P)$. Consider a process of the form $(\nu p)\,(*p?[x_1, \ldots, x_n].\,P \mid Q)$. Each time Q sends a tuple $[v_1, \ldots, v_n]$ along p, the process $[v_1/x_1, \ldots, v_n/x_n]P$ is executed. So, the process $*p?[x_1, \ldots, x_n].\,P$ works as a process definition. We write **let proc** $p[x_1, \ldots, x_n] = P$ **in** Q for $(\nu p)\,(*p?[x_1, \ldots, x_n].\,P \mid Q)$ below. For example, the following expression defines a recursive process that takes a pair consisting of an integer n and a channel r as an argument and sends n messages on r.

let proc $p[n, r] =$ **if** $n \leq 0$ **then 0 else** $(r![\,] \mid p![n-1, r])$ **in** $\cdots$

Example 3 (locks and objects). A concurrent object can be modeled by multiple processes, each of which handles each method of the object [13, 17, 24]. For example, the following process models an object that has an integer as a state and provides services to set and read the state.

$$(\nu s)\,(s![0] \mid *set?[new].\,s?[old].\,(s![new] \mid r![\,])$$
$$\mid *read?[r].\,s?[x].\,(s![x] \mid r![x]))$$

The channel s is used to store the state. The process above waits to receive request messages on channels set and $read$. For example, when a request $set![3]$ arrives, it sets the state to 3 and sends an acknowledgment on r.

Since more than one processes may access the above object concurrently, some synchronization is necessary if a process wants to increment the state of the object by first sending a $read$ request and then a set request. A lock can be implemented using a communication channel. Since a receiver on a channel is blocked until a message becomes available, the locked state can be modeled by the absence of a message in the lock channel, and the unlocked state can be modeled by the presence of a message. The operation to acquire a lock is implemented as the operation to receive a message along the lock channel, and the operation to release the lock as the operation to send a message on the channel. For example, the following process increment the state of the object using a lock channel $lock$.

$$lock?[\,].\,(\nu r)\,(read!\,[r]\,|\,r?[x].\,(\nu r')\,(set![x+1,r']\,|\,r'?[\,].\,lock![\,]))$$

3   A Simple Type System

In this section, we introduce a simple type system [7, 32] for our language. It prevents simple programming errors like: $*ping?\,[r].\,r![\,]\,|\,ping!\,[\mathbf{true}]$, which sends a boolean instead of a channel along channel $ping$, and $*ping?\,[r].\,r![\,]\,|\,ping!\,[x,y]$, which sends a wrong number of values on $ping$. Most of the existing programming languages that support concurrency primitives have this kind of type system.

In order to avoid the confusion between booleans and channels and the arity mismatch error above, it is sufficient to classify values into booleans and channels, and to further classify channels according to the shape of transmitted values. We define the syntax of types as follows.

$$\tau ::= \mathbf{bool} \mid [\tau_1, \ldots, \tau_n]\ \mathbf{chan}$$
$$\sigma ::= \tau \mid \mathbf{proc}$$

Type $\mathbf{bool}$ is the type of booleans, and $[\tau_1, \ldots, \tau_n]\ \mathbf{chan}$ is the type of channels that are used for transmitting a tuple of values of types $\tau_1, \ldots, \tau_n$. For example, if x is used for sending a pair of booleans, x must have type $[\mathbf{bool}, \mathbf{bool}]\ \mathbf{chan}$. A special type $\mathbf{proc}$ is the type of processes. The programming errors given in the beginning of this section are prevented by assigning to $ping$ a type $[\mathbf{bool}]\ \mathbf{chan}$.

An expression is called *well-typed* if each value is consistently used according to its type. The notion of well-typeness is relative to the assumption about free variables, represented by a *type environment*. It is a mapping form a finite set of variables to types. We use a meta-variable Γ to denote a type environment. We write $\emptyset$ for the typing environment whose domain is empty, and write $dom(\Gamma)$ for the domain of Γ. When $x \notin dom(\Gamma)$, we write $\Gamma, x : \tau$ for the type environment obtained by extending the type environment Γ with the binding of x to τ. We write $\Gamma \leq \Gamma'$ when $dom(\Gamma) \supseteq dom(\Gamma')$ and $\Gamma(x) = \Gamma'(x)$ for each $x \in dom(\Gamma')$. Intuitively, $\Gamma \leq \Gamma'$ means that Γ represents a stronger type assumption about variables.

$$\frac{b \in \{\mathbf{true}, \mathbf{false}\}}{\emptyset \vdash b : \mathbf{bool}} \quad \text{(ST-Bool)}$$

$$x : \tau \vdash x : \tau \qquad \text{(ST-Var)}$$

$$\frac{\Gamma' \vdash A : \sigma \quad \Gamma \leq \Gamma'}{\Gamma \vdash A : \sigma} \quad \text{(ST-Weak)}$$

$$\emptyset \vdash \mathbf{0} : \mathbf{proc} \qquad \text{(ST-Zero)}$$

$$\frac{\Gamma \vdash P : \mathbf{proc} \quad \Gamma \vdash Q : \mathbf{proc}}{\Gamma \vdash P \,|\, Q : \mathbf{proc}} \quad \text{(ST-Par)}$$

$$\frac{\Gamma, x : \tau \vdash P : \mathbf{proc} \quad \tau \text{ is a channel type}}{\Gamma \vdash (\nu x : \tau)\, P : \mathbf{proc}} \quad \text{(ST-New)}$$

$$\frac{\Gamma \vdash P : \mathbf{proc}}{\Gamma \vdash *P : \mathbf{proc}} \quad \text{(ST-Rep)}$$

$$\frac{\Gamma \vdash x : [\tau_1, \ldots, \tau_n]\ \mathbf{chan} \quad \Gamma \vdash v_i : \tau_i \ (\text{for each } i \in \{1, \ldots, n\})}{\Gamma \vdash x![v_1, \ldots, v_n] : \mathbf{proc}} \quad \text{(ST-Out)}$$

$$\frac{\Gamma \vdash x : [\tau_1, \ldots, \tau_n]\ \mathbf{chan} \quad \Gamma, y : \tau_1, \ldots, y : \tau_n \vdash P : \mathbf{proc}}{\Gamma \vdash x?[y_1 : \tau_1, \ldots, y_n : \tau_n].\, P : \mathbf{proc}} \quad \text{(ST-In)}$$

$$\frac{\Gamma \vdash v : \mathbf{bool} \quad \Gamma \vdash P : \mathbf{proc} \quad \Gamma \vdash Q : \mathbf{proc}}{\Gamma \vdash \mathbf{if}\ v\ \mathbf{then}\ P\ \mathbf{else}\ Q\ : \mathbf{proc}} \quad \text{(ST-If)}$$

Fig. 1. Typing rules for the simple type system.

We write $\Gamma \vdash A : \sigma$ if an expression A (which is either a value expression or a process expression) is well-typed and has type σ under the type environment Γ. The relation $\Gamma \vdash A : \sigma$ is defined by the set of inference rules shown in Figure 1.

Most of the rules should be self-explanatory for those who are familiar with type systems for sequential programming languages. The rule (ST-Weak) means that we can replace a type environment with a stronger assumption. It is equivalent to the usual weakening rule for adding an extra type binding to the type environment. We use (ST-Weak) since it is more convenient for extending the type system later. The rule (ST-New) checks that x is indeed used as a channel of the intended type in P.

The rule (ST-Out) checks that the destination channel x indeed has a channel type, and that each argument v_i has the type τ_i, as specified by the type of x. The rule (ST-In) checks that x has a channel type, and that the continuation part P is well-typed provided that each formal parameter y_i is bound to a value of the type τ_i as specified by the type of x. Those rules are analogous to the rules for function application and abstraction.

The above type system guarantees that if a process is well-typed, there is no confusion between booleans and channels or arity mismatch error.

4   A Type System with Input/Output Modes

Even if a program is type-checked in the simple type system in the previous section, the program may still contain a lot of simple programming errors. For example, the ping server in Example 1 may be written as $*ping?\,[r].\, r?[\,].\, \mathbf{0}$ by mistake. Then, clients cannot receive any reply from the server. Similarly, a client of the server may receive a message along *ping* instead of sending a message either by mistake or maliciously. In Example 3, a user of the object may receive a message along the interface channels *set* and *read* instead of sending a message.

We can prevent the above-mentioned errors by classifying the types of channels according to whether the channels can be used for input (receiving a value) or output (sending a value) [22]. We redefine the syntax of types as follows:

$$\tau ::= \textbf{bool} \mid [\tau_1, \ldots, \tau_n] \textbf{ chan}_M$$
$$M \text{ (mode)} ::= ! \mid ? \mid !?$$

A mode M denotes for which operations channels can be used. A channel of type $[\tau_1, \ldots, \tau_n] \textbf{ chan}_M$ can be used for output (input, resp.) only if M contains the output capability ! (the input capability ?, resp.). The wrong ping server $*ping? [r]. r?[]. \mathbf{0}$ is rejected by assigning to *ping* the type $[[] \textbf{ chan}_!] \textbf{ chan}_?$.

As in type systems for sequential programming languages, we write $\tau_1 \leq \tau_2$ when a value of type τ_1 may be used as a value of type τ_2. It is defined as the least reflexive relation satisfying $[\tau_1, \ldots, \tau_n] \textbf{ chan}_{!?} \leq [\tau_1, \ldots, \tau_n] \textbf{ chan}_?$ and $[\tau_1, \ldots, \tau_n] \textbf{ chan}_{!?} \leq [\tau_1, \ldots, \tau_n] \textbf{ chan}_!$. It is possible to relax the subtyping relation by allowing, for example, $[\tau_1, \ldots, \tau_n] \textbf{ chan}_!$ to be co-variant in $\tau_1, \ldots, \tau_n$ (see [22]). We do not do so in this paper for the sake of simplicity.

The binary relation $\leq$ on type environments is re-defined as: $\Gamma \leq \Gamma'$ if and only if $dom(\Gamma) \supseteq dom(\Gamma')$ and $\Gamma(x) \leq \Gamma'(x)$ for each $x \in dom(\Gamma')$.

The new typing rules are obtained by replacing only the rules (ST-OUT) and (ST-IN) of the previous type system with the following rules:

$$\frac{\Gamma \vdash x : [\tau_1, \ldots, \tau_n] \textbf{ chan}_! \qquad \Gamma \vdash v_i : \tau_i \text{ for each } i \in \{1, \ldots, n\}}{\Gamma \vdash x![v_1, \ldots, v_n] : \textbf{proc}} \quad \text{(MT-OUT)}$$

$$\frac{\Gamma \vdash x : [\tau_1, \ldots, \tau_n] \textbf{ chan}_? \qquad \Gamma, y : \tau_1, \ldots, y : \tau_n \vdash P : \textbf{proc}}{\Gamma \vdash x?[y_1 : \tau_1, \ldots, y_n : \tau_n]. P : \textbf{proc}} \quad \text{(MT-IN)}$$

5   A Linear Type System

The type system in Section 4 prevents a ping server from using a reply channel for input, but it does not detect a mistake that the server forgets to send a reply. For example, the process $*ping? [r]. \textbf{if } b \textbf{ then } r![] \textbf{ else } \mathbf{0}$ forgets to send a reply in the else-branch: Another typical mistake would be to send more than one reply messages: $*ping? [r]. (r![] \mid r![])$.

We can prevent the errors above by further classifying the channel types according to how often channels are used [14]. The syntax of types is redefined as follows:

$$\tau ::= \textbf{bool} \mid [\tau_1, \ldots, \tau_n] \textbf{ chan}_{(?m_1, !m_2)}$$
$$m \text{ (multiplicity)} ::= 0 \mid 1 \mid \omega$$

Multiplicities m_1 and m_2 in the channel type $[\tau_1, \ldots, \tau_n] \textbf{ chan}_{(?m_1, !m_2)}$ describes how often the channel can be used for input and output respectively. Multiplicity

$$\frac{\Gamma \vdash P : \mathbf{proc} \qquad \Delta \vdash Q : \mathbf{proc}}{\Gamma \,|\, \Delta \vdash P \,|\, Q : \mathbf{proc}} \quad \text{(LT-Par)} \qquad\qquad \frac{\Gamma \vdash P : \mathbf{proc}}{\omega\Gamma \vdash *P : \mathbf{proc}} \quad \text{(LT-Rep)}$$

$$\frac{\Gamma_i \vdash v_i : \tau_i \text{ for each } i \in \{1, \ldots, n\}}{(x : [\tau_1, \ldots, \tau_n] \; \mathbf{chan}_{(?0,!1)}) \,|\, \Gamma_1 \,|\, \cdots \,|\, \Gamma_n \vdash x![v_1, \ldots, v_n] : \mathbf{proc}} \quad \text{(LT-Out)}$$

$$\frac{\Gamma, y : \tau_1, \ldots, y : \tau_n \vdash P : \mathbf{proc}}{(x : [\tau_1, \ldots, \tau_n] \; \mathbf{chan}_{(?1,!0)}) \,|\, \Gamma \vdash x?[y_1 : \tau_1, \ldots, y_n : \tau_n].\, P : \mathbf{proc}} \quad \text{(LT-In)}$$

$$\frac{\Gamma \vdash v : \mathbf{bool} \qquad \Delta \vdash P : \mathbf{proc} \qquad \Delta \vdash Q : \mathbf{proc}}{\Gamma \,|\, \Delta \vdash \mathbf{if} \; v \; \mathbf{then} \; P \; \mathbf{else} \; Q : \mathbf{proc}} \quad \text{(LT-If)}$$

Fig. 2. Typing rules for the linear type system.

0 means that the channel cannot be used at all for that operation, 1 means that the channel should be used once for that operation, and ω means that the channel can be used for that operation an arbitrary number of times. By assigning to *ping* a type $[[] \; \mathbf{chan}_{(?0,!1)}] \; \mathbf{chan}_{(?\omega,!0)}$, we can detect programming errors like $*ping?\,[r].\,(r![]\,|\,r![])$ and $*ping?\,[r].\, \mathbf{if} \; b \; \mathbf{then} \; r![] \; \mathbf{else} \; 0$ above.

We define the binary relation $m_1 \le m_1'$ as the least partial order that satisfies $\omega \le 0$ and $\omega \le 1$. The subtyping relation is re-defined as the least reflexive relation satisfying the rule:

$$\frac{m_1 \le m_1' \qquad m_2 \le m_2'}{[\tau_1, \ldots, \tau_n] \; \mathbf{chan}_{(?^{m_1},!^{m_2})} \le [\tau_1, \ldots, \tau_n] \; \mathbf{chan}_{(?^{m_1'},!^{m_2'})}}$$

The subtyping relation allows, for example, a channel of type $[] \; \mathbf{chan}_{(?\omega,!\omega)}$ to be used as a channel of type $[] \; \mathbf{chan}_{(?1,!0)}$, but it does not allow a channel of type $[] \; \mathbf{chan}_{(?0,!1)}$ (which *must* be used once for output) to be used as a channel of type $[] \; \mathbf{chan}_{(?0,!0)}$ (which must not be used for output). We re-define $\Gamma \le \Gamma'$ by: $\Gamma \le \Gamma'$ if and only if (i) $dom(\Gamma) \supseteq dom(\Gamma')$, (ii) for each $x \in dom(\Gamma')$, $\Gamma(x) \le \Gamma'(x)$, and (iii) for each $x \in dom(\Gamma) \backslash dom(\Gamma')$, $\Gamma(x)$ is **bool** or a channel type of the form $[\tau_1, \ldots, \tau_n] \; \mathbf{chan}_{(?0,!0)}$. Note that $x : \tau, y : [] \; \mathbf{chan}_{(?0,!1)} \le x : \tau$ does not hold, since the type environment in the lefthand side indicates that y should be used for output.

Typing rules are shown in Figure 2 (Only the modified rules are shown: The other rules are the same as those of the previous type system). Notice the changes in the rules (LT-Out), (LT-In), (LT-Par), etc. In the rules (XX-Par) in the previous type systems, a type environment is shared by sub-processes. The sharing of a type environment is invalid in the linear type system, since the type environment contains information about how often channels are used. For example, if x has type $[] \; \mathbf{chan}_{(?0,!1)}$ both in P and Q, x is used *twice* in $P \,|\, Q$, and therefore x should have type $[] \; \mathbf{chan}_{(?0,!\omega)}$. The operation $\Gamma \,|\, \Delta$ in rule (LT-Par) represents this kind of calculation. It is defined by:

$$(\Gamma \mid \Delta)(x) = \begin{cases} \Gamma(x) \mid \Delta(x) & \text{if } x \in dom(\Gamma) \cap dom(\Delta) \\ \Gamma(x) & \text{if } x \in dom(\Gamma) \backslash dom(\Delta) \\ \Delta(x) & \text{if } x \in dom(\Delta) \backslash dom(\Gamma) \end{cases}$$

$$\mathbf{bool} \mid \mathbf{bool} = \mathbf{bool}$$

$$([\tau_1, \ldots, \tau_n] \, \mathbf{chan}_{(?m_1, !m_2)}) \mid ([\tau_1, \ldots, \tau_n] \, \mathbf{chan}_{(?m'_1, !m'_2)})$$
$$= [\tau_1, \ldots, \tau_n] \, \mathbf{chan}_{(?m_1 + m'_1, !m_2 + m'_2)}$$

$$m_1 + m_2 = \begin{cases} m_2 & \text{if } m_1 = 0 \\ m_1 & \text{if } m_2 = 0 \\ \omega & \text{otherwise} \end{cases}$$

The operation $\omega\Gamma$ in rule (LT-REP) is defined by:

$$(\omega\Gamma)(x) = \omega(\Gamma(x))$$
$$\omega\mathbf{bool} = \mathbf{bool}$$
$$\omega([\tau_1, \ldots, \tau_n] \, \mathbf{chan}_{(?m_1, !m_2)}) = [\tau_1, \ldots, \tau_n] \, \mathbf{chan}_{(?\omega m_1, !\omega m_2)}$$
$$\omega m = \begin{cases} 0 & \text{if } m = 0 \\ \omega & \text{otherwise} \end{cases}$$

In rule (T-IF), the type environment Δ is shared between the then-clause and the else-clause because either the then-clause or the else-clause is executed.

We can check that a ping server does not forget to send a reply by type-checking the server under the type environment $ping : [[] \, \mathbf{chan}_{(?0, !1)}] \, \mathbf{chan}_{(?\omega, !0)}$. On the other hand, the wrong server $*ping?[r]. \, \mathbf{if} \, b \, \mathbf{then} \, r![] \, \mathbf{else} \, 0$ fails to type-check under the same type environment: In order for the server to be well-typed, it must be the case that $\mathbf{if} \, b \, \mathbf{then} \, r![] \, \mathbf{else} \, 0$ is well-typed under the assumption $r : [] \, \mathbf{chan}_{(?0, !1)}$, but the else-clause violates the assumption.

Note, however, that in general the type system does not guarantee that a channel of type $[] \, \mathbf{chan}_{(?0, !1)}$ is used for output exactly once. Consider the process: $(\nu y)(\nu z)(y?[]. \, z![] \mid z?[]. \, (y![] \mid x![]))$. It is well-typed under the type environment $x : [] \, \mathbf{chan}_{(?0, !1)}$, but the process does not send a message on x because it is deadlocked. This problem is solved by the type system for deadlock-freedom in Section 7.

6   A Type System with Channel Usage

As mentioned in Section 2 (Example 3), a channel can be used as a lock. It, however, works correctly only if the channel is used in an intended manner: When the channel is created, one message should be put into the channel (to model the unlocked state). Afterwards, a process should receive a message from the channel to acquire the lock, and after acquiring the lock, it should eventually release the lock. The linear type system in Section 5 cannot guarantee such usage of channels: Since a lock channel is used more than once, it is given type $[] \, \mathbf{chan}_{(?\omega, !\omega)}$, which means that the channel may be used in an arbitrary manner. Therefore, the type system cannot detect programming errors like:

$$lock?[]. \, \langle critical\_section \rangle (lock![] \mid lock![])$$

$$!.U \xrightarrow{\{!\}} U \qquad \dfrac{U_1 \xrightarrow{\varphi_1} U_1' \qquad U2 \xrightarrow{\varphi_2} U_2'}{U_1 \mid U_2 \xrightarrow{\varphi_1 \uplus \varphi_2} U_1' \mid U_2'} \qquad \dfrac{U_2 \xrightarrow{\varphi} U_2'}{U_1 \,\&\, U_2 \xrightarrow{\varphi} U_2'}$$

$$?.U \xrightarrow{\{?\}} U \qquad \dfrac{U_1 \xrightarrow{\varphi} U_1'}{U_1 \,\&\, U_2 \xrightarrow{\varphi} U_1'} \qquad \dfrac{[\mu\alpha.U/\alpha]U \xrightarrow{\varphi} U'}{\mu\alpha.U \xrightarrow{\varphi} U'}$$

Fig. 3. Usage reduction rules.

which allows two processes to acquire the lock simultaneously, and

$$lock?[\,]. \langle critical\_section \rangle \mathbf{if}\ b\ \mathbf{then}\ lock![\,]\ \mathbf{else}\ \mathbf{0}$$

which forgets to release the lock in the else-clause.

We can prevent the errors above by putting into channel types information about not only how often channels are used but also *in which order* channels are used for input and output. We redefine the syntax of types as follows.

$$\tau ::= \mathbf{bool} \mid [\tau_1, \ldots, \tau_n]\ \mathbf{chan}_U$$
$$U\ (\text{usages}) ::= 0 \mid \alpha \mid ?.U \mid !.U \mid (U_1 \mid U_2) \mid U_1 \,\&\, U_2 \mid \mu\alpha.U$$

A channel type is annotated with a *usage* [15, 30], which denotes how channels can be used for input and output. Usage 0 describes a channel that cannot be used at all. Usage $?.U$ describes a channel that is first used for input and then used according to U. Usage $!.U$ describes a channel that is be first used for output and then used according to U. Usage $U_1 \mid U_2$ describes a channel that is used according to U_1 and U_2 possibly in parallel. Usage $U_1 \,\&\, U_2$ describes a channel that is used according to either U_1 or U_2. Usage $\mu\alpha.U$ describes a channel that is used recursively according to $[\mu\alpha.U/\alpha]U$. For example, $\mu\alpha.(0 \,\&\, (!.\alpha))$ describes a channel that can be sequentially used for output an arbitrary number of times.

We often write ? and ! for $?.0$ and $!.0$ respectively. We also write $*U$ and ωU for $\mu\alpha.(0 \,\&\, (U \mid \alpha))$ and $\mu\alpha.(U \mid \alpha)$ respectively. Usage $*U$ describes a channel that can be used according to U an arbitrary number of times, while usage ωU describes a channel that should be used according to U infinitely often.

We can enforce the correct usage of a lock channel by assigning the usage $! \mid *?.!$ to it. We can also express linearity information of the previous section: $(?^{m_1}, !^{m_2})$ is expressed by usage $m_1? \mid m_2!$ where $1U = U$ and $0U = 0$.

Before defining typing rules, we introduce a subusage relation $U \leq U'$, which means that a channel of usage U can be used as a channel of usage U'. Here, we define it using a simulation relation. We consider a reduction relation $U \xrightarrow{\varphi} U'$ on usages, where φ is a multiset consisting of ! and ?. It means that the operations described by φ can be simultaneously applied to a channel of usage U, and the resulting usage becomes U'. The reduction relation is defined by the rules in Figure 3. In the figure, $\uplus$ denotes the operator for multiset union.

We also define the unary relation $U^{\downarrow}$ as the least relation that satisfies the following rules:

$$0^\downarrow \qquad \frac{U_1^\downarrow \quad U_2^\downarrow}{(U_1 \mid U_2)^\downarrow} \qquad \frac{U_1^\downarrow \vee U_2^\downarrow}{(U_1 \,\&\, U_2)^\downarrow} \qquad \frac{([\mu\alpha.U/\alpha]U)^\downarrow}{\mu\alpha.U^\downarrow}$$

Intuitively, $U^\downarrow$ means that a channel of usage U need not be used at all. Using the above relations, the subusage relation is defined as follows.

Definition 2 (subusage relation). *The subusage relation $\leq$ is the largest relation that satisfies the following two conditions.*

1. *If $U_1 \leq U_2$ and $U_2 \xrightarrow{\varphi} U_2'$, then $U_1 \xrightarrow{\varphi} U_1'$ and $U_1' \leq U_2'$ for some U_1'.*
2. *If $U_1 \leq U_2$ and $U_2^\downarrow$, then $U_1^\downarrow$.*

For example, $U_1 \,\&\, U_2 \leq U_1$ and $! \mid ! \leq !.!$ hold. We re-define the subtyping relation so that $[\tau_1, \ldots, \tau_n]\ \mathbf{chan}_U \leq [\tau_1, \ldots, \tau_n]\ \mathbf{chan}_{U'}$ if $U \leq U'$. We write $\Gamma_1 \leq \Gamma_2$ if (i) $dom(\Gamma_1) \supseteq dom(\Gamma_2)$, (ii) $\Gamma_1(x) \leq \Gamma_2(x)$ for each $x \in dom(\Gamma_2)$, and (iii) $\Gamma(x)$ is either **bool** or a channel type of the form $[\tau_1, \ldots, \tau_n]\ \mathbf{chan}_U$ with $U \leq 0$ for each $x \in dom(\Gamma_1) \backslash dom(\Gamma_2)$.

The operations $\mid$ and ω on types and type environments are similar to those in the previous type system, except that for channel types, they are defined by:

$$([\tau_1, \ldots, \tau_n]\ \mathbf{chan}_{U_1}) \mid ([\tau_1, \ldots, \tau_n]\ \mathbf{chan}_{U_2}) = [\tau_1, \ldots, \tau_n]\ \mathbf{chan}_{U_1 \mid U_2}$$
$$\omega([\tau_1, \ldots, \tau_n]\ \mathbf{chan}_U) = [\tau_1, \ldots, \tau_n]\ \mathbf{chan}_{\omega U}$$

The new typing rules are obtained by replacing (LT-Out) and (LT-In) of the previous type system with the following rules:

$$\frac{\Gamma_i \vdash v_i : \tau_i \ (\text{for each } i \in \{1, \ldots, n\})}{\Gamma, x : [\tau_1, \ldots, \tau_n]\ \mathbf{chan}_{!.U} \vdash x![v_1, \ldots, v_n] : \mathbf{proc}} \qquad \text{(UT-Out)}$$

$$\frac{\Gamma, x : [\tau_1, \ldots, \tau_n]\ \mathbf{chan}_U, y : \tau_1, \ldots, y : \tau_n \vdash P : \mathbf{proc}}{\Gamma, x : [\tau_1, \ldots, \tau_n]\ \mathbf{chan}_{?.U} \vdash x?[y_1 : \tau_1, \ldots, y_n : \tau_n]. P : \mathbf{proc}} \qquad \text{(UT-In)}$$

In rule (UT-In), the assumption $\Gamma, x : [\tau_1, \ldots, \tau_n]\ \mathbf{chan}_U, y : \tau_1, \ldots, y : \tau_n \vdash P : \mathbf{proc}$ implies that the channel x is used according to U after the input succeeds. So, x is used according to $?.U$ in total. Similar ordering information is taken into account in rule (UT-Out).

Example 4. The process $lock?[\,].\,\mathbf{if}\ b\ \mathbf{then}\ lock![\,]\ \mathbf{else}\ 0$ is well-typed under the type environment $b : \mathbf{bool}, lock : [\,]\ \mathbf{chan}_{?.(!\&0)}$ but not under $b : \mathbf{bool}, lock : [\,]\ \mathbf{chan}_{?.!}$. It implies that the lock may not be released correctly.

Example 5. The wrong CML program in Section 1 is expressed as:

$$\mathbf{proc}\ f[x : \mathbf{int}, r : [\mathbf{int}]\ \mathbf{chan}_!] = (\nu y)\, y?[n].\, r![n + x].$$

The usage of y is inferred to be $?$. Therefore, we know that the process will be blocked on the input on y forever.

7 A Type System for Deadlock-Freedom

The type systems presented so far do not guarantee that the ping server eventually returns a reply, that a lock is eventually released, etc. For example, the type system in the previous section accepts the process

$$lock?[\,].\,(\nu x)\,(\nu y)\,(x?[\,].\,y![\,]\,|\,y?[\,].\,(lock![\,]\,|\,x![\,])),$$

which does not release the lock because of deadlock on channels x and y.

We can prevent deadlocks by associating with each input (?) or output usage (!) an *obligation level* and a *capability level*.[1] Intuitively, the obligation level of an action denotes the degree of the necessity of the action being executed, while the capability level of an action denotes the degree of the guarantee for the success of the action.

We extend the syntax of types as follows.

$$\tau ::= \mathbf{bool} \mid [\tau_1, \ldots, \tau_n] \ \mathbf{chan}_U$$
$$U ::= 0 \mid \alpha \mid ?^{t_o}_{t_c}.U \mid !^{t_o}_{t_c}.U \mid (U_1 \mid U_2) \mid U_1 \ \& \ U_2 \mid \mu\alpha.U$$
$$t \ (\text{level}) ::= \infty \mid 0 \mid 1 \mid 2 \mid \cdots$$

The two levels t_o and t_c in $!^{t_o}_{t_c}.U$ denote the obligation level and the capability level of the output action respectively. Suppose that a channel has the usage $!^{t_o}_{t_c}.U$. Its obligation level t_o means that a process can wait for the success of only actions with capability levels of less than t_o before using the channel for output. For example, if y has usage $!^2_0$ in $x?[\,].\,y![\,]$, then the capability level of the input on x must be 0 or 1. If the obligation level is 0, the channel must be used for output immediately. If the obligation level is ∞, arbitrary actions can be performed before the channel is used for output. The capability level t_c means that the success of an output on the channel is guaranteed by a corresponding input action with an obligation level of less than or equal to t_c. In other words, some process will use the channel for input before waiting for the success of an action whose obligation level is greater than or equal to t_c. If the capability level is ∞, the success of the output is not guaranteed. The meaning of the capability and obligation levels of an input action is similar.

Using the obligation and capability levels, we can prevent cyclic dependencies between communications. For example, recall the example above:

$$lock?[\,].\,(\nu x)\,(\nu y)\,(x?[\,].\,y![\,]\,|\,y?[\,].\,(lock![\,]\,|\,x![\,])),$$

Suppose that the usage of x and y are $?^{t_0}_{t_1} \mid !^{t_1}_{t_0}$ and $?^{t_2}_{t_3} \mid !^{t_3}_{t_2}$. From the process $x?[\,].\,y![\,]$, we get the constraint $t_1 < t_3$. From the process $y?[\,].\,(lock![\,]\,|\,x![\,])$, we get the constraint $t_3 < t_1$. Therefore, it must be the case that $t_1 = t_3 = \infty$. (Here, we define $t < t$ holds if and only if $t = \infty$.) Since the output on *lock* is guarded by the input on y, the obligation level of the output on *lock* must also be ∞, which means that the lock may not be released.

---

[1] They were called *time tags* in earlier type systems for deadlock-freedom [13, 15, 30].

Typing rules are the same as those for the type system in the previous section, except for the following rules:

$$\frac{\Gamma_i \vdash v_i : \tau_i \text{ (for each } i \in \{1,\ldots,n\}) \qquad \Delta \vdash P : \textbf{proc}}{(\Gamma_1 \mid \cdots \mid \Gamma_n \mid \Delta) = \Gamma, x : [\tau_1,\ldots,\tau_n] \textbf{ chan}_U \qquad t_c < \Gamma}{\Gamma, x : [\tau_1,\ldots,\tau_n] \textbf{ chan}_{!^{t_c}_{t_o} U} \vdash x![v_1,\ldots,v_n].P : \textbf{proc}} \quad \text{(DT-OUT)}$$

$$\frac{\Gamma, x : [\tau_1,\ldots,\tau_n] \textbf{ chan}_U, y : \tau_1,\ldots,y : \tau_n \vdash P : \textbf{proc} \qquad t_c < \Gamma}{\Gamma, x : [\tau_1,\ldots,\tau_n] \textbf{ chan}_{?^{t_c}_{t_o} U} \vdash x?[y_1 : \tau_1,\ldots,y_n : \tau_n].P : \textbf{proc}} \quad \text{(DT-IN)}$$

$$\frac{\Gamma, x : [\tau_1,\ldots,\tau_n] \textbf{ chan}_U \vdash P : \textbf{proc} \qquad rel(U)}{\Gamma \vdash (\nu x : [\tau_1,\ldots,\tau_n] \textbf{ chan}_U) \, P : \textbf{proc}} \quad \text{(DT-NEW)}$$

The side condition $t_c < \Gamma$ in the rules (DT-OUT) and (DT-IN) expresses constraints on obligation and capability levels. It means that t_c must be less than all the obligation levels appearing at the top level (those which are not guarded by ?. and !.).

The side condition $rel(U)$ in the rule (DT-NEW) means that all the obligation levels and the capability levels in U are consistent. For example, there must not be the case like $?^\infty_0 \mid ?^1_\infty$, where there is an input action of capability level 0 but there is no corresponding output action of obligation level 0.

The type system guarantees that any closed well-typed process is deadlock-free in the sense that unless the process diverges, no input or output action with a finite capability level is blocked forever.

Example 6. The usage of a lock is refined as $!^0_\infty \mid *?^\infty_t.!^t_\infty$. The part $!^0_\infty$ means that a value must be put into the channel immediately (so as to simulate the unlocked state). The part $?^\infty_t$ means that any actions may be performed before acquiring the lock and that once a process tries to acquire the lock, the process can eventually acquire the lock. The part $!^t_\infty$ means that once a process has acquired the lock, it can only perform actions with capability levels less than t before releasing the lock. Suppose that locks l_1 and l_2 have usages $*?^\infty_1.!^1_\infty$ and $*?^\infty_2.!^2_\infty$ respectively. Then, it is allowed to acquire the lock l_2 first and then acquire the lock l_1 before releasing l_2: $l_2?[].l_1?[].(l_1![] \mid l_2![])$, but it is not allowed to lock l_1 and l_2 in the reverse order: $l_1?[].l_2?[].(l_1![] \mid l_2![])$. Thus, capability and obligation levels for lock channels correspond to the locking levels in [5].

8   Putting All Together

In this section, we illustrate how the type systems introduced in this paper may be applied to programming languages. The language we use below does not exist. We borrow the syntax from ML [20], Pict [25], and HACL [16].

First, the ping server in Example 1 can be written as follows:

```
type 'a rep_chan = 'a chan(!o);
proc ping[r: [] rep_chan] = r![];
val ping = ch: ([] rep_chan) chan(*!c)
```

Here, the first line defines an abbreviation for a type. The part `!o` is the channel usage introduced in Section 6 and `o` means that the obligation level introduced in Section 7 is finite. In the second line, the type annotation for `r` asserts that `r` should be used as a reply channel. (In the syntax of ML, `[]` in the type annotation is `unit`.) The third line is the output of the type system. It says that `ping` can be used an arbitrary number of times for sending a reply channel, and it is guaranteed that the channel is received (`c` means that the capability level is finite) and a reply will eventually come back.

The following program forgets to send a reply in the else-clause:

```
proc ping2[b, r: [] rep_chan] = if b then r![] else 0;
```

Then, the system's output would be:

> *Error: r must have type [] rep_chan*
> *but it has type [] chan(!&0) in expression "if b then r![] else 0"*

The following program defines a process to create a new lock:

```
type Lock = [] chan(*?c.!o);
proc newlock[r: Lock rep_chan] = (new l)(l![] | r![l]);
val newlock: (Lock rep_chan) chan(*!c)
```

The process `newlock` takes a channel r as an argument, creates a new lock channel, sets its state to the unlocked state, and returns the lock channel through r. The system's output says that one can send a request for creating locks an arbitrary number of times, that the request will be eventually received, and that a lock will be sent back along the reply channel.

If a lock is used in a wrong manner, the program will be rejected:

```
(new r)(newlock![r] | r?[l].l?[].0)
```
> *Error: l must have type Lock*
> *but it has type [] chan(?) in expression "l?[].0"*

Since the lock `l` is not released in the program, the usage of `l` is not consistent with the type `Lock`.

9   Conclusion

In this paper, we gave an overview of various type systems for the π-calculus, from a simple type system to more advanced type systems for linearity, deadlock-freedom, etc. We have mainly discussed the type systems from a programmer's point of view, and focused on explaining how they can help finding of bugs of concurrent programs. For lack of space, we did not discuss extensions of the type systems for distributed and open environments, where one needs to introduce location-dependent types and some combination of static typing and dynamic typing [9, 27]. Other applications of type systems include formal reasoning about program behavior through process equivalence theories [14, 22, 23, 28, 33], analysis of security properties [1, 8, 10] and optimization of concurrent programs [11, 31].

We think that type systems for concurrent programs are now mature enough to be applied to real programming languages or analysis tools. To apply the type systems, several issues need to be addressed, such as how to let programmers annotate types, how to report type errors, etc. Some type systems have already been applied; Pict [25] incorporates channel types with input/output modes and higher-order polymorphism, and Flanagan and Freund [6] developed a tool for race detection for Java.

Integration with other program verification methods like model checking [3] and theorem proving would be useful and important. Recent type systems [2, 12] suggest one of such directions.

References

1. M. Abadi. Secrecy by typing in security protocols. *JACM*, 46(5):749–786, 1999.
2. S. Chaki, S. Rajamani, and J. Rehof. Types as models: Model checking message-passing programs. In *Proc. of POPL*, pages 45–57, 2002.
3. J. Edmund M. Clarke, O. Grumberg, and D. A. Peled. *Model Checking*. The MIT Press, 1999.
4. C. Flanagan and M. Abadi. Object types against races. In *CONCUR'99*, volume 1664 of *LNCS*, pages 288–303. Springer-Verlag, 1999.
5. C. Flanagan and M. Abadi. Types for safe locking. In *Proc. of ESOP 1999*, volume 1576 of *LNCS*, pages 91–108, 1999.
6. C. Flanagan and S. N. Freund. Type-based race detection for Java. In *Proc. of PLDI*, pages 219–232, 2000.
7. S. J. Gay. A sort inference algorithm for the polyadic π-calculus. In *Proc. of POPL*, pages 429–438, 1993.
8. A. D. Gordon and A. Jeffrey. Authenticity by typing for security protocols. In *Proceedings of the 14th IEEE Computer Security Foundations Workshop (CSFW 2001)*, pages 145–159. IEEE Computer Society Press, 2001.
9. M. Hennessy and J. Riely. Resource access control in systems of mobile agents. *Info. Comput.*, 173(1):82–120, 2002.
10. K. Honda and N. Yoshida. A uniform type structure for secure information flow. In *Proc. of POPL*, pages 81–92, 2002.
11. A. Igarashi and N. Kobayashi. Type reconstruction for linear pi-calculus with I/O subtyping. *Info. Comput.*, 161:1–44, 2000.
12. A. Igarashi and N. Kobayashi. A generic type system for the pi-calculus. In *Proc. of POPL*, pages 128–141, January 2001.
13. N. Kobayashi. A partially deadlock-free typed process calculus. *ACM Trans. Prog. Lang. Syst.*, 20(2):436–482, 1998.
14. N. Kobayashi, B. C. Pierce, and D. N. Turner. Linearity and the pi-calculus. *ACM Trans. Prog. Lang. Syst.*, 21(5):914–947, 1999.

15. N. Kobayashi, S. Saito, and E. Sumii. An implicitly-typed deadlock-free process calculus. In *Proc. of CONCUR2000*, volume 1877 of *LNCS*, pages 489–503. Springer-Verlag, August 2000.

16. N. Kobayashi and A. Yonezawa. Higher-order concurrent linear logic programming. In *Theory and Practice of Parallel Programming*, volume 907 of *LNCS*, pages 137–166. Springer-Verlag, 1995.

17. N. Kobayashi and A. Yonezawa. Towards foundations for concurrent object-oriented programming – types and language design. *Theory and Practice of Object Systems*, 1(4):243–268, 1995.

18. R. Milner. *Communicating and Mobile Systems: the Pi-Calculus*. Cambridge University Press, 1999.

19. R. Milner, J. Parrow, and D. Walker. A calculus of mobile processes, I, II. *Information and Computation*, 100:1–77, September 1992.

20. R. Milner, M. Tofte, R. Harper, and D. MacQueen. *The Definition of Standard ML (Revised)*. The MIT Press, 1997.

21. H. R. Nielson and F. Nielson. Higher-order concurrent programs with finite communication topology. In *Proc. of POPL*, pages 84–97, 1994.

22. B. Pierce and D. Sangiorgi. Typing and subtyping for mobile processes. *Mathematical Structures in Computer Science*, 6(5):409–454, 1996.

23. B. Pierce and D. Sangiorgi. Behavioral equivalence in the polymorphic pi-calculus. *JACM*, 47(5):531–584, 2000.

24. B. C. Pierce and D. N. Turner. Concurrent objects in a process calculus. In *Theory and Practice of Parallel Programming (TPPP), Sendai, Japan (Nov. 1994)*, volume 907 of *LNCS*, pages 187–215. Springer-Verlag, 1995.

25. B. C. Pierce and D. N. Turner. Pict: A programming language based on the pi-calculus. In G. Plotkin, C. Stirling, and M. Tofte, editors, *Proof, Language and Interaction: Essays in Honour of Robin Milner*, pages 455–494. MIT Press, 2000.

26. J. Reppy. *Concurrent Programming in ML*. Cambridge University Press, 1999.

27. J. Riely and M. Hennessy. Trust and partial typing in open systems of mobile agents. In *Proc. of POPL*, pages 93–104, 1999.

28. D. Sangiorgi. The name discipline of uniform receptiveness. *Theor. Comput. Sci.*, 221(1-2):457–493, 1999.

29. D. Sangiorgi and D. Walker. *The Pi-Calculus: A Theory of Mobile Processes*. Cambridge University Press, 2001.

30. E. Sumii and N. Kobayashi. A generalized deadlock-free process calculus. In *Proc. of Workshop on High-Level Concurrent Language (HLCL'98)*, volume 16(3) of *ENTCS*, pages 55–77, 1998.

31. D. T. Turner. The polymorphic pi-calculus: Theory and implementation. PhD Thesis, University of Edinburgh, 1996.

32. V. T. Vasconcelos and K. Honda. Principal typing schemes in a polyadic π-calculus. In *CONCUR'93*, volume 715 of *LNCS*, pages 524–538. Springer-Verlag, 1993.

33. N. Yoshida. Graph types for monadic mobile processes. In *FST/TCS'16*, volume 1180 of *LNCS*, pages 371–387. Springer-Verlag, 1996.

Author Index

Lecture Notes in Computer Science

For information about Vols. 1–2820
please contact your bookseller or Springer-Verlag

Vol. 2854: J. Hoffmann, Utilizing Problem Structure in Planning. XIII, 251 pages. 2003. (Subseries LNAI)

Vol. 2855: R. Alur, I. Lee (Eds.), Embedded Software. Proceedings, 2003. X, 373 pages. 2003.

Vol. 2856: M. Smirnov, E. Biersack, C. Blondia, O. Bonaventure, O. Casals, G. Karlsson, George Pavlou, B. Quoitin, J. Roberts, I. Stavrakakis, B. Stiller, P. Trimintzios, P. Van Mieghem (Eds.), Quality of Future Internet Services. IX, 293 pages. 2003.

Vol. 2857: M.A. Nascimento, E.S. de Moura, A.L. Oliveira (Eds.), String Processing and Information Retrieval. Proceedings, 2003. XI, 379 pages. 2003.

Vol. 2858: A. Veidenbaum, K. Joe, H. Amano, H. Aiso (Eds.), High Performance Computing. Proceedings, 2003. XV, 566 pages. 2003.

Vol. 2859: B. Apolloni, M. Marinaro, R. Tagliaferri (Eds.), Neural Nets. Proceedings, 2003. X, 376 pages. 2003.

Vol. 2860: D. Geist, E. Tronci (Eds.), Correct Hardware Design and Verification Methods. Proceedings, 2003. XII, 426 pages. 2003.

Vol. 2861: C. Bliek, C. Jermann, A. Neumaier (Eds.), Global Optimization and Constraint Satisfaction. Proceedings, 2002. XII, 239 pages. 2003.

Vol. 2862: D. Feitelson, L. Rudolph, U. Schwiegelshohn (Eds.), Job Scheduling Strategies for Parallel Processing. Proceedings, 2003. VII, 269 pages. 2003.

Vol. 2863: P. Stevens, J. Whittle, G. Booch (Eds.), «UML» 2003 – The Unified Modeling Language. Proceedings, 2003. XIV, 415 pages. 2003.

Vol. 2864: A.K. Dey, A. Schmidt, J.F. McCarthy (Eds.), UbiComp 2003: Ubiquitous Computing. Proceedings, 2003. XVII, 368 pages. 2003.

Vol. 2865: S. Pierre, M. Barbeau, E. Kranakis (Eds.), Ad-Hoc, Mobile, and Wireless Networks. Proceedings, 2003. X, 293 pages. 2003.

Vol. 2867: M. Brunner, A. Keller (Eds.), Self-Managing Distributed Systems. Proceedings, 2003. XIII, 274 pages. 2003.

Vol. 2868: P. Perner, R. Brause, H.-G. Holzhütter (Eds.), Medical Data Analysis. Proceedings, 2003. VIII, 127 pages. 2003.

Vol. 2869: A. Yazici, C. Şener (Eds.), Computer and Information Sciences – ISCIS 2003. Proceedings, 2003. XIX, 1110 pages. 2003.

Vol. 2870: D. Fensel, K. Sycara, J. Mylopoulos (Eds.), The Semantic Web - ISWC 2003. Proceedings, 2003. XV, 931 pages. 2003.

Vol. 2871: N. Zhong, Z.W. Raś, S. Tsumoto, E. Suzuki (Eds.), Foundations of Intelligent Systems. Proceedings, 2003. XV, 697 pages. 2003. (Subseries LNAI)

Vol. 2873: J. Lawry, J. Shanahan, A. Ralescu (Eds.), Modelling with Words. XIII, 229 pages. 2003. (Subseries LNAI)

Vol. 2874: C. Priami (Ed.), Global Computing. Proceedings, 2003. XIX, 255 pages. 2003.

Vol. 2875: E. Aarts, R. Collier, E. van Loenen, B. de Ruyter (Eds.), Ambient Intelligence. Proceedings, 2003. XI, 432 pages. 2003.

Vol. 2876: M. Schroeder, G. Wagner (Eds.), Rules and Rule Markup Languages for the Semantic Web. Proceedings, 2003. VII, 173 pages. 2003.

Vol. 2877: T. Böhme, G. Heyer, H. Unger (Eds.), Innovative Internet Community Systems. Proceedings, 2003. VIII, 263 pages. 2003.

Vol. 2878: R.E. Ellis, T.M. Peters (Eds.), Medical Image Computing and Computer-Assisted Intervention - MICCAI 2003. Part I. Proceedings, 2003. XXXIII, 819 pages. 2003.

Vol. 2879: R.E. Ellis, T.M. Peters (Eds.), Medical Image Computing and Computer-Assisted Intervention - MICCAI 2003. Part II. Proceedings, 2003. XXXIV, 1003 pages. 2003.

Vol. 2880: H.L. Bodlaender (Ed.), Graph-Theoretic Concepts in Computer Science. Proceedings, 2003. XI, 386 pages. 2003.

Vol. 2881: E. Horlait, T. Magedanz, R.H. Glitho (Eds.), Mobile Agents for Telecommunication Applications. Proceedings, 2003. IX, 297 pages. 2003.

Vol. 2883: J. Schaeffer, M. Müller, Y. Björnsson (Eds.), Computers and Games. Proceedings, 2002. XI, 431 pages. 2003.

Vol. 2884: E. Najm, U. Nestmann, P. Stevens (Eds.), Formal Methods for Open Object-Based Distributed Systems. Proceedings, 2003. X, 293 pages. 2003.

Vol. 2885: J.S. Dong, J. Woodcock (Eds.), Formal Methods and Software Engineering. Proceedings, 2003. XI, 683 pages. 2003.

Vol. 2886: I. Nyström, G. Sanniti di Baja, S. Svensson (Eds.), Discrete Geometry for Computer Imagery. Proceedings, 2003. XII, 556 pages. 2003.

Vol. 2887: T. Johansson (Ed.), Fast Software Encryption. Proceedings, 2003. IX, 397 pages. 2003.

Vol. 2888: R. Meersman, Zahir Tari, D.C. Schmidt et al. (Eds.), On The Move to Meaningful Internet Systems 2003: CoopIS, DOA, and ODBASE. Proceedings, 2003. XXI, 1546 pages. 2003.

Vol. 2889: Robert Meersman, Zahir Tari et al. (Eds.), On The Move to Meaningful Internet Systems 2003: OTM 2003 Workshops. Proceedings, 2003. XXI, 1096 pages. 2003.

Vol. 2891: J. Lee, M. Barley (Eds.), Intelligent Agents and Multi-Agent Systems. Proceedings, 2003. X, 215 pages. 2003. (Subseries LNAI)

Vol. 2893: J.-B. Stefani, I. Demeure, D. Hagimont (Eds.), Distributed Applications and Interoperable Systems. Proceedings, 2003. XIII, 311 pages. 2003.

Vol. 2895: A. Ohori (Ed.), Programming Languages and Systems. Proceedings, 2003. XIII, 427 pages. 2003.

Vol. 2897: O. Balet, G. Subsol, P. Torguet (Eds.), Virtual Storytelling. Proceedings, 2003. XI, 240 pages. 2003.

Vol. 2899: G. Ventre, R. Canonico (Eds.), Interactive Multimedia on Next Generation Networks. Proceedings, 2003. XIV, 420 pages. 2003.

Vol. 2901: F. Bry, N. Henze, J. Maluszyński (Eds.), Principles and Practice of Semantic Web Reasoning. Proceedings, 2003. X, 209 pages. 2003.

Vol. 2902: F. Moura Pires, S. Abreu (Eds.), Progress in Artificial Intelligence. Proceedings, 2003. XV, 504 pages. 2003. (Subseries LNAI).

Vol. 2905: A. Sanfeliu, J. Ruiz-Shulcloper (Eds.), Progress in Pattern Recognition, Speech and Image Analysis. Proceedings, 2003. XVII, 693 pages. 2003.